reflective
teaching

in schools

4th edition

Available and forthcoming titles in the *Reflective Teaching* Series

Series Editors: Andrew Pollard and Amy Pollard

Readings for Reflective Teaching in Schools (2nd edition), edited by Andrew Pollard

Reflective Teaching in Further and Adult Education (3rd edition), Yvonne Hillier

Forthcoming titles:

Reflective Teaching in Early Education, Jennifer Colwell *et al.*

Readings for Reflective Teaching in Early Education, edited by Jennifer Colwell and Andrew Pollard

Reflective Teaching in Higher Education, Paul Ashwin *et al.*

Reflective Teaching in Further, Adult and Vocational Education, Margaret Gregson, Yvonne Hillier *et al.*

reflective teaching

in schools

4th edition

Andrew Pollard

with Kristine Black-Hawkins, Gabrielle Cliff Hodges, Pete Dudley, Mary James, Holly Linklater, Sue Swaffield, Mandy Swann, Fay Turner, Paul Warwick, Mark Winterbottom and Mary Anne Wolpert

BLOOMSBURY

LONDON • NEW DELHI • NEW YORK • SYDNEY

Bloomsbury Academic

An imprint of Bloomsbury Publishing Plc

50 Bedford Square	1385 Broadway
London	New York
WC1B 3DP	NY 10018
UK	USA

www.bloomsbury.com

Bloomsbury is a registered trade mark of Bloomsbury Publishing Plc

First published 2014

British Library Cataloguing-in-Publication Data
A catalogue record for this book is available from the British Library.

ISBN: HB: 978-1-4411-4060-9
PB: 978-1-4411-9170-0
ePDF: 978-1-4411-3662-6
ePub: 978-1-4411-7539-7

Library of Congress Cataloging-in-Publication Data
A catalog record for this book is available from the Library of Congress.

Typeset by Fakenham Prepress Solutions, Fakenham, Norfolk NR21 8NN
Printed and bound in Great Britain

*This book is dedicated to Anne and Michael Pollard,
and to the generation who lived and worked in the 20th century to create
more productive, inclusive and balanced societies in the UK.*

*Beyond its prime audience of teachers and trainee teachers, it is also respectfully offered
to all politicians and others who need to understand why they must support and trust
education professionals if they really want to promote learning for the 21st century.*

Contents

Part four Reflecting on consequences

Part five Deepening understanding

WWW.

Supplementary chapters at **reflectiveteaching.co.uk**
- **Starting out** Learning as a newly qualified teacher
- **Improvement** Continuing professional development

Introduction

This book offers *two* levels of support for initial teacher education and continuing professional development.

- Comprehensive guidance is offered on key issues in classroom practice – including relationships, behaviour, curriculum planning, learning and teaching strategies, assessment processes and evaluation.
- Uniquely, the book also introduces evidence-informed 'principles' and 'concepts' to support a deeper understanding of teacher expertise.

Reflective Teaching thus supports both initial school-based training and extended career-long professionalism for both primary *and* secondary school teachers.

Developed over three decades, the book, companion reader and website represent the accumulated understanding of generations of teachers and educationalists.

Readings for Reflective Teaching in Schools provides a compact library which complements and extends the chapters in this book. It has been designed to provide convenient access to key texts and will be of particular help when library access may be difficult.

The associated website, **reflectiveteaching.co.uk**, offers an enormous range of supplementary resources including reflective activities, research briefings, advice on further reading and additional chapters. It also features a compendium of educational terms, a conceptual framework showcasing some of the UK's best educational research and extensive links to useful websites.

Underlying these materials, there are three key messages. The first is that it *is* now possible to identify teaching strategies which are more effective than others in most circumstances. Teachers therefore now have to be able to develop, improve, promote and defend their expertise by marshalling such evidence and by embedding enquiry and evaluation within routine practices. Second, all evidence has to be interpreted – and we do this by 'making sense'. In other words, as well as information about effective strategies we need to be able to discern the underlying principles of learning and teaching to which specific findings relate – we need to *understand* what is going on in this complex area of professional activity. Finally, we need to remember that education has moral purposes and social consequences. The provision we make is connected to our future as societies and to the life-chances of the children and young people with whom we work. The issues require very careful consideration.

Reflective activity is thus of vital importance to the teaching profession:

- it underpins professional judgement and its use for worthwhile educational purposes;
- it provides a vehicle for learning and professional renewal – and thus for promoting the independence and integrity of teachers;
- above all, it is a means to the improvement of teaching, the enhancement of learning and the steady growth in standards of performance for both schools and national education systems.

We hope that you will find these materials helpful in your professional work and as you seek personal fulfilment as a teacher.

A summary of the book follows.

Andrew Pollard
Bristol, Cambridge, London, June 2013

PART 1: BECOMING A REFLECTIVE PROFESSIONAL **introduces and structures the activity of becoming a teacher.** We start in Chapter 1 with a focus on the decision to teach and on the significance of the contribution we can make as professionals. Then comes an introduction to ways of understanding 'learning' (Chapter 2) – which is the foundation of expert teacher judgement. Despite much complexity, *learning* is what it is all about! The chapter on reflective practice (Chapter 3) discusses how such processes can improve the quality of our teaching. And then it gets really interesting, with a review of ten principles of effective teaching and learning (Chapter 4). These come from a major UK research and development programme and also draw on accumulated evidence from around the world. Measured effects of particular strategies are related to underlying principles.

 Two supplementary chapters are available on **reflectiveteaching.co.uk** – on school-experience and mentoring for initial training ('Mentoring') and on how to conduct small-scale enquiries to achieve an 'evidence-informed classroom' ('Enquiry').

PART 2: CREATING CONDITIONS FOR LEARNING **concerns the creation of classroom environments to support high quality teaching and learning.** We begin by considering the circumstances which impinge on families and schools (Chapter 5) – and we note the ways in which people contribute to and challenge such circumstances through their actions. We then move to the heart of classroom life with a focus on teacher–pupil relationships and inclusion (Chapter 6). Because such relationships are so crucial for classroom success, this is an extremely important chapter. Chapter 7 builds further and illustrates how positive cycles of behaviour can be created through firmness, fairness and engaging pupils in the curriculum. Finally, we consider a range of learning spaces in school and beyond (Chapter 8) and the affordances they offer for formal and informal learning. As well as the basic dimensions of classroom organisation, this chapter also addresses the use of technology, pupil organisation and teamworking with teacher assistants.

PART 3: TEACHING FOR LEARNING supports the development of practice across the three classic dimensions of teaching – curriculum, pedagogy and assessment. Chapter 9 starts us off with a review of curricular aims and design principles, before progressing to a review of national curricula in the UK and the role of subject knowledge. 'Planning' (Chapter 10) puts these ideas into action and supports the development and evaluation of programmes of study, schemes of work and lesson plans. Chapter 11 offers ways of understanding the art, craft and science of pedagogy – and the development of a pedagogic repertoire. 'Communication' (Chapter 12) extends this with an introduction to the vital role of talking, listening, reading and writing across the curriculum. Perhaps the core instructional expertise of the teacher lies in the skill of dialogic teaching? Finally, this part concludes by demonstrating how assessment can be tied into teaching and learning processes in very constructive ways (Chapter 13). In short, through principled strategies for sharing goals, pupil engagement, authentic feedback, self-assessment and responsive teaching, excellent progress in learning can be made.

PART 4: REFLECTING ON CONSEQUENCES draws attention to what is achieved, and by whom, in our classrooms – what are the consequences of what we do? Chapter 14 reviews big issues in assessment, with particular attention on how schools measure pupil achievement and manage accountability. Whilst some problems are raised, positive uses of summative assessment data are also promoted. 'Inclusion' (Chapter 15) asks us to consider various dimensions of difference and also the ways in which routine processes differentiate between people. However, the emphasis is on accepting difference as part of the human condition and on how to build more inclusive classroom communities.

PART 5: DEEPENING UNDERSTANDING, is the final, synoptic part of the book. It integrates major themes through discussion of teacher expertise and professionalism. 'Expertise' (Chapter 16) harvests and integrates powerful ideas from previous chapters into a holistic conceptual framework of enduring issues in teaching and learning. The chapter constructs a framework describing dimensions of expert thinking. In Chapter 17, 'Professionalism', we consider the role of the teaching profession in our societies and suggest how reflective teachers can contribute to democratic processes.

Supplementary chapters are available on the website, **reflectiveteaching.co.uk**, on succeeding as a newly qualified teacher ('Starting out') and on career and school development ('Improvement').

part one

Becoming a reflective professional

This part introduces and structures the activity of becoming a teacher.

We start with a chapter focused on ourselves and on the significance of the contribution we can make as professional teachers. Then comes an introduction to ways of understanding 'learning' (Chapter 2) – which is the foundation of teacher judgement. After all, despite much complexity, learning is what it is all about! The chapter on reflective practice (Chapter 3) discusses how such processes can improve the quality of our teaching. And then it gets really interesting, with a review of ten 'principles of effective teaching and learning (Chapter 4). These come from a major UK research and development programme and also draw on accumulated evidence from around the world.

Identity

Who are we, and what do we stand for?

1

Introduction

This chapter is concerned with the teachers, children and young people in classroom life, and with the feelings and perceptions we hold in relation to ourselves and others.

A key issue is that of our 'identities' as unique individuals and how these identities relate to the cultures and opportunities within classrooms and schools. However, to understand the identities of each other and ourselves we must recognise both social influences beyond the school and also development throughout each stage of life.

The first section of the chapter focuses on the professional vocation and work of teachers. We consider why people choose to become teachers and the values that might inform and sustain our practice. We introduce what is known about teachers' work, including how teachers respond to complexity and uncertainty. This section also reflects the belief that there are always things that we can do to improve the quality of educational provision for all learners. To this end, whilst celebrating vocational commitment, the chapter also acknowledges the professional resilience that is increasingly necessary.

Section 2 focuses on thinking about children and young people. We consider what we know about the particular identities and cultures of the young people with whom we work – in, and beyond, our schools. We challenge ourselves to consider how our values and pre-existing understandings may influence how we think about pupils and their learning.

Section 3 considers the ways in which children and young people develop and learn through their schooling. Social, physical and psychological factors are addressed. The agency of children and young people is then celebrated by tracing trajectories through primary and secondary education and into adulthood. Finally, our own biographies, and our commitment to teaching, are acknowledged. We again affirm the need to balance our personal and professional lives to achieve success.

TLRP principles

Two principles are of particular relevance to this chapter on identity and values in education:

Effective teaching and learning equips learners for life in its broadest sense. Learning should aim to help people to develop the intellectual, personal and social resources that will enable them to participate as active citizens, contribute to economic development and flourish as individuals in a diverse and changing society. This implies adopting a broad view of learning outcomes and ensuring that equity and social justice are taken seriously. (Principle 1)

Effective teaching and learning depends on teacher learning. The need for teachers to learn continuously in order to develop their knowledge and skills, and adapt and develop their roles, especially through classroom inquiry, should be recognised and supported. (Principle 9)

See Chapter 4

1 Understanding ourselves as teachers

1.1 Becoming a teacher

There are lots of reasons why people choose to enter the profession of teaching. Many are attracted because of a principled commitment to the education of children and young people – whether this is anticipated to be for a short period or, potentially, for a career. Teaching can certainly be a source of great fulfilment, and thus contribute to personal wellbeing. Teaching also, of course, offers secure and respected employment.

Commitment to 'working with children' is often particularly strong for those who choose to become primary or early years teachers. This was sensitively described by Nias whose classic study *Primary Teachers Talking* (1989) showed how identification with the role eventually became so strong for some that they saw themselves as 'persons-in-teaching' rather than just as people who happened to be employed as teachers. It has been argued that the commitment of primary teachers 'affirms feminine virtues such as caring and nurturance' (Burgess and Carter, 1992), but significant contributions are made by teachers of both sexes. Whilst the contemporary role is as challenging as in any other profession, there is no doubt that the opportunity to support the development of young children over time has considerable fascination and importance.

Studies of secondary school trainee teachers often find that a significant intrinsic factor is the opportunity to work within their subject specialism. This is either because of the perceived value of the subject itself or because of a desire to share their knowledge and enthusiasm with others (see, for example Younger, Brindley, Pedder and Hagger, 2004). For many too, there is a strong commitment to providing opportunities so that young people can fulfil their potential – as expressed in some of Richardson's books such as *Changing Life Chances* (2011). Secondary trainees may be very idealistic:

> I feel powerfully that everybody is deserving of equal chances to make their way in the world.

> You are influencing a whole generation, generations of people – and that's exciting.
> (Quoted in Younger et al., 2004, p. 249)

There is thus a well-established theme of idealism in the commitment of many aspiring teachers. The profession attracts those with a sense of moral purpose who decide that they want, through their work with children, students and young people, to make a contribution to the future of our societies. The 'passion for teaching' of many primary and secondary teachers as has been recorded many times in the past, and remains evident today (see Day, 2004; Gu, 2007, Reading 1.1).

Importantly however, the vocational commitment of trainees is not associated with complacency about the challenges of becoming a 'good teacher'. Most people, when beginning to learn how to become a teacher, are extremely aware of the challenges. Fortunately, with appropriate support, commitment can be nurtured until professional capabilities and self-confidence are secure. However, a slightly uneven journey, characterised by ups and downs and a lot of hard work, is not unusual – though guides, such as Turnbull's 'practical guide to empowerment' (2007) help considerably

The early years of classroom life for newly qualified teachers is crucial for career decisions. In a recent study of such experiences, McNally and Blake (2010) found that establishing good relationships with pupils and with teacher colleagues often assumes huge importance – and feelings about teaching and personal self-confidence ebb and flow (see also the **Research Briefing** on p. 11). The struggle to establish competence and acceptance could be overwhelming and feelings sometimes veered 'from anxiety and despair to fulfillment and delight'.

The significance of this research is that it highlights aspects of the journey that we all share as teachers. The feelings associated with our first few weeks in the profession may stay with us in some form – a keen sense of moral purpose; excitement because of the responsibility and opportunities; and awe, wonder and uncertainty about how to fulfill our ambitions for both ourselves as teachers and for the children and young people with whom we work. Gradually though, these commitments are tempered by experience, but it is to be hoped that they never fade completely.

Like the trainees in the research projects, much of our motivation and resilience will be associated with our personal qualities. Moreover, these qualities will develop and sustain us throughout our careers – and contribute to 'reflective practice'. The process of reflection acknowledges dilemmas and the need for expert judgement in teaching. It is entirely understandable to feel such challenges – see Richardson's classic 'Daring to be a Teacher' (1990). *Reflective Teaching in Schools* offers constructive ways of managing challenges in the short term whilst also building principled, career-long expertise.

Reflective activity 1.1

Aim: To reflect on your own decision to become a teacher.

Evidence and reflection: In Section 1.1 we explored the importance of early feelings in relation to motivation, aspiration and determination. Write for yourself a short piece, recollecting why you decided to train to become a teacher. If appropriate, also record your feelings at the point of qualifying.

Extension: Read what you have written and highlight where you have made reference to specific value commitments. List these, and try to identify personal experiences that informed why they were so important. (For example: to inspire people to want to discover the joy of literature – because of what my Year 7 English teacher did for me; to encourage every child to be confident enough to 'have a go' and persevere – because of the PE teacher who told me I'd never get picked for the football team.)

Share your thinking with colleagues and discuss the range of motivations which inform 'becoming a teacher'.

1.2 Values informing practice

As suggested above, the values we hold about the importance of education are critical to the decision to become teachers in the first place, and to sustaining our motivation and resilience through our career.

The values that inform our practice are not necessarily explicit but it is important to try to identify them for at least three reasons. First, being clear about values can help

Figure 1.1 Professional values as articulated by the General Teaching Councils of Scotland, Wales and Northern Ireland, and The Teaching Council, Ireland; for updates, see links on **reflectiveteaching.co.uk**.

GTC SCOTLAND

Professional Values and Personal Commitment

- Registered teachers show in their day-to-day practice a commitment to social justice, inclusion and caring for and protecting children.
- Registered teachers take responsibility for their professional learning and development.
- Registered teachers value, respect and are active partners in the communities in which they work.

GTC WALES

Code of Professional Conduct and Practice

Key Principles – professionalism and maintaining trust in the profession.

Registered teachers: base their relationship with pupils on trust and respect; have regard to the safety and wellbeing of pupils in their care; work in a collaborative manner with teachers and other professionals, and develop and maintain good relationships with parents, guardians and carers; act with honesty and integrity; are sensitive to the need, where appropriate, for confidentiality; take responsibility for maintaining the quality of their professional practice; uphold public trust and confidence in the teaching profession.

GTC NORTHERN IRELAND

Code of Values and Professional Practice – Core Values

The core values of the profession are: trust; respect; integrity; honesty; fairness; tolerance; commitment; equality and service.

A commitment to serve lies at the heart of professional behaviour. In addition, members of the profession will exemplify the values listed above in their working and in their relationships with others; recognising in particular the unique and privileged relationship that exists between teachers and their pupils. In keeping with the spirit of professional service and commitment, teachers will at all times be conscious of their responsibilities to others: learners, colleagues and indeed the profession itself.

TEACHING COUNCIL IRELAND

The Code of Professional Conduct for Teachers

The Code begins by setting out the ethical foundation for the teaching profession – respect, care, integrity and trust.

Respect: Teachers uphold human dignity and promote equality and emotional and cognitive development. *Care*: Teachers' practice is motivated by the best interests of the pupils/students entrusted to them. *Integrity*: Honesty, reliability and moral action are exercised through professional commitments, responsibilities and actions. *Trust*: Teachers' relationships with pupils/students, colleagues, parents, school management and the public are based on trust. Trust embodies fairness, openness and honesty.

us to assess whether we are consistent, both in what we as individuals believe, and in reconciling differences which may exist in a school between colleagues working together. Second, it can help us to evaluate and respond to external pressures and requirements – as 'creative mediators' of policy (see Chapter 3, Section 2.7). Third, it can help us to assess whether what we believe is consistent with what we actually do: that is, whether our value system or philosophy is compatible with our actual classroom practice.

As well an awareness of the values we held when we entered the profession (see Reflective activity 1.1), we are also required to work by values shared within our profession. In the British Isles, the three General Teaching Councils (GTC) (Scotland, Wales and Northern Ireland), Teaching Council (Ireland) and the Department for Education (England) articulate clear expectations regarding the values that should underpin teachers' work. These professional expectations are reflected in 'codes of conduct and practice for registered teachers', see Figure 1.1. In England, a similar statement is made in the documentation of Teachers' Standards.

Reflective activity 1.2

Aim: To compare your personal values (see Reflective activity 1.1) with the statements developed by the Teaching Councils.

Evidence and reflection: Were there values in your initial reflection that are not included in any of the national codes or standards? If so, why do you think this might be?

Are there ways in which the official codes and standards extend your value expectations? How? Which aspects of your practice do they relate to? For example, in your initial reflections, did you, like GTC Northern Ireland, highlight the value of 'service'?

Extension: Isolate and compare each element of the four statements of professional values. How would you explain the similarities and differences?

WWW.

For a supplementary approach to articulating values, aims and commitments see **reflectiveteaching.co.uk**

One of the arguments for developing codes or standards for professional practice is that they frame our practice and development in purposive ways. They are intended to encourage us to be reflective and responsible, to remind us of professional values, aims and commitments *and* to consider indicators of their implementation and effect. Only then will we be able to judge whether what we *really* do matches what we say we value. Gaps between aspirations, values and outcomes are common in many walks of life but for teachers it is particularly important to examine why this may occur. After all, failure to adapt and change may have significant effects on the lives of others.

Of course, self-improvement is often based, one way or another, on the collection and analysis of evidence. So the contemporary professional has to be willing to test his or her value positions and beliefs. Indeed, the reflective practitioner, as we will later see, is able to justify his or her practices and provide an explanation or 'warrant' for them.

An important step in developing as reflective practitioners is to understand how our own personal values, beliefs and practices are influenced by our previous experiences, circumstances and understanding. We need to become 'reflexive' and thus able to question ourselves. Such reflexivity is an important aspect of reflective practice. Whilst the latter addresses a wide range of social, organisational, pedagogic and other factors, reflexivity focuses directly on our self-awareness and ability to reflect on ourselves (Moore, 2004).

Beliefs, of course, can be particularly difficult to change since they may rest on significant cultural and material foundations. Indeed, we may even feel that our beliefs are representations of 'objective truths' and so that nothing more needs to be considered. Reflective practice requires an interesting combination of moral commitment and open-mindedness. Whilst being fully value committed, we must still aspire to learn and improve. We will explore this more fully in Chapter 3.

1.3 Teacher identities

What sort of a person do we think we are, and what sort of a teacher do we wish to become? In primary education, teachers often associate themselves with a pupil year or Key Stage, whilst in secondary identification with a subject or cluster of subjects is pretty much taken for granted.

The concept of 'identity' summarises the ways in which we think about ourselves. Our sense of personal identity forms through life and is particularly influenced by identification with 'significant others' such as parents, friends and, in due course, colleagues. But we often separate our thinking in terms of our 'personal' and 'professional' self and, in this section, we focus on the formation and development of professional identities as teachers.

As we have seen, most people enter the profession of teaching with a strong sense of personal commitment and such values are affirmed and expected as professional characteristics.

However, the progression from early idealism to long term professionalism is often not straightforward. At each stage, we must wrestle with the tension between vocational commitment and practical challenges.

Initial teacher education brings the first round of such challenges. Maynard and Furlong (1993) identified five typical stages of initial school experience – 'early idealism', 'personal survival', 'recognising difficulties', 'hitting the plateau' and, finally, 'moving on'. For example, it may well be rather dispiriting if you come into school to help children with their learning only to find that you cannot get them to pay attention and take you seriously! But it is also reassuring to know that most people do, with the support of others, work their way through these initial challenges – and as they do so, a more professional teacher identity begins to form.

For a full account of this and of helpful support, see the supplementary **Mentoring** chapter on **reflectiveteaching.co.uk**

In their few first years of teaching, teachers may experience a similar cycle. For example, Ewing and Manuel (2005) identified five stages from initial experiences to a more confident professionalism:

- early expectations and a sense of vocation;
- early days of the first teaching appointment;
- finding a place: the establishment phase;

- consolidating pedagogical content knowledge;
- building a professional identity and voice. (Ewing and Manuel, 2005)

This process is also similar to that described by McNally and Blake (2010) and must succeed if a long-term teaching career is to be established. The issue of achieving personal fulfilment from teaching is obviously of great significance in this. It is most likely when there is congruence between each teacher's personal commitments and the roles which they fulfil in school. If personal and professional identities align, then a long-term career is much more likely.

The classic study of teacher careers as a whole is Huberman's *The Lives of Teachers* (1993). He suggested that teacher careers typically develop through five stages. He saw initial training and early career learning as 'career entry' which, after five years or so, leads onto 'stabilisation' and then 'experimentation' for a long period which may last for 20 years or more. After that, he suggested, there is typically a period of wind-down into 'serenity and conservatism' followed by 'disengagement' and eventual retirement!

Day and Gu (2010, see also Reading 1.1) bring this analysis up to date for UK circumstances, as informed by a large-scale study on teachers' work and lives (see the **TLRP Research Briefing** on p. 11). They showed that the key contemporary factor in achieving satisfaction, commitment, wellbeing and effectiveness for teachers is the relative success with which various personal, work and external policy challenges are managed. In other words, given the challenges of teaching today, successful career teachers require strong personal and professional identities which derive coherence from underlying values and beliefs. Day et al. suggest that teachers who offer this combination of professional understanding and personal qualities are often particularly effective in terms of supporting pupil learning and are also better able to achieve a sustainable work-life balance. They are committed, but they also keep things in perspective.

Exploring a particular dimension of this, Hargreaves' (1998) has written on the place of emotion in teaching. He argues that:

> As an emotional practice, teaching activates, colours and expresses teachers' own feelings and actions as well as the feelings and actions of others with whom teachers interact. All teaching is inextricably emotional either by design, or by default. (p. 5)

Hargreaves reminds us that it is not only the values we go into teaching with that matter, but how we feel able to put these into practice. Affective responses to classroom situations invariably do influence our actions and the ways in which we express what we value. Moreover, in such interactions with pupils and others, our professional success often depends significantly on how we make others' feel. Becoming an effective teacher thus has a great deal to do with learning how to support, manage and develop oneself.

The nature of personal and professional identities is therefore of great significance for teachers. We each reflect the uniqueness of our past experiences and circumstances – and these influences, of course, have very significant effects on our self-perceptions. In school settings, the influence of other colleagues on the school staff is often considerable. They represent 'significant others' providing feedback to us in relation to our self-presentation.

Research Briefing

Teacher careers and effectiveness

A large-scale and comprehensive TLRP project on teachers' work, lives and effectiveness, VITAE, researched teachers' professional identities through career phases. Teachers' sense of professional identity is affected by tensions between: their personal values and life experiences; the situated leadership and cultures of their schools; and the impact of external policies on their professional work. Outcomes, in terms of wellbeing, commitment and resilience, and hence effectiveness, depend on teachers' capacity to manage interactions between personal, work and professional factors.

Commitment, Resilience and Effectiveness

Mediating Influences
(Stable/unstable/positive/negative scenarios)

Influencing Factors

Professional Life Phases

Personal

Situated   Professional

Influencing Factors

Professional Identities

Outcomes

Well-being,
Commitment
and Resilience

Effectiveness
• Perceived Effectiveness
• Pupil progress and attainment

Key findings:	Implications:
Pupil attainment: Pupils of teachers who are committed and resilient are likely to attain more than pupils whose teachers are not.	Policy makers, national associations and head teachers concerned with raising standards in schools need to consider the connections between teachers' commitment, resilience and effectiveness.
Professional identity: Teachers' sense of positive professional identity is associated with well-being and job satisfaction and is a key factor in their effectiveness.	Strategies for sustaining commitment in initial and continuing professional development programmes should distinguish between the needs of teachers in different phases of their professional lives.
Challenge: The commitment and resilience of teachers in schools serving more disadvantaged communities are more persistently challenged than others.	Schools, especially those which serve disadvantaged communities, need to ensure that their continuing professional development (CPD) provision is relevant to the commitment, resilience and health needs of teachers.
Experience: Teachers do not necessarily become more effective over time. Teachers in later years are likely to be less effective.	National organisations and schools need strategies for professional learning and development to support teachers in the later stages of their careers.
Sustainability: Sustaining and enhancing teachers' commitment and resilience is a key quality and retention issue.	Efforts to support and enhance teacher quality should focus upon building, sustaining and retaining their commitment and resilience.

Further information:
Day, C., Stobart, G., Sammons, P., Kington, A., Gu, Q., Smees, R,. Mujtaba, T. and Woods, D. (2006) *Factors that make teachers more effective across their careers.* TLRP Research Briefing No 20 (at **www.tlrp.org/pub**).
Day, C., Stobart, G., Sammons, P. and Kington, A. (2007) *Teachers Matter.* Maidenhead: Open University Press.
This TLRP Associate Project was funded by DfES and directed from the University of Nottingham.

Expert question

Effectiveness: are there improvements in standards, in both basic skills and other areas of curricular attainment, to satisfy society's educational goals?

This question contributes to a conceptual framework representing enduring issues and teacher expertise (see Chapter 16). The overall effectiveness of the school system is one of the outcomes to which the book as a whole contributes.

Our teacher colleagues, and others with roles in school and beyond, are likely to influence the development of our identities and self-confidence as teachers. If we don't relate well to them, that fact may inhibit our personal and professional development. On the other hand, collaboration with colleagues, when underpinned by open, trusting relationships, enables authentic development of professional identities. This has been demonstrated for many years by research on school effectiveness which identifies the benefits of schools supporting teachers in taking risks, exploring new practices and creating 'learning communities' (Lave and Wenger, 1991) in which teachers are also learners (MacBeath and Mortimore, 2001; MacGilchrist, Myers and Read, 2004; James et al., 2007).

In summary, for teachers, the personal and the professional interrelate to a considerable extent. The nature, resilience and development of our identity over time will make a significant contribution to our professional success.

1.4 Teachers' work

In terms of responsibilities, teachers' work can be described with some precision, and indeed, employment contracts do exactly this. Teachers have a right to receive particulars of employment setting out expectations for their role and, if full-time in England and Wales for example, they must be available for work for 195 days or 1,265 hours of 'directed time' each year. A minimum of 10 per cent of timetabled teaching time should be designated (without pupil contact) for planning, preparation and assessment. There will be provision addressing administration, breaks, leave, performance review, etc, etc.

However, whilst contractual conditions are extremely important, the most significant question concerns how we interpret both them and the role more generally. This question needs to be posed because, as we have already seen, teaching is a complex activity and contractual terms, whilst necessary, are not sufficient to validly represent it. Below, we offer a different but complementary approach.

Metaphor can enable us to understand complexity more clearly, and this certainly applies to interpretations of the nature of teaching. The most common metaphors used are 'the *art* of teaching' (e.g. Eisner, 1983; Egan, 2010), the *science* of teaching (e.g. Simon, 1985, Reading 11.3; Hattie, 2012, Reading 4.6), and the *craft* of teaching (e.g. Grimmett and Mackinnon, 1992; Brown and McIntyre, 1993; Day, 2005). Indeed, these metaphors are explicitly deployed in Chapter 11 to describe dimensions of teachers' pedagogic expertise (see also Reading 11.1).

The metaphor of 'art' emphasises the affective and creative aspects of teaching and learning as well as use of intuition in forming judgements. The 'science of teaching' conjures an image of the application of tested knowledge, whilst emphasis on the teacher's 'craft' affirms the particular significance of practical experience. There are many other common metaphors too, such as the 'teacher as gardener' which perhaps emphasises the personal development of learners, or the image of 'conductor' which foregrounds the teacher role in orchestrating multiple, simultaneous classroom activities.

The choice of metaphor thus foregrounds particular aspects of teachers' expertise, knowledge and decision-making – creating, instructing, directing, coordinating, facilitating, nurturing, etc.

Reflective activity 1.3

Aim: To develop insight into our identity and work as a teacher.

Evidence and reflection: The most established metaphors to describe teachers' work foreground the art, science and craft of teaching. Listed below are some additional metaphors that people have used to describe the work of teachers.

- architect
- conductor
- gardener
- engineer
- director.

Choose a couple of the metaphors discussed above and explore their strengths and limitations. For example, a conductor coordinates diverse contributions to create a symphony, but follows a score. A gardener nurtures and tends, but weeds …
Look over your lists. What does it reveal about how you understand the nature of teachers' work?

Extension: The issues raised could be discussed and analysed with colleagues. It might be helpful to try to identify aspects which are core to the role of teachers, and those which are more supplementary.

So far in this chapter, we have explored personal and professional values and demonstrated how teachers' own sense of identity is drawn on, and develops, during initial training and beyond. In a sense, the whole of this book is dedicated to helping us to analyse our own behaviour and its consequences. As we bring evidence to bear on our classroom practice, we can reflect on our value commitments and aspirations and on progress in the development of expertise (see Chapter 16).

We now move our focus onto children and young people who remain central to all our work.

2 Knowing children and young people as pupils

Developing an understanding of pupils requires a reflective teacher to empathise with their school experience as well as develop personal knowledge of and rapport with individual children. This is a foundation for establishing good behaviour and a positive learning atmosphere in the classroom – and is key to school practices.

2.1 Pupil views of themselves in school

The way that children think of themselves in school will directly influence their approach to learning, their 'learning disposition' (Dweck, 1986, Reading 2.6; Claxton, 1999, Reading 2.9). Some may be highly anxious and continually undervalue themselves. Others may seem overconfident and extremely resilient. Some may be very well aware of their own strengths and weaknesses whilst others may seem to have relatively naive views of themselves. Children and young people may be gregarious, or loners, or they may in fact be lonely. For instance, Pollard and Filer traced the home, playground and classroom experiences of small groups of children through their primary and secondary school careers (1996, 1999, 2007, Reading 1.2; see also Warin, 2010). Such studies show how pupils adopt particular strategies and identities as they manage relationships with peers and with teachers, and thus negotiate their way through schooling. These experiences contribute to each pupil's sense of identity and thence to confidence and achievement in learning. Qualitative research of this sort highlights the complexity of pupils' lives, and suggests that there are no simple explanations for how and why pupils respond to schooling as they do.

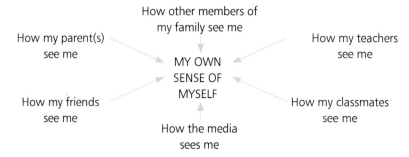

Reflective activity 1.4

Aim: To explore one of the features of 'growing up': the multiple and sometimes contradictory expectations that different people have of children and young people.

Evidence and reflection: These issues can be explored through 'picture maps' about themselves. Pupils can draw or write about each perspective.

How other members of my family see me

How my parent(s) see me

How my teachers see me

MY OWN SENSE OF MYSELF

How my friends see me

How my classmates see me

How the media sees me

Follow-up: The activity, as well as giving you insights into your pupils, may provide opportunities for discussion of how they could handle differing expectations of different people, and how it feels to feel uncertain of 'who we are'. You may also be able to discuss who they wish to become … and are becoming.

A central strategy in the development of positive self-concepts among the children and young people in school (Lawrence, 1987, Reading 6.6) lies in encouraging individuals to identify qualities within themselves which they can value. It is important to provide opportunities where a wide range of qualities can be appreciated. In classrooms where competitive achievement is greatly emphasised, some pupils may quickly come to regard themselves unfavourably, or else learn to resent and oppose the values of the teacher. It is, however, possible to create a climate where many different qualities are valued and where pupils are encouraged to challenge themselves to improve their own individual performance. In this way pupil dignity can be protected and individual effort and engagement rewarded (see Chapters 6 and 15 on inclusive practices). One of the ways of contributing to such a climate is to encourage pupils to evaluate their own work and to set their own personal goals – as in 'assessment for learning' (see Chapter 13). As we will see, it is important that such procedures are meaningful for students and worthy of their respect.

2.2 Pupil perspectives of teachers and school

Children's views of teachers have been studied for many years (Blishen, 1969; Meighan, 1978; Kyriacou, 2009; Pollard et al., 2000) – and also of trainees (Cooper and Hyland, 2000). Much of the evidence suggests that children like teachers who 'help them learn'. They expect teachers to teach, by which they seem to mean to take initiatives, to explain things clearly and to provide interesting activities. On the other hand, they also like teachers who are prepared to be flexible, to respond to the different interests of the individuals in the class and to provide some scope for pupil choice. Pupils dislike teachers who have favourites or who are unpredictable in their moods. Most children like a teacher who can sometimes 'have a laugh'. Overall, it seems that children like teachers who are firm, flexible, fair and fun, and who help them succeed as learners.

You could check these findings with some of the pupils you teach.

Reflective activity 1.5

Aim: To find out young people's criteria for a 'good teacher'.

Evidence and reflection: Hold a discussion (with the whole class, or in small groups which can then report back to the whole class) on what makes a 'good teacher'. Perhaps the discussion could be couched in terms of suggestions for a student on how to become a good teacher.

Discussions with pupils on such a topic must obviously be handled very carefully and only with the agreement of any teachers who are involved.

Follow-up: Such information can be interesting in two ways:

1 It reveals something of the young people's expectations of what it is to be a good 'teacher'.

2 It can contribute to reflection on our own effectiveness as teachers and in implementing our values, aims and commitments. It could also lead to a reconsideration of those values, aims and commitments.

The personal development of pupils implies that they take increasing responsibility and exercise more autonomy as learners. Indeed, extensive classroom research (Rudduck and Flutter, 2004, Reading 1.3; Rudduck and McIntyre, 2007, **Research Briefing** on p. 17) has shown that authentic consultation with pupils about teaching and learning is extremely worthwhile. It facilitates the development of relationships (see Chapter 6) and improves learning because of the higher quality feedback loops which are created (see Chapter 13). Such processes call for a degree of managed power-sharing between teachers and pupils. The most significant manifestation of pupil recognition lies in 'making visible' the learning objectives and success criteria which are in play. Hattie (2009, 2012, Reading 4.6), summarising one of the largest-ever international syntheses of research, put this in terms of two high level 'big ideas' which teachers should certainly adopt if they want to maximise effectiveness:

- I see learning through the eyes of my students
- I help students to become their own teachers.

Authentic consultation, engagement and transparency with pupils may seem risky for some teachers, since it involves opening up spaces and issues which might be contested. Ultimately however, understanding *has* to be constructed by learners so that, sooner or later, they simply have to take control of their learning. A reflective teacher embraces and constructively manages this process.

2.3 Pupil cultures

So far the focus has been on the teacher, the pupil and their mutual perceptions. However, it is most important to remember that, although the teacher is a central figure, classrooms are a meeting place for many children and young people – indeed, Jackson (1968, Reading 6.1) referred to 'the crowd' as being a salient feature of classroom life. How children learn to cope with being one of a crowd and how they relate to each other is of consequence. This can affect how well the children settle in the class socially, and, in turn, may affect their learning. There is, thus, a social dimension to classroom life.

Pupil culture has been described by Davies (1982, p. 33) as the result of children 'constructing their own reality with each other' and 'making sense of and developing strategies to cope with the adult world'. It thus reflects the children's collective perspectives and actions, many of which can be interpreted as defensive responses to adults.

Children's place is, therefore, an important means by which they can identify with each other, establish themselves as members of a group, try out different roles and begin to develop independence and responsibility. Young children often make friends with those who are immediately accessible and with whom they share common experiences (Rubin, 1980). Typically, their friends are children who live close by, who are in their class or who are the children of their parents' friends. When peer groups begin to form, each individual is likely to have to establish their membership of the group in a number of ways. For example, each member may be expected to contribute and conform to the norms which

Research Briefing — Consulting pupils about teaching and learning

TLRP's researcher/practitioner network on consulting pupils, led by Jean Rudduck, was influential in respect of policy on personalised learning. For example, 'pupil voice' was identified as enabling children to 'take ownership of their learning' and thus develop citizenship and a positive learning disposition. As the *2020 Vision* team put it in recommending effective pedagogies:

> Pupils are more likely to be engaged with the curriculum they are offered if they believe it is relevant and if they are given opportunities to take ownership of their learning. (DfES 2006, p. 26)

Many hundreds of teachers worked in Jean Rudduck's networks. They developed strategies for consulting pupils about teaching and learning in the classroom and for building pupil consultation into the organisation of the school. They found that pupil consultation on everyday, practical issues enhanced pupil self-esteem and also gradually changed the ways teaching and learning was thought about across the whole school. The figure below represents this impact.

PUPIL CONSULTATION AND PARTICIPATION

Yields practical agenda   Strengthens pupil self-esteem

ENHANCED COMMITMENT TO LEARNING AND SCHOOL

sustained by
transformation of teachers' knowledge of pupils
(greater awareness of their capacity for constructive analysis)

transformation of pedagogic and organisational practices

transformation of teacher-pupil relationships *(from passive to oppositional to more active and collaborative)*

Key findings:	Implications:
For pupils: Being consulted produces a stronger sense of engagement with learning, an enhanced sense of agency and of self as learner.	If pupils feel that they are respected in school, then they are more likely to commit themselves to learning.
For teachers: Consulting pupils leads to deeper insights into children's abilities and learning preferences, leading to more responsive teaching and giving greater responsibility to pupils individually and as a group.	Pupils' accounts of what helps and what hinders them in learning can provide a practical agenda for improving teaching and learning.
For schools: Consulting pupils strengthens school policy and priority development by including pupils in substantive rather than marginal or tokenistic ways.	Pupil testimony can feed powerfully into whole school policy and planning – where this is enabled to happen.
For national policy: Pupil engagement suggests new insights and practical tools for school self-evaluation, strategic planning and improvement.	Classroom and school practice engaging pupils can provide the basis for further systematic inquiry and policy development.

The U.N. Convention on the Rights of the Child (1989) included children's right to be heard as one of its four basic principles. It is seen as integral to the Citizenship curriculum and lifelong learning. How to listen and learn, as well as to teach and lead, is the challenge for teachers, schools and their communities.

Further information:
Rudduck, J., Arnot, M., Demetriou, H., Flutter, J., MacBeath, J., McIntyre, D., Myers, K., Pedder, D., Wang, B., Fielding, M., Bragg, S. and Reay, D. (2005) *Consulting Pupils about Teaching and Learning*. TLRP Research Briefing, No 5. Available at **www.tlrp.org/pub** (accessed 18 November 2013).
Rudduck, J. and McIntyre, D. (2007) *Improving Learning through Consulting Pupils*. TLRP Improving Learning series. London: Routledge.
This TLRP network was directed from the University of Cambridge.

Figure 1.2 Year 7
friendship groups

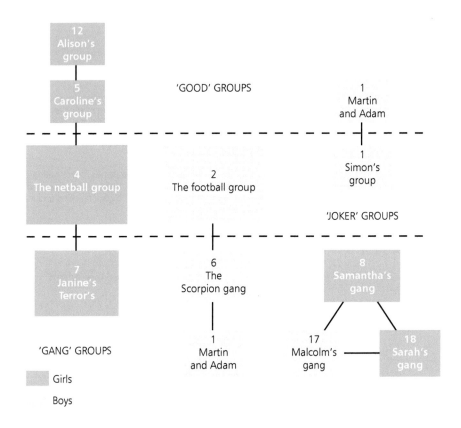

Figure 1.3
Perspectives of
Year 7 friendship
groups

	... good groups are ...	... joker groups are ...	... gang groups are ...
Good groups think ...	Sensible, quiet, honest, rare and friendly.	Nice, but they show off too much.	Stupid, rough, unfair, unkind, troublemakers.
Joker groups think ...	Quiet, boring, and they just wander about.	Good fun, friendly and sensible, good to play with.	Rough, thick, bossy, disgusting, silly, stupid babies, and they cause trouble.
Gang groups think ...	Goody-goodies, pathetic, soft, and they just talk and do what they're told.	Big-heads and show-offs, posh, rubbish.	(Own gang) great, fantastic, rough and tough. (Other gangs) cocky, rubbish, soft, stupid, thick, smelly, horrible, daft.

are shared by the group: for example, liking similar games, toys, television programmes; supporting the same football team or pop group; liking the same fashions. Group members will also be expected to be loyal to each other, 'stand up for their mates', play together and share things. For example, sociometric and interview data with Year 7 pupils produced the analysis in Figure 1.2 and the often lively perspectives on each other which are summarised in Figure 1.3. Pupil cultures do throw up challenges for teachers, but it is better to try to understand them than to pretend they do not exist.

Status is important in peer culture. As children and young people establish their individual identities among their peers, each will be valued in particular ways. For young children this value may be based on prowess in the playground in activities such as skipping, dancing, chasing or football as well having access to fashionable toys, clothes or activities. For secondary students, status may be earned through success at sport or even schoolwork for some. However, style is likely to be much more significant – such as wearing designer clothes, embracing fashionable music and even exploiting emergent sexuality.

The identities which students develop have serious implications for us as teachers because they often lead to significant differentiation as schools try to meet the apparent needs of particular student groups. Processes of differentiation start during the early years at school, perhaps with the practical organisation of group work, and have been found to increase during student's school lives (Breakwell, 1986; Pollard, 1996; Ireson and Hallam, 2001, Reading 15.4). Pupil responses may eventually lead to a polarisation of proschool and antischool cultures (Lacey, 1970) and this has been cited as of particular significance in the underachievement of boys, when to 'be good' in school is considered 'uncool' (Raphael Reed, 1996; Evans, 2007). Self-image and status within a peer group thus has significant consequences for development during the school years – and these often last into adult lives. This is further discussed in Chapter 15.

One particular issue which should be watched for, in relation to pupils' relationships with each other, is that of bullying (Elliott, 2002, Tattum and Lane, 1989, Robinson et al., 1995). This is an unacceptable aspect of young people's culture and often reflects both its tendency to emphasise conformity and its concern with status – as well as, frequently, the relative insecurity of the perpetrators. Thus children who are different in some way – new to school, overweight, or possibly have an unusual accent or simply a different culture – are picked on physically and verbally and are excluded by other pupils as their unacceptability for cultural membership is asserted or as a pecking order is maintained. In its worst forms this can degenerate into overt racism (Richardson and Miles, 2008), homophobia (DePalma and Atkinson, 2008) or sexual harassment (Lees, 1993).

Adult intervention must be firm, but also needs to be sensitive to the realities of the social situation. Everyone needs friends and to feel accepted by others. Very often then, the teacher's task is to stop the bullying whilst facilitating the entry of the 'victim' into an appropriate niche within the pupil cultures of the school (Cowie and Wallace, 2000). Complex issues are raised on which new teachers should seek advice from more experienced colleagues.

2.4 Understanding pupil needs

Just as we need to consider our personal identities and circumstances as teachers, so a similar kind of 'biographical' knowledge about each child is valuable in understanding them as individual people and as learners. We are likely to find that many characteristics are shared in common, but others will be more unique and individual. More 'personalised' forms of provision can thus be made (Department for Education and Skills (DfES), 2004b).

Many schools collect basic information about each child's medical history and educational progress, but such records, although sometimes helpful, rarely convey an impression of the 'whole child'. As a move in this direction, profiles, portfolios or 'records of achievement' used to be commonplace in schools. Increasingly, however, records tend to focus more narrowly on each child's progress and targets achieved in different subject areas, supplemented perhaps with examples of their work at different ages. However, they may be enhanced by including information about hobbies and interests, abilities and tastes and materials which reflect each pupil's social attitudes, behaviour, out of school achievements and family context. Students may also participate in decisions about what to include. Accessing such information can be done through a 'knowledge exchange' between home and school, as is modelled in the 'Home–school Knowledge Exchange' project (Feiler et al., 2007; Winter et al., 2009, see the **Research Briefing** on p. 107).

Such records may provide an excellent starting point for understanding each individual learner, in terms of their material, social and cultural circumstances as well as their development in school. They thus provide one sort of context for understanding children and young people in school. However, such records cannot replace the awareness which will come from personal contacts with pupils and, where appropriate, with their parents.

Reflective activity 1.6

Aim: To begin to construct a biographical understanding of a pupil.

Evidence and reflection:

- Take an interest in a pupil's general behaviour inside and outside the classroom. Consider how they interact with other pupils and how they tackle learning tasks.
- Present open-ended opportunities where the child can write, draw, talk or otherwise communicate about herself or himself. Discussions about friends, experiences, family or about favourite books or TV characters can be revealing. Make notes.
- If possible, discuss the pupil with parents and other teachers.
- Discuss the pupil's own perception of their individual needs with them.
- Summarise what you have learned.

Follow-up: Consider what implications your new understanding has for shaping the educational provision that is appropriate for the young person concerned.

It is often argued that the 'needs' of the learner should be seen as the starting point for teaching and learning policies. However, the notion of appropriate needs is not straightforward, since it begs questions about prior aims, and judgements about what is worthwhile (Barrow, 1984). Nevertheless, it may be valuable for us as reflective teachers to articulate what we see as the basic 'needs' of the learners to whom we commit ourselves.

The classic work of Maslow (1954) is interesting here, since he linked the drive to have needs met with motivation in learning. Maslow proposed a hierarchy of basic needs, and proposed that the lower level order of needs must be met before people could fulfil higher level needs. This argument is represented as a pyramid.

5 Self-actualisation needs

4 Esteem needs

3 Belongingness and love needs

2 Safety needs

1 Physiological needs

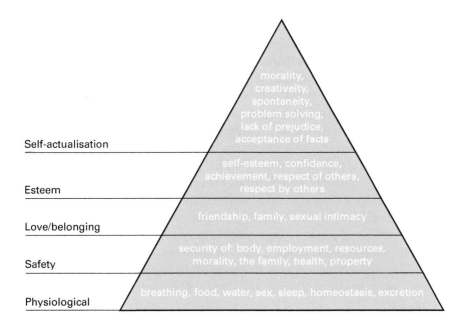

Figure 1.4
Maslow's hierarchy of needs

The lowest level (1) expresses our primary biological need for food, shelter, oxygen, water, etc. The second level (2) encompasses the need for security and freedom from anxiety. The third level (3) includes the need to feel that one belongs and to be loved and be able to love in return. The fourth level (4) addresses the need for prestige and status, to be successful and to feel good about oneself. The final level (5) might be seen as the ultimate goal of education – the need of people to fulfil their potential.

Teachers and pupils are no different in their humanity, and they therefore share the needs which each of these elements represent. To learn, and to work at teaching, physiological needs are basic – and we will explore one dimension of this in Chapter 8 when considering the physical qualities of classroom learning environments. More significantly, if a pupil is hungry or distressed, teaching and learning is unlikely to be

Expert question

Empowerment: is our pedagogic repertoire successful in enhancing wellbeing, learning disposition, capabilities and agency?

This question contributes to a conceptual framework representing enduring issues and teacher expertise (see Chapter 16). The empowerment of young people through teaching is one of the educational outcomes to which the book as a whole contributes.

effective. Successful schools and classrooms enable both teachers and pupils to feel safe, respected and valued. The experience of being in school thus supports developing towards mutual self-actualisation. We can all take pleasure from success.

2.5 Examining our perceptions of pupils

In the sections above, we have considered pupils' views of themselves, of teachers and of school. We have reviewed peer cultures and begun to understand the hierarchy of learner needs. How then, does this influence the expectations which we ourselves have about 'pupils'? (Jones, 2009, Reading 1.5)

All of us are likely to have views about what we would like children and young people to be like as pupils – polite, attentive, cooperative, hard-working, bright? And we also have ideas about the characteristics which may be less favoured. These conceptions tend to relate to the practical challenges of doing the job in the classroom. However, it has been found that teacher judgements are affected by the gender, ethnicity, or social class of the pupils and even by their names (Meighan and Siraj-Blatchford, 1981). If, as teachers, we hold such preconceptions without reflecting on them, it can result in treating particular individuals or groups of pupils in ways which may not be fair or just. When the pupils then respond, original preconceptions may be reinforced. Labelling, or stereotyping, can thus lead to a phenomenon known as the 'self-fulfilling prophecy' and thus result in considerable social injustices (Brophy and Good, 1974; Nash, 1976; Mortimore et al.,

1988; Hart, Dixon, Drummond and McIntyre, 2004, Reading 1.4). This is particularly the case if patterns emerge in official assessment outcomes (Stobart, 2008, Reading 13.6; Filer, 2000).

As reflective teachers, we must focus on supporting and enhancing the achievement of *all* pupils in our care. We therefore need to occasionally step back from our initial or routine reactions to pupils, and interrogate our conscious or unconscious processes of categorisation (see also Chapter 15, Section 1). For instance:

1   How does the school or classroom organisation differentiate between pupils, and what are the implications of this for teachers and pupils?

2   How do we personally acknowledge, categorise and label the pupils we work with?

3   How can we think about and work with pupils, moving beyond the labels?

Of course, teachers do have to develop ways of understanding, organising and grouping pupils in order to respond effectively to their educational needs. Within the classroom however, this should be done with regard for the purposes of each particular situation or learning activity (see Chapter 15 for extensive discussion of inclusive practice). An inflexible form of classroom organisation is almost bound to disadvantage some students unnecessarily.

Reflective activity 1.7

Aim To understand our perceptions of 'pupils'.

Evidence and reflection First, without referring to the register or any lists, write down the names of the pupils in your class or tutor group. Note which order you have listed them in and which names you found hard to remember. What does the order tell you about which students are more memorable than others, and for what reasons?

Second, use your complete class list to generate the 'personal constructs' which you employ. To do this, look at each adjacent pair of names and write down the word that you think indicates how those two pupils are most alike. Then write down another word which shows how they are most different.

When you have done this with each pair, review the characteristics that you have identified. What does this suggest to you about the concepts through which you distinguish children? What additional qualities do the children have which these constructs do not seem to reflect and which perhaps you do not use?

Extension Consider, perhaps with a colleague, the results of this activity and note any patterns that might exist: for example whether some of your ideas relate more to boys than girls, or to children from different class, ethnicity or religious backgrounds. There may be some constructs that relate to such things as academic ability, physical attributes or behaviour towards teachers or other children. How might this be problematic for the identities of those pupils within your class, or for your expectations of them as learners?

Reflecting on our own thinking and practices helps us to understand the complexity of the classroom choices and decisions that are faced routinely every day. It helps us to ensure that future actions can be justified; that we continue to be professionally accountable.

There are various 'tools' available to support reflective practice. One helpful one is Hart's *Framework for Innovative Thinking* (2000). The essence of this framework is that it invites us to break down, or interrupt, our routine thinking and to try new ideas. The latter are framed in constructive, enabling and inclusive ways. Figure 1.5 summarises Hart's 'five moves', and Reflective activity 1.8 invites us to try this out.

Figure 1.5 A framework for innovative thinking (adapted from Hart, 2000)

Five moves for innovative thinking	
Making connections	This move involves exploring how the specific characteristics of the child's response might be connected to features of the immediate and wider learning environment.
Contradicting	This move involves questioning the assumptions underlying a given interpretation by searching out a plausible alternative interpretation which casts the meaning of the situation in a new light. This helps to tease out the norms and expectations underlying the original interpretation so that it can be re-examined.
Taking a child's eye view	This move involves trying to enter the child's frame of reference and to see the meaning and logic of the child's response from the child's perspective.
Noting the impact of feelings	This move involves examining the part that our own feelings play in the meaning that we bestow on the situation and in leading us to a particular interpretation.
Postponing judgement in order to find out more	This move involves recognising that we may lack information or expertise needed to have confidence in our judgements. It involves holding back from further analysis and the attempt to arrive at judgements about the child's needs while we take steps to acquire further information.

Reflective activity 1.8

Aim: To review the learning of a pupil in the light of Susan Hart's Framework for Innovative Thinking.

Evidence and reflection: Think of a child or young person who is puzzling you, and review an example of their learning activities which surprised you or which you thought they might have done better.

Write a brief account of what happened.

Now use Hart's framework to reflect on what happened. Does it help in illuminating possible interpretations? What more would it be helpful to know? How might you find this out?

Extension: Share what you have written with a colleague who also knows the child or young person. How does their understanding match or contrast with yours? Why do you think this is? What teaching strategies seem most appropriate for the future?

3 Learning and teaching through life

Children and adults, pupils and teachers, occupy particular stages and roles through the lifecourse. We all pass through infancy, childhood and adolescence before establishing ourselves as young adults. We then, often imperceptibly, progress into 'middle age' (with its rather elastic definition) and on towards retirement. 'Old age' then beckons – with even more learning challenges. In one sense then, although relevant historic periods generate particular circumstances, we already know something of our pupils, for we once inhabited that role too. And although we may look upon children and young people as 'in need of a good education' it is upon them that we will one day come to depend.

This section draws on our common experience to acknowledge and empathise with processes of development, becoming and contributing over time.

3.1 Pupil development and career

There are many different theories and perspectives on what the years from birth to age 16 mean in our society.

We can start by acknowledging that 'childhood' and 'adolescence' are social constructions. For example, during particular periods of history and in different parts of the world, young people are considered to have 'grown up' sufficiently to assume responsibilities at widely varying ages (Aries, 1960; Boas, 1966; James and Prout, 1997; James and James, 2004). Indeed, for some, contemporary western childhood is seen as reflecting adult priorities and ambitions (Moss and Petrie, 2002) or adult sentiment and nostalgia (Gillis, 1997).

Thus whilst 'childhood' appears as a cultural feature of many societies, particularly in the western world, it is also possible to characterise young people simply as 'young people', rather than as 'children'. This suggestion is intended to disrupt the idea of children as *becoming* – with a focus on what the child is 'not yet'. On this argument, children and young people should thus be fully recognised as active and interactive agents (Jones, 2009, Reading 1.5; see also Mayall, 2002; Dahlberg, Moss and Pence, 1999) and as participants in society *during* childhood. Early phases of life have intrinsic value in themselves, not simply as preparations for future stages. This sort of approach can be illustrated by longitudinal studies of pupil learning and careers through primary and secondary school (Warin, 2010; Pollard and Filer, 1996, 1999, 2007, Reading 1.2). These sources provide detailed case studies of individual pupils as they develop through schooling, and document the ways in which relationships with family, friends and successive teachers influence the learning outcomes and the emergent identities of each child (see Figure 1.6).

Of course, there are extremely significant physiological changes too during infancy, childhood and adolescence. As we will see in Chapter 2, normal biological development is sequential. It follows that particular forms of educational provision are appropriate for children of different ages (a point which ambitious policymakers sometimes neglect). For example, it is implausible to require children to write until their fine motor control has

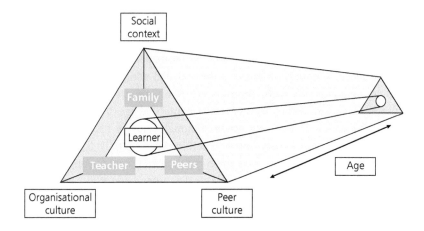

Figure 1.6 Social influences on learners through a school career

begun to develop. It is then possible to go with the flow of development to extend and refine that capability. This way of thinking is the source of the concept of 'readiness to learn', and has been applied in many domains. The problem of course, is that you might wait so long that teaching is neglected and children thus become disadvantaged. As with so many things in education, we need balanced judgement in the light of important ideas which pull in slightly different directions.

The physiological changes associated with puberty are many, and happen at different rates and stages. Such changes, whether early or late, can lead to a loss of self-confidence – for example, when a boy of 15 has not yet reached his growth spurt or broken voice, and still looks like a child whilst his peers look like young men. The scale and rate of physical changes in adolescence can sometimes lead to tiredness, clumsiness, moodiness and depression. It can also be a great boost to confidence, of course.

Neuroscientists are contributing more and more to our understanding of how the brain develops and functions and this is again explored in Chapter 2. For the moment, we can simply note that whilst infancy appears to be particularly significant, later development through childhood and adolescence is also extremely important. Cognitive capacity is enhanced through use, and schooling is the primary source of structured experience for most young people.

Other psychological features of childhood and adolescence relate to changes in cognition. Whilst the thinking of children tends to be relatively bounded by direct experience, older children and young people gradually become more sophisticated in their manipulation of abstract concepts and complex thought (Inhelder and Piaget, 1958). They develop the ability to 'de-centre' by empathising with others and can evaluate moral and ethical dilemmas (Kohlberg, 1976). Emotions and emotional states also play an important role in personal development – whether of children (Hyland, 2011) or even in teacher education (Shoffner, 2009).

All teachers thus have to consider and juggle with the developmental needs of learners in relation to curricular requirements and expectations.

It is now possible to see the consequences of these social and developmental factors within our education systems over time. The National Child Development Study (NCDS)

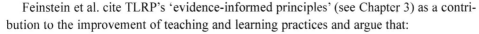

Mediating mechanisms

Education →
- Skills and competencies
- Social interactions
- Qualifications

→ **Wider benefits: Social productivity**
- Individual health and wellbeing
- Family functioning
- Community cohesion and flourishing
- Social cohesion, economic growth and equality

Figure 1.7
Mediating mechanisms for achievement of the wider benefits of learning (Feinstein, Vorhaus and Sabates, 2008)

has been following the lives of around 17,000 people born in Britain in one week in 1958 (see *Now We Are 50*, Elliot and Vaitilingam, 2008). Such longitudinal data has enabled analysis of the long-term consequences of early childhood and school experiences and analysis has begun to identify factors that reinforce positive and negative developments in people's lives. Other cohort studies have been established which will extend these analyses.

Feinstein, Vorhaus and Sabates (2008, Reading 1.6) draw on such studies in a Government Foresight Study on 'learning through life'. They note that there are significant 'economic returns' to investment in education but also that 'intrinsic motivations are also important in individual decision-making' (p. 23). In an important analysis of the 'wider benefits of learning' they demonstrate how education fosters skills, confidence and qualifications which lead to many other benefits in later life and across society (see Figure 1.7).

Feinstein et al. cite TLRP's 'evidence-informed principles' (see Chapter 3) as a contribution to the improvement of teaching and learning practices and argue that:

> Educational systems have a crucial role in equipping children and adults to withstand the economic, cultural and technological challenges they face in an increasingly globalised world. The fast pace of new technological developments and the intensification of economic pressures mean that the technical and academic skills of the working population are crucial for the UK economy. However, so are features of personal development such as resilience, self-regulation, a positive sense of self, and personal and social identity. The capability of individuals to function as civic agents with notions of personal responsibility, tolerance and respect depends on these wider features of identity which are strongly influenced by interactions with others in schools, workplaces, communities, neighbourhoods and through the media and other channels. (Feinstein, Vorhaus and Sabates, 2008, p. 35)

The implication of such research and of our brief consideration of pupil development and career in schools is to draw attention to the responsibility on us as teachers. Quite simply, our work contributes in significant ways to our national economy and cultures and, not least, to the future wellbeing of the country's citizens. Although daunting, this task echoes with the ambitions voiced by the trainee teachers discussed at the beginning of this chapter. Moreover, their commitment serves to remind

Expert question

Consequence: do assessment outcomes lead towards recognised qualifications and a confident sense of personal identity?

This question contributes to a conceptual framework representing enduring issues and teacher expertise (see Chapter 16).

us not just of the economic reasons for this endeavor, but also the moral. To participate in the process of education is to participate in civil society. As we engage children and young people in new learning, so we challenge ourselves, as reflective practitioners, to create new possibilities for all our futures.

3.2 Teacher development and career

Membership of the teaching profession represents a stage in the personal trajectory through life of each of us. For some, teaching will offer a long-term career. For others, our time as a teacher may be relatively brief, or even transitory. However, for all qualified teachers, official certification in that role affirms good knowledge of appropriate subject matter, understanding of learners and learning in school settings, and an important array of personal qualities. New teachers, in other words, are selected because of the competence they demonstrate and for the potential contributions which are anticipated.

The issues discussed above in relation to pupils also all apply again, albeit at different stages of life. Thus social relations, identity and self-confidence complement physical, psychological and neurological maturity to offer social, affective and cognitive capability. We are simply the children of yesteryear, who have now grown up.

As we saw in Section 1.2 above, Huberman (1993) proposed five stages of teacher development – career entry, stabilisation, experimentation, conservatism and disengagement. Day and Gu (2010) took this further in *The New Lives of Teachers* by linking the challenges of professional development with particular life and work scenarios. They argue that:

> The relative success with which teachers manage various personal, work and external policy challenges is a key factor in the satisfaction, commitment, well-being and effectiveness of teachers. The influences of school leadership, culture, colleagues and conditions are also profound, and relate directly to teacher retention and the work-life balance agenda. (Day and Gu, 2010, prelim, see also Reading 1.1)

The social influences on teachers through a professional career are thus not dissimilar to those which affect pupils as they progress through schooling. We all have basic needs which must be satisfied to create conditions for success. It is noticeable that, just as positive learning dispositions and resilience to new challenges are crucial to pupil success (see Claxton, 1999, Reading 2.9), so teacher commitment and resilience are essential to effectiveness over the whole of a career.

The finding in Day et al.'s (2006) study that: 'teachers do not necessarily become more effective over time' is challenging for us to think about. It draws attention to our own professional vulnerabilities and suggests that aspiration, good intentions or values are not enough. We also need to reflect on our practices, using evidence of various sorts to challenge ourselves in continuous cycles of improvement (see Chapter 3).

The notion 'warranted practice' has been used to emphasise the importance of progressive development in the work of teachers (Richardson, 1998). Ruthven (2005) used the term to describe the process teachers engage in to ensure continual improvement of provision, as well as meeting the demands of professional accountability. He suggests that educational reform depends on deeper understandings and flexible thinking about practice. For Ruthven, the term 'warranted' is used in two important senses. First, it provides reasoned grounds for the practice as intended; and second, it suggests that the practice as implemented in a particular setting is indeed likely to succeed in its aims. This perspective does not offer a 'cook book' prescription of 'what works', because teacher decision-making is seen as being contextual, dynamic and responsive to the needs of learners in each particular setting.

> **Expert question**
>
> **Warrant:** are our teaching strategies evidence-informed, convincing and justifiable to stakeholders?
>
> This question contributes to a conceptual framework underpinning professional expertise (see Chapter 16).

Our commitment to professionalism through a teaching career is expressed through our values, identities, and work as teachers. However, professionalism also needs to be under-pinned by processes which enable us to routinely review and improve our own practices (see Chapter 3).

Conclusion

This chapter celebrates the idealism and moral purpose of teachers, but also recognises the personal and professional challenges. It reviews the significant array of factors shaping pupil's lives, and suggests how such knowledge may be used to support effective teaching and learning. Finally, it describes the trajectories through life of pupils and teachers, and acknowledges our common humanity.

We saw that the process of reflecting on our aims and values as teachers can help us in developing a realistic personal *and* professional identity. Further, it was suggested that, by understanding the many influences on our teaching more explicitly, we can identify where we are being most successful and perhaps where values and intention, evidence and practice do not match as well as they might.

It was suggested that, by maintaining awareness of the cultures of children and young people, their views of us as teachers and their perspectives on themselves and each other, we are better able to take account of their needs when developing opportunities for learning. We do however need to keep under scrutiny the concepts which we ourselves use to understand pupils.

Finally, we considered the significance of teaching and learning in the lifecourse of pupils, and for ourselves.

Key readings

A classic introduction to the delights and challenges of teaching is:

> Richardson, R. (1990) *Daring to be a Teacher.* Stoke-on-Trent: Trentham Books.

A sensitive account of the values and commitment of primary school teachers, of relevance to secondary, is:

> Nias, J. (1989) *Primary Teachers Talking: a Study of Teaching at Work.* London: Routledge.

For an appreciative guide to being a teacher from a secondary perspective, of relevance to primary, see:

> Turbull, J. (2007) *9 Habits of Highly Effective Teachers. A Practical Guide to Empowerment.* London: Continuum.

On teacher development and commitment through careers and lives, the classic account is Huberman's. We also have excellent contemporary work from Day and Gu.

> Huberman, M. (1993) *The Lives of Teachers.* London: Cassell.
> Day, C. and Gu, Q. (2010) *The New Lives of Teachers.* London: Routledge. (see also Reading 1.1)

For a thorough exploration of how student teachers learn from the expertise of practising teachers, see:

> Hagger, H. and McIntyre, D. (2006) *Learning Teaching from Teachers – Realizing the Potential of School-Based Teacher Education.* Maidenhead: Open University Press.

There are many interesting books on children's culture, friendships and perspectives in primary and secondary schools. Devine promotes primary pupils 'speaking for themselves', whilst Rudduck and McIntyre summarise extensive cross-sectoral work on 'pupil consultation':

> Devine, D. (2003) *Children, Power and Schooling. The Social Structuring of Childhood in the Primary School.* Stoke-on-Trent: Trentham.
> Rudduck, J. and McIntyre, D. (2007) *Improving Learning Through Consulting Pupils.* London: Routledge. (see also Reading 1.3)

For detailed case studies of children's developing identities and careers through schooling, see:

> Pollard, A. and Filer, A. (1999) *The Social World of Pupil Career: Strategic Biographies through Primary School.* London: Cassell. (see Reading 1.2)

And for one of many analyses of secondary school experiences see:

Smyth, J. and McInerney, P. (2012) *From Silent Witnesses to Active Agents: Student Voice in Re-engaging with Learning.* New York: Peter Lang.

An important book which challenges all determinist ideas about 'ability' is:

Hart, S., Dixon, A., Drummond, M-J. and McIntyre, D. (2004) *Learning Without Limits.* Maidenhead: Open University Press. (see Reading 1.4)

The long-term consequences of schooling are quantified in:

Feinstein, L., Vorhaus, J., and Sabates, R. (2008) *Learning Through Life: Future Challenges.* Foresight Mental Capital and Wellbeing Project. London: The Government Office for Science. (Reading 1.6)

For a foretaste of the implication of the arguments in this chapter, try the readings in Chapter 17 of Readings for Reflective Teaching in Schools – such as:

Power, S. (2008) 'The imaginative professional', in Cunningham, B. (ed.) *Exploring Professionalism.* London: IOE Press. (Reading 17.5)

reflectiveteaching.co.uk offers additional professional resources for this chapter. These include *Further Reading, Reflective Activities,* useful *Web Links* and *Download Facilities* for diagrams, figures, checklists and activities.

Learning

How can we understand learner development?

2

Introduction

Learning can be considered as the process by which people acquire, understand, apply and extend knowledge, concepts, skills and attitudes. Children and young people also discover their feelings towards themselves, towards each other and towards learning itself. Learning is thus a combination of cognitive, social and affective elements. The teacher's recognition of what learners bring to their education is crucial.

TLRP principles

Three principles are of particular relevance to this chapter on learning:

Effective teaching and learning recognises the importance of prior experience and learning. Teaching and learning should take account of what the learner knows already in order to plan their next steps. This includes building on prior learning but also taking account of the personal and cultural experiences of different groups of learners. (Principle 3)

Effective teaching and learning promotes the active engagement of the learner. A chief goal of teaching and learning should be the promotion of learners' independence and autonomy. This involves acquiring a repertoire of learning strategies and practices, developing positive attitudes towards learning, and confidence in oneself as a good learner. (Principle 6)

Effective teaching and learning recognises the significance of informal learning. Informal learning, such as learning out of school, should be recognised as at least as significant as formal learning and should therefore be valued and used appropriately in formal processes. (Principle 8)

See Chapter 4

How we understand children and their learning affect the choices that teachers make, day by day, encounter by encounter in the classroom. There is a tendency to attribute differences between children's learning and attainments to deficits in the young people themselves. However, a new mindset is turning this deficit approach around, enabling teachers to take a 'credit approach', seeing all children as rich, strong, powerful learners, as long as conducive classroom conditions and compelling opportunities for learning are provided (see Hart et al., 2004; Swann et al. 2012, Reading 1.4). Reflective teachers taking the credit approach focus on what pupils can do, not on what they cannot do. They are more interested in young people's desire to understand than in gaps in their knowledge. If we see all learners as powerful then we are inescapably committed to the educability of every child, and to building and using our professional expertise to seek, understand and remove barriers to learning.

In this chapter we focus first on *processes of learning*, and introduce three perspectives which have particularly influenced education – behaviourism, constructivism and social constructivism. We then consider the classic debate about the relative roles of *'nature' and 'nurture'* in education through a review of biological, social and cultural factors – whilst emphasising the *agency* of learners and teachers.

1 Learning processes

Learning is a fascinating, but highly complex, aspect of human activity. In psychology, a distinction is often made between cognitive and affective development – contrasts being drawn between thought and feeling; rationality and emotion; and even some forms of knowledge and understanding. There are interesting interconnections of course – with a recent neuroscientific analysis entitled 'we feel, therefore we learn' (Immordino-Yang and Damasio, 2007, Reading 6.2). Indeed, attention, memory, decision-making and other cognitive capabilities are strongly influenced by affective disposition and feelings. The latter respond to characteristics of learning environments – such as homes, classrooms and even examination halls, as many of us will recognise.

Of course, humans learned for many thousands of years before anyone thought that a 'curriculum' and 'schooling' were necessary. Indeed, at its simplest, learning can be seen as the product of a continuous interaction between *development* and *experience* through life (Blyth, 1984, Figure 2.1). The professional teacher's job is to understand the process as well as possible and to offer children the benefit of that understanding.

For centuries, philosophers and psychologists have worked to analyse learning. The result is that there are many alternative theories which attempt to describe the process. We have simplified this complex field by identifying just three theories of learning which have been of particular influence on teaching and learning in schools. Each has merit in highlighting particular dimensions of learning.

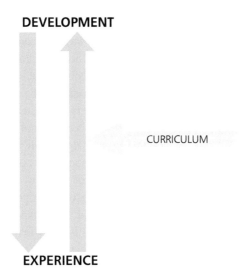

DEVELOPMENT

CURRICULUM

EXPERIENCE

Figure 2.1
Development, experience and curriculum

1.1 Behaviourism

This theory suggests that living creatures, animal or human, learn by building up associations or 'bonds' between their experience, their thinking and their behaviour. Thus, as long ago as 1911, Thorndike formulated two principles. First, the 'law of effect':

The greater the satisfaction or discomfort, the greater the strengthening or weakening of the bond.

Second, the 'law of exercise': the relationship between the frequency of the response and learning:

The probability of a response occurring in a given situation increases with the number of times that response has occurred in that situation in the past.

Thorndike confidently claimed that these 'laws' emerged clearly from 'every series of experiments on animal learning and in the entire history of the management of human affairs' (Thorndike, 1911, p. 244).

A variety of versions of behaviourism were developed and provided the dominant perspective on learning until the 1960s. Perhaps the most significant of these psychologists was Skinner (e.g. 1968, see Reading 2.1) who, through his work with animals, developed a sophisticated theory of the role in learning of stimulus, response, reinforcement and consequence.

The influence of behaviourist theory in education has been immense because, in the early part of the twentieth century, it provided the foundations of work on a 'science of teaching' based on whole-class, didactic approaches through which knowledge and skills were to be taught. The 'law of effect' was reflected in elaborate systems and rituals for the reinforcement of correct pupil responses. The 'law of exercise' was reflected in an emphasis on practice and drill.

Behaviourist learning theory casts the learner in a relatively passive role, leaving the selection, pacing and evaluation of learning activity to the teacher. Subject expertise can thus be transmitted in a coherent, ordered and logical way, and control of the class tends to be tight – because pupils are often required to listen. There is a problem though in whether such teaching actually connects with the learner's existing understanding.

Teaching which has been influenced by behaviourism can be seen in all schools. The importance of reinforcing children's work and effort is well established, and reflects the work of Skinner (e.g. 1953) in demonstrating the limited value of punishment as a means of supporting learning. The use of practice tasks is also well established, particularly for teaching aspects of the core curriculum such as numerical computation, spelling and writing, and this type of work reflects the influence of the 'law of exercise'. The use of teacher-controlled explanation and of question-and-answer routines are important parts of any teacher's pedagogic repertoire. They will be found, for instance, when new topics are being introduced and when taking stock of achievements. The idea of building progressive steps in learning (e.g. Gagné, 1965) is, of course, directly reflected in the organisation of the curriculum into 'stages' and 'levels'. Behaviourism has also been influential in work with children who experience emotional and behavioural difficulties (EBD), achieving significant success through reinforcement of appropriate actions (Wheldall, 1991).

Figure 2.2 represents the roles of children and adult in behaviourist-influenced teaching and learning processes.

Some particular points could be noted. First, there is a high degree of adult control in the process; deciding on the subject matter, providing instruction, pacing the lesson,

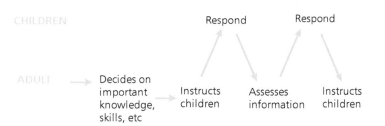

Figure 2.2
A behaviourist
model of roles
in the teaching–
learning process

correcting, assessing and reinforcing pupil responses. In principle, this makes it relatively easy for teacher expositions and explanations to be logical, coherent, linear and progressive as subject matter or skills are introduced to the pupils. However, there are also some difficulties with teaching in this way. The most important is the question of connecting with the existing understanding of the learner. In this respect, the strength of subject exposition can also be a weakness if a pupil does not recognise subject divisions as being relevant to daily experiences (see Chapter 9, Section 3.3). Such a mismatch can reduce motivation and achievement as the child cannot use the knowledge which is offered to build a meaningful understanding. In such circumstances, learning tends to be superficial and fragmented. This problem may be made acute when large groups are taught because it is very hard for a teacher to 'pitch' the lesson appropriately for all learners.

The influence of behaviourism has been greatest on what are commonly termed 'traditional' teaching methods, and particularly those associated with whole-class, subject-based teaching. Careful programmes of reinforcement can meet particular needs – for example, some computer programmes are particularly successful at exploiting these strengths. However, behaviourism is often oversimplified as a 'training' model and some in the media even seem to expect behaviourist assumptions to be applied to almost all teaching. Perhaps it is popular because of its association with tight discipline and strong subject teaching. However, the responsibility of teachers is to interact with pupils so that they actually learn, not simply to expose them to subject matter and drill. Teaching methods based on behaviourism must, therefore, be fit for their purpose.

1.2 Constructivism

This theory suggests that people learn through an interaction between thinking and experience, and through the sequential development of more complex cognitive structures. The most influential constructivist theorist was Piaget (e.g. 1926, 1950, 1961; see Reading 2.2) whose ultimate goal was to create a 'genetic epistemology' – an understanding of the origin of knowledge derived from research into the interaction between people and their environment.

In Piaget's account, when children encounter a new experience they both 'accommodate' their existing thinking to it and 'assimilate' aspects of the experience. In so doing they move beyond one state of mental 'equilibration' and restructure their thoughts to create another. Gradually then, children come to construct more detailed, complex and accurate understandings of the phenomena they experience.

Piaget proposed that there are characteristic stages in the successive development of these mental structures, stages which are distinctive because of the type of 'cognitive operation' with which children and young people process their experience. These stages are:

- the sensorimotor stage (approximately birth–2 years)
- the preoperational stage (approximately 2–7 years)
- the concrete operations stage (approximately 7–12 years)
- the formal operations stage (approximately 12 years onwards).

In each of the first three stages the role of the child's direct experience is deemed to be crucial. It is only in the formal operations stage that abstract thinking is believed possible. In the sensorimotor and preoperational stages children are thought to be relatively individualistic and unable to work with others for long. Children are believed to behave rather like 'active scientists', enquiring, exploring and discovering as their curiosity and interests lead them to successive experiences. Play and practical experimentation have a crucial role in the assimilation process at each stage (Piaget, 1951) – a point that is particularly well understood by early childhood educators (Moyles, 2005; Parker-Rees, 1999).

 The influence of constructivist theory in primary education was considerable following the report of the Plowden Committee (Central Advisory Council for Education (CACE), 1967, see also Reading 9.4) in which it was suggested that:

> Piaget's explanation appears to fit the observed facts of children's learning more satisfactorily than any other. It is in accord with what is generally regarded as the most effective primary school practice, as it has been worked out empirically.
> (CACE, 1967, para. 522)

The image of the active child as the agent of his/her own learning runs through Plowden. 'Child-centred' teaching approaches, based on interpretations of Piaget's work, were adopted with enormous commitment by many teachers in the late 1960s and 1970s. Great imagination and care was put into providing varied and stimulating classroom environments from which children could derive challenging experiences (e.g. Marsh, 1970). Sophisticated forms of classroom organisation, such as the 'integrated day' (Brown and Precious, 1968; Walton, 1971) were introduced and developed to manage the problem of providing individual children with appropriate direct learning experiences. Despite these efforts, empirical research showed that constructivist methods were not greatly reflected in the actual practice of teachers of older primary children (Galton, Simon and Croll, 1980). Constructivism has always been particularly influential in work with younger pupils with whom the benefits of working from children's interests, from play and from practical experience are relatively clear-cut (Anning, 1991; Dowling, 1992; Doddington and Hilton, 2007). However, Piaget's work has also influenced important research on the development of thinking skills and 'cognitive acceleration' in science and maths across the age range (Adey and Shayer, 1994).

There have been a number of criticisms of Piaget's work, particularly because of the way in which seeing the development of young people in sequential structured stages can lead to underestimation of their capacities. Psychologists, such as Donaldson (1978) and Tizard and Hughes (1984), demonstrated that children's intellectual abilities are far greater than those reported by Piaget. Their findings emerged when children were observed in situations that were *meaningful* to them. In such circumstances children also show considerably more social competence at younger ages than Piaget's theory allows (Dunn, 1988; Siegler, 1997). From a different perspective, sociologists such as Walkerdine (1983, 1988) have argued that Piaget's stages became part of child-centred ideology and a means through which teachers classify, compare and, thus, control children. Critics have also suggested that this form of constructivism over-emphasises self-discovery by the individual and ignores the social context in which learning takes place. In so doing, the potential of teachers, other adults and other children to support each child's learning is under-estimated.

Constructivist learning theory, as adapted by educationalists, casts the learner in a very active and independent role, leaving much of the selection, pacing and evaluation of the activity to the child to negotiate. There is considerable emphasis on pupil interests and some compromise on the specifics of curriculum coverage. In its place, there tends to be more emphasis on learning concepts and skills through work on pupil-chosen topics.

Teaching which has been influenced by constructivism can be seen in all schools. It is reflected in the provision of a rich, varied and stimulating environment, in individualised work and creative arts and in extended projects and investigations. Above all, though, the influence of constructivism is reflected in the ways in which teachers relate with children and young people. Perhaps this is an unintended legacy, but the nature of constructivism, with its close identification with the learner, provides many opportunities for teachers to share in pupil fascination and excitement when encountering new and meaningful experiences.

Figure 2.3 represents the roles of child and adult in constructivist-influenced teaching and learning processes.

Figure 2.3
A constructivist model of roles in the teaching–learning process

Note here the *negotiation* of pupil activity and the emphasis placed on direct experience in learning. Together, these have the enormous strength, in principle, of creating high levels of pupil motivation and engagement. In the right circumstances, creativity and other forms of pupil achievement can reach exceptional levels of excellence. However, coverage of a particular curriculum is hard to monitor and the diversity of individual pupil interests tends to produce relatively complex forms of classroom organisation as a range of activities is provided. Research shows that teachers then tend to be drawn into managing this complex environment rather than teaching itself.

As with behaviourist approaches, professional judgements about 'fitness for purpose' will guide decisions about the use of teaching methods based on constructivism.

1.3 Social cognition

This perspective on learning takes two main forms. On the one hand, it draws attention to the language and forms of understanding that are embedded in particular contexts and social practices – and sees these as important 'cultural resources' that are available to a learner from that setting. Studies with this emphasis are often referred to as *socio-cultural*. On the other hand, it draws attention to the key role of experienced participants in inducting less competent learners, and in 'mediating', 'scaffolding' and extending their understanding. Studies with this emphasis are known as *social constructivist*, because they retain the constructivist concern with learner activity, but also recognise the significance of social processes.

We might say then, that theories of social cognition affirm the importance of recognising and building on pupils' family and community knowledge, whilst also emphasising the role of teaching and instruction in extending such knowledge. The seminal writer on this approach was Vygotsky (1962, 1978, Reading 2.3) whose publications in Russian date from the 1930s. The increasing availability of Vygotsky's work in English coincided with reappraisals of the strengths and weaknesses of Piagetian theory. Psychologists such as Bruner (1986), Wood (1997) and Wertsch (1985) have been able to demonstrate the considerable relevance of Vygotsky's work to modern education. This complemented empirical work by other child psychologists, and curriculum-development initiatives by subject specialists.

As we have seen, a key insight concerns the role of the culture and the social context of the learner in influencing understanding (Wells (1999, Reading 2.5; Bruner, 1990, 2006, Reading 11.4; Pollard and Filer, 1997, Reading 1.2). This influence starts in informal ways from birth. Thus infants and young children interact with their parents and family and, through experiencing the language and forms of behaviour of their culture, also assimilate particular cognitive skills, strategies, knowledge and understanding (Dunn, 1988; Richards and Light, 1986). Cognition, language and forms of thought thus depend on the culture and social history of the learner as well as on any particular instruction which may be offered at any point in time. For example, Mercer (1992) shows how his daughter 'appropriated' new ways of playing from watching an older child. This influence of culture on learning continues throughout life; indeed, it is what makes learning meaningful. Ideas, language and concepts derived from interaction with others thus structure, challenge, enhance or constrain thinking.

An extremely practical conclusion from this is that teachers must engage with children's existing cultural and conceptual understandings (and misunderstandings) before attempting further instruction. A review from the United States (US) indicates that: 'if initial understanding is not engaged, students may fail to grasp new information and concepts, or may learn for the purposes of the test, but fail to transfer the learning to new situations' (Bransford et al., 1999, p. 25, Reading 4.1). As we will see later in this chapter, this argument for 'deep' and 'connected' learning is also linked to learner identity. Does the learner feel comfortable with new, school knowledge? Can they incorporate it and feel supported by the significant others in their lives (such as parents or their peers), or do they experience apathy or even disapproval?

The second major aspect of social cognition on which we will focus concerns the social constructivist mediation of understanding by more knowledgeable others. This is best illustrated through Vygotsky's concept of the 'zone of proximal development' (the ZPD) (1978, Reading 2.3). This is:

> the distance between the actual developmental level (of the child) as determined through problem solving and the level of potential development as determined through problem solving under adult guidance or in collaboration with more capable peers. (Vygotsky, 1978, p. 86)

The ZPD concerns each person's potential to 'make sense'. Given a learner's present state of understanding, what developments can occur if he or she is given appropriate assistance by more capable others? If support is appropriate and meaningful, then, it is argued, the understanding of children can be extended far beyond that which they could reach alone.

Such assistance in learning can come in many ways. It may take the form of an explanation by or discussion with a knowledgeable teacher; it may reflect debate among a group of children as they strive to solve a problem or complete a task; it might come from discussion with a parent or from watching a particular television programme. In each case, the intervention functions to extend and to 'scaffold' the child's understanding across their ZPD for that particular issue. An appropriate analogy, suggested by Bruner, is that of building a house. Scaffolding is needed to support the process as the house is gradually constructed from its foundations – but when it has been assembled and all the parts have been secured the scaffolding can be removed. The building – the learner's understanding – will stand independently.

The influence of social constructivism has grown steadily since the early 1980s. Perhaps this is because the approach seems to recognise both the needs of learners to construct their own, meaningful understandings and the strength of teaching itself. Indeed, a key to the approach lies in specifying constructive relationships between these factors. As Tharp and Gallimore (1988, Reading 11.4) suggest learning can be seen as 'assisted performance'.

Figure 2.4, elaborated from Rowland (1987), represents the roles of children and adults in social constructivist teaching and learning processes. Negotiation, focused perhaps on a National Curriculum topic, is followed by activity and discussion by children. However, the teacher then makes a constructive intervention to provide support and instruction – a role which Rowland named as that of the 'reflective agent'. This draws attention to the fact that any intervention must be appropriate. It must connect with the understandings and purposes of the learners so that their thinking is extended. If this is to happen, teachers need to draw on both their subject knowledge and their understanding of children and young people in general and of their class in particular. They must make an accurate judgement themselves about the most appropriate form of input. In this, various techniques

Figure 2.4
A social
constructivist
model of roles
in the teaching–
learning process

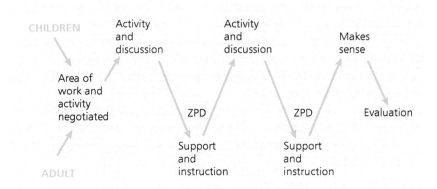

of formative assessment (see Chapter 13) are likely to be helpful. If such judgements are astute then the input could take the children's thinking forward, across the ZPD and beyond the level of understanding which they would have reached alone. Clearly there could be successive cycles of this process.

In recent decades, the influence of social constructivism has underpinned the work of curriculum associations and teacher-based curriculum innovation in all subjects. The role of language and of discussion is paramount in learning in each area.

Reflective activity 2.1

Aim: To consider the application of behaviourist, constructivist and social constructivist psychology in classroom practice.

Evidence and reflection: Review a selection of common learning situations and teaching methods, which your class or classes experience during a school day.

Note each learning situation, each teaching approach and then consider the psychological rationale for its use.

Learning situation	Teaching approach used	Psychological rationale for the teaching approach

Consider if you are drawing effectively on the strengths of each approach. Does this activity have any implications for the repertoire of teaching strategies that you use?

Extension: Consider the influence, strengths and weaknesses of each learning theory on teaching and learning in your school. Are the teaching approaches used 'fit for their purpose'?

Summary

Figure 2.5 provides a very simple summary of some key points in the previous discussions of teacher–learner interaction. Hopefully, the particular insights of each perspective on learning are apparent. We return to broader socio-cultural factors in Section 3.1 of this chapter.

Figure 2.5 Some features of behaviourist, constructivist and social constructivist models of learning in school classrooms

	Behaviourism in classrooms	Constructivism in classrooms	Social constructivism in classrooms
Image of learner	• Passive • Individual • Extrinsically motivated	• Active • Individual • Intrinsically motivated	• Active • Social • Socially motivated
Images of teaching and learning	• Teacher transmits knowledge and skills • Learning depends on teaching and systematic reinforcement of correct behaviours	• Teacher gives child opportunity to construct knowledge and skills gradually through experience • Learning can be independent of teaching	• Knowledge and skills are constructed gradually through experience, interaction and adult support • Learning comes through the interdependence of teacher and children
Characteristic child activities	• Class listening to an adult • Class working on an exercise	• Individuals making, experimenting, playing or otherwise doing something	• Class, group or individual discussion with an adult or other child/ren • Group problem-solving
Some characteristics	• Draws directly on existing subject knowledge in a logical, linear manner • When matched to existing understanding, can be a fast and effective way to learn	• Uses direct experience and allows child to explore in their own way at their own pace • Can build confidence and practical, insightful understanding	• Encourages collaboration and language development • By structuring challenges can clarify thinking and extending meaningful understanding
Some issues	• May not connect with existing understanding and may thus lead to superficiality • Difficult to motivate all children in class • Difficult to adapt structure of subject matter to varied pupil needs	• Has significant resource and organisational implications • Management of classroom often dominates actual teaching • Anticipates motivation and responsible autonomy from children	• Requires an appropriate, learning-oriented classroom climate • Requires a high level of adult judgement, knowledge and skill • Anticipates language, reasoning and social capability from children

So far in this chapter we have considered three major theoretical influences on learning and teaching processes in schools. We now move on to focus more specifically on children and young people as learners, and on factors which influence individual differences in learning.

2 *Nature*, nurture and agency

The next two sections provide an interconnected introduction to some of the factors which influence learning. Debate about the relative importance of 'nature' (biological factors) and nurture (environmental factors) has continued for centuries. The first section leads on nature, but shows how nurture also permeates. The second leads on nurture, but suggests that nature is similarly always present as an influence. So, to be clear, the interaction of nature and nurture is part of a cumulative, developmental process. As teachers, we need to understand them both.

These sections also consider 'agency'. This refers to the capacity of humans to act on the basis of their understanding. Although we are very signicantly influenced by our biology and circumstances, we are not determined by them. Indeed, in all circumstances, actions always make a difference of some sort. It is the responsibility of teachers to understand learners and then to ensure that they are supported and challenged to fulfil their potential and exercise their agency. This is the power of positive expectations, constructive thinking and professional commitment.

2.1 Personal development, health and wellbeing

Children's health and their physical and social development are crucial to their wellbeing and capacity to learn (Hugdahl, 1995; Cowie, 2012). The pioneering work of Tanner at the London Institute for Child Health (see Tanner, 1978) was influential in demonstrating patterns of normal development in children and it was on the basis of such work that mass-screening procedures were introduced into the United Kingdom. There is much more awareness now of diversity, but measures such as height and weight are still used as indicators of child health, for instance, through the birth to five 'Healthy Child Programme' in England, thus enabling problems to be identified and help offered if necessary. School nurses provide services for pupils at any age, including advice to young people during adolescence.

Health has always been strongly associated with social conditions (Rutter and Madge, 1976; Wilkinson and Pickett, 2009) and a general rise in average standards of living since the 1970s reduced the prominence of the issue for a time. However, more recently, UK poverty levels have steadily worsened and the circumstances of children in such families have been badly affected (see the index of poverty and social exclusion provided annually by the Joseph Rowntree Foundation; Ball, 2003, Reading 5.3; Department for Children, Schools and Families (DCSF), 2009, Reading 5.4). There have also been concerns about the mental health of children and young people – particularly in relation to anxiety caused by the frequency of assessment at school (Mental Health Foundation, 2005). Health across the UK as a whole remains an issue of considerable concern.

Young people develop physically at very different rates and such differences can affect both children's capacity for new learning and their self-confidence. Differential rates of development should therefore be carefully considered by teachers, particularly if National Curriculum and assessment procedures make little explicit allowance for such variations (Maude, 2001). In this context, there is concern that young children may sometimes be required to do things, such as controlling a pencil, before they are sufficiently physically developed. Similarly, adolescence sees variable spurts of hormonal and physical change, with significant implications for emotional and other forms of development. At all ages, levels of attainment may reflect present development rather than long-term learning capabilities, and this is a vital distinction.

Modern family lifestyles have also produced concerns about child health – arising particularly from the diet and lack of physical exercise of many children (National Audit Commission, 2001; Sustain, 2004). The general view, articulated for instance by Jamie Oliver, is that children consume too much fat, sugar and salt and that the exercise which they get is not sufficiently frequent or sustained to ensure healthy development of muscles and heart. Several cross-governmental schemes have existed to tackle the problem: Healthy Schools Programme, Food in Schools Programme, School Fruit and Vegetable Schemes, Physical Education, School Sport and Club Links are a few. Environmental issues such as toxicity in cities and the rapid development of child allergies are obviously additional concerns. More culturally related health problems of great seriousness include those associated with tobacco, alcohol, drugs and other abusing substances.

What, too, do children and young people think of their own health and health care at home and school? Mayall (1994) researched this question in London and found that they were both aware of many important health issues and capable of taking more responsibility than they were normally offered by adults. Those bodies had minds of their own, and wanted to be consulted!

Reflective activity 2.2

Aim To evaluate the exercises taken by pupils in your class/es.

Evidence and reflection We suggest that a simple daily record sheet is developed such as the one below. The task for an appropriate group of students could be to record their physical activity:

If you had any exercise at these times, please write in what you did.

- after getting up
- getting to school
- first lesson
- playtime
- second lesson
- dinner time

- third lesson
- getting home
- in the evening.

This could be completed retrospectively for one week.

Extension: Analyse your results. You will probably be able to see patterns in the type, amount and timing of activities. Perhaps there will be differences between boys and girls, or between children with gardens at home and those without. Do you judge that the amount of exercise is sufficient for healthy physical growth at the age of your sample of pupils?

2.2 Body and brain, mind and behaviour

The work of biologists and neurologists has attracted much attention in recent years and new knowledge is beginning to affect our understanding of human development and its implications for teaching (Dowling, 1999; Goswami, 2008; The Royal Society, 2011a, b, Reading 2.5). On the one hand, we have the extraordinary mapping of human DNA and some 30,000 genes from which each of our species is formed. Scientists now race to document the proteins within the body, which are arguably even more significant (see Morange, 2001). On the other hand, the implicit biological determinism of the concept of the 'selfish gene' (Dawkins, 1978) has developed into more wide-ranging socio-biological analyses which demonstrate the interaction of *genes* and *culture* (for an influential text, see Wilson and Lumsden, 1981). From the educational point of view, we must therefore accept the contribution of genetic variation whilst also affirming our responsibility with parents and others for helping each child to fulfil his or her potential in the context of specific social, cultural and economic opportunities. However, before exploring this further, we need to understand a little more about the brain itself.

The brain has three key biological elements:

- *the reptilian system*: a deep, core element that monitors basic survival needs, such as hunger, thirst, temperature, light, threat and risk;
- *the limbic system*: associated with emotions and long-term memory;
- *the neocortex*: located at the top of the brain, associated with more advanced mental functions and split into two hemispheres.

Learning is not effective if core survival needs are not met and, whilst this is particularly true for babies, it is a factor at any age – thus, for instance, justifying the provision of school breakfasts for young children in some communities and the establishment of stable and emotionally secure classroom climates.

Within the neocortex, parts of the left hemisphere have been found to be particularly significant for analytic capacities such as language, logic, pattern recognition and reflective thought; whilst much of the right hemisphere is associated with more intuitive and representational capabilities such as visualisation, imagination, rhyme, rhythm and expression.

There is a danger, however, in oversimplification of what is actually a complex, interacting cognitive system (Hellige, 1993).

Trillions of networks of neural cells are interconnected within the brain by 'synapses', and it is the number and complexity of these that affect the brain's capacity. There are two ways in which synapses are added to the brain – in part determined by biology, and in part by each child's experiences. First, in the early stages of development, the brain over-produces synapses but then selectively prunes out those which are not used. As Bransford et al. put it (1999, p. 104, see also Reading 4.1):

> the nervous system sets up a large number of connections. Experience then plays on these networks, selecting appropriate connections and removing inappropriate ones. What remains is a refined form that constitutes the sensory and cognitive bases for later phases of development.

The second way in which synapses are added is actually *driven* by experience, when additions occur as a biological consolidation of new learning. This process of adaption and development is known as 'plasticity', and operates throughout life. Such processes have enormous implications for teaching.

There is no doubt at all then, that children's mental capacities (or our own) are the product of the interaction of biological and environmental factors. In this context, it is helpful to distinguish between 'brain' (as a biological organ), 'mind' (the personal meanings which become embodied within a brain) and 'behaviour' (actions taken on the basis of thoughts and feelings). Of course, the mind strongly reflects the influence of culture. As leading neuroscientist Colin Blakemore (2000) wrote:

> if our behaviour were determined by our genes, we should be stuck in the world of the very first of our species who appeared some 100,000 years ago. But the extraordinary capacity of the brain to modify itself on the basis of its own experiences has fuelled a different form of evolution, the evolution of mind and culture.

So how do we help children to enhance their learning capacity? One answer to this has been provided by those promoting forms of 'brain-based learning', 'brain gym', 'brain-compatible classrooms', etc. Such initiatives aim to enable teachers to consider the implications of recent research so that it can be drawn into classroom practice. However, considerable caution is necessary because, as TLRP demonstrated (see the **Research Briefing** on p. 48) much scientific knowledge on the brain is not yet sufficiently robust to underpin the conclusions that are sometimes drawn for practice. There are rather too many neuro-myths in circulation at present and 'brain-based' schemes should be approached with great caution. The Royal Society has published summaries of existing knowledge with explicit warnings on these matters (2011a, b Reading 2.5). As they put it: 'much of neuroscience is still "upstream" of application' (2011b, p. 76).

Research
Briefing
Education and neuroscience

TLRP assembled leading practitioners, neuroscientists, psychologists and educationalists to review the impact of neuroscience on education. There was agreement about its enormous potential significance. There was also agreement that many recent applications were inappropriate and that some 'neuro-myths' in schools needed to be challenged.

Essentially, aspirations to apply 'brain science' too directly to 'practice' are misplaced. The model below represents the relationship between brain, mind and behaviour, and indicates the wide range of mediating environmental and intra-individual factors.

Examples of environmental factors	Examples of intra-individual factors	Factor affected
Oxygen Nutrition Toxins	Synaptogenesis Synaptic pruning Neuronal connections	BRAIN
Teaching Cultural institutions Social factors	Learning Memory Emotion	MIND
Temporary restrictions e.g. teaching tools	Performance Errors Improvement	BEHAVIOUR

A model of brain, mind and behaviour (from Morton and Frith, 1995)

Key findings:	Implications:
Nature/nurture: Biology is not destiny. Biology provides no simple limit to our learning, not least because our learning can influence our biology.	Teaching should aim to enable children's potential and to enrich their experience.
Neuro-myths: Education has invested an immense amount in 'brain-based' ideas that are not underpinned by recognisable scientific understanding of the brain. Many of these ideas remain untested and others are being revealed as ineffective, such as:	Professional judgement should be applied in respect of commercial 'brain-based' programmes
The belief that learning can be improved by presenting material to suit an individual's preferred 'learning style' is not supported by high quality evidence (Coffield et al., 2004).	Focusing on learning styles too narrowly could actually inhibit learner development more broadly.
Encouraging teachers to determine whether a child is left or right brained is misplaced. Performance at most everyday tasks, including learning activities, requires both hemispheres to work together in a sophisticated parallel fashion.	Right brain/left brain beliefs, particularly if linked to gendered assumptions, categorises children inappropriately.
Neuroscience: Some particular insights from neuroscientists and psychologists have broad implications for teaching and learning strategies which merit further exploration. For example:	There are grounds for 'cautious optimism'.
When we learn new information, the semantic links that form between this new information and our existing knowledge serve to make it meaningful. An area of the left hemisphere is a vital structure in this. (Fletcher et al., 2003).	The construction of meaning is a key to understanding and remembering information.
Mental visualisation of an object engages most of the brain circuitry which is activated by actually seeing it (Kosslyn, 2005).	'Visualisation' has considerable power and usefulness as a learning tool.
Cautious optimism: We are still at an early stage in our understanding of the brain. There are methodological limitations and the transfer of concepts between neuroscience and education requires caution. Nevertheless, the potential is great and there are grounds for optimism that interdisciplinary work will produce important, secure knowledge in years to come.	There is a growing need for research collaborations between neuroscience, psychology and education that embrace insights and understanding from each perspective.

Further information:
Howard-Jones, P. (ed.) (2007) *Neuroscience and Education: Issues and Opportunities.* A TLRP Commentary. London: TLRP. Available at **www.tlrp.org/pub**
Blakemore, S. J. and Frith, U. (2006) *The Learning Brain: Issues for Education.* Oxford: Blackwell.
Coffield, F., Mosley, D., Hall, E. and Ecclestone, K. (2004) *Learning Styles and Pedagogy: A Systematic and Critical Review.* London: ISRC.
The TLRP seminar series was coordinated by Paul Howard-Jones from the University of Bristol.

2.3 'Intelligence', attribution and expectations

Teachers meet the specific needs of children by knowing them well. In particular, teachers must build on, and extend, the prior cognitive ability, knowledge and skills of pupils. Indeed, perhaps unexpectedly, Hattie's (2009, Reading 4.6) meta-analysis of factors associated with different levels of achievement revealed a very high effect-size for prior abilities. It is thus right and proper that concepts to describe the attributes of pupils should exist. However, such concepts should be accurate, discriminating and capable of impartial application. Notions of 'intelligence' have a long history but, given what we now know about the capacity of people to develop themselves, there are also dangers of stereotyping and inappropriate generalisation.

Although the validity and measurement of the concept of intelligence has been in dispute among psychologists for many years, the idea was once taken for granted and has passed into our culture to denote a generalised form of ability. It is part of our language and it influences our ways of thinking about people. For instance, parents often talk about their children in terms of 'brightness' or 'cleverness', and teachers routinely describe pupils and classroom groupings in terms of 'ability'. The concept of intelligence is important too because it is often used in the rhetoric of politicians and the media when they communicate with the public. It is thus routinely assumed that there *is* both a generalised trait of intelligence and that it is possible to measure it objectively and use it to predict future achievement.

Of course, such beliefs underpinned the UK use in the 1950s and 1960s of intelligence tests, at 11-plus, to select students for secondary education. Belief in the context-free objectivity of such testing was severely undercut by studies at the time such as those by Simon (1953) and Squibb (1973). Indeed, research in areas where 11-plus was still used, such as in Northern Ireland, showed the lack of objectivity of the measurement. For instance, Egan and Bunting (1991) recorded gains of 30 to 40 per cent for a coached group of 11-year-olds compared with an uncoached group. The results showed clearly that children can be taught to do intelligence tests and that it is not possible to identify or measure some context-free generalised ability with any confidence.

To read more about this, including the work of Howard Gardner on 'multiple intelligence' and Goleman on 'emotional intelligence', see **reflectiveteaching.co.uk**

The debate about the notion of intelligence also continues. Psychologists such as Kline (1991) argue, on the basis of statistical factor analysis, that general ability remains a valid concept to describe an amalgam of inherited attributes. On the other hand, Howe (1990) used experimental and biographical evidence from different cultures to argue that there are many types of ability and that generalised measures, such as IQ scores, are misleading.

The concept of intelligence risks giving the impression that capacities are fixed (see Figure 2.6 for some 'labels' denoting abilities which are in everyday use). However, as we have seen, neuroscientists suggest that the brain is 'plastic' and can be moulded and developed by new experiences and

Expert questions

Validity: in terms of learning, do the forms of assessment used really measure what they are intended to measure?

Dependability: are assessment processes understood and accepted as being robust and reliable?

These questions contribute to a conceptual framework underpinning professional expertise (see Chapter 16).

Figure 2.6
Everyday language
embodying
labelling

opportunities. Indeed, many stories of 'the teacher who changed my life' concern professionals who believed in a child's capability, and helped them to succeed in a new field of learning.

Ability-based labelling can certainly restrict learner progress. For this reason Hart et al. (2004, see Reading 1.4) investigated alternative practices based on the pedagogies of nine teachers who challenged apparent differences in pupil ability. Instead they demonstrated that there is always potential for change as a result of what teachers and learners do in the present – 'transformability'. A second phase of research (Swann et al., 2012) explored what becomes possible when a whole school's staff act together to create a learning environment free from ability labelling. The research described how a school community became committed to transformability, and how the children became more powerful learners. Together, the staff worked to shape curriculum and pedagogy, and to build inclusion and social justice through their unshakeable commitment to the educability of *every* child.

Research by Dweck over many years (e.g. 1986, 1999, Reading 2.6) demonstrates why such challenges to fixed-ability thinking are so important. Dweck studied, in particular, how children think about, explain and 'attribute' their own capability. Those who adopt an 'entity theory' of intelligence tend to believe that their personal capability is fixed, and that they either 'can' or 'cannot' succeed at the new challenges that they meet in school. For this reason, they tend to adopt a form of 'learned helplessness' and dependency to accomplish school and this disposition tends to roll forward into adult life. However, those who adopt an 'incremental theory' of their capability believe that they are able

Sally communicates confidence, an understanding of progression and the need to practise to improve. Her pictures suggest that she has an 'incremental' view of her learning. Sally is on the way to becoming a 'lifelong learner' and a sound teaching goal would be to support her in finding new challenges.

Andrew's drawings seem to represent bewilderment, annoyance and anxiety, particularly about maths – and a retreat to sleep! Other pictures indicate how friends and the playground offer release. He appears to have an 'entity' model of his capacity in maths. It would be wonderful to be able to gradually help Andrew to develop a more positive view of himself as a learner of maths – but don't forget that he might be a splendid learner in other domains, including those out of school.

Figure 2.7 Sally and Andrew illustrate 'mastery' and 'helplessness' in learning

to learn and improve. They are thus likely to be more highly motivated, have greater engagement and take risks, exhibit 'resilience' (Claxton, 1999, Reading 2.9) and act independently. They exhibit 'mastery' rather than 'helplessness'. For instance, Figure 2.7 shows the drawings of two children who were asked to 'draw pictures of how they felt about school learning'.

Differences between young people certainly exist and prior opportunities and experiences also vary widely. The key question for teachers is *how to account for such differences*. Indeed, teacher expectations have been demonstrated to be very significantly related to pupil outcomes (Gipps and MacGilchrist, 1999, Reading 6.5).

- If teachers account for differences between learners by believing in unalterable variation in 'ability' (in other words, that some children simply *are* more clever than others – and that is that), then they may place limits on learning, albeit unintentionally.

- If they believe that each person's capacity to learn can be continually developed and shaped by working together, then a whole new, exciting and unpredictable world of opportunity is made possible as the teacher commits to supporting future learning.

Expert question

Expectation: does our school support high staff and student expectations and aspire for excellence?

This question contributes to a conceptual framework underpinning professional expertise (see Chapter 16).

The beliefs and values about learners and learning that teachers bring to learning encounters thus have profound effects, for better or for worse, on all children's opportunities to learn in school. Put crudely, are some pupils 'written off', or do we really try to do our job as professional educators?

There is thus an articulation of great consequence between teacher expectations and pupil beliefs.

In summary, it is worth remembering some simple points about 'intelligence' and learning:

- the use of generalised terms such as intelligence, ability, etc. is imprecise, insecure and unreliable – but, unfortunately, is often used in everyday interactions;

- there are many differences between children and young people, and one challenge for teachers is to identify, develop and celebrate such diverse attributes;

- whatever a learner's present capabilities, a teacher *can* influence the quality of pupil learning experiences and *can* thus influence future disposition and achievements.

As we have seen, whilst the influence of 'nature' is real, and intrinsic differences in capabilities do exist, these are profoundly mitigated by cultural factors and teacher/pupil actions. These impact on pupils' interpretation of performance and on their views of themselves as learners – and they thus merit our specific attention.

3 *Nurture*, nature and agency

In this section, we lead on the social and cultural factors which contribute to 'nurture' and the learning environment. At the same time though, we remain aware of biological factors and draw particular attention to the opportunities for teachers and pupils to take action to enhance learning.

3.1 Culture, language and disposition

Of course, it has always been thought that home background, peer relationships, the cultures of different schools and, increasingly, the media influence how children learn. However, the development of social constructivist and sociocultural psychology has led to a much greater understanding of the processes which are at work (Wells, 1999, Reading 2.4; Bruner, 1990; Mercer, 1995, 1992; see also Section 1.3 of this chapter.)

We can identify three particularly significant cultural influences on learning:

Cultural resources and experiences. Learning is a process of 'making sense' and whatever is taken as being meaningful ('makes sense') will be strongly influenced by the culture, knowledge, values and ideas of social groups which the learner has previously experienced. Such cultures provide an initial framework of understanding. Thus, each child's early learning will tend to elaborate and extend the knowledge which is embedded in their experienced culture. Sometimes this is talked about as 'situated learning' (Lave and Wenger, 1991).

The mediation of language. Language is the medium of thinking and learning and is created, transmitted and sustained through interaction with other people within the cultures of different social settings. These settings influence the range of 'languages' we use – the register, styles, dialects, etc. Language also embodies the 'cultural tools' through which new experiences are 'mediated' and interpreted as learners become inducted into the knowledge of their communities (Wertsch 1985, 1991). Sometimes this is known as 'cognitive apprenticeship' (Rogoff, 1990). See also Chapter 13.

Learning disposition. The term 'learning disposition' summarises the ways in which learners engage with any opportunity to learn. As defined by Carr (2001, p. 10), they are 'participation repertoires from which a learner recognises, selects, edits, responds to, resists, searches for and constructs learning opportunities'. When children start school, patterns in how they approach learning will probably already be discernible, and the role of the teacher is to encourage, and invite positive dispositions to form (Carr, 2008). In particular, opportunities (through tasks and activities) should be provided for positive engagement to be practised and learning disposition strengthened. Features of the classroom environment may invite or inhibit engagement, so the choices that teachers make are significant.

The approach to learning adopted by each child is crucial to educational outcomes. Will a learner be open or closed to experience and support, will they be confident or fearful, willing to take risks or defensive? What is their self-belief, their 'identity' as a learner? Can they overcome setbacks, and will they become a 'lifelong learner'? The origins of disposition and learner identity reflect the learning cultures which each child has experienced (Pollard and Filer, 1996, see Reading 1.2), yet schools continue the process as the first formal institution which is experienced in a sustained way.

The major sources of such cultural influence are commonly seen as family and community, peers, the school and the media. We will consider each in turn.

Family and community. Family background has been recognised as being of crucial significance in educational achievement for many years. This occurs not just in material ways, depending on the wealth and income of families, nor simply because of ownership or otherwise of overt forms of 'cultural capital' (Bourdieu and Passeron, 1977). The most significant issues for school learning

Expert question

Connection: does the curriculum engage with the cultural resources and funds-of-knowledge of families and the community?

This question contributes to a conceptual framework underpinning professional expertise (see Chapter 16).

concern what the culture of the family and community provides in terms of frameworks of existing understanding, language for further development and the child's disposition regarding learning.

Peers at school. Peer group culture is important to children as a way of both enjoying and adapting to school life (Davies, 1982). Some peer cultures favour school attainment and are likely to reinforce teacher efforts to engender a positive approach to learning. Other peer cultures derive meaning from alternative values, and young people who are influenced by such cultures may approach school with minimal or even oppositional expectations. Such children will still be constructing understanding, but it may not be the type of understanding for which teachers would have aimed.

The school. Schools have their own unique cultures, created by those who work there and those who are associated with them. A school culture must be seen as a learning context which is at least as important as the bricks and mortar, books and equipment which make up the material environment of a school (see, for instance, Nias, Southworth and Campbell, 1992). Again, we have to ask how this culture influences the framework for understanding which is offered to students, the language in which teaching and learning is transacted and the stance which pupils adopt (Rudduck and McIntyre, 2007,

> **Expert question**
>
> **Culture:** does the school support expansive learning by affirming learner contributions, engaging partners and providing attractive opportunities?
>
> This question contributes to a conceptual framework underpinning professional expertise (see Chapter 16).

Reading 1.3). For instance, are children and young people encouraged to take risks in their learning?

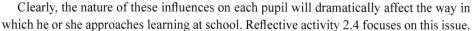

The media and new technologies. The influence of the media is very considerable and has been extensively researched (Marsh, 2005; Buckingham, 2008, see also Kress, 2010, Reading 8.6). Some people have been concerned about the effects of such experience. With reading from paper in relative decline, children and young people watch many hours of television each week and use screens and mobile technologies in toys as well as in phones and tablets. Play and lifestyles are influenced by advertising and popular media, including the internet and social networking. Such experiences can be extremely educational in new ways. Key issues for learning include whether the stance adopted is passive or active, and how new cultural experiences are interpreted and used. Engagement with new media creates powerful opportunies for many, but there are access problems for others where technologies and support are not available.

Clearly, the nature of these influences on each pupil will dramatically affect the way in which he or she approaches learning at school. Reflective activity 2.4 focuses on this issue.

Reflective activity 2.4

Aim: To map the influence of culture on the learning disposition of a pupil.

Evidence and reflection: This activity is directly based on the text of Section 3.1. It provides an opportunity to review the range of influences on a child and their capacity as a learner. Drawing up a table, as illustrated below, is a helpful way of organising thoughts.

	Cultural resources and experiences	The mediation of language	Learning disposition
The influence of family and community			
The influence of peers and friends at school			
The influence of the school			
The influence of the media and of new communication technologies			

Think of a child or young person whom you know well. Consider the way culture and experiences influence the child's understanding, the language he or she uses and the learning disposition he or she adopts. Complete each cell of the table, as far as you can, to map what you know about the sources of influence on that child.

If you have time it would be valuable to talk to the pupil and others – parents, peers and teachers – to improve the quality of your evidence.

Extension: Repeat this exercise with different pupils, or compare the results of similar activities by colleagues. What insights are produced by comparisons of children of different sex, ethnicity, religion, social class, attainment? You can see some examples of this sort of analysis in the final chapters of Pollard and Filer (1996, 1999).

In summary, children and young people are both reproduced by their culture, and produce new forms of it. However, culture and language always mediate thought, interpretation and learning. Thus success or failure through curriculum tasks and short-term performance is given particular significance by the cultural interpretations that are made of it (Filer and Pollard, 2000, Reading 14.7). In these ways, culture both structures learning attainment and shapes the self-belief of the learner. What then, are the consequences for the personality, identity and motivation of the child?

3.2 Personality, motivation and identity

Psychologists' understanding of personality has, according to Hampson (1988), derived from three contributory strands of analysis. The first is the *lay perspective* – the under-standings which are implicit in common-sense thinking of most of us about other people. This is evident in literature and in everyday action. It is a means by which people are able to anticipate the actions of others – ideas about the character and likely actions of others are used for both the prediction and explanation of behaviour.

Such understandings have influenced the second strand of analysis – that of *trait theorists*. Their work reflects a concerted attempt to identify personality dimensions and to objectively measure the resulting cognitive and *learning styles*. Among the most frequently identified dimensions of cognitive style are impulsivity/reflexivity (Kagan, 1964) and extroversion/introversion (Eysenck, 1969). Such early work has been synthe-sised by Riding and Rayner (1998) into two orthogonal families – wholist/analytic and verbal/imager. Other accounts identify more general learning styles such as the concrete/abstract/sequential/random offered by Butler (1998) and the visual/auditory/tactile of Sarasin (1999). However, whilst a learning style approach is important in recognising patterns of individual difference, it is not straightforward to translate it into specific classroom provision. Indeed, a systematic review of such research concluded that the scientific basis of 'learning styles' is weak (Coffield et al., 2004, see also the **Research Briefing** on neuroscience on p. 48). Further, this is another occasion where we need to be wary of inappropriately limiting the expectations that we make of children. Perhaps, in other circumstances, they would sometimes surprise us.

A third strand of personality analysis has become prominent in recent years, and Hampson calls this the *self-perspective*. This approach sees the development of personality in close association with that of self-image and identity. Crucially, it draws attention to the capacity of humans to reflect on themselves, to take account of the views of others and to develop. The social context in which children grow up, their culture, interaction and experiences with significant people in their lives, is thus seen as being very important in influencing their views of self and consequent patterns of action.

A key aspect of this concerns the meaning which learning has for a child. In one sense, such motivation issues can be seen as being technical and related to specific tasks. Certainly, when children fail to see any purpose or meaning in an activity it is unlikely to be productive, however well intended and carefully planned. Sadly, as we saw in Chapter 1, a very common perception of children regarding schools is that lessons are 'boring' and, for this reason, engendering enthusiasm often requires sensitivity, flexibility, spontaneity and imagination from the teacher. The nature of this challenge is represented in Figure 2.8, which plots the relationship between new learning challenges and existing skills, knowledge and understanding. If too great a challenge is set for a child, then the situation of risk may produce withdrawal. Conversely, if the challenge is too little, then boredom and inappropriate behaviour may ensue. Targeting the effective learning in which the child will be highly motivated requires considerable skill and knowledge of both the subject matter and the child. Of course, motivation can stem from a wider range

Figure 2.8 Risk, boredom and motivation

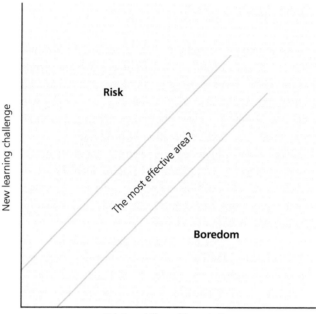

of factors too, from 'intrinsic' and 'extrinsic' interest, to a fear of receiving negative sanctions.

However, the most enduring form of motivation is connected to the evolving identity of each person and to their 'framework of meaningfulness' (National Research Council, 1999). For example, Pollard and Filer (1999, Reading 1.2) tracked two cohorts of English children from starting school at age 5 to GCSEs at age 16. They documented 'strategic biographies' or each child as they adapted to successive teachers and classrooms. In some settings, particular children felt affirmed as they developed new skills, appropriated new knowledge and fulfilled their learning identities *through* the school curriculum. Other settings were less conducive to such processes and the children felt little personal connection to the curriculum. It became something that was done to them, that they had to endure, rather than an activity through which they could experience personal development and understanding. For us all, deep and enduring learning only occurs when new knowledge has relevance and connects meaningfully with the personal narratives through which we make sense of life.

Similar ideas have been endorsed by some UK governments after many years of singleminded pressure for 'performance'. For example, 'personalised learning' has been suggested as a new concept for educational provision (Teaching and Learning Review Group, 2006, Reading 10.7).

Expert questions

Personalisation: does the curriculum resonate with the social and cultural needs of diverse learners and provide appropriate elements of choice?

Relevance: is the curriculum presented in ways which are meaningful to learners and so that it can excite their imagination?

These questions contribute to a conceptual framework underpinning professional expertise (see Chapter 16).

We also need to remember that learning can be emotionally challenging, and is certainly not simply cognitive and rational. Frijda (2001) suggests that emotions are subjective responses to events that are important to individuals. Positive or negative emotions reflect the affirmation or threat to previous understandings and 'meaning structures' – or indeed, implications for a learner's personal identity, self-esteem or social status. Whilst it can be 'embarrassing' for a child to succeed, it is often humiliating to fail. Learning can thus be stressful at several levels (Lazarus, 1991, 1999).

One way of overcoming this two-pronged challenge is to become more effective at 'learning how to learn', and it is to this powerful set of ideas that we now turn.

3.3 Metacognition and thinking skills

Humans have the unique capacity to reflect on their own thinking processes and to develop new strategies. This capacity for self-awareness regarding one's own mental powers is called 'metacognition' (Flavell, 1970, 1979). It has received strong endorsement and extension in recent years through the refinement of practical ways of developing 'thinking skills' (e.g. Fisher, 2008, Reading 2.7; McGuinness, 1999; McGregor, 2007).

Metacognition is a particularly important capacity once children start to attend schools. Prior to this, at home, learning is largely self-directed and thinking tends to be embedded in immediate personal experience (Donaldson, 1978); at school, the agenda for learning increasingly becomes directed by teachers. Thinking is challenged to become more disciplined and deliberate; tasks are set, problems posed and instructions given; criteria for success and failure become more overt. The result of all this is that a new degree of self-control is required and, in order to achieve this self-control, new forms of reflective self-awareness become essential.

Vygotsky (see Section 1.3) believed that learners, in working to understand and cross their 'zones of proximal development', could be supported by their own disciplined and reflective thinking. Tharp and Gallimore (1988, Reading 11.4) provide a particularly good illustration of this, with their four-stage theory of 'assisted performance'. The concept of 'Building Learning Power' (Claxton, 2002, 2004, 2011, Reading 2.9; Deakin Crick, 2006) is a contemporary development of these ideas. Indeed, experience has shown that guidance to children on how to review their learning needs to be direct.

> There is a need to be explicit about what we mean by better forms of thinking. If students are to become better thinkers – to learn meaningfully, to think flexibly and to make reasoned judgements – then they must be taught explicitly how to do it.
> (McGuinness, 1999, p. 3)

TLRP's project on 'learning how to learn' (James et al., 2006, 2007, Reading 2.8) has been extremely influential and takes an expansive approach to the issues. The project explored the conditions in classrooms, schools and networks which enable pupils and teachers to engage in new practices which are conducive to learning how to learn. These extend the principle of using assessment and feedback to support learning, as we will see in Chapter 13.

4 Taking stock of learning

4.1 Key factors in learning

This section offers a simple summary of the key factors that affect learning and motivation (see Figure 2.9). The interaction of nature and nurture, and the potential for agency, is readily apparent in the figure. Teachers, and pupils, can make a difference.

Figure 2.9 Factors affecting learning engagement (adapted from Bransford, 1999)

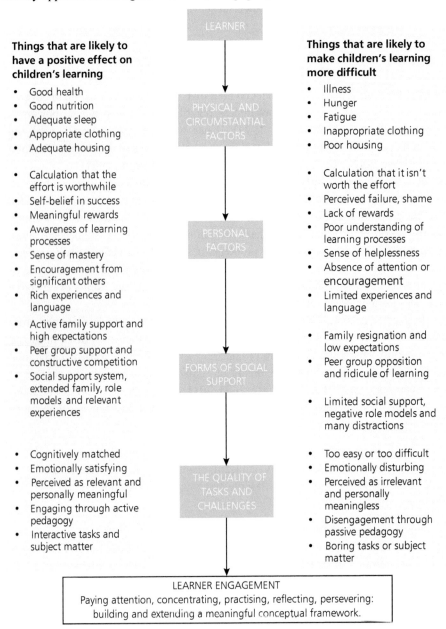

LEARNER

Things that are likely to have a positive effect on children's learning

PHYSICAL AND CIRCUMSTANTIAL FACTORS
- Good health
- Good nutrition
- Adequate sleep
- Appropriate clothing
- Adequate housing

PERSONAL FACTORS
- Calculation that the effort is worthwhile
- Self-belief in success
- Meaningful rewards
- Awareness of learning processes
- Sense of mastery
- Encouragement from significant others
- Rich experiences and language

FORMS OF SOCIAL SUPPORT
- Active family support and high expectations
- Peer group support and constructive competition
- Social support system, extended family, role models and relevant experiences

THE QUALITY OF TASKS AND CHALLENGES
- Cognitively matched
- Emotionally satisfying
- Perceived as relevant and personally meaningful
- Engaging through active pedagogy
- Interactive tasks and subject matter

Things that are likely to make children's learning more difficult

- Illness
- Hunger
- Fatigue
- Inappropriate clothing
- Poor housing

- Calculation that it isn't worth the effort
- Perceived failure, shame
- Lack of rewards
- Poor understanding of learning processes
- Sense of helplessness
- Absence of attention or encouragement
- Limited experiences and language

- Family resignation and low expectations
- Peer group opposition and ridicule of learning
- Limited social support, negative role models and many distractions

- Too easy or too difficult
- Emotionally disturbing
- Perceived as irrelevant and personally meaningless
- Disengagement through passive pedagogy
- Boring tasks or subject matter

LEARNER ENGAGEMENT
Paying attention, concentrating, practising, reflecting, persevering: building and extending a meaningful conceptual framework.

Our understanding has moved a long way beyond simple theoretical models. We now know that the most effective, deep, long-term learning is meaningful and conceptual. This is hugely important for teaching, and Reflective activity 2.5 encourages you to apply these insights to children in your class.

Reflective activity 2.5

Aim: To review and apply knowledge about factors affecting learning.

Evidence and reflection: Try to take stock of the issues that have been raised in this chapter. Although they are complex, they directly affect individuals such as the children in your class.

Consider a boy and a girl with contrasting motivation towards learning. Using the structure provided by Figure 2.9, make notes on the factors which, in your opinion, affect their engagement with learning. Record physical and circumstantial factors, personal factors, forms of social support, and the quality of tasks and challenges which they typically meet in school.

Does such a review help in understanding and making better provision for such children?

Extension: To what extent have such factors affected your own engagement as a learner through your educational career? Over time, could you use this understanding to develop your personal learning effectiveness?

4.2 Metaphors of learning

Within our cultural history, theories about learning have come and gone. And although, as we have seen, contemporary sciences are gradually accumulating more stable knowledge, the field remains complex. It is helpful therefore to consider the resonance of two metaphors which attempt to make sense of this cultural variability and scientific complexity.

We draw here on the work of Sfard (1998) whose paper was entitled: 'On Two Metaphors for Learning and the Dangers of Choosing Just One'. Sfard suggests that metaphors provide a deceptively simple way of representing our tacit frameworks of understanding. In particular, they reach between culturally embedded intuition and more formal knowledge. As she put it: 'they enable conceptual osmosis beween everyday and scientific discourses' (p. 4).

Learning as 'acquisition'

'Since the dawn of civilisation', human learning has been 'conceived as the acquisition of something' writes Sfard (p. 5) whether this be knowledge *per se* or conceptual development. In either case, the image is of the 'human mind as a container to be filled with certain materials and of the learner becoming an owner of these materials' (p. 5). These entities may include knowledge, concepts, skills, facts, understanding, meaning, attitudes, etc. They are to be acquired through remembering, internalisation, construction, appropriation, development, etc, and with the help of teachers who guide, support, deliver, explain, mediate, test, etc. Once acquired, the capabilities can be applied, transferred, shared with others, etc. We discuss all of these aspects extensively in this book, for the metaphor is a fine representation of an established view of 'education'. National education systems rest on the foundation of this metaphor, and are designed in systematic ways to provide the conditions, support and instruction which will maximise learner attainment at each stage of development.

Learning as 'participation'

This alternative metaphor is more recent but is rapidly growing in significance in the contemporary world. The emphasis is on the learner as 'a person interested in participation in certain kinds of activities' (Sfard, 1998, p. 6). So this is learning through activity; through direct, authentic engagement in an applied situation – learning through practice as a participant. With the support of parents, family and friends, a child might learn to 'play games', 'go shopping', identify with a football team – or to become a bit more independent by 'sleeping over', etc, etc. Another obvious example is the priority given in contemporary teacher education to direct, participatory school experience. And there are many others. The metaphor thus affirms direct experience with participants or practitioners in real situations. Instead of prioritising formal knowledge, one becomes a participating member of a practice community (see Lave and Wenger, 1991). The metaphor has particular resonance in respect of informal and tacit learning (Thomas and Pattison, Reading 2.9) – including through use of new technologies (Buckingham, 2005; Kress, 2010, Reading 8.6). Indeed, in addition to the unbounded flow of information which is now available, social networking opens up a vast range of opportunities for participation. The potential for learning in entirely new participatory ways, building on global diversity, appears to be exponential. Figure 2.10 summarises these descriptions.

Figure 2.10 Two metaphors for learning (edited from Sfard, 1998)

	Acquisition metaphor	Participation metaphor
Learning process	Acquisition of something	Becoming a participant
Student role	Recipient, constructor	Participant, apprentice
Teacher role	Provider, facilitator	Expert practitioner
Form of knowledge	Possession, commodity	Activity, practice
Form of knowing	Having, possessing	Belonging, communicating

We may wish to debate the relative advantages and disadvantages of these two metaphors for learning – and, when you look for it, such debate is a constant theme in popular culture. However, a reflective teacher should carefully note Sfard's argument that the metaphors represent two very important ways through which learning occurs. Put another way, the acquisition of capabilities through formal education is necessary but not sufficient, and the same can be said for participation in communities of practice. Acquisition alone, risks bookish knowledge which can't easily be applied. Participation alone, risks contextually bounded thinking. For analytic power and personal effectiveness which can be applied in and through practice, we need both forms of learning. As we see below, this is not always easy to provide.

4.3 Applying learning beyond school

We move towards a conclusion in this chapter by drawing attention to a major problem of school learning. In the 'real world' outside, it is hard to actually *apply* the knowledge that has been learned in classrooms. This seems to be because of the very different frames of reference that structure thinking in the different settings – and echoes of our discussion about the metaphors of 'acquisition' and 'participation' will be readily apparent.

Routine activities at home, parks, shops or street are accomplished using a quite different set of procedures and forms of knowledge than the procedurally constrained requirements of school (for an indication of the potential, see Thomas and Pattison, 2007, Reading 2.10). Whilst the former tend to be pragmatic and informal, the latter are very carefully structured and formally assessed. The result, sadly, is that children often find it hard to make connections between their learning in these two worlds. For instance, Hughes et al. (2000) documented the gap between the abstract, formal knowledge of school mathematics and the authentic contexts in which it might have been applied (but often remained unused). Similar findings exist across the curriculum, from doing geography tasks in school, to getting lost when travelling; and from doing well in spelling tests, to being unable to write a real letter about something important.

Learning, in this sense, is about *making connections* between different forms of knowledge and across the two metaphors (see also the **Research Briefing** on home–school knowledge exchange in Chapter 4, p. 107). However, this is particularly difficult when understanding and skills are being developed and have not yet been confidently appropriated into identity and self-belief.

From a teacher perspective, we need to acknowledge that children probably know a lot more than we think they know. If only we could tap into the funds of knowledge that are sustained in the social practices of families, communities and networks, then pupils' learning might become much more authentic, flexible and sustained.

We thus have yet another topic on which a reflective and aware teacher can be really effective – this time in encouraging children to think about what they know, how they know it, how it fits into their lives and how they can apply such knowledge in the future.

Expert question

Connection: does the curriculum engage with the cultural resources and funds-of-knowledge of families and the community?

This question contributes to a conceptual framework underpinning professional expertise (see Chapter 16).

Conclusion

Learning is an immensely complex topic and this chapter has simply touched the surface of some of the many issues which are involved. In one sense, perhaps the provisional nature of our understanding is no bad thing, because, if we knew it all, then one of the greatest sources of fascination and fulfilment in teaching would be diminished. The vocation of teaching will certainly always include this element of intellectual challenge as teachers seek to understand what children understand, and then to provide personalised support.

In this chapter we reviewed three influential theories on children's learning and related these to school practices. We then considered how physical and biological factors in the body and brain interact with the social and cultural factors of family, community and the broader society elements of a long-established 'nature–nurture' debate. Whilst acknowledging consequential differences between learners, we emphasised the agency of both teachers and pupils and their power to act in the present. Commitment to the learning capacity of all children is seen as a professional responsibility and a precondition for enhancing children's lives and system-wide improvement. Whatever pupil circumstances may be, teachers have the precious opportunity to influence their learning and their lives for the better.

Key readings

On psychological approaches to learning, Wood offers a splendid account, including reference to behaviourism, constructivism and, in particular, social constructivism. He discusses the implications for learning in school.

Wood, D. (1997) *How Children Think and Learn: The Social Contexts of Cognitive Development.* London: Wiley-Blackwell. (see also Readings 2.1, 2.2 and 2.3 on Skinner, Piaget and Vygotsky)

Research and debate on the implications of the neurobiology of the brain is growing, though caution is appropriate in such a new field of research. For an expert introduction, see:

Goswami, U. (2008) *Cognitive Development: The Learning Brain.* Hove: Psychology Press. (see also Reading 2.5)

Bruner's work has extended for over 50 years now and has powerfully promoted a 'cultural psychology' focused on the creation of understanding. See, for example:

Bruner, J. (1990) *Acts of Meaning.* Cambridge, MA: Harvard University Press. (Reading 11.1)

Across the world, there are significant attempts to take stock and review everything that is known about learning and schooling. Bransford, Brown and Cocking's book is one influential outcome:

Bransford, J. D., Brown, A. I. and Cocking, R. R. (eds) (2000) *How People Learn: Brain, Mind, Experience and School*. Washington, DC: National Academy Press. (Reading 4.1)

Whilst 'intelligence' remains a powerful concept, the ways in which capability is interpreted, towards 'mastery' or 'helplessness', is now receiving particular attention. For an accessible account, see:

Dweck, C. S. (2006) *Mindset: The New Psychology of Success*. New York: Ballantine. (Reading 2.6)

The idea of 'Building Learning Power' through developing resilience, resourcefulness, reflectiveness and reciprocity is worth considering. See:

Claxton, G. (2002) *Building Learning Power: Helping Young People Become Better Learners*. Bristol: The Learning Organization (TLO). (Reading 2.9)

Among many interesting books on the development of metacognitive and thinking skills, see:

Fisher, R. (2008) *Teaching Thinking: Philosophical Enquiry in the Classroom*. London: Continuum. (Reading 2.7)

For perhaps the most influential British study of recent years on learning in schools, see:

James, M., McCormick, R., Black, P., Carmichael, P., Drummond, M-J., Fox, A., MacBeath, J., Marshall, B., Pedder, D., Procter, R., Swaffield, S., Swann, J. and Wiliam, D. (2007) *Improving Learning How to Learn: Classrooms, Schools and Networks*. London: Routledge.
James, M., Black, P., Carmichael, P., Conner, C., Dudley, P., Fox, A., Frost, D., Honour, L., MacBeath, J., McCormick, R., Marshall, B., Pedder, D., Procter, R., Swaffield, S. and Wiliam, D. (2006) *Learning How to Learn: Tools for Schools*. London: Routledge. (Reading 2.8)

An interesting book on the informal learning out of school is:

Thomas, A. and Pattison, H. (2007) *How Children Learn at Home*. London: Continuum. (Reading 2.10)

reflectiveteaching.co.uk offers additional professional resources for this chapter. These may include *Further Reading*, illustrative *Reflective Activities*, useful *Web Links* and *Download Facilities* for diagrams, figures, checklists and activities.

Reflection

How can we develop the quality of our teaching?

3

Supplementary chapters at reflectiveteaching.co.uk is:

- **Mentoring** Learning through mentoring in initial teacher education
- **Enquiry** Developing evidence-informed practice

Introduction

This book is based on the belief that teaching is a complex and highly skilled activity which, above all, requires classroom teachers to exercise judgement in deciding how to act. High-quality teaching, and thus pupil learning, is dependent on the existence of such professional expertise.

The process of reflective teaching supports the development, maintenance and extension of professional expertise. We can conceptualise successive levels of expertise in teaching – those that student teachers may attain at different stages in their courses; those of the new teacher after their induction to full-time school life; and those of the experienced, expert teacher. And as teaching is a dynamic and responsive process, it is a profession in which development and learning are continuous.

The process of reflection thus feeds a career-long spiral of professional development and capability (see Figure 3.1).

Figure 3.1 The spiral of professional development

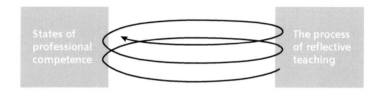

Reflective teaching should not only be personally fulfilling for teachers but should also lead to a steady increase in the quality of the education provided for children – teaching requires a sense of moral purpose. Indeed, we would argue that because it is evidence-based, reflective practice supports initial training students, newly qualified teachers, teaching assistants and experienced professionals in satisfying both external performance requirements and the intrinsic commitments to education to which most teachers subscribe.

TLRP principles

Two principles are of particular relevance to this chapter on reflective practice for the improvement of teaching:

Effective teaching and learning fosters both individual and social processes and outcomes. Learning is a social activity. Learners should be encouraged and helped to work with others, to share ideas and to build knowledge together. Consulting learners about their learning and giving them a voice is both an expectation and a right. (Principle 7)

Effective teaching and learning depends on teacher learning. The need for teachers to learn continuously in order to develop their knowledge and skills, and adapt and develop their roles, especially through classroom inquiry, should be recognised and supported. (Principle 9)

See Chapter 4

This chapter has three main parts. The first introduces some of *the dilemmas and challenges* which teachers and teaching assistants face; these are linked briefly to the idea of professional standards. In the second part, the meaning of reflective teaching is explored; seven major characteristics of reflective teaching are then identified and discussed. In exploring these characteristics, particular emphasis is placed on teaching as an evidence-informed profession and on the ways in which teachers might support one another's reflective practice. In the final part, we draw some conclusions that might inform the future actions of teachers and teaching assistants.

1 Dilemmas, reflection and effectiveness

1.1 Dilemmas and challenges in classroom life

The complicated nature of educational issues and the practical demands of classroom teaching ensure that a teacher's work is never finished. One need only review the foci of the various chapters in this book to gain a sense of the breadth of professional concerns that are within the purview of every teacher. Thus, when practicalities, performance standards, personal ideals and wider educational concerns are considered together, the job of reconciling the numerous requirements and possible conflicts may seem to be overwhelming. As a primary teacher explained to us:

> 'I love my work but it's a constant struggle to keep it all going. If I focus on one thing I have to neglect another. For instance, if I talk to a group or to a particular child then I have to keep an eye on what the others are doing; if I hear someone read then I can't be in position to extend other children's language when opportunities arise; if I put out clay then I haven't got room for painting; if I go to evening courses then I can't prepare as well for the next day; if I spend time with my family then I worry about my class but if I rush around collecting materials or something then I feel guilty for neglecting the family. It's not easy … but I wouldn't do anything else.'

And a secondary teacher's concerns highlight the tension that appears between the numerous facets of their professional and personal lives:

> 'I have to say that I find teaching immensely rewarding, but it should be appreciated that it's all-encompassing. My work with my science classes across several year groups, departmental responsibilities, form group pastoral care and role as assessment leader all take considerable time, care and attention. I'm not sure that I know of any teacher who feels that they're doing a good job all round, but some say that's the sign of a teacher who cares don't they? … acknowledging that you can always do better. But don't even talk to me about 'work-life balance'!'

These quotes illustrate that the 'job' of becoming a teacher involves, amongst other things, learning a complex set of technical skills and understandings; positioning yourself within a larger community of practice; managing emotional dimensions of 'personal development'; and connecting, integrating and reconciling various sources of theory and experiences of practice. For beginning teachers, it is first necessary to reconcile the realities of school experience with prior personal beliefs about children, subjects, teaching and learning (Luehmann, 2007).

Such dilemmas and tensions are frequently expressed. A classic analysis of the dilemmas which teachers face was provided by Berlak and Berlak (1981). The framework that they developed is simple but powerful. Its strength derives from the fact that, although they studied only three schools in detail, they took great care to relate their analysis of the dilemmas which arose in the 'micro' world of the classroom to the major factors, beliefs and influences in society as a whole. Such factors, they argued, influence, structure and constrain the actions of teachers, children and parents. However, they do not do so in ways which are consistent, because of existing complexities and contradictions within school and education systems – hence the dilemmas which have to be faced. The resolution of

Figure 3.2
Common dilemmas faced by teachers

Treating each child as a 'whole person'	Treating each child as a 'pupil'
Organising the children on an individual or group basis	Organising pupils as a class
Giving pupils a degree of control over their time, their activities and their work standards	Maintaining purposeful control over children's use of time, their activities and their work standards
Seeking to motivate the children through intrinsic engagement and enjoyment of activities	Offering reasons and rewards so that students are extrinsically motivated to tackle tasks
Providing a curriculum structure that enables children to feel in control of their learning	Providing a curriculum structure that reflects what the children need for them to understand and take a place in society
Showing connections in teaching and learning across subject boundaries	Maintaining the integrity of subject content in teaching and learning
Aiming for quality in school work	Aiming for quantity in school work
Focusing on the development of basic skills across the curriculum	Focusing on expressive and creative elements of subject and topic learning
Trying to build up cooperative and social skills	Developing self-reliance and self-confidence in individuals
Inducting the children into a 'common culture'	Affirming the variety of cultures in a diverse, multi-ethnic society
Allocating teacher time, attention and resources equally among all the children	Paying attention to the special needs of particular children
Maintaining consistent rules and understanding about behaviour and schoolwork	Being flexible and responsive to particular situations and individuals
Presenting oneself formally to the children	Being more open with the children
Working with 'professional levels' of application and care for the children	Considering one's personal needs as well as one's professional responsibilities

such dilemmas calls for teachers to use professional judgement to assess the most appropriate course of action in any particular situation.

But what are the major dilemmas that have to be faced?

Figure 3.2 presents some of the dilemmas and challenges faced by teachers in primary and secondary schools. There are also phase-specific dilemmas and challenges that are not listed, and you may like to consider what is particularly important to you, or what you would add?

Reflective activity 3.1

Aim: To review experienced dilemmas.

Evidence and reflection: Think about your own situation and classroom experiences. Look carefully at Figure 3.2 and see whether any of the identified dilemmas provide a realistic reflection of those you are experiencing. Are there other dilemmas that relate to your specific context?

Having carried out this exercise, try to identify the three most pressing dilemmas that you are facing. Think carefully about each of these and consider whether there are any measures that you might take to help mitigate them (for example, discussions with relevant colleagues about developing approaches to behaviour management; changing classroom assessment practices in line with recent CPD events; researching the classroom behaviour of individuals/groups in order to have the evidence for curriculum developments, etc.)

The important point here is to start with one dilemma and consider what evidence you need to be able to address it effectively, and where that evidence might come from. Progress will often be slow and incremental, but such professional development has powerful potential for change.

Extension: Note that this reflective activity may well lead to a more formalised piece of classroom-based research; this is considered in Reflective activity 3.2 below.

This book provides a practical guide to ways of reflecting on such issues. Indeed, it offers strategies and advice for developing the necessary classroom expertise to resolve them. Resolution of such dilemmas will always be based on teacher judgement. However, in contemporary education, performance data and other evidence are now routinely used to augment (and sometimes challenge or refine) such judgements.

1.2 Reflection and evidence-informed practice

Three main sources of evidence are available to teachers.

School performance or benchmark evidence, generated from assessment, inspection or intake data, is often made available to schools to support improvement strategies. Such data may also be provided to parents to inform school choice. It is also now very significant to school managers who must respond if trends appear, and for inspection teams and others who make judgements about school *and* teacher effectiveness. There are now sophisticated management information systems which enable, for instance, tracking of pupil progress and school self-evaluation in preparation for inspection (See Chapter 14, Section 3.3, also Readings 14.3 and 14.4). There are various systems for data collation, target setting and national comparison – such as, in England, RAISEonline. In secondary education, most exam boards also provide feedback systems. Measures of pupil outcomes may be used in annual reviews of teacher performance – which will certainly personalise the challenge of achieving appropriate validity and reliability. At the other end of the scale, international, system-wide comparisons are also made with countries in Europe, the Americas and parts of Asia and Australasia through surveys such as the Programme for International Student Assessment (PISA) and Trends in International Mathematics and Science Study (TIMSS).

A second source of evidence comes from educational research and, in particular, from research reviews and summaries which interpret such research. The research centre for Evidence-Policy and Practice in Education (eppi.ioe.ac.uk) pioneered systematic reviews of available evidence, whilst the Teaching and Learning Research Programme produced User Summaries, Research Briefings and Practitioner Applications for its major school findings (**tlrp.org**). The British Educational Research Association is the largest UK body for specialist researchers in the field (**bera.ac.uk**). The National Foundation for Educational

Research (**nfer.ac.uk**) continues to provide a range of independent evidence to support teaching and learning. However, establishment of a trustworthy UK aggregating service to enable access to the range of valuable work has proved difficult in recent years. An 'evidence centre' and other collaborative initiatives have been debated and trialled and

the best contemporary resource in the 'toolkit' at **educationendowmentfoundation.org.uk**. For a 2010 review and analysis of sources of research on education, see **sfre.ac.uk**. Further guidance is provided in Chapter 16, and up-to-date advice and links are maintained on **refectiveteaching.co.uk**.

The third source of evidence is, arguably, the most important for reflective practitioners for it suggests that teachers themselves collect their own classroom and school evidence. It suggests, in other words, that teachers take control of their own research and development. This builds on the long tradition of action research which was established by Lawrence

Stenhouse (Reading 3.3). The General Teaching Councils in Northern Ireland, Scotland and Wales and the Teaching Council of Ireland (see Reading 17.3) are particular advocates of this sort of work (as was the GTC for England, until its closure in 2011). Indeed, the GTC for Northern Ireland actively promotes 'The Reflective Teacher' and encourages the

professional community to 'take ownership'. The GTC for Scotland has been supporting professional development since 1966. Following Donaldson (2010), there are new developments for career-long professional review through a system of 'professional update'. The GTC for Wales has awarded significant funds to promote professional development and teacher research, and is a significant voice for teachers. More widely, teacher unions and organisations such as Educational International (ei-ie.org) support research activities that inform teaching and learning in various countries across the globe.

The model at Figure 3.3 summarises the relationship between classroom practice and enquiry. It suggests that a practical *problem* in the classroom can helpfully be considered in terms of the *issues* which might underlie it. Some careful thinking might help! As we saw above, this foregrounds an appreciation of classroom *dilemmas* – the challenge of

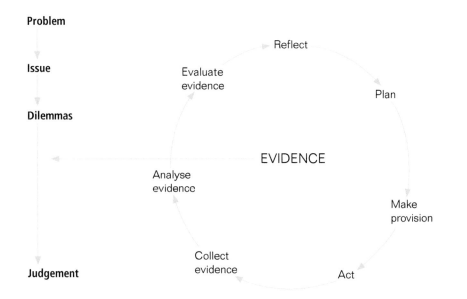

Figure 3.3
Evidence-informed
practice

deciding what to do when there are a number of competing possibilities. The essence of professional expertise in teaching is being able to make high-quality practical *judgements* (Heilbronn, 2010, Reading 3.6) to resolve such dilemmas. Figure 3.3 shows how evidence from classroom enquiry and other research sources can enhance such judgements.

For example, pupils' inappropriate classroom behaviour might result in an immediate response from a teacher to assert control. However, later reflection might promote consideration of a number of possible longer-term issues. Are teacher–pupil relationships beginning to go awry for some reason? Do the children respect teacher authority and accept his or her actions as fair? Is the curriculum engaging the students, or causing them to become bored? Are the lessons well planned, offering focus, interest, progression and successful learning experiences? Each of these topics, and others, could merit further investigation through classroom enquiry.

Of course, the sources of evidence we have reviewed – using performance or benchmark data, interpreting educational research and professional enquiry by teachers themselves – actually complement each other. Reflective professionals should thus be able to draw on, or contribute to, many sources of evidence, and use them to inform their teaching practices. However, evidence in education must always be critically evaluated, as in other fields of social science or professional practice, because absolute 'truth' is not available, given the difficulties of research on people and teaching/learning processes. Further, because education is imbued with values, it would also be inappropriate to entirely base educational decisions on evidence. This is the reason why the term 'evidence-informed' is preferred over 'evidence-based'. It shares an assertion of the importance of evidence in decision-making, but does not make inappropriate claims for precedence. Judgement remains essential for practitioners in classrooms and schools, just as it is necessary for administrators and politicians in relation to policy.

1.3 Standards for effectiveness and career development

In recent years, competency criteria and 'standards' have been set by governments in many countries to provide a framework for teacher training and further professional development. The evolution of such standards can take a considerable time and is often predicated on the political perspectives of particular governments. In most cases, such standards provide a statutory framework for continuing professional development and performance management, as well as for initial teacher education.

Broad standards and competences can be helpful in defining goals for students, mentors, headteachers, tutors and others who are engaged in teacher education and professional development. They can:

- set out clear expectations;
- help teachers to plan and monitor development, training and performance;
- maintain a focus on improving the achievement of pupils and educational quality;
- provide a basis for the professional recognition of teacher expertise.

However, we need to be clear about the status of such models and criteria. Those required where a centralised national curriculum and legally defined assessment procedures exist may well differ from those which are called for where teachers and schools are more

Figure 3.4
Regulations for the education of pupil teachers, 1846

Regulations respecting the education of pupil teachers.
Minutes of the Committee of Council on Education, 1846.

Qualifications of candidates:

To be at least 13 years of age.

To not be subject to any bodily infirmity likely to impair their usefulness.

To have a certificate of moral character.

To read with fluency, ease and expression.

To write in a neat hand with correct spelling and punctuation, a simple prose narrative read to them.

To write from dictation sums in the first four rules of arithmetic, simple and compound: to work them correctly, and to know the table of weights and measures.

To point out the parts of speech in a simple sentence.

To have an elementary knowledge of geography.

To repeat the Catechism and to show that they understand its meaning and are acquainted with the outline of Scripture history. (Where working in schools connected with the Church of England only.)

To teach a junior class to the satisfaction of the Inspector.

Girls should also be able to sew neatly and to knit.

engaged with a greater degree of partnership; for example, there is a substantial difference in the character of the standards in the different countries of the UK, in different states in North America and in various countries of the European Union. Those called for where class sizes are large and resources scarce (as in many parts of the world) may vary from those needed when much smaller classes or groups are taught with good access to suitable equipment. Further, it is worth considering that the standards required at any particular period in history are unlikely to remain constant. To illustrate this point, it is interesting to consider the requirements made of apprenticed 'pupil teachers' in England almost 170 years ago (see Figure 3.4).

We have to remember then, that officially endorsed standards are historically and contextually specific. Despite the moderating influence of available research, they are likely to be strongly influenced by the cultures, values and the priorities of decision-makers who happen to be in power at the time of their construction. During a 40-year career, a teacher is likely to experience many such systems, and historical or comparative reflection will help keep them in perspective. Indeed, Hay McBer's influential report on teacher effectiveness cautioned against over-conformity when they emphasised that 'teachers are not clones' and asserted that professionals always have to use their judgement about circumstances, pupils, contexts and teaching approaches (2000, para 1.1.4). The central point to be made here, then, is that whilst standards provide a framework for teacher actions and responsibilities, they are not a substitute for the practical judgements that are the central element of reflective and evidence-informed teaching (see Calderhead, 1994, Reading 3.5 for an elaboration of the complexities of teaching).

2 The meaning of reflective teaching

The concept of reflective teaching stems from Dewey (1933, Reading 3.1 who contrasted 'routine action' with 'reflective action'). According to Dewey, routine action is guided by factors such as tradition, habit and authority, and by institutional definitions and expectations. By implication it is relatively static and is thus unresponsive to changing priorities and circumstances. Reflective action, on the other hand, involves a willingness to engage in constant self-appraisal and development. Among other things, it implies flexibility, rigorous analysis and social awareness.

Reflective action, in Dewey's view, involves the 'active, persistent and careful consideration of any belief or supposed form of knowledge in the light of the grounds that support it' (1933, p. 9). Teachers who are unreflective about their teaching tend to accept the *status quo* in their schools and simply 'concentrate on finding the most efficient means to solve problems that have largely been defined for them' by others (Zeichner and Liston, 1996, p. 9). Of course, routine action based on ongoing assumptions is necessary, but Dewey argued that it is insufficient on its own. In Dewey's view, reflection 'enables us to direct our actions with foresight' (1933, p. 17).

Donald Schön (1983, Reading 3.2; 1987) extended these ideas in analysing the actions of many different professional occupations – medicine, law, engineering, management,

Expert question

Reflection: is our classroom practice based on incremental, evidence-informed and collaborative improvement strategies?

This question contributes to a conceptual framework underpinning professional expertise (see Chapter 16).

etc. Schön emphasised that most professionals face unique situations that require the use of knowledge and experience to inform action. This is an active, experimental and transactional process which Schön called 'professional artistry'. It is the 'kind of professional competence which practitioners display in unique, uncertain and conflicted situations of practice' (1987, p. 22) – a form of 'knowing-in-action'. Schön thus came to distinguish between 'reflection-on-action', which looks back to evaluate, and 'reflection-in-action', which enables immediate action. Both contribute to the capabilities of a reflective teacher.

Others, such as Solomon (1987), have made a powerful case for reflection as a social practice, in which the articulation of ideas *to others* is central to the development of an open, critical perspective. The support of colleagues and mentors is thus extremely helpful in building understanding – ideas which have been extended further with the concepts such as 'culture of collaboration', 'community of enquiry' and 'network learning' (see Reading 3.7).

Such ideas about what it is to be a reflective professional, when developed and applied to teaching, are both challenging and exciting. In this section, we review their implications by identifying and discussing seven key characteristics of reflective practice. These are that it:

1 implies an active concern with aims and consequences, as well as means and technical efficiency.

2 is applied in a cyclical or spiralling process, in which teachers monitor, evaluate and revise their own practice continuously.

3 requires competence in methods of evidence-informed classroom enquiry, to support the progressive development of higher standards of teaching.

4 requires attitudes of open-mindedness, responsibility and wholeheartedness.

5 is based on teacher judgement, informed by evidence and insights from other research.

6 along with professional learning and personal fulfilment, they are enhanced through collaboration and dialogue with colleagues.

7 enables teachers to creatively mediate externally developed frameworks for teaching and learning.

Each of these characteristics will now be considered more fully.

2.1 Aims and consequences

Reflective teaching implies an active concern with aims and consequences as well as means and technical competence

This issue relates first to the immediate aims and consequences of classroom practice for these are any teacher's prime responsibility. However, classroom work cannot be isolated from the influence of the wider society and a reflective teacher must therefore consider both spheres.

An example from the history of educational policy-making in England will illustrate the way in which changes outside schools influence actions within them. Following the initiation of a 'Great Debate' by Prime Minister Callaghan (1976) many of the 'taken-for-granteds' in education were progressively challenged during the 1980s and 1990s. Successive Conservative governments introduced far-reaching and cumulative changes in all spheres of education. Many of these reforms were opposed by professional organisations (see for example, Haviland,1988; Arnot and Barton 1992) but with no noticeable effect on political decision-making. Indeed, the allegation was made that educational policy was being influenced by a closed system of beliefs – an 'ideology' deriving from a small number of right-wing politicians and pressure groups. Meanwhile, teachers and pupils worked to implement the new forms of curriculum, assessment, accountability, management and control which had been introduced, despite the fact that the profession at the time was largely opposed to the principles on which the reforms were based (see Osborn et al., 2000; Pollard et al., 1994).

Such a stark example of the contestation of aims and values in education raises questions concerning the relationship between professionals, parents and policymakers, and mirrors current developments in many countries around the world. It is possible to start from the seemingly uncontroversial argument that, in democratic societies, decisions about the aims of education should be 'democratically' determined. However, it has also been suggested (for instance, by *Education International* representing 400 education organisations across the world) that teachers should adopt a role as active 'interpreters' of political policy. Indeed, that most teachers accept this argument is shown by the ways in which they have implemented legislation about which they had reservations. For example, where prescribed national curricula are to be implemented, the 'official' rationale may not match up to the day-to-day experience of classroom teachers. Reflective teachers are likely to use their initiative to adapt the curriculum so that it is more suitable for the pupils in their care (Ball, Maguire and Hoskins, 2011).

This stance accepts the authority of governments regarding educational goals, but asserts the need for practical judgement regarding implementation. It is thus very different from the idea of the wholly autonomous professional with which many teachers once identified. Yet it can be argued that the existence of unconstrained autonomy is only reasonable and practical if ends, aims and values are completely uncontroversial. However, as soon as questions about educational aims and social values are seriously raised, then the position changes. In a democratic society, the debate appropriately extends to the political domain and this, of course, is what has happened in recent years in many countries.

This does not mean though, that teachers, even as interpreters of policy, should simply 'stand by' in the procedure. Indeed, there are two important roles that they can play. In the case of the first, an appropriate metaphor for the teacher's role is, as both White (1978) and Sachs (2003) have suggested, that of 'activist'. This recognises that school teachers are individual members of society who, within normal political processes, have rights to pursue their values and beliefs as guided by their own individual moral and ethical concerns. They should thus be as active as they wish to be in contributing to the formation of public policy. Second, whilst accepting a responsibility for translating politically determined aims into practice, teachers should speak out, as they have done many times in the past, if they view particular aims and policies as being professionally impracticable, educationally unsound or morally questionable. In such circumstances the professional experience, knowledge and judgements of teachers should be brought to bear on policymakers directly – whether or not the policymakers wish for or act on the advice which is offered (for interesting developments of this argument, see Thompson, 1997). Indeed, it is important that, within a modern democratic society, teachers should be entitled to not only a hearing, but also some influence, on educational policy. Sectoral and subject associations in the UK, such as the Association for the Study of Primary Education and the Geographical Association, together with the General Teaching Councils of most parts of the UK and teacher unions (whose influence may be particularly significant), provide collective forms of organisation for such voices.

 The reflective teacher should thus be aware of the political process and of its legitimate oversight of public educational services. They should also be willing to contribute to it both as a citizen and as a professional (see also Chapter 17 and Readings 17.2, 17.5 and 17.7).

2.2 A cyclical process

Reflective teaching is applied in a cyclical or spiralling process, in which teachers monitor, evaluate and revise their own practice continuously

 This characteristic refers to the process of reflective teaching and provides the dynamic basis for teacher action. It is clearly evident in the thinking of Dewey, Schön and others, though the specific conception of a classroom-based, reflexive process stems from the teacher-based, action-research movement of which Lawrence Stenhouse was a key figure. He argued (1975, Reading 3.3) that teachers should act as 'researchers' of their own practice and should develop the curriculum through practical enquiry. Various alternative models have since become available (Carr and Kemmis, 1986; Elliott, 1991; McNiff, 1988) and, although there are some significant differences in these models, they all preserve a central concern with self-monitoring and reflection (see also Pring, 2010, Reading 3.4).

Teachers are principally expected to plan, make provision and act. Reflective teachers also need to monitor, observe and collect data on their own, and the children's, intentions, actions and feelings. This evidence then needs to be critically analysed and evaluated so that it can be shared, judgements made and decisions taken. Finally, this may lead the teacher to revise his or her classroom policies, plans and provision before beginning the process again. It is a dynamic process which is intended to lead through successive cycles, or through a spiralling process, towards higher quality standards of teaching. This model is simple, comprehensive and certainly could be an extremely powerful influence on practice. It is consistent with the notion of reflective teaching, as described by both Dewey and Schön, and provides an essential clarification of the procedures for reflective teaching.

Figure 3.5 represents the key stages of the reflective process.

Figure 3.5 The process of reflective teaching

Reflective activity 3.2

Aim. To explore how improvement can come from collecting evidence of our teaching.

Evidence and reflection. The key to this process is to create a focus and to consider what evidence is required in order to make judgements about how to proceed. For example, you may be considering the progress of a particular child in a specific curriculum area, or analysing the effectiveness of a method for encouraging group dialogue. Whatever your focus, the stages you'll consider are:

1 Which facet of classroom life should be investigated and why?
2 What evidence to collect, and how?
3 How can we analyse, interpret and apply the findings?

This may seem rather formal, but these are all things you'll be thinking about in any situation where you are evaluating your classroom.

To start with, pick a small issue or dilemma (see Section 1.1 and Reflective activity 3.1) and see if you can construct a plan for evidence gathering, on which you can base subsequent action.

Extension. Generally, teachers focus their first classroom-based research and development activity on an individual child or group of children. Is there a whole-class intervention that you would like to trial? How will the evidence base change for such work?

For detailed support on these three processes of classroom enquiry, see the supplementary chapter on Enquiry at **reflectiveteaching.co.uk**

2.3 Gathering and evaluating evidence

Reflective teaching requires competence in methods of evidence-informed classroom enquiry, to support the progressive development of higher standards of teaching

We can identify four key skills here: reviewing relevant, existing research; gathering new evidence; analysis; and evaluation. Each of these contribute to the cyclical process of reflection (see Section 2.2).

Reviewing relevant, existing research. The issue here is to learn as much as possible from others. Published research on the issue of concern may be reviewed. Internet-based search techniques make this an increasingly straightforward task as do other resources – including the *Key Readings* which conclude all chapters of this book and its associated book of linked **Readings**. Going into yet more depth, *Notes for Further Reading*, chapter-by-chapter, are offered on **reflectiveteaching.co.uk**.

Gathering new evidence. This relates to the essential issue of knowing what is going on in a classroom or school as a means of forming one's own opinion. It is concerned with collecting data, describing situations, processes, causes and effects with care and accuracy. Two sorts of data are particularly relevant. 'Objective' data are important, such as descriptions of what people actually do. Pupil performance data comes into this category of course (Ofsted, 2008, Reading 14.4), but is only part of the picture. Additionally, it is also vital to collect more subjective data which describe how people feel and think – their perceptions. The collection of both types of data calls for considerable skill on the part of any classroom investigator, particularly when they may be enquiring into their own practice.

Analytical skills. These skills are needed to address the issue of how to interpret descriptive data. Such 'facts' are not meaningful until they are placed in a framework that enables a reflective teacher to relate them one with the other and to begin to theorise about them.

Evaluative skills. Evaluative skills are involved in making judgements about the educational consequences of the results of the practical enquiry. Evaluation, in the light of aims, values and the experience of others enables the results of an enquiry to be applied to future policy and practice.

Increasingly the teaching community is engaged, at a classroom or school level, in enquiries into teaching and learning, in order to inform subsequent practice and the developmental priorities of a school. Many of such enquiries exhibit characteristics of case study and action research (Pring, 2010, Reading 3.4; Carr and Kemmis, 1986; Hamilton and Corbett-Whittier, 2013). The 'case' is often a class, a year group or the school cohort in which spiral of action research develops. A range of data collection methods may be used, focusing on pupil perspectives, direct observations, interpretations of attainment data, etc.

Expert question

Warrant: are our teaching strategies evidence-informed, convincing and justifiable to stakeholders?

This question contributes to a conceptual framework underpinning professional expertise (see Chapter 16).

Such work can both develop and legitimate school and classroom policies – and thus provide sound answers to challenges where at teacher or school is required to justify their practice.

However, such competence is not sufficient in itself for a teacher who wishes to engage in reflective teaching. Certain attitudes are also necessary and need to be integrated and applied with enquiry skills.

Further practical advice on how to carry out classroom enquiries is offered in supplementarymaterial on **reflectiveteaching.co.uk**. This includes guidance on publicly available sources of research evidence and, being web-based, is updated regularly.

2.4 Attitudes towards teaching

Reflective teaching requires attitudes of open-mindedness, responsibility and whole-heartedness

In this section we draw directly on the thinking of Dewey.

Open-mindedness. As Dewey put it, open-mindedness is:

> An active desire to listen to more sides than one, to give heed to facts from whatever source they come, to give full attention to alternative possibilities, to recognise the possibility of error even in the beliefs which are dearest to us. (1933, p. 29)

Open-mindedness is an essential attribute for rigorous reflection because any sort of enquiry that is consciously based on partial evidence, only weakens itself. We thus use the concept in the sense of being willing to reflect upon ourselves and to challenge our own assumptions, prejudices and ideologies, as well as those of others – no easy task. However, to be open-minded regarding evidence and its interpretation is not the same thing as declining to take up a value position on important social and educational issues. This point brings us to the second attribute which Dewey saw as a prerequisite to reflective action – 'responsibility'.

Responsibility. Intellectual responsibility, according to Dewey, means:

> To consider the consequences of a projected step; it means to be willing to adopt these consequences when they follow reasonably ... Intellectual responsibility secures integrity. (1933, p. 30)

The position implied here is clearly related to the question of aims that we discussed in 2.1 above. However, in Dewey's writing the issue is relatively clearly bounded and he seems to be referring to classroom teaching and to school practices only. Tabachnick and Zeichner (1991) take this considerably further. Moral, ethical and political issues will be raised and must, they argue, be considered so that professional and personal judgements can be made about what is worthwhile. It clearly follows that a simple instrumental approach to teaching is not consistent with a reflective social awareness.

Wholeheartedness. 'Wholeheartedness', the third of Dewey's necessary attitudes, refers essentially to the way in which such consideration takes place. Dewey's suggestion was that reflective teachers should be dedicated, single-minded, energetic and enthusiastic. As he put it:

There is no greater enemy of effective thinking than divided interest. … A genuine enthusiasm is an attitude that operates as an intellectual force. When a person is absorbed, the subject carries him on. (1933, p. 30)

Together, these three attitudes are vital ingredients of the professional commitment that needs to be demonstrated by all those who aim to be reflective teachers. Echoes with the issues discussed in Chapter 1 will be readily apparent.

In modern circumstances, these attitudes of open-mindedness, wholeheartedness and responsibility are often challenged, as a result of continual change from the political centre in many countries. Halpin (2001) argues that maintaining 'intelligent hope' and imagining future possibilities are essential for committed educationalists. Beyond simple optimism, this requires 'a way of thinking about the present and the future that is permeated by critique, particularly of the kind that holds up to external scrutiny taken-for-granted current circumstances' (p. 117). Maintaining a constructive engagement, a willingness to imagine new futures, and a self-critical spirit are thus all connected to reflective practice.

2.5 Teacher judgement

Reflective teaching is based on teacher judgement, informed by evidence and insights from other research

Teachers' knowledge has often been criticised. For instance, Bolster (1983) carried out an analysis of teachers as classroom decision-makers and suggested that, since teacher knowledge is specific and pragmatic, it is resistant to development. Bolster argued that teacher knowledge is based on individual experiences and is simply believed to be of value if it 'works' in practical situations. However, this gives little incentive to change, even in the light of evidence supporting alternative ideas or practices. On this analysis there is little need for teacher judgement, since teachers will stick to routinised practices.

For an alternative view we can again draw on Donald Schön's work (Schön, 1983, Reading 3.2) on the characteristics of 'reflective practitioners'. Schön contrasted 'scientific' professional work such as laboratory research, with 'caring' professional work such as education. He called the former 'high hard ground' and saw it as supported by quantitative and 'objective' evidence. On the other hand, the 'swampy lowlands' of the caring professions involve more interpersonal areas and qualitative issues. These complex 'lowlands', according to Schön, tend to become 'confusing messes' of intuitive action. He thus suggested that, although such 'messes' tend to be highly relevant in practical terms, they are not easily amenable to rigorous analysis because they draw, as we have seen, on a type of knowledge-in-action. It is spontaneous, intuitive, tacit and intangible but, it 'works' in practice.

Schön's ideas have received powerful empirical support in recent years, with the sophistication of teachers' classroom thinking and 'craft knowledge' being increasingly recognised and understood by both researchers (Calderhead, 1988b, Reading 3.5; Brown and McIntyre, 1993; Warwick, Hennessy and Mercer, 2011) and some organisations with an influence on policymakers (OECD, 2005; Barber and Mourshead, 2007). It is clear that effective teachers make use of judgements all the time, as they adapt their teaching to the ever-changing learning challenges which their circumstances and pupils present to them. There has also been much greater recognition of the role of intuition in the work of experienced teachers (Atkinson and Claxton, 2000; Tomlinson, 1999a and 1999b) and decision-making. Of course, reflective teachers need to recognise potential bias in their judgements as a result of their diverse experiences, and this again emphasises the need for open-mindedness.

Educational researchers' knowledge may be based on comparative, historical or philosophical research, on empirical study with large samples of classrooms, teachers, pupils or schools, on innovative methodologies, or on developing theoretical analyses. Many researchers certainly regard it as their duty to probe, analyse and evaluate – particularly with regard to the impact of policy – even though this is not always popular with governments! Whatever its character, such educational research has the potential to complement, contextualise and enhance the detailed and practical understandings of practising teachers.

In recent years, considerable effort has been made to improve the relevance, significance and impact of educational research, and to engage with practitioners and policymakers. Indeed, the best work is of very high quality and is an important source of ideas and evidence on teaching, learning, policy and practice.

Over 100 selections of such work are provided in **Readings** and further advice (with regular updates) is offered through **reflectiveteaching.co.uk**.

Politicians' knowledge of education has often been criticised. However, governments have a democratic mandate and are appropriately concerned to ensure that educational services meet national needs. Teachers would thus be unjustified if they ignored the views of politicians, though independence, experience, judgement and expertise remain the defining characteristics of professionalism. Indeed, where politicians' views appear to be influenced by fashionable whims, media panics or party considerations rather than established educational needs, then a certain amount of 'professional mediation' may be entirely justified (see Section 2.7).

Taken as a whole, we strongly advocate attempts to maximise the potential for collaboration between teachers, researchers and politicians. For such collaboration to be successful it must be based on a frank appreciation of each other's strengths and weaknesses. While recognising the danger of unjustified generalisation, we therefore identify these strengths and weaknesses (see Figure 3.6).

We arrive then, at a position that calls for attempts to draw on the strengths of the knowledge of teachers, researchers and politicians or policymakers. By doing this, we may overcome the weaknesses which exist in each position. This is what we mean by the statement that reflective teaching should be based on 'informed teacher judgement'. The implied collaborative endeavour underpins this whole book.

Figure 3.6
A comparison
of teachers',
researchers'
and politicians'
knowledge

	Strengths	Weaknesses
Teachers' knowledge	Often practically relevant and directly useful Often communicated effectively to practitioners Often concerned with the wholeness of classroom processes and experiences	May be impressionistic and can lack rigour Usually based in particular situations which limits generalisation Analysis is sometimes over-influenced by existing assumptions
Researchers' knowledge	May be based on careful research with large samples and reliable methods Often provides a clear and incisive analysis when studied May offer novel views of situations and issues	Often uses jargon unnecessarily and communicates poorly Often seems obscure and difficult to relate to practical issues Often fragments educational processes and experiences
Politicians' knowledge	Often responsive to issues of public concern. May have a democratic mandate May be backed by institutional, financial and legal resources	Often over-influenced by short-term political considerations Often reflects party political positions rather than educational needs Is often imposed and may thus lack legitimacy

2.6 Learning with colleagues

Reflective teaching, professional learning and personal fulfilment are enhanced through collaboration and dialogue with colleagues

The value of engaging in reflective activity is almost always enhanced if it can be carried out in association with other colleagues, be they trainees, teaching assistants, teachers, mentors or tutors. The circumstances in schools, with very high proportions of contact-time with children, have constrained a great deal of such educational discussion between teachers in the past – though this is gradually changing as whole-school or even inter-school professional development assumes a greater priority. On teacher-education courses, despite the pressure of curricular requirements, reflection together in seminars, tutor groups and workshops, at college or in school, should bring valuable opportunities to share and compare, support and advise in reciprocal ways. Indeed, school settings are a particular example of the development of 'communities of practice', which Wenger analysed (1999, see also Reading 3.7). This concept of workplace communities of practice has also been powerfully developed beyond schools through the use of teacher networks.

Whether professional conversations occur between experienced teachers, as in lesson study in the UK (see Chapter 10), or between novice and experienced teachers as in school-based initial teacher education, consideration of professional ethics and structuring will ensure that the participants derive the maximum benefit from activity. For example:

- agreement about roles and relationships within such arrangements must be clear;
- the central focus of discussions should be on the benefits for children's learning that derive from the joint reflection;
- in cases where the focus is on developing the teaching of one person involved in the discussion, clear parameters for any teaching observations and subsequent conversations need to be agreed;
- decisions on future targets should be agreed together before discussion concludes.

It is important, of course, that trust between teachers and others is really secure – for without this, the sharing of ideas, concerns and challenges can seem threatening. Interestingly, Kettle and Sellars (1996), when studying developing reflective practice with trainee teachers, found that work with peers encouraged challenge to existing theories and preconceived views of teaching whilst modelling a collaborative style of professional development.

More practical advice on mentoring is offered on **reflectiveteaching.co.uk**

This sort of work can be extremely engaging. For instance, a group of teachers investigated 'talk in science' in their school ... and the implications spread through the school. A sense of excitement is palpable in the lead teacher's report of the project:

> 'After a year of classroom analysis we, as the research group, have a wealth of data and we are now in a position to talk with enthusiasm and authority to other professionals about what we have learned about establishing a classroom climate which values this approach and encourages talk which is exploratory, responsive and relevant to individual needs. We are also able to extend our knowledge and understanding to influence future developments.' (Flitton, 2010; see also Flitton and Warwick, 2012)

Wherever and whenever it occurs, collaborative, reflective discussion capitalises on the social nature of learning (Vygotsky, 1978, Reading 2.3). This is as significant for adults as it is for children and it works through many of the same basic processes. Aims are thus clarified, experiences are shared, language and concepts for analysing practice are refined, the personal insecurities of innovation are reduced, evaluation becomes reciprocal and commitments are affirmed (see also Pring, 2010, Reading 3.4). Moreover, openness, activity and discussion gradually weave the values and self of individuals into the culture and mission of the school or course. This can be both personally fulfilling and educationally effective.

Given the enormous importance of coherence and progression in school provision, collaborative work is also a necessity. Work on school leadership suggests the imperative of senior management working actively and positively with staff to find institutional solutions to teaching dilemmas and challenges. Yet more detailed work on the nature of school cultures and the development of the 'intelligent school', whilst affirming the enormous value of whole-school staff teams working and learning together, has also shown the complexity and fragility of the process (MacGilchrist et al., 2004). Beyond schools, the development of 'networked learning communities' and other forms of

Expert question

Culture: does the school support expansive learning by affirming learner contributions, engaging partners and providing attractive opportunities?

This question contributes to a conceptual framework underpinning professional expertise (see Chapter 16).

web-supported activity are very exciting, though are not always sustained. Professional, subject and phase-based associations, together with the existing UK General Teaching Councils, often provide important opportunities for collaborative work.

Whatever their circumstances, reflective teachers are likely to benefit from working, experimenting, talking, and reflecting with others (for a proven systematic approach, see Reflective activity 3.3). Apart from the benefits for learning and professional development, it is usually both more interesting and more fun!

Reflective activity 3.3

Aim: To deepen collaboration with colleagues.

Evidence and reflection: One way of doing this is through implementing regular Lesson Study lessons.

Lesson Study is a highly specified form of classroom action research focusing on the development of teacher practice knowledge. Stemming from practice over many decades in Japan, lesson study offers a well developed set of principles and procedures for supporting the professional development of teachers, focusing on the collective planning and analysis of 'research lessons'. It has several components:

- identifying themes and groups
- formulating hypotheses and goals
- joint research lesson planning
- post research lesson discussion
- passing on the knowledge gained.

Lesson Study involves groups of teachers collaboratively planning, teaching, observing and analysing learning and teaching in specified lessons. Essentially, Lesson Study provides a way of looking in detail at something teachers want to try out in a lesson series – this can be a big thing (e.g. developing dialogic group work) or a smaller thing (e.g. an approach to lesson introductions). There is a specific and agreed lesson study focus and observations relate to the children's experience of the intervention; this is different from many 'normal' lesson observations (which usually have a range of different foci and in which the focus of observation is usually the teacher). A Lesson Study consists of a series of 'research lessons' that are *jointly* planned, taught/observed and analysed by a Lesson Study group. A series is usually three lessons, though it can be longer; a minimum of two is absolutely essential to ensure that the teacher learning from the first lesson can be used in the second.

Extension: You may wish to develop this approach across your cluster of schools in order to share innovations and developments more widely.

This approach to collaborative professional development is applied to curriculum planning in Chapter 10, Section 5.2. See also Pete Dudley's website: **http://lessonstudy.co.uk/**

WWW.

2.7 Reflective teaching as creative mediation

Reflective teaching enables teachers to creatively mediate external requirements

'Creative mediation' involves the interpretation of external requirements in the light of a teacher's knowledge of his or her pupils, values and educational principles. A study of change in education (Osborn et al., 2000) identified four different kinds of 'creative mediation' deployed by teachers to interpret such situations.

- *Protective mediation* calls for strategies to defend existing practices which are greatly valued (such as the desire to maintain an element of spontaneity in teaching in the face of assessment pressure).

- *Innovative mediation* is concerned with teachers finding strategies to work *within* the spaces and boundaries provided by new requirements – finding opportunities to be creative.

- *Collaborative mediation* refers to teachers working closely together to provide mutual support in satisfying and adapting new requirements.

- *Conspirational mediation* involves schools adopting more subversive strategies where teachers resist implementing those aspects of external requirements that they believe to be particularly inappropriate.

Such forms of mediation exemplify major strategies in the exercise of professional judgement (see also Chapter 17 and Readings 17.2, 17.3 and 17.5). Clearly they need to be carefully justified – but the irony is that creative mediation is often the source of essential forms of innovation for future development. Indeed, innovative schools and teachers are often sought out by charities, think-tanks, teacher associations and even government agencies in the constant quest for improvement in the quality of educational services.

All education systems need to be able to guarantee consistency in entitlements to provide opportunities for all – but they also require some capacity for innovation and change. In applying principles and evidence through their practice, and making this public when appropriate, reflective teachers have a significant role in providing such leadership.

> ### Expert questions
>
> **Effectiveness**: are there improvements in standards, in both basic skills and other areas of curricular attainment, to satisfy society's educational goals?
>
> **Empowerment**: is our pedagogic repertoire successful in enhancing wellbeing, learning disposition, capabilities and agency?
>
> These questions contribute to a conceptual framework underpinning professional expertise (see Chapter 16).

Conclusion

In this chapter we have considered the spiral of professional development and the potential to raise standards of teaching through evidence-informed judgement. We have outlined the seven key characteristics of reflective teaching.

Some readers may well be wondering if this isn't all just a bit much to ask. How is the time to be found? Isn't it all 'common sense' anyway? Two broad responses may be made. First, it is certainly the case that constantly engaging in classroom enquiry and reflective activities of the sort described in this book would be impossible. The point, however, is to use them as *learning experiences* which are undertaken from time to time in a 'mindful' and purposive way. Such experiences should lead to conclusions which can be applied in more routine circumstances. This is how professional expertise is actively developed. Second, there is certainly a good deal of 'common sense' in the process of reflective teaching. However, when reflective teaching is used as a means of professional development it is extended far beyond this underpinning. The whole activity is much more rigorous – carefully gathered evidence replaces subjective impressions, open-mindedness replaces prior expectations, insights from reading or constructive and structured critique from colleagues challenge what might previously have been taken for granted. 'Common sense' may well endorse the value of the basic, reflective idea but, ironically, one outcome of reflection is often to produce critique and movement beyond the limitations of common-sense thinking. That, in a sense, is the whole point, the reason why reflection is a necessary part of professional activity. The aim of reflective practice is thus to support a shift from routine actions rooted in common-sense thinking to reflective action stemming from professional understanding and expertise.

Expert question

Reflection: Is our classroom practice based on incremental, evidence-informed and collaborative improvement strategies?

In summary, evidence-informed reflection makes an important contribution throughout professional life. Novice teachers, such as those in initial teacher education, may use it to improve on specific and immediate practical teaching skills. Competent teachers, such as those who are newly qualified, may use reflection as a means of self-consciously increasing understanding and capability, thus moving towards a more complete level of professionalism. Expert teachers will work at a higher level, understanding the various issues concerning children, curriculum, classroom and school so well that many decisions become almost intuitive (see Chapter 16 and Eaude, 2012, Reading 16.3). Reflective activity thus can be seen as making a central contribution throughout a professional career.

Key readings

The dilemmas in educational decision-making, which suggest that reflection is a continually necessary element of teaching, are analysed in:

Berlak, A. and Berlak, H. (1981) *Dilemmas of Schooling.* London: Methuen.

On the potential gains from self-evaluation, classroom research and enquiry, see:

Stenhouse, L. (1975) *An Introduction to Curriculum Research and Development.* London: Heinemann. (Reading 3.3)

A classic work by Dewey which has strongly influenced the development of reflective practice is:

Dewey, J. (1933) *How We Think: A Restatement of the Relation of Reflective Thinking to the Educative Process.* Chicago: Henry Regnery. (Reading 3.1)

For analyses on the nature of professional knowledge and its potential to enhance learning, see:

Schön, D. A. (1983) *The Reflective Practitioner: How Professionals Think in Action.* London: Temple Smith. (Reading 3.2)

Heilbronn, R. and Yandell, J. (2011) *Critical Practice in Teacher Education: A Study of Professional Learning.* London: IOE Press. (Reading 3.6)

Timperley, H. (2011) *Realising the Power of Professional Learning.* Maidenhead: Open University Press. (Reading 16.6)

For an overview of different forms of research in education, including the contribution of school-based action research, see:

Pring, R. (2010) *Philosophy of Educational Research.* London: Continuum. (Reading 3.4)

More specific guidance on conducting classroom and school research is on reflectiveteaching.co.uk and includes:

Menter, I., Elliot, D., Hall, J., Hulme, M., Lewin, J. and Lowden, K. (2010) *A Guide to Practitioner Research in Education.* Maidenhead: Open University Press.

Mitchell, N. and Pearson, J. (2012) *Inquiring in the Classroom. Asking the Questions that Matter about Teaching and Learning.* London: Continuum.

The significance of learning and developing practice with colleagues is elaborated in:

Wenger, E. (1999) *Communities of Practice: Learning, Meaning and Identity.* Cambridge: Cambridge University Press. (see also Hodkinson et al., Reading 3.7)

McLaughlin, C., Black Hawkins, K., Brindley, S., McIntyre, D. and Taber, K. (2006) *Researching Schools: Stories from a Schools-University Partnership.* Maidenhead: Open University Press.

Sachs provides arguments for morally informed and socially aware teachers:

Sachs, J. (2003) *The Activist Teaching Profession.* Buckingham: Open University Press. (see also Reading 17.5 and 17.7)

reflectiveteaching.co.uk offers additional professional resources for this chapter. These may include *Further Reading*, illustrative *Reflective Activities*, useful *Web Links* and *Download Facilities* for diagrams, figures, checklists and activities.

Principles

What are the foundations of effective teaching and learning?

4

Introduction

This chapter is focused on ten 'evidence-informed educational principles' which have been specifically identified to support the development of teachers' professional judgement – and, indeed, as a contribution to education policy-making. Whilst the previous chapter focused on the *process* of reflective teaching, this one highlights some of the *enduring issues* with which teaching and learning are concerned.

The ten principles were conceptualised by the UK's Teaching and Learning Research Programme (2000–12) by reviewing the outcomes of its many research projects, consulting with UK practitioners in each major educational sector, and comparing these findings with other research from around the world (see James and Pollard, 2012).

The TLRP funded educational research for over a decade and involved over 100 projects and other initiatives. It represented a new style of social science which insists on engagement of potential users throughout the research process (Pollard, 2007). TLRP project teams thus worked closely with teacher practitioners and, in some cases, with policymakers. TLRP identified major themes, such as learning, teaching, assessment, etc, to analyse across its projects – and this process finally enabled the distillation of ten evidence-informed principles. They represent a holistic summary, prepared for application, of 'what we think we know' about effective teaching, learning and education.

The same period has seen the development of meta-analyses of measured effects of specific teaching strategies. John Hattie's work has been groundbreaking (Hattie, 2009, Reading 4.6; 2012, Reading 10.7), and is complemented by a new programme of randomised trials in England funded by the Education Endowment Foundation (EEF). This work is consolidated and presented to schools in the Sutton Trust-EEF Teaching and Learning Toolkit (**educationendowmentfoundation.org.uk/toolkit**). The Toolkit is particularly focused on disadvantaged pupils and the improvement of attainment through the use of specific teaching strategies.

TLRP's holistic principles and studies of effect sizes complement each other. It is vital to know which teaching strategies are likely to be most effective, and it is also essential to be able to interpret and understand teaching and learning processes, and to set them in the context of more wide-ranging educational purposes. We are thus developing, step by step, the means of really improving educational standards and life-chances for pupils. In the final part of the chapter we return to the theme of international knowledge accumulation.

1 Evidence-informed principles

Each of the ten principles which are described in this chapter has an extensive research base – they are 'evidence-informed'. They do not, however, seek to tell teachers what to do. Indeed, each principle is expressed at a level of generality which calls for contextual interpretation by a teacher in the light of his or her knowledge of the educational needs of pupils and the circumstances of the school in which he or she works. The principles are thus intended as a guide and support for teachers in making the professional judgements which they are uniquely positioned, and required, to make.

TLRP's approach promotes contextualised, evidence-informed teacher judgement. Other experts take similar positions:

> Bureaucratic solutions to problems of practice will always fail because effective teaching is not routine, students are not passive, and questions of practice are not simple, predictable, or standardised. Consequently, instructional decisions cannot be formulated on high then packaged and handed down to teachers. (Darling-Hammond, USA, 2007)
>
> TLRP 'insists that the articulation of evidence-informed pedagogic principles, which can inform teacher and policy-maker judgements rather than detailed instructional prescriptions that tell teachers what to do, is the most useful way to improve classroom practice at scale. This is surely right: teaching and learning are deeply contextual and highly contingent. Certainly our experience in Singapore strongly supports this claim, particularly if backed up by contextually appropriate, iterative, authentic and extended professional learning experiences (Hogan, Singapore, 2012, p. 97).
>
> The Teaching and Learning Toolkit will be most useful when in the hands of professionals. The aim of the Toolkit is to support teachers to make their own informed choices and adopt a more 'evidence-based' approach. The evidence it contains is a supplement to rather than a substitute for professional judgement; it provides no guaranteed solutions or quick fixes. (Higgins *et al.*, UK, 2013)

TLRP's ten principles are an attempt to pick out prominent patterns from the complexity of teaching and learning, and to shed light on them. They are statements of what we think we understand, at this point in time. The evidence-informed principles offer reference points, thus making it easier to take stock and review progress in educationally sound ways. But when particular classroom dilemmas arise, the principles will not actually determine a specific decision, for that is the job of the reflective teacher.

Our overarching guide is Principle 1, which is concerned with the most enduring objectives and moral purposes of education. A cluster of principles on curriculum, pedagogy and assessment then take us to the heart of teacher expertise, whilst a further group highlights the personal and social processes which underpin learning. Finally, two principles draw attention to enabling conditions for success in practice and policy.

In the following section, we introduce and illustrate the ten principles as a whole. Issues associated with each principle are also discussed and elaborated in relevant chapters of the book (as indicated in Figure 4.1), and we return synoptically to them in new ways in Chapter 16 when reviewing the various dimensions of teacher expertise.

Figure 4.1, overleaf, represents the ten principles holistically.

> **Expert question**
>
> **Principle**: is our pedagogy consistent with established principles for effective teaching and learning?
>
> This question contributes to a conceptual framework underpinning professional expertise (see Chapter 16).

Effective teaching and learning

10 Effective teaching and learning demands consistent policy frameworks with support for teaching and learning as their primary focus. Policies at national, local and institutional levels need to recognise the fundamental importance of teaching and learning. They should be designed to create effective learning environments in which all learners can thrive. (Chapters 5, 8, 9, 14, 16 and 17)

1 Effective teaching and learning equips learners for life in its broadest sense. Learning should aim to help people to develop the intellectual, personal and social resources that will enable them to participate as active citizens, contribute to economic development and flourish as individuals in a diverse and changing society. This implies adopting a broad view of learning outcomes and ensuring that equity and social justice are taken seriously. (Chapters 1, 9 and 15)

9 Effective teaching and learning depends on teacher learning. The need for teachers to learn continuously in order to develop their knowledge and skills, and to adapt and develop their roles, especially through classroom inquiry, should be recognised and supported. (Chapters 1, 3, 16 and 17)

2 Effective teaching and learning engages with valued forms of knowledge. Teaching and learning should engage with the big ideas, facts, processes, language and narratives of subjects so that learners understand what constitutes quality and standards in particular disciplines. (Chapters 9 and 10)

8 Effective teaching and learning recognises the significance of informal learning. Informal learning, such as learning out of school, should be recognised as at least as significant as formal learning and should therefore be valued and used appropriately in formal processes. (Chapters 2, 5, 8 and 15)

3 Effective teaching and learning recognises the importance of prior experience and learning. Teaching and learning should take account of what the learner knows already in order to plan their next steps. This includes building on prior learning but also taking account of the personal and cultural experiences of different groups of learners. (Chapters 2 and 10)

7 Effective teaching and learning fosters both individual and social processes and outcomes. Learning is a social activity. Learners should be encouraged and helped to work with others, to share ideas and to build knowledge together. Consulting learners about their learning and giving them a voice is both an expectation and a right. (Chapters 3, 6, 7, 12 and 15)

6 Effective teaching and learning promotes the active engagement of the learner. A chief goal of teaching and learning should be the promotion of learners' independence and autonomy. This involves acquiring a repertoire of learning strategies and practices, developing positive attitudes towards learning, and confidence in oneself as a good learner. (Chapters 2, 7, 11 and 13)

5 Effective teaching and learning needs assessment to be congruent with learning. Assessment should help to advance learning as well as determine whether learning has taken place. It should be designed and carried out so that it measures learning outcomes in a dependable way and also provides feedback for future learning. (Chapters 13 and 14)

4 Effective teaching and learning requires teachers to scaffold learning. Teachers should provide activities which support learners as they move forward, not just intellectually, but also socially and emotionally, so that once these supports are removed, the learning is secure. (Chapters 6, 11 and 12)

Figure 4.1 Ten evidence-informed educational principles for effective teaching and learning

2 TLRP's principles

2.1 Education for life

Commitment to broad educational objectives has existed for a very long time in the UK and Republic of Ireland. For example, in a recent manifestation, the general requirements of Section 78 of the Education Act 2002 state that a maintained school in England or Wales must offer:

> A balanced and broadly based curriculum which promotes the spiritual, moral, cultural, mental and physical development of pupils at the school and of society, and prepares pupils at the school for the opportunities, responsibilities and experiences of later life.

Similar statements apply in Scotland and Northern Ireland. However, despite such affirmation, goals of this type have been historically vulnerable to erosion by the narrowing effects of high-stakes assessment and accountability.

TLRP also embraced a wide definition of educational values and purposes. The importance of attainments as measured by national tests and qualifications was recognised, but there was also interest in other outcomes. These included learner engagement, participation, skills, dispositions and the development of learning identities and autonomy. Such outcomes have the potential to contribute to a wide range of educational aims including those linked to economic productivity, social cohesion, cultural development, personal fulfilment and environmental sustainability. These are all important in a contemporary developed society.

The UK's long-standing commitment to broad, rich and inclusive forms of education thus gave rise to the first of TLRP's ten principles.

Principle 1: Effective teaching equips learners for life in its broadest sense.
Learning should aim to help individuals and groups to develop the intellectual, personal and social resources that will enable them to participate as active citizens, contribute to economic development and flourish as individuals in a diverse and changing society. This means adopting a broad conception of worthwhile learning outcomes and taking seriously issues of equity and social justice for all.

reflectiveteaching.co.uk
features a video on this principle: Teaching should equip learners for life.

TLRP worked with the Philosophy of Education Society of Great Britain to examine the way in which this principle might inform policy and, by extension, practice. The philosophers argued that empirical evidence is not sufficient for decision-making in policy or practice, for it is always complemented by values. For example, Bridges suggested:

> We should be more explicit about the educational and wider political values which frame policy and practice, and be more ready to subject these to careful scholarly, as well as democratic, scrutiny and criticism. (2009, p. 3)

There are many examples of the influence of values in policy-making at the highest level. For example, consider the speech made by the English Secretary of State for Education, Michael Gove, when moving the second reading of the 2011 Education Bill in the Westminster Parliament:

This Bill provides an historic opportunity for this country. It will help to guarantee every child a high quality education, which will equip them for the technological, economic, social and cultural challenges of the next century. Throughout history, the opportunities we give to our young people have far too often been a matter of time and chance. Accidents of birth or geography have determined children's fate, but education can change all that. Education allows each of us to become the author of our own life story. Instead of going down a path determined for us by external constraints, it allows each of us to shape our lives and the communities around us for the better. (Hansard, 8 February 2011)

A strong commitment to opportunity is clear, but such rhetoric has to be reconciled with the realities of the rapidly expanding academies programme in England, which the bill was designed to promote. It has been predicted by some that this policy will in fact reinforce inequality (see, for example, Benn, 2011). Time will tell. In any event, as in all walks of life, the relationship between espoused goals and actual consequences has to be considered.

Vision and values are arguably even more important at other levels of the education system. When they engage with pupils, teachers can, without doubt, change lives – as we discussed in Chapter 1 of this book (see Gu, 2007, Reading 1.1). Qualitative sociologists have demonstrated how learners perceive and make sense of their school experiences. For example, one series of projects tracked two cohorts of children from age 4 to age 16 (Pollard and Filer, 1999, Reading 1.2). That work recorded how pupils progressively develop strategies to cope with the challenges of schooling over time, and how secure forms of learning become embedded in personal narratives and identities. It suggested that where school curricula fail to make meaningful connections with the learner, pupil performance and capability are likely to be shallow and transitory. Similar ideas were reflected in other TLRP projects. A developed example was provided by a study of further education experiences – *Transforming Learning Cultures* (James and Biesta, 2007) – which recognised the way in which institutional conditions enable or constrain opportunities for independent learning. Another was that of Crozier and colleagues (2010) who analysed disjunctions in the experiences of working-class students entering higher education. However, the analysis was developed most thoroughly by the *Learning Lives* project (Biesta et al., 2010) which studied learners across the lifecourse using a combination of evidence from a large-scale cohort study and case study interviews reviewing learning careers over time. This study was important for its lifelong reach and demonstration of the durability of attitudes deriving from early school experiences. In particular, it reported how narratives about learning and educational experiences are used as frameworks of interpretation in the development of identity, self-confidence and agency in later life. Other quantitative studies reinforce this analysis to demonstrate the 'wider benefits' of learning

(Feinstein et al., 2008, Reading 1.6).
Education, in other words, makes an enormous difference to the people we become. Teachers, have a unique privilege and responsibility to shape the next generation. That is why this principle of 'education for life' is so important. Teaching has moral purpose.

Reflective activity 4.1

Aim To reflect on the moral purposes of education in relation to learner development.

Evidence and reflection Typically, this issue has particular resonance when applied to people who we know well – parents, partners or even ourselves. Think deeply about a person whose early upbringing and school education you know something about. How did those experiences influence the person they became? Can you see traces of adult qualities in those earlier experiences, or even identify patterns of development? Were there any particular critical incidents which made a difference in the life you are considering? Were there relationships of particular significance? Thinking of teachers, what specific memories arise? How would you summarise this review, in relation to the first TLRP principle?

Extension The next step is clearly to imagine the trajectories through life of some of the children and young people whom you teach. Consider the potential lifelong consequences of day-by-day experiences at school.

2.2 Valued knowledge

Principle 2: Effective teaching and learning engages with valued forms of knowledge. Teaching and learning should engage with the big ideas, facts, processes, language and narratives of subjects so that learners understand what constitutes quality and standards in particular disciplines.

There has always been debate about what a curriculum should consist of, how it should be organised, what constitutes valued knowledge in a subject or field, how such knowledge can be represented and communicated to learners, and how learners' knowledge, understanding and skills can be identified and evaluated (see Chapter 9). Such debates reflect the priorities in our culture and the capacity of particular stakeholders to promote their views. Analysts of such processes characterise the curriculum as a contested, social construction, with any particular settlement being influenced by the balance of power of the time. The early work of Young (1971) and Bernstein (1971) established this approach and the history of UK curriculum 'reform' in recent years demonstrates the significance of the perspective.

However, from a different direction, the development of curricula has also involved philosophers, cognitive psychologists, subject specialists, curriculum developers and assessment experts – many of whom bring a far greater awareness of the distinctive character of particular bodies of knowledge. England's National Curriculum Review recognised that such experts bring: 'a view of disciplinary knowledge as a distinct way of investigating, knowing and making sense with particular foci, procedures and theories, reflecting both cumulative understanding and powerful ways of engaging with the future. In this sense, disciplinary knowledge offers core foundations for education, from which the subjects of the curriculum are derived' (Department for Education (DfE), 2011).

Interestingly, the later work of Young (2008, Reading 9.2) has contributed significantly to the commitment to 'bring knowledge back in'.

But the level at which the curriculum is applied is the domain of practising teachers for it is they who put the 'curriculum into action' (Stenhouse, 1975, Reading 3.3). In the UK, it is common to think of curriculum 'elements' such as knowledge, concepts, skills and attitudes (Her Majesty's Inspectors, 1985) and a commitment to learning skills as well as content is firmly established. Indeed, some curricular innovations promote a particular emphasis on skills or competencies (e.g. the Royal Society of Arts (RSA)'s 'Opening Minds', or Claxton's 'Building Learning Power', 2011). In balancing these elements, Ryle's classic distinction between 'knowing that' and 'knowing how' (1945) has been particularly influential. Teachers know that both knowledge and skills are vital.

Building on the work of Polanyi (1958), Eraut's contribution to TLRP (2007) also argued for the significance of 'personal knowledge'. This type of knowledge foregrounds understanding and skills acquired during acculturation, social interaction and reflection on experience. Eraut argued that: 'A person's performance nearly always uses these kinds of knowledge in some integrated form, and is influenced by both context and feelings.' Such informal ways of 'making sense' have considerable significance for understanding and misunderstanding in schools. We will consider informal learning again in discussion of Principle 8.

TLRP's emphasis on 'valued forms of knowledge' has been described as 'an immensely important principle' by a leading educationalist in the Asia–Pacific region – David Hogan. However, work in Singapore has:

> focused a lot more analytical attention on the intellectual quality of the instructional and assessment tasks that students are asked to work on, and the extent to which the knowledge practices they engage in are informed by, and are consistent with, domain specific forms of disciplinary knowledge and epistemic norms. (2012, p. 103)

Hogan argues that the most important single factor in determining the quality of teaching, learning and outcomes lies in the nature of instructional tasks (see also Reading 4.2). Hattie's meta-analysis of global research makes the same point: 'what teachers *get students to do* in the class is the strongest component of the accomplished teacher's repertoire, rather than what the teacher specifically does' (2009, p. 35, Reading 4.6, also 16.5).

Subject knowledge is undoubtedly of enormous significance in teacher effectiveness (see Chapter 9). This is one reason why 'lesson study' has become so well established in the Far East and why similarly focused approaches are developing rapidly around the world (see Chapter 10, Section 5.2).

2.3 Prior experience

reflectiveteaching.co.uk
features a video on this principle: Teaching should build on prior experience.

Principle 3: Effective pedagogy recognises the importance of prior experience and learning. Pedagogy should take account of what the learner knows already in order for them, and those who support their learning, to plan their next steps. This includes building on prior learning but also taking account of the personal and cultural experiences of different groups of learners.

Whilst the nature of knowledge to be learned is important, few people now think that children arrive at school as 'empty vessels' to be filled. The principle of starting where children are and helping them to move on is widely recognised. The scientific foundation of this principle lies in the practical philosophy of Dewey and the constructivist psychology of Piaget and Vygotsky (see Chapter 2 and Readings 2.2 and 2.3). International evidence is also very extensive, including from synoptic reviews by the American Psychological Association (1997) and by European researchers (Dochy, Segers and Buehl, 1999). A famous quote by Ausubel put this clearly:

> If I had to reduce all of educational psychology to just one principle, I would say this:
> 'The most important single factor affecting learning is what the learner already knows.
> Ascertain this, and teach him accordingly.' (1968, p. vi)

One reason for affirming the importance of prior learning is cognitive, and has been demonstrated in subjects such as science where early misconceptions create barriers to later learning. Such misunderstandings need to be identified and addressed. One TLRP project developed and evaluated sequences for teaching science concepts and complemented this with banks of diagnostic questions to identify misconceptions (Millar et al., 2006). The researchers found that carefully designed probes can illuminate pupils' understanding of key concepts, and can thus inform judgements about 'next steps' in teaching. They also found that the level of pupils' understanding of many fundamental science ideas increases only slowly with age, so that pitching an appropriate level of challenge is essential. Of course, work of this sort influences the sequencing of content knowledge within national curricula.

A second rationale for focusing on prior learning is concerned with motivation and providing appropriate opportunities to learn. Here, it is essential to take account of the knowledge, understandings, skills and attitudes derived from the other worlds that pupils inhabit: from their homes, communities and peer groups. For example, a number of TLRP projects, ranging between those working with young children to others concerned with further and higher education, found benefits in teachers making more deliberate and positive use of the informal knowledge and understanding that children and young people acquire.

However, because of the extent of social inequality and difference within the UK (see Chapter 5), children and young people have extremely variable experience before and during their schooling. For some, there are continuities between home and school, whilst for others there are disjunctions. This has great significance for teaching and learning, and in building identities. This aspect of effective pedagogy will be revisited in discussion of Principles 7 and 8 on personal and social processes and relationships.

Whatever the merits of the case, with large classes it can be difficult to determine each pupil's prior knowledge. Indeed, some barriers to learning undoubtedly stem from teachers' misplaced assumptions about pupils. However difficult, expert teachers are committed to seeking to understand learners so that appropriate starting points are identified. In summary, understanding pupils' prior experience from previous teaching and learning, from home and from their communities is difficult, but can significantly improve teacher judgements and thereby enhance pupils' confidence in learning.

2.4 Scaffolding understanding

reflectiveteaching.co.uk
features a video on this
principle: Teachers should
scaffold learning with
appropriate tools.

Principle 4: Effective pedagogy requires learning to be scaffolded. Teachers, trainers and all those, including peers, who support the learning of others, should provide activities and structures of intellectual, social and emotional support to help learners to move forward in their learning. When these supports are removed the learning needs to be secure.

Scaffolding in teaching can be compared to building work; scaffolding supports the construction until the house (or the learner's understanding) is strong enough to stand on its own. The idea was implicit in Vygotsky's work but was taken further in a classic paper by Wood, Bruner and Ross (1976; see also Tharp and Gallimore, 1988, Reading 11.4). Vygotsky's conception of learning emphasises the importance of active choice and use of cultural tools, especially language, in learning. The role of the 'more expert other' in helping the novice to make progress beyond the level of their present understanding is equally crucial (see discussion of the zone of proximal development in Chapter 2). When these two elements are brought together, the pertinence of the concept of scaffolding becomes evident.

A major contribution to such scaffolding derives from teachers' understanding of both curricular knowledge and of how children and young people learn. They thus recognise when they should intervene to help the pupil move on to a higher level of understanding. For example, the TLRP's project on *InterActive Education* (Sutherland, Robertson and John, 2009, Research briefing, p. 217) concluded that ICT in the classroom will not help learning on its own. As the research team put it: 'without a teacher carefully crafting and orchestrating learning, the incorporation of ICT into the classroom is likely to tip over into learning which is at odds with what the school intends students to learn' (2009, p. 206).

It is also worth drawing attention to the fact that TLRP's principle picks out provision of 'intellectual, social *and* emotional support'. It does this because discussion of these issues tends to focus on cognitive forms of scaffolding alone. However, the TLRP proposition is that social and emotional factors are also important, such as those associated with social expectations and feelings of personal security for example (see Immordino and Damasio, 2007, Reading 6.2). Because learning is intrinsically personal, intellectual progress is enabled or constrained by such factors and reflective teachers will consider how to provide for each of the three dimensions (see rows 3.1, 3.2 and 3.3 of the conceptual framework in Chapter 16, and discussion of Maslow in Chapter 1, section 2.4).

A crucial contribution to scaffolded learning derives from dialogue between teacher and learners, and through the feedback loops that this makes possible. To be effective, teacher support must be carefully matched to the current understanding or capabilities of the learner and must thus be informed by feedback from the student. As Hattie puts it, there should be explicit 'visibility' in the teaching–learning process.

> The teacher must know when learning is correct or incorrect; learn when to experiment and learn from the experience; learn to monitor, seek and give feedback; and know to try alternative learning strategies when others do not work. ... It is most important that

teaching is visible to the student, and that learning is visible to the teacher. The more the student becomes the teacher and the more the teacher becomes the student, then the more successful are the outcomes. (Hattie, 2009, p. 25)

Dialogue is the most practical way of creating such visibility. The dialogic approach proposed by Alexander (2001, 2006, Reading 12.3) comprises a three-part repertoire informed by dialogic principles (see also Chapters 11 and 12). The repertoire consists of 'learning talk' (narrating, explaining, questioning, answering, analysing, speculating, imagining, exploring, evaluating, discussing, arguing, justifying and negotiating), 'teaching talk' (rote, recitation, exposition, discussion, dialogue) and 'interactive strategies' (whole-class teaching, teacher-led group work, pupil-led group work, one-to-one pupil discussion, one-to-one discussion between pupil and teacher). The principles that inform this repertoire are that genuine dialogue is collective, reciprocal, supportive, cumulative and purposeful. According to Alexander, the most vital of these is cumulation: that teachers and pupils build on their own and each other's ideas and chain them into coherent lines of thinking and enquiry.

The expert teacher facilitates, focuses, listens, analyses, contributes *and* teaches. This brings us to the role which assessment can play in learning.

2.5 Assessment for learning

Principle 5: Effective pedagogy needs assessment to be congruent with learning. Assessment should be designed and implemented with the goal of achieving maximum validity both in terms of learning outcomes and learning processes. It should help to advance learning as well as determine whether learning has occurred.

reflectiveteaching.co.uk features a video on this principle: Assessment should support learning.

TLRPs *Learning How to Learn* project (James et al., 2007, Reading 2.8, **Research Briefing** on p. 356) elaborated the highly influential proposition that assessment should be used to 'advance learning' as well as measure it. The project built on work by the UK Assessment Reform Group which demonstrated that 'assessment for learning' practices can lead to improved learning and achievement (Black and Wiliam, 1998; Black et al., 2003). The project found that four clusters of practices were necessary to support such learning, all of which are based on dialogue. They are: developing classroom talk and questioning to elicit understanding; giving appropriate feedback; sharing criteria of quality; and peer- and self-assessment (which incorporate elements of the three previous clusters). These assessment practices helped teachers to promote 'learning how to learn', which in turn enabled pupils to become more autonomous learners. The project found that classroom practice thus becomes better aligned with the educational values expressed by teachers, and less driven by a culture of performativity. Chapter 13, picks up on this analysis, when guiding principles and practical implications are discussed at length.

However, changes in practice are not easy to establish and the project demonstrated that, although advice on specific techniques is useful in the short term, longer-term development and sustainability depends on re-evaluating beliefs about learning, reviewing the way learning activities are structured, and rethinking classroom roles and relationships.

A related element of Principle 5: 'Assessment should be designed and implemented with the goal of achieving maximum validity both in terms of learning outcomes and learning processes' was addressed by other projects and thematic initiatives. Traditionally, the quality of assessments is judged by their reliability and their validity, which together indicate whether the inferences drawn from assessment results are dependable (see Chapter 14, Broadfoot, 2007, Reading 14.1). Often more attention is paid to reliability for two reasons. First, there are clear technical procedures for enhancing reliability. Second, the publication of unreliable results can have immediate and far-reaching political and personal consequences where data is used for accountability purposes. However, there is a sense in which even reliable assessment results have no worth if they are not valid – if they do not represent authentic learning.

One of TLRP's associated projects (Filer and Pollard, 2000, Reading 14.7) focused on assessment encounters from a sociological point of view. Children and young people develop their identities through successive experiences as they move through schooling, and experiences of assessment are shown to be among the most powerful of these. Assessment can thus be seen as a social process with significant consequences. Indeed, pupil performance is strongly influenced by the contexts and circumstances in which assessments take place, and results take meaning from social and cultural interpretation. If learners' sense of agency and identity is to be nurtured, the case for maintaining the validity of both assessment events and the inferences drawn from them is therefore overwhelming. But this is not easy to do when assessment data is also used as an indicator of school performance.

These problems occur wherever high-stakes assessment exists. For example, Singapore has testing at the end of Primary school (Year 6), the end of Secondary school (Year 10) and the end of Year 12. As Hogan explains:

> By virtue of the tight nexus between social mobility patterns and national high stakes assessments, and the commitment of the government to 'meritocratic' sorting and allocation through national high stakes assessments, reliability remains the over-riding issue for parents and the government. This constrains the ability of the system to develop assessments that have greater authenticity and validity. At the same time, the character and logic of classroom instruction is directly shaped by national high stakes assessment – in Singapore, as they do elsewhere, teachers teach to the test. ... In effect, although it places a floor on student learning, the national high stakes assessment system in Singapore places a ceiling on it as well. (2012, p. 105, Reading 4.2)

At the heart of the matter are concerns about fitness for purpose, and TLRP contested the common view that a single set of assessments could serve several purposes without distorting one purpose or another (Mansell and James, 2009, Reading 14.5). Above all, it was argued that assessment systems must be congruent with the overarching purpose of education systems to advance learning.

'Assessment should help advance learning as well as determine whether learning has taken place', says TLRP's principle. This may sound obvious, but many teachers know that assessment requirements can militate against good learning. When staff end up 'teaching to the test' rather than teaching to the principles to which they are professionally committed, something is not right.

2.6 Active engagement

reflectiveteaching.co.uk features a video on this principle: Learning should involve and engage the learner.

Principle 6: Effective pedagogy promotes the active engagement of the learner.
A chief goal of teaching and learning should be the promotion of learners' independence and autonomy. This involves acquiring a repertoire of learning strategies and practices, developing positive learning dispositions, and having the will and confidence to become agents in their own learning.

Almost all TLRP research projects affirmed the importance of developing active engagement, positive learning dispositions, self-confidence and learning awareness (see also Chapter 2, section 3). Indeed, the programme developed in an era characterised within much of the UK by central control over curriculum, pedagogy and assessment, so that the motivation and engagement of under-performing learners had become an increasingly pressing contemporary issue. It remains a difficult judgement to ensure that national requirements provide enough guidance to ensure entitlements whilst also providing sufficient scope and support for teachers to respond to needs of the particular pupils for whom they are responsible (see Chapter 9). Concern for the quality of learning experiences is a further driver of this concern with active engagement.

However, the most pragmatic reason for emphasising active engagement is simply that it is essential for learning. As we saw in Chapter 3, Piaget's constructivist psychology emphasised processes of accommodation and assimilation through which learning takes place, and the example of Armstong's work (1980) highlights the 'appropriation' of knowledge. Sociocultural analysts envisage a learner whose capability and confidence are greatly influenced by others, and who develops independent agency and meaning within networks of social relationships. This capacity to sustain active engagement in purposive ways is encapsulated in Guy Claxton's conception of 'building learning power' through resilience, resourcefulness, reflection and reciprocity (2011, see also Reading 2.9 and the discussion in Chapter 9, section 2.4)

More traditionally, psychological questions concerning the active engagement of learners have been framed in terms of motivation, with emphasis being placed on ways of involving individual learners in particular tasks. The work of Carol Dweck for instance, on 'mastery' and 'learned helplessness' as orientations to new learning challenges, has

been very influential (1999, Chapter 3, Section 2.3, Reading 2.6). The promotion of learner independence and autonomy has thus been seen as essential to the effectiveness of learning.

In a commentary on TLRP's ten principles, Allal (2012) highlighted the ways in which this principle of active engagement links back to the scaffolding of understanding. In particular, she argued that this requires what she termed, 'co-regulation':

> Scaffolding is a process that is elaborated on the basis of what the learner does and says (given his or her current developmental level), rather than a pre-existing support structure that an expert prepares, introduces and later withdraws. The elaboration of scaffolding cannot take place without the active engagement of the learner. (2012, p. 65)

There is a resonance here with Hattie's call for 'visible' teaching and learning (2008, Reading 4.6) and with Alexander's emphasis on dialogue (2008, Reading 12.3). They each make the point that the guidance provided by teacher scaffolding can only be accurately deployed and taken up except through the active engagement of the learner. In this way, and many more, TLRP principles are interconnected.

Nor indeed, should we forget that when pupils are positively engaged in learning activities, behavioural problems tend to be very minor. We explore this more fully in Chapter 7.

2.7 Social relationships

reflectiveteaching. co.uk features a video on this principle: Social relationships are vital to learning.

Principle 7: Effective pedagogy fosters both individual and social processes and outcomes. Learners should be encouraged and helped to build relationships and communication with others for learning purposes, in order to assist the mutual construction of knowledge and enhance the achievements of individuals and groups. Consulting learners about their learning and giving them a voice is both an expectation and a right.

Learning is a social as well as an individual activity. It flourishes through interaction with other minds, when the conditions are right. Good teacher–pupil classroom relationships underpin such conditions. Or, to put it another way, teacher–pupil respect is the foundation of discipline, order *and* learning (see Chapters 6 and 7). More broadly, some TLRP projects used the concept of social capital (Putnam, 1995) to analyse available opportunities, whilst noting the formative role that school and classroom processes and peer relations can play in such accumulation. Social processes, at many levels, create conditions for individual learning.

TLRP's studies on group work (Baines et al., 2008), teacher learning (James et al., 2007) and inclusion (Ainscow et al., 2006), among others, show that when schools function as genuine learning communities, students and teachers thrive both collectively and as individuals. For example, pupils who worked effectively in groups also did measurably better on individual exams than those who had other forms of teaching and learning. The SPRinG (Social Pedagogic Research into Group-work) and Scottish SPRinG projects found that, in Key Stages 2 and 3, children who worked effectively together made gains in their inferential thinking and their higher cognitive understanding (see the **Research Briefing** on p. 316). Group work also improved social relationships among pupils and between pupils and teachers. Experiments carried out with older students, using concept-mapping software, also showed that opportunities for students to discuss their maps with others was the significant factor in raising attainment (Bevan, 2007).

Going further, Principle 7 suggests that 'consulting learners is both an expectation and a right'. In parallel with psychological research on pupil agency and learning, this reflects the humanistic tradition in British education drawing on the practitioner enquiry movement initiated by Stenhouse (1975, Reading 3.3). TLRP's network on *Consulting Pupils about Teaching and Learning* was a manifestation of this commitment to practical theorising and improvement. The network directly engaged teachers, children and young people in reflection on their classroom practices and school experiences (Rudduck and McIntyre, 2007, Reading 1.3, see the **Research Briefing** in Chapter 1, p. 17). Indirectly, it connected with thousands more pupils in building from the UN Convention on the Rights of the Child (United Nations, 1989, see also Reading 17.6) to affirming the quality and constructive nature of feedback about teaching and learning that pupils were able to offer. Outcomes included enhanced commitment to learning and improved teacher–pupil relationships. Pupils were more likely to be engaged with schooling when they were consulted and their views treated with respect.

Here then we see the social awareness of a significant cluster of TLRP projects, and their attention to the construction of pupil meaning in relation to circumstances. It also concerns the realisation of rights, formation as a person, manifestation of citizenship and, ultimately, the contribution of individuals to history.

At its core though, consulting pupils strengthens pupils' engagement with learning, gives teachers deeper insights into pupils' abilities and learning preferences and strengthens school policy and planning. Giving pupils a 'good listening to' challenges old habits.

2.8 Informal learning

PRINCIPLE 8: Effective pedagogy recognises the significance of informal learning. Informal learning, such as learning out of school or away from the workplace, should be recognised as at least as significant as formal learning and should therefore be valued and appropriately utilised in formal processes.

This principle can be stated simply, but has profound implications and challenges. Recognition of the social and cultural dimensions of learning in many TLRP projects produced a heightened awareness of learners, relationships and contexts (see also Chapter 2, Section 3). Over several years, researchers struggled with how to study, analyse and represent the learning that took place beyond formal educational settings.

UK Governments have recognised the significance of social context in relation to children and young people. For example, in England from 2003, the *Every Child Matters* agenda and integration of national health, social and educational provision into Children's Services across the whole country were evidence of holistic analysis and of attempts to promote inclusion through the coordination of services.

TLRP's own work in these areas was at rather different levels, whether in workplace, university or school education. Regarding school education, two areas of research stand out – on home–school relationships and the influence of new technologies.

The *Home–school Knowledge Exchange* project (see Hughes and Pollard, 2000, **Research Briefing**, p. 107), investigated how the home and school environments for learning might complement each other. Focusing upon literacy and numeracy in these two worlds, the team helped teachers, parents and children to find new ways of exchanging knowledge between home and primary school, using videos, photographs, shoeboxes of artefacts, etc. For example, primary pupils took photos to show the maths and literacy activities they were doing at home. Maths activities included cooking, shopping, playing board games, setting timers and consulting timetables. Children were also asked to collect a 'shoebox' of artefacts from home, *All about Me*, which offered teachers and other pupils insights into their interests and opportunities. The project team then investigated how this process of knowledge exchange could enhance learning and ease the transition to secondary school.

Explicit home–school knowledge exchange activities produced impact on outcomes but this was mediated by social class, gender and attainment – factors that underline the importance of considering the character of informal learning with sensitivity in order to avoid negative consequences for particular groups of pupils (Thomas and Pattison, 2007, Reading 2.10).

TLRP's work on technology began with a project on the integration of ICT into everyday classroom practices. The *InterActive Education* project (Sutherland, Robertson and John, 2009) worked with primary and secondary school teachers to study how subject-knowledge could be used in teaching through the use of new technologies (see the Research Briefing at p. 217). The use of mobile and other forms of technology is now so pervasive and so embedded within the cultures of children and young people that it provides a very strong illustration of the knowledge and experiential resources that exist beyond formal educational settings (Buckingham, 2008; Kress, 2010, Reading, 8.6). Access and knowledge are uneven, however, making the affordances of mobile devices difficult to harness in schools. The project found that technology could be particularly effective at enhancing subject knowledge when teachers were able to bridge between the idiosyncratic and the intended curricular learning using tailored software. The software was seen, in sociocultural terms, as a mediating tool in support of the teaching–learning process.

Reflecting back on the project, Robertson and Dale (2009) write that there is a 'tendency to view schools as islands, loosely connected to society. ... What young people learn in

Enhancing home–school knowledge exchange

Engaging parents and carers in their children's education is expected to make a major contribution to the development of personalised learning. As *2020 Vision* puts it:

> *Mothers and fathers are children's first teachers. There is compelling evidence that parental aspirations, expectations and involvement have a major impact on their children's attainment. (DfES, 2006, p. 23)*

Children learn in two different worlds, home and school. Yet the knowledge which exists in each of these worlds is often not fully recognised or understood in the other. Martin Hughes and his TLRP colleagues worked with teachers, parents and children to find new ways of exchanging knowledge between home and primary school. They looked in particular at how this process of knowledge exchange could enhance children's learning in literacy and mathematics and through the transition from primary to secondary school. The social and emotional aspects of learning, and of pupil identity, cannot be separated from academic performance. The child's home and school experiences are thus intimately connected in relation to learning.

Key findings:	Implications:
Exchange activities: Home–school knowledge exchange activities can have a positive impact on teachers, parents and children, and on attainment in literacy and mathematics. At primary–secondary school transfer, they can help to avoid the common post-transfer dip in pupil performance.	Greater priority should be given to exchanging knowledge between home and school, as a means of improving home–school relationships, raising attainment in literacy and mathematics and facilitating learning during primary–secondary school transfer.
Funds of knowledge: There are substantial 'funds of knowledge' in homes and communities which can be used to support children's learning. They are often embedded in national and ethnic cultures, and in the experience of family members. Popular culture is an important influence on children's funds of knowledge.	Schools need to recognise these funds of knowledge and find ways of making them more visible in the classroom and in the school. Exchange of videos, photographs and 'shoe-boxes' of significant items can be used to make this knowledge more tangible.
School transfer: Teachers, parents and children all have significant 'funds of knowledge' which can be drawn on to support transfer. Parents know about children's out-of-school lives while primary teachers have extensive knowledge of the children they have taught. This knowledge is often ignored by secondary teachers who want children to have a 'fresh start'.	Parents, teachers and children need to find ways of sharing and exchanging their different funds of knowledge. Transfer 'passports', photographs of out-of-school life and videos of secondary school can all be used. Drama activities can help children and parents share their hopes and fears about transfer.
At risk children: Some groups of children are particularly likely to be 'at risk' when transferring from primary to secondary school. These include children who are considered to be 'gifted and talented' as well as children whose families are considered to be 'hard to reach'.	Schools need to consider how they will provide support for these 'at risk' groups. More clearly targeted strategies at the start of secondary school can help to prevent later disengagement and under-performance.

Schools which take on the challenges of home-school knowledge exchange are likely to see a range of benefits for teachers, children and parents. Teachers can appreciate the additional knowledge they acquire about children's out-of-school lives and can use it to enrich their curricula. Parents can acquire a greater understanding of what is happening to their children in school, gain a greater appreciation of teachers' professional skills, and realise how they can complement the work of the school at home. Children can appreciate when aspects of their out-of-school lives are valued and respected in school, and when their work at school is better understood at home. As one parent commented about her child: 'I think she likes to show people things about herself and I think she really enjoys that…yeah I think she really liked to do that'.

Further information:
Hughes, M. *et al.*(2007) *Enhancing Primary Literacy and Mathematics through Home–School Knowledge Exchange.* TLRP *Research Briefing* No 22. London: TLRP.
Hughes, M. *et al.*(2008) *Supporting Primary-Secondary Transfer through Home-School Knowledge Exchange.* TLRP *Research Briefing.* London: TLRP. Available at **www.tlrp.org/pub** (accessed 18 November 2013).
Feiler, A., Andrews, J., Greenhough, P., Hughes, M., Johnson, D., Scanlan, M. and Yee, W. (2007) *Improving Primary Literacy: Linking Home and School.* London: Routldge.
Winter, J., Andrews, J., Greenhough, P., Hughes, M., Salway, L. and Yee, W. (2009) *Improving Primary Mathematics: Linking Home and School.* London: Routledge.
This project was directed from the University of Bristol.

other places and spaces has little currency in the classroom ... and ... schools are represented as enduring features of the landscape, immune to change' (p. 155). They suggest that schools reflect an 'assemblage' of social relations, assumptions and organisational arrangements with significant effects on pupils, teachers, parents and others. Change, they suggest, is inevitable, as the impact of new technology and of learning beyond school accumulates. Their book concludes:

> Maybe it is time to consider young people's out-of-school knowledge and cultures not as 'distractions' from the main business of schooling, but as rich, complex, diverse and powerful sources for learning and as an important place to start in designing education for the twenty-first century. (p. 176)

There is a significant resonance here with our earlier discussion of the metaphor of 'learning as participation' (see Chapter 2, Section 4.2).

Reflective activity 4.3

Aim: To review TLRP's principles on engagement, relationships and informal learning (Sections 2.6, 2.7 and 2.8).

Evidence and reflection: This group of principles concern how teaching makes *connections* with the learner. Emphasising the construction of meaning, they acknowledge personal and social influences on children and young people in schools and beyond – as realised through both formal and informal learning processes. Once again, these are enduring issues – they are forever with us.

However, such principles imply wide-ranging awareness on the part of teachers, and speak to recognition of the 'participation metaphor' of learning as well as that of 'acquisition' (see Chapter 2, Section 4.2). How far do you feel that the role of the teacher can, or should, embrace such issues? Traditionally, the formal teacher role has been defined narrowly – though many teachers have stepped beyond this, sometimes routinely. How though, do you see the role today, and in the future?

Discuss the issues with colleagues. How can teaching and learning in school contribute to and draw on the learning which takes place beyond school? How can we, as teachers, make better connections with the frameworks of meaning and relationship which are of particular importance to the children and young people in our classrooms?

Extension: An excellent development of this activity would be to explore the issues directly through discussion with selected pupils or even with parents or other stakeholders in the community. How do learners' lives, as a whole, relate to experiences in and benefits from schooling?

2.9 Teacher learning

Principle 9: Effective pedagogy depends on the learning of all those who support the learning of others. The need for lecturers, teachers, trainers and co-workers to learn continuously in order to develop their knowledge and skill, and to adapt and develop their roles, especially through practice-based inquiry, should be recognised and supported.

This principle provides the rationale for this book as a whole – we need to be reflective, and thus commit to our own learning, because this enhances our effectiveness in supporting pupils.

Teacher learning is concerned with both what we do *and* how we think (see Wiliam, 2009, Reading 16.4). Put another way, the most effective forms of teaching depends not only on behavioural change and the acquisition of new knowledge about pedagogy, but also on the development of values and understanding. With the right school leadership and support, such learning is particularly effective in the workplace and through participation in collaborative activities with other teachers (see Chapters 3 and 16, in particular).

These conclusions began to emerge early in the life of TLRP. A summary of common themes by Mary James suggested:

1. Learning involves the acquisition of knowledge and skills *and* participation in social processes. Thus the development of supportive professional cultures is vitally important. Within schools, especially secondary schools, the focus is often the department or team. However, the very cohesion of these groups can create insularity and inhibit change. Rich and dynamic learning environments need to provide opportunities for boundary crossings, and to encourage learning from others in different communities of practice (see Chapter 3, Section 2.6).

2. Teachers are most ready to accept ideas for change if they resonate with their existing or previous beliefs and experience. However, this does not necessarily make them 'right' or appropriate. Teachers need to develop knowledge and skills to evaluate evidence and the confidence to challenge taken-for-granted assumptions, including their own. This is difficult (see Hargreaves, 2008, Reading 16.2) and it is often helpful to involve outsiders, perhaps researchers from universities or visiting teachers from other schools. Teachers need to be assured that it is acceptable and often fruitful to take risks – so a culture of trust and openness is crucial.

3. Evidence from research about effective practice is not always sufficiently accessible for teachers to use as a basis for action. Findings often need to be transformed into practical and concrete strategies that can be tried out. This may involve the production of concise and user-friendly materials, although ideas are often mediated best by talk and personal contacts with other teachers who have had some success in using them. (James, 2005, pp. 107–8)

Later TLRP studies emphasised the interaction of teacher characteristics (e.g. knowledge, attitudes and behaviour), cultural factors (e.g. school communities or professional networks) and structural factors (e.g. policy contexts). Where these were seen to be aligned as, for example, they have been recently in Finland, then teacher learning was likely to be most effective (see Sahlberg, 2012, Reading 4.3).

The character of teachers' professional lives was the particular focus of a TLRP associate project, *Variations in Teachers' Work, Lives, and their Effects on Pupils* (VITAE) (Day et al. 2007, Chapter 1, Section 1.3, Reading 1.1 and the **Research Briefing** on p. 11). This longitudinal study of 300 teachers provided a new perspective on teachers' quality, retention and effectiveness over the whole of their careers.

The project found that:

1. pupils of teachers who are committed and resilient are likely to attain more highly than pupils whose teachers are not;

2. teachers' sense of positive professional identity is associated with wellbeing and job satisfaction, and this is a key factor in effectiveness;

3. the commitment and resilience of teachers in schools serving more disadvantaged communities tend to be persistently challenged;

4. teachers do not necessarily become more effective over time – a minority risk becoming less effective in later years;

5. sustaining and enhancing commitment and resilience is key to teachers' career decisions to continue or leave the profession.

The project thus concluded that strategies are needed for meeting the needs of teachers in each phase of their professional lives, and in particular communities. Learning with colleagues in school is particularly influential in creating commitment, resilience and wellbeing. These factors are also correlated with pupil outcomes – thus affirming the significance of teacher learning in effective education systems.

2.10 Policy frameworks

Principle 10: Effective pedagogy demands consistent policy frameworks with support for learning as their primary focus. Organisational and system level policies need to recognise the fundamental importance of continual learning – for individual, team, organisational and system success – and be designed to create effective learning environments for all learners.

There is growing international awareness of the significance of the coherence, or otherwise, of national systems. Curriculum requirements must articulate with assessment processes and qualifications; these must be supported by teacher education, recruitment, promotion and retention policies; which in turn must be linked to school priorities, leadership, organisation and pedagogic culture; and provision for funding and accountability to parents, community and other stakeholders must contribute appropriately too. Above all, all of these forms of provision must be focused on the contribution they can make to effective learning (Schmidt and Prawat, 2006). The system must be an educationally principled system – simply being tightly controlled is insufficient.

The coherence of national systems is manifested at several levels, and we will here identify three – school, locality and nation.

At school level

There has been an enormous amount of work in recent decades on school effectiveness and improvement. MacGilchrist, Myers and Reed (2004) argued that the four most important characteristics of an effective school are: high quality leadership and management, a concentration on teaching and learning, a focus pupils' rights and responsibilities, and the development of the school as a learning organisation. TLRP projects certainly found similar patterns. For example, within the *Learning How to Learn* project, Swaffield and MacBeath (2005) found that school leaders who prioritised developing a sense of purpose, supporting professional development, auditing expertise and supporting networking were significantly more effective in fostering learning how to learn in classrooms. Similarly, the *Pupil Consultation* project found that support and commitment of school leaders was vital to ensure that consultation led to changes in actual classroom practices (Rudduck and McIntyre, 2007).

In the locality of the school

The work which teachers and schools do is in service of the children, young people, families and employers within their community – though, of course, this can be a very complex set of relationships. Indeed, most schools, particularly in urban areas, serve several communities and provide for social groups in widely different circumstances.

Ideally, connections between schools and their communities are close, because of the significance of informal learning at home and in other out-of-school settings. Indeed, teachers are often well known in their communities. The school curriculum may even be explicitly tailored to local expectations about important knowledge, and those with significant roles in the community may contribute to the life of the school – for instance, as helpers, fund-raisers or governors. The RSA has been advocating and trialling just such an 'area based curriculum' (Thomas, 2010, Reading 10.4).

Teachers and schools also have to demonstrate professional accountability and to be willing to justify pedagogic judgements and decisions. The established way of doing this is through the governing body of the school and the accountability structures of the local education authority. However, in England, local authorities now have very limited powers and most secondary schools, and a significant number of primaries, have assumed a new status as independent 'academies' or 'free schools'. Many schools are now directly funded by the DfE. It is not yet clear how this will affect the overall coherence and quality of national provision.

Nationally

The case for coherent, principled education policy is strong and there are some excellent examples of countries which seem to achieve this. Finland is the most often quoted (Sahlberg, 2012, Reading 4.3) but Section 3, below, illustrates work from New Zealand, Singapore, Australia and the USA too, amongst many others. However, history suggests that this is not easy to achieve in large, complex societies.

For example, in 2003 the Labour Government in England published its *Every Child Matters* agenda which highlighted the importance of five wide-ranging outcomes for the education system: being healthy; staying safe; enjoying and achieving; making a positive contribution; and achieving economic wellbeing. And yet there was a tension between meeting these broad objectives, with which few disagreed, and focusing on narrow performance targets which that particular government also prioritised. Indeed, educationalists sometimes felt that progress was being made despite government policy rather than because of it. However, there have been exceptions and one might pick out policy for early years education which has been strongly influenced by research, including that of TLRP's associate project, EPPE (Sylva et al., 2010; Siraj-Blatchford et al., 2013).

There is thus still much work to do to make policy better informed by research evidence, as the work of the UK *Strategic Forum for Research in Education* (**sfre.ac.uk**) demonstrated. This is an area which is ripe for development and new initiatives can be anticipated (see the web-links at **reflectiveteaching.co.uk**).

But values are always contested in a democracy, particularly in very unequal societies such as those in the UK (see Chapter 5, Green and Janmaat, 2011, Reading 5.2). Further, our education systems are also complex and only partially integrated across sectors. There are thus several structural reasons why coherence is difficult to achieve.

We need to be both realistic and optimistic about this goal. Although achieving *principled* educational coherence is difficult, incremental progress can be, and is being, made as governments realise its significance. It remains important that all those with an interest in effective teaching and learning – pupils, parents, teachers, researchers, policymakers and the public at large – continue to strive together to establish socially just policies that truly support learning for the diverse needs of all learners in our communities.

Reflective activity 4.4

Aim: To consider the roles of teacher learning and public policy development in educational improvement.

Evidence and reflection: People in particular roles or structural positions tend to develop shared perspectives, and these perspectives tend to reflect their material interests. So, politicians must struggle for power and then demonstrate that they can rule decisively? And teachers must achieve professional status and defend their authonomy and working conditions? But in fact, of course, both policymakers and teachers would claim that they: 'act in the public interest'.

The truth is that the public interest cannot be fulfilled without the complementary efforts of all stakeholders working together. TLRP's principles were designed to offer a simple framework of educationally sound ideas on which to base such cooperation.

What scope do you see, on whatever scale, for developing your own learning as a teacher, and for constructively engaging with school, local or government decision-makers? (See Chapter 17 for further ideas on this.)

Extension Working with some colleagues, consider some recent government policies on education which you know about. Are they coherent with other contemporary national policies? How do they relate to the evidence-informed principles proposed by TLRP?

3 International knowledge accumulation

In this chapter so far, we have reviewed TLRP's ten evidence-informed principles for effective teaching and learning. These were developed in and for the UK. However, the extent of international collaboration in understanding education is now enormous – and indeed, is part of the role of academic researchers. Teams form, propositions are tested, papers are exchanged, findings debated, books written, etc, etc. From such processes, new frameworks of understanding are created.

In North America, there is an extensive and very well established body of work. There are many contributions from the US in particular. For example, Linda Darling-Hammond and Ann Lieberman have added to the accumulative understanding over many years, and their review of *Teacher Education Around the World* (2012) is simply a recent contribution. See also, in particular, Darling-Hammond (1996, 2008). An influential synthesis of US work is, *How People Learn: Brain, Mind, Experience and School.* (Bransford et al., 2000, Reading 4.1). This was produced by the Committee on Developments in the Science of Learning for the US National Academy of Sciences. In Canada, innovative efforts to embed educational research within policy and practice have been made by Ben Levin and his team. For instance, *How to Change 5000 Schools* (2008) synthesises evidence whilst remaining grounded in the quality of teaching and learning in classroom and school practices.

Research in Australia, New Zealand and parts of the Far East has also made significant contributions. For example, Bob Lingard and colleagues' longitudinal work on school reform and 'productive pedagogies' in Queensland, Australia, which has generated a lot of interest (see Linguard, Hayes, Mills and Christie, 2003). *Best Practice Syntheses* from New Zealand have made a great contribution (eg, Alton-Lee, 2003; Timperley et al., 2007, Reading 16.6) and from Singapore, work by David Hogan and colleagues (2013, Reading 4.2) has codified and measured instructional systems for improvement of teaching in core subjects. Hong Kong has harvested work from around the world and introduced its school curriculum through a consultative process over a ten year period.

The case of Finland as documented, for instance, by Hannele Neimi et al. (2012) and Pasi Sahlberg (2012, Reading 4.3), has been much cited and demonstrates how educational principles can be applied in a sustained developmental way to achieve coherence across a national system. Reading 17.4 illustrates such thinking in the case of the Republic of Ireland's teacher education.

Comparative study remains a much debated subject with significant concern in relation to 'policy borrowing'. Robin Alexander's tour de force, *Culture and Pedagogy* (2000) provided an exceptionally rich analysis of the interaction of culture, power, schools, curriculum and pedagogy in five countries – thus analysing both unique and common features. Reviews by international agencies, such as *The Nature of Learning* (Dumont et al. for the OECD, 2010,

Reading 4.4), draw together research from a wide range of disciplines, and PISA survey analyses provide hugely influential feedback on national performance. However, they also inevitably mask many inter-cultural subtleties (Sturman, 2012, Reading 14.6). PISA ranks the performance of countries, subject to significant methodological qualifications, and analysis of these data has suggested a formula for success requiring high expectations combined with significant school autonomy to enable improvement practices to become embedded.

The National Foundation for Educational Research (NFER) provided a useful 'mapping of seminal reports on good teaching' from 2007–12 (Rowe, Wilkin and Wilson, 2012,

Reading 4.5). The review collates overlapping conclusions in respect of the 'teaching environment', 'teaching approaches' and 'teacher characteristics' – see Figure 4.2. The authors draw attention to the need to 'understand the principles that underpin practice' and note that, whilst awareness of strategies and techniques is valuable, 'they are not enough, in themselves, to change practice' (p. 26). Indeed, it is interesting to see how the 'teaching approaches' resonate closely with TLRP's ten principles.

The most comprehensive and systematic synthesis of recent years has been the work of John Hattie (2009, Reading 4.6). He has developed techniques to measure 'effect sizes' across multiple research studies, thus ranking findings for significance.

This work is now cogently expressed in *Visible Learning for Teachers* (Hattie, 2012). Hattie summarises by proposing eight 'mind frames' for teachers. If, he suggests, they were established as 'theories of practice', then significant impacts on learning should

follow (see Reading 10.7). These 'mind frames' again overlap with TLRP's principles in interesting ways.

Three cover dimensions of knowledge, learning, pedagogy and assessment.

- Teachers/leaders want to talk more about the learning than the teaching.
- Teachers/leaders engage in dialogue not monologue.
- Teachers/leaders see assessment as feedback about their impact.

Two others address engagement and relationships, whilst also reaching into informal settings to draw significant others into the learning process.

- Teachers/leaders believe that it is their role to develop positive relationships in classrooms/staffrooms.
- Teachers/leaders inform all about the language of learning.

Teaching environment	Teaching approaches	Teacher characteristics
• Calm, well-disciplined, orderly • Safe and secure • An ethos of aspiration and achievement for all • Positive emotional climate • Purposeful, stimulating • Bright, attractive and informative displays • Clean, tidy and well organised • New or redesigned buildings and spaces • Lower class sizes	• Interactive (e.g. working and learning together – social constructivism) • Use of teacher–pupil dialogue, questioning • Monitoring pupil progress (including the use of feedback) • Pupil assessment (including assessment for learning) • Pupil agency and voice (active engagement in their learning) • Enquiry-based • Effective planning and organisation • Scaffolding learning • Building on the prior experience and learning of pupils • Personalisation, responding to individual needs • Home–school learning, knowledge exchange • Use of new technology and ICT • Collaborative practice • Good use of teaching assistants • Creative use of visits and visiting experts	• Good subject knowledge • Self-efficacy and belief • High expectations • Motivational • Provides challenge • Innovative and proactive • Calm • Caring • Sensitive • Gives praise • Uses humour as a tool • Engenders trust and mutual respect • Flexible (where appropriate) • Builds positive relationships with pupils • Self-reflecting

Figure 4.2 Key features in a repertoire of effective teaching (Rowe, Wilkin and Wilson, 2012)

The final three of Hattie's 'mind frames' relate to teacher learning and commitment.

- Teachers/leaders believe that their fundamental task is to evaluate the effect of their teaching on students' learning and achievement.

- Teachers/leaders believe that success and failure in student learning is about what they, as teachers or leaders, did or did not to.

- Teachers/leaders enjoy the challenge and never retreat from 'doing their best'.

> ### Expert question
>
> **Warrant**: are our teaching strategies evidence-informed, convincing and justifiable to stakeholders?
>
> This question contributes to a conceptual framework underpinning professional expertise (see Chapter 16).

The overlaps between synoptic studies of different sorts give confidence to the process of international knowledge accumulation. It remains very unlikely that we will ever be able to state exactly 'what works' in all specific educational contexts. However, as evidence accumulates, informed teachers and others can refine their understanding and improve their judgement. We are progressively able to say 'what is *likely* to work' (see, for example the EEF Toolkit (**educationendowmentfoundation. org.uk/toolkit**). This growing confidence reflects the development of knowledge and expertise.

It is thus becoming entirely reasonable that we should, as teachers, be able to justify (or 'warrant') our practices to others through the use of evidence of various sorts. It is also, of course, increasingly reasonable to expect governments to take note, so that policy is well aligned with knowledge about learning and teaching.

Conclusion

In this chapter we have reviewed TLRP's ten evidence-informed principles which were developed to support the judgements of teachers and others in working towards high-quality teaching and learning.

Each principle focuses attention onto particular dimensions of teaching and learning. However, the principles should be seen as being interconnected. TLRP represented them 'in the round' to assert holism and to facilitate consideration of inter-relationships (see Figure 4.1). The salience of particular principles may change in relation to the specific circumstances or issues which a teacher faces, but none of them is likely to recede entirely.

The ten principles are used to structure reflection within this book because they tap into the enduring issues which teachers must face. At various points within the book, the text thus draws attention to particular principles in relation to the issues under consideration. The principles offer a framework for our understanding. They are also complemented through the book by the introduction of powerful concepts and 'expert questions' for analysing teacher expertise. We will take stock of these elements as a whole in Chapter 16.

The principles have a particular cutting edge when used to evaluate or review actual policy or practice. When that is done, there is often a gap between aspiration and achievement. This gives pause for thought, and can lead to new insights and developments. Why not apply the principles to interrogate a government policy document or, at the other end of the scale, to review some aspect of school provision, or a dimension of your classroom practice that has been concerning you?

As we have seen, TLRP's work is part of a continuing international effort to harvest, evaluate and synthesise global knowledge about teaching and learning. TLRP's principles represent a holistic understanding of teaching, learning and education. They complement more specific analyses of the measured effects of particular teaching strategies.

We conclude this chapter with a statement from the Chief Executive of the General Teaching Council for England which once again asserts the role of evidence-informed, principled judgement:

> As professionals, teachers use expert judgement to recognise and resolve the dilemmas in teaching and learning which they face every day in the classroom. At their best, teachers are able to reflect on and evaluate their practices, and to make rationally and ethically defensible judgements that go beyond compliance, pragmatic constraints or ideological preferences. (Bartley, 2010, p. 2)

This book is designed to support the development of such judgement, and TLRP's ten principles are offered as contributions to that goal.

Key readings

Simple summaries of TLRP's findings are available in the form of a teacher guide, poster, DVD and Commentary at: **tlrp.org/findings** or on **reflectiveteaching.co.uk/links**. The Commentary is:

James, M. and Pollard. A. (2006) *Improving Teaching and Learning in Schools.* London: TLRP.

For an extended academic review of the principles and international commentaries see:

James, M. and Pollard, A. (2012) *Principles for Effective Pedagogy: International Responses to Evidence from the UK Teaching and Learning Research Programme.* London: Routledge.

Synoptic reviews of cumulative evidence on teaching and learning include:

Bransford, J. (ed.) (1999) *How People Learn: Brain, Mind, Experience and School.* Washington, DC: National Academy Press. (Reading 4.1)

Muijs, D. and Reynolds, D. (2011) *Effective Teaching. Evidence and Practice.* London: SAGE. (Reading 8.7)

Good, T. and Brophy. J. (2008) *Looking in Classrooms*. Boston: Pearson.

Darling Hammond, L. (1996) *The Right to Learn: A Blueprint for Creating Schools that Work*. San Francisco: Jossey-Bass.

Globally influential work drawing on development in Austalia, Canada, Singapore and Finland is:

Hayes, D., Mills, M., Christie, P. and Linguard, R. (2006) *Teachers and Schooling Making a Difference.* Sydney: Allen and Unwin.

Levin, B. (2008) *How to Change 5000 Schools.* Cambridge, MA.: Harvard Eduction Press.

Hogan, D., Chan, M., Rahim, R., Kwek, D., Aye, K. M., Loo, S. C., Sheng, Y. and Luo, W. (2013) 'Assessment and the logic of instructional practice in Secondary 3 English and Mathematics classes in Singapore.' *Review of Education*, 1 (1), 57–106. (see Reading 4.2)

Sahlberg, P. (2012) *Finnish Lessons: What Can the World Learn from Educational Change in Finland?* Boston: Teachers' College Press. (Reading 4.3)

An OECD attempt to summarise the implications deriving from what is known about learning from across the world is:

Dumont, H., Istance, D. and Benavides, F. (2010) *The Nature of Learning. Using Research to Inspire Practice.* Paris: OECD. (Reading 4.4)

A UK synopsis of contemporary studies on effective teaching is:

Rowe, N., Wilkin, A. and Wilson, R. (2012) *Mapping of Seminal Reports on Good Teaching.* Slough: NFER. (Reading 4.5)

Two synopses of quantitative research, encouragingly consonant in general with the results of qualitative research and teacher experience, are:

Hattie, J. (2009) *Visible Learning: A Synthesis of Meta-Analyses Relating to Achievement.* London: Routledge. (Reading 4.6)

Marzano, R. J. (2009) *Designing and Teaching Learning Goals and Objectives.* Bloomington: Solution Tree.

For a UK website harvesting international evidence on particular teaching strategies and summarising knowledge from a programme of randomised trials in England, see:

educationendowmentfoundation.org.uk/toolkit

For more specialist insights, the handbook below indicates the range of scientific disciplines engaging with contemporary understanding of teaching and learning, and the nature of their contributions.

Sawyer, R. K. (2006) *The Cambridge Handbook of the Learning Sciences.* Cambridge: Cambridge University Press.

The insights from international research are also played out in particular ways in relation to learners of different ages, and thus for each sector of education. Among the most significant recent sectoral reviews are:

Early Childhood: The Effective Pre-School and Primary Education Project: Sylva, K., Melhuish, E., Sammons, P., Siraj-Blatchford, I. and Taggart, B. (2010) *Early Childhood Matters.* London: Routledge.

This book summarises the first large scale multi-level longitudinal study of young children's development and underpinned a significant expansion in early years provision in the UK. See www.ioe.ac.uk/eppse <http://www.ioe.ac.uk/eppse>.

Cambridge Primary Review: Alexander, R. (ed.) (2010) *Children, Their World, Their Education*, Final Report and Recommendations. London: Routledge.

The CPR was funded in 2006 by Esmee Fairbairn Foundation to evaluate the current state of primary education by combining 'retrospective evidence with prospective vision'. The final report, based on extensive research, drew together over 30 interim reports. Its website is can be found at www.primaryreview.org.uk.

Nuffield 14–19 Review: Pring, R., Hayward, G., Hodgson, A., Johnson, J., Keep, E., Oancea, A., Rees, G., Spours, K. and Wilde, S. (2009) *Education for All: the Future of Education and Training for 14–19 Year Olds in England and Wales.* London: Routledge.

In 2003, the Nuffield Foundation funded a major Review of every aspect of 14–19 provision to be led by Richard Pring. The final Report was supported by a wide range of research papers, and these remain available on its website (www.nuffieldfoundation.org/nuffield-review-14–19-education-and-training-0)

Inquiry into the Future of Lifelong Learning: Schuller, T. and Watson, D. (2009) *Learning Through Life.* London: National Institute for Adult Continuing Education (NIACE).

This Inquiry was set up in 2007 by the National Institute of Adult Continuing Education, and informed by over 250 evidence submissions. The Report is 'nested' in 30 supplementary papers published on www.lifelonglearninginquiry.org.uk. The primary focus is on adult learning but the crucial continuity with early childhood and schooling is drawn out.

Mental Capital and Well Being Report: Feinstein, L., Vorhaus, J., Sabates, R. (2008) *Learning through Life: Future Challenges*. London: Government Office for Science. (Reading 1.6)

The Office for Science's Foresight Programme advises the Government on how to achieve the best possible intellectual development for everyone. This Report considered factors which could affect 'learning through life' in future decades. The report is available at foresight.gov.uk

part two

Creating conditions for learning

This part concerns the creation of classroom environments to support high-quality teaching and learning.

We begin by considering the circumstances which impinge on families and schools (Chapter 5) – and we note the ways in which people contribute to and challenge such circumstances through their actions.

We then move to the heart of classroom life with a focus on teacher–pupil relationships and classroom climate (Chapter 6). Because 'good relationships' are so enabling, this is an extremely important chapter.

Chapter 7 builds further and illustrates how positive cycles of behaviour can be created through firmness, fairness and engaging pupils in the curriculum.

Finally, we consider a range of learning spaces (Chapter 8) in school and beyond and we consider affordances they offer for formal and informal learning. As well as the basic dimensions of classroom organisation, this chapter also addresses the use of technology, pupil organisation and teamworking with teacher assistants.

Contexts
What is, and what might be?

5

Introduction

This chapter provides a brief review of some of the contextual factors which are important in education, and of how teachers, children and families respond. The influence of social context pervades everything that happens in schools and classrooms, and awareness of such issues is therefore an important contributing element of reflective teaching. This influence is felt at many levels – from the 'big picture' of government policies in Scotland, Wales, England, Northern Ireland, the Republic of Ireland or elsewhere, to the detail of community, school and family cultures and particular individual circumstances.

A second purpose of the chapter is to establish some principles concerning the relationships of individuals and society. Indeed, the chapter is very deliberately in two parts. The first, 'Social context', emphasises the ideas, social structures and distribution of resources which *structure* action in various ways. The second part, 'People and agency', is concerned with the factors which, in various senses, *enable* action by individual teachers and children.

A particular theoretical position thus underpins this chapter and, indeed, the book as a whole. At its core is the conception of a dialectical relationship between society and individuals. This suggests the existence of a constant interplay of social forces and individual actions (see, for example, Giddens, 1984). On the one hand, the decisions and actions which people make and take in their lives are constrained by social structures and by the historical processes which bring about such structures. On the other hand, each individual has a unique sense of self, derived from his or her personal history or biography. Individuals have a degree of free will in acting and in developing understandings with others. Sets of these understandings, which endure over time, form the basis of cultures. Such understandings can also lead to challenges to established social structures and thus to future changes.

The ways in which these processes play out is significantly influenced by the circumstances of various social groups in terms of power, wealth, status and opportunities (Reid 1998, Halsey, 1986). Individuals, each with their own background and sense of self, will react to such factors in a variety of ways. Some in powerful positions might wish to close ranks and defend themselves by suggesting that their position is inherited by right or earned by merit. Some among those who are less fortunate may accept the social order or even aspire to success in its terms. Others may try to contest it – for of course, to be able to question existing social arrangements is a fundamental right in our democratic societies.

The particular historical era in which we happen to live also makes a significant difference. Following the Second World War, the UK economy was still the third largest in the world (after the US and Soviet Union). Since then our living standards have trebled and life-expectancy has steadily risen. However, relative to some other countries such as Germany and the US, our growth has been relatively faltering and unbalanced. In the future, growth and competition from countries such as China, India and Brazil will continue to force structural changes in our economy. In recent decades, these global forces have resulted in increasingly interventionist education policies from governments of both left and right. The form of intervention differs, but intervene they do. Educational provision, in other words, cannot escape its circumstances.

There is thus an enduring ebb and flow in social change – a process of tension and struggle. It is the product of a constant interaction between agency and circumstance, voluntarism and determinism, biography and history (Mills, 1959, Reading 5.1).

New priorities may emerge in future (see Collarbone, 2009, Reading 16.1). For instance, given the environmental challenges facing the world, it would not be surprising if schools were one day required to play a major role in introducing more sustainable ways of life to new generations. At the moment, governments sometimes appear to merely pay lip service to this issue, but events could make it a much higher priority. We cannot predict the future and the roles which education may be called upon to fulfil.

A reflective teacher has responsibilities within this process which should not be avoided.

The interaction of structure and agency can thus be seen in education, as in other fields of life. Amongst the many ways in which they may be realised, they can be seen to influence both national policy frameworks and everyday informal learning.

TLRP principles

Two principles are of particular relevance to this chapter on the broader contexts in which teaching and learning take place:

Effective teaching and learning recognises the significance of informal learning. Informal learning, such as learning out of school, should be recognised as at least as significant as formal learning and should therefore be valued and used appropriately in formal processes. (Principle 8)

Effective teaching and learning demands consistent policy frameworks with support for teaching and learning as their primary focus. Policies at national, local and institutional levels need to recognise the fundamental importance of teaching and learning. They should be designed to create effective learning environments in which all learners can thrive. (Principle 10)

See Chapter 4

---

1 Social context

We now consider four aspects of the social context which are particularly significant for practice in schools: ideology, culture, opportunity and accountability. The influence of each can be traced at national, regional, local and school levels so that, although such issues sometimes seem distant, they shape classroom activity in very real ways.

1.1 Ideology

A dictionary definition of ideology states that it means a 'way of thinking'. However, particular sets of ideas are often used, consciously or unconsciously, to promote and legitimise the interests of specific groups of people. Indeed, if a particular way of thinking about a society is dominant at any point in time, it is likely to be an important influence on education and on teachers' actions. It may determine the types of schools which are created, produce a particular curriculum emphasis and even begin to frame the ways in which teachers think about their work and relate with children and young people.

For instance, in the US of the 1950s and the Cold War, anti-communist feeling was so great that it not only led to the now discredited inquisitions of the McCarthy Committee but also to a range of nationalistic practices in schools, re-interpretations of history and pressures to compete with the 'enemy', particularly after the 1957 launch of the Russian *Sputnik* satellite. Similarly, in the USSR and Eastern Bloc countries, before the revolutionary changes which swept Eastern Europe in 1989, pupils were taught highly selective views of history, of the values and achievements of their societies. They too were encouraged to compete, particularly to sustain exceptional international achievements in areas such as science and sport. In both cases, despite widely differing circumstances, it can be seen that the ideologies of key political elites interacted with the 'commonsense thinking' of the wider population to create particular ideological climates (see the work of Gramsci, 1978, for an analysis of such hegemonic phenomena). Although the influence of these ideological periods was enormous, they passed.

 International comparison also enables us to place the 'taken for granted' into perspective and consider alteratives. A study by the LLAKEs research centre in London (Green and Janmaat, 2011, Reading 5.2) analysed the values and assumptions underpinning education policies in the western world. They identify three main positions:

- **Liberal** – with core beliefs in individual opportunities and rewards based on merit (English speaking countries, particularly UK and US);

- **Social Market** – with solidarity depending more on the state and less on civil society (North West continental Europe, including Belgium, France, Germany, Netherlands);

- **Social Democratic** – with egalitarian and solidaristic values and higher levels of social and political trust (Nordic countries, such as Denmark, Finland, Norway, Sweden).

Particular beliefs and values permeate perception and decision-making in these societies, and throw up a wide range of issues. For instance, a common question in some parts of the UK is: Why do we widely admire the achievements of the Nordic countries but in reality do so little to emulate them?

The ideologies which influence education in the UK also come and go.

For example, there have been very different beliefs over the years about what kinds of schools should be provided and who should go to them. After the Second World War, it was thought that the most appropriate way of organising secondary education was to have different types of school – grammar schools, technical schools and secondary moderns. Pupils would be selected for each of these schools on merit, based on how they performed in '11-plus' tests. However, it was not long before this 'tripartite' system came to be criticised for favouring well-off families rather than widening educational opportunities. This led to proposals for the introduction of a system of secondary schools, which would be 'comprehensive' in that there was to be no selection of students. By the 1960s this view had become the new orthodoxy and, with support from all major political parties, comprehensive schools supported by local education authorities became the norm in most of England, Scotland and Wales. The commitment to the meritocratic ideal of 'opportunities for all' was distinctive, but comprehensives were criticised in the 1990s for being too complacent or, as an English Minister once put it, 'bog standard'. The Coalition Government in England from 2010 urged that schools should become responsive to their clientele by breaking free from local authorities and establishing themselves as independent 'academies'. A mix of competition and collaboration between such schools is expected to improve the performance of the system overall.

Some historians have argued (for example, Simon, 1992) that forms of school organisation can best be understood in terms of the reproduction of social class structures and patterns of advantage and disadvantage. Indeed, authors such as Althusser (1971) saw education systems within capitalist societies as forms of an 'ideological state apparatus' designed to achieve broader social control in the interests of powerful elites. On the other hand, sociologists such as Collins (1977), Kogan (1978) and Archer (1979, Reading 17.1) have argued that educational policies and provision are the product of competing interest groups and that control and power is more diffuse.

Unfortunately, ideologies flourish in education about the curriculum, teaching methods, assessment requirements and many other issues. In the postwar years, civil servants had tended to moderate political manifestations of popular ideas – though this was, in itself, a reflection of their own 'assumptive world' (McPherson and Raab, 1988). However, in more recent decades there has been a considerable struggle for control between politicians, civil servants and professionals over education policy (Ball, 1990; Bowe, Ball and Gold, 1992, Reading 17.7). As they should in democracies, politicians gradually prevailed – but the tension can still be seen in animated media debates and moral panics about education issues, uneasy relationships between researchers and policymakers, and regular 'shake ups' of government education departments. In recent years politicians have taken to claiming that their policies are 'evidence based' – though the academic community is sometimes rather sceptical of this assertion. However, the commitment in principle to the use of evidence to inform policy and practice is a very important development. Significant work has been done on this through organisations such as the Economic and Social Research Council, the British Academy and, in education, the UK Strategic Forum for Research in Education (SFRE), Campaign for Evidence-Based Education (CEBE) and British Educational Research Association (BERA).

Even at national levels, ideologies interact with culture and identity as well as with material interests. For example, in England, as we will see in the discussion of accountability later in this chapter, the big story of the last 30 years has been the growth of centralised control over the education system. But this is not quite the same in Scotland, Northern Ireland or Wales, where devolution has enabled the centralist tendencies of the English system to be significantly moderated. No ideology is

> **Expert question**
>
> **Warrant**: are our teaching strategies evidence-informed, convincing and justifiable to stakeholders?
>
> This question contributes to a conceptual framework underpinning professional expertise (see Chapter 16).

all-powerful, and countervailing ideas emerge over time, based on their own power-bases and social movements.

The Scottish Parliament now ensures that education policy responds to Scottish, rather than English, priorities. Similarly, the National Assembly for Wales and the Northern Ireland Assembly, with more limited powers, act to interpret primary legislation and to develop their own new policy initiatives. However, such measures are influenced by *different* sets of beliefs and power relations. In Wales, for instance, the *Curriculum Cymreig* and the compulsory teaching and learning of the Welsh language are particularly distinctive. Debate over the future of Northern Ireland's grammar schools continues, as it has for decades, though the 11-plus transfer test has recently been abolished. Although integrated education has been expanding, over 90 per cent of Northern Ireland's pupils still attend either Catholic or Protestant schools. Meanwhile, as we will see in more detail later in this chapter, Scotland has taken distinctive positions, for instance on student fees, the *Curriculum for Excellence* and professional development matters. The Republic of Ireland has been fully independent since 1922, and its education system has evolved considerably over the period.

The relationships between the four major parts of the UK have always been complex and, of course, they will continue to evolve. Whilst such complexity has increased since devolution, the basic educational issues to be tackled remain much the same. Education is inevitably concerned with the future, with opportunities and life-chances, with produc-tivity, wealth, community, identity and fulfilment. It is not surprising that it is contested. If possible, reflective teachers should develop their understanding at this enduring level.

In summary, the ideas, perspectives or beliefs which prevail at a particular point of time are likely to be reflected in public debate and education policy. Whilst the basic issues being contested are likely to remain much the same, the settlements reached will change and change again over a teaching career. At some point in time, critique and experience lead to evaluation, counter proposal, development and change (Bowe, Ball and Gold, 1992, Reading 17.7). Societies and dominant ideologies are never static, but awareness of the concept of ideology makes it more likely that reflective teachers will be able to evaluate the values or interests that may lie behind new ideas, policies or practices.

It is important to remember that no one, including ourselves, is immune to the influ-ences of ideologies. For instance, professional ideologies are always likely to remain strong among teachers – they represent commitments, ideals *and* interests. Reflective teachers should be open-minded enough to constructively critique their own beliefs, as well as those of others.

1.2 Culture

Cultures can be seen as sets of shared perspectives. They often develop from collective activity and from the creative responses of groups to situations. Furthermore, cultures endure over time and thus represent sets of perspectives, values and practices into which individuals are likely to be socialised. The playground cultures of young children provide an example here. In one sense, children in friendship groups develop unique and particular ways of perceiving school life. Indeed, they use these as a means of understanding school and coping with it (Clarricoates, 1987; Davies, 1982; Pollard, 1987b). Yet at the same time, continuities in children's culture, from generation to generation, provide a context which young children absorb (Opie and Opie, 1959; Sluckin, 1981). For older students, pupil cultures are strongly influenced by films, television, games, popular music, mobile phones and other styles and technologies – but they are played out through students' collective agency.

The community within the school provides another cultural context. This will influence and be influenced by the perspectives of parents, children and teachers. However, few communities can be characterised as single, united entities. Among the many divisions which may exist are those relating to ethnicity, language, religion, social class, gender, sexuality and to political or personal values. The existence of such cultural diversity is particularly important in many inner-city schools and reflective teachers are likely to explore the relationship between cultures in young peoples' homes, communities and school very carefully indeed (Vincent, 2000). A great deal of research has shown problems arising when working-class cultures are regarded as being deficient by those in schools (for example, Lareau, 1989; Sharp and Green, 1975; Ball, 1981a). Similarly, institution-alised forms of racism are likely to result if teachers fail to appreciate the perspectives of ethnic groups (Troyna and Hatcher, 1992; Wright, 1992; Mac an Ghaill, 1988; Gillborn, 1995). Stereotypical perceptions of teachers may also have gender or sexuality dimensions that could impinge in a number of ways on the educational opportunities of both girls and boys (for example, Thorne, 1993; Kehily, 2002; Skelton, 2001, Mac an Ghaill, 1994).

There are also likely to be cultures among the adults within each school. Primary school staffrooms provide a backstage area where tensions are released, feelings are shared and understandings about school life are developed. This is the territory of the classroom teacher, and the resulting relationships usually provide a source of solidarity and sympathy when facing the daily pressures of classrooms (Nias et al., 1989). While colleagues may be stimulating and supportive of experimentation, they can also become protective of existing practices and inhibit innovation (Pollard, 1987a; Sedgwick, 1988). Within secondary schools, teachers' allegiances and identities tend to be strongly influ-enced by subject departments, but may also reflect the pastoral system of year group teams or a range of sporting or supplementary school activities (Power, 1996). Whilst the complexity of secondary schools creates more opportunities for sub-groups to form within the staff, headteachers will be concerned to maintain a shared understanding of 'the way we do things here'.

Devolution has had a particularly significant effect as cultural differences become reflected in education policies. After 1999, with the establishment of the Scottish Parliament, the National Assembly for Wales and the Northern Ireland Assembly, a high degree of political autonomy was established in each home country. Scotland and Northern Ireland took responsibility for legislation for education and training, and Wales took executive control for the implementation of shared English–Welsh legislation. There were initially many similarities between the four systems (Raffe et al., 1999) with the same broad institutional structure of schools and many other arrangements. As time has passed, notable differences have developed. Of particular note is the role of the Welsh language and the *Curriculum Cymreig* in asserting a strong Welsh identity. In Scotland, education has been seen as 'lying at the heart of Scottish identity' (Paterson, 1998), with teachers as significant cultural leaders. The *Curriculum for Excellence* is a uniquely Scottish creation for 3 to 18-year-olds (see also Reading 14.2). It has strong recognition of lifelong learning and identifies 'four capacities' to complement 'curriculum areas and subjects'. In Northern Ireland, the challenge of achieving political agreement delayed the creation of a streamlined Education and Skills Authority and selective secondary education has been retained despite the fact that the 11-plus exam has been abolished. The influence of the churches also remains an enduring feature of education. However, the Council for the Curriculum, Examinations and Assessment (CCEA) has developed an innovative *Northern Ireland Curriculum* and has facilitated some exceptional uses of new technologies to support schools. There are thus both important differences and enduring similarities in educational provision across the UK. Particular priorities and institutional arrangements are likely to become increasingly distinct.

Cultures have a huge impact on learning and behaviour, as is being progressively demonstrated by the rapidly developing field of 'cultural psychology' (Wells, 2011, Reading 2.4; Bruner, 1986, 1990, Reading 11.1; see also Chapter 2). For instance, Wertsch (1991) argues that the thinking of any learner is dependent on the 'cultural tools' that they deploy. These concepts and artefacts frame and mediate understanding and thus shape development. They will thus certainly have a direct impact on school performance. Similarly, new learning may affect, or even change, the sense of identity of individuals, and such changes may or may not feel viable to them within their home culture. For instance, a classic study (Jackson and Marsden, 1962) showed the unease of working-class boys on being sent out of their communities to a grammar school, and similar problems may affect the performance of children from minority ethnic groups today. It has been argued that organisations like schools can helpfully be seen as 'communities of practice' (Wenger, 1999) which evolve and maintain strong norms of behaviour and thought. New members must learn how to conduct themselves and there may be a process of 'cognitive apprenticeship' (Rogoff, 1990) as new understanding is acquired. However, depending on the social, cultural and economic background of a new pupil or teacher, such induction may or may not be comfortable. Cultures can thus be exclusive as well as inclusive, particularly when organisations feel the need to assert a narrow range of goals. Sadly, exclusion from school has become a significant issue in recent years.

There is thus a sense in which cultures can both enable and constrain learning. Indeed, they are likely to afford different opportunities for particular individuals and groups. It is to these issues that we now turn.

Expert question

Culture: does the school support expansive learning by affirming learner contributions, engaging partners and providing attractive opportunities?

This question contributes to a conceptual framework underpinning professional expertise (see Chapter 16).

1.3 Opportunity

It has been said that 'education cannot compensate for society' (Bernstein, 1971) – and yet the opportunities which teachers and others aspire to create for their pupils make an important contribution to the meritocratic ideal to which most contemporary societies subscribe. However, the challenge of creating such opportunities through education is not to be underestimated.

Although there are substantial differences in Scotland, Wales, Northern Ireland and in England's regions, the UK as a whole is very wealthy in terms of global criteria – but at the same time there is significant inequality in the distribution of income and wealth. For instance, in 2008/9 the bottom fifth of households received under £5,000 in annual income before tax and benefits, whilst the top fifth had £73,800 or more – 15 times higher. Such differences have existed for many centuries and tangible evidence of this is available in the contrasts of our buildings, estates and landscape in both urban and rural settings – or even in

Expert question

Consequence: do assessment outcomes lead towards recognised qualifications and a confident sense of personal identity?

This question contributes to a conceptual framework underpinning professional expertise (see Chapter 16).

the windows of estate agents (bearing also in mind that increasing numbers of households do not own their homes). Indeed, it may seem extraordinary, but 3.8 million UK children (29 per cent) live in poverty as defined by the Department for Work and Pensions (2011). In many instances, these children are concentrated in particular communities in which 'cycles of disadvantage' (Rutter and Madge, 1976) are remarkably resistant to change (DCSF, 2009, Reading 5.4).

International comparison shows that health, social and educational problems are closely related to inequality within wealthy countries (Wilkinson and Pickett, 2009), as illustrated in Figure 5.1 below.

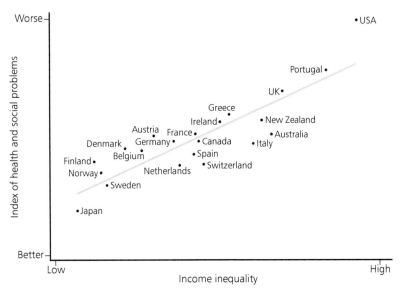

Figure 5.1
Health and social problems in relation to inequality (Wilkinson and Pickett, 2009)

These relative positions are measured regularly by international agencies and draw from data within each country on issues such as social relations, life expectancy, mental health, obesity and, not least, educational performance.

In the case of the UK, there was a substantial rise in inequality during the 1980s and in recent years the incomes of top earners have continued to race away (Sibieta, 2011). Economists speculate about the causes of these trends and debate factors such as changes in employment opportunities, returns from high-level skills and education, regional differences and demographic patterns. The direct consequences of government policies on tax and benefits may moderate such structural factors, but the UK's recent experience is of a low level of inter-generational mobility (Blanden, Gregg and Machin, 2005). In other words, the circumstance of parents tends to be reproduced for their children.

In summary, affluence and poverty are both growing and becoming 'locked in' (Crawford et al., 2011; DCSF, 2009, Reading 5.4). The social differences in our societies tend to be reproduced from generation to generation. How then does this process of reproduction occur?

An illuminative analysis of this has been provided by a French sociologist, Pierre Bourdieu (1977). Whilst recognising exceptional cases, he argued that overall social status is significantly affected by three forms of 'capital' – each of which can be transferred from one generation to another. 'Economic capital' concerns access to material assets. 'Social capital' focuses on relationships in the family, community or wider society which offers contacts, networks and support. 'Cultural capital' relates to the understanding, knowledge and capabilities of individuals to act within particular social settings. The seeds of difference are sown in the ways in which young children are brought up (see

Ball, 2003, Reading 5.3). For instance, Lareau (1989) contrasts the 'concerted cultivation' of middle-class families with the assumption of 'natural growth'. The latter causes less aware families to interact with their children in quite different ways – with particularly significant consequences for language development. Reay (2000) illuminates how mothers in different circumstances deploy 'emotional capital' to support their children, and she suggests that generational reserves are built up over time.

Families thus provide economic, social, cultural, linguistic and emotional resources. These affect the experiences, opportunities and expectations which are made available to the next generation.

These factors are particularly transparent in relation to school choice, with the private sector offering to reinforce advantages for the children of parents who can afford their fees. Sociologists fear that the quasi-market in schooling, which has been extended in England through the roll-out of independent academies, will further embed inequality (Ball, 2008). Whilst the Government promotes the 'freedom' of such schools from local authorities, the new structures of provision are expected by others to undermine education as a public good and render it as a 'market-controlled commodity' (Benn, 2011).

Using very large data-sets and innovative statistical techniques, it is now possible to measure the relative influence of neighbourhood, school, family and personal influences on a child's education (Leckie, Pillinger, Jenkins and Rasbash, 2010). This shows that family and personal factors are by far the most significant, which puts the work of schools into perspective (see the **Research Briefing** on p. 133).

School, family, neighbourhood: which is most important to a child's education?

Children grow up in complex social environments. The influences on a child's development are many, and many-layered. The school they go to, the family around them, and the neighbourhood they grow up in are often highlighted as particularly important for children's educational achievements. But, which is the most important?

- families account for 40% of the overall variation between children in their academic progress during secondary schooling;
- the wider shared environments of primary school (9%), secondary school (10%), neighbourhood (2%) and Local Education Authority (LEA) (1%) account for a total of 22%;
- children themselves account for the remaining 38%.

From a school effectiveness point of view it is interesting that the family effect is just as important as the child effect. However, this does not necessarily imply that interventions to improve child academic outcomes are best implemented at the family level. While primary and secondary schools appear less important than families, they still make reasonably substantial contributions; and it is at these levels that many educational policies are likely to be most effective. It is easier for governments to intervene in the running of schools than to change parenting practices within families.

The research
Our knowledge of the impact of schools, neighbourhoods and families comes from studies that look at each of these influences separately, and therefore little is known about their relative importance. For example, school effectiveness studies attempt to measure the importance of schools on children's academic progress, but nearly always ignore the role of family. Family research using siblings, on the other hand, attempts to quantify the importance of genetic and environmental family influences, but nearly always ignores the role of the wider shared environment of schools and neighbourhoods. Knowledge of the relative effects of schools, neighbourhoods and families is needed to help inform decisions about the allocation of government resources to programmes and policies that will support children's learning.

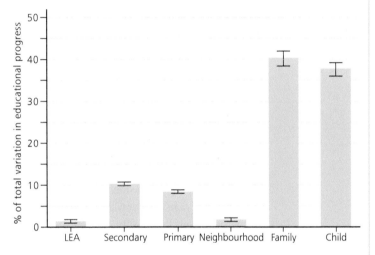

The importance of different influences on educational progress, with 95% credible intervals.

Research design
We follow half a million English school children through secondary schooling. We use cross-classified multilevel statistical models to estimate the impact of the different influences of children's complex social environments on their academic progress.

Our final model decomposes the variation in children's progress into effects attributable to six influences: Local Education Authorities (LEAs), secondary schools, neighbourhoods, primary schools, families and children. This is an improvement on previous school effectiveness studies because it differentiates, for the first time, between the effects of the family and of the pupil; and it is an improvement on previous family research because it estimates the influence of the family-shared environment separately from those of the wider shared environments of schools and areas. Thus, we unite school effectiveness studies and family research under a single framework and therefore disentangle the various influences on children's progress.

Further information
References for practitioners, journalists and policymakers
Leckie, G., Pillinger, R., Jenkins, J. and Rasbash, J. (2010). *School, family, neighbourhood: which is most important to a child's education? MethodsNews:* Newsletter from the ESRC National Centre for Research, Summer, 4.
Leckie, G., Pillinger, R., Jenkins, J. and Rasbash, J. (2010). *School, family, neighbourhood: which is most important to a child's education? Significance,* 7, 67–72.

This work was carried out at the University of Bristol.

University of BRISTOL

It is absolutely clear then, that it is impossible for education to 'compensate for society'. And yet the particular needs of the pupils before us still have to be met, and this is a moral imperative as well as a professional responsibility. Whatever the nature of the overall context around us, teachers must focus on providing the best possible educational opportunities for their pupils. Indeed, beyond the overarching statistics, there are many examples of people whose lives have been transformed through the influence of teachers.

The resources which are available in a school make a big difference in the creation of learning opportunities, and we will distinguish four types here: people, buildings, equipment and materials.

Many people are involved in the life of a successful school and, for this reason collaboration and teamwork are needed, irrespective of status. Apart from the head and the teaching staff, there are many others, such as cleaners, dinner supervisors, cooks, secretaries, classroom ancillaries and caretakers, who all have very important supportive roles to play. However, from the educational point of view, the expertise of classroom teachers is the key factor in determining the quality of provision. Teachers themselves are the most important resource, which puts a premium on the recruitment, development and retention of excellent staff. Class size is perceived as a major factor in determining practice and research has supported this proposition for many years (e.g. Glass, 1982; PateBain et al., 1992; Blatchford, 2003).

Buildings are also an important influence on what goes on in schools. At its most obvious, buildings constrain decisions about numbers and types of classes because of the number and nature of the classrooms which are available. This often affects class sizes and forms of curriculum and teaching organisation. The quality of the school environment will also be influenced by aesthetic considerations, and schools vary considerably in terms of the degree of consideration that is given to this issue. Reflective teachers are likely to be concerned about the quality of the learning environment within their classrooms, departments and school and will aim to maximise the learning potential of the spaces which they have available (see Chapter 8).

Equipment and materials enable teachers to provide learning experiences of various sorts. For example, for primary schools maintaining a broad and balanced curriculum across all subjects, the needs range from hall and playground requirements to instruments for music-making, artefacts for historical work and specific resources associated with curriculum progression in English, mathematics and science. In secondary school subject departments, equipment and materials are even more specialised and are likely to be tuned to particular exam syllabi as well as reflecting more generic educational objectives.

The most challenging form of equipment for schools to maintain relates to information technology. This is fast moving in terms of both hardware and software, and variation in provision between schools is often considerable.

UK schools have locally managed budgets in which income from national taxation is distributed annually on the basis of a formula. This allocates a certain amount for each pupil on roll, plus allowances in respect of social disadvantage or special educational needs. The way this is organised varies. For instance, in Scotland three year budgets are managed through the 32 local authorities that are responsible for provision in their areas, whilst in England secondary academies receive an annual grant directly from the national government. The total cost of such funding is very considerable. For example, during 2010/11 English schools had expenditure of £35.8 billion. Of this, 0.7 per cent (£263.8 million) was spent by local authority maintained nursery schools; 47.8 per cent (£17.1 billion) by primary schools; 46.1 per cent (£16.5 billion) by secondary schools and 5.4 per cent (£1.9 billion) by special schools.

Expenditure is the responsibility of the headteacher and governors. However, once fixed costs are taken out of the overall budget, school managers often have relatively small sums to spend at their discretion. Indeed, the salaries of teachers and other staff often amount to around 75 per cent of the budget, followed by costs of building maintenance and school running costs. Only a relatively small percentage is left for books, equipment, materials and discretionary expenditure.

The key factor in school budgets remains the number of pupils on roll. Each school's position in the quasi-market for pupil enrolments in its area is thus crucial to its resource base – hence the pressure for performance in formal assessments and in developing a positive local reputation.

Resources thus structure the material conditions in which teachers work and the opportunities they can provide for pupils. However, the actions they take are also likely to be influenced by the degree of autonomy which they feel they have. For this reason, we now focus on the issue of accountability.

1.4 Accountability

Teachers are paid to provide professional services. However, the degree of accountability and external control to which they have been subject has varied historically.

In the early years of state provision, education was managed through 'payment by results'. Teacher salaries were dependent on the results of annual visits by inspectors to test pupils in reading, writing and arithmetic. Indeed, when introducing the Revised Code for Education of 1862, its proposer Robert Lowe made the famous boast that: 'If it is not cheap, it shall be efficient, if it is not efficient, it shall be cheap'. Although superseded in the first part of the nineteenth century, the approach left a legacy in the form of imposed performance requirements. However, from the 1920s teachers began to develop greater professional autonomy (Lawn and Ozga, 1986). In particular, the independence of headteachers within their schools and of class teachers within their classrooms emerged to become established principles. After the Second World War, as professional confidence grew, this independence extended into the curriculum to the extent that, in 1960, the curriculum was described by Lord Eccles, Minister for Education, as a 'secret garden' into which central government was not expected to intrude. Such confidence was probably at a high point in the early 1970s.

In 1977, a speech at Ruskin College, Oxford, by Prime Minister Callaghan reflected a changing ideological, economic and political climate. This resulted in teachers coming under increasing pressure to 'increase their accountability' and to demonstrate competent performance against centrally defined criteria. These developments were presented by Margaret Thatcher's Conservative government during the 1980s as a necessary reduction in the influence of the 'producers' (seen as teacher unions, administrators and theorists) and thus to enable educational provision to be shaped by the 'consumers' (seen as parents and industry, though with little direct reference to children and young people themselves). Later, under Tony Blair's New Labour administration, the emphasis was in terms of applying modern personnel and performance management systems so that nationally prescribed curricula and pedagogies could be delivered – for instance, as set out in England through the National Curriculum and Literacy and Numeracy Strategies.

In the contemporary, devolved UK and in Ireland, a wide range of approaches is now evident. Each country has its national curriculum and inspection system but the form and role of these vary considerably.

With effect from 2014, England adopted a new National Curriculum which requires primary schools to focus on core knowledge in English, mathematics and science, whilst also expecting provision of a 'broad and balanced' education. Subject to these constraints, schools are to make their own judgements about the 'school curriculum' as a whole. Secondary schools have been particularly encouraged to leave the state system to become independent 'academies', for which the statutory requirements of the National Curriculum do not formally apply. In relation to assessment and qualifications, formal testing remains at age 11. GCSEs were 'reformed' to increase rigour and A Level exam syllabi continue to frame school provision but now with input from universities. The accountability measure for secondary schools was expanded to include progress in eight subjects, thus endorsing the value of a broad curriculum. League tables will continue to be produced – despite the technical difficulties of doing so (Leckie and Goldstein, 2009). The English model remains one of schools being required to directly account for themselves to stakeholders, in competition with other schools in their locality. The direction of policy by successive governments has been to use market forces to hold schools to account.

Expert question

Effectiveness: are there improvements in standards, in both basic skills and other areas of curricular attainment, to satisfy society's educational goals?

This question contributes to a conceptual framework underpinning professional expertise (see Chapter 16).

However, England retains a powerful interventionist capacity in the form of the Ofsted inspection system (e.g. Ofsted, 2012). Ofsted contracts teams of inspectors to make a structured report on every individual school in a regular cycle. Comparative data from schools serving similar socio-economic communities and baseline data from the school being inspected are used to evaluate levels of performance and improvement. The strongest sanction available to Ofsted is that a school be placed in 'special measures'. This means that it is deemed to have been failing to meet expected performance standards under the present management. Support or even an alternative leadership team may be provided. 'Failing schools' can be closed by order of the Secretary of State.

Scotland has taken a very different approach and, in 2011, established *Education Scotland* which aims to coordinate almost all of Scotland's provision for curriculum, pedagogy, assessment, leadership, self-improvement, professional development and inspection. It seeks to support quality and improvement by working 'in partnership alongside the full range of bodies and organisations active in Scottish Education'. In addition to schools themselves, this includes local authorities, further and higher education, third sector organisations and parent groups. Improvement is thus expected to come from processes of personal and institutional self-development, local collaboration and a collective sense of national purpose.

In 2011, as if to highlight these differences, England's General Teaching Council was abolished whilst GTC Scotland was granted full independence from the government (effective April 2012) as a self-regulating, professionally-led body – the first in the world. The establishment of the GTCS was strongly influenced by the model provided by the General Medical Council. It is thus based, at root on trust in the teaching profession's capacity to regulate and improve its own professional standards.

The GTC for England published a policy paper on these issues just before their abolition (2011, Reading 5.5). They argued that accountability is by nature 'relational' because it is associated with actions by both the account-holder and the account-giver. Particular forms of accountability thus influence behaviour and provision. A question then arises about the effects of accountability in relation to overarching educational objectives. On this, the GTCE argued that in England there had been insufficient focus on teaching quality. Rather, the foundations of professional collaboration and enduring school improvement had been undermined by measurement of narrow, short-term perfor-mance and by punitive inspection. In place of this, they suggested, the teaching profession needs systems which support the development of expertise and record how professional responsibilities are discharged. Ultimately, the profession needs to regulate itself. On this latter point, at the time of writing, a Royal College of Teaching in England is being actively discussed.

In Wales, Northern Ireland and Ireland, GTCs maintain professional standards of conduct and practice, register teachers and support professional development. Like the GTCE, they were established by legislation in the late 1990s and are largely reliant for core functions on income from annual teacher registration. However, since numbers of registered teachers are relatively small in Wales and Northern Ireland, this is challenging. It raises a question about the extent to which teachers should themselves pay for professional regulation or whether it should be funded by governments in the public interest.

The issue of accountability thus crystallises many issues concerning the relationship between education and society. Should education be a relatively autonomous system or should it be under tight forms of control? Should teachers simply carry out centrally determined instructions, or should they develop and exercise professional judgement? What, indeed, is the role of local democratic institutions in this? And who should pay for the accountability system? The history of our education system provides many fascinating instances of attempts to reconcile such dilemmas (Silver, 1980) and there are plenty of related current issues which a reflective teacher might consider.

In particular, though, and following the dialectical model of social change which we discussed at the beginning of this chapter (Readings 5.1 and 17.5), the issues of account-ability, autonomy and control pose questions of a personal nature for reflective teachers. How should each individual act? To whom do you feel you should be accountable – to children, parents, colleagues, your headteacher, local or national government, the media, inspectors, or yourself?

Reflective activity 5.1

Aim: To review and explore the significance of ideology, culture, opportunity and accountability.

Evidence and reflection: Arrange to meet with a small group of work colleagues. In preparation, share out study of each section of Chapter 4 so that ideology, culture, opportunity and accountability are each covered.

In a meeting, each sub-group should explain the issues raised in their section of the chapter, and should relate them to your work context. How, in particular, is your school affected by the context in which it exists?

Extension: What other contextual factors are particularly significant in determining the circumstances of your school?

---

2 People and agency

We now turn to the individual and personal factors which are the second element in the dialectical model which underpins this book. For instance, classroom life can be seen as being created by teachers and children as they respond to the situations in which they find themselves. Thus, as well as understanding something of the factors affecting the social context of schooling, we also need to consider how teachers and children respond. Such responses reflect subjective perceptions, beliefs, values, commitments, identities, life narratives and imagined futures. This is the exercise of agency and voice – and recognition that our actions are not simply determined by our circumstances.

We begin by focusing on teachers.

2.1 Teachers

The importance of high-quality teaching is now understood by governments across the world (Barber and Mourshed, 2007; OECD, 2005; Chapter 4). This has significantly increased the attention being given to teaching as a profession, and to the individuals within it.

Teachers are people who happen to hold a particular position in schools. No apologies are made for asserting this simple fact, for it has enormous implications as we saw in the first chapter of this book. Each person is unique, with particular cultural and material experiences making up his or her 'biography' (Sikes, Measor and Woods, 1985). This provides the seedbed for their sense of 'self' and influences their personality and perspectives (Mead, 1934; Gu, 2007, Reading 1.1). The development of each person continues throughout life, but early formative experiences remain important. Indeed, because personal qualities, such as having the capacity to empathise and the confidence to project and assert oneself, are so important in teaching. Indeed, much of what particular teachers will be able to achieve in their classrooms will be influenced by them. Of even greater importance is the capacity to know oneself. We all have strengths and weaknesses and most teachers would agree that classroom life tends to reveal these fairly quickly (Turnbull, 2007). Reflective teaching is, therefore, a great deal to do with facing such features of ourselves in a constructive and objective manner and in a way which incorporates a continuous capacity to change and develop.

The particularly human capability of being able to review the relationship of 'what is' and 'what might be' is one which teachers often draw on when considering their aims and examining their educational values and philosophies. While there has always been a good deal of idealism in commitment to teaching, there has also always been a concern with practical realism. Indeed, a very important factor which influences teachers' perceptions in the classroom is that the teacher has to 'cope', personally as well as professionally, with the classroom situation (Pollard, 1982; Woods, 1990; Sachs, 2003). For this reason, we would suggest that a fundamental element of classroom coping, or survival, is very deeply personal, for it involves teachers, with a particular image of their self, acting in the challenging situation which classrooms represent. In this, it is important to remember that what it is possible to do in classrooms is constrained by the basic facts of large numbers of children, limited resources, compulsory attendance, curriculum and assessment frameworks and other external expectations which exist about what should and should not take place. The 'social work' role of teachers in supporting children, young people and their parents or carers in some communities is also considerable – particularly in primary schools (Webb and Vulliamy 2002).

In such circumstances, teachers face acute dilemmas between their personal and professional concerns and the practical possibilities (Berlak and Berlak, 1981; Eaude, 2012, Reading 16.3). They are forced to juggle with their priorities as they manage the stress which is often involved (Cole and Walker, 1989; Dunham, 1992; Sikes, 1997) and as they come to terms with classroom situations.

And yet the espoused goal of contemporary policy is for the lightening of constraint on teachers so that they are enabled to exercise professional judgement in a wider range of circumstances. This is particularly significant in England where, at the time of writing, Government Ministers have declared an intention to rely on teacher judgement in respect of the 'school curriculum' (excepting, e.g. the core subjects), pedagogy (excepting, e.g. phonics for early reading) and assessment (excepting, e.g. end of Key Stage tests and formal examinations). The exceptions are extremely important qualifiers of course. Diversity of school provision will reflect innovation by teachers as they exploit new opportunities. Reflective teachers will of course want to consider the nature of this innovation and its social as well as educational consequences.

In recent years considerable attention has been paid to providing stronger continuity in professional development, so that the situation of a trainee, newly qualified teacher, established teacher, advanced skills teacher and headteacher is now well defined. This may offer a sense of continuity for a career professional, and certainly enabling governments to provide more systematic forms of support and direction. Arguably the most cogent UK example of such thinking is 'Teaching Scotland's Future' (Donaldson, 2010).

We also need to consider the position of teachers as employees, for as such they have legitimate legal, contractual and economic interests to maintain, protect and develop (Lawn and Grace, 1987). For example, as we saw in Chapter 1, teachers in England and Wales are contracted to work up to 1,265 hours per year 'directed time' over 195 working days. Morning and afternoon breaks count as directed time, and a midday break for lunch is also protected. Teachers may be required to undertake activities which are additional to basic classroom teaching such as attendance at staff planning meetings and parents' evenings, and extracurricular activities such as sport, clubs, choirs, orchestras and drama productions. Given such activity, surveys of working hours regularly record that teachers work far in excess of their contractual obligation. Such efforts may not be sustainable and a balance has to be struck between educational expectations and what it is reasonable to ask of people who happen to earn their living from teaching. Indeed, headteachers have a duty to manage the school's workforce with regard to their wellbeing. It should never be forgotten that teachers also have their own personal lives outside the classroom and their own independent identities – however challenged these may be by work and the complexities of modern society (Maclure, 2000). Many teachers also have significant family responsibilities, as well as other interests which may be important to them.

Expert question

Empowerment: is our pedagogic repertoire successful in enhancing wellbeing, learning disposition, capabilities and agency?

This question contributes to a conceptual framework underpinning professional expertise (see Chapter 16).

Notwithstanding such considerations, teaching attracts people to it who have a sense of moral purpose. There is thus, in general terms across the profession, a principled commitment to providing high-quality education that meets the needs of learners. It is this value commitment which causes teachers to 'go the extra mile' on behalf of children and young people.

2.2 Pupils

As with the personal factors associated with teachers, the most important point to make about children and young people is that they are thinking, rational individuals (Corsaro, 2011; James, Jenks and Prout, 1998; Jones, 2009, Reading 1.5). Each one of the ten million UK school pupils has a unique 'biography', and the ways in which they feel about themselves, and present themselves in school, will be influenced by their understandings of previous cultural, social and material experience in their families and elsewhere (Bruner, 1986). Through their compulsory education, from age 5 to 16, most children develop a relatively clear sense of their identity as learners (Warin, 2010; Pollard and Filer, 1996, Reading 1.2). Indeed, preschool experience and social processes in the primary school lead them to perceive themselves as relative school failures or successes. The foundations of their 'learning disposition' and stance as a 'lifelong learner' become established, and there is no doubt that this is the crucial age phase for educational investment (Karoly et al., 1998) as demonstrated by initiatives such as Sure Start and the development of Children's Centres.

As children progress through secondary schools, with their complex systems of setting, banding, options and 'pathways', these self-perceptions are further reinforced or modified (see also Lawrence, 1987, Reading 6.6). At the point of leaving schooling and entering the worlds of college or work, children's life trajectories are thus likely to be well established. Teachers should thus not lose sight of the fact that, in their daily work, they are shaping long-term life-chances and identities, as well as working towards immediate targets for performance (Feinstein et al., 2008, Reading 1.6).

Pupils at school embody and are influenced by a huge range of circumstances and prior experiences. These include factors, such as sex, social class, race, language development, learning disposition, health and type of parental support. As we saw earlier in this chapter in the discussion of opportunities, patterns of advantage and disadvantage are very significant. However, such factors do not determine consequences.

The key issue is how children and young people respond to their circumstances – and in this, teachers can have a crucial role in supporting them.

Pupils have to survive in classroom situations in which they may well feel insecure (Jackson, 1968, Reading 6.1). Peer culture and the support of friends are considerable resources in this. However, this can also pose dilemmas in class when pupils attempt to please both their peers and their teacher. Creative strategies are called for and these may cover a range from conformity through negotiation to rejection. The agency of young learners is thus played out in the immediacy of the classroom and teachers thus have unique opportunities to influence factors such as motivation, approaches to learning and to subject knowledge (Rudduck and McIntyre, 2007; see also Reading 1.3).

Above all, though, we must never forget that children are placed in the role of 'pupils' for only part of each day. It is no wonder that families, friends, relationships, television, film, computer games, music, fashion, sport, etc., are important to them. A reflective teacher, therefore, must aim to work with an understanding of the culture of young people. Indeed, it is very unwise to try to do otherwise and, if connections can be made, then pupil culture can itself provide an excellent motivational hook into schoolwork.

Parents and carers can play a particularly important role in supporting the learning of children and young people. They are often thought of as supplementary teachers, with an advantageous one-on-one teaching ratio, and such support is certainly a major factor in pre-school development and early literacy.

However, perhaps the most important role for parents and carers today is in providing a source of stable emotional support for each child as he or she encounters new challenges in school. Reay (2000) has provided a fascinating analysis of this as a form of 'emotional capital'. Schools are increasingly pressured places, and there is a need for someone to really nurture the developing child

Expert question

Connection: does the curriculum engage with the cultural resources and funds-of-knowledge of families and the community?

This question contributes to a conceptual framework underpinning professional expertise (see Chapter 16).

from day to day, year to year. It is not necessary to be well off financially to do this, indeed, the most valuable contributions are probably time, patience, understanding and affection. There is also an increasing understanding that all families and communities, including those that may seem disadvantaged, have 'funds of knowledge' that should be tapped to enhance children's learning (Moll and Greenberg, 1990). Social circumstances do, however, radically affect participation (Crozier and Reay, 2005; Ball, 2003, Reading 5.3; Vincent, 1996, 2000) and the voices of young people can sometimes be inadequately

recognised (Crozier, 2000). However, if processes for supportive knowledge exchange between such parents and teachers could be established, the potential for enhancing learning is enormous (Hughes and Pollard, 2000; Desforges with Abouchaar, 2003).

Reflective activity 5.2

Aim: To consider the meaning and significance of 'agency', both for teachers and for learners.

Evidence and reflection: Reflective activity 5.1 reviewed circumstances, and this activity focuses on how people respond and act in relation to these. In particular, it is about the human spirit and the possibilities which always exist whatever the circumstances.

An interesting way of approaching this is to share one's educational biography with a colleague with whom one feels secure. Taking it in turns, take time to provide a narrative of how you moved through your education, meeting different teachers, growing up, finding some learning difficult but succeeding in others … Identify and focus on some key episodes or turning points which enabled you to progress. Explore if you can the actions you took and the encouragement or support you received from others.

Does consideration of such narratives and key moments enable you to see the significance of agency, in the form of your determination to succeed or the judgement by others to encourage you?

Extension: You might like to consider the learning of a small number of pupils you know at school. To what extent are they able to exercise agency in relation to their circumstances and goals, and might you be able to help?

Conclusion

The intention in this chapter has been to discuss the relationship between society as a whole and the people who are centrally involved in education. This is because school practices and classroom actions are influenced by the social circumstances within which they occur. However, it has also been argued that individuals can, and will, have effects on future social changes as they exercise their personal agency – though the degree of influence ebbs and flows depending on the roles occupied and at different phases of history.

A theoretical framework of this sort is important for reflective teachers because it establishes the principle that we can all 'make a difference' within our society. Professional commitment is therefore very important and we should not accept an ascribed position as passive receptors of externally determined prescription. The provision of high-quality education is enhanced when social awareness complements high levels of teaching skills, and when individual responsibilities for professional actions are taken seriously.

This fundamental belief in the commitment, quality and constructive role of teachers underpins the book. The analysis is optimistic. High-quality education depends on the professionalism of teachers.

Key readings

We begin with the theoretical framework which informs this book, with its juxtaposition of social context and individual agency.

Mills, C. W. (1959) *The Sociological Imagination.* Oxford: Oxford University Press. (Reading 5.1)

The English Department for Education and Science exercised its own imagination to produce:

Teaching and Learning Review Group (2006) *2020 Vision: Report of the Teaching and Learning in 2020 Review Group.* London: DfES. (Reading 10.7)

For a comparative analysis of educational values in different countries, their effects on provision and on what seems possible, see:

Green, A., Preston, J. and Janmaat, J. G. (2006) *Education, Equality and Social Cohesion: A Comparative Analysis.* London: Palgrave. (see also Reading 5.2)

Devolution has enabled distinctive policies to develop in each part of the UK. For an authoritative account, see:

Mitchell, J. (2012) *Devolution in the United Kingdom.* Manchester: Manchester University Press.

For comprehensive reviews of contemporary issues facing primary and secondary education in England see:

Alexander, R. (ed.) (2010) *Children, Their World, Their Education. Final Report and Recommendations of the Cambridge Primary Review.* London: Routledge.

Pring, R. (2012) *The Life and Death of Secondary Education for All.* London: Routledge.

The work of Pierre Bourdieu has influenced ways of understanding different forms of cultural, social and emotional capital, alongside the economic, though which social differences are perpetuated. See:

Bourdieu, P. and Passeron, J. C. (1977) *Reproduction in Education, Society and Culture.* London: SAGE.

Stephen Ball has documented policies and practices in the reproduction of social class and other forms of differentiation, with particular reference to secondary education. A collection is:

Ball, S. (2006) *Education Policy and Social Class.* London: Routledge. (see also Reading 5.3)

On the challenges of working in schools to overcome disadvantage, see:

Department for Children, Schools and Families (2009) *Breaking the Link between Disadvantage and Low Attainment.* Nottingham: DCSF Publications. (Reading 5.4)

An important international study of the consequences of inequality is:

Wilkinson, R. and Pickett, K. (2010) *The Spirit Level: Why Equality is Better for Everyone.* London: Penguin.

The contextual factors which affect education so significantly are the central focus of the field of Education Studies. See, for example:

Ward, S. (ed.) (2012) *A Student's Guide to Education Studies.* London: Routledge.

Bates, J. and Lewis, S. (2009) *The Study of Education: An Introduction.* London: Continuum.

Bartlett, S. and Burton, D. (2012) *Introduction to Education Studies.* London: SAGE.

To review the contemporary challenges and pleasures of being a teacher, see:

Day, C. and Gu, Q. *(2010) The New Lives of Teachers.* London: Routledge. (see also Reading 1.1)

For an understanding of modern childhoods and schooling, and an appreciation of the value of engaging with pupils, take a look at:

Blundell, D. (2012) *Education and Constructions of Childhood.* London: Continuum. (see also Reading 1.5)

Rudduck, J. and McIntyre, D. (2007) *Improving Learning Through Consulting Pupils.* London: Routledge. (see also Reading 1.3)

The challenges of parents and teachers working together in partnership to support learners are explored in practical ways in:

Crozier, G. and Reay, D. (2005) *Activating Participation: Parents and Teachers Working Towards Partnership.* Stoke-on-Trent: Trentham Books.

reflectiveteaching.co.uk offers additional professional resources for this chapter. These may include *Further Reading*, illustrative *Reflective Activities*, useful *Web Links*, and *Download Facilities* for diagrams, figures, checklists, activities.

Relationships
How are we getting on together?

6

Introduction

The existence of teacher–pupil relationships in classrooms is extremely important. Basically, it underpins and enables both 'order' and 'learning' – and is thus the foundation for success as a teacher. However, a 'good relationship' is not something which can be assumed.

The basic problem is that classrooms tend to be potentially threatening to both teachers and pupils because of their very structures and purposes, as Waller's classic study of 'latent conflict' illustrated so vividly (1932). In simple terms, the teacher faces relatively large numbers of children and is expected to educate them, while each child faces the evaluative power of the teacher and is expected to learn (see Jackson, 1968, Reading 6.1). There are significant challenges for both parties, so that teachers and pupils put considerable efforts into developing ways of coping with the situation.

How then, is a way forward found? There are only two basic possibilities: either order is imposed by teachers using their power, or there is negotiation between teachers and pupils so that understandings to define ways of collaborating together are constructed. These understandings are the basis of 'good relationships'.

As we have seen, for instance in Chapter 1, teachers normally have a strong moral purpose and place great emphasis on establishing good relationships with children.

However, it is not unusual for teachers or student teachers who lack negotiating skills to attempt to impose themselves. Although the strategy may work in the short term, it can have unfortunate side effects. When teachers 'become angry', 'go mad' or 'get eggy' they may be seen by children as being unfair. Children then report being 'picked on', 'shown up', 'done over' and humiliated – and such feelings do not create appropriate conditions for effective learning (Immordino-Yang and Damasio, 2007, Reading 6.2). Pupils are quick to discern when the expectations of them and the sense of order in the classroom begin to be based more on the use of teacher power than on a sense of fairness and respect.

Fortunately however, a shared sense of the moral order of the classroom, with social conventions, expectations and tacit rules, and thus a sense of what is 'right', is the normal outcome of a successfully conducted round of classroom negotiations. Such codes and principles of interaction have wider and longer-term significance in contributing to the social, ethical and moral education of children. In a sense, good relationships and 'citizenship' in the classroom can act as a model for responsible, active citizenship in later life.

See Chapter 4

TLRP principles

Two principles are of particular relevance to this chapter on classroom relationships as a foundation for learning:

Effective teaching and learning requires teachers to scaffold learning. Teachers should provide activities which support learners as they move forward, not just intellectually, but also socially and emotionally, so that once these supports are removed, the learning is secure. (Principle 4)

Effective teaching and learning fosters both individual and social processes and outcomes. Learning is a social activity. Learners should be encouraged and helped to work with others, to share ideas and to build knowledge together. Consulting learners about their learning and giving them a voice is both an expectation and a right. (Principle 7)

This chapter is structured in four main parts.

It begins with detailed discussion of classroom relationships and the roles of rules, routines and fairness. This understanding is then directly applied to teaching and learning processes through consideration of curriculum, teacher and pupil actions, and developmental cycles in class relationships over time. We then move on to discuss teacher expectations and professional skills – particularly for maintaining classroom authority. Finally, the outcome of all this is considered in terms of 'classroom climate'. This includes specific sections on emotional security, self-esteem and inclusion.

Then, In Chapter 7, we focus more directly on managing classroom behaviour.

1 Classroom relationships

Classroom order and discipline should be based on good relationships and a sense of engagement in learning. The concept of 'working consensus' focuses on such 'agreed ways of getting on together' (Hargreaves, 1972).

1.1 The working consensus

Good classroom relationships are based on recognition of the legitimate interests of others and on a mutual exchange of dignity between the teacher and pupils in a class. There evolves, in other words, a reciprocal, but often tacit, recognition of the needs of the other in coping with classroom life (Pollard, 1985, Reading 6.3).

Expert question

Relationships: are teacher–pupil relationships nurtured as the foundation of good behaviour, mutual wellbeing and high standards?

This question contributes to a conceptual framework underpinning professional expertise (see Chapter 16).

In a classroom, teachers and pupils have the capacity to make life very difficult for each other and a pragmatic basis for negotiation thus exists. However, shared understandings about working together will not just appear. To a very great extent, the development and nature of relationships will depend on initiatives made by teachers, as they try to establish the rules, understandings, routines and rituals which will structure behaviour in their classrooms.

Children and young people expect such initiatives from teachers and they are unlikely to challenge their teacher's authority, as long as the teacher acts competently and in ways which pupils regard as 'fair'.

1.2 Rules and 'initial encounters'

Pupils will normally expect the teacher to set boundaries and expectations, and these may helpfully be expressed in a small number of formal, overt rules – tailored, of course, for the age of the pupils. Often, these can (and should) be derived from whole-school policy and practices. We might, for instance, promote three overarching rules on:

- treating others as we would want to be treated (e.g. respect, support, empathy);
- committing ourselves to learning in school (e.g. positive thinking, effort, resilience);
- behaviour in school and classroom (e.g. noise levels, movement, teacher respect).

Chaplain (2003, Reading 6.4) makes the important point that such overarching rules offer pupils a sense of personal and psychological safety. They should demonstrate and affirm that the classroom will be secure, thus contributing to the conditions for future learning (Immordino-Yang and Dmasio, 2007, Reading 6.2). They also provide a foundational form of moral principles for interpersonal relationships in the classroom – and should be expressed in a forward looking, positive way.

The first few weeks of contact with a class, the period of 'initial encounters' (Ball, 1981b), is a particularly important opportunity during which a teacher can take initiatives and introduce rules and understandings. This is often a 'honeymoon period' when teachers attempt to establish their requirements and the children opt to play a waiting game. However, both the behavioural expectations and the teacher's capacity to enforce them are normally tested by the pupils before long, for children usually want to find out 'how far they can go' and 'what the teacher is like' when pressed.

1.3 Classroom routines

Classroom routines enable us to operationalise overarching rules and apply their principles to concrete activities. Each teacher will have their own favoured routines and they will certainly vary by age of pupil in primary and by subject in secondary schools. Chaplain offers secondary examples such as:

- entering the classroom

- getting attention
- getting out materials
- changing activities
- going to the toilet
- dealing with interruptions
- dealing with latecomers
- keeping pupils on-task
- finishing the lesson.

Routines to manage versions of the same issues will be found in primary settings. Additionally, among many others, are likely to be routines for:

- register
- carpet time
- asking and answering questions
- tidying up time
- play time
- getting ready for assembly
- changing for PE
- story time
- going home time.

Routines, in other words, are multi-purpose procedures which put rules and understandings into practice. When they are established, a switch-signal may be given (maybe a teacher announcement, a sound, or hand-signal) and hardly anything needs to be said! But the expectations which are embedded in the routines do always need to be patrolled and maintained. If this is not done, then understandings will decay and children may take advantage of the situation. Routines are thus a major focus of negotiation as the working consensus develops.

1.4 Identifying routines and understandings

Awareness of routines and tacit understandings is particularly important for a trainee teacher who is likely to be working with children who have already established a set of understandings with their normal class teacher. Reflective activity 6.1 is designed to help with this.

Reflective activity 6.1

Aim: To identify the overt and tacit content of classroom rules, routines and understandings.

Evidence and reflection: Asking the pupils is an obvious first step. With care, this can be done either in discussion or might be introduced as a written activity. Young children might be asked to make up stories about 'naughty children at school' and to explain things that they might have done or 'should have done'. Students usually enjoy such activities, and they may make it possible to increase awareness of tacit understandings. Another interesting method is to focus notes on key routines, for instance, at transitions points in classroom processes through the day. Try to identify the 'switch signals' and notice the way the teacher monitors the effectiveness of the routine and renegotiates or asserts if it begins to fray.

Extension: A further way to gather information on tacit expectations is to study the patterns which exist in what people do. Observation, using a notebook to record such patterns, is one possibility. A more explicit method is to record the events which lead to pupils being reminded of 'the way we do things here' or to being 'told off'. These could be noted during observation, or a video recording could be made of a session for later analysis.

Having developed an understanding of key expectations, we may of course wish to review and evaluate them. Do they enable us to fulfil our educational intentions and to teach in the ways which we favour? Which need reinforcement, or adjustment – and how might we prioritise such developments?

However, notwithstanding any future developments we may anticipate, a basic and prior requirement is that teacher actions are regarded as being fair.

1.5 Being 'fair'

In the negotiation of the working consensus and establishment of 'good relationships', there is nothing more important than being seen, by pupils, to have acted with fairness. This occurs because of their ultimate vulnerability to teacher power, and they therefore need to be assured that teachers will act reasonably. Children have to survive the challenges of the classroom – the crowds, praise and power, as Jackson (1968, Reading 6.1) put it.

If a teacher or student teacher acts without consideration of existing rules, routines and understandings this is likely to produce a negative response from the children and young people, because actions which they regard as incompetent or unfair will almost inevitably be made.

> ## Reflective activity 6.2
>
> *Aim*: To check that we are acting in ways which are regarded as being 'fair'.
>
> *Evidence and reflection*: Again, the only really valid source of information on this is from the pupils themselves. Whilst it is possible to discuss the issue openly with them or to approach it through story or drama, it is probably less contentious and as satisfactory to watch and note their responses to teacher actions. This should be a continuous process for teachers who are sensitive to the way their children feel about school, but it is worthwhile to focus on the issue from time to time. Both verbal and non-verbal behaviour could be noted and interpreted – the groans and the expressions of pleasure, the grimaces and the smiles. From such information, and from the awareness to be gained from such an activity, it should be possible to analyse classroom actions in terms of the classification which is discussed below.
>
> One obvious point to note here is that not all the children will feel the same about teacher actions. Patterns in such responses may be significant (see section 2.4, p. 156 below).
>
> *Extension*: The feedback which this activity should produce could contribute to the smooth running of the classroom and to the maintenance of the working consensus. If rules and understandings which were previously established are being broken by a new teacher, then the children may become resentful if change is not explained. If classroom routines are not being maintained and enforced by the teacher, then the pupils may well consider the teacher to be 'soft' and may try some 'playing-up' at his or her expense.

The discussion above highlights the development of mutually shared understandings about classroom life and emphasises their legitimacy. This, whilst acknowledging the leadership role of the teacher, is the basis of a good classroom relationship.

2 Relationships for learning

Perhaps the most important strategy in establishing good relationships with pupils is to establish some sort of connection with them as people. Each of us welcomes recognition of our individuality and responds to a smile, a kind word, or any other expression of interest – and so it is with children and young people in schools. Many teachers have these 'soft skills' and an authentic interest in the children for whom they have responsibility – after all, significant personal fulfilment in teaching comes through the success of others. If pupils feel this open, positive regard (Rogers, 1961) and understand that it has to be framed by the requirements of school, then the foundations for good relationships for learning exist.

2.1 Curriculum and relationships

Teaching can only be regarded as successful if the learners are learning. When this happens, both teachers and pupils feel fulfilled and the quality of their relationship is enhanced. Good relationships thus contribute to the conditions which make learning possible, but are also reinforced by success.

A major contribution to good classroom relationships is thus the provision of an interesting and appropriate curriculum, with suitable learning experiences and high-quality feedback. Issues concerning curriculum, pedagogy and assessment are thus never far away. However, the way in which such provision is made is particularly significant for the development of relationships.

Educationalists taking stock of such issues and looking to the future, such as those contributing to *2020 Vision* (Teaching and Learning Review Group, 2006, Reading 10.7), recommend a more 'personalised' curriculum in which learners are directly involved. Research on 'pupil voice' has made a valuable contribution to this (Rudduck and McIntyre, 2007, Reading 1.3; see also the **Research Briefing**, p. 17).

It is thus valuable to consult children on how they feel about classroom activities. This information supplies a basic type of feedback on children's motivation and can be set alongside other diagnostic information about learning achievements and difficulties.

The method suggested in Reflective activity 6.3 below involves direct comparison between classroom activities in different areas of the curriculum. Such comparisons are useful because they often highlight hidden issues.

Reflective activity 6.3

Aim: To gather information on how pupils feel about curricular activities which they undertake in school.

Evidence and reflection: One method, suitable for children or young people for whom writing is not difficult, is simply to ask them to write a comparison of two activities which you choose. It may be worth structuring this at the beginning by suggesting notes are made under headings such as the ones below:

	Good things	Bad things
Activity 1		
Activity 2		
Activity 3, etc.		

An alternative method would be to carry out a similar exercise verbally. There is no

---

reason why even very young children cannot participate in discussions about the activities which they like and dislike. Fairly open questions might be used, such as, 'Can you tell me about the things that you like doing best at school?' and 'Can you tell me about the things which you don't like doing?'. These, if followed up sensitively by further enquiries to obtain reasons (and the results recorded), should soon show up the children's criteria and patterns in their opinions about your provision. The recording is important, for when there is no record to reflect on it is very easy to fail to fully appreciate the messages one may be being offered.

Extension This activity should yield data of considerable importance for future planning and provision, and should be analysed to identify any patterns in the children's perspectives. If some children seem to be poorly motivated, to lack interest or to dispute the value of an activity, then the situation must be reconsidered and remedial measures taken.

2.2 Pupil perspectives of teachers

Another aspect of pupil perspectives is their views on their own teacher. This is a fairly well-researched issue and enquiry into it can yield good summary data on the way young people feel about the quality of relationships and education in their classroom. Obviously, for professional and ethical reasons, teachers should only collect such information in their own classroom, or with the permission of other people who may be concerned (Wilson and Powell, 2001).

Research has consistently shown that students like teachers who are kind, consistent, efficient at organising and teaching, patient, fair and who have a sense of humour. They dislike teachers who are domineering, boring, unkind, unpredictable and unfair. Strict/soft are two common constructs which children use, with 'strict but fair' often being positively valued. 'Softness' is usually regarded as a sign of weakness.

Predictability is also usually important and children and young people are often expert interpreters of the 'moods' of their teachers. Indeed, more generally, pupil feedback to teachers has been found to be both relatively accurate and reliable.

2.3 Teacher and pupil actions

Figure 6.1 provides a simple model for reflecting on the types of action which teachers and children make in classrooms when a working consensus exists.

The most important distinction is between actions which are bounded by the understandings which have been negotiated and those which are not. Five basic 'types of action' can be identified.

Conformity. These actions, by teachers or children are 'as expected'. They are according to the tacit conventions and agreements of the working consensus.

Figure 6.1
A classification
of types of
teacher and pupil
classroom action

Teacher Acts				Pupil Acts
Unilateral	Within the working consensus			Unilateral
Non-legitimate censure	Legitimate routine censure	Conformity	Legitimate routine deviance	Non-legitimate rule-framed disorder

Routine deviance. This is the type of mischief or petty misdemeanour which is accepted as being part of normal pupil behaviour. Talking at inappropriate times, 'having a laugh' and 'day dreaming' might be examples. Such activities are partly expected by teachers and are not normally intended as a challenge. They are thus within the bounds of the working consensus. It is important for support staff to also be aware of such boundaries.

Routine censure. This is the typical teacher response to routine deviance – a mild reprimand. It will be regarded by the pupils as legitimate, in so far as such a reprimand will not threaten the dignity of a child nor be employed inappropriately. Censures of this type are also within the bounds of the working consensus – they are expected. The teacher is doing his or her job.

Non-legitimate disorder. This is a type of pupil action which teachers dislike and find hard to understand. It often occurs when a child or a group of pupils seek to disrupt a classroom situation. They are particularly prone to do this if pupils perceive themselves to have been treated 'unfairly' or feel that their dignity has been undermined. Action of this type usually reflects the cultural rules of peer groups and can be used to build up a type of 'solidarity' or an alternative source of positive self-esteem.

Non-legitimate censure. This is the type of adult action which pupils dislike and cannot understand. It often occurs when a teacher loses his or her temper or feels under great pressure. The effect of such actions is that the children feel attacked and unable to cope. They perceive teacher power being used without justification. Such actions lie outside the bounds of the working consensus and are likely to lead to a breakdown in relationships.

The central argument is that 'good relationships' are based on the existence of a negotiated sense of acceptability and fairness which teachers and children share.

2.4 Patterns in pupil actions

We suggested above that children's actions might range from conforming to rules, engaging in routine deviance and mischief or, by stepping beyond this, to acting in unilateral and disorderly ways.

These patterns are indeed commonly found in classrooms – as in other walks of life. After all, they simply reflect strategies of agreement, negotiation or challenge. Etzioni (1961), in a classic analysis of compliance, documented how these dimensions recur in most social settings as people interact together.

In a teacher-research study, Pollard (1985) identified three types of friendship groups among 11-year-olds. 'Goodies' were very conformist, fairly able but considered rather dull. 'Jokers' liked to negotiate and 'have a laugh' with their teachers. 'Gang' group members were willing to disrupt classes, had low levels of academic achievement and were thought of as a nuisance. If we relate characteristic pupil actions to such types of pupil friendship group, then we can represent the range of behaviour, as indicated in Figure 6.2.

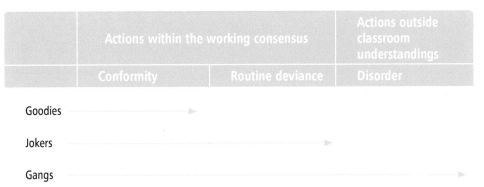

Figure 6.2
Parameters of
pupil behaviour

Figure 6.2 simplifies significant complexities, but it does highlight some important social consequences of classroom relationships. If the quality of both interpersonal relationships *and* curriculum provision is high, then the parameters of pupil actions are likely to move to the left of the diagram and both behaviour and engagement are likely to improve. If interpersonal relationships are poor and curriculum provision is inappropriate, then the parameters are likely to move to the right of the diagram. The result is likely to be an increase in disruption, a decrease in learning and the growth of dissatisfaction with school. Overall, social differentiation and exclusion are likely to increase, as the teacher acts to deal with disruptive children – who may then become 'labelled' as such.

2.5 Positive and negative cycles

Changes in relationships with a class can be *felt* through day-to-day experience over a period of time in one's work with a class. They can also be represented for reflection. For instance, consider the model of a positive cycle of teaching and learning in Figure 6.3, a model seen from the pupil perspective.

In this model it is first suggested that teacher initiatives lead to learners enjoying a sense of their own dignity and value. Second, it is postulated that children are stimulated by the curriculum or learning activities provided for them by the teacher. These are judged to be interesting and appear likely to satisfy their interest-at-hand in learning. Third, the situation is regarded as being fair. There are two aspects of fairness here, relating to the way the children are ordered and controlled and to the nature of the tasks which they are presented with. Regarding the first, let us assume that the students and teacher are operating within established organisational and social frameworks and that thus they

Figure 6.3
A positive cycle of
teaching, learning
and relationships

Figure 6.3
A positive cycle of
teaching, learning
and relationships

Dignity
Stimulation
Interest

Learning

Employment

Expert question

Relationships: are teacher–pupil
  relationships nurtured as the foundation
  of good behaviour, mutual wellbeing and
  high standards?

This question contributes to a conceptual
framework underpinning professional
expertise (see Chapter 16).

have both negotiated and both understand the parameters of permissible action. Order thus has a secure base. The other aspect of fairness concerns the appropriateness of the match between the task which the children are faced with and their ability and motivation to do it. If the task is well matched and attractively presented, then pupils are likely to accept its challenges and attempt to grapple with them vigorously. The result of the existence of this sense of dignity, stimulation and fairness is postulated in the model as being enjoyment and learning. This is brought about essentially because the children's interests are satisfied by teacher provision and action from the start. The further, and crucial, result of this child enjoyment and learning is that teacher interests are thereby satisfied. Order is maintained, instruction is effective and teacher self-esteem can flourish, with the likely result that the teacher will feel able to inject further energy and care with which to again project the dignity, stimulation and fairness to fuel another cycle. A cyclical process of reinforcement is created which can then spiral upwards into a higher and higher quality of learning experiences. Sometimes teaching goes just like this.

On the other hand, we must also recognise the existence of negative cycles which, instead of spiralling upwards, can lead to a decline into suspicion, hostility and unpleasantness. Again this can be represented by a model seen from the child perspective (Figure 6.4).

In this model it is suggested that teacher initiatives threaten children's interests on three counts. First, they represent an affront to children's dignity as people. Teacher actions may be seen as being dismissive, high-handed or even aggressive. Second, the learning activities provided for the children are seen as being boring. In other words, they are badly matched to the ability and concerns of the children. They are too hard, too easy or too disconnected from children's interests to provide significant motivational attraction. Third, teachers may be seen to be acting unfairly. In other words they do not abide by negotiated

Figure 6.4
A negative cycle of
teaching, learning
and relationships

understandings about their behaviour or that of the children. They use their power to act unilaterally. The children will, in a situation of this sort, feel and express a great deal of frustration. Their interests, far from being satisfied, are being ignored or threatened while at the same time they are relatively powerless to defend themselves. And yet they do have a degree of defensive power which comes from their numbers. friendships and peer-group membership, and this collective solidarity is likely to be used to neutralise the damage done by their teacher (with a shrug of the shoulders or a wink to 'mates') or to respond in kind with forms of resistance such as mischief, mucking about and having a laugh at the teacher's expense. Work evasion, rather than learning, is a probable outcome.

Ironically, the further result of this, which completes the cycle, is likely to be damage to the teacher's interests. Order in the classroom will constantly be challenged if it is essentially oppressive. Attempts at instruction will not be matched by quality in learning if children have not been offered an appropriate motivation to learn. The children's deviant responses will constantly threaten the teacher's self-esteem and autonomy. Such resistance is likely to further reduce the teacher's enjoyment but increase the stress and the potential workload which that teacher faces.

Fortunately there are not many classrooms where this situation endures, but it is worth being watchful and monitoring one's own provision. In such reflection on classroom relationships, if things seem to be deteriorating, it is tempting to perceive the causes of disruption as being exclusively to do with particular children. However, reflection on our own actions in respect of the working consensus and the quality of curriculum provision may provide another set of issues for consideration. These issues are, to a great extent, within our own control as teachers.

3 Teacher thinking and professional skills

3.1 Teacher perspectives

So far in this chapter, a number of suggestions have been made about how a teacher can take account of the perspectives, feelings and position of pupils. Now it is time to change the focus onto ourselves as teachers for, as was discussed in Chapter 5, the self-image of a teacher is just as important to maintain as the self-image of the child. Good teaching has never been easy, for to some extent it has always meant placing the learner's needs before our own. However, classroom relationships are a very special and subtle phenomenon. On the one hand, the nature of the working consensus is related to disciplinary issues and problems which are likely to confront the teacher. On the other hand, the quality of the relationships can, potentially, provide a continuous source of personal pleasure and self-fulfilment for a teacher.

If our own feelings as teachers are also an important factor in maintaining a positive working consensus, then ways of monitoring our feelings may be useful. Reflective activity 6.4 suggests keeping a personal diary. This has been used by classroom researchers over many years (Dadds, 1995) and is a tried and tested way of reflexively taking stock of life as it unfolds. Talking with colleagues and friends can also be immensely valuable and supportive. The point is a simple one – to care for others, we must also look after ourselves (see also the **Research Briefing** on teacher commitment and resilience, Chapter 1, p. 11, and Turnbull, 2007).

Reflective activity 6.4

Aim: To monitor and place in perspective our own feelings on classroom relationships.

Evidence and reflection: Probably the best way to do this is by keeping a diary. This does not have to be an elaborate, time-consuming one, but simply a personal statement of how things have gone and of how we felt.

The major focus of the diary in this case will obviously be on relationships. It is very common for such reflections to focus in more detail on particular disciplinary issues or on interaction with specific individuals. It should be written professionally, with awareness of ethical issues and the feelings of other classroom participants.

Diary-keeping tends to heighten awareness and, at the same time, it supplies a document which can be of great value in reviewing events.

Extension: Once a diary has been kept for a fortnight or so, you might set aside some time to read it carefully and to reflect upon it with a view to drawing reasonably balanced conclusions regarding yourself and your future planning for the classroom. It would be better still to discuss the issues which are raised with a colleague or friend.

3.2 Expectations of others

The expectations of teachers for the learners in their charge have long been recognised as contributing to pupil achievements in school. The classic study of this, by Rosenthal and Jacobson (1968), suggested that a 'selffulfilling prophecy' could be set up, in which children who were believed to be 'bright' would do well but, where negative expectations existed, then children would underperform. Indeed, although the ways in which teacher expectations influence pupil behaviour and attainment is highly complex, there is a broad consensus that high expectations can have a very positive effect (Gipps and MacGilchrist, 1999, Reading 6.5).

However, other research has shown differences in teachers' expectations of children from different social class backgrounds (e.g. Hartley, 1985; King, 1978; Sharp and Green, 1975). Similar issues have been raised in relation to gender (Delamont, 1990) and race (Wright, 1992). This raises a very important issue for reflective teachers who will want to ensure that they do not unwittingly favour some children over others. Two particularly comprehensive studies of links between expectations, behaviour and performance were carried out in London and considered differences in terms of gender, social class, race, etc. (Mortimore *et al.*, 1988; Tizard *et al.*, 1988, see also Richardson, 2009, Reading 15.1).

Whilst teachers should aim to raise their expectations and look for positive points for potential development in their pupils, there are also dangers from the existence of negative expectations. For instance, stereotyping is the attribution of particular characteristics to members of a group, and is often used negatively. Thus sex role stereotyping might be found, say, in an infant classroom with girls being encouraged to become 'teacher helpers'. Perhaps they might also play domestic roles in the 'home corner' while boys engage in more active play such as using construction equipment. Some research (e.g. Murphy, 2001) suggests that gendered play might be related to later differences in learning styles. However, as Walkerdine and other feminists have shown, girls in such situations can assert power through the adoption of an appropriate discourse (Walkerdine, 1981). Stereotyping should be avoided, but it is never absolute in its effects.

> **Expert question**
>
> **Expectation:** does our school support high staff and student expectations and aspire for excellence?
>
> This question contributes to a conceptual framework underpinning professional expertise (see Chapter 16).

Bias is a further source of unequal treatment of pupils. It might refer to images and ideas in books and in other resources which suggest the superiority or inferiority of certain groups of people (see Chapter 8). However, educational procedures can also be biased in themselves. For example there has been a longstanding debate about bias in intelligence tests and such questions are recurring with regard to aspects of national assessment procedures. This debate has focused on class, gender and cultural bias at various times and is closely associated with the ways in which disadvantages can be 'institutionalised'. The institutionalisation of disadvantage refers to situations in which social arrangements and procedures are established and taken for granted, despite the fact that they may systematically disadvantage a particular social group. Epstein has provided a particularly clear analysis of this with regard to racism (Epstein, 1993).

For a practical enquiry to try at this point, you could revisit Reflective activity 1.7. This explores teacher perceptions of children in class and the possibility of patterned differences in the ways in which particular groups of children are viewed.

3.3 Professional skills

The specific ways in which teachers act, and their effectiveness, are a focus for professional learning and refinement over many years. An experienced teacher can seemingly act with minimal effort, and the extent of practice and reflection may not be apparent.

There are several levels at which such skills may be considered (Chaplain, 2003a/b).

At the most basic, we might focus on non-verbal behaviour such as facial expression, use of eye contact, posture, gesture and movement. Pupils in classrooms monitor their teachers almost continuously for indications of their intentions or to pick up on changes in mood which might be of consequence. A skilful teacher thus is thus aware of, and manages, their non-verbal behaviour as a form of communication to pupils. It is thus possible, without saying a word, to convey confidence or anxiety, calmness or tension, satisfaction or displeasure through the ways in which we present ourselves.

Verbal capabilities represent another group of skills. Most obviously there is the capacity to project one's voice within a classroom environment. This is not necessarily to do with volume, but is certainly related to clarity in both the form and content of what is said. Pitching one's voice appropriately, so that it is not strained but can be heard, is extremely important and can be developed to improve effectiveness. When under pressure or anxious, people tend to speak more quickly and with a higher pitch – and this may need to be explicitly countered. Voice training should certainly be considered if difficulties are encountered. Through the *ways* in which we speak, we are also able to convey feelings of enthusiasm, confidence, concern, etc. so that the form of the presentation will, hopefully, reinforce the substantive message we intend to communicate.

An equally important skill is the ability to listen to and interpret what is said by pupils. The most significant dimension of this is to maintain openness to what is said, rather than 'hearing what we expect to hear'. This is by no means easy. But it is an essential skill if an effective feedback loop from pupils to teacher is to be maintained. Without it, we cannot learn from pupil perspectives and the appropriateness of our teaching will inevitably be impaired.

The ways in which teachers behave, speak and listen must, in aggregate, combine authority and accessibility. It is essential that pupils respect the role and knowledge of their teachers, but also that they feel able to engage openly with them.

Expert teachers monitor this balance and are able, drawing on their professional skills, to make ongoing and

Expert question

Reflection: is our classroom practice based on incremental, evidence-informed and collaborative improvement strategies?

This question contributes to a conceptual framework underpinning professional expertise (see Chapter 16).

contextually appropriate adjustments. In such ways, they establish classroom climates which are effective for learning.

3.4 Classroom authority

Teachers enact their role on behalf of parents and others in society more broadly. In that sense, the powerful position we hold is socially ascribed. But the main point of developing good relationships with the class as a whole is that this authority should be accepted by the children and young people themselves (Bennett, 2012, Reading 7.3). Only then, can the power of a teacher be converted into an authentic and practically useful 'authority'. Authority, in other words, is based on acceptance of the superior role of the teacher by those who are subject to them – on the legitimation of teacher power.

The understandings of the working consensus provide the moral foundation from which teacher power can be asserted and classroom authority can be established. This is vital to the work of every teacher and we therefore refocus on it in Chapter 7, Section 2. There, in the context of managing pupil behaviour, we review the role of positive expectations, confident self-presentation, measured use of language and the development of a repertoire of strategies.

Classroom authority will be most secure when good relationships (as discussed in this chapter) are combined with constructive strategies for managing behaviour and building engagement (as discussed in Chapter 7).

4 Enhancing classroom climate

In this chapter so far, we have focused on classroom relationships from pupil and teacher perspectives, on the interaction between them and on the professional capabilities which are called for. It is now time to consider overall outcomes in terms of the classroom as an environment for learning. This is summarised through the concept of 'classroom climate'. In this section, we will also review how the classroom environment can support pupil self-esteem and make inclusive provision for all children.

4.1 Classroom climate and emotional security

The influence of classroom environments on teachers and children has been a research topic for many years. One obvious question which emerged was how to define the 'environment'. In a classic study, Withall (1949) answered this by highlighting the 'socio-emotional climate' as being particularly significant.

Contemporary advances in neurobiology draw connections between social, emotional and cognitive and biological factors. For example, authors of an article entitled: 'We feel, therefore we learn' explain that:

Modern biology reveals humans to be fundamentally emotional and social creatures.
... The relationship between learning, emotion and body state runs much deeper than
many educators realise. It s not that emotions rule our cognition, nor that rational
thought does not exist. It is rather, that the original purpose for which our brains
evolved was to manage our physiology, to optimise our survival and to allow us to
flourish. ... But there is another layer to the problem of surviving and flourishing, [for]
as brains and the minds they support became more complex, the problem became not
only dealing with one's own self but managing social interactions and relationships.
... The physiology of emotion and its consequent processes of feeling have enormous
repercussions for the way we learn. (Immordino-Yang and Damsio, 2007, pp. 3–9,
Reading 6.2)

Put another way, the feelings which pupils develop about classroom life, about their
teachers and about learning itself have profound educational implications (Hascher, 2003).
We are unlikely to 'open up' for learning unless we feel personally secure.

Building on such ideas and in work on school and community networks, West-Burnham,
Farrar and Otero (2007) have argued that 'all learning is relational' and that new ways of
thinking about learning relations in local communities are necessary. In this perspective,
relationships both within and beyond the school make social, emotional *and* cognitive
contributions to learning. The significance of this is attested by the strength of the association of home circumstances and pupil outcomes, as we saw in Chapter 5. And yet, despite
what is known about such relational factors, 'life in classrooms' remains dominated by the
themes of 'crowds, praise and power' (Jackson, 1968, Reading 6.1).

There are thus good reasons why reflective teachers attend to the social and emotional
dimensions of pupil experience. They are a foundation for the development of a sense of
belonging and they engender constructive approaches to learning.

Attempts have been made to measure classroom climate by studying the perceptions of teachers and children (see Frieberg, 1999). Indeed, Fraser and Fisher (1984)
developed a 'My Classroom Inventory' for teachers to use in their own classrooms
(see Reflective activity 6.5). This can give structured feedback on pupil feelings about
classroom life and might be used, for example, at the beginning and end of a school
year. However, such techniques arguably fail to grasp either the subtleties of the interpersonal relationships to which many school teachers aspire, or the dynamic complexity
of teacher–pupil interaction. Asking pupils to simply 'draw a picture of important things
in their classroom' can also be extremely revealing, and may be more appropriate for
younger children.

Reflective activity 6.5

Aim: To 'measure' overall classroom environment at a particular point of time.

Method: Each child will need a copy of the inventory below. As a class (or in a group) pupils should be asked to circle the answer which 'best describes what their classroom is like'. The items could be read out in turn for simultaneous, but individual, responses. Scoring of answers can be done using the teacher's column. 'Yes' scores 3 and 'No' scores 1 except where reversed scoring is indicated (R). Omitted or indecipherable answers are scored 2.

There are five scales, made up by adding various items, as follows:

Satisfaction (S)	Items 1, 6, 11, 16, 21
Friction (F)	Items 2, 7, 12, 17, 22
Competitiveness (CM)	Items 3, 8, 13, 18, 23
Difficulty (D)	Items 4, 9, 14, 19, 24
Cohesiveness (CH)	Items 5, 10, 15, 20, 25

Follow-up: Mean scores for each scale will indicate the nature of the overall classroom climate and may raise issues for further consideration, particularly if repeated some time later. (It should be noted that the inventory reproduced here is a short form of a longer instrument and is not a reliable measure of the feelings of individuals.)

NAME ....

What describes your classroom?   Circle your answer

1	The pupils enjoy their school work in my class	Yes No	
2	Children are always fighting with each other	Yes No	
3	Children often race to see who can finish first	Yes No	
4	In our class the work is hard to do	Yes No	
5	In my class everybody is my friend	Yes No	
6	Some pupils are not happy in class	Yes No	R
7	Some of the children in our class are mean	Yes No	
8	Most children want their work to be better than their friend's	Yes No	
9	Most children can do their schoolwork without help	Yes No	R
10	Some people in my class are not my friends	Yes No	R
11	Children seem to like the class	Yes No	
12	Many children in our class like to fight	Yes No	
13	Some pupils feel bad when they don't do as well as the others	Yes No	
14	Only the smart pupils can do their work	Yes No	
15	All pupils in my class are close friends	Yes No	
16	Some of the pupils don't like the class	Yes No	R
17	Certain pupils always want to have their own way	Yes No	
18	Some pupils always try to do better than others	Yes No	
19	Schoolwork is hard to do	Yes No	
20	All of the pupils in my class like one another	Yes No	
21	The class is fun	Yes No	
22	Children in our class fight a lot	Yes No	
23	A few children in my class want to be first all of the time	Yes No	
24	Most of the pupils in my class know how to do their work	Yes No	R

Enduring insights on the social and emotional foundations of secure relationships are provided by the work of Rogers on counselling (1961, 1969, 1980). He suggested that three basic qualities are required if a warm, 'person-centred' relationship is to be established – acceptance, genuineness and empathy. If we apply this to teaching, it might suggest that acceptance involves acknowledging and receiving children 'as they are'; genuineness implies that such acceptance is real and heartfelt; whilst empathy suggests that a teacher is able to appreciate what classroom events feel like to pupils. Rogers introduced the challenging idea of providing 'unconditional positive regard' for his clients and perhaps this can also provide an ideal for what teachers should offer children and young people. Good relationships are, according to Rogers, founded on understanding and on 'giving'.

Rogers' three qualities have much in common with the three key attitudes of the reflective teacher, discussed in Chapter 3. Being able to demonstrate acceptance and genuinely empathise requires 'open-mindedness' and a 'wholehearted' commitment to the children in our care. It also necessitates 'responsibility' when considering the long-term consequences of our feelings and actions. However, this analysis is not really adequate as a guide to classroom relationships because additional factors are involved. For a number of reasons, the warmth and positive regard which teachers may wish to offer their class can rarely be completely 'unconditional'. In the first place, we are constrained by our responsibility for ensuring that the children learn adequately and appropriately. Second, the fact that teachers are likely to be responsible for relatively large numbers of pupils means that the challenges of class management and discipline must always condition our actions. Third, the fact that we ourselves have feelings, concerns and interests in the classroom means that we, too, need to feel the benefit of a degree of acceptance, genuineness and empathy if we are to give of our best.

> ## Expert question
>
> **Culture:** does the school support expansive learning by affirming learner contributions, engaging partners and providing attractive opportunities?
>
> This question contributes to a conceptual framework underpinning professional expertise (see Chapter 16).

Good relationships in classrooms and schools must then be based on each teacher having earned the respect of children and young people by demonstrating empathy and understanding *and* by establishing a framework of order and authority. It is a finely judged balance between two necessary elements.

If, as reflective teachers, we are to take full account of the social and emotional climate in our classrooms, we need a form of analysis which recognises this subtlety. It must recognise both the importance of interpersonal understandings and also the inevitable power struggle between teachers and pupils.

4.2 Supporting children's confidence and self-esteem

Children often feel vulnerable in classrooms, particularly because of their teacher's power to control and evaluate. This affects how children experience school and their openness to new learning. Indeed, it is often suggested that children only learn effectively if their self-esteem is positive (Roberts, 2002). A considerable responsibility is thus placed on teachers to reflect on how they use their power and on how this use affects children.

There are two basic aspects of this. First there is the positive aspect of how teachers use their power constructively to encourage, to reinforce appropriate child actions and to enhance self-esteem (Lawrence, 1987, Reading 6.6: Merrett and Wheldall, 1990, Reading 7.6). Indeed, the importance of maintaining 'high expectation' of children cannot be over-emphasised (Gipps and MacGilchrist, 1999, Reading 6.5). Second, however, there is the potential for the destructive use of such power. This particularly concerns the manner in which teachers act when 'rules' are broken. This can be negative and damaging, but skilful and aware teachers will aim to make any necessary disciplinary points yet still preserve the dignity of each child. Activities are suggested below to monitor each of these aspects, starting with 'being positive'.

'Being positive' involves constant attempts to build on success. The point is to offer suitable challenges and then to make maximum use of the children's achievements to generate still more. This policy assumes that each child will have some successes. Sometimes a child's successes may be difficult to identify. Such difficulties often reveal more about the inability of an adult to understand and diagnose what a child is experiencing. As the psychologist Adler argued many years ago (Adler, 1927), irrespective of the baseline position, there is always an associated level of challenge – a target for learning achievement – which is appropriate and which can be the subject of genuine praise (Butt, 2011, Reading 14.3). It may range from correctly forming a letter of the alphabet to producing a vivid story; from sustaining personal lesson concentration to beginning to master the subject as a whole; from joining in sporting activities to breaking a school record, etc. The appropriateness of the achievement is a matter for a teacher to judge, but the aim should be to encourage all children to accept challenges and achieve successes (Merrett and Wheldall, 1990, see also Chapter 10, Section 4 on lesson planning for differentiation).

This brings us to 'avoiding destructive action'. This is the second aspect of the teacher's use of power – the way in which control is used. On this issue, we want to focus on the dangers of 'flashpoints' in classrooms – situations in which teachers 'lose their head' and start to act unilaterally. All teachers would probably agree that a class of children has to be under control if purposeful and productive activities are to take place. However, a teacher's power can be exercised in many ways. In most situations teachers try to be calm, firm and fair – they act within the bounds of the working consensus and use positive statements and various types of legitimate 'routine censure' to maintain discipline.

Unfortunately, there is a well-documented tendency for teachers to reprimand children over-personally when telling them off in the heat of the moment, rather than focusing positively on the activity in which they should have engaged. The effect of this reactive strategy can be that the children may feel attacked and humiliated so that, rather than conforming more, the children 'want to get back at' the teacher who has 'picked on' them 'unfairly'. Here, the problem is that the teacher's action is 'unilateral' and lies outside the understandings of the working consensus. A recommended way of enforcing authority, whilst at the same time protecting the self-esteem of each child, is to focus on the action or behaviour of the children for condemnation rather than on the children themselves (Hargreaves, Hestor and Mellor, 1975; Robertson, 1996). Reprimands can then be firmly given, but the self-image of each child is left relatively intact. Each child can then conform with dignity if he or she so wishes, and the incident is contained within the bounds of the working consensus. This will be discussed further in Chapter 7 where we focus on classroom management and other aspects of discipline and behaviour.

Thus, reflective teachers are likely to attempt to use their power positively and constructively, and they will be particularly aware of the potential damage to relationships which can be done by overhasty reactions to some classroom crises.

A further type of reflection on relationships concerns the degree of involvement by children, which brings us to the notion of what we have called the 'inclusive classroom'.

4.3 Developing an inclusive classroom

An inclusive classroom is one which is consciously designed to enable each child to act as a full participant in class activities and also to feel themselves to be a valued member of the class (Kershner, 2009, Reading 15.6). This is what all of us wish for but there is plenty of evidence that, in the context of curriculum pressures, relatively large class-sizes and the requirements of many assessment procedures, it is difficult to achieve.

One feature which often causes problems is that there are variations in both the quantity and quality of teacher attention that is given to different categories of children. Sadly, this is a clear example of variations in expectation (Gipps and MacGilchrist, 1999, Reading 6.5). There are many categories around which such differentiation is often found (West and Pennell, 2003; see Chapter 15, Section 1) – for example: ability (e.g. Alur and Hegarty, 2002; Iveson and Hallam, 2001; Mortimore et al., 1988), gender (e.g. Delamont, 1990; Francis, 2000), race (e.g. Connolly, 1998; Troyna and Hatcher, 1992) and social class (e.g. Rist, 1970; Sharp and Green, 1975; Reay, 1998). Age could also be an important factor particularly in mixed-age classes. In addition, it is necessary to analyse and to be aware of the responses to school life of individual children. It is very understandable if teachers tend to deal first with children whose needs press most or whose actions necessitate an immediate response. However, the problem which then arises is that some other children may be consistently passed over (Collins, 1996). Whilst we may have to accept that the needs of all the children in a class cannot be satisfied simultaneously by any teacher, they may be met more consistently through the skilled work of support staff. Croll and Moses (2000) provide a challenging analysis of this in relation to children with special educational needs, but we have a responsibility to ensure that teacher effort is distributed in proportion to the needs of all the pupils.

Expert question

Inclusion: are all learners treated respectfully and fairly in both formal and informal interaction?

This question contributes to a conceptual framework underpinning professional expertise (see Chapter 16).

Classes also vary in the degree to which differences between children and their abilities are valued. Such differences between people must inevitably exist (see Pollard, 1987a, Reading 15.2), but a contrast can be drawn between classes in which the strengths and weaknesses of each child are recognised and in which the particular level of achievement of each child is accepted as a starting-point (see, for example Thorne, 1993, Reading 15.5), and classes in which specific qualities or abilities are regarded as being of more value than others in absolute terms. Sadly, in the case of the latter, the stress is often on levels of attainment rather than on the effort which children may have made. Indeed, relative attainments become institutionalised through inflexible 'ability' grouping systems; the ethos becomes competitive rather than cooperative; and the success of some children is made possible only at the cost of the relative failure of others. The overall effect is to marginalise and exclude some children whilst the work of others is praised and regarded as setting a standard to which other children should aspire. This can have very negative consequences for children's perceptions of themselves as learners (Dweck, 1986, 1999, Reading 2.6).

Quality of work and standards of achievement are crucially important considerations, but there are also many other factors to bear in mind. For instance, we would suggest that an inclusive classroom will produce better classroom relationships and more understanding and respect for others than one which emphasises the particular success of a few. Such issues are particularly significant when specific assessment knowledge is gathered. In the United Kingdom the outcomes of both teacher assessment and national testing now produce relatively formalised 'results' and must be handled very carefully if they are not to threaten the self-esteem of lower achieving children (Reay and Wiliam, 1999). Of course, children who are less academically successful may have considerable other strengths and achievements and these can be recognised and celebrated.

Thus, there are some central questions about how children are valued which should be answered by a reflective teacher. Among them are those which are suggested in Reflective activity 6.6 below. This time they take the form of a checklist.

Overall then, teachers wishing to sustain an inclusive classroom will set out to provide opportunities for children to feel valued, to 'join in' and to believe in themselves as learners. At the same time they will attempt to eliminate any routines or practices which would undercut such aims by accentuating the relative weaknesses of some children (Putnam and Burke, 1992; McDermott, 1996; see also Clegg and Billington, 1994, Reading 8.3).

For more extensive elaboration of issues associated with inclusion, please see Chapter 15.

Conclusion

Good relationships are intimately connected to pupil wellbeing, classroom learning and effective discipline. They give pleasure to the participants, provide a foundation for learning and pre-empt trouble. No wonder that positive classroom relationships are a considerable source of teacher and pupil fulfilment.

Perhaps, too, an expectation of being caring towards each other may spread among the children and young people and be of longer-term benefit for society more generally.

We end this chapter with a note of caution, of particular relevance to trainee teachers.

There are sometimes children with whom very specific efforts to develop good relationships may need to be made. Such cases might include particularly able children who may

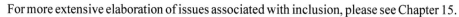

become bored; children who find schoolwork difficult and may become frustrated; children who have special educational needs; children who are new to the class or school; and children who have been upset by events in their lives over which they have little control, such as a bereavement, a breakup of their parents' marriage, parental unemployment or even sexual or physical abuse. Such children need very sensitive and empathic attention and may require special help to express their feelings, to place these in perspective, to realise that their teacher and others care about them and to feel that they have tangible and appropriate targets to strive for in their lives. Such care may enable a child to take control of the situation, with the support of their teacher, to the extent that this is possible.

However, teachers should guard against being amateur therapists. Child psychologists and social workers are available and they should be invited to give advice if circumstances require their help.

Key readings

Philip Jackson's classic text featuring 'crowds, praise and power' in classrooms is:

Jackson, P. (1968) *Life in Classrooms*. New York: Holt Rinehart and Winston. (Reading 6.1)

The interpretive approach to classroom relationships which has informed much of this chapter is discussed in detail in:

Pollard, A. (1985) *The Social World of the Primary School.* London: Cassell. (Reading 6.3)

For helpful advice applying psychological knowledge on a wide range of issues in classroom relationships and management including professional social skills and classroom rules, routines and rituals see:

Chaplain, R. (2003) *Teaching Without Disruption in the Primary School*. London: Routledge.
Chaplain, R. (2003) *Teaching Without Disruption in the Secondary School*. London: Routledge. (Reading 6.4)

The best book on 'pupil consultation' and 'voice' is:

Rudduck, J. and McIntyre, D. (2007) *Improving Learning Through Consulting Pupils*. London: Routledge. (see also Reading 1.3)

One of a number of classic books by Carl Rogers on 'person-centred' theory is:

Rogers, C. (1969) *Freedom to Learn*. New York: Merrill.

The significance for learning of relationships within and beyond the school is described in:

West-Burnham, J., Farrar, M. and Otero, G. (2007) *Schools and Communities: Working Together to Transform Children's Lives*. London: Continuum.

More general overviews of research on classroom relationships are provided by:

Watkins, C. (2004) *Classrooms as Learning Communities*. London: Routledge.

Humphreys, T. (1995) *A Different Kind of Teacher*. London: Cassell.

Pianta, R. C. (1999) *Enhancing Relationships Between Children and Teachers*. Washington, DC: American Psychological Association.

Ingram, J. and Worrall, N. (1993) *Teacher–Child Partnership: The Negotiating Classroom*. London: David Fulton.

On children's confidence and self-esteem, Lawrence provides a research review and practical ideas:

Lawrence, D. (1987) *Enhancing Self-esteem in the Classroom*. London: Paul Chapman. (Reading 6.6)

A fascinating and impressive research guide to 'classroom environment' is:

Fraser, B. (1986) *Classroom Environment*. London: Routledge.

reflectiveteaching.co.uk offers additional professional resources for this chapter. These may include *Further Reading*, illustrative *Reflective Activities*, *Web Links* and *Download Facilities* for diagrams, figures, checklists, activities.

Engagement
How are we managing behaviour?

7

Introduction

Behaviour management is of perennial concern to all teachers because of the numbers of children in a typical classroom, as Jackson (1968, Reading 6.1) indicated. This means that, in a sense, the teacher is always dealing with a 'crowd'. Control of that crowd must, therefore, be a priority. For many student teachers in particular, this concern initially displaces almost all other aims as they take on the challenge of coping with 'the class'. In such circumstances, relationships with individuals – a vital building block – may even be displaced.

'Good behaviour' is most easily obtained and maintained by establishing appropriate relationships (Chapter 6), providing clear expectations and ensuring that pupils are fully engaged in learning activities. The focus of attention should therefore be directed at achieving a positive climate for learning and at the prevention of managerial problems, so that crises are avoided. This is by no means easy, since classrooms are such complex places where events can unfold very quickly. Doyle's analysis of the 'multi-dimensionality, simultaneity and unpredictability' of this is excellent (1977, Reading 7.1).

It is easy, and understandable, for classroom management objectives to take precedence over learning requirements. Moreover, even where teachers have control of the classroom, pupils may remain unclear about the aims of learning tasks set for them. As Galton (1989), suggests, the consequence is a sense of ambiguity and risk, which then undermines the quality of children's engagement with learning. Holt (1982) made this idea more controversial by suggesting that pupils 'learn to be stupid' in schools. They do this when teachers' requirements for conformity with managerial rules, structure and order override the pupils' need for understanding and engagement in high quality learning tasks. The vital message for us is that classroom management is a necessary means to an end – but it is not the end itself. TLRP's principles on pedagogy build on, and extend, this point.

TLRP principles

Two principles are of particular relevance to this chapter on achieving an ordered classroom through pupil engagement:

Effective teaching and learning promotes the active engagement of the learner. A chief goal of teaching and learning should be the promotion of learners' independence and autonomy. This involves acquiring a repertoire of learning strategies and practices, developing positive attitudes towards learning, and confidence in oneself as a good learner. (Principle 6)

Effective teaching and learning fosters both individual and social processes and outcomes. Learning is a social activity. Learners should be encouraged and helped to work with others, to share ideas and to build knowledge together. Consulting learners about their learning and giving them a voice is both an expectation and a right. (Principle 7)

See Chapter 4

Before starting work in a new school, reflective teachers will ensure that they know and understand something about the ethos and values of the school and department/s they are about to join. At the very minimum they will ask to see copies of the school's behaviour policies and talk with mentors and other teaching and support staff about how those policies are put into practice.

This chapter has been structured in six sections. We begin by affirming the significance of behavioural issues both for teachers and policymakers, and also review some sources of professional support which are available. Section 2 analyses how to establish classroom authority. Section 4 focuses on practical teaching skills for engaging pupils, whilst Section 5 looks at how to manage typical classroom episodes. Finally, we consider positive and negative cycles, tying back to Chapter 5 on relationships, and provide a summary.

1 Understanding classroom behaviour

There are a great many explanatory theories about children's behaviour, whether in or out of school. Three elements are typically posed:

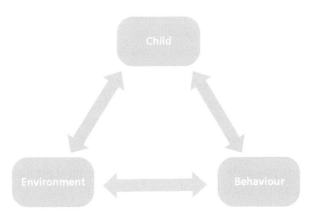

Figure 7.1 Child, environment and behaviour

The terminology above is that of Chaplain (2003) who draws on the social learning theory of Bandura (1995). Bronfenbrenner (1979, Reading 8.1) has a similar conceptualisation (see Chapter 8, Section 1). Symbolic interactionist sociology would tend to speak of 'children', 'contexts' and 'strategic action'. Such nuanced distinctions can certainly be drawn.

The basic point though, is that the actions taken by anyone relate both to the person they are and to the situation they are in.

From the teacher perspective then, to understand classroom behaviour, we must first appreciate the circumstances of the children and young people for whom we have responsibility; and we must then really think hard about the educational provision which we make for them in school. The latter constitutes the environment – the context, to which pupil behaviour is a response.

1.1 Children and young people

Expert question

Connection: does the curriculum engage with the cultural resources and funds-of-knowledge of families and the community?

This question contributes to a conceptual framework underpinning professional expertise (see Chapter 16).

We need here to take stock of the issues raised in Chapters 1, 2 and 4 of this book and to recognise that pupils in the same classroom may have very different home circumstances. Contemporary societies are seeing extreme differences in wealth and in the associated forms of cultural capital. Many families maintain a conventional, two-parent structure, whilst others sustain more diverse relationships. Some children will start school with great eagerness to learn, whilst others may feel deeply uneasy or even be frightened. As they get older, some pupils will receive significant support and interest from parents or carers, whilst others will find that their efforts may be treated as being of little consequence. Many will find that the language of instruction is their mother tongue and will be familiar with typical teacher discourse. Others may find that they need to adapt to the use of their second language in the school setting, or that some patterns of their home language are frowned upon at school.

It is very easy to succumb to stereotypes in seeking to make sense of the complexity of children's lives, but this really should be resisted. Being 'poor' does not denote a lack of commitment to one's children, just as being 'well off' certainly doesn't in itself produce valuable support. Each form of social difference – social class, gender, ethnicity, disability, etc. – is simply a circumstance which needs to be understood. The question then, despite the patterns which research and experience might suggest, becomes: 'What do people make of their circumstances?'.

In summary, teachers need to do what they can to understand prior experiences of the children and young people that they teach.

1.2 Providing an engaging environment

The school environment is crucial to establishing positive behaviour amongst pupils. Watkins has suggested that this is associated with proactive policies, a strong sense of community, teacher collaboration and promotion of pupil autonomy (2011, Reading 7.2).

There are four dimensions of the classroom environment which teachers must review with particular care:

Curriculum – it is clearly crucial that pupils find the curriculum of interest. If they do, then that commitment will engender more engaged behaviour. If they don't, then they may seek diversions. This can be particularly tricky where basic skills need to be mastered over many years, and teacher creativity to find interesting ways of teaching these is imperative. Chapters 9 and 10 focus on curriculum.

Pedagogy – pupils tend to be particularly aware of how they are being controlled – of the rules, routines and rituals of the classroom, the fairness which should underpin them and the security which they offer. Beyond this, they will hope for pedagogies which are participatory, make the subject matter interesting, support success in learning and enable fun, laughter and enjoyment. Chapters 11 and 12 address such issues.

Assessment – anxiety about being judged by others is commonplace, and for children and young people school may be the first place in which they experience formal assessment. On the one hand, feedback which enables progress in learning is likely to be greatly welcomed. It indicates that the teacher has taken an authentic interest (see Chapter 13). On the other hand, the experience of more formal assessment may not be a happy one, and certainly needs to be managed with great care (as discussed in Chapter 14).

Relationships with others – this dimension is essentially about relationships between peers, which can be fraught and challenging for some children. Feeling accepted by a peer group is very important for surviving in school and is manifested in 'having friends'. But children can also be unkind and some children may become isolated or even be bullied. Teachers need to create classroom rules and a climate in which everyone is valued, but must then be watchful to ensure that the experienced environment lives up to these expectations (see Chapters 1 and 6).

> **Expert question**
>
> **Engagement:** do our teaching strategies, classroom organisation and consultation enable learners to actively participate in and enjoy their learning?
>
> This question contributes to a conceptual framework underpinning professional expertise (see Chapter 16).

Where a classroom environment provides for such high-quality curriculum, pedagogy, assessment and relationships, poor behaviour is likely to be minimised.

Or, to put this another way, if poor behaviour arises, as well as thinking about the needs and perspectives of the child or children themselves, it is very valuable to review one's classroom provision. Might it be possible to engage the children more effectively?

1.3 Progression in behaviour

In principle, an effective teacher will expect to make progress during the school year in classroom control and the stability of pupil behaviour. And a similar progression may be experienced when a student teacher takes a class over a sustained period of time. It is helpful to try to see this positively in terms of 'leading learning activities', so that control itself is a by-product.

Figure 7.2, on p. 179 overleaf, comes from Chaplain (2003, see also Reading 6.4) and highlights some of the characteristic processes which are likely to be found in 'early encounters' and 'later stages'.

The model shows how pressures of establishment and active negotiation are gradually replaced by greater levels of trust. With this, most importantly, comes teacher encouragement for pupils to take more control of classroom situations and exercise more self-control. Of course, such agency remains framed by the understandings which have been established and honed over time. For many teachers, a summer term, unless dominated by tests or examinations of one sort or another, is a time when they feel able to give pupils more freedom to explore their interests and potential.

Reflective activity 7.1, below, invites a 'stock take' on classroom behaviour and engagement.

Reflective activity 7.1

Aim: To understand pupil behavior in our classroom circumstances.

Evidence and reflection: Reflect on the proposition that pupil actions relate both to the person they are and to the situation they are in (as discussed above).

- Review Section 2.1 and consider: how far do you really understand, and make connections with, the circumstances of your students' lives?
- Review Section 2.2 and consider: do pupils feel engaged by the curriculum, pedagogy, assessment and relationships you are providing?
- Review Sections 2.3 and consider: how are things going in terms of the *progression* of classroom relationships and behaviour over time?

It would be very valuable to discuss these issues with a colleague, so that there is an exchange of insights.

Extension: It would be excellent to make a visual recording of some periods of classroom practice to review and discuss in terms of the questions above.

Having developed a deeper understanding, the question becomes: What to do next? It is often helpful to map scenarios for consideration. Such analysis provides a foundation for successful behavioural strategies.

But this is an endpoint, and we must always start with establishing authority.

2 Establishing authority

Establishing authority over a class is partly about self-belief, in the sense of acting with confidence as a teacher – and it is also partly about capability, in the sense of being professionally competent in the core skills of teaching and, in particular, in being able to interpret and analyse classroom events as they develop so that adjustments are possible. Underlying these qualities, as we saw in Chapter 6, is the relationship which one develops with pupils and, in particular, being seen to act fairly.

The best teachers are competent, reflective and understanding – and thus become confident. Pupils respect these qualities and thus trust their teacher. Bennett suggests that these qualities are associated with justice, courage, patience, wisdom and compassion

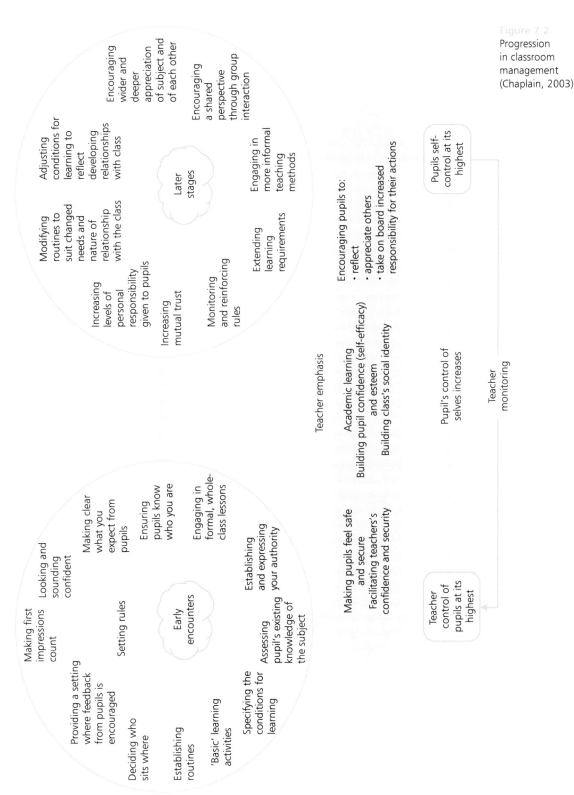

Figure 7.2
Progression
in classroom
management
(Chaplain, 2003)

(2012, Reading 7.3) and that there is a need for visualisation and self-belief. One has to 'take the stage'.

The difficulty is that competence and understanding take time to develop – and whilst advice can support such processes, there is no substitute for direct experience. So trainee teachers face the difficult challenge of working on their competence and understanding whilst groups and classes still need to be taught.

In this section, we focus on four issues which support the establishment of classroom authority – expectations, self-presentation, use of language and strategic repertoire.

2.1 Expectations

Children and young people are, just like most of us, extremely good at sensing the beliefs, motivations and dispositions of others. Teachers who appear to presume that pupils are 'up to no good' and 'cannot be trusted' are likely therefore to engender similarly guarded responses. On the other hand, if a teacher is able to convey a set of expectations which presumes capability and projects realistic goals towards success, then it is likely that pupils will try to respond. A classic study by Hargreaves, Hester and Mellor (1975) characterised the former as 'provocative' teachers, and the latter as 'insulative'.

Teachers therefore need to take control of their own expectations, and to review these carefully – particularly in relation to personal theories about pupil behaviour. Beliefs of any sort evolve in the light of experience, but can also be culturally and personally embedded. Indeed, as we saw in Chapter 1, section 3, contrasting ideas of children as inherently 'good' or 'bad' have long histories within contemporary cultures – and may also be found within some staffrooms. To establish authority, teachers need to be cautious about unquestioned beliefs, in whatever form they may emerge. In the long term, neither being too 'soft' nor being too 'strict' will work. The most realistic and effective strategy is to consistently convey presumption of the best from pupils, whilst watching carefully for signs of the worst.

Expectations for behaviour in respect of classroom rules should thus be made explicit through discussion and then reinforced. Whenever things begin to slide, or if established understandings are challenged, then such rules need to be reasserted. But the trick here is to achieve the reassertion in an incorporative way, without precipitating a negative reaction. As discussed in Chapter 2 on learning, it helps to 'credit' pupils with what they do, rather than focus on deficits and failures.

Setting high expectations about behaviour, as for learning, is thus an important foundation for establishing teacher authority. This is greatly helped if the expectations we seek to establish are congruent with whole-school policies and culture, and Reflective activity 7.2 suggests ways of exploring this.

> **Expert question**
>
> **Expectation:** does our school support high staff and student expectations and aspire for excellence?
>
> This question contributes to a conceptual framework underpinning professional expertise (see Chapter 16).

Reflective activity 7.2

Aim To explore and understand a school's policies and practices with regard to behaviour management.

Evidence and reflection: Answers to the following sequence of questions may be found by studying your school's behaviour policies and through talking to staff at various levels within the school.

1 What are the school's primary aims and values?
2 What principles about discipline and bahaviour are derived from these?
3 What are the implicit and explicit 'school rules'?
4 What reinforcements and sanctions are accepted?
5 What are the greatest challenges in implementing the school's policies?
6 How can I appropriately reflect the schools disciplinary principles and rules in my classroom organisation?
7 Where and in what way should I ask for support if things go wrong?

Add other questions to the list as they occur to you.

Extension Having gathered information, the next process is to relate this to your own expectations and strategic repertoire for managing behaviour. How does the school support you, or qualify your original intentions?

2.2 Self-presentation

In this section, we consider self-confidence, judgement and various professional skills including an ability to 'act out' the teacher role.

Teachers who are able to project themselves so that pupils take for granted that they are 'in charge' have a valuable capability. There is an important element of self-confidence in this and student teachers, in particular, may sometimes find it difficult to enact the change from the student role to the teacher role. Perhaps this is not surprising, for a huge transition in rights and responsibilities is involved. The first essential, then, is to believe in oneself as a teacher.

Judgement is needed about self-presentation because the process of establishing authority, as we saw in Chapter 6, is essentially one of negotiation between the teacher and the class. Authenticity is an important contribution to any negotiation and it is likely that, in the challenges of the classroom, attempts by novice teachers to bluff, and to pretend that they are hugely experienced, will be found out. Whilst necessary skills and understanding develop, it is therefore normally wise to progress carefully and 'with' the students if at all possible. This does not mean that one should not act the part and fulfil the 'teacher role' (see below) – indeed, the pupils will expect this. But it is best to recognise that establishing authority requires careful reflection on, and management of, the complementary roles and relationships between teacher and pupils.

Professional skills, as reviewed in Chapter 6, Section 3.3, come into their own here – for they are all related to demonstration of classroom competence. *Non-verbal skills* relate to such things as gesture, posture, movement, position in the room, facial expression, etc. These will be actively interpreted by children. The intended impression might be one of confidence and competence, but the reflective teacher will need to consider how effectively this is achieved. How do you feel? How do you move within the classroom? *Voice control* is particularly crucial, for changing the pitch, volume, projection and intensity can convey meaning. If one's voice is to be used in this way then it will require some training and time to develop. Teachers, like singers and actors, can learn to use their diaphragm to project a 'chest voice', to breathe more deeply and speak more slowly so that their voice and their message is carried more effectively. And, of course, the skill of really *listening* to pupils and understanding what they have to say is also critical to the establishment of authority – for this is the basis of its legitimacy. Learning pupil names is extremely important. It helps the build-up of confidence and establishes the groundwork for positive relationships with individual children.

A final and more general area of presentational skill is that of 'acting' – as though on a stage. In this sense it is the ability to convey what we mean by 'being a teacher', so that expectations are clear and relationships can be negotiated. Do not underestimate the power of turning your class into an audience when appropriate. As an audience they will feed your self-presentation and, if you actively observe and listen to your audience, you will know exactly where your efforts are succeeding or misfiring.

Acting is also an enormous strength for teachers for one other particular reason. When one is acting, one is partially detached from the role. It is possible therefore to observe oneself, to analyse, reflect and plan. Acting, in other words, is controlled behaviour which is partially distanced from self. In the situations of vulnerability which sometimes arise in classrooms this can be a great asset.

The skills which have been reviewed above are necessary but are not sufficient. They have no substantive content or merit in their own right. A self-confident performer who lacks purpose and gets practical matters wrong (for example has ill-defined objectives, mixes up children's names, plans sessions badly, loses books, acts unfairly, etc.) will not be able to manage a class. A teacher has to be purposive as well as skilled and must understand the ends of education as well as the means.

2.3 Language

Sometimes, our primary purpose in speaking to pupils is to ensure that they correct some aspect of their behaviour. We may, quite simply, need to be assertive. But in so doing, as the adult and as the teacher, we also need to bear in mind our broader educational purposes. Every time we speak to pupils, for whatever purpose, we have educational opportunities. In relation to behaviour, the aim is to keep them 'on track' as effectively as possible as a means to educational ends.

Rogers (2011, p. 83) identifies seven ways in which language should be used to support good discipline:

1 keep corrective interaction as 'least-intrusive' as possible;

2 avoid unnecessary confrontation;

3 keep a respectful, positive tone of voice wherever possible;

4 keep corrective language positive where possible;

5 restore working relationships with a reprimanded pupil as quickly as possible;

6 follow up with children on matters beyond the classroom context;

7 if we need to communicate frustration, or even anger, do so assertively rather than aggressively.

In his final point, Rogers is warning teachers not to get 'out of control'. Pupils do have ways of describing this – the teacher has 'flipped', 'gone mad' or 'lost it'. This is the 'non-legitimate censure' discussed in Chapter 6, Section 2.3 – and the images of teacher insanity are not there by chance. Such uncontrolled use of power is a long way from establishing legitimated authority and respect.

Standing back from this a little, the basic point is that to establish our authority as teachers, even with the pressure of the busy classroom, we must carefully think about what we say and how we say it. In principle, teacher language to build good discipline should:

- *connect personally* with relevant pupil/s;
- *identify the behaviour* which needs to change;
- *encourage re-engagement* with curricular intentions;
- *minimise disruption* to others;
- *follow through* to ensure conformity.

For example:

- A simple, routine and individual primary example might be: 'Sally' (teacher gains her attention with a neutral tone of voice and then sustains eye contact), 'that's enough talking for now', 'let's see if you can complete your story before playtime' (teacher watches beneficially, and makes that clear, to see that Sally goes back on task).

- Scaling this up a little in a secondary context: 'Sean' (teacher moves to stand closer to pupil, but without threatening), 'it really isn't fair to take Alan's book without asking him', 'please give it back and we will find you another' (teacher checks return of Alan's book, provides another and checks that Sean understands the activity and is able to begin his work).

- In a routine whole-class, primary situation the teacher might say: 'Now everybody' (gain attention, perhaps with a clap or other sign), we have been becoming rather noisy this afternoon and this isn't good for concentrating on our work', 'I'd like us to try really hard now so that we can all focus on what we have to learn', 'and then nobody will fall behind' (teacher presents the learning goals for the session and moves actively within the classroom to reinforce the request using proximity).

- If secondary students become more challenging, which should not be assumed, a more assertive strategy may be necessary – but the five points above remain a sound guide. For example, the teacher might try: '4C, we need to talk about those of you who are arriving late to lessons. This is not acceptable because it is making it impossible to cover the syllabus and, in the end I'm afraid, you may all suffer from that', 'we need to review the reasons, and then agree how to avoid lateness in future' (teacher and pupils discuss issues and agree ways forward. Teacher monitors progress over successive lessons to establish a new expectation).

Put another way, measured and constructive assertiveness combined with provision of an interesting curriculum can sustain and reinforce good order – and thus help in the establishment of authority (Canter and Canter, 1992). Intemperate use of language can fuel poor discipline by undermining authority.

Although audio recordings never seem flattering, recording a lesson introduction or some other whole-class episode can be a useful way of seeing how much your verbal repertoire is developing.

2.4 Strategic repertoire

Expert question

Repertoire: is our pedagogic expertise sufficiently creative, skilled and wide-ranging to teach all elements of learning?

This question contributes to a conceptual framework underpinning professional expertise (see Chapter 16).

Experienced teachers are aware of a repertoire of strategies on which they can draw to establish and maintain appropriate pupil behaviour. Rogers (2011) reviews a range of strategies and suggests that teachers should minimise their 'intrusion'. The proposal is closely tied to the existence of tacit classroom understandings, as described in Chapter 6. So good classroom relationships provide a sort of 'moral order' in the classroom which underpins behaviour. When this exists, it seems almost invisible – but don't be taken in! Teachers work continuously to maintain such relationships.

Teacher strategies become more intrusive when we feel the need to draw on our authority and assert our power. They are least intrusive when we are able to rely on the tacit understandings of the 'working consensus'.

Strategies identified by Rogers can be considered in three groups. These reflect *minimal, routine* and *assertive* levels of teacher action.

Minimal intrusion strategies

The efficacy of these strategies rests on the existence of well understood rules and good classroom relationships. Good behaviour can thus be achieved with simple reminders. Three of Rogers' minimal strategies are:

- Tactical ignoring – the teacher is aware of, but temporarily ignores, minor misdemeanors whilst focusing on and affirming positive behaviours. Pupils then come into line.

- Incidental language – reminders of classroom rules are given without attributing blame to anyone. Because rules are established and accepted, pupils self-adjust to conform. 'We have a rather messy classroom at the moment, and we can't go out if it's like that can we?'
- Take-up time – after a rule reminder or request, the teacher moves away to give pupils time to cooperate. In so doing, she communicates trust (though she might also keep an eye on progress!)

Routine strategies

This group of strategies reflects the ebb and flow of teacher–pupil interaction and the fact that relationships are always dynamic. A little jostling and testing of boundaries is thus to be expected. The strategies below are typical of those which teachers use to frame and control classroom situations, particularly when children or young people may have non-curricular activities in mind.

- Behavioural direction – expected behaviours are directly, positively and briefly communicated. 'All paying attention to me now please.'
- Rule reminder – rather than 'picking on' a particular transgressor, the teacher reminds everyone of a rule. 'Now what are our rules about getting ready for PE?'
- Prefacing – with awareness of potential misbehaviour, this strategy can be used to anticipate and frame activities without being too heavy-handed. At appropriate moments, the teacher interacts with relevant pupils to show awareness, to nip unwanted aspects in the bud, and to redirect attention back to curricula goals.
- Distraction – this contrarian strategy involves deliberately drawing attention to something that is going well and thus by-passing something which might be problematic. With the class refocused, the difficulty fades away or can be quietly dealt with.
- Direct questions – such questions challenge pupils to justify themselves and to take responsibility. 'What should you be doing now? Where should you put the ...?' Such questions may be the starting point for discussion and clarification of rules.
- Directed 'choices' – these are pupil options which are circumscribed by established rules and routines. 'Yes, you can go in the play area once you've finished your story.' 'When you have made notes on your homework, you can certainly go out for break.'

Assertive strategies

The strategies in this group depend on the teacher asserting their authority and 'standing up' to pupils in various ways. Whilst, they are more categoric, they still make reference to established understandings and rules. However, they leave pupils in no doubt that the teacher is in charge.

- Blocking – this is an important strategy to maintain focus on important behavioural issues in the face of all sorts of distraction tactics which may be deployed by pupils. 'Hold on. Now let's get to the point about what really happened – and I'll hear you one at a time. John. … Sam …'

- Assertion – this strategy calmly deploys verbal and non-verbal skills and draws on reserves of self-confidence to defend and promote a principle about behaviour which has been threatened. 'It is not OK to hit people in school, at any time at all.' 'Language of that sort is unacceptable.' The stance should be non-aggressive, so that the teacher is clearly holding the moral high-ground. We thus demonstrate to the class as a whole that our action is responsible and legitimate – which erodes support for transgressors, re-asserts more routine expectations and gradually calms things down. It is quite possible, in some situations, that there may need to be a sequence of blocking and assertion moves as the complexity of pupil feelings, explanations and actions is worked through. Judgement is needed in what to block so that progress can be made, whilst also dealing with the issues which are felt to be important. From the pupil perspective, an overall judgement will eventually be made about the 'fairness' of the teacher in dealing with the incident.

- Command – a direct instruction. To be effective, a command needs to be delivered with clarity and confidence, and to be followed up immediately. 'Louise, put down the hose pipe NOW.' Eye contact, proximity and firm tone of voice will all convey the seriousness of teacher intentions. This strategy is one of direct intervention and should not be common in classroom use. If it is, it may be a sign that relationships are breaking down. The plight of a student teacher ineffectually demanding things from an alienated class of children is not a pretty sight. Thus, to be effective, commands still draw on mutual respect, for pupils will conform best when they trust the teacher – just as army officers command the respect of their troops.

We have reviewed a repertoire of strategies for managing behaviour and Cowley (2010, Reading 7.4) offers yet more. The moral foundation of these strategies rests, in all cases, on classroom relationships, as described in Chapter 6. Teachers' power is always circumscribed but, as responsible adults, we have the task of analysing and interpreting what is going on – and taking action if necessary. To do this, it is important to be able stand back a little.

> ### Reflective activity 7.3
>
> *Aim* To review the repertoire of strategies for managing behaviour which we typically use.
>
> *Evidence and reflection* Brainstorm, perhaps with a group of colleagues, on the strategies which you use to manage behaviour – just get a list. Use the ideas above from Rogers, or harvest from other sources if this is helpful. Then maybe refine it a bit, to eliminate overlaps.
>
> Now see if you can sort your strategies into categories based on the degree of intrusion. Which rest on tacit understandings? Which contribute to routine patrolling? Which demand really assertive activity?
>
> *Extension* Having expanded and analysed your strategic repertoire for managing behaviour, it is good to try it out. Acting mindfully, look for opportunities to experiment! In the light of your experience, refine your repertoire.

3 Skills for engagement

In this section, we look at a magnificent seven management skills which relate to the maintenance of classroom engagement: 'gaining attention', 'framing', 'withitness', 'overlapping', 'pacing', 'orchestration' and 'consistency'. Such skills enable lesson plans to be put into action successfully (see Chapter 10, Section 4).

3.1 Gaining attention

This is often one of the first problems to confront a student teacher. With children in the classroom, talking, moving around, playing or whatever, how do you get them to stop what they are doing and turn their attention to you? Established teachers are likely to have at least one routine for this. Thus a single, sharp clap of the hands may cut through the noise and produce a short pause which creates an opportunity to take the initiative. On a sports field where speech may not carry well, a whistle is the conventional tool. In some primary contexts, teachers use a signal requiring children to raise both arms and face the teacher. This has the considerable merit of making it very obvious which children are now paying attention, and which are not. An equivalent in a very ordered secondary classroom might be to establish a routine in which students file into the room, move to their established places, take out their books for the subject and look to the front. Sadly, things are not always so simple and gaining attention often has to be worked for.

To understand why this is, it is worth considering what is at stake. When children or young people are milling about, talking and playing amongst themselves, they are free of adult constraints and able to indulge in all the excitements and diversions of peer culture. The switch signal given by the teacher is an interruption in this freedom. It is an assertion, based on the teacher's authority, that the time has now come for the children to assume the role of 'pupils' again. They are to set aside what they were previously doing, and must now accept the rules, routines and expectations of the classroom.

As with so many aspects of teaching, it is helpful to think of building up a repertoire of ways of gaining attention so that various strategies are available. Whilst a clear, firm command may be effective from time to time, is important to avoid uncontrolled shouting, or indeed, to take any other action which could be interpreted as desperation or weakness. Pitch of voice and speed of talking need to be watched. For student teachers, it is very good practice to study the strategies used by established teachers and to discuss their routines with them. Acting confidently, which such consultation will enable, will communicate competence so that, hopefully, success builds on success.

Gaining attention is a crucial test of authority. If we have earned the respect of the pupils as their teacher, and they know that we are likely to offer them an interesting curriculum, then they will normally pay attention when asked appropriately.

3.2 Framing

Understandings about classroom behaviour are not static. Indeed, even if an expected behaviour is well established, pupils are expert at gauging the degree to which they need to conform and the extent to which they might be able to 'get away' with something. To do this, they interpret the mood and intent of their teacher by monitoring their actions, statements and movements. For example, an active, purposeful entry to a classroom is a clear signal that a teacher 'means business' and will normally tighten the frame immediately. As long as something substantive and interesting follows, things should be fine. Conversely, acting rather casually, or withdrawing into conversation with a visiting adult, will usually cause behavioural expectations to weaken and may result in children relaxing in their approach to activities

Framing thus indicates the extent to which situations or events are structured by expectations. It may apply in particular settings, or from moment to moment within a lesson. For instance, one might compare the strong frame which often exists in a hushed library, with the weak framing which often exists in classrooms during wet dinner breaks. For some purposes, such as during the introduction to a teaching session, one might want the frame to be strong thus ensuring tight control and attention. On other occasions, such as for group problem-solving discussions, a weaker overall frame may be perfectly acceptable and may enable children to take initiatives which are necessary to fulfil learning objectives. Situations of difficulty often arise where strong framing is expected by a teacher but children act as if the framing is weak. If this happens, a teacher has to act quickly to redefine the rules in play.

The ability of a teacher to manage the strength of behavioural framing over time has a great deal to do with classroom discipline. It sustains expectations, and avoids a lurch from routine to routine. In particular, skilful management provides a means of pre-empting serious difficulties through giving clear expectations about acceptable behaviour. By its very nature, though, the development of such understandings cannot be rushed and frequently needs to be explicitly reviewed by teachers and children.

3.3 Withitness

This is a term coined by Kounin (1970, Reading 7.5) to describe the capacity of teachers to be aware of the wide variety of things which are simultaneously going on in a classroom. This is a constant challenge for any teacher and can be a particular strain for a new teacher until the skill is acquired.

Teachers who are 'with-it' are said to 'have eyes in the back of their head'. They are able to anticipate and to see where help is needed. They are able to nip trouble in the bud. They are skilful at scanning the class whilst helping individuals, and they position themselves accordingly. They are alert; they can pre-empt disturbance; and they can act fast. They can sense the way a class is responding, re-establish the framework of expectations if necessary and act to maintain a positive atmosphere.

3.4 Overlapping

This is another of Kounin's terms and describes the skill of being able to do more than one thing at the same time. This is similar to the popular term 'multitasking'. Most teachers work under such pressure that they have to think about and do more than one thing at a time. Decisions have to be made very rapidly. It has been calculated that over 1,000 interpersonal exchanges a day typically take place between each teacher and the children in their care. Frequently scanning the class, even whilst helping one individual, should enable the teacher to identify and reinforce appropriate behaviour or to anticipate and intervene at the first signs of trouble. As Kounin (Reading 7.5) points out, if children perceive that the teacher is 'with-it' enough to know what is going on, they are more likely to remain on task and achieve the appropriate learning objectives.

3.5 Pacing

Pacing involves making appropriate judgements about the timing and phasing of the organisation and content of teaching–learning sessions. Organisational decisions have to be made about when to begin and end an activity and how much time to leave for tidying up or a plenary discussion. It is very easy to get involved in activities, forget about the clock and suddenly to find that it is break time. More complex educational judgements are necessary in relation to learning activities and the various phases of a typical session. For example, the motivation generated at the start of an activity has to be sustained or managed throughout. There may also be a need for 'incubation' and 'developmental' phases in which children think about the activities, explore ideas and then tackle tasks. From time to time there may be a need for a 'restructuring phase' where objectives and procedures may need to be clarified further. Finally, there may be a 'review phase' for reinforcing good effort or for reflecting on overall progress. (For more detailed discussion on the pacing of content delivery, questions and answers, etc. see Chapter 12, Section 2).

In England, strict lesson structures were once imposed on teachers and learners through 'national strategies' for literacy and numeracy, but scope for flexibility and exercising judgement about pacing are vitally important. They depend crucially on being sensitive to how children are responding to activities. If they are immersed and productively engaged, then one might decide to extend a phase or run the activity into the next session. If the children seem to be becoming bored, frustrated or listless, then it is usually wise to retain the initiative, to restructure or review the activity or to move on to something new. If the children are becoming too 'high', excited and distracted, then it may be useful to review and maybe redirect them into an activity which calms them down by rechannelling their energies. As will be discussed in the next section, working with a class of individuals may involve being able to respond to many, if not all, of their responses at the same time.

3.6 Orchestration

We use the term 'orchestration' to refer to the way in which a teacher works with the whole class rather like a conductor controls an orchestra or a standup comedian 'plays' an audience. Whether the teacher is adopting whole-class, individual or group teaching strategies, part of their job is to maximise the time that all the individuals in the class are on task and paying attention. Involving all the children in the learning activities of a classroom involves developing the sensitivity to be able to 'read' how individuals or groups are responding and to be able to anticipate the most effective way of maintaining interest or re-engaging attention. Bored, listless behaviour might be engendered because a task is too easy or too difficult (see Chapter 10 on differentiation). On the other hand some children may be highly motivated by an activity which others find tedious and dull. In all cases the teacher has to be aware of everything that is happening in their classroom and be prepared to act accordingly. This may involve a differentiated response in which some children are allowed to continue with what they are doing whilst a new focus is found for others. Certainly, teachers have to be aware of a range of ways of motivating all the individuals in the class (Gilbert, 2002).

3.7 Consistency

We identify one final, overarching skill for maximising learner engagement. This concerns the maintenance of consistency in the promotion of classroom rules, routines and expectations.

After all, in the domain of the classroom, the teacher often acts as government, police, judge and jury all rolled into one. Pupils are one of the crowd and remain subject to the teacher's right to evaluate and power to punish (cf. Jackson, 1968, Reading 6.1). Teacher inconsistency, if it occurs, reduces the integrity of the working consensus and the sense of fairness on which it is based. This, in turn, can lead to a variety of subsequent control difficulties and to risk-avoidance strategies so that new learning is compromised.

Pupils will feel vulnerable unless they can rely on teacher consistency and fairness. However, with such security, children and young people are more likely to open themselves up to the challenges and risks of new learning. Teacher consistency thus provides an underlying structure for high-quality pupil learning.

Reflective activity 7.4

Aim: To investigate one's classroom management skills.

Evidence and reflection: Ask a colleague to observe you in a teaching session and to make notes on the way in which you manage the children. They could watch out for examples of gaining attention, framing, withitness, overlapping, pacing, orchestration and maintaining consistency. Discuss the session together afterwards.

Alternatively, set up a video camera to record a session which you take. Analyse the playback in terms of the issues above.

Sometimes people only see what seems to be going wrong! If there is a danger that you are becoming negative about your management skills and judgements then adopt the 'three to one rule'. This rule states that you can only identify one negative thing after you have identified three positives. When you run out of positives you have to stop. (This strategy also works with children who have been asked to evaluate their own work or that of others!)

Extension: Such analysis should increase self-awareness of management skills. Try to identify possible improvements which could be made. These can be practised and worked on. Give yourself time to develop your expertise.

---

4 Managing classroom episodes

'Flow' is a summary criterion which can be used to describe the consequences of classroom management over time. It highlights the degree of continuity and coherence achieved in a learning session, and implies steady, continuous progression. The suggestion is thus that we should work with the children to develop a coherent sense of purpose within our classes; organise our classrooms in ways which are consistent with those purposes; and manage the children, phases and events so that learning objectives are cumulatively reinforced. Consistency and reinforcement of desirable behaviours can be important here, as Merrett and Wheldall (1990, Reading 7.6) emphasised.

In this section we discuss five issues which pose particular management challenges to the flow of sessions. We discuss 'beginnings' of sessions; their 'development'; 'transitions' between phases of sessions or between sessions themselves; and the 'endings' of sessions. We also consider strategies for dealing with 'the unexpected'.

4.1 Beginnings

Just as, for curriculum, it is essential that pupils understand what they are expected to learn so, for behaviour, it is helpful that there should be clarity concerning how they should behave.

The beginning of a session is often seen as important because of the way in which it sets a tone and clarifies intent. Simple strategies such as being in the classroom to receive the children help to establish that you are receiving them on your territory and, by implication, on your terms (Laslett and Smith, 1992).

The next important goal is usually to: introduce and interest the children in the planned activities; provide them with a clear indication of the learning objectives of the session, a clear understanding of what they are expected to do; and structure the activity in practical, organisational terms. See Reflective activity 11.2.

Reflective activity 7.5

Aim: To evaluate the beginning of a session and to consider areas for improvement.

Evidence and reflection: Video record a session you have taught or observe someone else's lesson. Consider what happened in terms of the following questions.

- How did the teacher attract the children's attention?
- Did the teacher explain the objectives of the session?
- What did the teacher use as a stimulus at the start of the lesson and how effective was this?
- Were the instructions to the class clear?
- Did the children know why they were doing this activity?
- Did the children know what they were going to learn from it?
- Did the children know if any follow-up is expected?
- Did the children know on what criteria their work was to be assessed?
- Did the children know how this activity links with other work they had done or would do next?

Extension: What specific actions could be taken for improvement? What general skills need to be worked on?

4.2 Development

This issue calls for careful thought. However carefully the session begins, how does it develop? Pupils will expect to find some progression which will maintain their interest and engagement with curricular tasks. This is a clear example of how good behaviour can be seen as a product of good teaching – in this case, of appropriate curriculum planning (see Chapter 10).

4.3 Transitions

Transitions are a regular cause of control difficulties, particularly for trainee teachers. This often arises when expectations about behaviour concerning one activity have to be left behind and those of the new one have yet to be established. In these circumstances, a skilled teacher is likely to plan carefully, involve available support staff, take an initiative early and structure the transition carefully.

For example, it would be a challenging prospect if a whole range of creative, artistic activities were in full flow when primary school children suddenly had to get changed for a physical education session in the hall. We would suggest that it is important to break down a transition such as this into three discrete stages. The skill lies in first, anticipating problems before they arise; second, in pre-structuring the next phase; and finally in interesting the children in the next phase so that they are drawn through and into it. These principles (anticipate, pre-structure and engage) apply to any transition.

> ## Expert questions
>
> **Progression:** does the curriculum-as-delivered provide an appropriate sequence and depth of learning experiences?
>
> **Engagement:** do our teaching strategies, classroom organisation and consultation enable learners to actively participate in and enjoy their learning?
>
> These questions contribute to a conceptual framework underpinning professional expertise (see Chapter 16).

> ## Reflective activity 7.6
>
> *Aim* To monitor periods of transition in your own teaching.
>
> *Evidence and reflection* Consider a transition phase in your own teaching in the light of the following questions.
>
> - Did you give an early warning of the transition?
> - Did you give clear instructions for leaving existing work?
> - Did you give the children clear instructions for the transition and for any movement that was necessary?
> - Did you arouse the children's interest in the next phase?
>
> *Extension* Reviewing your performance as a whole, what are the major points for improvement? Do you see these as technical, as personal, or as associated with other factors? What might you try next time?

4.4 Endings

Ending a session is a further management issue and four aspects will be reviewed. The first is a very practical one. At the end of any session equipment must be put away and the classroom must be tidied up ready for future sessions. The second aspect relates to discipline and control. Children and young people can sometimes get a little 'high' at the end of a session when they look forward to whatever follows. This, combined with the chores of tidying up, can require a degree of awareness and firmness from the teacher. The procedures that are called for here are similar to those for transitions.

The two other aspects involved in ending sessions have more explicit and positive educational potential. One of these concerns the excellent opportunities which arise, for example in the plenary of a literacy lesson, for reviewing educational progress and achievements, for reinforcing good work and for contextualising activities which have been completed. This is complemented by the opportunities that also arise for asserting the membership of the class as a communal group. Shared experiences, teamwork and cooperation can be celebrated and reinforced through the enjoyment of poetry, singing, games, stories, etc. Moreover, there are lots of very productive opportunities at the ends of sessions and even an odd space of unexpected time, perhaps waiting for a bell, which can be used constructively.

Overall, a carefully thought-out and well-executed ending to a session will contribute to the flow of activities by providing an ordered exit, by reinforcing learning and by building up the sense of 'belonging' within the class as a whole.

Reflective activity 7.7

Aim: To review the end of a session and identify areas for improvement.

Evidence and reflection: Reflect back on a session you taught recently in the light of the following questions.

- Did you give early warning of the end of the session?
- Did you give clear instructions for tidying up?
- Did you reinforce those instructions and monitor the tidying up?
- Did you take opportunities to reinforce the educational achievements, efforts and progress made?
- Did you take opportunities to build up the sense of the class as a community?
- Did you praise the children for what they did well?
- Did you provide for an ordered exit from the room?
- How might you respond differently in future?

Extension: You could very usefully ask a mentor or an experienced colleague to observe your session and offer specific comments. Before you do, highlight the particular issues on which you want feedback. This might also be a good moment to do some reading about the principles of class management.

4.5 The unexpected

As Doyle (1977, Reading 7.1) identified, unpredictability is one of the most salient features of the classroom for trainee teachers. It is difficult to predict children's reactions to questions or how they will respond to specific activities. Similarly, it is difficult to predict how long it will take for a class to complete an activity. These are skills which are acquired over time and with experience. However, in any classroom there is the continuous possibility of internal and external interruptions; for example, there may be changes in the normal schedule or a potential breakdown in equipment. Skilled teachers learn to plan ahead, to anticipate potential difficulties and to have a range of strategies for dealing with the unexpected. In this section we consider how teachers might deal with the unexpected in terms of both learning outcomes and 'crises'.

In line with a social constructivist approach to learning, teachers are encouraged to ask open-ended questions which can be interpreted and answered in a number of different ways (see Chapter 7, Section 1.3 and Chapter 13, Section 1.2 for further discussion). As appropriate answers are not predetermined, teachers may be surprised by the children's responses. Where the answer is unexpected the teacher then faces the dilemma of wanting to acknowledge the legitimacy of the response without being drawn too far away from the teaching point being made. Consider, for example, the following situation. A teacher introduces her class of 7-year-olds to the subject of soil erosion and, assuming that the class are following her discussion, asks how grass might help to control this process. Unfortunately, several members of the class remember an earlier lesson about the oxygen cycle and want to discuss the idea that grass is important to humans because it releases oxygen into the atmosphere. As a skilled practitioner the teacher affirms the children for remembering the previous lesson before returning to her original topic. Being able to handle the unexpected in a way which reinforces children's prior learning and yet remains true to the original learning objective is the mark of a skilled teacher. (Note also the role of teacher knowledge in making this possible, as discussed in Chapter 8, Section 3.)

On a more practical level, a classroom 'crisis' is a clear example of the unexpected. Crises can come in many forms, from a child being sick or cutting a finger, to students (or perhaps a parent) challenging the teacher's authority and judgement. Despite the wide-ranging issues which are raised, there are three fairly simple principles which can be applied from the classroom-management point of view.

The first priority is to *minimise the disturbance*. Neither a child who is ill or hurt, nor a parent or child who is upset, can be given the attention which they require by a teacher who has continuing classroom responsibilities. Help from support staff, the school secretary, an ancillary helper, or other teacher should be called in either to deal with the problem or to relieve the class teacher so that they can deal with it. In this way disturbance to the classroom flow can be minimised and those in need of undivided attention can receive it. The school should have an identified procedure for how to handle crises. Of course, a student teacher usually has a full-time teacher upon whom to call.

The second step for handling a crisis is to *maximise reassurance*. Children can be upset when something unexpected happens and it may well be appropriate to reassert the security of their classroom routines and expectations. A degree of caution in the choice of activities for a suitable period might therefore be wise.

The third strategy, which is appropriate when a crisis arises, concerns *pausing for sufficient thought* before making a judgement on how to act. Obviously, this depends on what has happened and some events require immediate action. However, if it is possible to gain time to think about the issues outside the heat of the moment, then it may produce more authoritative and constructive decisions.

Reflective activity 7.8

Aim: To monitor responses to a classroom crisis.

Evidence and reflection: After a crisis has arisen, a diary-type account of it and of how it was handled could be written. This might describe the event, and also reflect the feelings which were experienced as the events unfolded. It might be valuable to encourage children to record and talk about a similar account and reflection after the event, so that you can gain an insight into why they behaved as they did.

The following questions might be asked:

- Did you minimise disturbance?
- Did you maximise reassurance?
- Did you make appropriate judgements on how to act?

Extension: Having examined your actions and the children's responses to the crisis it would probably be helpful to discuss the event and the accounts with a friend or colleague. An interesting reading would be David Tripp (1993) on 'critical incidents'.

---

5 Cycles of behaviour

5.1 Towards engagement and independence

Here we revisit the discussion in Section 2.5 of Chapter 6. Positive relationships between teacher and pupils are sustained if teachers' act thoughtfully, constructively and fairly towards their pupils but also, most particularly, by the quality and appropriateness of the curriculum and educational experience which is on offer. Children and young people are alert to this. They want to be interested and they want to learn. School can otherwise be 'so booooorrrring ….'. Pupil engagement will be high if tasks and activities are clearly introduced, appropriately chosen and well- matched to pupil needs. If this is done, success is possible and a sense of achievement can be gained.

So, to summarise, in terms of dealing with behavioural problems the most effective strategy is, without doubt, to try to prevent them from happening in the first place. Certainly, the incidence of inappropriate behaviour is likely to be significantly reduced by following some basic rules of thumb to improve pupil engagement (see Checklist 7.1).

Unfortunately, whilst such strategies should significantly reduce the incidents of misbehaviour they may not prevent it in all circumstances. Consequently, a prudent teacher will develop in their repertoire a range of strategies for dealing with inappropriate behaviour … before it develops into anything worse.

> ### Checklist 7.1
>
> Aim To pre-empt general misbehaviour and improve engagement.
>
> 1 Be clear about general class rules and what constitutes acceptable behaviour.
> 2 'Catch 'em being good', and 'give credit' for appropriate behaviour.
> 3 Select tasks and activities that offer appropriate challenge and interest, but which also enable pupils to achieve success.
> 4 Have clear learning objectives and make sure pupils understand these.
> 5 Explain the activity or task clearly and be sure that everyone knows what to do and how to do it.
> 6 Be supportive of any problems encountered and provide feedback.
> 7 Show approval of appropriate work and reward effort.
> 8 Be consistent and be positive.

5.2 Managing challenging behaviour – avoiding a negative cycle

Although, hopefully, crises will be rare, there may be behavioural problems which gradually erode good relationships and threaten classroom order. In this section we present them in terms of recurring challenges which even the most experienced teacher may have to deal with. The aim, of course, would be to anticipate undesirable behaviour and to 'nip it in the bud' so that it does not lead to a negative cycle (see Chapter 6, Section 2.1). Nevertheless, difficulties are bound to occur from time to time and prudent teachers are likely to want to think through possible strategies in advance so that they can act confidently in managing such situations.

If behavioural problems are serious or repeated it would be appropriate to consider the strategies listed below. Suggestions are offered for five progressive stages. The emphasis should remain on prevention, and you should bear in mind that, whilst the 1997 Education Act enables teachers to restrain pupils with 'such force as is reasonable in the circumstances', corporal punishment in any form is illegal.

1 If inappropriate behaviour occurs only once and seems relatively minor:
   - Indicate that you have noticed and disapprove of the behaviour – eye contact and a shake of the head.

2 If repeated:
   - Make sustained eye contact, use more empahtic non-verbal gestures.
   - Move towards the child.
   - Invite the child to participate – ask a question or encourage a comment, direct the focus onto work to be done.

3 If persistent, in addition to the responses above:
   - Name the child firmly and positively.

- Move to the child.
- Stop the action.
- Find out the facts if the situation is ambiguous; avoid jumping to conclusions.
- Briefly identify the inappropriate behaviour, comment on the *behaviour* (not the child), keep voice low and controlled, avoid nagging/lecturing.
- Clearly state the desired behaviour, and expect a compliant response.
- Distance the child from the situation – avoid a contagious spread, a public clash and an 'audience' which can encourage 'showing off'.
- Focus on the principal individual involved; don't be drawn into discussion with a group; followers will conform if you control the leader.
- Deal with the situation as quickly and neatly as possible; don't be drawn into long arguments; don't let the situation distract your attention from the rest of the class and the goals of your lesson.

4   If punishment is judged to be necessary:
- Ensure that the punishments you consider are consistent with school policies and established classroom norms.
- Be sure that the punishment you decide upon is appropriate and will be seen to be 'fair'.
- Avoid indiscriminate punishment of class or group which would be deemed 'unfair'.
- Be confident that you can implement the punishment as announced.

5   Closure/after the event:
- Take those involved to one side, perhaps individually, and present them with 'the problem' – preserve their dignity, avoid 'supporters' chipping in.
- Encourage the child to identify what had been wrong, thus sharing responsibility.
- If you have acted inappropriately in any way, then apologise, so you are seen to be fair.
- Invite the child to draw up a 'contract' for the future.
- If privileges are to be withdrawn, show how they can be earned back.
- Provide new opportunities to earn praise.
- Conclude with 'peace terms' which are clear to all parties.

The point of all this is to be 'firm but fair'. You, as the teacher, are responsible and must take control. But you have to act appropriately and negotiate a new foundation for future conformity and a sustainable, positive relationship (see also Chapter 6).

Other problems can also exist in any classroom. These may be associated with an individual child who has particular difficulties. These need to be understood rather than lead to condemnation. To do this, it is important to record and analyse the behaviour and try to identify the possible causes before major action is taken. In keeping a diary of events one might record the conditions, characteristics and consequences of the behaviour and thus produce evidence for future action.

Checklist 7.2

Aim: To record incidents of ongoing 'problem' behaviour.

Conditions: When exactly does the disruption occur?

- Is it random or regular?
- Is there a pattern with a particular child?
- Is there a pattern regarding a particular task?
- Is there a pattern with a particular teacher?

Characteristics: What exactly happens?

- Is it a verbal reaction?
- Is it a physical reaction?

Consequences: What are the effects?

- On the child, the teacher?
- On the class, the school?
- Do others join in, ignore, retaliate?

Such major, persistent problems are best discussed with other colleagues and a common strategy worked out in line with the school's behaviour policy. In some circumstances, this might also involve the parents, if necessary, so that a consistent approach can be adopted.

Whether a problem is associated with an individual child or most of the class, a consistent, balanced, firm and constructive approach is essential and would, hopefully, provide security for pupils as well as support for the teacher. It must be remembered that children and young people respond to situations and experiences. We, as teachers, structure such experiences. Thus, if students respond problematically, we must reflect on the experiences that we provide rather than simply trying to apportion blame elsewhere. As we have seen, teachers can be 'provocative' or 'insulative' (Hargreaves, Hester and Mellor, 1975). Which are you? Can you find ways to manage behaviour which draw on and sustain a positive cycle in your classroom relationships?

Expert question

Reflection: is our classroom practice based on incremental, evidence-informed and collaborative improvement strategies?

This question contributes to a conceptual framework underpinning professional expertise (see Chapter 16).

For consideration of whole school issues and a summary checklist of principles for classroom management deriving from the Elton Report, see the supplementary material for Chapter 7 on **reflectiveteaching.co.uk**

Conclusion

This chapter has examined aspects of behaviour management which help to establish and sustain conditions for successful learning. Such issues are of great concern to us as teachers, because they underpin our effectiveness.

However, most of us gradually grow in confidence and competence with such challenges. Indeed, 'good discipline' is, above all, the product of professional expertise (see Chapters 1 and 16).

Student teachers should allow themselves time to learn, experiment, and learn some more. We all make mistakes too, but it is important to see these as learning opportunities. Direct experience is irreplaceable in developing competence, but there is also much to be said for sharing ideas, problems and successes through discussion with colleagues and mentors.

Key readings

For a sophisticated and influential analysis of classroom environments and engagement of pupils in learning tasks, see:

Doyle. W. (1986). 'Classroom organization and management', in M. C. Wittrock (ed.), *Handbook of Research on Teaching* (3rd edn). New York: Macmillan. (Reading 7.1)

There are many books which provide practical advice on classroom strategies to achieve good behaviour. For example:

Bennett, T. (2011) *Mastering the Art and Craft of Teaching*. London: Continuum. (Reading 7.3)
Cowley, S. (2010) *Getting the Buggers to Behave*. London: Continuum. (Reading 7.4)

Robertson, J. (1996) *Effective Classroom Control: Understanding Teacher–Pupil Relationships*. London: Hodder and Stoughton.
Rogers, B. (2011) *Classroom Behaviour*. London: SAGE.

Watkins, C. (2011) *Managing Classroom Behaviour*. London: ATL (Reading 7.2)

For a layered model for managing pupil behaviour, based on psychological research (Reading 6.4), see:

Chaplain, R. (2003) *Teaching Without Disruption in the Primary School*. London: Routledge.
Chaplain, R. (2003) *Teaching Without Disruption in the Secondary School*. London: Routledge.

For a book which provides many insights on classroom management, and which has become a classic, see:

Kounin, J. S. (1970) *Discipline and Group Management in Classrooms.* New York: Holt Rhinehart and Winston. (Reading 7.5)

The classic on assertive discipline is:

Canter, L. and Canter, M. (1992). *Assertive Discipline: Positive Behavior Management for Today's Classroom.* Santa Monica, CA: Canter and Associates.

On 'positive teaching' see:

Merrett, F. and Wheldall, K. (1990) *Identifying Troublesome Classroom Behaviour.* London: Paul Chapman. (Reading 7.6)

It is crucial to hold on to management issues in the context of broader educational objectives and with awareness of the overall effect on a classroom. On this, with a useful scale for analysing the 'working atmosphere', see:

Haydn, T. (2007) *Managing Pupil Behaviour.* London: Routledge.

Taking this even further, for a philosophical account see:

Straughan, R. (1988) *Can We Teach Children to be Good? Basic Issues in Moral, Personal and Social Education.* Buckingham: Open University Press.

From time to time public concern is expressed about behaviour in schools. The outcome of one such episode led to the Elton Report. This is a balanced summary of the factors and issues, and is well worth consulting:

DES (1989a) *Discipline in Schools,* Report of the Committee of Enquiry chaired by Lord Elton. London: HMSO.

reflectiveteaching.co.uk offers additional professional resources for this chapter. These may include *Further Reading,* illustrative *Reflective Activities,* useful *Web Links* and *Download Facilities* for diagrams, figures, checklists, activities.

Spaces
How are we creating environments for learning?

8

Introduction

Pupils in primary and secondary schools routinely experience many 'learning spaces', yet how do spaces become effective learning environments? In this chapter we consider a number of key issues.

The core space for a teacher is, of course, the classroom, and a central concern of teachers in any phase of schooling is whether both the classroom and the class are organised in a manner that facilitates teaching and learning. For teaching and learning to succeed, it seems clear that the physical and human resources of the classroom need to be marshalled to reinforce the teacher's values, aims, curriculum and syllabus demands – and of course, as we will see, there are some important differences between primary and secondary schools.

But classrooms are not the only spaces where pupils learn. Pupils spend most of their time in environments other than school, many of which have the potential to contribute to their learning. In addition to routine learning spaces such as home, street or park, institutions such as museums and nature reserves now offer more formalised 'out of the classroom' learning experiences. Television, new media, mobile technologies and specific 'virtual learning environments' often now play a significant role in supporting learning. Above all though, the home remains the most significant influence on pupils' attitudes, and is a resource for learning that might be further exploited (Mayall, 2009).

All of these spaces have 'affordances' for learning. The term, with its origins in Gestalt psychology, was first coined by Gibson (1977), in developing an ecological approach to perception. It has been widely adopted in education, particularly in relation to educational technologies (see Edwards, 2012, Reading 8.5), to express the inherent potential for learning which an environment or tool offers. For such potential to be realised, it has to be identified by the user. Thus, for example, a pencil may have affordance for drawing as a means of expression with variable use of line, shading and pattern – whilst another person may perceive it simply as a tool for writing. Even then though, it has important affordances, such as its susceptibility to a rubber for alterations. And the other side of affordances is the idea of constraints – there are some things about an environment, space or tool that are likely to frame learning potential in particular ways. Reflective teachers need to be aware of the affordances and constraints of the environments and resources with which they work.

See Chapter 4

TLRP principles

Two principles are of particular relevance to this chapter on learning environments:

Effective teaching and learning recognises the significance of informal learning. Informal learning, such as learning out of school, should be recognised as at least as significant as formal learning and should therefore be valued and used appropriately in formal processes. (Principle 8)

Effective teaching and learning demands consistent policy frameworks with support for teaching and learning as their primary focus. Policies at national, local and institutional levels need to recognise the fundamental importance of teaching and learning. They should be designed to create effective learning environments in which all learners can thrive. (Principle 10)

In this chapter we will see that not only are there a range of possible spaces for learning, but that they each have affordances and constraints for particular purposes, which may be different at primary and secondary level. Exploiting the affordances and constraints of an environment can be achieved by good organisation and management. However, this should not be taken to imply rigidity; for if the rules and routines of the classroom are clear and agreed, good organisation can increase freedom for a teacher or educator to teach and the learner to learn. In particular, it should give them more time to create a sense of 'learning community' (Watkins, 2004) – to diagnose pupils' learning difficulties, to listen to pupils and to teach. This is more preferable, in classrooms in particular, than having to spend too much time on 'housekeeping' (Hastings and Wood, 2001).

1 Environments for learning

1.2 What is a learning environment?

In considering the creation of a learning environment, with the learner at the centre, it is useful to begin by looking more generally at the complex 'layers' which exist within and around any learning space, and which can affect a person's development. The ecological

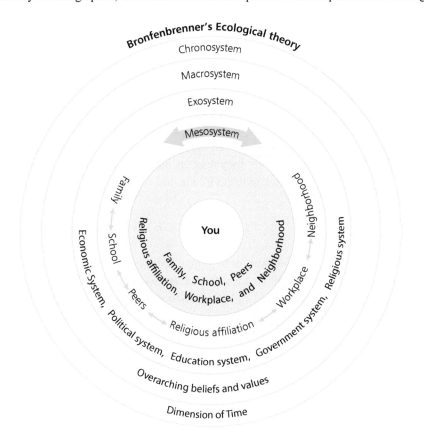

Figure 8.1
Bronfenbrenner's
ecological theory

systems theory of Bronfenbrenner (1979; 1993, Reading 8.1) gives a useful way to think about these layers. He represented a pupil at the centre, and layers of environment expanding in concentric circles, as shown in Figure 8.1. Immediately around the learner, he defines a layer comprising their own 'biology' and the relationships they have with their immediate surroundings. For example, a young person's peers may affect his or her beliefs and behaviour (and vice versa) and talking to his teacher may support his learning. The next layer is defined as the connections between the components of the previous layer; the relationship between a pupil's parents and her teacher would be included here. Beyond this lies the larger social system, in which the pupil does not directly function, but which may affect them. Parental work schedules are one example; a pupil has no role in them, but may be affected by increased pressure in the family home as a result of one parent being frequently absent. Finally, the outermost layer describes the wider cultural values, customs and laws within which the child is developing.

Thinking about a pupil's environment in this way makes it clear that no learning space can be considered in isolation. There are connections between the various settings and communities involved in a pupil's life. Of course, these interconnections change over time and the ways in which people, resources and space typically interact in early, primary, secondary and further education have some similarities but are also distinct.

Whilst recognising the significance of learning in a wide range of settings, it is important for an educator to understand what they can influence, manage and organise, and those influences to which they can only respond.

> **Expert question**
>
> **Connection:** does the curriculum engage with the cultural resources and funds-of-knowledge of families and the community?

Sometimes a teacher will want to make a significant change to a pupil's immediate environment to support their learning. This could involve separating groups of pupils into different teaching groups; it may involve talking to their parents to influence the learning environment at home to encourage homework completion; or it could involve rearranging the tables for group work. At other times, they may encourage pupils to work in less formal learning environments.

1.2 Formal and informal learning environments

The classroom provides a structured and formal learning environment, which can be subject to a number of constraints. Less formal environments (such as museums and outdoor learning spaces) can provide opportunities to work outside such constraints. They can provide:

- an immediate and novel context for learning;
- an alternative source of curriculum delivery, allowing repackaging of the curriculum through e.g. a museum's object collections;
- a chance to ensure that the curriculum does not restrict pupils' learning;
- objects and environments that can form the basis for enquiry and knowledge

building, allowing pupils the chance to follow and explore their interests, and encouraging a mastery approach to learning;

○ pupils with the chance to develop more engagement and autonomy in knowledge building, through handling and questioning objects.

Working successfully within less formal environments can be a challenge for a teacher, who is usually constrained by curriculum demands, and working off the school site in particular can involve extra organisation (a useful website which supports such planning is at **schooltrip.com**). Any use of a learning space outside the classroom by a teacher and their class needs to be considered from the pragmatic considerations of organisation, and from pedagogical perspectives on what will enable effective learning in these spaces. It is useful to note that such spaces can also provide distractions from learning.

However, children's learning is not all intentional and planned. Children learn through everyday experience, from their peers in the playground, at home, and as part of their communities.

Peer group culture is important to children as part of adapting to school life (Davies, 1982). As children get older, the culture of boys and girls tends to become more distinctive and the culture of the playground also starts to mirror both academic achievement within school and social factors outside the school, such as social class and ethnicity. Such differentiation is particularly important to gendered patterns in motivation and learning disposition (Murphy, 2001). Some peer cultures favour school attainment and are likely to reinforce teacher efforts to engender a positive approach to learning. Other peer cultures derive meaning from alternative values, and children who are influenced by such cultures may approach school with minimal or even oppositional expectations. Such children will still be constructing understanding, but it may not be the type of understanding for which teachers would have aimed.

The interaction between home and school is also important for learning (Hughes and Pollard, 2000, see the **Research Briefing** in Chapter 4, p. 107). Indeed, much of children's lifestyle at home can have an influence on their learning. Children watch many hours of television each week, or spend many hours on the computer, and their play and lifestyles are influenced by advertising, social media and the internet. Young people may identify with particular 'imagined communities' (Anderson, 1991), but also virtual communities. As Buckingham (2000) has argued, electronic media provide an alternative environment within which enduring questions are played out. How much they learn will depend on whether children are passive or active in their stance and how new cultural experiences are interpreted and used.

As well as the home, the wider community also has key opportunities for learning. A 'community' can mean different things, but usually refers to either a community of locality, or a community of identity. Having said that, a locality can be important to someone's identity, and can provide a network of support and a sense of belonging. Collective identities can also be important to children, and may be based on wider regional variations or looser groupings. The way in which values, beliefs and common experience define such communities can be very important to pupils' learning.

Explicit opportunities provided for learning within a community can include youth clubs, toddler groups, education–business partnerships (which provide schools with links to local business), learning resource services such as libraries, and organisations like the Scouts, Brownies or Guides. Such activities may also be mediated by specialist informal educators who will explore and enlarge experiences.

2 Organising the classroom for learning

2.1 The classroom as a learning environment

Organising the classroom environment is important, because research suggests that disorganised classrooms predict poor attainment and poor behaviour (Pointon and Kershner, 2000). Such research reinforces the view that the environment in a classroom should: be tidy; be aesthetically pleasing; stimulate pupils interest; set high standards in the display and presentation of pupils' work; and be created in such a way that it is practical to maintain. In addition, however, reflective teachers should aim to structure the environment so that opportunities are taken to reinforce their overall purposes, both in general terms, and for particular lessons/lesson activities. This applies equally in a primary classroom, as well as in a subject-teaching room at secondary school. Research suggests that the physical aspects of the classroom environment interact with the teacher's intentions for learning, and that careful consideration of the interaction of these elements is necessary in creating an 'inclusive classroom' (Lucas and Thomas, 2000).

In considering the physical environment of the classroom you may find the questions in Checklist 8.1 helpful. These focus on the use of displays to support learning.

Checklist 8.1

Aim: To examine the classroom environment.

1. *Design*. What are the main design features of the room, and how do they affect its aesthetic feel?
2. *Affordances*. What are the possibilities and constraints for active learning in the classroom? Can you move the tables to enable discussion? What are the possibilities and issues for display on walls, on windows, on flat surfaces, off the ceiling?
3. *Purposes*. Do displays stimulate and inform? Do they provide opportunities for pupils to interact with them, for example, by posing questions? Do displays only show finished products or do they also reveal processes and value hard work, for example, displaying drafts and then finished products. Do they provide a stimulus for discussion (such as thinking walls, or a periodic table in a chemistry lesson), sharing problems, or giving mutual support and advice? Do they provide a stimulus for structuring enquiry, from devising questions to testing ideas?

---

4. *Quality*. Do classroom displays show that the pupils' work is valued? Does it provide a model which pupils may apply to their own work? Is there a 'working wall' which enables ongoing contributions by pupils?

5. *Practicality*. Is the classroom environment as practical as it can be to maintain?

Other research suggests that environmental factors, such as classroom temperature, acoustics, and lighting may affect pupils' ability to engage in learning (Woolner et al., 2007; Winterbottom and Wilkins, 2007). There is a limit to what individual teachers can do to control such factors, but maintaining good ventilation, preventing 'over-lighting' of pupils' workstations, and ensuring pupils sit where they cannot see a 'glare spot' on the interactive whiteboard are all important.

2.2 Use of resources

A good supply of appropriate resources is essential, given the importance of direct experience and practical activities to pupils' learning. Such resources may differ between primary and secondary. For example, at primary level, you will be more likely to find resources which provide direct and active learning experiences. However, at all levels, resources can:

- motivate, inspire and focus pupils' attention;
- provide a basis for discussion, or be designed to enable pupils to learn independently;
- explain, instruct, or demonstrate procedures and ideas;
- enable pupils to access information;
- enable pupils to learn in manageable steps;
- help pupils to recall, consolidate and extend their learning;
- support assessment of pupils' understanding, perhaps by providing a structure for recording responses.

In some ways, organising resources is a straightforward matter, but it also requires careful thought and attention to detail. For instance, it is all too easy to discover that the paint has dried out in a Year 1 classroom, or that insufficient chemicals have been ordered for the Year 9 chemistry syllabus. Likewise, even with centrally managed resources, laptops may have run out of charge, the printer may have run out of ink, or the laptops may update themselves for five minutes before they can be used. It may take several days for new software to be installed on the computers by the ICT technicians. It is also common in schools that shared resources are not put back where they are usually stored; a sense of collective responsibility for the care and use of such centralised resources is therefore essential.

When considering employing resources for pupils' learning, four possible criteria might be considered:

- *Appropriateness*. What resources are needed to support the learning processes which are expected to take place?
- *Availability*. What resources are available? What is in the classroom, the school, the community, businesses, libraries, museums? Are there cost, time or transport factors to be considered?
- *Storage*. How are classroom resources stored? Which should be under teacher control? Which should be openly available to the pupils? Which are stored by the technician? Are they clearly labelled and safely stored?
- *Maintenance*. What maintenance is required? Is there a system for seeing that this is done? In the case of ICT and specialist equipment, where is the expertise and technical support located and how can this be accessed?

Reflective activity 8.1

Aim: To plan resources to support specific learning activities.

Evidence and reflection: Identify the objective for a proposed lesson activity, then consider the resources and classroom organisation which are required, using the four criteria listed above as a starting point:

Activity:
Objectives:
Resources required:
  - Appropriateness:
  - Availability:
  - Storage:
  - Maintenance:

Extension: Together with another teacher, either from a different subject or a different year group, analyse the classroom(s) in which you both teach most often. Each of you should have one or more particular learning activities in mind, and you should work together to analyse each other's classrooms. Share the problems and issues that are pertinent to your circumstances.

2.3 Use of space

The way a teaching space is organised has considerable impact on the teaching strategies that can be deployed, the attitude of the learners and thus the quality of learning. Space in a classroom is always limited; yet what space there is must be utilised in such a way that it allows a teacher to change organisational strategies, for instance between whole-class teaching, group work, or pair work, with associated implications for seating. The use of interactive whiteboards and personal laptop computers in classrooms also creates particular demands on classroom space. Such technologies enable exciting new forms of whole-class and individualised learning but should be deployed in relation to educational purposes rather than just because of their availability.

Because primary teachers tend to occupy the same classroom for all of their teaching, it is often possible to use space flexibly, and to move tables and desks as appropriate for the learning activity. However, notwithstanding the constraints of e.g. fixed science-benches, secondary teachers can also benefit by examining the requirements of the learning activity, and adapting the classroom space in response.

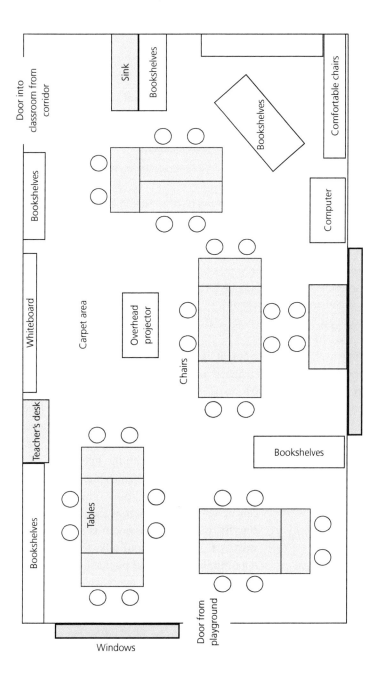

Figure 8.2 Plan of a Key Stage 2 classroom

When thinking about the most effective use of classroom space, consider developing a classroom plan, either on card, by using classroom design software (e.g. **http://teacher. scholastic.com/tools/class_setup/**) or using the drawing toolbar on a word processor (see Figure 8.2 for a primary example and consider Reflective activity 8.2). Using such a plan, it is possible to explore the affordances and constraints of each teaching space when organising for teaching and learning.

Reflective activity 8.2

Aim: To produce a classroom plan.

Evidence and reflection: A simple plan should be made of the fixed points in the classroom – walls, windows, doors, sinks, pegs, benches, gas taps, etc. It is relatively easy to produce a plan 'to scale' on computer (e.g. using **http://teacher.scholastic. com/tools/class_setup/)**, or by using squared paper.

Major existing items of furniture should be represented by shapes to the same scale as the classroom plan.

The furniture can be moved around on the plan to experiment with different classroom layouts.

Extension: Careful analysis is needed of the space requirements of each classroom activity and of each activity in relation to the others. It is therefore worth considering the arrangement of the classroom for very different types of activity – e.g. in secondary foreign language lessons, paired conversational work and whole-class question and answer sessions.

When planning a classroom layout, it is important to consider how to promote and manage dialogue between the teacher and class and between pupils in groups and pairs (Mercer and Littleton, 2007, Reading 11.6). For example, interactive whiteboards can be effective tools to promote dialogic teaching at a whole-class level (Warwick, Hennessy and Mercer, 2011). However, in this case the teacher must consider whether the screen is accessible to all pupils, and whether the classroom is organised to promote high-quality discussion at such a whole-class level with the interactive whiteboard as a stimulus. Likewise, when trying to promote small group discussion, sitting in rows may not be conducive. It can be tempting to merely focus on the logistics of an activity, but if the classroom is not organised in such a way as to promote pupil talk, then a teacher may miss opportunities to support pupils' learning (Higgins, 2003).

Finally, whatever approach is taken to resource management or classroom layout, it is still important to have one eye on health and safety implications; it is easy for aisles to be blocked by bags, or for bottlenecks of pupils to build up in particular areas of the classroom.

Expert question

Dialogue: does teacher–learner talk scaffold understanding to build on existing knowledge and to strengthen dispositions to learn?

This question contributes to a conceptual framework underpinning professional expertise (see Chapter 16).

2.4 Use of time

Notwithstanding all the other dimensions of teaching, research has shown that the amount of time during which pupils are fully engaged in targeted instructional tasks is closely related to outcomes (Berliner, 1991, Reading 8.4; Heuston and Miller, 2011). This is affected by the length of the school year, day and timetabling, as well as by the effectiveness of classroom routines and organisation.

However well-organised a classroom is, and however good one's organisation of resources, when pupils start to use that space, it can lead to a significant amount of 'evaporated time', and may require some re-analysis of the way in which space and resources, and pupils' use thereof, are designed and managed. For example, in primary schools, Campbell and Neill (1992) showed that almost 10 per cent is lost as 'evaporated time' in classroom-management activities. A similar study in secondary schools found that secondary teachers only spent 46 per cent of their allocated lesson time actually teaching pupils. Minimising this evaporated time is important, but even within the remaining 'instructional' time, it is still important to ensure pupils are engaged and motivated for them to learn effectively (Goswami and Bryant, 2010). This is not necessarily always achieved. Findings from the primary-based Oracle study (Galton et al., 1999) showed considerable variations between different classrooms in the proportions of pupil time with high levels of engagement. Overall, Key Stage 1 pupils were task-engaged for about 60 per cent of classroom time, distracted for about 20 per cent of the time and organising themselves or being organised for the remaining 20 per cent. Hence, in this section, we consider two aspects: pupils' use of the space and resources to maximise the time available for curriculum activity, and the time actually spent in active learning.

Time available for curriculum activity is the remaining time in each teaching/learning session, once it has properly started, excluding interruptions and time to pack up at the end of the lesson. The time available is clearly related to a number of organisational strategies. The most obvious of these are the routine procedures which are developed within the classroom space that, for example, help to avoid queues and bottlenecks. These help to manage the pressure which might otherwise be placed on the teacher by the pupils and they contribute to producing a positive, structured classroom environment. Reflective activity 8.3 may be helpful in reviewing classroom organisation and procedures, and thus increase the time available for curriculum activities.

Reflective activity 8.3

Aim: To evaluate routine activities to maximise time for teaching and learning.

Evidence and reflection: Use this list as a starting point for considering the routines that affect your lessons, and how you may improve your use of space and / or resources to reduce wastage of time. The list is generic, and applicable to both primary and secondary school – you will need to add to the list to match your type of school and (in secondary school) your curriculum subject. Identify any aspects of organisation you can deal with in advance of the lesson (for example, moving the tables, or distributing resources before pupils enter the room). Can you improve your own routines (for example, preventing bottlenecks by asking pupils to unpack before putting their bags away, or by distributing resources around the room). Are you planning far enough ahead or practising crisis management (for example, do you often find yourself hunting for resources in the cupboards, or running to the prep room or office for resources you've forgotten?). Can you actively involve pupils, giving them routine responsibility for specific aspects of resource organisation (for example, giving automatic responsibility to particular pupils to give out books or materials at the start of the lesson)?

Purpose of procedure	Procedure	Evaluation of procedure	Possible improvement
Entering the classroom			
Leaving the classroom			
Completing the register			
Collecting in homework			
Issuing homework			
Distributing learning resources			
Collecting learning resources			
Going to the toilet			
Tidying up			

Extension: Teachers and Teaching Assistants build up a useful repertoire of strategies for these organisational matters. A good extension would be to share and exchange ideas with a 'critical friend'.

Encouraging pupils to take on more responsibility for organising themselves, their classroom and their resources is important, as it can enhance their learning time, reduce their reliance on the teacher, and give the teacher more time to focus on pupils' learning. Indeed, the aim is for the classroom to run itself. For this to happen effectively, it is important to ensure that the locations of all resources are labelled, or that resources are visible and obvious, so that pupils can fetch them with ease where it is safe to so. This is easier to do in primary school, as pupils tend to spend all their time in one room. However, over time, and with established departmental practices, it is relatively straightforward to encourage in secondary classrooms as well. Alternatively, a teacher may adopt different strategies to try to maximise time available for learning. These could include asking pupils to hand out resources to the rest of the class, or individuals or groups moving between workstations, with resources remaining fixed to such locations.

Time spent in active learning is the second key issue. Whilst this can be assessed at any point, it may also be seen as providing summative information: a product of the overall learning environment which is provided for the pupils. Reflective activity 8.4 helps in analysing the amount of time pupils spend actively learning.

Reflective activity 8.4

Aim To monitor an individual pupil to estimate active learning time.

Evidence and reflection Watch a chosen pupil during a teaching/learning session. Judge the times at which:

1. The pupil is 'on task' (i.e. *actively* engaged in the given task and learning objectives)
2. The pupil is doing other necessary activities related to the task (e.g. logging into a computer, fetching equipment)
3. The pupil is 'off task' (i.e. appears distracted or disengaged).

Calculate the total amounts and proportions of learning time in each category:

'On-task' time	[… minutes], [… %]
'Task-management' time	[… minutes], [… %]
'Off-task' time	[… minutes], [… %]

Extension Are there any changes in classroom organisation or management strategies which could help to maximise active learning time?

To maximise learning in which pupils are actively engaged, it is also important to ensure there are a *variety* of *stimulating* tasks over time. Teachers should try to avoid 'satiation' (i.e. letting the pupils get bored by monotonous or repetitive activities). Although such variety is closely related to the teaching and learning strategies a teacher employs, explicitly reflecting upon the planned activities to ensure variety is an organisational issue, the aim being to ensure that each pupil will remain engaged and motivated throughout (see Reflective activity 8.5).

Reflective activity 8.5

Aim To evaluate the variety of learning objectives, tasks and activities, and the extent to which they engage pupils.

Evidence and reflection This evaluation could be carried out by an observer who focuses on a particular pupil for a lesson or teaching episode. All activities should be recorded in terms of their motivational appeal, explicit purpose and what the pupil was required to do. Alternatively, tasks could be monitored, by the teacher, for a longer period. Some questions which might be asked could include:

a) Is there a planned highlight for each lesson or teaching episode?
b) Are there long sequences of the same type of task?
c) Is there variety between active and passive tasks?
d) Is there variety between pupils working alone, in small groups, and as a whole class?

Extension Consider the findings from this exercise, and try to deduce the reasons for any patterns you identify. If you judge it appropriate, what could you do to increase the stimulus and variety of learning objectives, tasks and activities?

---

3 Using technology for learning

As we have seen, the classroom environment consists of its physical environment and social systems, informed by the prevailing values and culture of the school. The ways in which resources are organised and used will reflect these interlinked elements. This is true too of ICT resources, which are now integral to teaching and learning.

3.1 ICT in formal school settings

Expert question

Culture: does the school support expansive learning by affirming learner contributions, engaging partners and providing attractive opportunities?

This question contributes to a conceptual framework underpinning professional expertise (see Chapter 16).

The organisation and use of ICTs afford or constrain opportunities for learning. We begin with some organisational considerations, but move swiftly to consider teachers' pedagogic intentions.

The general availability of ICT resources in the classroom is increasingly important and can be a strong determinant of whether technology will be readily used by pupils to support their learning. The use of computer suites is decreasing because, although they may still be helpful for some purposes, they are not accessible at all times. Mobile equipment, owned by children, may also have potential for use too, though this also clearly raises coordination, technical and access issues among others. In any event, simply having ICT in the classroom does not determine its effective use for pupils' learning.

ICT brings opportunities for teaching in particular subject and topic areas. Although uninspiring 'drill' programmes still exist, the quality of educational software and web-resources is increasing. For example, **numbergym.co.uk** offers an excellent range of mathematically engaging activities for learners of any age to achieve 'fluency' and confidence with number. There are many more software and website resources for particular curricular purposes and collaboration and exchange of ideas with colleagues and through subject and sectoral associations will be helpful in identifying them.

New technology also enables new processes of teaching and learning. In recent research, Kennewell and his colleagues (2008) considered the practices of primary and secondary teachers using ICT in the context of 'interactive' teaching approaches (Moyles et al., 2003). Here, the teachers might be characterised as being 'dialogic' in their orientation to teaching and learning, being advocates of the idea that communication is 'central to the meaning making process and thus central to learning' (Mortimer and Scott, 2003). So how does ICT use 'fit' here?

The bottom line is that teachers are absolutely crucial to exploiting the potential of classroom technologies (Sutherland, John and Robertson, 2007, see the TLRP **Research Briefing** on p. 217).

A good example is that of the interactive whiteboard (IWB), now familiar in many countries; they provide a digital hub through which other technologies can be channelled,

Research Briefing   Teaching and learning with new technology

UK governments see enormous potential in the use of technology for schools, college, university, workplace and lifelong learning (for instance, see DfES, 2005b or DENI, 2004). Provision starts in nurseries and stretches forward towards the elderly. It will be a very important part of our future.

The evolution of the terminology is instructive. 'IT', 'ICT' and 'e-learning' were in common usage for some years, but progressed to 'technology-enhanced learning' (TEL). This denotes an important change. In particular, it is now understood that the fundamental factors in learning endure whether new technology is involved or not. Appropriate technology can 'enhance' some learning (though probably not all), but works best when it is combined with contributions from skilled and knowledgeable teachers, parents or others. Thus we have the concept of 'blended learning' which combines old and new methods, each playing to their strengths.

TLRP's two major projects on the use of new technology in schools have contributed to these developments – one based on learning in nursery schools and the other focused on the teaching of specific subjects in secondary schools. In both instances, the research showed that the affordance of the technological tools to support effective learning is not drawn out consistently without teacher expertise guiding the learner on how to interpret and make sense of his or her experiences. Technology can enhance learning and can complement teaching, but it is unlikely to replace the role of a more knowledgeable other in discussion, guidance and feedback.

Key findings:	Implications:
Equipment: New technological equipment is, in itself, not terribly useful in enhancing learning.	The key to enhancing learning concerns the use to which technological tools are put.
Guided interaction: Learners' encounters with new technology are enhanced when practitioners use guided interaction to support them.	Professional development should aim to enhance the capability of teachers and others in using new technology to scaffold new understanding.
Essential teaching: Effective teaching and learning with new technology involves building bridges between 'idiosyncratic' and 'intended' learning.	Authentic new knowledge is not embedded in the technology. Effective learning depends on teacher contributions to shape, amend or reinforce emerging understanding.
Multiple experiences: Providing experience of a broad range of new technologies promotes opportunities for learning.	Experience of many technologies builds confidence and positive attitudes to technology enhanced learning and its use.
Formal and informal learning: There is a two-way exchange of knowledge between home and school use of new technology, which impacts on learning in school.	Students can be beneficially encouraged to build on their out-of-school learning within school, and to continue their school learning at home.

Among the 'subject design initiatives' underpinning the InterActive project were:

Learning to spell: 10–11-year-old students used WordRoot, a multimedia sound and word package, and the presentation package PowerPoint, to analyse the structure and etymology of 'hard words'. Students' spelling improved, as shown by paper and pencil tests.

Learning to write in a foreign language: 13–14-year-old students used drop-down menus in Word to support their writing in German. They wrote more in the foreign language and took more risks with grammar. Students' writing on paperwas also enhanced after this exercise.

Learning mathematical proof: 13–14-year-old students used dynamic geometry software and presentation software to learn about geometrical proof. They worked in groups and presented their work to the class for feedback on the validity of the proofs they had produced.

Using computers for shared writing: 9–10-year-olds in pairs composed an extra chapter of Alice in Wonderland, writing direct to screen. Analysis of pupils' interactions and writing suggests that the computer affords a more visual way of conceptualising the narrative voice and structure of a text than pen and paper. This challenges traditional notions of the writing process.

Further information:
Plowman, L. (2006) *Supporting Learning with ICT in Pre-school Settings.* TLRP Research Briefing 15. London: TLRP.
Sutherland, R. et al. (2006) *Using Computers to Enhance Learning.* TLRP Research Briefing 19. London: TLRP.
Sutherland, R., John, P. and Robertson, S. (2007) *Improving Learning with ICT.* TLRP Improving Learning series. London: Routledge.
The full research briefings are downloadable at **www.tlrp.org/pub**. 'Practitioner Applications' on the TLRP website suggest classroom activities to explore issues raised by these projects.
These project were directed from the University of Stirling and University of Bristol.

as orchestrated by the teacher and the pupils (see Beauchamp and Kennewell, 2013). Tools such as this offer a range of affordances and constraints for learning. These are determined by two things – the functionality of the device(s) and how both teachers and pupils see that functionality as providing opportunities for, or barriers to, learning. This relates substantially to the pedagogical perspective of the teacher (Hennessy, Warwick and Mercer, 2011).

Consider Diane, a primary teacher, and Lloyd, a secondary history teacher. Both are committed to an interactive, dialogic pedagogy, with its emphasis on engaging pupils in active, self-regulated and collaborative learning (see **http://dialogueiwb.educ.cam. ac.uk/**). As a result, their use of the interactive whiteboard is often calculated to stimulate discussion, set the scene for collaborative group work or enable their pupils to 'take over' the use of the board in whole-class or group work. They see the board's multimodality (providing sound, text, still images and video) and ability to act as a 'hub' as providing the flexibility they need to teach according to their pedagogical intentions. In their classrooms, a visitor might expect to see the whiteboard being used by the teacher or the pupils for:

- annotating still images, using input from pupil groups or talk pairs;
- revisiting resources – e.g. annotated pictures, audio recordings – to reignite understanding, reinforce learning and, through discussion, compare perspectives over time;
- creating or listening to sound files, sometimes associated with text or images;
- considering work from particular pupil, shown using the visualiser and annotated on the interactive whiteboard screen;
- group presentation of work, through the use of pictures, scanned objects, text, etc.;
- groups working directly at the interactive whiteboard on tasks that contain multimodal elements;
- the use of the internet to pick up instantly on pupils' contributions to discussion;
- use of the interactive whiteboard with other resources, such as where simulations are used alongside actual group experiments in science;
- building pages of ideas from different groups in a plenary, in order to continue the trajectory of learning in the next lesson;
- communicating with other classes in the school or elsewhere through video links to support ongoing work.

None of these ideas are particularly technically challenging, but such uses of the whiteboard are unlikely to be seen in a classroom where the teacher has little concern with pupils being active and self-regulated in their learning, or with developing a collaborative learning ethos. In such classrooms, by contrast, the whiteboard might simply be used to present illustrations of a story being told by the teacher. Thus a teacher who adopts an interactive, dialogic pedagogy will perceive the affordances and constraints of particular hardware and software very differently from a teacher who favours a more didactic pedagogy. This does not mean that the teacher's role in teaching and organising learning is less in either case – but it is significantly different.

The same points apply to software packages, as Reflective activity 8.6 explores.

Expert question

Dialogue: does teacher–learner talk scaffold understanding to build on existing knowledge and to strengthen dispositions to learn?

This question contributes to a conceptual framework underpinning professional expertise (see Chapter 16).

Reflective activity 8.6

Aim To consider the affordances and constraints of a particular piece of software.

Evidence and reflection Pick a particular program that you use a lot (such as, for example, Notebook or Activ software for a whiteboard) or that you encourage the pupil to use – it can be on any device. What do you consider to be the particular affordances for learning that it has? (Or, to put it another way, how does it help pupils to learn?) What are the particular constraints of the same program, in your view?

Extension Do you think that the pupils share your view of the affordances and constraints of the program? Whether 'yes' or 'no', what makes you think so?

The constraints on the uses of ICT in classrooms derive not only from the pedagogic intentions of teachers or the availability of ICT hardware and software, but from other features of the learners or the setting. The fundamental question for the teacher has to be 'will this use of ICT in the lesson enhance the pupils' learning?' Checklist 8.2 suggests pedagogical and practical considerations to consider:

Checklist 8.2

Aim To consider the pedagogical and practical implications of the classroom use of ICT.

- Has e-safety been considered? In particular, do all devices you plan to use have appropriate internet site blocking? Can pupils easily access the sites you want them to use?
- Is some direct teaching in relation to e-safety a necessary feature of the lesson? (see **http://Ofsted.gov.uk/resources/safe-use-of-new-technologies**)
- Have you considered how the use of ICT resources may impact on the time management of your lesson (e.g. set-up time, time on task)?
- Have you planned for the procedural aspects of ICT use in the lesson (e.g. numbers of pupils to a computer, physical placement of computer resources, possible circulation of groups to a single resource such as the IWB)?

- Are any password systems, used to access devices, clear for the pupils?
- Are the devices fully charged? (This is a particularly important consideration where laptop or mobile device charging units may not be in your classroom).
- Is the right version of the software that you plan to use actually on each of the devices the pupils will be using?
- Have you considered whether the pupils are able to store their own work in progress, and know how to do so?

3.2 ICT beyond schools

Much educational activity and learning now takes place in the digital world, with many pupils using learning platforms to store their work, respond to learning tasks, complete homework and communicate with their teacher and their peers (Sutherland, John and Robertson, 2007; Facer et al., 2003). There is, as Kress (2010, Reading 8.6) put it, a 'revolution in communication'.

Schools and the systems they operate within are relatively traditional places, and they are likely to be profoundly challenged by new screen-based technologies and access to social media. A strategic issue will be to develop through the adoption of controlled learning platforms or to branch out through the use of more open technologies and social media. Whilst the practical and technical issues are complex and uncertain given the rate of innovation, there clearly are massive potential opportunities from the use of new technologies.

With the increasing availability of smartphone and tablet computers, this engagement between the teacher's pedagogical intentions and the pupils' everyday activity on such devices at home and elsewhere is now generating enormous potential. The use of such devices – providing easy access to the internet, video and audio material, games for learning, applications with specific foci, social communication and e-books – contributes to the idea that their use for learning is 'natural', both in school and at home (Banister, 2004).

The consequence is a shift in emphasis here from 'teaching' to more informal learning, and from the product to the process of learning.

A note of caution concerning accessibility should be sounded here. Recent work (Grant, 2011; Jewitt and Parashar, 2011) has suggested that many pupils and parents see school and home as separate domains and significant numbers of pupils are unable to access technology at home. Boundary crossing homework may not be acceptable for some and could deepen inequalities for others. However, for low income families where the school has facilitated the introduction of ICT resources into the home, there is evidence of increased pupil time engaged in homework and independent learning, and pockets of increased parental engagement with their pupils' learning.

Expert question

Connection: does the curriculum engage with the cultural resources and funds-of-knowledge of families and the community?

This question contributes to a conceptual framework underpinning professional expertise (see Chapter 16).

4 Managing pupils and adults

The people in a classroom need to be organised and managed in ways which are most appropriate for supporting the learning activities which have been planned. This involves pupils, classroom assistants, other support staff, parents and carers, both in classrooms and through connections with informal learning at home.

4.1 Organising pupils

Our choices in organising pupils for teaching purposes must be made with regard to both pedagogical and practical considerations and with the over-riding principle of 'fitness for purpose'. Pedagogical considerations include the general aims of the teacher that inform classroom ethos and procedures, as well as any particular learning objectives for the task and pupils. Practical factors include the number of pupils, the size of the room and the availability of resources. A secondary school science laboratory, for example, is a very different working space to a primary classroom, and provides different affordances and constraints on the ways in which pupils might be organised for activities.

Here we set out the three basic organisational choices available to us – class work, group work and individual work – identifying the main characteristics of each. For further discussion of the pedagogic strategies associated with each of these three forms of organisation, see Chapter 11.

> ### Expert question
>
> **Repertoire:** is our pedagogic expertise sufficiently creative, skilled and wide-ranging to teach all elements of learning?
>
> This question contributes to a conceptual framework underpinning professional expertise (see Chapter 16).

Class work

This is the strong form of organisation for: starting and ending a lesson; giving out administrative instructions; introducing learning objectives, tasks and activities; the direct teaching of specific concepts and knowledge; demonstrating; and extending and reviewing work. Whole-class elements to lessons should be seen as part of the flexible repertoire that a teacher has with respect to pupil organisation, to be used as appropriate.

Whole-class activity is generally assumed to be teacher-centred, and what most whole-class activities have in common is that the teacher generally remains the focus of control. But there is a continuum of teacher dominance even when the whole class is involved in the same activity, and these sessions can be highly interactive (see, for example, Muijs and Reynolds, 2011, Reading 8.7). At one end of the continuum is the situation where the teacher talks and the pupils listen, take notes or copy from the board. At the other, the teacher may plan to give control of the activity to the pupils who may 'teach' by, for example, reporting what they have learned, demonstrating the result of an activity, offering solutions for problem-solving, discussing alternative or conflicting ideas, and asking questions.

These activities can create a sense of class identity and shared endeavour. Again, it is the teacher's pedagogic framework that will determine how whole-class elements of lessons proceed; some will encourage pupils' active participation in *all* elements of a lesson, whilst others may be reticent to do so.

Using whole-class organisational procedures may give the teacher a chance to teach the class more directly and economically than when working with groups. For instance, he or she may be able to stimulate pupils' thinking by sharing lesson objectives, exploring ideas, asking more 'probing' questions, modelling quality answers and supporting review, assessment and reflection on their learning. Hopkins et al. (2000) weigh the benefits of whole-class teaching and cooperative group work, considering just such ideas. However, class work can challenge both the teacher and the listener. It is difficult to match the instruction appropriately to pupils' differing needs. There is a tendency for teaching to be pitched at the 'middle', potentially failing those capable of more and those needing support. Whilst some believe that one of the strengths of whole-class teaching is that it 'pulls along' the less able, others recognise that engagement can be uneven, with some pupils 'opting out' even though they retain an apparent 'listening posture' (Cordon, 2000). Some pupils may be reluctant to face the risks involved in contributing to the whole class, whilst the ability of listeners to remain focused on one speaker is limited and affected both by the listeners' motivation and the speaker's skill. There is evidence of teachers addressing questions only to pupils in a V-shaped wedge in the centre of the room, or to particular groups or individuals (Wragg, 2000). An awareness of these potential difficulties should help teachers to tailor the length and nature of whole-class elements of lessons to the learning needs of their pupils.

Group work

Group work is often recommended for developing social and language skills and as a means by which pupils can support, challenge and extend their learning together, as in computer-based problem-solving (Wegerif and Dawes, 2004), work on a creative task or in subjects such as Design and Technology or Science where practical work is required. Group work can provide teachers with opportunities to observe pupils' learning more closely and, through questioning or providing information, to support them as they move forward. This approach draws particularly on social constructivist psychology (see Chapter 2 for a discussion of the theoretical understanding behind this approach).

Groups are likely to exist in some form in most classrooms. However, their form and function may vary considerably (Kutnick, Blatchford, and Baines, 2002; Baines et al., 2008; Kutnick, Ota, and Berdondini, 2008; see the **Research Briefing** in Chapter 11, p. 316). Five types of group work can be identified according to the purpose they are intended to serve:

- *Task groups*. The teacher decides on a group of pupils to work together on a particular task or learning objective. Pupils in the group may or may not normally sit or work together and are likely to be given specific group roles, such as recorder or researcher.

- *Teaching groups*. Groups can also be used for 'group teaching' purposes, where the teacher instructs pupils who are at the same stage, doing the same task, at the same time. This may be followed by the pupils working individually. Such a system can be an economical use of teacher instruction time and resources. The teaching may be directive or be based on a problem-solving activity.

- *Seating groups*. This is a very common form of grouping, where a number of pupils sit together around a table, usually in a four or six. Such an arrangement is flexible, allowing pupils to work individually and to socialise when appropriate. The central question for the teacher here is, 'if the pupils are not actually working together, is this arrangement beneficial to their learning?'

- *Collaborative groups*. This is used where there is a shared group aim, work is done together and the outcome is a combined product – perhaps in the form of a model, completed experiment, story or problem solved. Importantly, it involves pupils working and talking together, sharing their ideas and explaining their reasoning (Mercer and Littleton, 2007, Reading 11.6). The collaboration can also lead to a number of different outcomes from individuals or pairs.

- *Reciprocal teaching.* This form of collaboration occurs when pupils work in pairs, one taking the role of 'teacher partner', offering evaluation, and feedback. This approach is particularly evident in subjects like PE, drama and languages which involve 'performance'. The teacher supports by intervening to develop the quality of the evaluation and feedback.

Interestingly, genuinely collaborative group work is rather rare in schools (Galton, 2007); despite the fact that it is probably the most productive form of group work for learning, it requires rather more organisation on the part of the teacher than other forms of group work, together with a genuine commitment to the active involvement of pupils in their own learning. In particular, it is crucial that pupils share an understanding of the task and of the ground rules for their collaborative activity. These need to be explicit (Baines et al., 2008).

Reflective activity 8.7

Aim To consider the pros and cons of group working.

Evidence and reflection Either closely observe pupils working in groups in two lessons, or reflect on group work activities that you have initiated in your classroom over the last week. Use these questions as a starting point for your reflections:

- What were the successful elements of the group work?
- What was less successful?
- Can you identify why a particular group activity was successful or unsuccessful?
- What would you do differently next time?

Extension Had the pupils in the groups been guided and trained in how to work productively for learning in this way? Do you consider that this would have enhanced the group work?

Teachers have identified a number of problems associated with group work. Some appear concerned about motivating the pupils and helping them to recognise that being in a group is for the purposes of work rather than a chance to 'just have fun'. The monitoring of group work can also pose problems, especially if the group is intended to work collaboratively on their own without a teacher. And the management of groups, in terms of numbers, membership and workspaces, may pose dilemmas.

Identifying criteria by which groups may be formed may help to clarify some of the key issues. Possible criteria may include:

- *Age groups*. These are occasionally used as a convenient way of grouping for some activities. They are much less useful as a basis for specific teaching points because of the inevitable spread of attainment interests and needs.

- *Attainment groups*. Groups based on attainment levels can be useful for setting up specific and well-matched tasks; Hallam et al. (2002) discuss this issue in some depth. They are divisive if used as a permanent way of grouping.

- *Interest groups*. It is important to enable pupils with shared interests to work together from time to time. There may be particular advantages for the social cohesion of the class when pupils are of different attainment, sex, race, social class.

- *Friendship groups*. These provide opportunities for social development. Awareness of the needs of any isolated and marginal pupils is necessary, as is some attention to the possibility that friendship groups can set up divisive status hierarchies among the pupils, or reinforce stereotypes about gender, race or abilities.

Group work most frequently fails where pupils do not have a clear sense of purpose and appropriate skills to work together effectively. The work of the *Thinking Together* group shows that pupils have to be taught how to talk productively in groups, developing their capacity to use what Barnes (2008) and Mercer (2000) call 'exploratory talk' (see **thinkingtogether.educ.cam.ac.uk**).

Individual work

Whether or not pupils are *seated* in groups, they spend a great deal of classroom time working individually. They may be learning via tasks which require them to work alone or demonstrating the results of their learning in individual outcomes. Individual work is thought to be particularly useful for developing pupils' ability to work independently and autonomously.

Working individually may be the dominant mode in many lessons, but does not mean that the pupils are working without support. The teacher's role in supporting activity and scaffolding learning (van de Pol et al., 2010) is probably even more intense than it is when pupils are working in groups, but it does have the potential advantage that such support and scaffolding is targeted on the specific learning needs of an individual. As a result, it is likely to be highly productive for learning (see Chapter 12).

However, there are potential problems. A teacher who relies heavily on setting individual work in lessons may find that similar teaching points have to be explained on many separate occasions. An emphasis on working with each individual separately inevitably means that only a limited amount of time can be spent with any one pupil, and it has been shown that most of this time is spent monitoring pupils' work, rather than in developing their understanding (Galton et al., 1999). It is particularly important to think of individual work, as with whole-class work, as part of the repertoire of organisational alternatives open to a teacher at particular points in a lesson. So a teacher must ask themselves 'what am I hoping to achieve by getting the pupils to work individually at this point in the lesson? Is this the best form of organisation for the task, or for my intended outcomes?'

Professional judgement is essential in ensuring that, whatever organisational strategy is being considered – whole-class, group or individual – it is consistent with learning goals and evidence of effectiveness. Each approach within the teacher's repertoire has a different purpose and specific potential. Whilst each has its justifiable place in the classroom, they should be used to fulfil educational purposes.

We now go onto consider how teachers can liaise and work with other adults, including parents and support staff, in and beyond the classroom.

> **Expert question**
>
> **Reflection**: is our classroom practice based on incremental, evidence-informed and collaborative improvement strategies?
>
> This question contributes to a conceptual framework underpinning professional expertise (see Chapter 16).

4.2 Working with adults

Parents and carers

Involvement by parents and carers is particularly significant in work with young pupils, whilst their potential as 'expert contributors' and specialist helpers (such as with ICT) is embraced in many secondary schools. Whilst the most important support for learning offered by parents and carers is in the home (Harris et al., 2009), the educational benefits of home–school liaison are well documented.

Inspectors in England, in surveying schools of all types, found that, 'joint working between the home and the school led to much better outcomes for pupils' (Ofsted, 2011, p. 5). Examples of good practice included not only working in classrooms, but the institution of parent councils or forums. In general though, as Desforges with Abouchaar (2003) found eight years earlier, the various skills, qualifications, experience and insights of parents were found to be underused by schools; this was particularly the case in secondary schools.

A wide range of patterns of parental involvement exist, but we will identify three:

- *Parents as consumers*: receiving the services of the school but maintaining a discrete separation of parent and teacher responsibilities (e.g. where involvement is through formal parents' evenings, and other 'managed' school events).

- *Parents as resources*: providing a range of help, for example in support of the school or in providing direct assistance based upon their skills.

- *Parents as partners*: recognised as a partner in each pupil's all-round development, e.g. discussing the curriculum and each pupil's response; contributing as parent governors; having open access to the classroom and regular informal contacts with teachers (Crozier and Reay, 2005).

Expert question

Connection: does the curriculum engage with the cultural resources and funds-of-knowledge of families and the community?

This question contributes to a conceptual framework underpinning professional expertise (see Chapter 16).

If the interest and expertise of parents or carers is to be drawn on, perhaps three basic things need to be done. The first is to find time for adequate discussion with parents to find out what they have to offer and to help them engage with the school environment. The second is to think carefully about how they can be most educationally productive when they are in the school. Third, if parents and carers are to work in classrooms, it is necessary to negotiate clear ground rules on issues such as classroom roles, confidentiality and access to areas of the school such as the staff room. Finally, it is obviously crucial to discuss whether they will interact with their own child and, if so, what the ground rules will be.

It seems that parents and carers, teachers and pupils have mixed feelings on the question of parental involvement in classrooms. Pupils in one study expressed strong views about protecting the privacy of their home life and were against their parents coming into school (Edwards and Alldred, 2000). Some parents may feel anxious about working in a school because of their own 'bad' experiences of school; because they do not feel they have anything to offer the 'expert' teacher; or because they are unsure about how to relate to pupils in the school situation. Further, parents are often only available for short and specific periods of the day and may find it difficult to fit into school routines. Other parents may be resistant to approaches from a school or teacher, feeling that it is the teacher's job to do the teaching. Teachers may also have reservations, perhaps feeling vulnerable in case something happens in class which could undermine their status in the eyes of the parents; or having a more principled perspective that acknowledges parental help can become a socially divisive factor, giving greater advantages to comparatively advantaged middleclass pupils whose parents are most likely to participate in such schemes.

Despite such challenges, the clear message is that the creation of stronger partnerships between home and school are likely to be of considerable advantage to pupils' learning.

Support staff

The number of support staff in schools has increased considerably throughout the UK. For example, in 2011, 43 per cent of the mainstream school workforce in England was comprised of support staff, with over half being teaching assistants (TAs). Their duties were wide-ranging. Some 'Higher Level Teaching Assistants' regularly take over a full teaching role during teachers' planning, preparation and assessment time, and are involved in staff meetings and staff training. Many support staff are involved in other 'teaching-related' activities, for example recording pupils' progress and contributing to the assessment of pupils' work. Assistants, whatever their title, are often involved in working with pupils with learning and behaviour difficulties.

In this context, Blatchford et al. (2011) assessed the impact of teaching assistants and their role in the English education system. Their conclusions are pertinent both nationally and internationally. When looking at results for 8,200 pupils over the five years to 2011, the authors found that, despite much innovative and effective practice, pupils who received the most support from TAs consistently made *less* progress than similar pupils who received less TA support. They argue that this is fundamentally a question of how TAs are used and prepared for their work, rather than any fault of the TAs themselves. They note 'a drift toward teaching assistants becoming, in effect, the primary educators of lower-attaining pupils and those with special educational needs', and state that 'the more support pupils get from TAs, the less they get from teachers', separating these pupils from the teacher and the curriculum. Thus, they state, 'it is perhaps unsurprising then that these pupils make less progress.'

It seems that what is important is the way in which the school and the individual classroom teacher handles relationships with support staff (Sood, 2005) and prepares them for their role in the classroom. In particular, Blatchford et al. (2011) note the nature and extent of the pedagogical role of the teaching assistant as being at the heart of whether they will be effective in supporting pupil learning. They suggest:

- TAs should not routinely support lower attaining pupils and those with Special Educational Needs (SEN);
- teachers should deploy TAs in ways that allow them to 'add value' to their own teaching;
- schools have a formal induction process for TAs;
- there should be more joint planning and feedback time for teachers and TAs.

It is particularly important for the individual teacher to note that the quality of classroom teaching and learning can be greatly enhanced if all the adults in a classroom plan together, so that they understand and carry out specific activities in a coordinated and coherent fashion. Certainly it is the case that that, whenever they are asked, teaching assistants of all kinds state that they greatly appreciate it when teachers work *with* them, sharing learning intentions and expectations of their classroom roles on a lesson by lesson basis (O'Brien and Garner, 2001). The skill and dedication of such support staff cannot be doubted, but their effective deployment in helping to promote pupils' learning is clearly the responsibility of the school and the class teacher.

Conclusion

In this chapter, two major points about learning spaces have been made.

First, all contexts and settings (whether directly experienced or virtual) provide conditions which influence learning. Some will enable learning to flourish, whilst others may inhibit such development. These differences in 'affordance' are similar to the patterns in any ecological context. So, when we organise our own classroom learning environments, we should consider the likely overall effect on our objective of supporting learning (Bransford et al., 1999, Reading 8.2).

Second, classrooms are far from being isolated entities. Rather, they are contextualised by many other influences on pupil lives. Among the most obvious are the school as a whole, the family and community. But these factors are also encompassed by wider cultural, economic, technological, social and political conditions.

Effective classroom organisation thus requires consideration of the physical environment, resources, technologies, structures, routines, processes and people that are intended to progress pupil learning. Such factors, as well as the organisation of pupils themselves, must be considered in relation to their capacity to enable or constrain learning.

Awareness of the range of influences on pupil learning and appropriate organisation of classroom provision is a hallmark of an expert teacher.

Key readings

Understanding of the conditions which enable learning, development and performance have been enhanced by ecological analyses which trace contextual influences. Classics are:

Baker, R. G. (1968) *Ecological Psychology: Concepts and Methods of Studying the Environment of Human Behaviour.* Stanford: Stanford University Press.

Bronfenbrenner, U. (1979) *The Ecology of Human Development: Experiments by Nature and Design.* Cambridge, MA: Harvard University Press. (Reading 8.1)

Influences on the development of children and young people have been extensively studied. A good summary is:

Corsaro, W. A. (2011) *The Sociology of Childhood.* London: SAGE.

There are many excellent studies of home–school relations:

Rogoff, B., Goodman Turkanis, C. and Bartlett, L. (2001) *Learning Together: Children and Adults in a School Community.* Oxford: Oxford University Press. (see also Reading 2.10)

Crozier, G. and Reay, D. (2005) *Activating Participation: Parents and Teachers Working Towards Partnership.* Stoke-on-Trent: Trentham.

As all practitioners know, circumstances vary in different classrooms and judgement
has to be applied to select appropriate forms of classroom organisation for the purposes
which the teacher has in mind. For insights into these challenges and opportunities, see:

Hopkins, D., Harris, A., Singleton, C. and Watts, R. (2000) *Creating the Conditions
for Teaching and Learning.* London: David Fulton.

Display within school and classroom environments can convey important messages. On
this, see:

Andrew-Power, K. and Gormley, C. (2009) *Display for Learning.* London:
Continuum (see also Reading 8.3)

The classic paper on the effective use of time in classrooms is:

Berliner, D. (1991). 'What's all the fuss about instructional time?', in M. Ben-Peretz
and R. Bromme (eds), *The Nature of Time in Schools: Theoretical Concepts,
Practitioner Perceptions*. New York: Teachers College Press. (Reading 8.4)

For more general guidance on classroom organisation in primary and in secondary
classrooms, see:

Dean, J. (2008) *Organising Learning in the Primary School Classroom.* London:
Routledge.

Mercier, C., Philpott, C. and Scott, H. (2012) *Professional Issues in Secondary
Teaching.* London: SAGE.

For insights into working with ICT across the curriculum, see:

Beauchamp, G. (2012) *ICT in the Primary School: From Pedagogy to Practice.*
Harlow: Pearson

Edwards, A. (2012) *New Technology and Education.* London: Continuum (Reading
8.5)

Sutherland, R., Robertson, S. and John, P. (2008) *Improving Classroom Learning with
ICT.* London: Routledge.

On the potential influence of technology and new media from beyond school, take a
look at:

Buckingham, D. and Willett, R. (eds) (2006) *Digital Generations: Children, Young
People and the New Media.* London: Routledge.

Facer, K. (2011) *Learning Futures: Education, Technology and Social Change.*
London: Routledge.   ·

Kress, K. (2012) *Literacy in the New Media Age.* London: Routledge. (see
Reading 8.6)

On interactive and dialogic teaching, see:

Mercer, N. and Hodgkinson, S. (2008) (eds) *Exploring Talk in School*. London: SAGE. (Reading 11.6)

Muijs, D. and Reynolds, D. (2011) *Effective Teaching: Evidence and Practice*. London: SAGE. (Reading 8.7)

For a practical introduction to effective group work, including consideration of issues related to ability grouping, see:

Baines, E., Blatchford, P. Kutnick, P., Chowne, A., Ota, C. and Berdondini, L. (2009) *Promoting Effective Groupwork in the Classroom*. London: Routledge. (TLRP **Research Briefing**, p. 316)

Ireson, J. and Hallam, S. (2001) *Ability Grouping in Education*. London: SAGE. (see also Reading 15.4)

On Teaching Assistants, Blatchford et al.'s study has powerful messages for classroom deployment, whilst Dillow records the experience of working in the role.

Blatchford, P., Russell, A. and Webster, R. (2011) *Reassessing the Impact of Teaching Assistants*. London: Routledge.

Dillow, C. (2010) *Supporting Stories: Being a Teaching Assistant*. Stoke-on-Trent: Trentham Press.

A powerful analysis of the design of learning environments is provided by:

Bransford, J., Brown, A. L., and Cocking, R. (eds) *How People Learn: Brain, Mind, Experience, and School*. Washington, DC: National Academy Press. (Reading 8.2)

reflectiveteaching.co.uk offers additional professional resources for this chapter. These may include *Further Reading*, illustrative *Reflective Activities*, useful *Web Links* and *Download Facilities* for diagrams, figures, checklists and activities.

part three

Teaching for learning

This part supports the development of practice across the three classic dimensions of teaching – curriculum, pedagogy and assessment.

Chapter 9 starts us off with a review of curricular aims and design principles, before progressing to a review of national curricula in the UK and the role of subject knowledge. 'Planning' (Chapter 10) puts these ideas into action and supports the development and evaluation of programmes of study, schemes of work and lesson plans.

Chapter 11 is offers ways of understanding the art, craft and science of pedagogy – and the development of a pedagogic repertoire. 'Communication' (Chapter 12) extends this with an introduction to the vital role of talking, listening, reading and writing across the curriculum. Perhaps the core instructional expertise of the teacher lies in the skill of dialogic teaching?

Finally, this part concludes by demonstrating how assessment can be tied into teaching and learning processes in very constructive ways (Chapter 13). In short, through principled strategies for sharing goals, pupil engagement, authentic feedback, self-assessment and responsive teaching, excellent progress in learning can be made.

Curriculum
What is to be taught and learned?

9

Introduction

The existence of national curricula is common across the world. Such provision ensures coverage of a particular range of knowledge, thus providing pupil entitlements and satisfying national aspirations. However, there is also awareness that centrally imposed requirements can inhibit local curricular adaption and, in particular, could stifle teacher innovation. A balance thus has to be struck.

In this chapter we introduce enduring concepts and principles of curriculum design on which innovation and curriculum development can be based. We thus hope to equip the reflective teacher for career-long engagement with curricular issues.

TLRP principles

Three principles are of particular relevance to this chapter on curricular requirements:

Effective teaching and learning equips learners for life in its broadest sense.
Learning should aim to help people to develop the intellectual, personal and social resources that will enable them to participate as active citizens, contribute to economic development and flourish as individuals in a diverse and changing society. This implies adopting a broad view of learning outcomes and ensuring that equity and social justice are taken seriously. (Principle 1)

Effective teaching and learning engages with valued forms of knowledge.
Teaching and learning should engage with the big ideas, facts, processes, language and narratives of subjects so that learners understand what constitutes quality and standards in particular disciplines. (Principle 2)

Effective teaching and learning demands consistent policy frameworks with support for teaching and learning as their primary focus. Policies at national, local and institutional levels need to recognise the fundamental importance of teaching and learning. They should be designed to create effective learning environments in which all learners can thrive. (Principle 10)

See Chapter 4

To begin, we briefly review three ways of thinking about 'curriculum'.

The official curriculum. This is the explicitly stated programme of learning, and will probably incorporate a national curriculum which has been endorsed by government. Such a course of study is likely to have three elements. First, there will be the intended curriculum content. This will have been consciously planned and, in many cases, will be specified in terms of subject syllabi – though the identification of integrative topics remains popular in primary education. Second, the official curriculum will normally require a particular sequence and progression, thus framing the content into scheduled programmes of study. Third, courses and other provision will be designed with the intention of challenging pupils appropriately and of enabling achievements to be recorded by teacher assessment, test or examination. For example, as we will see in more detail later, for many years national curricula within the UK have been structured by Key Stage programmes of study for core and foundation subjects in combination with attainment targets for particular 'levels', national assessment and examination requirements. However, things do change. Whilst it has sometimes been hard to introduce curriculum activities to reflect school and community priorities, this is now explicitly encouraged across the UK. In England at the time of writing, radical changes to assessment requirements are also proposed, including abandoning use of 'levels'. The official school curriculum thus reflects a historically specific combination of national requirements and local commitments and decisions.

The hidden curriculum. This concept focuses attention on tacit learning during schooling. It highlights how children and young people come to understand such things as teacher and pupil roles and attitudes towards learning and schooling. Children may also acquire ideas about the ways boys or girls 'should' behave, or about differences 'because' of being black or white, middle class or working-class. Such ideas reflect the way in which values are conveyed through the interaction and language associated with teaching and learning processes. The hidden curriculum is thus implicit within regular school procedures and curriculum materials, and can exert a powerful influence on pupils through its influence on self-image and expectations (see Jackson, 1968, Reading 6.1 for a classic study).

The experienced curriculum. This way of conceptualising the curriculum draws attention to the parts of the curriculum, both official and hidden, which connect most meaningfully with children and young learners. Adults can plan all they like, and do so with the best of intentions, but what sense do learners actually make of this provision? Arguably, it is this experienced curriculum that has the most educational impact. Thinking about curricular provision from the perspectives of a deliberately wide range of learners is a helpful check when we review our planning, whether it is for a single lesson, series of lessons or even for a whole school.

The 'school curriculum', when seen as a whole, is thus considerably more than an aggregation of lessons. It is the totality of the substantive provision and experience offered to pupils, as Male and Waters demonstrate (2012, Reading 9.1).

1 Principles for curriculum provision

1.1 Knowledge, development and curriculum

The educational role of curricular provision relates to three basic, enduring considerations. They are fundamental to all curricular deliberation:

- the *nature of knowledge*
- the *needs of learners*, and crucially
- the *interactions* between them.

These elements were highlighted in the first chapter of an Expert Panel report on England's National Curriculum (DfE, 2011). An edited version is reproduced below:

> Subject knowledge can be seen as representing the accumulated experience of the past and a representation of this for the future. The concepts, facts, processes, language, narratives and conventions of each subject constitute socially refined forms of knowledge – knowledge that is regarded as 'powerful' in our society (Young, 2008, Reading 9.2). Established knowledge is highly codified, with disciplines, associations, professions and specialist institutions. Many contemporary bodies of knowledge are more mobile, with innovation and change being characteristic features.
>
> However, education is also about the development of individual learners – in schools, as pupils. There are many dimensions to such development including the personal, social and emotional as well as the physical, neurological and cognitive. For young children in particular, such factors are of great significance because they provide the foundation for learning. The significance of the development of individuals over time has increasingly been recognised in recent years. Longitudinal research has demonstrated the lasting consequences of high-quality early learning experiences (Sylva et al., 2001) and a Foresight Report (Feinstein et al., 2008, Reading 1.6) affirms the trajectories of 'learning through life' and the economic and wider benefits of such learning.

> Education can thus be seen, at its simplest, as the product of interaction between socially valued knowledge and individual development. It occurs through learner experience of both of these key elements. Education, through the school curriculum, mediates and structures these processes. The core expertise of teachers is to reach between and facilitate a productive interaction of knowledge and development. As James and Pollard (2012) put it, effective teaching 'engages with valued forms of knowledge' and also 'equips learners for life in its broadest sense' .
>
> Some people emphasise subject knowledge and discount the significance of more developmental aspects of education. And there are also many who foreground the development of skills, competencies and dispositions whilst asserting that contemporary knowledge changes so fast that 'learning how to learn' is all that is necessary. But these are unhelpful polarisations, for it is impossible to conceptualise 'learning to learn' except in relation to some substantive purpose. Our position is therefore that *both* elements – knowledge and development – are essential considerations in relation to curricular provision.
>
> The two elements are not, however, equally significant at every age. In particular, developmental aspects and basic skills are more crucial for young children, while appropriate understanding of more differentiated subject knowledge, concepts and skills becomes more important for older pupils. Curricular provision for early years, primary, secondary and further education is thus distinct, although the underlying issues endure.

This argument is represented in Figure 9.1 overleaf, and the TLRP principles are further discussed in Chapter 4 of this book:

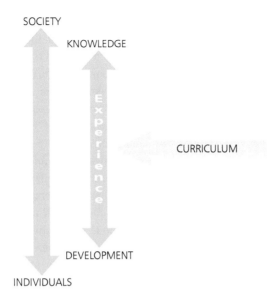

Figure 9.1
Education: the
interaction of
knowledge,
development and
curriculum

1.2 Aims and values

When creating, adapting or implementing a curriculum, or any element within it, it is crucial to be very clear about the purposes the provision is expected to serve.

At a high level, legislation may define overall educational goals. For example, in England, Section 78 of the Education Act 2002 states that school curriculum should be 'balanced and broadly based' and should:

> promote the spiritual, moral, cultural, mental and physical development of pupils at the school and of society, and prepare pupils at the school for the opportunities, responsibilities and experiences of later life.

This is a foundational statement for consideration of the school curriculum as a whole and represents value commitments about the nature of an appropriate 'education' which can be traced back to at least the 1944 Education Act. Similar high level statements set expectations for the curricular frameworks in Scotland, Wales, Northern Ireland, and can be found in many countries internationally including the Republic of Ireland. They are essentially ethical, moral and political statements, which make transparent the values and ambitions to which a nation aspires.

Historical study and international comparison (Meyer et al., 1992; National Foundation for Educational Research, 2011) reveal some common themes in relation to what can broadly be termed social, economic, personal, cultural

Expert questions

Breadth: does the curriculum represent society's educational aspirations for its citizens?

Balance: does the curriculum-as-experienced offer everything which each learner has a right to expect?

These questions contribute to a conceptual framework underpinning professional expertise (see Chapter 16).

and environmental goals. This can also be illustrated by comparison of the educational aims proposed within four sectoral reviews from England (see over).

The representation in Figure 9.2 risks over-simplification, but does demonstrate some key points. First, it suggests that knowledge and skill, developed in age-appropriate ways, are of enduring importance in satisfying social and economic goals in all sectors. Of course, these are always prominent concerns for policy-makers, industry and the media. Second, there is also a very strong emphasis on personal development in all sectors, which is often a particular commitment for parents and educationalists. The table also shows the awareness which exists about citizenship during schooling and it suggests that environmental concern is emerging. In the case of the early years, the particular importance of personal goals is further asserted by identifying 'prime' (italicised) and 'other' areas for learning. Such factors remain crucial in 'primary' education but gradually give way to 'secondary' education's need to focus on knowledge and skill in preparation for formal examinations and the social and economic demands of the workplace.

In whatever sector or circumstance one works, it is appropriate for reflective teachers, schools and their stakeholders to deliberate on educational purposes on a regular basis. Whilst positions on social, economic, personal, cultural and environmental issues might be expected, the particular priorities, expression and provision should reflect the values, judgement, debate and resolution of each school community. In this way, specific *connections* can be created to the culture and aspirations of those served by each school (see also Chapter 10).

The outcomes of such deliberation on purposes should, of course, be published on websites and in school brochures. After all, the outcomes of education are of enormous significance and learners of any age, and their parents or carers too, have a right to expect that teachers will approach their work from a considered and morally justifiable position.

Further, without such clarity, it is not possible for a fully *coherent* and holistic curriculum to be offered (see Chapter 10) or for appropriately aligned and *congruent* assessment practices to be developed (see Chapters 13 and 14).

This brings us to the level of detailed application, where educational aims are chased through school policies and into specific programmes of study, lessons and everyday provision. This is likely to be of particular interest to student teachers too, and is considered in some detail in Chapter 10. As we will see there, the existence of clarity and transparency in educational goals makes it more likely that intentions will be communicated to learners – and there is mounting international evidence that this

Figure 9.2 A comparison of educational aims across sectors in England

	Expert Panel Report for the National Curriculum Review (DfE, 2011)	Early Years Review (Tickell, 2011)	Cambridge Primary Review (Alexander, 2010)	Nuffield 14–19 Review (Pring et al., 2009)
Social and Economic	Provide opportunities for participation in a broad range of educational experiences and the acquisition of knowledge and appreciation in the arts, sciences and humanities, and of high-quality academic and vocational qualifications Satisfy future economic needs for individuals and for the workforce as a whole, including the development of secure knowledge and skills in communication, literacy and mathematics and confidence in acquiring new knowledge and skills	Communication and language Expressive arts and design Mathematics Understanding the world	Exploring, knowing, understanding and making sense Fostering skill	Knowledge and understanding Practical capabilities
Personal	Support personal development and empowerment so that each pupil is able to develop as a healthy, balanced and self-confident individual and fulfil their educational potential	Personal, social and emotional development Physical development	Wellbeing Engagement Empowerment Autonomy	Personal fulfilment Moral seriousness
Cultural	Appreciate national cultures, traditions and values, whilst recognising diversity and encouraging responsible citizenship		Empowering local, national and global citizenship Celebrating culture and community	Community relatedness
Environmental	Promote understanding of sustainability in the stewardship of resources locally, nationally and globally		Promoting interdependence and sustainability	

is reflected in enhanced outcomes. Indeed, clarity informs evaluative review of provision and increases accountability.

Reflective activity 9.1

Aim: To examine statements of aims and values presented in National Curriculum and school documentation.

Evidence and reflection: Are aims and values explicitly stated within the National Curriculum and school documentation at your disposal?

If so, are the aims consistently supported by the stated underlying values? What vision of education do you derive from reading these statements?

If not, can you derive some of the core aims and values from an examination of the curriculum advice presented in the documentation?

Extension: How do the aims, values and vision connect with the particular communities that the school serves? To what extent do the explicit or implicit aims and values reflect your own views of what should inform an appropriate school curriculum? Is there anything missing? Is there anything that shouldn't be there? Why?

---

2 Elements of learning

This section discusses the building blocks of a curriculum for learning – knowledge, concepts, skills and attitudes. This framework derives from Her Majesty's Inspectorate (HMI) (1985, Reading 10.1) whose classic booklet, *The Curriculum for 5 to 16*, was designed to encourage and refine professional discussion of curriculum matters. They introduced the four elements in the following terms:

Knowledge: Selections of that which is worth knowing and of interest. As HMI put it: 'The criteria for selecting content should be in the aims and objectives which a school sets for itself. That which is taught should be worth knowing, comprehensible, capable of sustaining pupils' interest and useful to them at their particular stage of development and in the future'.

Concepts: The 'big ideas' which inform a subject, or generalisations which enable pupils to classify, organise and predict – to understand patterns, relationships and meanings, e.g. flow, change, consequence, temperature, refraction, power, energy.

Skills: The capacity or competence to perform a task, e.g. personal/social (listening, collaborating, reflecting), physical/practical (running, writing, cutting), intellectual (observing, reasoning, imagining), communication (oracy, literacy, numeracy), etc.

Attitudes: The overt expression of values and personal qualities, e.g. reliability, initiative, self-discipline, tolerance, resilience, resourcefulness, etc.

2.1 Knowledge

Understandings about the nature of knowledge underpin all curricula. Three basic positions are well established – with roots back to the philosophy, psychology and sociology of education.

1 There are those who argue that particular 'forms of knowledge' exist. These are thought to be distinguishable, philosophically, by the different ways of thinking and kinds of evidence which are employed in investigating them (Hirst, 1965; Peters, 1966). These forms are thought to be based on *a priori* differences, i.e. logical and inherent differences. Such a view has been referred to as 'rationalist' (Blenkin and Kelly, 1981) and is often used to legitimate traditional curriculum subjects (Wilson, 2000, Reading 9.3).

2 There are those who emphasise the ways in which knowledge is socially constructed, and learned, by individuals and groups in interaction together and with their environment, and by successively restructuring their understanding through these experiences (Berger and Luckman, 1967, Light and Littleton, 1999). This view has resonance with the psychology of Piaget, Vygotsky and Bruner (see Chapter 2 and Readings 2.2, 2.3 and 9.5).

3 Knowledge can be seen in sociological terms as being defined by powerful groups who define certain types of understanding as being important or of high status. They may attempt to control access to some forms of knowledge, particularly those associated with power (Young, 1971; Bernstein, 1971), but they may also try to insist on the exposure of pupils to particular forms of knowledge which are deemed appropriate.

Of course, these views of knowledge are not discrete and any one person's perspective may draw on several of them, or even on them all. Michael Young (2013, Reading 9.2) makes an important distinction between 'powerful knowledge' (see position 1 above) and 'knowledge of the powerful' (position 3 above). The former is associated with specialist understanding which is capable of application in a wide variety of contexts. He argues that providing access to such powerful knowledge is the main purpose of schooling, whilst knowledge of the powerful must sometimes be challenged in democratic, egalitarian societies.

The important point is that the different emphasis which is placed on particular views of knowledge tends to reflect social values, and these *can* and often *do* influence the structure and content of the curriculum.

A recent manifestation of such debates arose through a National Curriculum Review in England between 2011/13. Government Ministers were particularly influenced by the 'core knowledge curriculum' of E. D. Hirsch (1987), an American scholar. This sets out a specified sequence of topics to teach in each subject and promises thereby to enhance both standards and opportunities. Incremental progression was anticipated based on the logic of each subject, research and experience of typical learning sequences and comparison with the ordering of knowledge in successful jurisdictions internationally. The policy was caricatured in terms of proposing 'regurgitation of facts – as in the 1950s'. In an extreme form, such subject specification does indeed risk constraining the capacity of teachers to respond to specific pupil needs through the exercise of professional judgement. On the other hand, there is no doubt that, as TLRP's Principle 2 states, 'effective pedagogy engages with valued forms of knowledge' (see Chapter 4). To do this successfully, expert teachers do have to master the content of each subject and consider the learning challenges associated with that domain, but they must also understand the specific needs and circumstances of their pupils and feel empowered to use their expertise to design appropriate classroom tasks and activities. From Singapore we know that, 'the highest quality of teaching occurs when there is a focus on the intellectual quality of the instructional and assessment tasks that students are asked to work on' (Hogan, 2012, Reading 4.2). As we saw in Chapter 4, this position is confirmed by much international research and it reaffirms the necessary interaction between knowledge and development with which this chapter began. Neither one, nor the other, can stand alone. In Scotland's *Curriculum for Excellence*, this is recognised through the consideration of curriculum subjects in terms of 'experiences and outcomes'.

Reflective activity 9.2

Aim: To consider the influence of views of knowledge on a part of a national or school curriculum.

Evidence and reflection: This is a potentially large activity which needs to be made specific to keep it within bounds. We suggest that national or school documentation for a *single* subject is selected for study – history or geography may be good choices.

Consider, how is knowledge viewed? To what extent is it seen as an established body of subject content and skills to be transferred to learners, and to what extent is knowledge seen as something to be created through experiential engagement in tasks and activities? Can you see opportunities for synergies between these approaches?

Extension: Is this view of knowledge consistent with the aims and values of the curriculum that you investigated in Reflective activity 8.1?

Expert question

Progression: does the curriculum-as-delivered provide an appropriate sequence and depth of learning experiences?

This question contributes to a conceptual framework underpinning professional expertise (see Chapter 16).

Notwithstanding debates on how subject knowledge is actually used, a high degree of consistency has been established on the ways in which subjects provide the organisational frameworks for national curriculum requirements in countries round the world. In reviewing the comparative work of Meyer and Kamens (1992), Ross (2001) suggests that 'local variations have been ironed out as a pattern of international conformity has prevailed' (p. 129). Ross indicates that national curricula generally feature the following subjects: one or more national languages; mathematics; science; some form of social science; and aesthetic education in some form, though this is less firmly established than the other four areas. A contemporary archive on international curriculum and assessment frameworks is hosted by National Foundation for Educational Research (NFER) and confirms the breadth and subject-based organisation of knowledge in countries around the world (see **inca.org.uk**).

This however, as we will see in due course, says little about the ways in which the curriculum of a school or classroom can or should actually be presented to pupils and many variations emerge at the level of practice (Alexander, 2008, Reading 12.3).

2.2 Concepts

Concepts enable the most important ideas and deep structure of knowledge and understanding in each subject to be presented in concise ways. This avoids long lists of curriculum content which sometimes bedevil attempts to represent a subject domain, and which can seem overwhelming to both teachers and pupils.

For example, in 2012 the Geographical Association proposed a curriculum for schools based on 'thinking geographically'. As they put it:

> A few large, organising concepts underlie a geographical way of investigating and understanding the world. These are high level ideas that can be applied across the subject to identify a question, guide an investigation, organise information, suggest an explanation or assist decision making. They are the key ideas involved in framing the unique contribution of geography as a subject discipline. The three main organising concepts for geography are place, space and environment. There are further basic ideas in geography that run across this overarching framework, such as connection, inter-relation, scale and change. Using these ideas carefully and accurately is a key component of what we mean by thinking geographically. (Geographical Association, 2012)

Such 'big ideas' reveal the powerful analytic core of subject disciplines. The potential of concepts in designing curriculum provision was specifically identified by Schools Council projects during the 1970s and early 1980s. For example, Elliott (1976) made the case in terms of:

> *The information explosion* – which generates new facts at such a rate that it is futile to try to keep up. An alternative is thus to select facts to support conceptual development.

> *Concepts for learning* – for new situations are rarely entirely novel and we are able to use our store of conceptual understanding to interpret and make sense of new experiences.

> *Concepts as organisers* – because they 'provide a map of knowledge' which break down the randomness of experience and enable us to understand it.

> *Concepts as anchorage points* – in providing stability for exploration of the subject and enabling cumulative understanding by learners.

Alan Blyth was one of the first serious researchers on primary education and emphasised the need to maintain the integrity of school subjects in the teaching of young children. This philosophy was realised through a number of curriculum development projects, with *Time, Place and Society 8–13* (Blyth et al., 1976) providing an outstanding example. In the case of this integrated humanities work, the key concepts were: communication; power; values and beliefs; conflict and consensus; continuity and change; similarity and difference; causes and consequences.

The work of the Association for Science Education provides another example. Their '*Principles and Big Ideas of Science Education*' (Harlen and Bell, 2010) provides comprehensive conceptual framework for teaching science and for curricular provision throughout schooling.

And the arts are, arguably, even better prepared for a conceptually-based curriculum through the legacy of analysis and connoisseurship which distinguishes quality. Music and art have conceptual languages accumulated over hundreds of years. In some cases, such powers of discrimination have been codified – as in the case of dance and movement where Rudolf Laban (1879–1958) developed an exceptional analysis based on the concepts of body, effort, shape and space.

Through the provision of a robust and valid framework of key concepts, it is thus possible to maintain the integrity of subjects and their parent disciplines in very concise ways. The subject associations, which are often sub-divided in relation to particular sectors, play an invaluable role here.

Beyond the significance of concepts as a useful device in the toolkit of curriculum planning and provision, they really earn their place because of their capacity to illuminate and render accessible the deep structure of subject knowledge. This point has been made by scholars focusing from early years and through to higher education. Thus Aubrey (1994), in a classic collection of papers on the role of subject knowledge in the early years of schooling, emphasised 'the ways in which subject knowledge is acquired and the organisation of teaching to promote the learner's construction of meaning'. Recent research in higher education, such as that by Entwistle (2009) has documented 'ways of thinking and practising in the subject' (WTPS) and the development of 'deep under-standing' through making transparent the conceptual frameworks of each discipline. 'Threshold concepts', which unlock disciplinary understanding, have been identified, as have the barriers posed by forms of 'troublesome knowledge' (Meyer and Land, 2008).

Nor should we perhaps fail to notice that this book on reflective teaching is itself explicit in offering a set of principles (Chapter 4) and a conceptual framework (Chapter 16) in an attempt to support deep understanding of teaching. Whilst providing practical guidance on 'how to survive in the classroom', the book also aspires to support professional analysis and the development of expertise throughout a career.

Concepts then, to return to HMI's definition, enable learners to classify, organise and predict – and to understand patterns, relationships and meanings within subjects. They are epistemological tools in support of high-quality, authentic learning.

2.3 Skills

Put simply, a skill is 'the capacity or competence to perform a task' (HMI, 1985, p. 38) but in the context of curriculum planning, use of the term has become more complex. Several uses can be identified:

'Physical skills' normally refers to bodily coordination such as running, catching, etc., and to fine motor skills such as writing, sewing, drawing or typing,

'Basic skills' usually refers to communication, literacy and numeracy, and sometimes includes the use of technology.

'Personal skills' is the most fundamental and typically includes capabilities such as self-awareness, reflection, thinking and problem solving; as well as interpersonal awareness, cooperation and leadership with others. 'Thinking skills' are discussed in Chapter 2.

'Study skills' tends to be a specific set of capabilities focused on managing one's own learning, such as observing, interpreting, classifying, memorising, prioritising.

'Subject skills' highlights particular capabilities required for learning in subject domains, such as mapping in geography, experimenting in science and empathising in drama.

'Vocational skills' identifies requirements for particular avenues of potential employment and career, such as nursing, business, computer programming, farming, etc.

Although skills identified in these classifications often overlap, the salient point is that there are sets of capabilities which complement and extend a curriculum which is expressed in terms of subject knowledge. An innovative contemporary project on this is that of *Opening Minds* promoted by the Royal Society of Arts. This competence framework focuses on citizenship, learning, relating to people, managing situations and managing information and 'emphasises the ability to understand and to do, rather than just the transmission of knowledge'.

One way of thinking about this is in terms of a classic distinction between declarative knowledge and procedural knowledge. If the former sets out that which is known, the latter describes how it is developed and used. This distinction between 'knowing that' and 'knowing how' was drawn by Gilbert Ryle (1945). His argument asserts the significance of skills, procedures and learning activities in the development of knowledge. He also shows how, in terms of moving beyond the dry recitation of facts towards application and relevance to life, capabilities to apply knowledge are vital. There is no doubt then, that skills provide a distinct and valuable element of curriculum provision.

However, as we have seen, bodies of knowledge and associated conceptual tools represent the accumulated understanding of our societies and therefore demand attention. Skills alone therefore, are unlikely to justify presentation as a complete curriculum. But skills add enormous value to engagement with subjects. Indeed, they support the development of subject knowledge, are realised through it and contribute to its transfer and application into practice.

Systematic and embedded provision for skill development is thus a vital element of learning within any curriculum. It is often planned for and reviewed in cross-curricular terms, and such provision can be made at classroom, school or national levels – and most helpfully at all three.

When the National Curriculum was first introduced in England, the National Curriculum Council (NCC) published guidance on *The Whole Curriculum* (NCC, 1990) which drew teachers' attention to cross-curricular dimensions, skills and themes. More recently in Wales, the *Skills Framework for 3–19 Year-olds* (Welsh Assembly Government, 2008, Reading 10.5) updates this approach for a twenty-first century curriculum. Scotland's *Curriculum for Excellence* also provides a carefully developed skills framework offering 'Skills for Learning, Skills for Life and Skills for Work' (Scottish Government, 2009). Figure 9.3, below, illustrates the four 'capacities' which have been conceptualised and prioritised in Scotland. There is strong emphasis on the responsibilities of *all* educators to support such learning through all sectors and a framework of National Qualifications offers accreditation.

Figure 9.3 The four capacities of Scotland's *Curriculum for Excellence*

Successful learners

with
- enthusiasm and motivation for learning
- determination to reach high standards of achievement
- openness to new thinking and ideas

and able to
- use literacy, communication and numeracy skills
- use technology for learning
- think creatively and independently learn independently and as part of a group
- make reasoned evaluations
- link and apply different kinds of learning in new situations

Confident individuals

with
- self-respect
- a sense of physical, mental and emotional well-being
- secure values and beliefs

and able to
- relate to others and manage ourselves
- pursue a healthy and active lifestyle
- be self-aware
- develop and communicate their own beliefs and view of the world
- live as independently as they can
- assess risk and take informed decisions
- achieve success in different areas of activity

To enable all young people to become

Responsible citizens

with
- respect for others
- commitment to participate respons- ibly in political, economic, social and cultural life

and able to
- develop knowledge and understanding of the world and Scotland's place in it
- understand different beliefs and cultures
- make informed choices and decisions
- evaluate environmental, scientific and technological issues
- develop informed, ethical views of complex issues

Effective contributions

with
- an enterprising attitude
- resilience
- self-reliance

and able to
- communicate in different ways and in different settings
- work in partnership and in terms
- take the initiative and lead
- apply critical thinking in new contexts
- create and develop
- solve problems

2.4 Attitudes

Attitudes were regarded by HMI as 'the overt expression, in a variety of situations, of values and personal qualities' (1985, p. 41). Examples given were honesty, reliability, initiative, self-discipline and tolerance which 'may be encouraged in the formal curriculum and the informal, and in the general life of the school'. Clearly, this affirms the significance of the 'hidden curriculum' to which we drew attention at the beginning of this chapter. Indeed, the process of induction of the young into the values of their society has always been one of the classic roles of schools.

In recent years, there has been particular awareness of citizenship – as reflected in our earlier discussion of educational aims. Attitudes to health, exercise and diet have been prominent too, and it is predictable that pressure will grow for schools to introduce children and young people to issues concerning environmental sustainability. Specific values and priorities thus reflect particular social, cultural and economic priorities. Over the years of a teacher's career, these will ebb and flow with changing governments and social norms. They may also vary depending on the particular circumstances and ambitions of the communities which a school serves, thus enabling local variation.

This brings us back to the issues raised in Chapter 2, Section 3.1). There, we saw how culture and language frame the interpretation of experience, and how attitudes are influenced by family, community, peers, school and the media. The overall effect is that children and young people form, or are socialised into adopting, attitudes which reflect the influence of significant others in their lives.

HMI also emphasised that schools should 'seek to promote positive attitudes through the attention they give to content and method' (1985, p. 41). Here we begin to focus on the educational issues which, in contemporary terms, might be termed 'dispositions to learn'. There is, after all, probably nothing more important for lifelong learning than the confidence of learners in tackling new learning challenges. In Chapter 2, again, we saw how important it is for learners to believe in their potential to learn and to improve – to adopt an 'incremental' theory of their own capability, as Dweck (1986, Reading 2.6) put it (see p. 51).

Claxton has cogently argued that it is possible to 'build learning power' in schools by nurturing attributes such as resilience, resourcefulness, reflection and reciprocity (Claxton, 2002, Reading 2.9; 2011). As he puts it:

- *Resilience* covers aspects of the learner's emotional and experiential engagement with the subject matter of learning.

- *Resourcefulness* embraces the main cognitive skills and dispositions of learning.

- *Reciprocity* covers the social and interpersonal side of learning.

- *Reflectiveness* covers the strategic and self-managing sides of learning. (Claxton et al., 2011, p. 40)

Through such careful attention to learning itself, a 'supple learning mind' can be created (see Figure 9.4 overleaf).

Figure 9.4
The supple
learning mind
(from Claxton et
al., 2011)

The Supple Learning Mind

Reflectiveness

- Planning: working learning out in advance
- Revising: monitoring and adapting along the way
- Distilling: drawing out the lessons from experience
- Meta-learning: understanding learning, and yourself as a learner

Reciprocity

- Interdependence: balancing self-reliance and sociability
- Collaboration: the skills of learning with others
- Listening/Empathy: getting inside others' minds
- Imitation: picking up others' habits and values

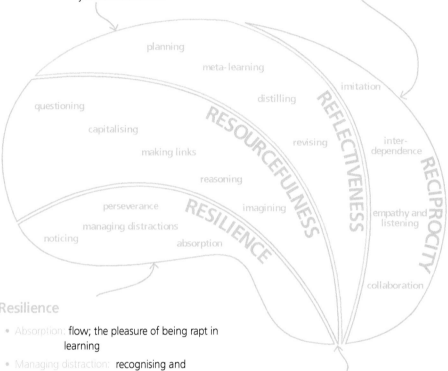

Resilience

- Absorption: flow; the pleasure of being rapt in learning
- Managing distraction: recognising and reducing interruptions
- Noticing: really sensing what's out there
- Perseverance: stickability; tolerating the feelings of learning

Resourcefulness

- Questioning: getting below the surface; playing with situations
- Making links: seeking coherence, relevance and meaning
- Imagining: using the mind's eye as a learning theatre
- Reasoning: thinking rigorously and methodically
- Capitalising: making good use of resources

These attributes are closely associated with 'learning how to learn' (James et al., 2007, Reading 2.8) and are viewed by many as being essential for learning in the twenty-first century. For example, the *2020 Vision* report for the DfES in England (Teaching and Learning Review Group, 2006, Reading 10.7), anticipated the necessary characteristics of future teaching and aspired to 'design a new school experience'. Key elements were identified as Personalisation, assessment for learning, learning how to learn, pupil voice and engaging parents and carers in their children's education. Underpinning all this was a commitment to pupil engagement in a meaningful curriculum and authentic learning for life.

> ## Expert question
>
> **Engagement:** do our teaching strategies, classroom organisation and consultation enable learners to actively participate in and enjoy their learning?
>
> This question contributes to a conceptual framework underpinning professional expertise (see Chapter 16).

2.5 A balanced curriculum

The analytic power of the distinction between knowledge, concepts, skills and attitudes is particularly useful in curriculum design. A rounded curriculum will provide balance between them, ensuring that each has its place. This is important for those who frame national curricular frameworks, but it is also an enormous help in the creation of the School Curriculum and in terms of classroom provision.

Reflective activity 9.3 suggests a way of mapping the elements of learning within an area of curriculum provision.

Reflective activity 9.3

Aim: To consider knowledge, concepts, skills and attitudes in schemes of work.

Method: Select topics within a programme of study in a subject area. Working on your own or preferably with a colleague, identify and list the knowledge, concepts, skills and attitudes which are targeted for development.

TOPICS	Knowledge	Concepts	Skills	Attitudes

Follow-up: How easy was it to identify elements in the four categories? Which were explicit, and which implicit?

Has the activity led you to refine or extend your plans? How could the framework be used to take stock of pupil learning in your classroom?

---

3 National curricula

Structured national curricula have many attractions. For example:

Aims and objectives for each stage of education can clarify what both pupils and teachers are expected to do (see Section 1.2 above)

Curriculum breadth and balance can be considered 'as a whole' (see Chapter 10).

Curriculum progression and continuity can be planned and monitored both from class to class and on transfer between schools (see also Chapter 10).

Training and professional development programmes for teachers can be tailored to known National Curriculum needs (see Chapter 17).

Resources for teaching and learning programmes can be developed on a large scale and in organised, cost-effective ways (see Chapter 8).

Assessment and inspection systems can be used to reinforce intentions (see Chapter 14).

Parents, employers and other stakeholders have the opportunity to know and understand what is being taught and may be able to offer support more effectively (see Chapter 5).

Coherence, alignment and improvement of the system as a whole can be developed through evaluation processes, research and refinement (see Chapter 4).

However, there are a number of dilemmas in the design of national curricula. For example, how should the value of coherence and progression in subject knowledge be compared with the benefits of applied understanding through more integrated study or work focused on particular topics? How can a National Curriculum framework guarantee curricular entitlements and guide the work of teachers whilst also enabling them to exercise professional judgement when responding to particular learning needs?

These questions illustrate the challenge posed by two of TLRP's principles. Effective teaching and learning 'engages with valued forms of knowledge' (Principle 2), but it also 'recognises the importance of prior experience and learning' (Principle 3) (see Chapter 4).

3.1 UK curricular structures

Secondary education

When reviewing the curricula of each of the four countries of the UK, provision in secondary education is particularly variable because of differences in examination and certification arrangements, school, college and academy structures, links to vocational provision and employment, and changes in the duration of compulsory education and training. 'Valued forms of knowledge' reflect national circumstances, government priorities and school choices to a considerable extent – for example, at the time of writing, newly established academies and free schools in England are not formally required to follow National Curriculum requirements.

Across the UK, differences in examination and award structures appears to be growing. The distinctiveness of Scotland's 'Highers' is now joined by new, 'more rigorous' GCSEs to be progressively introduced in England from 2014. It may be necessary to adjust provision in Wales and Northern Ireland if comparability is sought. AS levels have been deemed equivalent to Scottish Highers, but are to be abolished in England. A levels remain in England, Wales and Northern Ireland, with a growing influence of universities on their content. Many vocational qualifications in England are no longer accredited (see section 3.4 below) and in Scotland, Wales and Northern Ireland reviews continue.

Debate concerning optimal transitions points contributes to instability in some national qualification structures. For example, from 2015, young people in England will remain in full-time education or training to age 18, though statutory assessment through GCSEs is to age 16. Kenneth Baker (2013), a former Secretary of State for Education, makes a strong case for the National Curriculum to end with a new qualification at age 14, with a 'new vision' of more diverse courses to meet particular needs from 14–18. English education is, he argues, 'fixated' on exams at age 16.

However, GCSEs have been extremely important and have demonstrated steadily improved pupil outcomes. For example, in England's 1997 results, only 36 per cent of pupils achieved five or more A–C GCSEs including English and Maths, but this exceeded 50 per cent by 2011. The 'English Baccalaureate' was introduced in 2010 as a way of recognising the traditional 'academic' curriculum in school league tables (the proportions of pupils attaining GCSE grade C or better in English, maths, a language, history or geography, and two sciences). However, from 2014, secondary schools in England will report on GCSE performance of pupils in English and mathematics and must publish a 'progress measure' indicating pupils' achievement across eight subjects (including EBacc, other academic, arts or vocational).

Policy on these issues develops continuously and, for updated information, please consult **reflectiveteaching.co.uk**.

Primary education

In relation to primary education, there is a little more stability and rather more similarities in UK systems – as there are around the world (Meyer and Kamens, 1992; DfE, 2011).

In Figure 9.5 it can be seen that subject areas and cross-curricular skills show remarkable consistency. In each country, the primacy of 'basic capability' in literacy and numeracy is emphasised. However, this is done in interestingly different ways.

Figure 9.5 UK curricula structures for primary education (2012)

ENGLAND	WALES	NORTHERN IRELAND	SCOTLAND
'Subjects'	**'Subjects'**	**'Areas of Learning'**	**'Curricular Areas'**
ENGLISH	ENGLISH *(except in KS1 Welsh-medium classes)*	LANGUAGE AND LITERACY	LANGUAGES
	Welsh *(in Welsh-medium schools)*	Irish *(in Irish-speaking schools)*	Gaelic *(to support first language speakers)*
MATHEMATICS	MATHEMATICS	MATHEMATICS AND NUMERACY	MATHEMATICS
SCIENCE	SCIENCE		SCIENCES
HISTORY	HISTORY		
GEOGRAPHY	GEOGRAPHY	THE WORLD AROUND US	SOCIAL STUDIES
DESIGN and TECHNOLOGY	DESIGN and TECHNOLOGY		TECHNOLOGIES
ICT (Computing from 2014)	ICT		
ART and DESIGN	ART and DESIGN	THE ARTS	EXPRESSIVE ARTS
MUSIC	MUSIC		
PHYSICAL EDUCATION	PHYSICAL EDUCATION	PHYSICAL EDUCATION	HEALTH AND WELLBEING
LANGUAGES from 2014 at Key Stage 2			
Religious education*	Religious education*	Religious education*	RELIGIOUS AND MORAL EDUCATION
Skills across the curriculum:	**Skills across the curriculum:**	**Thinking skills and personal capabilities:**	**Skills for learning, skills for life, skills for work:**
	Developing thinking	Thinking, problem solving and decision-making	Thinking
		Self-management	Employability, enterprise and citizenship
		Working with others	
		Managing information	
		Being creative	
		Cross-curricular skills:	
Language and literacy	Developing communication	Communication	Literacy
Mathematical fluency	Developing number	Using mathematics	Numeracy
	Developing ICT	Using ICT	Health and wellbeing;
Personal, social and health education	Personal and social education	Personal development and mutual understanding	

(Key: UPPER CASE – statutory provision; * a statutory requirement to be taught in accordance with locally agreed syllabi; lower case – non-statutory provision)

In England's primary provision from 2014, exceptional priority has been given by the Coalition Government to English, mathematics and science (deemed 'core subjects' and the focus of detailed, year-by-year programmes of study). 'Other foundation' subjects remain statutory but have very condensed content coverage and minimal assessment requirements. Whilst the core subjects are felt to be essential for future learning and work, other subjects are seen as contributing to a broad and balanced curriculum. Assessment and inspection arrangements reinforce this impression. However, the minimalist specifications for foundation subjects are intended to remove constraint from teachers and thus enable innovation. Official programmes of study are mainly concerned with knowledge and, to a lesser extent, with concepts. They almost exclusively leave consideration of subject-related and cross-curricular skills and attitudes to teachers. In principle, a unique 'school curriculum' can be constructed. However, each school must publish its curriculum on a year-by-year basis.

In Wales, curriculum structures mirrored those of England for many years although the distinctiveness of Wales was expressed through the *Curriculum Cymreig* (ACCAC, 2003). This remains a statutory requirement on the cultural, economic, environmental, historical and linguistic characteristics of Wales. In 2008, a more radical development introduced a new School Curriculum for 3 to 19-year-olds to provide a 'more learner-centred and skills-focused curriculum for the twenty-first century' (Welsh Government, 2008). This is reflected in 'Skills Across the Curriculum' and qualifications through 'Essential Skills Wales' (see Reading 10.5), although conventional subjects remain the basic unit of curriculum planning in schools and national Literacy and Numeracy Frameworks are being introduced. For young children, the Foundation Phase is structured in terms of 'areas of learning'.

In Northern Ireland's primary curriculum, subjects are set aside in favour of six 'areas of learning', and teachers are encouraged to 'integrate learning across the six areas to make relevant connections for children' (Council for Curriculum, Examinations and Assessment (CCEA), 2007). In addition, cross-curricular skills, thinking skills and personal capabilities are emphasised. Guidance is offered on broad approaches to teaching and 'ideas for connecting learning'. Thus, for example: 'Children learn best when learning is interactive, practical and enjoyable. Teachers should make use of a wide range of teaching methods, balancing whole-class, group and individual activities, to engage children in effective learning' (CCEA, 2007, p. 9).

Integrated approaches are also encouraged in Scotland's primary education, where the *Curriculum for Excellence* has been carefully built around the aspiration that learners from 3 to 18 should achieve the 'four capacities' of 'successful learners', 'confident individuals', 'responsible citizens' and 'effective contributors' (see Figure 9.3 above). Eight 'curriculum areas' then structure programmes of expected 'experiences' and required 'outcomes' and reflect explicit consideration of the contribution of each area to the four overall curricular purposes (see Scottish Government, 2006). Subjects are recognised as 'an essential feature of the curriculum, particularly in secondary school', but schools 'have the freedom to think imaginatively about how the experiences and outcomes might be organised and planned for in creative ways which encourage deep, sustained learning and which meet the needs of their children and young people' (Scottish Government, 2008).

Expert questions

Breadth: does the curriculum represent society's educational aspirations for its citizens?

Balance: does the curriculum-as-experienced offer everything which each learner has a right to expect?

These questions contribute to a conceptual framework underpinning professional expertise (see Chapter 16).

In summary, within the UK's secondary and primary schools, there are both similarities and differences in the particular curricular structures and requirements of each country, and these vary too over time. Whichever sector, country or era you work or study in, the important thing to note is that curriculum arrangements are social constructions. Although they may seem 'set in stone', they actually do change and teachers are likely to see quite a few in the course of a career. Whilst they reflect the history, culture, ideologies and political context of their construction, the basic elements of learning (knowledge, concepts, skills and attitudes) endure.

3.2 Teaching, learning and national curricula

TLRP's third principle, states that: 'Effective teaching and learning recognises the importance of prior experience and learning'.

This poses a significant dilemma for highly structured national curricula: How can a specified curriculum, at one and the same time, set out a specific framework for required content and progression and yet remain flexible enough to draw on the interests, experiences, approaches to learning and physical and intellectual capabilities of individual children? Is there a risk that some pupils will feel excluded by the specified content? And how, if content is too specified, can innovation occur?

As we have seen, England's recent National Curriculum Review produced a tight specification of the core curriculum in terms of both content and structure. Detailed, year-on-year programmes of study were set out for core subjects building on the ideas of E. D. Hirsch (1987). To a large extent then, the curriculum for schools was placed in a linear form within core subjects – and this was, of course, backed up by formal assessment procedures.

There are several disadvantages in this approach. First, psychologists such as Bruner (1977, see Reading 9.5) suggest that children can learn most things at *most* ages if they are taught in meaningful ways and revisited at more advanced stages – thus coining the term 'spiral curriculum'. Some children may thus experience and become interested in things which a linear National Curriculum does not anticipate – and teachers may feel constrained in following up those interests. Perhaps indeed, children's learning is driven by developmental considerations (e.g. Katz 1998; Pollard et al., 2000) which subject-based national curricula may lack the flexibility to accommodate. Second, we now know that learners do not often acquire understanding in a simple, linear way, with a step-by-step progression (Gagné, 1965), as some behaviourist psychology might have had us believe. Other learning theorists, influenced by Vygotsky (see Chapter 2, Section 1.3, Reading 2.3) suggest that children learn when they are able to 'make sense' of some experience, particularly when they have an imaginative insight or are supported by more experienced or knowledgeable teachers, parents or peers (Tharp and Gallimore, 1988, Reading 11.4). As we have seen, this is one rationale for the 'personalisation' agenda – to respond more effectively to individual need (Teaching and Learning Review Group, 2006, Reading 10.7).

Nor do subject specialists suggest progression through a particular sequence of substantive knowledge without considerable flexibility. Building also on psychological understanding, the recommendation is that a curriculum specification should leave sufficient flexibility to enable teachers to use their judgement in support of *conceptual* development and application. Ernest made the point particularly clearly over 20 years ago in relation to mathematics. He wrote:

Expert question

Personalisation: does the curriculum resonate with the social and cultural needs of diverse learners and provide appropriate elements of choice?

This question contributes to a conceptual framework underpinning professional expertise (see Chapter 16).

> One of the greatest dangers in stipulating a statutory curriculum in mathematics at (several) levels of attainment is that it becomes a barrier which may deny a youngster access to higher concepts and skills when he or she is ready for them … The major flaw in this scheme (is) the mistaken assumption that children's learning in mathematics follows a fixed hierarchical pattern … This is nonsense. (Ernest, 1991, p. 50)

The over-riding message is perhaps that learning is not always predictable or linear, and any curriculum that diminishes the opportunity for teachers to respond to pupil needs is less likely to promote meaningful learning.

At the classroom level, talking with pupils goes a long way in resolving this dilemma. Children and young people are perfectly capable of accepting that there is nationally expected curriculum coverage, but will welcome teacher efforts to make appropriate connections with their prior knowledge, emergent understanding and their experience. This is the only way through which a curriculum can, operationally, 'make sense' to learners.

WWW. ⟳

To read a more extended discussion, including Pollard's resignation from a government role on this issue, see the supplementary material for Chapter 9 on **reflectiveteaching.co.uk**

3.3 Subject-based and integrated curricula

A subject-based curriculum is one which maintains high boundaries, distinction and specialisation between subjects. The resulting curriculum has been seen as being typical of secondary education. It has been called a 'collection curriculum' (Bernstein, 1971) because the learner acquires their overall education through the accumulation of under-standing in different domains. Progression within each separate subject is intended to be strong, though coherence of learning across subjects may be weaker. 'Cross-curricular themes' are often used to forge lateral links, but tend to be hard to sustain.

An integrated curriculum, on the other hand, is one which draws across subject boundaries to construct a more holistic and, it is hoped, meaningful focus for study (Turner-Bisset, 2000, Reading 10.3). For many years, this approach has been associated with primary education and, in particular, with provision for younger children. 'Topic work' is one classic manifestation and another rationale reflects beliefs about the value of 'play' itself (Central Advisory Council on Education (CACE), 1967, Reading 9.4).

Arguments for the desirability of an integrated curriculum include the suggestion that the curriculum must draw on authentic pupil experiences (rather than 'artificial' subjects) if effective learning is to take place. A second argument proposes that a higher priority can be given to generic processes, key skills and attitudes if the emphasis on subject knowledge is lessened.

However, caricatures of differences between primary and secondary education do not stand, for there are many examples of exceptional integrated work in secondary education, and of skilful subject teaching in primary schools. Indeed, this is once again an example of an educational dilemma in which both positions have some merit. It is not surprising therefore, that the best schools find ways of drawing on the strengths of each approach. The same principle can be applied at a classroom level by varying the ways in which curricular activity is presented to pupils.

The need for breadth in curriculum, to provide a range of learning experience, is well established. Indeed, international comparison shows curricular breadth being maintained in many countries to age 16 and beyond, far longer than is typical in the countries of the UK. There has been a particular tendency in England for political concern to 'raise standards' in core subjects to drive out opportunities for quality engagement with the arts, humanities and vocational subjects.

And so we learn that, to offer an effective educational experience, the 'basics' have to be balanced with other curricular areas in responsive ways (see Chapter 10, Sections 2 and 3, for discussion of the principles of curriculum planning).

The same dilemmas are faced in Scotland, Wales and Northern Ireland and indeed, the Republic of Ireland, but at the time of writing government requirements are significantly less prescriptive than in England. Creative teachers in any setting will use their expertise to present the curriculum to pupils in meaningful ways. In so doing, the advantages and disadvantages of focusing on particular subjects or on integrating knowledge across them always has to be weighed. There are good arguments for both.

> **Expert questions**
>
> **Breadth:** does the curriculum represent society's educational aspirations for its citizens?
>
> **Balance:** does the curriculum-as-experienced offer everything which each learner has a right to expect?
>
> These questions contribute to a conceptual framework underpinning professional expertise (see Chapter 16).

3.4 Academic and vocational education

In secondary education, as preparation begins for employment or for further or higher education, there have been significant differences of opinion in relation to the most appropriate curriculum. These go back in history for many decades. The 1944 Education Act, for instance, made provision for 'technical', 'secondary modern' and 'grammar' school provision – thus reinforcing the principle of distinct programmes of study for particular purposes and for selected groups of students based on assessment of aptitude and ability. However, the Newsom Report of 1963 recorded the poor quality of education provided to many disadvantaged pupils who were not in grammar schools, and bemoaned that 'half our future' was being wasted. When comprehensive schools were introduced and adopted in most parts of the UK, provision for pupils with different needs was made within each school, through vocational and academic 'pathways'. Distinct courses, work experiences and qualifications were created alongside conventional examinations, and were subject to a great deal of innovation, change and confusion over the years.

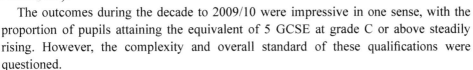

In England, the Tomlinson Report of 2004 proposed a radical overhaul of this complexity, with GCSEs, A levels and vocational qualifications to be replaced by a single, four-level diploma ranging from pre-GCSE to beyond A level and enabling mixed-aged classes as students progressed through modules of study at their own rates. An interesting feature of this proposal was that both academic and vocational learning was to be assessed on the same scale, and in principle was thus to have party of esteem. But the proposal proved too radical, and the scheme was not adopted.

Parallel provision of academic and vocational pathways and qualifications thus continued to be provided – with vocational education still somewhat undervalued officially, despite the unique opportunities it offered to many (Unwin, 2009, Reading 9.6).

The outcomes during the decade to 2009/10 were impressive in one sense, with the proportion of pupils attaining the equivalent of 5 GCSE at grade C or above steadily rising. However, the complexity and overall standard of these qualifications were questioned.

In 2009, an independent review of education and training for 14–19 year olds in England and Wales was published, the Nuffield Review (Pring et al., 2009). In some ways, this echoed elements of Tomlinson. For instance, it asserted 'a broad vision of education in which there is a profound respect for the whole person, irrespective of ability or cultural and social background, in which there is a broader vision of learning and in which the learning contributes to a more just and cohesive society' (p. 4). The report recommended that:

A new curriculum framework should introduce all young people to:

- forms of understanding which enable them to make sense of their physical and social worlds;
- opportunities to excel and to have a sense of achievement;
- practical and economically relevant capabilities;
- issues of profound social and personal concern;
- information, advice and guidance for future career, training and education;
- knowledge, skills and experience which are relevant to the wider community.

A unified and inclusive qualifications framework should be developed that embraces different forms of learning and promotes more effective choice and greater breadth of study. (2009, p. 11)

Expert question

Congruence: are forms of assessment fit for purpose in terms of overall educational objectives?

This question contributes to a conceptual framework underpinning professional expertise (see Chapter 16).

A very different analysis by Wolf (2011) was adopted by the Coalition Government. This viewed the breadth, range and complexity of post-16 vocational courses as 'leading to dead-ends' rather than being of intrinsic value, and saw their expansion in recent years as a product of school strategies to improve their standing in league tables. A radical simplification was therefore implemented, with slimming down of qualifications, reassertion of required standards in English and maths, and expansion of apprenticeships. In parallel with these developments, the 'English Baccalaureate' was introduced (see Section 3.1, above) to promote a more academic curriculum.

What we thus see in the case of vocational education, is an area of educational policy which has been historically unstable. Despite the strength of the case (Unwin, 2009, Reading 9.5), a consensus about the role and status of vocational education does not exist in England – certainly not in the way in which it does in countries such as Switzerland or Germany. It is not surprising that the Nuffield Review urged a debate to clarify values and intentions, or that practical decision-making in secondary, vocational and further education is so challenging. The dilemmas between common or distinct institutions, courses, qualifications and standards are acute.

Similar issues have been rehearsed in the Scottish Government's *Review of Post-16 Education and Vocational Training* (2011a). Interestingly however, the direction of policy is to 'seek a broad consensus and to create a truly coherent system with the individual learner at its heart'. Progress towards a fully integrated system, building from the *Curriculum for Excellence* is proposed.

4 Subject knowledge

Teachers with good subject knowledge are able to make more secure judgements about the *appropriate* teaching of knowledge, concepts, skills and attitudes. Indeed, international research studies such as the meta-analysis of Hattie (2009, Reading 4.6) suggest that the subject knowledge of teachers is an extremely important influence on pupil attainment. Perhaps this is not surprising, but simply having a lot of specialist knowledge is *not* sufficient for effective teaching.

The most influential analysis of subject knowledge in education was provided by Shulman (1986, Reading 9.7). He identified three forms of subject knowledge:

- *Content knowledge* – knowledge of the subject held by the teacher.
- *Pedagogic content knowledge* – knowledge of how to use content knowledge for teaching purposes.
- *Curricular knowledge* – knowledge of curriculum structures and materials.

4.1 Content knowledge

Content knowledge refers to the kind of knowledge that teachers gain from their own schooling, university and college courses or from personal research and interest. It can be sub-divided into two aspects, the substantive and syntactic, as defined by Schwab (1978).

- The *substantive* aspect of subject matter knowledge relates to a foundational understanding of facts, concepts and principles of a subject and the way in which they are organised.
- The *syntactic* aspect relates to knowledge about why such knowledge is deemed important and is justified.

Knowledge of the social structure of Tudor England and of how various political influences affected the lives of people during this period would be an example of substantive knowledge in history. Knowing how this knowledge has been arrived at through the use of primary and secondary evidence and an understanding of the relative validity of such evidence would be an example of syntactic knowledge of history.

When planning for pupil learning, primary school teachers must draw on their substantive knowledge from across all the subjects they teach – the main curricular challenge is one of breadth. The quote below from a reception teacher demonstrates how she drew on substantive knowledge she had gained during her initial teacher education course when planning a lesson on counting:

> When I was planning this lesson I drew on my knowledge of the pre-requisites for counting: knowing the number names in order, one to one correspondence, the cardinal principle, being able to count objects that cannot be moved/touched and counting objects that cannot be seen e.g. sounds or beats. These developmental stages formed the progression and structure to the lesson.

Such knowledge is not always accessible from memory, and the reflective teacher will seek to refresh and develop their substantive knowledge of topics before planning and teaching. For example, when planning to teach a topic on 'Egypt', one might research both ancient and modern Egypt drawing on geographical and historical resources. Such sources might include schemes of work, text books, a library or the internet. Topics such as this may only be taught annually or even bi-annually and committed teachers will refresh and develop their substantive knowledge each time they occur in order to invigorate their own interest and pass on enthusiasm to pupils.

Secondary teachers are appointed to teach a subject and they have subject expertise which is the foundation of their professional identities. Subject curricula are expressed in terms of the knowledge, concepts and skills associated with that particular discipline. Their main challenge is thus one of subject depth – for the secondary teacher may have to work across a wide range of syllabi and classes. Whilst it might be reasonably assumed that the more teachers know about a subject the more their pupils will achieve, studies have not found this straightforward correlation (Dunkin and Biddle, 1974). You may find echoes of this in your personal experience. Can you recall an occasion when an 'expert' tried to explain something to you with little success? To be a successful teacher of a subject requires *both* sorts of knowing – knowing the subject 'inside out' *and* knowing how best to present it so that it can be learned.

4.2 Pedagogical content knowledge

Pedagogical content knowledge is Shulman's (1986, Reading 9.7) second form of subject knowledge, which he described as 'subject matter knowledge *for teaching*'. It does not simply reflect understanding of a subject, or even of how to teach. Rather, it is knowledge of *how to combine both* in relation to a particular domain. It is thus a specific category of teacher knowledge.

Teachers draw on their pedagogical content knowledge when deciding how they will introduce a new idea or develop pupils' knowledge or skills in relation to a specific aspect of a subject. For example, when teaching the scientific topic of 'our solar system', a primary teacher might decide to represent the sun and planets with different sized spheres and to take pupils out onto the school field in order to demonstrate the relative distances between objects in the solar system. When teaching about life in Victorian times, a secondary teacher might borrow domestic artefacts from a local Victorian collection and ask pupils to consider for what purpose they were used. These teachers would not only have drawn on their knowledge of the subject matter and on their general knowledge of how children of a particular age learn; they would also have drawn on knowledge of how children learn in the particular subject. In science, much use is made of analogies since it is not always possible to demonstrate concepts concretely. In the case above, the teacher might have used an orange and a marble as analogies for the Earth and moon. Artefacts are often used for historical topics when trying to help children understand how people lived in earlier times.

Teaching another person what you know thus involves finding ways of *representing* subject matter to assist their learning, as well as being aware of the new representations that are subsequently developed. Our earlier discussion of concepts as significant elements of learning (see Section 2.2 of this chapter) resonates here. Shulman highlights new conceptual developments as 'transformations'. These transformations take many forms and are:

> The most powerful analogies, illustrations, examples, explanations and demonstrations – in a word, the ways of representing and formulating the subject that make it comprehensible to others. (1986, p. 9)

With experience, teachers develop a 'representational repertoire' for the subject they teach which may itself enrich and extend their own subject understanding – it's a truism that a good way to understand something is to try to teach it. This repertoire is part of the result of 'thinking like a teacher' about a subject and is, of course, significantly helped by the teachers own conceptual understanding. In any one lesson a teacher may use a number of different strategies of this kind. The successes and failures of our transformations in making learning meaningful for our pupils, individually and as a group, add to our knowledge – of the subject and of how it may be learned, in particular of subject-specific difficulties which pupils experience. Reflective activity 9.4 is designed to help think about this.

Aim To consider the idea of *transformations* when preparing to teach.

Method For a particular lesson or series of lessons focus specifically on what you know about the content and what you want your pupils to learn about the content. If teaching materials are prescribed, review them in the light of your understanding of the subject matter.

How do you represent your personal understanding of this content? How might you make it meaningful for your pupils? Consider some ways in which you might *transform* the content. How might you introduce ideas/concepts/principles? How can you best move pupils from what is known or familiar to new knowledge? Are there any strategies, activities or tasks which seem particularly appropriate? What makes you think they will work? Are there parts of the learning where pupils may misunderstand or be mislead? How might you avoid this? What language will you use? How will you approach any subject-specialist language?

If possible discuss your ideas for *transformations* with another teacher or student teacher.

Follow-up Teach the lesson and try out your *transformations*. How did they work? Is there anything from the lesson that you will to add to your representational repertoire?

4.3 Curricular knowledge

'Curricular knowledge' is Shulman's third form of teacher knowledge and perhaps the simplest.

It relates to: programmes of study, syllabi, schemes of work, resources, technologies and instructional materials through which curricular objectives may be realised. The selection of such material is often structured by school policies, but rests on teacher judgement in respect of more specific activities and lessons.

For most teachers, curricular knowledge is much easier to acquire than content knowledge or pedagogic content knowledge. Indeed, some would argue that, whilst curricular knowledge can be obtained from text books, the internet, or from school and National Curriculum documentation, the acquisition of content knowledge calls for sustained study and pedagogical content knowledge requires extensive experience.

Whilst there may be some truth in this view, confidence is enhanced by being clear about the nature of the expertise being developed. The elegance of Shulman's categorisation may help in this respect. In particular, for the reflective teacher, it should be possible to analyse the nature of the subject knowledge which one has in relation to the role one is required to fulfil. If there are discrepancies, then the new challenges can be faced.

For discussion and advice on the practical development of subject knowledge, see the supplementary material for Chapter 9 on **reflectiveteaching.co.uk**

4.4 Applying subject knowledge

As we have seen, having decided what it is that pupils should learn, the reflective teacher draws on their subject matter knowledge and their pedagogical content knowledge in relation to a particular group of pupils in order to decide what they need to do in a lesson.

For example, when teaching the skill of overarm throwing, the teacher must be sure of what this involves – subject matter knowledge. They might decide that the best way to teach this would be by demonstrating it themselves before asking pupils to practise – pedagogical content knowledge. They will certainly want their pupils to try overarm throwing for themselves rather than just reading about it or watching a teacher demonstration since their syntactic knowledge of PE informs them that physical action is necessary for learning in this subject. The reflective teacher will consider the difficulty that some pupils might have with this and perhaps break the movement down into smaller actions for some pupils to practice – knowledge of pupils. Therefore, in order to decide what they need to do and what their pupils need to do in order to learn how to throw overarm, the reflective teacher draws on a number of categories of knowledge for teaching.

Pedagogical content knowledge might be considered to be the key to effective teaching and the reflective teacher will give careful consideration to how they 'represent and formulate the subject to make it comprehensible to others'. In the teaching of mathematics, the choice of examples (Watson and Mason, 2005), the use of representations (Drews and Hansen, 2007) and the making of connections (Askew et al., 1997) have all been found to be important aspects of pedagogical content knowledge.

More generally, experienced teachers with thorough subject knowledge have been found to be more likely to adapt and modify text books and other published materials where they find the organisation of content and the representations of concepts unsatisfactory (Hashweh, 1987). Teachers with deep subject knowledge are also more likely to identify where learners might misunderstand, to recognise dawning insights and to see where connections might be made within the subject and with other subject areas.

Rowland, Turner, Thwaites and Huckstep (2009) formalised this understanding through the development of what they call a 'knowledge quartet'. Their framework has its empirical origins in observations of trainee and beginning teachers teaching mathematics (Rowland, Huckstep and Thwaites, 2005; Turner, 2009). The 'quartet' highlights four aspects of subject knowledge.

Expert question

Coherence: is there clarity in the purposes, content and organisation of the curriculum and does it provide holistic learning experiences?

This question contributes to a conceptual framework underpinning professional expertise (see Chapter 16).

Foundation – content knowledge in substantive and syntactic forms, which enables and circumscribes the available teaching repertoire.

Transformation – the capacity to re-present content knowledge in ways that are pedagogically powerful, as described above.

Connection – the expert teacher's awareness of the structures and sequencing of knowledge, so that particular elements can be related to a more holistic understanding.

Contingency – the teacher's capacity to respond to classroom events and pupil actions in ways which, though unexpected, still build towards understanding.

This work on mathematical content knowledge found that trainee and beginning teachers did not always use the most appropriate representations in their teaching and did not always make connections that would support the mathematical understanding of their pupils. However, when helped to reflect on the mathematical content of their teaching using the knowledge quartet framework as a tool, teachers often identified such limitations in their practice and suggested how they might make improvements (Turner, 2009).

Conclusion

National curricula provide a significant means of attempting to fulfil national objectives and of attempting to provide coherence and progression in the learning of pupils. They also clarify the aims and role of teachers. Even when, as in England, significant numbers of secondary schools in the independent and academy sectors are formally exempt, national curricula influence exam boards and thus schools.

However, by the very act of setting out 'requirements', a 'framework' or a set of 'guidelines', the architects of national curricula select *particular* content for teaching, study, learning and assessment. This material tends to cater for the majority, but must inevitably be more suitable and interesting for some learners than for others. Children and young people with particular special needs, or coming from disadvantaged backgrounds, may not relate well to such curricula and alternative provision may suit them better.

Indeed, the specification of a National Curriculum raises the immediate question, 'Whose curriculum is it?' Any curriculum reflects values, views of knowledge and of learning. Reflective teachers will recognise that dominant opinions and influence can change over time and that they are not always clear-cut or coherent. Ambiguities and dissonances within and between the different agencies that govern education are also commonplace. Where teachers have views on such matters, perhaps based on study, experience, evidence and reflection, to make their voices heard in educational debates is a valuable professional contribution. Subject, phase or other professional associations are important vehicles for this.

Nor should we forget the clarification with which we began this chapter. The official curriculum of any country is a very different thing from the whole school curriculum, which includes the hidden curriculum and the curriculum-as-experienced by pupils. There is enormous scope for creativity, adaption and extension in the School Curriculum.

At the end of the day, teachers must use their expertise to manage a constructive interaction between the knowledge society deems to be important, and the specific needs of children and young people.

In the next chapter we focus on the practical implementation of the curriculum through whole school policies, programmes of study, schemes of work, lesson planning and evaluation.

Key readings

A balanced and highly influential overview of the nature, scope and design of school curricula is:

Her Majesty's Inspectors (1985) *The Curriculum from 5 to 16.* Curriculum Matters 2. An HMI Series. London: HMSO. (Reading 10.1) (available at educationengland. org.uk)

Extending common principles across primary and secondary education (Reading 9.1) are:

Male, B. and Waters, M. (2012) *The Primary Curriculum Design Handbook.* London: Continuum.
Male, B. and Waters, M. (2012) *The Secondary Curriculum Design Handbook.* London: Continuum.

The ways in which curriculum design has been developed in England, Northern Ireland, Scotland and Wales is described and analysed in:

Wyse, D., Baumfield, V., Egan, D., Hayward, D., Mulme, M., Menter, I., Gallagher, C., Leitch, R., Livingston, K. and Lingard, R. (2012) *Creating the Curriculum.* London: Routledge.

For sophisticated analysis and proposals on the primary curriculum, see:

Alexander, R. (ed.) (2010) *Children, Their World, Their Education. Final Report and Recommendations of the Cambridge Primary Review.* London: Routledge.

An incisive history of the development of aims, values and structures in the secondary curriculum is presented in:

White, J. (2011) *The Invention of the Secondary Curriculum.* London: Palgrave Macmillan.

The distinction between the 'knowledge of the powerful' and 'powerful knowledge' for all is drawn in:

Young, M. (2008) *Bringing Knowledge Back In.* London: Routledge. (Reading 9.2)

Shulman provided the classic text analysing key dimensions of subject knowledge:

Shulman, L. S. (1986) 'Those who understand: knowledge and growth in teaching', *Educational Researcher*, 15, 4–14. (Reading 9.7)

A strong case for developing personal capabilities, dispositions and skills through contemporary curricula has been through the work of Guy Claxton, such as:

Claxton, G., Chambers, M., Powell, G. and Lucas, B. (2011) *The Learning Powered School: Pioneering 21st Century Education.* Bristol: TLO. (see also Reading 2.9)

The classic argument for young children learning through direct experience was expressed in the Plowden Report:

Central Advisory Council for Education (1967) *Children and their Primary Schools.* London: HMSO. (Reading 9.4)

A wonderful book making the point that any curriculum must take full account of learning and developmental processes remains:

Bruner, J. S. (1966) *Towards a Theory of Instruction.* Cambridge, MA: Harvard University Press. (see also Reading 9.5)

English secondary education is undergoing a period of considerable change at present, with new school, examination and accountability structures. For interesting overviews with constructive proposals, see:

Baker, K. (ed.) (2013) *14–18: A New Vision for Secondary Education.* London: Bloomsbury.

The Academies Commission Report (2013) *Unleashing Greatness: Getting the Best from an Academised System.* London: RSA/Pearson.

For a wonderful supply of ideas and innovation from UK subject associations, see the regular flow of practical journals on various subjects for teachers. These include:

British Journal of Religious Education (Professional Council for Religious Education)

British Journal of Teaching Physical Education (Physical Education Association of the United Kingdom)

Mathematics Teaching (Association of Teachers of Mathematics)

School Science Review and *Primary Science* (Association for Science Education)

Teaching English (National Association for the Teaching of English)

Teaching History and *Primary History* (The Historical Association)

The Journal of Design and Technology Education (Design and Technology Association).

Reference to official websites for UK countries that provide information about national curricula and links to subject can be found on reflectiveteaching.co.uk.

reflectiveteaching.co.uk also offers additional professional resources for this chapter. These may include *Further Reading*, illustrative *Reflective Activities*, useful *Web Links* and *Download Facilities* for diagrams, figures, checklists, activities.

Planning
How are we implementing the curriculum?

10

Introduction

This chapter discusses the implementation of curriculum planning by moving through three successive levels of detail, considering the same issues which teachers or trainee teachers must review when planning their teaching programme. It then focuses on processes for evaluation and further development.

In case all this sounds over-structured, we must once again affirm the uniquely enriching role of the creativity and imagination of individual teachers in providing high-quality, responsive curriculum experiences for pupils in their classes. Qualities of experience which may be produced – excitement, surprise, awe, spontaneity, concentration, humour, amazement, curiosity, expression, to name but a few – are created through the rapport and interaction between a teacher and his or her class. From the pupil's point of view, this brings the curriculum 'alive'.

But it is easier to be imaginative and responsive if you are also secure. Good planning is thus enabling.

TLRP principles

Two principles are of particular relevance to this chapter on providing high-quality curricular experiences:

Effective teaching and learning engages with valued forms of knowledge.
Teaching and learning should engage with the big ideas, facts, processes, language and narratives of subjects so that learners understand what constitutes quality and standards in particular disciplines. (Principle 2)

Effective teaching and learning recognises the importance of prior experience and learning. Teaching and learning should take account of what the learner knows already in order to plan their next steps. This includes building on prior learning but also taking account of the personal and cultural experiences of different groups of learners. (Principle 3)

See Chapter 4

A valuable set of conceptual tools for thinking about the curriculum is embedded in the various sections of this chapter – breadth, balance, coherence, connection, relevance, progression, Personalisation and differentiation. Most of these concepts derive from HMI (DES, 1985, Reading 10.1) and have been at the heart of national curriculum planning in each UK country for many years (Wyse et al., 2012).

The particular formulation of conceptual tools for analysing curricular provision offered here contributes to the holistic analysis of teacher expertise, which is the subject of Chapter 16.

1 The school curriculum

There are many similarities in the curricula offered by schools, but also important differences of emphasis. The statutory requirements of the National Curriculum in each country assert pupil entitlements, but schools have significant scope to develop their own approach to curriculum whilst remaining constrained by assessment and inspection conditions and by parental expectations. In any event, after decades of centralised prescription in each country of the UK, the trend of public policy is towards granting schools more curricular autonomy (see Chapter 9, Section 3). For example, in England from 2014, maintained primary schools are invited to develop their *own* School Curriculum – as long as they also satisfy statutory requirements.

Governance: The governing body of each school has legal responsibility for the curriculum and will receive and approve curricular proposals from the headteacher or senior leadership team. The governors should ensure that the review, development and articulation of the school's curriculum is carried out to a high standard. Many governing bodies have a curriculum and standards committee with responsibility for making sure that professionals within the school review and update subject and curriculum policies in accordance with the school's aims and in the light of its recent performance, parental expectations, professional judgement and statutory requirements.

The development of national curricula in recent decades has drawn attention to the need for progression and coherence from year to year, but also for the responsibility on schools to provide a broad and balanced curriculum experience (see Male and Waters, 2012, Reading 9.1 and Section 2.2 below).

Aims: Irrespective of national requirements (see Chapter 9, Section 1.2), curriculum planning should be influenced by the overall philosophy and specific aims of a school. Many schools emphasise personal development and state their aim to ensure that each child achieves his or her potential and that each becomes a well rounded, successful, caring and knowledgeable person. For example, many English schools have been influenced by the agenda of 'Every Child Matters' (DfES, 2003). This made the commitment that every child:

- is safe, feels safe and knows how to stay safe;
- is healthy and can look after his or her own health;
- enjoys their childhood, their learning and achieves well;
- makes a positive contribution to school life and to the wider community;
- is prepared well in order that s/he can achieve economic and personal wellbeing.

Policies: School policy statements reflect the overall philosophy and aims of a school but provide more detailed guidance for practical implementation. They are likely to address significant aspects of the life of the school (e.g. special educational needs and equal opportunities) and may also frame the school's schemes of work for particular areas or subjects within the curriculum. They must be endorsed by school governors, with dates set for review.

Figure 10.1
School philosophy,
policies, schemes
of work and
teacher planning

Aims and values of the curriculum.
Nationally derived, institutionally adopted
and adapted by the school.

Policies: subject, cross-subject and management based.
Providing purposes, rationale and broad guidelines. Regular
review by school staff and governors.

Long term plans.
Broad framework of curricular provision. Coverage of curriculum
subjects, review of 'blocked' and 'continuing' units of work.

Medium term plans.
Detailing objectives, activities, assessment opportunities and
resource/health and safety considreations for termly/ half-termly
units of work. Inclusion of cross-curricular considerations.

Weekly plans.
Providing an overview of the 'curriculum
in action' across curriculum subjects.

Lesson plans.
Providing lesson objectives, procedures,
differentiation strategies and assessment criteria.

Assessment and evaluation, which feeds back into
all levels of planning and informs policy change.

The timetable: The configuration of the timetable is a particularly important planning decision. Indeed, once constructed, a timetable enables or prohibits aspects of planning. The first step then, is to define the basic framework. What should be the pattern of the teaching week? How long is a teaching session? Where do the breaks come? How long are the breaks? When does school start and finish? Making decisions about start and finish times may involve considerations of pupils' travelling time, the operation of school buses, before and after school activities, etc. Length and positioning of breaks will involve thinking about providing food, the rhythm of the day, pupil and staff stamina. Other decisions about school organisation (for instance, in mixed classes, bands, streams or sets) will also be reflected in the timetable and may also enable or constrain it. These decisions have very significant consequences for the time which is available for pupil learning.

Time frames for planning: In most schools, curriculum planning is managed in three time frames:

- long term (whole Key Stages)
- medium term (yearly, termly or half-termly) and
- short term (fortnightly, weekly or for specific lessons or sequences of teaching)

Figure 10.1 provides a model of the links between national and school policies and the subsequent levels of curriculum planning. We will consider these levels in more detail through this chapter.

Review: Curriculum planning is not a once-and-for-all affair. The curriculum needs to reviewed and revised from time to time to make sure it is relevant, up to date and enabling all children to achieve their potential. Good practice is to tie this review process closely in with school improvement planning.

2 Long-term planning

2.1 Programmes of study

Long term planning of programmes of study must develop with awareness of national and organisational requirements.

In primary education, national curricula frameworks may provide guidance on the specific knowledge, concepts and skills which should be covered in each subject. Sometimes this is organised by Key Stage, sometimes by year. More detailed requirements tend to be produced for core subjects such as English, mathematics and science. For example, following a curriculum review in England, the primary school curriculum is tightly prescribed for these core subjects whilst other 'foundation subjects' (art and design, design and technology, geography, history, computing, music, physical education and foreign languages) focus only on 'essentials'. This is intended to leave scope for the development of particular school curricula as locally determined. Programmes of study for each subject must, however, be organised by academic year and published.

Secondary teachers at Key Stage 4 and Post-16 have a particularly strong frame for their work in the shape of the specifications (or syllabi) which are set by the examination boards. Schools and subject teams select appropriate accredited courses and, once selected, specifications are provided which teachers use to create specific programmes of study. Some exam boards offer large quantities of support materials for schools. However, teachers and departments need to decide how to respond to such provision. Whilst academies in England are not constrained by the National Curriculum, they must still respond to national systems for qualifications and accountability so the specifications set by exam boards remain extremely influential.

2.2 Breadth and balance

As we also saw in Chapter 9, Section 1.2, the requirement that the curriculum in England and Wales should be broad and balanced is longstanding. It was affirmed in the Education Act, 2002 and through the curriculum review for England of 2011–13. It is expressed with reference to 'spiritual, moral, cultural, mental and physical development' and preparing pupils for 'the opportunities, responsibilities and experiences of adult life'. Similar statements apply to Scotland, Northern Ireland and Wales. Taken seriously, breadth and balance address holistic questions about educational provision (see TLRP's first principle, Chapter 4). Thus, whilst the statutory curriculum contributes an important part, it should not be seen as the whole educational experience. This is the reason why most countries try to achieve balance in the knowledge, concepts, skills and attitudes which are expected across the curriculum as a whole – and argument explicitly made, for example, in the Welsh Assembly Government's *Skills Framework for 3–19 Year-olds* (2008, Reading 10.5).

Inspection reports in all parts of the UK have, for decades, testified that children are likely to achieve most progress in the core skills or literacy and numeracy if they learn in a rich, broad and balanced curriculum which provides them with stimulating content to talk, read and write about and to explore mathematically, scientifically, socially or creatively. The same point is revealed by international evidence which found that a broad curriculum was a distinctive feature of high performing jurisdictions (DfE, 2011). Following this through, reference to provision for 'spiritual, moral, social and cultural development' occurs no less than three times in the criteria of Ofsted's 2012 inspection framework.

However, it is sometimes necessary to have a concerted focus on certain aspects of the curriculum, particularly if children have for some reason fallen behind. Sustained efforts to keep cohorts of children together so that they are 'ready to progress' from year to year is again a feature of high performing counties such as Singapore and Finland (DfE, 2011).

Expert questions

Breadth: does the curriculum represent society's educational aspirations for its citizens?

Balance: does the curriculum-as-experienced offer everything which each learner has a right to expect?

These questions contribute to a conceptual framework underpinning professional expertise (see Chapter 16).

2.3 Connection and coherence

Connection. The concept of 'connection' draws attention to the extent to which curricular experiences are meaningful to pupils. The advent of national curricula has arguably improved provision of entitlements, but this success brings with it a degree of standardisation. For some, the school curriculum simply fails to make connections with other parts of their lives. The extent of disengagement in schooling is disproportionately concentrated among children from poorer backgrounds, with lower outcomes at all ages. Parents in some communities can also lack confidence in approaching those in schools. And yet, as one of TLRP's projects emphasised, there are 'funds of knowledge' (Moll, 1970) in all communities and progress may be found if methods of 'home–school knowledge exchange' can be established (Hughes and Pollard, 2000, **Research Briefing** on p. 107). Engagement with their communities has been a traditional strength of rural schools and there are many exemplary cases in urban settings too.

Curriculum innovation is thus an established response by schools to the problem of disengagement (Rawling, 2006). This has been encouraged by governments across the UK, within the parameters of their national requirements. For instance, a former curriculum authority for England, the Qualifications and Curriculum Authority, promoted a 'big picture' curriculum (QCA, 2007) to encourage flexibility and connectedness between different forms of knowledge and areas of experience. Schools have tried skills-led programmes, such as *Opening Minds* (RSA, 2013).

An explicit attempt to explore the potential for greater connection between schools and their communities is the *Area Based Curriculum* which has been promoted by the RSA (Thomas, 2010, Reading 10.4). This approach encourages teachers to begin with the formal curriculum through connections to the pupils' locality and lives outside school, and to expand their pedagogic repertoire to use resources, people and opportunities from beyond the classroom. The overall idea is to do everything possible to create authentic learning experiences which enable pupils to apply more abstact knowledge in ways which are contextually meaningful to them.

Coherence. This concept refers to the extent to which the various parts of a planned curriculum relate meaningfully together to reinforce the knowledge, skills, concepts or content being learned. The opposite would be fragmentation and confusion.

Clearly this is an important issue if we conceive of learning as a process of 'making sense' (Haste, 1987; Watkins, 2003). Indeed, Gestalt psychologists such as Lewin (1935) established the significance which developing an overarching frame of reference has on learning. People tend to enjoy learning more when they understand it as a whole. They feel more in control and are more willing to think independently and take risks. On the other hand, perceptions of incoherence can lead to feelings of frustration and to strategies such as withdrawal.

Coherence is often sought across subjects and this,

> **Expert question**
>
> **Connection:** does the curriculum engage with the cultural resources and funds-of-knowledge of families and the community?
>
> This question contributes to a conceptual framework underpinning professional expertise (see Chapter 16).

Expert question

Coherence: is there clarity in the purposes, content and organisation of the curriculum and does it provide holistic learning experiences?

This question contributes to a conceptual framework underpinning professional expertise (see Chapter 16).

of course, has been a prime goal of integrated curricula (Turner-Bisset, 2000, Reading 10.3) and of cross-curricula planning of themes and skill development (e.g. Siraj-Blatchford and Siraj-Blatchford, 1995). However, coherence is also necessary, and is not assured, within *single* subjects. The ability to convey such understanding is, as we saw in Chapter 9, Section 4, likely to be associated with the extent of subject confidence and expertise of the teacher.

The quality of the teacher's content knowledge and pedagogic content knowledge are thus clearly significant variables in achieving coherence, but coherence ultimately derives its force from the sense, or otherwise, which the *pupils* make of the curriculum which is provided.

3 Medium-term planning

3.1 Schemes of work

Schemes of work provide a practical curriculum plan for each subject or area of learning. If schools commit to publishing their year-by-year curriculum for parents, schemes of work are likely to underpin such documentation.

Schemes of work describe how the curriculum may be taught by individual teachers and thus, in aggregate, represent the work of the staff team as a whole. They are likely to incorporate, but may also adapt and supplement, the Programmes of Study of the National Curriculum. Schemes of work may draw on other published resources and are frequently modified in the light of both experience and curriculum initiatives. A key intention is that such schemes of work should give a clear view of how *progression* and *depth* in learning is provided in relation to each subject or area of learning. Teachers will also be concerned to ensure that the curriculum is presented in ways that are *relevant* to the pupils. We will return to these themes.

It is recommended that each scheme of work should address four basic issues:

- *What do we teach?* To outline knowledge, concepts, skills and attitudes to be developed, links between subjects and cross-curricular elements.

- *How do we teach?* To cover how the curriculum and learning processes are to be organised, units of work, learning activities and processes, forms of grouping to provide differentiation, resources needed, time allocations and opportunities for assessment.

- *When do we teach?* To address the issues of curriculum continuity and progression throughout appropriate Key Stages.

- *How do we know that children are learning?* To monitor progress and attainment, and to set future learning targets.

This level of planning is usually undertaken in secondary schools by teachers working in subject teams and departments, and in primary schools by class teachers, individually or in year group teams, and with the support subject specialists. It is likely to be updated, as with all planning, on the basis of teachers' views on the quality of activities, performance data, and changes in school or year group organisation.

Schemes of work are thus each teacher's essential medium-term planning tool, but need to be developed in the light of the policies and priorities of the school as a whole. Without such plans we have little basis on which to define the purposes of teaching sessions, or to assess pupil progress.

There are many ways of setting out a scheme of work, but they tend to begin by recording the following:

Class/subject details. Brief details are provided of the year group, Key Stage, time period in which the work will be carried out, and the subject/curriculum areas encompassed in the plan. Medium-term plans may be shared with colleagues, and such details enable the context of the document to be understood.

Learning objectives. Objectives express what we intend the pupils to learn in terms of knowledge, concepts, skills and attitudes. More tangibly, 'learning outcomes' may also be used to state what the children will be 'able to do' as a result of the teaching and learning programme. Such statements may be used to formulate sequences or 'ladders' of success criteria on a gradient of complexity or 'difficulty'. Teachers and children can thus use these to review their progress and to help in understanding the level of challenge in a task. A further refinement could be to specify 'must', 'should' and 'could' criteria as a bridge between curriculum planning and assessment for learning (see Chapter 13).

Activities. This section indicates what the pupils will be doing in order to satisfy the stated objectives. Only a very brief description of activities is required at this stage of planning, and this may well be set out in a tabular form with each row being assigned for a lesson-by-lesson or week-by-week description of topics and activities. Other columns may record links back to objectives, necessary resources and key assessment points. For example:

Lesson/ Week	Topic/s	Activities	Link to objectives	Resources	Assessment
1					
2					
3					
Etc ...					

This layout provides a holistic overview of the teaching programme and makes it possible 'at a glance' to review whether activities are appropriately varied and therefore likely to maintain pupil interest. It is also possible to begin to plan where activities will need to be differentiated for different year groups or for children of different attainment in the same class. With such planning, resources which need preparation or pre-ordering can be organised.

Reflective activity 10.1 suggests learning more about schemes of work by working with a colleague.

Reflective activity 10.1

Aim: To consider the quality of activities in schemes of work.

Evidence and reflection: Work with a colleague to compare the activities presented in a selection of schemes of work, either for your own class or for a specific age range. What are the strengths and weaknesses of the layouts used? Are the anticipated activities incremental in terms of pupil learning? What is the balance of types of activity? Are activities likely to enthuse and motivate pupils? Are outcomes clearly articulated? Is success in key learning points described?

Extension: Which activities would you replace, what with, and why?

When planning schemes of work, a reflective teacher should remember, as we saw in Chapters 2 and 9, that learning does not necessarily occur in a smooth, upward fashion. Unpredictable developments of insight and understanding may be experienced, just as occasional plateaux may occur and be needed. A reflective teacher thus needs to monitor activities closely to try to ensure the best balance between boredom from too easy tasks, frustration from tasks that are too hard, comfort from consolidation tasks and excitement from tasks that are challenging but not too daunting. The scheme of work is an excellent tool when taking stock of such issues.

3.2 Progression

'Progression' is a powerful concept in the analytic toolkit of reflective teachers (Haynes, 2010, Reading 10.6) – however, it is used in several significant ways.

First, in HMI's conception (1985), progression is linked to providing continuities in children's development as learners. They write:

> Children's development is a continuous process and schools have to provide conditions and experiences which sustain and encourage that process while recognising that it does not proceed uniformly or at an even pace. If this progression is to be maintained, there is a need to build systemactically on the children's existing knowledge, concepts, skills and attitudes, so as to ensure an orderly advance in their capabilities over a period of time. Teaching and learning experiences should be ordered so as to facilitate pupils' progress, with each successive element making appropriate demands and leading to better performance.' (Her Majesty's Inspectors, 1985, p. 48)

This understanding of progression recognises variation, diversity and uncertainty in learning and urges teachers to personalise the curriculum in relation to pupils' existing knowledge.

Second, a rather more generic application can be illustrated through by National Curriculum 'levels'. Using the case of England prior to 2014, Male and Waters (2012) provide an example from the geography curriculum in which we can see recognition of the need to balance subject matter and intellectual challenge to achieve positive learning outcomes. They write:

> If we look at the elements of the national geography currculum that refer to places, we find:
>
> Level 2 – to *describe* the places they visit.
> Level 3 – to make *comparisons and contrasts* between one place and another.
> Level 4 – to begin *to recognise patterns* and make *generalisations*.
> Level 5 – to give geographical *explanations* for those patterns.
> Level 6 – to take account of *different sources* of evidence.
> Level 7 – to *explain relationships* between causes.
>
> These are criteria that apply to any topic within geography. Whether students are engaged in a fieldwork study of a local village or the analysis of another country, they could be working at one of the above levels. These are intellectual levels that are concerned with the ways in which students process the knowledge they are acquiring. In turn the way they are processing extends and deepens that knowledge. (2012, p. 162)

A third, and rather different, emphasis comes from those who are concerned in the first place with the integrity of subject knowledge, for they tend to expect more specific progression in the substantive and logical dimensions of each domain. For example, Hirsch's *Core Knowledge Curriculum*, based on *Cutural Literacy: What Every American Needs to Know* (1988) and which had a considerable influence on the latest version of the curriculum in England, orders information to be learned in great detail but leaves pedagogic implications for teachers to determine. The English review harvested national curricula from around the world and built up its programmes of study from a process of comparison, drafting and consultation about such knowledge (DfE, 2013). So the outcome offers progression and very high expectations, but is primarily justified in subject terms rather than in terms of the learning of that subject knowledge.

A final use of progression focuses at more detailed level on the cognitive challenge of each curricular element. In Scotland, promotion of the concept of 'depth' gives particular prominence to this issue. We will explore it further in Section 4.1 below, when discussing Bloom's taxonomy of educational objectives in relation to planning learning tasks and activities.

> **Expert question**
>
> **Progression:** does the curriculum-as-delivered provide an appropriate sequence and depth of learning experiences?
>
> This question contributes to a conceptual framework underpinning professional expertise (see Chapter 16).

3.3 Relevance

Relevance is of vital importance in the selection of content.

There is little doubt that children and young people learn most effectively when they understand the purposes and context of the tasks and challenges with which they are faced. When a pupil complains that an activity is 'pointless', is 'boring' or that they 'don't see what it's for', then the curriculum is failing to satisfy the criterion of relevance.

In such circumstances, motivation may fall and with it may go concentration, commitment and quality (see Watkins, 2003; Teaching and Learning Review Group, 2006, Reading 10.7; Pollard and Triggs, 2000). Progress and standards of work are thus likely to decrease unless the teacher can justify the activity and bolster motivation. Indeed, even when an activity could have great relevance, this may not have been adequately explained to or appreciated by learners. One long-running finding regarding teaching has been that, very often, pupils have not known why they are doing an activity – hence the need to make learning 'visible' (Hattie, 2010, Reading 4.6; 2012, Reading 16.5).

A key consideration here is the value of incorporating practical activities and first-hand experience into the teaching programme through the scheme of work. This should be done in ways which are appropriate to the age of the pupils, but is an essential part of curriculum provision. If this is ever doubted, try asking your pupils.

> ### Expert question
>
> **Relevance**: is the curriculum presented in ways which are meaningful to learners and so that it can excite their imagination?
>
> This question contributes to a conceptual framework underpinning professional expertise (see Chapter 16).

> ### Reflective activity 10.2
>
> *Aim:* To explore the extent to which sharing learning intentions or success criteria influences feelings of engagement for pupils.
>
> *Evidence and reflection:* The simple method here is to ask the pupils. Having taught a lesson, or seen one taught (pupils will often 'open up' more to someone who is not their own teacher), select a small group of children – ask them some or all of the following:
>
> - What was the lesson mainly about?
> - What did they think that they were supposed to be learning and what did they think that they learned?
> - Do they see any connections with other work that they have done in the same subject?
> - Do they see any connections with work that they have done in other subjects?
> - Did they enjoy the lesson?
> - If the lesson was being taught again to a similar group how could it be improved?
>
> *Extension:* Review what you have learned about the pupils' views. Share your findings with the class teacher if they were not 'your' pupils. What are the implications for the future?

4 Short-term planning

4.1 Lesson plans

When devising lesson plans, reflective teachers will be aware of relevant programmes of study and schemes of work. They will also consider the existing understanding and motivation of their pupils so that specific objectives can be refined and provision can be differentiated.

Against this background, a particular learning session can be planned effectively. Of course, such plans provide a teacher with structure and security and it should not be forgotten that the resulting confidence can be used to be responsive to the children during the session. Good planning underpins *flexibility*.

Elements of a lesson plan are likely to include:

a) Context

b) Learning intentions

c) Phases of the lesson

d) Learning tasks

e) Success criteria

f) Resources, ICT and safety

g) Supporting adults.

Figure 10.2 sets this out as a form and each element is discussed below.

Elements of a lesson plan	The lesson plan
a) Context	
b) Learning intentions	
c) Structure of the lesson/s	
d) Learning activities and tasks	
e) Success criteria	
f) Resources, ICT and safety	
g) Supporting adults	

Figure 10.2
Elements of a lesson plan

a) *Context*

It is helpful for an initial section to summarise basic organisational information such as:

- the class and any groups within it;
- the date and duration of the lesson/s;
- the subject/s and focus of the session/s.

Second, it is essential to take stock of, and carefully consider, the existing understanding of the learners. This should be recorded in an appropriate way.

- What are the present capabilities, knowledge and experience of the pupils?

b) *Learning intentions*

It sounds obvious, but it is important to be clear what pupils are expected to learn! Within the broader context of overall schemes of work, objectives for a lesson sequence or single lesson should be relatively focused. Clear learning intentions enable appropriate practical decisions to be made, for instance in selecting learning activities and tasks.

It is useful to give some thought to how learning intentions are expressed. One frequently used formulation adopts the opening phrase: 'By the end of this lesson pupils will be able to ...' which certainly encourages precision. The things pupils 'will be able to do' should be observable so it is useful to select active verbs such as 'list, describe, compare, identify, explain, solve, apply, discuss, evaluate, demonstrate the ability to, or demonstrate an understanding of ...' Alternatively, objectives can be expressed more developmentally. Pupils might be expected, for example, to: 'be aware of, have had practice in, been introduced to, have considered, developed the ability to, gained increased insight into, improved performance in, have considered, have an understanding of, begun to analyse ...'. As well as general objectives for the class, we may want or need to define objectives for particular groups or individuals.

As we saw in Chapter 1, it is good practice on appropriate occasions to consult with pupils and to share learning intentions (Rudduck and McIntyre, 2007, Reading 1.3), and also to discuss appropriate criteria to for judging success. Clarke (1998) coined the acronym 'WILF' (what I'm looking for) and has emphasised 'active learning through formative assessment' (2008), whilst Hattie (2009) has assembled international evidence on the significance of 'visible' teaching and learning (see Readings 4.6 and 16.5). Clear success criteria shared with pupils also help them to get a good fix on the object of their learning and what it will look and feel like when they have accomplished it. Thus it can empower pupils to monitor, regulate and feedback on their own and each others' progress. Some years earlier, Gage and Berliner (1975) made a similar point by identifying the power of 'advance organisers'. This simply means offering learners a clear explanation of what is going to happen, why, and what is expected of them.

Expert question

Congruence: are forms of assessment fit for purpose in terms of overall educational objectives?

This question contributes to a conceptual framework underpinning professional expertise (see Chapter 16).

• Are the key learning objectives clear, and how may they be shared with pupils?

c) *Structure of the lesson/s*

Thinking through the structure of a lesson or lesson sequence is one of the most important aspects of planning. Of course it involves thinking about the specific pupils in the class and the lesson objectives, but also, in particular, it requires the application of pedagogical content knowledge (see the discussion in Chapter 9, Section 4.3).

However, before becoming too daunted by the detail, it is worth considering the overall strategy to be adopted. Barnes et al. (1986) identified three approaches to teaching: 'closed', 'framed' and 'negotiated'.

> *Closed*: Content controlled by the teacher; pupils accept teachers' routines; typical methods – teacher exposition, worksheets, note-giving, copying, individual exercises, routine practical work; teacher evaluates.

> *Framed:* Content defined by the teacher, criteria for activities and tasks made explicit for pupils; pupils operate within teacher's framework, join in teacher's thinking, make hypotheses, set up tests; typical methods – teacher exposition with discussion eliciting pupil ideas; individual or group problem-solving; lists of tasks given, discussion of outcomes; teacher adjudicates.

> *Negotiated:* Content discussed, joint decisions; pupils involved in discussion of goals and methods, share responsibility for frame and criteria; typical methods – group and class discussion and decision-making, pupils plan and carry out work, make presentations, evaluate outcomes.

Each approach arguably has a place in a teacher's repertoire and in combination could certainly provide variety. It may be worth considering the use of these approaches in different parts of a lesson.

Expert question

Repertoire: is our pedagogic expertise sufficiently creative, skilled and wide-ranging to teach all elements of learning?

This question contributes to a conceptual framework underpinning professional expertise (see Chapter 16).

Reflective activity 10.3

Aim: To structure teaching and learning in a curriculum area.

Method: For a topic you plan to teach, think about how the knowledge might be presented and how teaching might be sequenced. Using your pedagogic subject knowledge and understanding of your pupils, what steps or 'chunks' might you plan for?

Review the appropriate use of closed, framed and negotiated teaching strategies.

Identify possible tasks and activities. Experiment with the scheduling of activities to arrive at your first draft plan.

Examine the structure you are considering and identify where there will be teacher input, where pupil activity? What does the balance look like? Where are the opportunities for interaction?

> Think about the ways in which your selection provides for progression (see Section 3.2 above), differentiation and Personalisation (see Sections 4.2 and 4.3 below).
>
> Think about time. How many sessions will you need? Have you got enough? How does the programme divide into lessons? Will you need to keep pupils together or is it possible to plan for fast and slow tracks?
>
> Identify the elements of your proposed curriculum which are likely to be seen as highlights by the pupils. Do they come at appropriate places?
>
> Are there opportunities for you to take stock with the pupils to share what has been achieved, what is working well and what barriers they are encountering?
>
> Revise your programme as necessary.
>
> *Follow-up:* Keep structure under review as you plan. Make it a focus of your evaluation and adjust your planning accordingly.

d) *Learning activities and tasks*

A mark of good teaching is the ability to transform what has to be learned into manageable tasks and activities, which are matched in size, complexity and depth to learners' existing capabilities. In this way, pupils are both stimulated and able to cope – and thus they succeed.

Judgements about progression and depth of cognitive challenge in tasks are particularly significant. Indeed, such judgements are probably the most important that a teacher makes. The international research, certainly says this. For example:

> Powerful and accomplished teachers are those who focus on students' cognitive engagement with the content of what it is that is being taught … (Hattie, 2012, p. 19, New Zealand, Reading 16.5)

> We have come to the conclusion, that the design of instructional and assessment tasks is the fundamental determinant of the quality of teaching and learning in the classroom. (Hogan, 2012, p. 103, Singapore, Reading 4.2)

> Our key point is that it is the intellectual demands embedded in classroom tasks that influence the degree of student engagement and learning. (Newmann, Bryk and Nagaok, 2001, p. 31, USA)

Expert question

Progression: does the curriculum-as-delivered provide an appropriate sequence and depth of learning experiences?

This question contributes to a conceptual framework underpinning professional expertise (see Chapter 16).

Central to the idea of cognitive challenge is the proposition that there are different forms of thinking. Bloom's Taxonomy of Educational Objectives (1956) identified six different kinds of thought processes: recall; comprehension; application; analysis; synthesis; evaluation.

The taxonomy implies a hierarchy. Thus recall and comprehension are basic forms of knowing. Application and analysis come when knowledge is put to use. Synthesis and evaluation are only possible with deeper

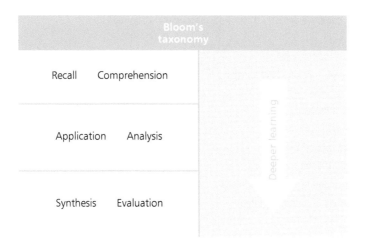

Figure 10.3
Bloom's taxonomy
and deeper
learning

forms of understanding. Much of the work derived from Bloom is concerned with developing 'higher-order' and 'deeper' thinking in pupils through activity or teacher questioning.

Bloom's classification (or variations on it) have been used to analyse the range and variety of activities and tasks in both primary and secondary schools. For instance, in a study conducted in infant schools, researchers distinguished between five types of task demands:

Incremental: which introduces new ideas, concepts, procedures and skills which are acquired during a task.

Restructuring: which requires children to invent or discover for themselves, so that existing skills, knowledge and concepts are advanced.

Enrichment: through which, by using familiar ideas, concepts, procedures, knowledge and skills on new problems, learning is applied.

Practice: which reinforces ideas, concepts, procedures, knowledge and skills which are assumed to be already known.

Revision: which reactivates known skills, concepts, knowledge, etc., which may not have been used for some time. (Bennett et al. 1984)

The study found that 60 per cent of tasks set in Language and Maths were intended as short-term practice, 25 per cent were 'incremental', 6 per cent were enrichment, 6 per cent were intended as long-term revision and only 1 per cent were intended as 'restructuring'. Practice tasks may be useful in confirming knowledge or skills, but one also has to consider at what point such tasks might become boring and counter-productive.

A secondary study was undertaken in five comprehensive schools and focused on first year mixed ability classes (Year 7). As indicated in Figure 10.4, tasks were designated 'low-level' or 'high-level' for cognitive demand (Kerry 1984).

Figure 10.4 The cognitive demand of common secondary school tasks

Low-level tasks	High-level tasks
Reinforcing or practice of a skill already learned	Imaginative tasks – includes writing poems, stories
Copying from the board	Collecting evidence, problem-solving, deducing, reasoning, such as devising questions to be answered and finding answers
Drawing and colouring in	
Reading aloud around the class	
Silent reading; listening; watching	Application tasks – using knowledge gained in a new situation
Memorising – learning dates/vocabulary	
Observing results of a demonstrated experiment or replicating a demonstration	Analysis tasks – find out why, differentiate facts from hypotheses, find patterns, clarify relationships
Note-taking with information supplied in textbook, worksheet or by teacher	Synthesis tasks – reorganising ideas in a new statement, developing plans to test ideas, discovering relationships, proposing changes or improvements
Looking up factual information	
	Evaluation tasks appraise, assess, criticise against justified criteria

Expert question

Expectation: does our school support high staff and student expectations and aspire for excellence?

This question contributes to a conceptual framework underpinning professional expertise (see Chapter 16).

Analysis of tasks set suggested that 85 per cent of tasks were low-level and only 15 per cent high-level. Of the low-level tasks, the three most frequent were: reinforcing/practising (16 per cent), copying (16 per cent) and drawing and colouring (14 per cent).

The findings are strikingly similar to those from the infant school study. The concern raised by both studies is the comparative rarity with which pupils met with stimulating and demanding tasks.

The difficulty here is that there is a tendency for teachers and pupils to interact together in comfort zones. Routinised teaching produces drift in pupil learning and, through this mutual accommodation, everyone gets through the day (see Pollard, 1985). But such coping strategies are exactly the reason why inspectors, government ministers and others persist in challenging the profession to have 'high expectations'.

One way of approaching this is to review the stimulus and variety of tasks over time.

Reflective activity 10.4

Aim To evaluate the stimulus and variety of tasks and activities.

Method This evaluation could be carried out by an observer, by yourself or by involving the pupils.

It can be carried out by focusing on a particular pupil for a relevant period, or on an analysis of whole-class or group provision.

The tasks in which pupils engage should be considered in terms of their motivational appeal, cognitive challenge and activity (write, read, talk, draw, listen, watch, move, sing, etc.).

Some questions which might be asked could include:

- How were the pupils introduced to the activity?
- Was there a motivational highlight?
- Was the level of cognitive challenge appropriate?
- How much writing were pupils required to do?
- What is the balance between active and passive tasks?
- What is the balance between collaborative and individual activity?

Follow-up Consider the findings from this exercise and try to deduce the reasons for any patterns you identify. How do you evaluate the results? Discuss your thoughts with others. If you judge it appropriate, what could be done to increase the stimulus and variety of activities and tasks?

e) *Success criteria*

Assessment forms a vital element of every stage of planning. Without assessment and the consequent re-evaluation of planning, effective teaching cannot be developed and maintained. When preparing a lesson plan, it is good practice to think through and record appropriate *success criteria* for the lesson. Objectives are then much more likely to be borne in mind when explaining tasks, interacting with pupils and in providing feedback.

For example, a lesson objective for a Year 2 class might be:

- Pupils should be able to understand the operation of subtraction and its related vocabulary with numbers up to 20.

Success criteria should specify evidence of progress/success with respect to the objective. Of course, the anticipated outcomes will be influenced by the age of the pupils, by previous assessments of their capabilities, and by the precise nature of the activity. Thus, this objective is likely to lead to very different anticipated outcomes in a Year 1, Year 2 or Year 3 class. For example, anticipated outcomes for the above objective might lead to the following success criteria in a Year 2 lesson plan:

- Work demonstrates an understanding that subtracting zero leaves a number unchanged.

- In discussion, pupils demonstrate an understanding of the terms 'take away' and 'find the difference between'.

Such clarity of thinking at the planning stage allows the teacher to share with the pupils not only the broad lesson objectives but also to clarify specific expectations, targets and outcomes. Teacher feedback to pupils can be much more precise. Furthermore, if pupil involvement in assessing their own work is desirable, and Chapter 13, Section 2.1 argues strongly that it is, then explicating success criteria is a powerful tool in helping teachers to develop self-assessment as part of the pupil learning process (Clarke, 2001; Muschamp, 1994, Reading 13.4).

f) Resources, ICT and safety

The use of checklists (actual or mental depending on experience) is highly recommended for making absolutely sure that all the practical necessities for a successful lesson are in place. This is basic, but essential.

Safety considerations should be considered and there should be no short cuts in recording the issues anticipated and the provision made. If something does go wrong, such records assume considerable significance.

If the use of ICT is important for the lesson, a specific part of the lesson plan may be devoted to it. Clearly it would be impossible to outline how an interactive whiteboard was to be used in each phase of a lesson, though there may be phases of the lesson where its use by pupils, or its combined use with other resources for demonstration purposes by the teacher, merits a reference in the lesson plan

g) Supporting adults

Effective planning is essential to get the benefits from teaching assistants, volunteer parents or any one of a range of other adults who may be contribute to classroom work. It is important that the teacher shares the nature of lesson activities with any supporting adult, and make it clear which pupil or pupils should be the focus of their attention. Above all however, it is also vital to share the learning intentions for an activity if the supporting adult is to play a full part in promoting learning (see Chapter 8, Section 4.2 for a fuller account of the effective use of adult learning support). Some teachers do this verbally, but many have a record to which supporting adults can refer that defines the lesson learning intentions, the activity and their role.

The topics above are likely to feature in effective lesson plans, whatever variations there may be in their presentation. Degrees of detail will vary between the novice and more experienced teachers, between exploratory and established lessons and in relation to teacher confidence generally.

Reflective activity 10.5

Aim   To review existing lesson planning.

Evidence and reflection   For trainee teachers, we suggest that you select one lesson plan that you were responsible for creating. Review the plan in the light of the seven topics discussed above. To what extent does your plan reflect these elements and the issues associated with them? What might be done to improve your specific plan or the next plan in the teaching sequence? Compare your planning with that of another trainee or with another teacher in a different teaching team in your school. What are the similarities and differences? How might your planning be improved?

Extension   Most teachers will agree that planning becomes more streamlined with experience. From the perspective of school inspectors, clearly stated objectives, task differentiation strategies and assessable outcomes are key features that are looked for in any plan.

Review some lesson plans over at least three curriculum areas. Are these features clear in your planning?

There are, of course, numerous lesson plans available on the internet and as published materials. Whilst many materials are of high intrinsic quality, there are a lot of weaker publications. Any resource should therefore be carefully evaluated before use in school, with due consideration given to its appropriateness to *your school's* aims, *your objectives and methods*, and perhaps most importantly to the overall suitability for the specific needs, motivations and circumstances of *your pupils*.

We move now to consider two issues which underlie all elements of lesson planning. These concern *differentiation* and *Personalisation*. Put another way, they concern how we can design lessons which maximise meaningful connections between the knowledge to be taught and the children and young people who are to learn. Beyond the specific details of planning, what are the underlying issues?

4.2 Differentiation

The concept of differentiation highlights the cognitive demands which a curriculum or an activity make of the learner (Haynes, 2012, Reading 10.6). This is of enormous importance, as David Ausubel asserted:

> If I had to reduce the whole of educational psychology to just one principle, I would say this: 'The most important single factor influencing learning is what the learner already knows. Ascertain this and teach him accordingly'. (Ausubel, 1968, p. vi, cited in Hattie, 2012, Reading 16.5)

In terms of lesson planning, differentiation relates to the appropriateness, or otherwise, of particular tasks and activities to the learner's existing understanding and needs. How well

Expert question

Differentiation: are curriculum tasks and activities structured appropriately to match the intellectual needs of learners?

This question contributes to a conceptual framework underpinning professional expertise (see Chapter 16).

'matched' are pupil and task? To achieve differentiation, teacher expertise is required at four key stages:

- establishing the intentions of the teacher and the pupil;
- identifying the pupil's existing knowledge, concepts, skills and attitudes;
- observing and interpreting the process by which the task is tackled;
- analysing and evaluating the outcomes from the task,

so that appropriate plans can be made for future learning opportunities.

A mismatch could occur at any (or all) of the stages. To take an example at the first stage, a teacher could set a task for a particular purpose but, if this was not explained appropriately, then the pupil might misunderstand. Any task might be done 'wrongly', or it may be done 'blindly', i.e. without seeing the point of it. There could also be a mismatch at the second stage. The task may be too hard for a pupil because it requires certain knowledge or skills which they do not have. A mismatch at the third stage can be illustrated by a task which may be set with an instruction to use certain apparatus, or to present the outcome in a certain way. However, the apparatus may not be necessary and may actually confuse the pupil, or the style of presentation may assume some skill which the pupil has not yet acquired. Additional problems could also arise from a mismatch at the fourth stage. For instance, teachers often mark the end product of children's learning. However, a high percentage of 'errors' cannot necessarily be assumed to relate to 'bad' work or 'poor' learning. Indeed, errors can provide important clues about where misunderstandings may have occurred.

Various differentiation strategies can be used in lesson planning – and Kerry and Kerry (1997) identified no less than 15 different methods. However, the classic distinction is between differentiation by task and differentiation by outcome.

> *Differentiation by task* requires lesson plans in which, for all or part of the lesson, particular groups of children will be engaged in different activities. This may be because the pupils are grouped according to their attainment in a subject, or because it has been judged appropriate for particular children to focus on different topics. In such cases, the lesson plan should specify the particular groups, activities and objectives.

> *Differentiating by outcome* calls for lesson plans in which the same basic task can be tackled in many ways – thus making it possible for students to respond in ways which are appropriate to their present level of knowledge, skill or understanding. A lesson plan might specify overall learning objectives but define differentiated outcomes in terms of what 'all', 'most' or 'some' pupils will be expected to accomplish.

Experience will show of course that the neat distinction between differentiation by task and outcome is, in reality, often blurred.

It is worth bearing in mind that there are dangers in relying on differentiation by outcome too much because it can become a euphemism for 'just seeing how well they do'. It allows teachers to avoid going through the vital process of envisaging what success will look like for particular groups of learners within the class.

However it is achieved, the cognitive challenge of tasks in your lessons should be matched to the cognitive needs of the learners in your class.

4.3 Personalisation

'Personalisation' is a relatively new educational concept which reflects both cumulative international understanding about learning and contemporary commitment to reducing inequalities in outcomes. Whilst echoing the cognitive issues associated with differentiation, it extends and broadens these to also embrace the social, emotional and motivational dimensions of learning (see the Research briefing on p. 291).

The idea was cogently expressed by the Chief Inspector of Schools for England in a report setting out 'A Vision for Teaching and Learning in 2020'. She wrote:

> **Expert question**
>
> **Personalisation:** does the curriculum resonate with the social and cultural needs of diverse learners and provide appropriate elements of choice?
>
> This question contributes to a conceptual framework underpinning professional expertise (see Chapter 16).

Personalising learning means taking a more structured and responsive approach to each child's learning, so that all pupils are able to progress, achieve and participate. This will be evident in high-quality, challenging teaching that engages pupils and helps them to take ownership of their learning. Better assessment, whether of learning or for learning, will promote the progress of every child and young person. All children will experience an engaging curriculum that helps them to develop the knowledge, skills, understanding and attitudes they need to thrive throughout their lives. (Teaching and Learning Review Group, 2006, p. 41, Reading 10.7)

2020 Vision drew on a US research review (Bransford et al., 2000, Reading 4.1) to declare that:

Personalising learning is learner-centred and knowledge-centred ...
Close attention is paid to learners' knowledge, skills, understanding and attitudes. Learning is connected to what they already know (including from outside the classroom). Teaching enthuses pupils and engages their interest in learning: it identifies, explores and corrects misconceptions. Learners are active and curious: they create their own hypotheses, ask their own questions, coach one another, set goals for themselves, monitor their progress and experiment with ideas for taking risks, knowing that mistakes and 'being stuck' are part of learning. Work is sufficiently varied and challenging to maintain their engagement but not so difficult as to discourage them. This engagement allows learners of all abilities to succeed, and it avoids the disaffection and attention-seeking that give rise to problems with behaviour.

... and it is assessment-centred

Assessment is both formative and summative and supports learning: learners monitor their progress and, with their teachers, identify their next steps. Techniques such as open questioning, sharing learning objectives and success criteria, and focused marking have a powerful effect on the extent to which learners are enabled to take an active role in their learning. Sufficient time is always given for learners' reflection. Whether individually or in pairs, they review what they have learnt and how they have learnt it. Their evaluations contribute to their understanding. They know their levels of achievement and make progress towards their goals.

On this definition, personalised learning can be seen as a synoptic concept, drawing together many threads of good practice. However, it does this by particularly emphasising the engagement of 'children, young people and their parents as respected users of the education service, giving them choices about how they access learning, listening to what they think about the service they receive and even designing those services with them' (Teaching and Learning Review Group, 2006, p. 39).

The emphasis on engagement and on meeting the needs of individual learners can seem daunting until one realises that the needs of many children and young people are shared in common. This is picked up elsewhere in this book, for instance on learning how to learn (Chapter 2), pupil consultation (Chapters 1 and 6), parental involvement and new technologies (Chapter 8), and assessment for learning (Chapter 13).

In the context of lesson planning, the concept of personalised learning can be used to review what has been planned and to pose questions for oneself regarding the likely efficacy of the provision. In addition to tasks being appropriately differentiated, will they really engage pupils, connect with their culture and expectations, and support their learning?

However it is achieved, Personalisation should enable learners to identify with classroom activities in meaningful ways – a point which may have to be asserted (see the **Research Briefing** on p. 291).

5 Evaluating curricular provision

In this section we begin by considering three generic questions which can be used to interrogate our own practice, with a particular focus on the application of subject knowledge in the curriculum. Addressing them will illuminate some issues on which personal improvement can be focused.

We then move on to consider 'lesson study' – a systematic approach to curricular improvement in collaboration with other colleagues. The latter is attracting a lot of international attention as a process to support high-quality teaching, learning and professional development.

These approaches illustrate, in different ways, TLRP's principle that 'pupil learning depends on teacher learning' (see Chapter 4, Section 2.9).

Research Briefing   Personalising learning

In January 2004, David Miliband, then Schools Minister in England, suggested that personalised learning included: 'high expectation of every child, given practical form by high quality teaching based on a sound knowledge and understanding of each child's needs' (North of England Conference Speech). Building on this, the DfES *2020 Vision* expansively emphasised children 'taking ownership' of their learning:

> *Personalising learning means taking a more structured and responsive approach to each child's learning, so that all pupils are able to progress, achieve and participate. This will be evident in high quality, challenging teaching that engages pupils and helps them to take ownership of their learning. All children will experience an engaging curriculum.* (2006, p. 41)

However, the English teacher training agency was restrictively focused on performance and national standards:

> *The term 'personalised learning' means maintaining a focus on individual progress, in order to maximise all learners' capacity to learn, achieve and participate. This means supporting and challenging each learner to achieve national standards and gain the skills they need to thrive and succeed.* (TDA Standards, 2007)

TLRP analysed the concept of personalised learning as it emerged, and published a Commentary identifying four particular challenges.

Key TLRP questions and findings:	Implications:
Conceptualisation: Are the components of personalised leaning and the relationships between them empirically supported and sufficient? There is a tension between expansive interpretations and restrictive definitions. Personalisation could be about the development of learner identities and dispositions – but it could also be about more pupil assessment and target setting.	A really powerful concept sounds attractive, is intellectually coherent and practically robust. The many versions of 'personalised learning' could make implementation difficult, but also provide considerable scope for professional interpretation.
Authenticity: Is this initiative really about learning? Or is it, despite the title, still primarily about teaching and curriculum delivery? By drawing attention to the personal, and to learning rather than teaching, 'personalised learning' enlists a softer vocabulary than that of targets, performance and delivery. But can a simple reconciliation be achieved? It seems unlikely where high-stakes assessment remains.	Personalisation is in some tension with the commitment, in England, to regular and end of key stage assessment. The rhetoric may be perceived as an ideological 'smoke screen'. Things may be easier in Wales, Scotland and Northern Ireland.
Realism: Are the ambition and rhetoric over-reaching themselves? The school system has been subject to deep and wide change in recent years. There are questions about the system's ability to cope with further innovation. Nor is it safe to assume that practices which prove effective in some places will succeed in others.	The problem of scaling up is considerable and workforce reform introduces fresh challenges. Personalisation represents a huge challenge to the teaching profession. Whilst innovative schools show the way, can others follow?
Risks: What are the major difficulties likely to be and how can they be managed? The concept of personalised learning continues to be interpreted in many ways. The response of the profession is a major risk factor and concerns about workload are important. Personalisation challenges the mutual accommodations which often grow up in routine teacher–pupil classroom practices and calls for high expectations, positive responses and new forms of learner-aware pedagogy.	The profession should contribute actively to the definition of personalised learning. Continued constructive negotiation on workloads is likely to be necessary. Appropriate support for teachers will be needed. Government agencies should work to achieve consistency.

Further information:
James, M. and Pollard, A. (2004) *Personalised Learning: A TLRP Commentary.* Swindon: ESRC. Available at **www.tlrp.org/pub** (accessed 18 November 2013).
Sebba, J., Brown, N., Steward, S., Galton, M. and James, M. (2007) *An Investigation of Personalised Learning Approaches used by Schools.* (Research Report RR843). London: DfES.

5.1 Key evaluation questions

All plans, at whatever level, should be open to modification and change depending on their success in aiding the development of learning in the classroom. A reflective teacher clearly understands the intimate links between the processes of planning, teaching, assessment and evaluation (see Figure 3.5, Chapter 3).

Three evaluation questions may be posed:

- Did pupils learn what was expected, and why?
- How did teacher knowledge support learning?
- How did classroom activities facilitate learning?

Question 1: Did pupils learn what was expected, and why?
'Assessment' and 'evaluation' are often confused because they are intricately entwined.

For example, the question, 'Did pupils learn what was expected?' focuses on both the learner and the teaching intentions. In order to answer the question, the reflective teacher needs assessment information on pupil performance. This information comes from formative assessment (see Chapter 13). *Assessment* thus involves collecting evidence about *how* pupils related to particular teaching/learning experiences and *what* (if any) knowledge, understanding or skills were developed. Evaluation, on the other hand, considers *why* the particular teaching and learning experience supported or did not support intended or unintended learning.

Assessment and evaluation thus go 'hand in hand' since it is not possible to consider the *why* without the *how* and the *what*. Evaluation of *why* pupil performance took the form it did is likely to lead to deeper analysis of teacher action – hence our other two questions.

Question 2: How did teacher knowledge support learning?
Evaluation of knowledge for teaching includes consideration of both content knowledge and pedagogical content knowledge (see Chapter 9, Section 4) and whether these were sufficient to support learning. The reflective teacher will have given some thought to these issues when planning. However, it may only be possible to fully answer this evaluation question after the teaching/learning has taken place. The reflective teacher will consider how well learning was supported by their knowledge of the subject and how to make this accessible to learners. Specific questions to ask include:

- Did I use appropriate and accurate language?
- Did I need to rely on text books or other sources of content matter?
- Did pupils give responses to questions or make suggestions about which I was uncertain?
- Had I predicted what pupils would find easy or difficult and any misconceptions they might have?
- Did my explanations and/or demonstrations aid pupils' understanding of the content?

- Did I use the most appropriate examples and representations?
- Did I introduce ideas in an order which enabled understanding to be built?
- Did I make connections between ideas presented in the lesson and with pupils' learning more generally?

This is not intended to be a definitive list but gives an idea of the sorts of questions reflective teachers might ask which relate to their own knowledge for teaching.

The precise nature of evaluative questions to ask about their own knowledge for teaching will vary depending on the subject matter of the teaching/learning experience being evaluated. For example, in a Religious Education lesson a teacher might ask 'did the artefacts I used portray accurate information about the religious rites?' Of essence here, is that the reflective teacher considers whether their pedagogical content knowledge facilitated learning. That is, did they know enough about not only the subject but also about how to teach the subject – so that pupils were able to learn?

The purpose of evaluating knowledge for teaching is not to identify limitations in teacher knowledge. Rather, it is to understand better how to meet the learning needs of pupils. Having evaluated our use of language, ability to respond to pupils, sequencing of content, etc., this analysis can be used to inform our own learning and future teaching. Focusing on the way in which subject matter knowledge and pedagogical content knowledge supports learning, facilitates the development of knowledge for teaching (Turner, 2013). In this way future teaching and learning are enhanced.

Question 3: How did classroom activities facilitate learning?
The evaluation of classroom activities thus requires careful analysis of *how* children respond to activities, *what* they learn from them and *why* that learning takes place.

Certain pupil and/or teacher activities may facilitate learning of some types of subject content better than others, and understanding this is important if the teacher is to develop their repertoire of teaching strategies for particular subjects.

It is also necessary to focus on individual pupils. For example, analysis of an activity might suggest that some children learned from physically manipulating objects while explaining what they were doing, whilst other children learned from watching and listening. Yet other children may have failed to learn through listening, but then physically manipulated the objects and learned for themselves. There are many possibilities.

Analysis of *why* activities are successful for different types of content and with different pupils may lead to more generic pedagogical learning. Like the other two key evaluative questions, the answer to this question is only useful to the teacher if it leads to developments in their planning for teaching and learning. Provided that careful analysis is carried out, it is possible to learn about how to develop planning for teaching and learning both from activities that worked well and those that did not.

> **Expert question**
>
> **Reflection**: is our classroom practice based on incremental, evidence-informed and collaborative improvement strategies?
>
> This question contributes to a conceptual framework underpinning professional expertise (see Chapter 16).

Reflective activity 10.6

Aim: To evaluate a teaching session with particular reference to the appropriate application of subject knowledge.

Evidence and reflection:

1 Plan to teach a session involving some new learning. In doing so, consider: what you want pupils to learn; what knowledge you need in order to support their learning; and what classroom activities are most appropriate. Having thought about the possibilities be prepared to respond to pupil input.

2 Obtain some sort of record of what happens. For instance, you could set up a video, make an audio recording or ask a colleague to observe you. In the case of the latter, try to get your colleague to make detailed notes on what is said by both you and the children.

3 Teach the session.

4 Analyse what happened under headings of the three key evaluative questions:
   - Did pupils learn what was expected, and why?
   - How did teacher knowledge support learning?
   - How did pupil and teacher activities facilitate learning?

Extension: Discuss your findings with a colleague and consider the consequences of what you have learned.

In the discussion of lesson study below, we see that this sort of evaluation activity can be made more systematic, collaborative and cumulative.

5.2 Evaluation through Lesson Study

Lesson Study blends teacher creativity with scientific rigour to establish systematic processes for teacher learning about classroom practice. It has a long history in Japan, and has spread across Asia and into the West. It can be seen as a rigorous form of evaluation, with direct developmental implications.

The *creative* element is found in the fact that teachers work together to refine, innovate or create new teaching approaches or curricular designs. The *scientific* element is found in the ways in which these teachers gather from research evidence, information about teaching approaches that could be effective and then, equally systematically, gather evidence of their pupils' learning (from their observations as well as from the perspectives of the pupils themselves) as they try out, refine, re-try and re-refine their new teaching approaches. This process of trialling and refining is carried out over a cycle of mini, group enquiries called 'research lessons' (RL). In these research lessons the group will study how the pupils are learning, in order to tease out ways of teaching the approach they are trialling that have the biggest effect on pupil learning.

Whatever teachers learn, they then make public. Learning and development does not remain the property of that classroom or school. Japanese teachers are culturally very collaborative and teacher knowledge is viewed with the same importance as medical knowledge in the West. Japanese teachers read the accounts of other teachers' lesson studies with interest as part of the literature they consult before engaging in their own classroom research. When they have completed a lesson study they will also invite colleagues to their classrooms for 'open house' events where they teach their new approach or an aspect of their new curriculum *in public* in front of an invited audience from local schools or colleges, before discussing it with their guests (and their pupils).

Lesson Study groups work best if they have several perspectives on the lesson and also include teachers with a range of experiences. A minimum of three is preferable, though in Japan such groups are often very much larger. Sometimes a Lesson Study group will include a teacher from outside the school who has particular expertise in the pedagogical or curriculum area under focus and who can bring this expertise to bear. Alternatively the group may include a member who has participated in lesson studies that have successfully developed new approaches in similar aspects of teaching.

There are productive ways in which trainee and newly or recently qualified teachers can gain most from participation in Lesson Study. These are explored in detail in Dudley and Gowing (2012).

What do you do in a Lesson Study?

A Lesson Study involves collaboratively planning (in great detail) a lesson, teaching the lesson with colleagues present, and observing the pupil learning that occurs – and then, immediately afterwards, analysing the evidence collected by the group members. This is done over a number of 'research' lessons so that there is comparison, refinement and cumulation in the pedagogy which is adopted.

Lesson study has itself evolved over a long period and a number of deliberate steps have become established. These are:

1 Members of a lesson study group will draw up or agree to observe a protocol which ensures that the group come together as equals in learning and enquiry and that whatever experience individual members bring to the process, it is treated with respect as an equal contribution to the group's collective endeavour.

2 The group will agree their focus – which can usefully be expressed as a research question – although it always takes a similar form 'How can we teach X more effectively to Y in order to improve their learning?' (where X will be an aspect of curriculum or subject knowledge and Y will be a learner group such as 'Year 5' or 'boys in Year 4 who have fallen behind in narrative writing').

3 Members will investigate what is 'out there' in terms of evidence of successful approaches developed elsewhere in relation to their focus. They will meet to pool their research findings. They may also plan their first research lesson. They will need to agree whose class will be used. They will often identify a small number of 'case pupils' who will be the subject of particular attention in the lesson study. Case pupils represent or typify learner groups in the class. They may, for example, represent high, middle and lower attaining pupils.

4   When planning the research lesson, the lesson study group plans for the whole class but pays specific attention to the planned learning for the case pupils. The group predicts and sets out what they hope each case pupil will achieve by the end of the research lesson (very like success criteria) and they also list what they hope each of the pupils will be doing at each stage of the lesson.

5   One of the teachers then teaches the research lesson. The others observe the class taking note of everything that goes on but paying particular attention to the case pupils and noting what they do. Observation notes are made on copies of the lesson plan which the teachers use as an observation proforma.

6   After the lesson the teachers interview a sample of pupils in order to ascertain their perspective on the research lesson – what worked more or less well and how it could be improved next time.

7   After the lesson and pupil interviews, the teachers discuss what they observed as soon as they can after the lesson is over – and preferably on the same day. The discussion should always follow the following structure:

   a   Sharing what each member observed of the *learning* of each of the case pupils compared with the predictions the group had made for the case pupil, and a discussion about why such differences may have occurred.

   b   Discussion about the *learning* of the class as a whole.

   c   The discussion will then turn to the lesson itself and the teaching – but this is after much discussion about the learning and is always based on observed evidence of the learning that took place.

   d   Discussion about what to do in the next research lesson to address issues from the one just taught.

8   The group then plans the next research lesson.

9   After a sequence of three or more research lessons, the group has usually had a chance to reassess some of the pupils whose learning they will now understand in much greater detail. They will also usually have agreed some changes to the teaching or to the lesson designs that are to be adopted in the future and shared with colleagues. And so progress is made.

Figure 10.5 summarises the lesson study cycle diagrammatically.

Participating teachers tend to feel that, because the research lessons are jointly planned and analysed, they are the property of the group, rather than of the person who happens to teach the lesson. Therefore, if something goes wrong it is part of the whole group's learning and not something for the individual teacher to worry about. Teachers say that as a result of this they are more prepared to take risks and to tackle aspects of the curriculum or subjects which they feel least secure with (Dudley, 2011).

Furthermore, in a lesson study teachers are learning from and with each other while focused on a common endeavour – that of improving the learning of pupils and improving the quality of their teaching. This helps even experienced teachers to see their classrooms, their teaching and their pupils' learning with fresh eyes. They thus become more aware

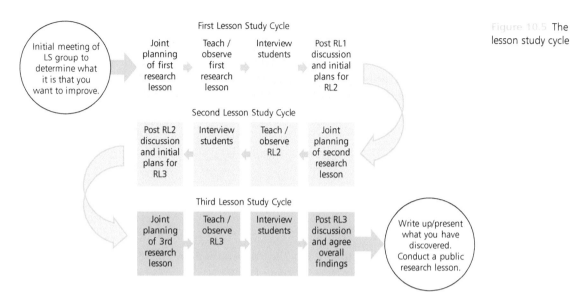

Figure 10.5 The lesson study cycle

of familiar or habitual practices that are not normally noticed but which, because they are suddenly more visible, can be changed and improved.

An ongoing lesson study programme of curriculum review and renewal can help a school to ensure that the structure and content of its curriculum is constantly evaluated and improved in terms of the learning and teaching that it generates. Furthermore, such improvements are passed on to other teachers and schools for further critique and adaption, thus generating a second wave of professional learning. In this way the curriculum is kept alive and appropriate progression, relevance, differentiation and Personalisation are renewed.

In Japan, lesson study is also used as a key tool within a much wider-ranging and longer-term cycle of whole school curriculum review and renewal. Many Japanese schools are very explicit about the kinds of person they want their education to create as well as the type of learners they hope their pupils will become. This means their school aims extend well beyond knowledge, skills and understanding – to the values, attributes, personal qualities and characteristics of their learners that will help them in adult life and help society as well. Kuno (2011) demonstrates how collaborative Lesson Study can be deployed for such whole-school development and for the promotion of breadth, balance, connection and coherence.

Conclusion

Curriculum planning is a highly skilled activity underpinned by understanding of key principles (Her Majesty's Inspectors, 1985, 10.1; Hattie, 2012, Reading 16.5). Whilst it requires awareness of curriculum requirements at national level and of whole-school policies, this must be complemented by understanding of the prior knowledge of pupils, of subject knowledge and pedagogic knowledge.

As we have seen, these forms of expertise must be combined with sound practical organisation to deliver an interesting and appropriately challenging set of learning experiences. In the hands of a skilled and sensitive teacher, structure and purpose will be tempered by flexibility and intuition, and enriched by imagination and commitment.

Key readings

For the classic statement of a planned whole curriculum framework and introduction to the conceptual tools of breadth, balance, coherence, progression, relevance and differentiation, see:

Her Majesty's Inspectors (1985) *The Curriculum from 5 to 16.* HMI Series, Curriculum Matters No 2. London: HMSO. Reading 10.1 (available at educationengland.org.uk)

Excellent overviews of curriculum planning issues, including the significance of breadth and balance, are provided in:

Male, B. and Waters, M. (2012) *The Primary Curriculum Design Handbook.* London: Continuum.

Male, B. and Waters, M. (2012) *The Secondary Curriculum Design Handbook.* London: Continuum. (Reading 9.1)

The importance of subject domains is addressed in Chapter 9, Section 4, and in Young (2008, Reading 9.2) and Wilson (2000, Reading 9.3). This is complemented by the case for study of topics across subjects and for cross-curricula planning. A committed argument is made by Turner-Bissett and by Hunter and Scheirer, whilst the Siraj-Blatchfords explore specific strategies for cross-curricula provision.

Turner-Bissett, R. (2000) 'Reconstructing the primary curriculum', *Education 3–13: International Journal of Primary, Elementary and Early Years Education*, 28 (1), 3–8. (Reading 10.3)

Hunter, R. and Scheirer, E. A. (1988) *The Organic Classroom: Organizing for Learning 7 to 12.* London: Falmer.

Siraj Blatchford, J. and Siraj Blatchford, I. (1995) *Educating the Whole Child: Cross-curricular Skills, Themes and Dimensions.* Buckingham: Open University Press.

Establishing curricular connections and relevance for the lives of pupils is a constant challenge for teachers. To help in meeting this need there have been calls for more use of local resources within the curriculum and attempts to personalise provision in a range of ways.

Thomas, L. (2010) *The RSA Area Based Curriculum: Engaging the Local.* London: RSA. (Reading 10.4)

Teaching and Learning in 2000 Review Group. (2006) *2020 Vision: Report of the Teaching and Learning in 2020 Review Group*. London: DfES. (Reading 10.7)

On lesson planning, Haynes provides accessible and practical guidance. Hattie draws implications from his exceptional synthesis of international evidence on effective lesson design and teaching practices.

Hattie, J. (2012) *Visible Learning for Teachers: Maximising Impact on Learning.* London: Routledge. (Reading 16.5)

Haynes, A. (2010) *The Complete Guide to Lesson Planning and Preparation.* London: Continuum. (Reading 10.6)

The link between curriculum planning and assessment is further elaborated in Chapter 13.

Systematic and open evaluation of lessons is key to improvement, as Hattie's work has shown, and the Lesson Study approach suggests practical ways of framing this in collaboration with colleagues. On this, see

Dudley, P. (2011) *Lesson Study: a Handbook.* Cambridge: Dudley. (Available at lessonstudy.co.uk)

For stimulating views on the principles that underpin curriculum planning and design, and stressing learner engagement, see:

Egan, K. (1988) *An Alternative Approach to Teaching and the Curriculum.* London: Routledge.

Eisner, E. (1996) *Cognition and Curriculum Reconsidered.* London: Paul Chapman.

reflectiveteaching.co.uk offers additional professional resources for this chapter. These may include *Further Reading*, illustrative *Reflective Activities*, useful *Web Links* and *Download Facilities* for diagrams, figures, checklists and activities.

Pedagogy
How can we develop effective strategies?

11

Introduction

Pedagogy can be seen as the skilful interplay of teachers' craft knowledge and their creative responsiveness to specific classroom situations, as informed by theory and research. Teachers move between these different sources of experience, strategic judgement and understanding, as they take decisions 'in action'. In this chapter, we use case study vignettes to represent decision-making in action.

Figure 11.1 The science, craft and art of pedagogic expertise

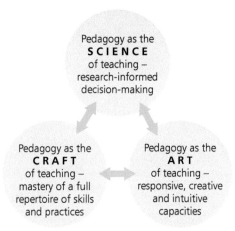

As Figure 11.1 shows, the art, craft and science of teaching each contribute to the overall concept of pedagogy (GTC E, 2010, Reading 11.2). Craft is seen as the repertoire of teachers' accumulated skills, strategies, methods, approaches and practices from which they select and to which they continue to add through experience. Art is seen as teachers' moment-by-moment responses to what is happening in the classroom in ways that are secure, grounded, creative or innovative, as the occasion demands. Science is seen as teachers' knowledge, understanding of and engagement in evaluation, reflection and research, in search of evidence to inform the professional choices and decisions they make. This approach to pedagogy can be contrasted with understandings of 'folk pedagogy' which unfortunately still exist in contemporary cultures (Bruner, 1996, Reading 11.1). Indeed, to establish the profession of teaching, it is vital to move beyond folk pedagogy to establish the nature of teachers' expertise.

Pedagogic judgement enables teachers to reach between subject knowledge of the curriculum and their understanding of the needs of learners. In particular, teachers develop a repertoire of skills to 'scaffold' and extend learners' understanding and to support engagement in learning.

Two principles are of particular relevance to this chapter on teacher strategies and pedagogic repertoire:

Effective teaching and learning requires teachers to scaffold learning. Teachers should provide activities which support learners as they move forward, not just intellectually, but also socially and emotionally, so that once these supports are removed, the learning is secure. (Principle 4)

Effective teaching and learning promotes the active engagement of the learner. A chief goal of teaching and learning should be the promotion of learners' independence and autonomy. This involves acquiring a repertoire of learning strategies and practices, developing positive attitudes towards learning, and confidence in oneself as a good learner. (Principle 6)

See Chapter 4

In discussing pedagogy, we also acknowledge the crucial importance to pedagogy of *subject knowledge*, which we take to mean the concepts, knowledge and understanding, within and between domains of learning, on which teachers' subject-specific planning and teaching draws. For detailed discussion of subject knowledge, see Chapter 9, Section 4. Of course, this is complemented by the need for understanding about *learning*. Whatever aspirations or expectations may exist, it is essential to take account of the existing knowledge, experience and understanding of children and young people. For more detailed discussion of learning, see Chapter 2. Pedagogic expertise, as you can see, draws on a wide range of understanding and capabilities – which is what makes it so interesting.

In this chapter, we begin with a case study vignette enabling us to see the 'pedagogy in action' of a successful student teacher. A short discussion of how thinking about pedagogy has developed is then provided, for its significance to the profession has not been fully established in the UK until recently. Section 3 is focused on pedagogic judgements to support learner development, and we then return to the issue of pedagogic repertoire. This is illustrated through a discussion of the use of talk to 'scaffold' student understanding through whole-class, small group and individual teaching. Finally, we look at the way in which pedagogy develops over time, as can be seen even through a short series of lessons.

1 Enacting the art, craft and science of pedagogy

1.1 Art, craft and science in action

We offer a vignette as a starting point for thinking about how pedagogy, as defined in the previous section, might be enacted in the classroom.

Case study 11.1 Studying teenage magazines

Fiona, an English trainee teacher, is working with a diverse Year 7 class. They have been exploring broadsheet and tabloid newspaper design and language and are now moving on to focus on magazines. They have all brought in a magazine of their choice which they have already thought about for homework. The students arrive in dribs and drabs at the start of the lesson. Fiona welcomes them individually and encourages them to settle quickly, using a variety of strategies such as her warm tone of voice and reminders of customary routines to achieve quiet. A partially completed spider diagram on teenage magazines is projected onto the whiteboard and students are rapidly engaged in trying to add to it. One boy wonders aloud: 'What do girls read?' When the students become over-excited and start to interrupt one another, Fiona re-gains the whole class's attention by a range of means, in particular through: showing that she is listening to people's suggestions with genuine interest; asking students to extend their contributions; insisting students attend to one another's points of view; and collating suggestions clearly on the board for them to respond to. Furthermore, Fiona helps students develop their ideas by contextualising them in terms of marketing and publishing. Another slide on the board reveals that the terms unique selling point (USP) and target audience are important ideas for this lesson. Fiona then projects images of the front covers of two popular magazines on the board: one on football apparently targeting boys, and one about pop music apparently geared towards girls. Immediately, the students demonstrate some of their differing values as they comment on aspects of the covers such as the selection of celebrities featured and their forthright attitudes about them, and the free gifts being offered as marketing ploys. Fiona skilfully weaves in this unsolicited information to expand students' learning about USPs and target audiences, moving on to even more detailed analysis and using specialist terms from the discourse of magazine publishing such as 'persuasive' and 'promotion', words which some students then appropriate themselves. The discussion turns to the magazines each individual has brought in, including how much they cost and how they are displayed in newsagents and supermarkets to catch the attention of their target audiences. At this point, the students are learning about different magazines than the ones they read themselves (and the boy who wondered what girls read is getting some answers). Fiona, too, is learning things about her class such as their reading preferences, their interests, their spending power. She now asks them to apply what they have been learning about USPs and target audiences. The task is to imagine they have been asked by a publishing executive board to market one of the company's teenage magazines. They can either create a new one or use the one they have brought with them. One student has brought along a weekly supplement produced by one of the main broadsheet newspapers. Fiona holds it up for the class to see whilst the student reports on how and why she would persuade teenagers to read it. From her report, and from some probing questions by Fiona, it is clear that although the supplement is intended for adult readers of the broadsheet, it is also of some interest to younger readers than its target audience. During the student's contribution, Fiona realises that one of the boys has given in to the temptation of reading what he has brought in himself – a copy of a Simpsons' magazine – rather than listening to what is being said. Without interrupting the student who is speaking, Fiona quietly walks over to his desk, picks up the Simpsons magazine and returns to the front of the class. Having responded to the first student's ideas, she engages the boy whose magazine it is by making a virtue of the fact she now has two magazines in her hand. Fiona invites the watching class good-humouredly to compare and contrast the two very different magazines in terms of target audiences and USPs, not in order to say whether one is better than the other, but to reflect on how differently they are being marketed. A misdemeanour is transformed by Fiona into a positive and purposeful teaching point. Everyone benefits.

1.2 Analysing pedagogy

It is interesting to look at this vignette of Fiona's lesson in the light of the introductory definition above in order to analyse how it exemplifies her pedagogy. Her craft is apparent everywhere: the interactions with students she uses to settle them and engage their attention; preparation of pre-written material on attractive and legible slides projected on the whiteboard; deftness in collating ideas in writing on another board, as they emerge from discussion; choice of language and use of features such as warmth, interest and firmness to simultaneously steer, control and encourage students' work. However, the structure and intent of the lesson do not occur by chance. Both are informed by science, by theories of planning, teaching and learning which Fiona has encountered in her prior experience as a learning support assistant and her teacher training. The way she relates to individual students and orchestrates whole-class discussion draws on theories of dialogic teaching and learning, for example the power of what Alexander calls 'reciprocal' and 'cumulative' teaching (2008a, p. 113) which incorporates the ideas students contribute that are new to her but have the potential to extend everyone's learning about magazines. Although it is predominantly a whole-class lesson with some opportunities for pair and individual work, there is a clear sense that Fiona sees herself as the teacher who has specific knowledge and understanding which she wants students to be learning. Her plan for the lesson is differentiated accordingly. She acknowledges that not all students' understanding is at the same stage and that she will be working in the relevant Vygotskyan zone of proximal development with different students (see Chapter 2).

The way Fiona handles her realisation that a boy is not attending to the class discussion but reading his Simpsons' magazine nicely exemplifies the art of her pedagogy. Although she appears to act intuitively, her quick-thinking enables her to seize the opportunity to transform a confiscated magazine into material for learning. She also understands the way in which a firm but encouraging tone of voice can engage students such as these, communicating that she enjoys discovering their views about the topic. Furthermore, she assumes an understanding that they, in return, are interested in her ideas. The students do, indeed, react in a lively way to her responses: dismissive of the celebrities who appear on the magazine covers she has chosen. They learn that she is genuinely surprised and can see how her new knowledge goes on to shape the rest of the lesson. Fiona's and the students' attitudes towards the magazines and their marketing are not, therefore, neutral. Instead, the unit of work is deeply connected with societal attitudes and values, including monetary values, and there is considerable potential for students to be dismissive of one another's selections. However, a spirit of genuine enquiry permeates the lesson: even though the stated objectives and outcomes are framed in terms of what students will know, understand and do, the enacted lesson takes on several features of an exploration.

In terms of her subject knowledge, Fiona has studied English at Advanced Level, has a good English literature degree and is training as an English teacher. During her teacher education course, she has learnt about studying a wide range of texts from literary, linguistic and media perspectives, including mail order catalogues, newspapers, magazines, websites and TV programmes. She has good conceptual knowledge and understanding of this area of English studies, a range of well-honed analytical skills and a confident meta-language to steer her through the unit of work. She is well positioned to review the English department's existing work on magazines and select from it as she deems appropriate. She is also able to draw on her own personal history of reading magazines herself, past and present. With her fellow student teachers, she has had the chance to explore some of the magazines young people like her Year 7 class read, though not the idiosyncratic variety of this particular class. What we see, however, is Fiona's substantive content knowledge (see Chapter 9, Section 4) being transformed for teaching this particular class, not merely transmitted to them raw, and her pedagogical content knowledge giving shape to the lesson overall.

Although the above vignette and analysis focus only on a tiny part of Fiona's pedagogy, they are designed to show that pedagogy is multifaceted and constantly shifting, hence the need for all teachers not only to try and identify what constitutes their pedagogy but also to keep it under constant review. Whilst this example illustrates pedagogy in action within a single lesson, later in the chapter we will look at the pedagogy of a teacher focusing on the learning of an individual child and, finally, on pedagogy within a sequence of lessons.

Reflective activity 11.1

Aim: To identify aspects of the craft, art and science of pedagogy in our teaching.

Evidence and reflection: Think back to a lesson you have taught very recently. On a blank piece of paper, make a rough sketch of the diagram in Figure 11.1 above. In each circle, note down anything from the lesson you can identify as aspects of the craft, art and science of your pedagogy. What is the balance between the different aspects? At what stage of the lesson were different aspects prevalent? How might you account for any difference in emphasis?

Extension: Add to your sketch instances where you feel your subject knowledge related to these aspects of your pedagogy.

2 Pedagogy, knowledge and learning

2.1 The development of pedagogic principles

How is pedagogy represented in a selection of the literature? In the introduction to the TLRP commentary, *Professionalism and pedagogy: A contemporary opportunity*, we are reminded that 'the relative lack of reference to pedagogy in educational discussion within the UK, compared with practice in many other successful countries, has been the focus of academic debate for the best part of thirty years' (GTC E, 2010, p. 4, Reading 11.2). The origin of concern about this lack is traced to Brian Simon's thought-provoking chapter written in the 1980s entitled 'Why no pedagogy in England?' (Simon, 1981) (Reading 11.3). In this text, Simon defines the term pedagogy as the 'science of teaching' (Ibid., p. 124), arguing that although the concept of pedagogy has long been revered in many European countries, in England it has been shunned. The chief reason is:

> the practice and approach of our most prestigious educational institutions (historically speaking), the ancient universities and leading public schools. Until recently, and even perhaps today, these have been dominant, both socially and in terms of the formation of the climate of opinion. It is symptomatic that the public schools, in general, have until recently contemptuously rejected the idea that a professional training is in any way relevant to the job of a public schoolmaster. (Ibid., p. 125)

The view that education of teachers was only needed for those teaching in the elementary schools, meant that education 'as a subject of enquiry and study, still less a "science", has had little prestige in this country' (Ibid., p. 128). Teachers in the public schools thus only needed a good knowledge of their subject rather than professional training. However, the challenges for teachers working in the elementary schools did eventually force school boards to take a more systematic approach and a science of teaching emerged which could be incorporated into teacher education. Hence, there began to be some recognition of the importance of pedagogy. Simon's challenging question has been revisited on numerous occasions from different perspectives, not least because the concept of pedagogy has continued to carry uncertain weight and meaning. It remains the case that teachers working outside the maintained sector are not required to have qualified teacher status, although many, of course, do.

However, whilst Simon argued that the development of teaching was dominated by a concern with the individual differences between learners and groups of learners, and how to respond to them, he also offered an interesting, but contrasting, viewpoint:

> To develop effective pedagogy means starting from the opposite standpoint, from what children have in common as members of the human species; to establish the general principles of teaching and, in the light of these, to determine what modifications of practice are necessary to meet specific individual needs. (Ibid., p. 141)

It was on the basis of Simon's appeal, to the establishment of 'general principles of teaching' that TLRP began its work on the principles which underpin effective teaching and learning (see Chapter 4).

Despite numerous government interventions in education in England during the two decades following Simon's seminal essay, Alexander was able to write an article over 20 years afterwards entitled 'Still no pedagogy? Principle, pragmatism and compliance in primary education' (2004). Although teachers were, by then, required to pay more attention to pedagogy, Alexander argued that the concept was very narrowly conceived, unlike the continental view of pedagogy which:

> especially in northern, central and eastern Europe, brings together within the one concept the act of teaching and the body of knowledge, argument and evidence in which it is embedded and by which particular classroom practices are justified. (Alexander, 2004, p. 10)

Expert questions

Repertoire: is our pedagogic expertise sufficiently creative, skilled and wide-ranging to teach all elements of learning?

Warrant: are our teaching strategies evidence-informed, convincing and justifiable to stakeholders?

These questions contribute to a conceptual framework underpinning professional expertise (see Chapter 16).

From a wide-ranging comparative study, Alexander argues that pedagogy involves teachers engaging with the complexity of domains which include what is to be taught, to whom and how, along with attention to the effect of policy and institutional contexts within which teaching takes place *and* the culture and values of all those involved, whether schools, teachers or students, acknowledging this complex dynamic of pedagogy is what marks 'the transition from teaching to education' (Alexander, 2008a, p. 49, Reading 12.3). Indeed, more recently, this view has led Alexander to describe pedagogy as 'the heart of the enterprise [which] gives life to educational aims and values, lifts the curriculum from the printed page, mediates learning and knowing, engages, inspires and empowers learners – or, sadly, may fail to do so' (Alexander, 2010, p. 307).

The concept of pedagogy has thus, over the years, become transformed from Simon's notion of a science of teaching to a much more holistic idea, one which requires teachers to reflect on whether and how their pedagogy develops from established principles. We now review some of these developments.

2.2 Perspectives

Critical pedagogy: In some parts of the world educators have used the concept of pedagogy to challenge the status quo. One of the most well-known of those educators is the Brazilian, Paulo Freire, whose central argument in *Pedagogy of the Oppressed* (2000) is that pedagogy is the means by which the most oppressed people can be taught to reflect critically on their oppression and actively participate in liberation from it. Freire's notion of pedagogy is of teaching through which the oppressed learner becomes literate and gains the power of self-direction, rather than merely adopting the forms of education offered by the oppressor or, indeed, being filled up like an empty vessel. Instead, he views the literacy process as a dynamic one in which 'reading the world always precedes reading the word, and reading the word implies continually reading the world' (Freire, 2000, p. 37). Education of this kind means making connections between language and life so that each illuminates the other. Freire's pedagogy, often referred to as critical pedagogy to indicate the expectation that some form of action will arise out of the stance being adopted, stems from very particular attitudes and values but resonates with educators in many different parts of the world. In writings about his work it is possible to identify aspects of craft, science and art that he believes teachers command, integrally related to their subject knowledge.

Theories of mind: Meanwhile, other prominent educators, for example Jerome Bruner in the United States, have viewed pedagogy from the perspective of educational psychology with different consequences again. Bruner, strongly influenced by the work of Vygotsky, is interested in how theories of the human mind affect teachers' practice. As we saw above, in his analsyis of 'folk pedagogy' (1996, Reading 11.1), he demonstrates that the way teachers perceive learners' minds affects how they teach, a powerful argument for a science of teaching which would enable us to understand the workings of the mind as clearly as possible. Drawing connections between 'models of mind and models of pedagogy' (1996, p. 53), he demonstrates how a theory of mind which holds that learners acquire knowledge through imitation will lead to a very different pedagogy than a theory of mind which privileges learning through inter-subjective exchange. Bruner is not arguing for one model over and above another; rather, he suggests that what is needed is the forging of different perspectives on learning into 'some congruent unity, recognised as parts of a common continent' (1996, p. 65). Echoes of Dweck and Sfard are clear (see Chapter 2).

Pedagogical discourse: Deborah Britzman, an American critical ethnographer with a keen interest in teacher education, likewise argues the need for teachers to learn how theoretical perspectives inform their pedagogy. In *Practice Makes Practice: A Critical Study of Learning to Teach* (2003), she explores how it is not just important to identify and reflect critically on theoretical perspectives but also on different discourses which can crucially affect the way in which teachers, teaching and pedagogy are construed:

> every curriculum, as a form of discourse, intones particular orientations, values, and interests, and constructs visions of authority, power, and knowledge. The selected knowledge of any curriculum represents not only things to know, but a view of knowledge that implicitly defines the knower's capacities as it legitimates the persons who deem that knowledge important. This capacity to privilege particular accounts over others is based upon relations of power. (Britzman, 2003, p. 39)

Teachers therefore need to remain keenly aware of the way different discourses shape their thinking and that of their students. Discourses which characterise learners as 'Level 4s' or 'C/D borderlines' need to be defamiliarised and challenged, as they are by the UK team who conducted the 'learning without limits' research (Hart et al., 2004, see Reading 1.4). The researchers and the teachers with whom they worked set out to explore what changed when students' potential achievements were viewed as 'limitless', modifying their perspective to 'formulate the teaching task not primarily in terms of opposition to something negative, but as one of commitment to something positive: transforming the capacity to learn' (2004, p. 262).

Pedagogical thoughtfulness: One of the four aspects of pedagogy being discussed in this chapter is the art of pedagogy. Defined in TLRP terms as the teacher's 'responsive, creative and intuitive capacities' (Pollard, 2010, p. 5), it is not surprising to find it sometimes characterised as something a teacher either has or does not have, rather than as an aspect of pedagogy which teachers can be taught. However, the art of being attentive and responsive is certainly a quality that can be developed. A key exponent of such capacities is Max van Manen, a Canadian who has written extensively about what he calls pedagogical 'thoughtfulness' (van Manen, 1991, Reading 11.5). Considering parents and teachers simultaneously, he draws comparisons between how they relate to young people. His aim is to emphasise that their roles are equally important, but different. A particularly interesting angle from which he explores the concept of pedagogy is from the student's viewpoint (van Manen, 1999). In an early work, *The Tact of Teaching: The Meaning of Pedagogical Thoughtfulness* (1991), he urges the need for teachers to attend closely to individual children, exercising pedagogical 'tact' in how they engage with the young people they teach by which he means the constantly shifting everyday classroom dynamics through which learning happens and the 'thoughtfulness' with which they reflect on their practice (van Manen, 1991). (For further examples, see Chapter 2.) Explicitly seeking out and researching students' perspectives on pedagogy is rare, but van Manen's selection of student descriptions of their own classroom experiences in a later work serves as a vital reminder that pedagogy is not the province of the teacher alone; students – their values, attitudes, responses, prior knowledge – are a key aspect of pedagogy, too.

Learning and experience: As van Manen's ideas remind us, pedagogy is inextricably linked with learning. Pedagogy is concerned – but not solely concerned – with the subject matter or topic being learned; it is also concerned with children and young people's learning much more broadly. John Dewey, the great American philosopher of education working in the early years of the twentieth century, is highly critical of any form of instruction which merely instils facts in learners' minds but does not encourage genuine thinking. In his key work, *Democracy and Education* (1916), he makes this point forcefully:

> There can be no doubt that a peculiar artificiality attaches to much of what is learned in schools. It can hardly be said that many students consciously think of the subject matter as unreal; but it assuredly does not possess for them the kind of reality which the subject matter of their vital experiences possesses. They learn not to expect that sort of reality of it; they become habituated to treating it as having reality for the purposes of recitations, lessons and examinations. That it should remain inert for the experiences of daily life is more or less a matter of course. The bad effects are two-fold. Ordinary experience does not receive the enrichment which it should; it is not fertilised by school learning. And the attitudes which spring from getting used to and accepting half-understood and ill-digested material weaken vigour and efficiency of thought. (Dewey, 1916, p. 155)

Early years and primary teachers are particularly well-placed to understand children's learning holistically. They spend much of their time each day with the same group of children and are often therefore aware of the interconnections children may make between ordinary experience and school learning. However, the case study enactments of this chapter also demonstrate how secondary teachers can likewise increase effectiveness by drawing on students' learning beyond the classroom and the school.

3 Enacting learner development

3.1 Building from prior learning

The extent to which ordinary experience may be enriched or 'fertilised' (to use Dewey's metaphor from the previous section) by school learning is explored in the vignette which follows. It exemplifies TLRP Principle 3 which links teaching to prior experience and learning and 'includes building on prior learning but also taking account of the personal and cultural experiences of different groups of learners' (James and Pollard, 2006, p. 8). In it, we see an early years trainee teacher, Siobhan, carrying out focused observations and analysis of an individual child, Alfie, and how both of these form part of her pedagogic practice.

Case study 11.2 Studying a child's reading development

Siobhan, an early years trainee teacher, conducts a study into 6-year-old Alfie's reading development over the course of a six-week school placement. At the start of the placement she collects evidence of the child's current attitudes to, and attainment in, reading from:

1. classroom observations of the child reading in a variety of situations;
2. reading to and with the chosen child;
3. a reading interview;
4. a running record;
5. observations and assessments of phonics lessons and guided reading lessons.

During the placement she continues to gather observational and assessment evidence from phonics and reading lessons and repeats the initial activities towards the end.

From her initial observations of the child reading in a variety of situations, Siobhan notes that Alfie frequently chooses to read during 'independent' time in the classroom, selecting a range of texts from *Beano* comics to factual books about dinosaurs and poetry books about monsters. He often engages other children in what he is doing, attempting to tell them what the book is about and asking them to read with him. He reads aloud to his peers in an excited and animated fashion, making sound effects and loud exclamations. It is evident that he has read many of the texts in the book corner. Siobhan elects to conduct a running record on a book about monsters and this he reads with confidence and fluency. Whether reading books with his peers, or on a one-to-one basis with an adult, Alfie enjoys the opportunity to share his enthusiasm and to discuss

---

texts. In contrast, during phonics and guided reading sessions Alfie appears distracted and not engaged in the content of the sessions or the books, only becoming so when phonics sessions contain images of monsters or when the content of the book in guided reading sessions captivates him. When asked about books he doesn't like reading, he states, 'the ones at guided reading are so boring'. His parents have contacted the school to say that the books that are being sent home are not engaging him and he has committed them to memory.

The reading interview elicits further information about Alfie's attitudes to reading. He confidently asserts, 'I like reading a lot' but with the caveat 'not when we have to read on the carpet and my legs get itchy and I can't see the pictures. I like seeing the pictures'. At home he reads with his older brother, and his dad sometimes. He makes frequent reference to his older brother and how he reads his 'chapter books', especially his monster books and also his *Beano* comics.

3.2 Analysing pedagogy

Siobhan's study enables her to make reflective observations about Alfie's learning and demonstrates how focused observations and analysis of an individual child are central to pedagogy (see Chapter 2 for further examples). Siobhan comments on the holistic nature of young children's learning and development and reveals how a teacher's pedagogy is underpinned by knowledge of the individual learner, both in school and beyond, and their responses to a wide variety of classroom interactions. Alfie's keen interest in reading is not evident from his responses in guided reading and phonics sessions but is apparent through the observations Siobhan makes of him reading independently and with his peers and also from the comments he makes during the one-to-one reading interview. He benefits greatly from having adults and peers share his enthusiasm and read with him individually and the impact on his self-esteem and his attitude to reading in contrast with his behaviours during more structured reading sessions is notable. Alfie's comments about his discomfort on the carpet and frustration about not being able to 'see the pictures' indicate the pedagogic value of listening to young children's individual voices and taking account of their physical and emotional needs. Finally, we see through the notable influence of Alfie's older brother on his reading, the crucial impact of home literacy experiences on school learning and the potential this has to fertilise learning and teaching.

Expert questions

Reflection: is our classroom practice based on incremental, evidence-informed and collaborative improvement strategies?

Empowerment: is our pedagogic repertoire successful in enhancing wellbeing, learning disposition, capabilities and agency?

These questions contribute to a conceptual framework underpinning professional expertise (see Chapter 16).

4 Pedagogic repertoire

The idea of pedagogy is multifaceted and needs to be constantly refined through teachers' reflections on their classroom experience from their own and their students' perspectives. We need to question whether our pedagogic expertise is sufficiently creative, skilled and wide-ranging and whether our teaching strategies are evidence-informed, convincing and justifiable. Some aspects of pedagogy may appear to be more visible and, possibly, more urgent than others but ultimately all of them need to be in play.

A key step is to link the learning intentions of a lesson with appropriate teaching strategies. The planning of lessons is discussed extensively in Chapter 10, Section 4, and particular emphasis is placed on differention and Personalisation so that the cognitive and motivational appropriateness of planned activities can be maximised. Being able to draw on a range of strategies complements this by enabling the selection of effective teaching/learning processes. Overall intentions can then be shared with pupils (Hattie, 2012, Reading 16.5). In summary, to be most effective, aims and methods should be matched *and* understood.

As Robin Alexander argues, 'teachers need a repertoire of teaching approaches from which they can select on the basis of fitness for purpose in relation to the learner, the subject-matter and the opportunities and constraints of context' (Alexander, 2008a, p. 109, Reading 12.3).

Alexander's analysis of pedagogic repertoire concentrates on three broad aspects: the organisation of interaction (see also Chapter 8, Section 4.1), talk for teaching, and talk for learning (Alexander, 2008a).

We focus here on talk for teaching and on some of the research informing it. For those relatively new to teaching, it is pedagogy as craft, and talk as a key feature of that craft, which often makes the most immediate and pressing demands. We therefore explore this aspect of the pedagogic repertoire in some depth.

4.1 Using talk for whole-class, small group and individual teaching

As Alexander (2008a, Reading 12.3) stresses, choices about when, how and to what extent to interact with the whole class underpin a teacher's pedagogic craft. A paradox in teaching is that whilst teachers use talk as the main tool of their trade, many are not aware of the range of ways they *could* use it when interacting with students. Broadly speaking, as teachers we use talk to provide information, check understanding and maintain control. However, there is much we can also do such as link present activities to past experience, set up future activities, relate existing ideas to new educational frames of meaning and model ways of using language (Mercer and Littleton, 2007, Reading 11.6; see also Chapter 8). One interesting way of thinking about and reflecting on different teacher and learner interactions is to use categorisations such as those suggested by Mortimer and Scott (2007). They divide whole-class interactions into four types of communicative approach along two dimensions, the first representing a continuum between dialogic and authoritative talk and the second between interactive and non-interactive talk:

> *Interactive/dialogic:* the teacher and students explore ideas, generating new meanings, posing genuine questions and offering, listening to and working on different points of view.
>
> *Non-interactive/dialogic:* the teacher considers various points of view, setting out, exploring and working on the different perspectives.
>
> *Interactive/authoritative:* the teacher leads students through a sequence of questions and answers with the aim of reaching one specific point of view.
>
> *Non-interactive/authoritative:* the teacher presents one specific point of view.
> (Mortimer and Scott, 2007, p. 39)

The first two approaches allow for whole-class dialogue where the teacher engages pupils and elicits their ideas, gets extended responses and allows pupil contributions to shape the dialogue. However, in the second pair, through authoritative talk, the teacher pursues a direction or 'story', presents new information for children to consider and/or learn and is unlikely to seek extended contributions. We return to the concept of dialogic talk more extensively in Chapter 12, but in relation to pedagogy, a reflective teacher will consider the affordance these different types of whole-class interactions offer to particular learning situations.

The findings of one large investigation into classroom talk, the Observational Research and Classroom Learning Evaluation (ORACLE) research, showed that approximately 80 per cent of teachers' time, in Key Stage 2 classrooms, was spent in talk between the teacher and children – 56 per cent with individuals, 15 per cent with the whole class, 7 per cent with groups (Galton, Simon and Croll, 1980). In a more recent study Galton et al. found that 'for the typical pupil, 75 per cent of all pupil–teacher exchanges are experienced as a member of the class, exactly as they were twenty years ago' (1999, p. 84). Interestingly, a similar large project, the Primary, Assessment, Curriculum and Experience (PACE) research, found that in Key Stage 1 classrooms, the proportion of whole-class work was also very high, with a lower figure for individual work (Pollard and Triggs, 2000). Reflective teachers may want to consider their own pedagogy in the light of such findings.

There is a strong body of research in the past 30 years, both internationally and recently in the UK, which supports the view that by working in groups and interacting with others, students' academic performance and attitudes to learning can be improved. Galton (2007) summarises the key benefits of training students to work in groups as follows:

> First, the process promotes *independent thinking,* such that pupils gain a sense of control over their learning. Second, it can develop *speaking and listening skills*, allowing pupils to share feelings and ideas. Third, it can encourage *positive self-esteem*, allowing pupils to build confidence in their own abilities. Fourth, it can improve classroom *relationships*, enhancing pupils' sense of social responsibility. (Galton, 2007, p. 110)

Considerations about the organisation of collective and collaborative group work and activity between students are therefore part of a teacher's pedagogic repertoire, as the enactments in this chapter demonstrate.

An example of a project which also demonstrates how teachers aim to enhance the learning potential of pupils working in classroom groups (at Key Stages 1–3) is the SPRinG project (Baines et al., 2008). It began in 2000 and continues in a number of ways. It actively involved teachers collaborating with researchers in a programme designed to raise levels of group work during typical classroom learning activities and to enhance students' skills of listening, explaining, sharing ideas, building trust and respect, planning, organising and evaluating. The project also aimed to develop the skills of the teacher in group work through supporting, guiding, monitoring, fostering independence and providing classroom management. Findings from the study have important implications for pedagogy (see the TLRP **Research Briefing** on p. 316). Involvement in SPRinG had positive effects on pupils' academic progress in relation to usual classroom practices. In Key Stage 1, benefits were seen in reading and mathematics. In Key Stage 2, group work benefited all types of knowledge in science but especially conceptual understanding and inferential thinking, while at Key Stage 3 the success depended on the type of topic but appeared to benefit higher cognitive understanding. Across the three Key Stages, pupils were more likely to sustain high level interactions, engaging in more autonomous learning relative to comparison pupils, and teachers were more likely to monitor interactions between pupils and engage less in direct teaching.

Expert questions

Engagement: do our teaching strategies, classroom organisation and consultation enable learners to actively participate in and enjoy their learning?

Dialogue: does teacher–learner talk scaffold understanding to build on existing knowledge and to strengthen dispositions to learn?

These questions continbute to a conceptual framework underpinning professional expertise (see Chapter 16).

Research
Briefing   Improving pupil group work

This project, SPRinG, was designed to develop principles and strategies to improve the quantity and effectiveness of group work. Teachers and researchers collaborated to develop children's capacity to work in groups (listening, explaining, sharing ideas, building trust and respect, planning, organising, evaluating), and to develop the role of the teacher in group work (support, guide, monitor, fostering independence, providing classroom management) (see the Improving Practice workbook by Baines *et al.*, 2008 below).

An experimental design was used so that the success of the intervention programme could be evaluated against a control group who were not exposed to the intervention. Pupil progress in the experimental and control groups were monitored over a school year and measures of attainment, motivational, attitudinal and behavioural evidence were recorded.

Key findings:	Implications:
Integrating group work: Thoughtful and committed teachers successfully implemented structured group work into mainstream curriculum areas in primary and secondary schools and across the whole curriculum.	Children need to be *actively taught* group work skills and encouraged to appreciate supportive relationships. A whole school approach to group work is desirable, with CPD on teaching strategies.
Pupil attainment: Involvement in structured group work had positive effects on pupil's academic progress and higher conceptual learning.	There is a need to rethink pedagogic strategies which favour teacher-led situations and individual work. The effectiveness of peer-based co-learning has been relatively neglected.
Pupil behaviour: Involvement in the structured group work had positive effects on pupil behaviour through an increase in active on-task interactions, more equal participation in learning, sustained interactions and higher level discussions.	Given the space and time to develop pupils' group-working skills, teachers can bring about a transformation in the learning environment.
Relationships: Personal relationships between teachers and the class and between pupils within the class improved, provided teachers take time to train pupils in the skills of group working.	Teachers were freed up to engage with learning rather than being sidetracked by classroom management. Beneficial groupwork strategies were also applied by children beyond the classroom.

Previous research had indicated that there can be positive learning and social effects of cooperative group work. But this evidence did not provide teachers with the basis for adopting group work for everyday classroom life. The SPRinG project was distinctive in providing a general programme that applies group work across the curriculum, over the school year, and when a range of learning tasks may be undertaken simultaneously.

The main impetus for the SPRinG project was thus to address the wide gap between the potential of group work and its limited use in schools.

A new approach was needed in order to integrate group work into the fabric of the school day. We therefore embarked on an ambitious project in which we worked with teachers to develop a programme of group work that could be successfully integrated into school life. This programme was then systematically evaluated by examining pupil progress over a full school year, and in comparison to a control group in terms of attainment, motivation for group working, and within-group interactions.

Further information:
Blatchford, P., Galton, M. and Kutnick, P. (2005) *Improving Pupil Group Work in Classrooms.* TLRP Research Briefing 11. London: TLRP.
Baines, E., Blatchford, P. and Kutnick, P. (2008) *Promoting Effective Groupwork in Primary Classrooms.* TLRP Improving Practice Series. London: Routledge.
A helpful website can be found at: **www.spring-project.org.uk.** 'Practitioner applications' on the TLRP website offer ideas for developing group work skills.
This project involved the universities of London, Brighton and Cambridge.

Although such studies demonstrate the benefits of group work, a consistent finding in research since the 1970s is that whilst pupils may sit *in* groups they rarely work *as* groups (Alexander, 2008b) so that this arrangement is not as productive as could be. Amongst factors which Galton (2007) identifies as causing teachers to desist from setting up group work are the perception of a loss of teacher control over the learning environment and the difficulty in ascertaining whether talk in groups is on-task. Issues that can impede effective group work are constructing tasks appropriate for the arrangement and the degree of structure required. Size and composition of groups can also create difficulties. (These aspects of group work will be discussed further in Chapter 12.)

Whatever the challenges in setting up effective group work, from a cognitive perspective, the social constructivist ideas of Vygotsky point to the benefits of establishing group work as part of a repertoire of strategies. In the same way that a more knowledgeable adult can help a student move through the zone of proximal development, so too more knowledgeable peers can support learning. However, it is not unusual to see teachers setting up group work and then almost immediately beginning to circulate and check understanding and give comments. Galton and Williamson (1992) found that when a teacher's intervention occurs too early in the group's deliberations, then students can quickly feel a loss of ownership and control over discussion. Judgements therefore need to be made about when it is appropriate to scaffold discussion. It is to this aspect of pedagogic craft that we now turn.

4.2 Scaffolding whole-class, small group and individual learning

Scaffolding is a term that is often used loosely to describe all kinds of support that teachers may offer (Pea, 2004). However, in the sense that the term was used by Wood, Bruner and Ross (1976) in their seminal paper, the concept offers much more than this. They described scaffolding as the support given to a less experienced learner by a more experienced adult or peer – which Tharp and Gallimore (1988) refer to as assisted performance (Reading 11.4). In scaffolding learning, teachers actively, temporarily and contingently provide learners with just the right amount of cognitive support to bring them closer to independence. Over time, an adult, or more experienced other, can reduce the degree of freedom to make a complex task more manageable for the student so that they can achieve independent competence. Their idea of scaffolding can thus be seen to develop the work of Vygotsky and the concept of the 'zone of proximal development' (ZPD) (see Chapter 2 and Reading 2.4).

Established conceptualisations of scaffolding see it as an interactive process occurring between teacher and student in which both participate actively and where learners are 'guided by others' (Stone, 1998, p. 351) to develop understandings that would be problematic for them to achieve unaided. Van de Pol, Volan and Beishuizen (2012) discuss literature around scaffolding and argue that its characteristics are threefold. The first of the characteristics is 'contingency', which suggests that the teacher's scaffolding approaches are tailored to the specific needs and current levels of performance of the learners. The second characteristic is 'fading', whereby scaffolding is gradually withdrawn according to the learner's developing understanding and competence. Thirdly, transfer of responsibility occurs. In considering how, where and when to scaffold learning a teacher therefore needs to take into account:

- how approaches are tailored to the specific needs and current levels of performance of learners;
- how the level of scaffolding can be withdrawn depending on the learner's progress;
- how learners can take responsibility for their learning.

Teachers are often urged to use modelling as a way to scaffold learning. Recently, for example, it has been a key feature of the recommended teaching sequence for writing in primary classrooms where teachers are encouraged to demonstrate the skills of an expert writer to the class. The basis for the approach was set out in the joint United Kingdom Literacy Association (UKLA) / Primary National Strategy (PNS) publication, *Raising Boys' Achievements in Writing* (2004). However, when a teacher models something in the classroom, the children should not be expected simply to imitate it. As Bruner says:

> what the teacher must be, to be an effective competence model, is a day-to-day working model with whom to interact. It is not so much that the teacher provides a model to *imitate*. Rather, it is that the teacher can become a part of the student's internal dialogue – somebody who respects what he wants, someone whose standards he wishes to make his own. (Bruner 1966, p. 124)

Expert question

Repertoire: is our pedagogic expertise sufficiently creative, skilled and wide-ranging to teach all elements of learning?

This question contributes to a conceptual framework underpinning professional expertise (see Chapter 16).

Scaffolding, which includes modelling, is thus a dynamic interaction that needs to be finely tuned to the learner's ongoing progress. Support given by the teacher depends on the characteristics of the situation, for example the type of task and the responses of the student. Scaffolding strategies therefore need to be adapted for each classroom situation, which is what makes it a key part of teachers' pedagogic repertoire.

5 Enacting a series of lessons

5.1 The art, craft and science of pedagogy over time

In the following vignette of a trainee English teacher studying a novel with a Year 7 class, the reader is once again invited to consider ways in which aspects of the science, craft and art of pedagogy are played out, this time over a sequence of lessons. It is also an opportunity to reflect on the extent to which in this example the pedagogic expertise is skilled and creative and what evidence appears to inform the teaching.

Case study 11.3 Learning in the graveyard

A Year 7 class is reading Neil Gaiman's The Graveyard Book *(2008) with Nadia, a trainee English teacher. She has planned a unit of work to last several weeks during which time they will read the whole novel and undertake creative writing. In one lesson, she plays them Saint-Saëns' tone poem, 'Danse macabre', dimming the classroom lights to create a more ghostly atmosphere. Chapter 5 of Gaiman's novel revolves around the concept of the danse macabre and Nadia explains the traditional 'dance of the dead' to the class, embellishing her explanation with the idea of the violin being the devil's instrument. Nadia projects a traditional image of the devil and dancing skeletons on the board, writing up suggestions from the class for words and phrases to describe the music. One student's idea is skeletons using their rib cages as instruments. Nadia's lesson evalua-tions show that although students find it challenging to write from music as distinct from pictures or objects, their responses make her realise she could have afforded to include more information about resonances of the danse macabre. She also ponders the issue of how far students learn their own use of literary language by adopting the author's usage for themselves. In another lesson, Nadia focuses more on devising characters using language alone, afterwards evaluating what happens when, as she puts it, 'I am putting in input, giving instructions, disseminating ideas and criteria, and students are on the receiving end of this, left alone with their thoughts and imagination to act as the "furnace" for this input, galvanising ideas, making things their own, applying it to their thoughts and producing a character'. She is mindful of an element of competition between students creeping in. Although it is probably because they are eager to please her it is not something she wants to encourage. Indeed, she is very aware of a particular student, Damian, who appears comparatively passive and negative and she realises she needs to be more proactive in encouraging him to contribute and praise him explicitly when he does.*

A high point of the unit of work is the lesson in which Nadia takes the class on a seven-minute walk to the church graveyard in order to undertake some creative writing in a very concrete setting. She has remembered from her PGCE subject studies the value of making sure students have something specific to write about. The advice has merged with a school-based professional studies session about the benefits of learning outside the classroom. Nadia has enlisted the support of the class teacher for the graveyard trip, but has undertaken all the planning and preparation herself including: trying out the walk to the site to check the route and the timing; sending a letter home to parents; leaving a note on the classroom door to inform anyone who might drop by where they have gone; acquiring a whistle to take with her as a way to re-gather the group. Her plan for the lesson includes precise instructions to the class about behaviour and safety regulations and a word about respect: she reminds students that they are ambassadors for the school whenever they leave the premises and 'it's even more important in a cemetery, a place where people are sensitive'.

The day is an uncharacteristically warm English spring day, a point which makes a difference to the learning the students do. On arriving in the graveyard, they sit in a circle underneath a yew tree ready to begin their writing lesson. Now Nadia tells them they are like 'field scientists collecting data for their hypotheses back in the lab'. On this occasion, they are hunting for words to create a sense of the atmosphere of the graveyard as

> *well as the headstones and tombs within it. The students collect words avidly but more important for their learning is the change to their perceptions about graveyards. To date, they have tended to characterise graveyards as 'dank, creepy and mysterious'. This trip has shown them how much more like a garden such places may be. At the start of the visit, the students sit and write what they can see, hear, smell, and feel: birdsong, the rustling of leaves, the distant hum of cars, the sound of a chainsaw, wheels of a baby buggy being pushed along. They also write about the feeling of fresh air, the animals and insects they can see, the smell of recently cut grass. However, aspects of the gothic genre also prevail for example as students peer into a stone tomb and claim to be able to see real bones inside and afterwards their writing still includes references to twisted trees and deadly air.*
>
> *Back in the classroom the following lesson, Nadia offers a model poem for students to explore and use as a basis for their own writing, the popular but anonymous 'I saw a peacock' poem. The first half of each line begins 'I saw …' the second half of the line describing what was seen. One student suggests, in the light of their work in the graveyard, that they might begin each line with one of the five senses, not just 'I saw', an idea that Nadia welcomes and includes in the lesson.*

5.2 Analysing pedagogy

This brief glimpse of Nadia's planned unit of work based on *The Graveyard Book* and students' associated creative writing, affords further reflection on the pedagogy involved. In this instance, the focus is on continuity and progression between lessons. Planning a whole unit of work involved Nadia bringing together different strands of subject knowledge, in particular a literary novel written for young people which draws heavily on the gothic genre as well as English history, Christian iconography, murder mystery and suspense. Nadia had not focused on gothic literature within her English degree, but said most of her knowledge was gleaned from popular culture. She was, however, steeped in other aspects of literary knowledge from both the study and the production of texts. She was, therefore, able to select ideas from a variety of approaches to creative writing and think more broadly about the possible relationships between models of literary writing such as Gaiman's book and how inexperienced writers learn. She is drawing, therefore, on longstanding traditions linking reading with writing: most children's authors when asked what advice they would offer to aspiring writers will say 'read, read read!'. Educational theorists make the same claim for the influence of the reader in the development of the writer, drawing on research as warrant (see for example Barrs and Cork, 2001, Reading 12.5). Because Nadia is a trainee teacher, her lesson plans and evaluations make very explicit the craft of her pedagogy as she manoeuvres between each lesson, reflecting on the last and looking ahead to the next. Whether designing the sequence of activities and giving shape to her literary and creative plans for the class, or reflecting on what to try next to engage students who remain unenthused, Nadia scans her growing repertoire to select and justify what she judges to be the best options. Although she has planned very carefully, the unforeseen arises and needs responding to. She had not anticipated quite how difficult it might be to retain the concentration of a whole class of interested students when out in the open air of the graveyard and surrounded by enticing distractions. Precisely because of the richness of the environment, there were unexpected challenges to the anticipated outcomes of the lesson. However, whilst the craft of her pedagogy enabled her to retain firm control of the lesson, the art of her pedagogy ensured she was responsive to what students were actually learning; for example, the realisation that their assumptions about a typical graveyard were being overturned, or the way they wanted to adapt the firm poem structure she had suggested they use when they spotted a more appropriate framework.

Reflective activity 11.3

Aim: To explore how principles about pedagogy relate to our own planning and teaching.

Evidence and reflection: Review a sequence of three lessons you have recently planned and taught. Identify as many different aspects of pedagogy as possible within and between the three lessons, explaining and justifying them in the light of what you have just read. What is the balance between the different aspects (science, craft and art) and how do you account for it? What challenges did the sequence present in terms of your subject knowledge?

Extension: What implications are there for classroom interactions and teachers' scaffolding of students' learning in this series of lessons?

Conclusion

In this chapter we have explored the interconnected aspects of pedagogy: art, craft and science. We have also shown how they are closely related to teachers' subject knowledge and awareness of learning processes. As our readings, discussion and enactments show, pedagogy is a rich and fascinating concept, constantly being shaped and re-shaped by teachers. At times some elements of pedagogy will appear more pressing than others. Nevertheless, how we teach and respond to learners will be crucially informed by our understanding of pedagogy as a whole. Whilst some ideas about teaching and learning endure, others change and are transformed, not only as new research is undertaken by teachers in classrooms or professional researchers but also because teaching and learning are human enterprises and hence are never static. No two teachers are the same; no two learning contexts are the same. We all need, therefore, to reflect on our pedagogy as and when our own understanding is further developed by experience. At all times, we need to juggle our concern with subject knowledge and the need to consider learners holistically. As the vignette of Alfie above demonstrates, the importance of listening to students' individual voices cannot be underestimated.

Key readings

TLRP's overall school findings, including 'ten principles for effective teaching and learning', are discussed in Chapter 4 of this book. For a simple explanation of the idea of pedagogy seen as science, craft and art, and an exposition of 'conceptual tools' for tackling enduring educational issues, see:

Pollard, A. (ed.) (2010) *Professionalism and Pedagogy: A Contemporary Opportunity.* London: TLRP. (Reading 11.2) (see also Chapter 16)

Alexander's comparative analysis of pedagogic issues has generated a strong conceptual framework which is applicable to any setting. See:

Alexander, R. (2000) *Culture and Pedagogy. International Comparisons in Primary Education.* Oxford: Blackwell.
Alexander, R. (2008) *Essays on Pedagogy.* London: Routledge. (Reading 12.3)

An influential application of a synthesis of global research is:

Hattie, J. (2012) *Visible Learning for Teachers.* London: Routledge. (Reading 16.5)

A classic summary of research on teaching is provided in a US handbook, and many other overviews are also available:

Anderson, P. M. (2008) *Pedagogy. A Primer.* New York: Peter Lang.
Joyce, B., Weil, M. and Calhoun, E. (2009) *Models of Teaching.* New York: Pearson.
Muijs, D. and Reynolds, D. (2011) *Effective Teaching.* London: SAGE. (Reading 8.7)
Richardson, V. (2001) *Handbook of Research on Teaching.* Washington: AERA.

There are many excellent guides to practical teaching strategies and skills. Among the best are:

Kyriacou, C. (2009) *Effective Teaching in Schools: Theory and Practice.* Cheltenham: Nelson Thornes.
Petty, G. (2009) *Teaching Today: A Practical Guide.* Cheltenham: Nelson Thornes.
Sotto, E. (2007) *When Teaching Becomes Learning.* London: Continuum.

An exceptional collection of readings on pedagogy is cited below. In this volume, Leach and Moon explore the interplay between 'school knowledge', 'subject knowledge' and 'pedagogic knowledge'.

Leach, J., and Moon, B. (1999). *Learners and Pedagogy.* London: SAGE.

To explore the particular significance of dialogue in classroom pedagogy, see:

Mercer, N. and Littleton, K. (2007) *Dialogue and the Development of Children's Thinking.* London: Routledge. (Reading 11.6)

There is a long tradition of thinking about teaching as a creative and organic process. This approach emphasises how teaching must connect with the learner as a person and with their construction of meaning. See:

Bruner, J. (1996) *The Culture of Education*. Cambridge, MA: Harvard University Press. (Reading 11.1)

Dixon, A., Drummond, M. -J., Hart, S. and McIntyre, D. (2004) *Learning Without Limits*. Maidenhead: Open University Press. (see also Reading 1.4)

For consideration of more radical approaches to pedagogy, try:

Kincheloe, J. L. (2008) *Critical Pedagogy Primer*. New York: Peter Lang.

Leach, J. and Moon, B. (2008) *The Power of Pedagogy*. London: SAGE.

In one way or another, most of *Reflective Teaching*'s chapters are concerned with pedagogy and, for readings on more specific issues – such as relationships, engagement, behaviour, assessment, etc. – please consult the relevant chapter.

reflectiveteaching.co.uk offers additional professional resources for this chapter. These may include *Further Reading*, illustrative *Reflective Activities*, useful *Web Links*, and *Download Facilities* for diagrams, figures, checklists, activities.

Communication
How does use of language support learning?

12

Introduction

In this chapter we address speaking, listening, reading and writing as crucial forms of classroom communication between all teachers and their students, and consider some of the ways in which each is vital to learning. In order for teachers to deepen their understanding, we consider what it is helpful to know about spoken and written language, discussing some essential ideas about grammar, dialect and standard English. We show how teachers model, respond to and engage knowledgeably with the many varieties of language and modes of communication that are used in their classrooms every day. We focus on different kinds of texts that students may read or write, whether verbal, visual or multimodal. Furthermore, we outline some of the key features involved in supporting students who have English as an additional language (EAL).

The idea of communication always includes purpose, audience, context and style, a notion first drawn to teachers' attention by James Britton and colleagues in their classic research study, *The Development of Writing Abilities (11–18)* (Britton et al., 1975). Why are these four ideas so important for teachers and learners? Although much of the time language is taken for granted, when we reflect on it we realise that these four elements are always in play. For example, communication in the playground often involves children talking together to negotiate how they play and their choice of language is informed by the fact that they are with their peers in a very familiar context. Hence, their talk will be informal in style. By contrast, in a whole-school assembly, communication could involve talk in a very formal style by an adult addressing an audience of students about the topic of road safety with a didactic purpose. In both instances, the purpose, audience, context and style determine the characteristics of the communication, as is the case in any authentic communicative interactions, whether spoken, written or visual.

TLRP principles

Two principles are of particular relevance to this chapter on the use of language in teaching and learning:

Effective teaching and learning requires teachers to scaffold learning. Teachers should provide activities which support learners as they move forward, not just intellectually, but also socially and emotionally, so that once these supports are removed, the learning is secure. (Principle 4)

Effective teaching and learning fosters both individual and social processes and outcomes. Learning is a social activity. Learners should be encouraged and helped to work with others, to share ideas and to build knowledge together. Consulting learners about their learning and giving them a voice is both an expectation and a right. (Principle 7)

See Chapter 4

These ideas about the social and interactive nature of communication underpin the whole of this chapter.

1 Characteristics of classroom communication

There are many aspects of classroom communication which have an impact on how effectively teachers and students communicate in early years, primary and secondary classrooms. For example, it is valuable to remember that high-quality communication is important across the whole curriculum, not just in English. The Bullock Report (DES, 1975) advocated the importance of paying attention to language across the curriculum to underline the argument that educationally productive talk is the responsibility of all teachers, not solely English teachers. Thirty-five years later, the final report of the Cambridge Primary Review (Alexander, 2010) emphasised high-quality talk as fundamental to effective teaching and learning, including the character, quality and uses of reading, writing and talk and the development of students' understandings of the distinct registers, vocabularies and modes of discourse of each subject. Alexander asserts, 'oracy must have its proper place in the language curriculum. Spoken language is central to learning, culture and life and is much more prominent in the curricula of many other countries' (2010, p. 24).

Language skills are fundamental to communication but the interpersonal nature of communication also calls for significant social skills. A great deal of what we say is conveyed by non-verbal means. Tone, pitch, volume and how we project our voice are all part of the communication process. Non-verbal language such as facial expression, effective eye contact, posture, gesture and interpersonal distance or space, is usually interpreted by others as a reliable reflection of how we are feeling (Nowicki and Duke, 2000). However, non-verbal signals may also confuse or contradict what we are trying to communicate. This may be particularly so in communication between people from different cultures and backgrounds. Siraj-Blatchford argues that 'language involves more than learning a linguistic code with which to label the world or to refer to abstract concepts; language also involves learning how to use the code in socially appropriate and effective ways' (2000, p. 20).

> ## Expert question
>
> **Coherence**: is there clarity in the purposes, content and organisation of the curriculum and does it provide holistic learning experiences?
>
> This question contributes to a conceptual framework underpinning professional expertise (see Chapter 16).

> ## Reflective activity 12.1
>
> *Aim* To investigate who speaks and how much during a lesson.
>
> *Evidence and reflection* We recommend that you begin with an audio recording of part of a lesson. You may want to gather data on your own teaching.
>
> Now sit back, relax and listen … Consider:
> - How much speaking is there?
> - Who is doing the speaking?
> - Which pupils speak?

- When does the teacher speak?
- When do the pupils speak?

Reviews of this kind can highlight the pattern of talk in a classroom. It can often reveal aspects which surprise us, because it is so difficult to be aware of how much we talk, to whom and when, whilst we are engrossed in the process of teaching itself.

Extension: Having identified the pattern of talk, we need to decide whether what we do is consistent with our aims. You might like to see if you can develop the way you teach in the light of what you have learned in this activity. You could also use a similar approach to investigate different aspects of classroom interaction, e.g. teacher–pupil interaction in group work; pupil–pupil interaction, generally or in small group work. You will find suggestions for other observations in subsequent Reflective activities in this chapter.

Since communication in classrooms is often focused on some meaningful topic, it requires appropriate cognitive capacities in addition to language and interpersonal skills. It requires knowing something about the subject under consideration and being able to think about and process what we want to communicate to others as well as what they are trying to communicate to us. Nor can the attitudes of the participants be forgotten: developing the cognitive relationship between them and the context itself is also very important if they are to remain motivated to learn. Furthermore, when students consciously examine these relationships, their metacognitive capacities will come into play (Whitebread et al., 2010).

A great many skills and processes therefore are in play in good classroom communication. In this chapter, we focus chiefly on talk, listening, reading and writing, but it is helpful to bear these other facets in mind.

2 Talking and listening

Expert questions

Repertoire: is our pedagogic expertise sufficiently creative, skilled and wide-ranging to teach all elements of learning?

Dialogue: does teacher–learner talk scaffold understanding to build on existing knowledge and to strengthen dispositions to learn?

These questions contribute to a conceptual framework underpinning professional expertise (see Chapter 16).

As discussed in Chapter 11, teachers' pedagogic repertoire crucially includes classroom talk (Alexander, 2008a, Reading 12.3). In classroom situations, teachers and students act as both speakers and listeners. In the following section we outline some of the key literature which informs teachers' thinking and practice, emphasising in particular the notion of achieving a strategic balance between authoritative and dialogic discourse (Mortimer and Scott, 2007).

We begin by discussing the impact of teacher-initiated talk on students' learning, for example through questioning, responding, instructing and explaining, and then move to discuss more overtly collaborative forms of spoken communication, whether between teachers and students or amongst small groups of students themselves.

2.1 Questioning, responding, instructing and explaining

How good are we at asking questions? Questions can be used for a wide range of purposes and are a vital tool for teaching and learning. They can be thought of in terms of the level of demand they make on children's thinking and can be broadly divided into two main categories: lower-order and higher-order questions. Lower-order questions are often closed or literal requiring relatively brief, factual answers which are either right or wrong. Higher-order questions invite a range of possible answers and require children to apply, reorganise, extend, evaluate or analyse information. A useful way of thinking about categorising types of questions is Bloom's taxonomy (1956). This identifies six levels of cognitive processes: knowledge, comprehension, application, analysis, synthesis and evaluation (see also the discussion at p. 163). It also provides examples of questions which can elicit different types of thinking.

Asking questions can provide teachers with immediate feedback on students' thinking: on what they know and, most importantly, how they can improve its quality. However, research shows that teacher-led patterns of talk are overwhelmingly prevalent (Mortimer and Scott, 2007) rather than interchanges which elicit higher-order thinking from students. Kyriacou and Issitt (2008) argue that when teachers' use of talk is linked to good learning outcomes, they use strategies other than closed question exchanges and help students appreciate the value of dialogue for learning. Moreover, Rojas-Drummond and Mercer's research (2003) shows that the most effective teachers are those who use question and answer sequences, not just to test knowledge but also to guide the development of children's understanding.

Questioning and response interactions have often been characterised as initiation-response-evaluation(IRE) or initiation-response-feedback (IRF). In the former, the teacher initiates an exchange by posing a question, the student responds with a brief answer and the teacher acknowledges the answer and moves on to the next question. In the context of IRE, teachers ask many questions but too often they are 'closed', requiring only short responses and not enough of the kinds of questions that get children thinking or encourage extended answers. Smith, Hardman, Wall and Mroz (2004) found that in literacy and numeracy lessons most of the questions asked were of a low cognitive level designed to funnel students' responses towards a required answer that the teacher already knows. In a worthwhile IRF exchange, on the other hand, the teacher makes an evaluation of the student's response, gives

Expert questions

Relationships: are teacher–pupil relationships nurtured as the foundation of good behaviour, mutual wellbeing and high standards?

Engagement: do our teaching strategies, classroom organisation and consultation enable learners to actively participate in and enjoy their learning?

These questions contribute to a conceptual framework underpinning professional expertise (see Chapter 16).

feedback or elaborates on the answer and this pattern then often becomes a more positive chain of interactions between a teacher and an individual student (Mortimer and Scott, 2007). The process can thereby help a class construct a common basis of knowledge and provide vital information about where learners are in their understanding (see Chapter 13). As Dawes (2004) suggests, learners benefit from having their ideas rephrased and elaborated. Critically though, the value of these exchanges depends on the quality of the feedback. Wells (1999) evaluates the IRF sequence and argues that the teacher's feedback can also be used to clarify, exemplify, expand, explain or justify a student's response and can help students to plan ahead for a task they are about to carry out or review and generalise from lessons they have already learnt. Wragg and Brown (2001) note the teacher's response should provide reinforcement, feedback and encouragement. It is important that all answers are considered and here non-verbal features of communication such as a teacher's body language, gesture and facial expression also come in to play. An atmosphere of trust in which students are not afraid of saying the wrong thing is essential.

In analysing the kinds of questions teachers use, Nystrand et al. (1997) (Reading 12.1) distinguish between test questions and authentic questions. Of course test questions have their place but they are retrospective rather than prospective and do not take forward students' thinking. Nystrand's findings have made a particular contribution to understanding about the nature of classroom discourse and its effect on student learning. However, he argues that the relationship cannot be simply reduced to measuring 'authentic' versus 'recall and display' questions; the inappropriate use of authentic questions can be counter-productive and the skilful use of a lecturing style can, on occasion, be effective. A concise, clear exposition by the teacher may be a more efficient way of explaining the nature and purpose of the task and authentic questions unrelated to the objective of the lesson are unlikely to develop students' understanding. What matters most is not the frequency of particular types of exchange but how far students are treated as active participants in the construction of their own knowledge.

Expert question

Authenticity: do learners recognise routine processes of assessment and feedback as being of personal value?

This question contributes to a conceptual framework underpinning professional expertise (see Chapter 16).

Diagnostic questions take time and thought to devise but elicit valuable information about students' learning. Some whole-class questioning skills that have long been understood as being effective in eliciting thoughtful and informative responses include pausing, prompting, asking for further clarification and relating students' contributions to other relevant aspects of their learning (Perrot, 1982, Reading 12.2). In Wolf, Crosson and Resnick's (2004) research into talk about literary texts, effective strategies included: teachers reformulating and summarising what students say, providing opportunities for other students to build on these ideas; teachers encouraging students to put the main idea in their own words; and teachers pressing the students for elaboration of their ideas, e.g. 'How did you know that?' 'Why?'. As well as those questions asked by teachers, Harlen (2006) highlights the importance of students asking questions because these can show what they neither know nor understand, demonstrating the limits of their understanding and the nature of their own ideas. Students can also gain satisfaction and motivation for learning when they are given the opportunity to investigate their own questions (Hodgson and Pyle, 2010).

Although it may seem an obvious point to make, students need to have time to answer questions. In the ORACLE study of group work in the 1980s, Galton and his colleagues found that that the average time teachers allowed children to respond was two seconds before either repeating the question, rephrasing it, redirecting it to another child, or extending it him- or herself (Galton, Simon and Croll, 1980). Without 'wait time' children will give less well-formulated answers than they may otherwise have done or even have no answer to give. According to Alexander (2008b), increasing the wait time from three to seven seconds resulted in an increase in: 1) the length of student responses; 2) the number of unsolicited responses; 3) the frequency of student questions; 4) the number of responses from less capable students; 5) student–student interactions; and 6) the incidence of speculative responses. Another shortcoming in teacher questioning is not distributing questions around the class. One strategy which Harrison and Howard (2009) propose to alleviate this is to have a no-hands-up policy. This conveys the message that all children are expected to have an answer and ensures that the child who thrusts his or her hand up enthusiastically is not always chosen.

Reflective activity 12.2

Aim: To identify question and response patterns in a lesson.

Evidence and reflection: For this activity you could either choose to audio/video record a lesson you teach or, with her or his agreement, observe a colleague's lesson. Choose three five-minute periods in the teaching sessions (e.g. at the beginning, middle and end) and note the questions asked. Identify the questions which are closed and those which are open. How many follow either an IRE or an IRF pattern? Were there opportunities for children to formulate their answers because they were given wait time?

Extension: Were there opportunities for children to ask questions themselves, of you and of each other?

2.2 Dialogic teaching and learning

As discussed in Chapter 11 and above, research shows that teachers do the majority of speaking in the classroom. Drawing in the main on the theoretical ideas of Bakhtin and Vygotsky however, a number of authors have advocated the potential of teacher–student communication which enables students to play a more active part in shaping classroom discourse. Wells (1999, see also Reading 2.4) formulates the concept of dialogic inquiry, in which knowledge is co-constructed by teachers and students as they engage in joint activities, stressing the potential of collaborative group work and peer assistance. Nystrand et al. (1997) describe dialogic instruction, characterised by the teacher's uptake of

Expert questions

Engagement: do our teaching strategies, classroom organisation and consultation enable learners to actively participate in and enjoy their learning?

Dialogue: does teacher–learner talk scaffold understanding to build on existing knowledge and to strengthen dispositions to learn?

These questions contribute to a conceptual framework underpinning professional expertise (see Chapter 16).

students' ideas, authentic questions and the opportunity for students to modify the topic, making a strong case for the effectiveness of dialogically-organised instruction over a monologic approach. He argues that classroom talk should require students to think, not just to report someone else's thinking.

Whilst the term *dialogic teaching* is increasingly used in education discussions, it is helpful to be aware of its origins if it is to be understood and implemented. Alexander (2008b, Reading 12.3) argues that dialogic teaching demands a balance of talk, reading and writing; management of classroom space and time; a productive relationship between speaker and listener; and attention to the content and dynamics of talk itself. Dialogic teaching, he suggests, is characterised by five key criteria. It is:

- *collective*: teachers and children address learning tasks together, as a group or as a class;

- *reciprocal*: teachers and children listen to each other, share ideas and consider alternative viewpoints;

- *supportive*: children articulate their ideas freely, without fear of embarrassment over 'wrong' answers, and they help each other to reach common understandings;

- *cumulative*: teachers and children build on their own and each other's ideas and chain them into coherent lines of thinking and enquiry;

- *purposeful*: teachers plan and steer classroom talk with specific educational goals.
  (Alexander, 2008b, p. 28)

The main pedagogic implication for reflective teachers is an emphasis on the importance of social learning through teacher–student and student–student dialogue. A dialogic approach to teaching and learning requires teachers and students to build actively on each other's ideas, posing questions and constructing shared interpretations and new knowledge. For teachers, it involves using open-ended, higher-order questioning, feeding in ideas and reflecting on and interpreting students' contributions to a lesson. For learners, it encourages articulation and justification of personal points of view, appreciating and responding to others' ideas and taking turns in whole-class and group interactions (Mercer and Littleton, 2007, Reading 11.6). In contrast to a teacher-led, transmission approach, a dialogical pedagogy signals the co-presence of the teacher as a member of a community of learners, available to guide and coach the learner, modelling the exploratory nature of dialogue. However, as Mortimer and Scott

Expert questions

Personalisation: does the curriculum resonate with the social and cultural needs of diverse learners and provide appropriate elements of choice?

Relevance: is the curriculum presented in ways which are meaningful to learners and so that it can excite their imagination?

These questions contribute to a conceptual framework underpinning professional expertise (see Chapter 16).

(2007) discuss (see Chapter 11), teachers need to make decisions about where and when a transmissive approach may in fact be appropriate to guide learners.

In all this, we emphasise the need for teachers to be aware of the individuals in their classroom and how meaningful contexts and audiences for developing students' talk and listening are key. Alexander (2008b) stresses that ensuring the ethos and the conditions of the classroom are conducive is essential in order for dialogic teaching and students' learning to take place.

2.3 Inter-thinking and group work

All forms of classroom communication call for particular types of awareness about the rules of communication. Student behaviour in small groups largely mirrors the discourse modelled by, and the expectations communicated by, their teachers (Webb et al., 2006). In communicating with students therefore, the reflective teacher needs to model appropriate discourse and expectations. In order to participate productively, the rules must be clear and each participant must understand and accept these rules. In the 'Thinking together' project, Mercer and Littleton (2007, Reading 11.6) show how children and teachers collectively construct and agree some ground rules for good, productive discussion. Critically, these rules are not predefined and imposed but emerge from collective discussion and consideration and therefore can expose the particular concerns of children, taking account of their own perspectives of group work. Having been negotiated and agreed, ground rules can then be summarised and displayed so that they can be referred to by the children and the teacher when appropriate.

As discussed in Chapter 11, cooperative group work can, at its best, be a particularly good context for learning. It fits well with Vygotskyan ideas about the importance and meaningfulness of the social context in which the learner acts (see Chapter 2). In Johnson and Johnson's (1997) review of 378 studies, collaborative learning activities were shown to benefit learning and conceptual development, especially for complex tasks. So too, in a research survey for the Cambridge Primary Review (Howe and Mercer, 2007), talk in groups was shown to be good for children's learning. Mercer and Littleton (2007) argue that by talking together, students do more than interact: they 'interthink'. This means that they engage in collective thinking which enables them to share strategies, construct new strategies together, examine others' strategies and make decisions only once all group members are satisfied. It also helps them learn to think better on their own.

A series of *Thinking Together* projects, reported by Mercer and Littleton (2007), assessed the impact of dialogue-based intervention on students' educational attainment, indicating that students who had been taught using this approach made better, more rapid progress in both maths and science. Other school-based studies have provided convincing evidence for the educational value of talk in collaborative learning, but only when guided and organised by teachers (Kyriacou and Issitt 2008; Howe, 2010).

What then is the role of the teacher in facilitating and contributing to group work and what kinds of interaction among students are necessary to achieve its potential? Clarity of goals, the appropriateness of the task, the composition of the group and the degree of help students have been given in developing group-work skills are significant. Bains et al. (2008) argue that teachers need to adapt grouping practices for different purposes and learning tasks and that adults should support and guide groups, monitoring progress in ways that encourage independence rather than directly teaching students. Above all, teachers should ensure that the talk used in group work is productive.

Mercer and Littleton (2007, Reading 11.6) characterise three different ways in which students in classrooms talk together as 'disputational', 'cumulative' and 'exploratory'. They argue that exploratory talk constitutes a powerful way for students to think and reason together. Its effectiveness is due to three main reasons. First, participants appropriate successful problem-solving strategies and explanatory accounts from each other; secondly, they jointly construct new, robust, generalisable explanations; and thirdly, participation in external dialogue promotes internal dialogue. According to Mercer, Dawes, Wegerif and Sams (2004) in their study of science learning, students with experience of exploratory talk achieve significantly better than students without this experience.

Reflective activity 12.3

Aim: To analyse and categorise an example of classroom talk.

Evidence and reflection: After seeking and gaining permission, record a group discussion and make a transcript. Analyse the transcript, categorising the types of talk using Mercer and Littleton's three categories: disputational, cumulative and exploratory talk. (See Reading 11.6 for examples) Reflect on which of the three were most commonly in use. How would you account for this?

Extension: With reference to Mercer and Littleton's ideas about interthinking, what might be the next steps in developing students' capacity to think together?

2.4 Creative talk

A key aspect of talking and listening is how it can encourage creative thinking and learning in the classroom (Cremin, 2009). Reflective teachers work to extend students' abilities as speakers and listeners and help them express themselves effectively to create and critically evaluate their own work. Through creative talk, Cremin argues, teachers can foster students' curiosity, capacity to make connections, take risks and innovate. What do we mean by 'creative' talk? Some examples might be oral storytelling or drama techniques including role play, hot-seating and freeze-frame.

Oral storytelling and retelling is a powerful way for students to take ownership of their own narratives, enabling them to make choices about words and phrases. As Hardy (1977) argued, narrative is a primary act of mind. Cremin (2009) writes persuasively about the role oral narrative has in fostering the creative sculpting of language, imaginative engagement in learning and the oral confidence and competence it develops. Personal oral stories have their place in the curriculum. Rosen (1988) and Zipes (1995) have shown the significance of autobiography and of individual and collective memory in the formation of identity. More recently, in a book-making project with children in post-war Bosnia, Darvin (2009) discusses how, through storytelling, the social nature of this literacy event helped the children begin to explore the vital concepts of preservation, friendship and peace and to construct and see themselves in relation to others. In addition to personal oral narratives, Grainger et al. (2005) have shown how experience of retelling well-known and traditional tales can make a rich contribution to children's writing.

As with storytelling, drama incorporates the use of talk and self-expression and has been shown as a strong form of communication in its own right as well as a successful precursor to invigorate successful writing, allowing students to experience and explore situations with their teacher and peers and to organise their thoughts orally. According to Woolland (2010), drama can raise the self-esteem of even the most disaffected of children. Because it is rooted in social interaction, Winston (1998) argues that drama is a powerful way to help children relate positively to each other, experience negotiation, gain confidence and raise self-esteem.

In drama, a number of forms of talk are used – as well as gestures, facial expressions and movements – to create meaning. Learners adapt speech for different purposes and can reflect upon language choices to contribute to their growing command of the spoken word. In many classrooms, teachers use role play to offer students crucial opportunities to enact, imitate, imagine, confront, review and understand the social world they inhabit as well as to use their knowledge and understanding in different areas of the curriculum (Cremin et al., 2006).

There are many different drama conventions which can be exploited to promote creative talk and learning in the classroom (Neelands and Goode, 2000). A particularly effective strategy is hot-seating in which students or teachers take on the role of a character to be questioned about their behaviour and motivation. Characters may be hot-seated individually, in pairs or in small groups. The technique is very effective for helping students to engage with characters, both fictional and real, and also for developing students' questioning techniques. Another useful strategy is freeze-frame where the action in a play or scene is frozen, as in a photograph or video frame. This requires students to share and negotiate ideas, discussing as a group how best to convey a moment in time. Thoughts can then be interrogated through thought-tracking, where individuals in the freeze-frame are tapped on the shoulder and asked to speak their thoughts or feelings aloud. There are therefore multiple opportunities for students at all stages of schooling to deepen their learning through creative talk.

3 Reading

In this next section, we turn our attention to reading as one of the main forms of communication through which students learn. Being able to read involves making meaning from texts; it is not simply a matter of learning to decode letters and words. Making meaning from texts enables people to construct and explore other worlds, whether real or imagined, to engage in debates and to encounter different forms of knowledge. From texts, readers learn how writers communicate with readers, and readers with writers.

Teaching children to read and ensuring young people acquire a habit of lifelong reading are amongst the highest aims to which any teacher aspires. How reading is taught is a much discussed and debated topic. Here, we focus on just a few issues that are helpful to think about. Reflective teachers, whether working with children in the early years or at any stage thereafter, will constantly find reasons for reading (Cliff Hodges, 2010) and want to develop their own understandings about why reading is so important (Harrison, 2004, Reading 12.4).

There are many reasons why we read. However, if children only learn to read but not what reading is for, they will not make progress. Maryanne Wolf's thought-provoking book, *Proust and the Squid: The Story and Science of the Reading Brain*, reminds us why this is:

> Reading is one of the single most remarkable inventions in history; the ability to record history is one of its consequences. Our ancestors' invention could come about only because of the human brain's extraordinary ability to make new connections among its existing structures, a process made possible by the brain's ability to be shaped by experience. The plasticity at the heart of the brain's design forms the basis for much of who we are, and who we might become. (Wolf, 2007, p. 3)

If human beings are not genetically disposed to read but must actively learn how to do so, then there are extremely important implications for how reading is taught in the classroom:

> To acquire this unnatural process, children need instructional environments that support all the circuit parts that need bolting for the brain to read. Such a perspective departs from current teaching methods that focus largely on only one or two major components of reading. (Ibid., p. 19)

Wolf's point makes clear the need for teachers to approach reading from a wide variety of perspectives, ensuring that at the same time as learning to decode text, children become increasingly aware of the many pleasures and purposes that reading might hold for them.

3.1 Teaching reading

The teaching and development of reading skills and knowledge are deeply rooted in approaches from which children and young people learn the social, cultural, aesthetic and practical pleasures of reading. Although the development of reading skills and knowledge involves teaching and learning how to decode written language, it includes much else besides (Meek, 1988). For example, it includes inference or prediction both of which require knowledge about the distinctiveness of different texts such as picturebooks and recipes, or about different media, for example films and posters, as well as knowledge about the world. When students leave school, they need reading to be something they can use to learn and respond to an infinite variety of texts and media. Being able to read in versatile and sustained ways greatly enhances the scope of what people may be able to learn. So what underlying principles can help all teachers to support their students' reading development?

3.2 Theories of reading

One suggestion comes from reader-response theory. Louise Rosenblatt, an American academic working with university students over several decades of the twentieth century, developed ideas about reading that remain extremely valuable to teachers today (Rosenblatt, 1978, 1994). She argues that reading forms a transaction between the reader and the text. Each transaction results in a unique reading. The uniqueness of the reading derives from the fact that readers bring with them their own prior knowledge which they use in their encounter with the text to make meaning. Her ideas chime with recent research into young people's *funds of knowledge* and the value of using what is learnt at home as a foundation of what is learnt in school in all areas of the curriculum (Gonzalez, Moll and Amanti, 2005).

> **Expert question**
>
> **Personalisation:** does the curriculum resonate with the social and cultural needs of diverse learners and provide appropriate elements of choice?
>
> This question contributes to a conceptual framework underpinning professional expertise (see Chapter 16).

In addition to each reading being different depending on the individual reader, Rosenblatt also argues that what each reader gains from the reading depends on why they are reading. Readers will adopt different stances towards the text depending on whether they are reading for the feelings a text evokes or for the information it may yield, or both. For example, reading a text about the First World War soldiers in the trenches may primarily generate what Rosenblatt calls an *aesthetic* response such as feelings of revulsion or fear, or it may generate an *efferent* response (from the Latin word *effere,* meaning to carry away), a response more concerned with information that remains after the reading (Rosenblatt, 1978, 1994) such as details of how trenches were constructed or statistics about unsanitary conditions. Of course, a reader may also shuttle back and forth between aesthetic and efferent responses, the one informing the other. Because a text is never read in quite the same way by two readers, it can be very valuable for students in a classroom to make their individual readings available for discussion, learning to justify or modify their readings in the light of other people's. As well as what they learn from the reading, they are also learning about what it means to read *per se*, to question facts, interpret ideas and take up a critical position whilst the teacher, too, gains insight into how different students understand the same text.

3.3 Reading and engagement

National and international reports are clear about the need to do more than merely teach young people to decode text if they are to engage with and enjoy reading (Kirsch et al., 2002). What such reports argue strongly is the need for a culture of reading and the development of policies to promote literacy across the curriculum and reading for many types of enjoyment. If choice is a key factor in promoting reader engagement (Clark and Pythian-Sence, 2008), we need to find ways to develop freedom of choice both within and beyond the curriculum. An ongoing and crucially important task for teachers is to be as familiar as possible with the breadth of literature available for children and young people and to know what the specific individuals we teach are reading, both at school and at home. In-depth surveys such as Hall and Coles's *Children's Reading Choices* (1999) are illuminating not just in terms of actual texts cited by young people but also what kinds of texts they enjoy. Contrary to the popular impression of young people's reading preferences, especially the assumption that boys prefer non-fiction, this survey found that between the ages of 10–14, 'Overwhelmingly both boys' and girls' book reading at all ages is narrative fiction' (Hall and Coles, 1999, p. 85). If that is the case, and if such texts also enable readers not just to learn facts but experience feelings, then classroom reading of literary and non-fiction narratives should be a vital part of every teacher's subject knowledge for teaching. Across the whole age range and curriculum, such reading offers young people different viewpoints from which to reflect on the world they live in. As Peter Hollindale argues, 'stories are very important. They take us across the bridge from the thinkable, where we are, to the imaginable, where we need to be' (2011, p. 110).

> **Expert question**
>
> **Engagement:** do our teaching strategies, classroom organisation and consultation enable learners to actively participate in and enjoy this learning?
>
> This question contributes to a conceptual framework underpinning professional expertise (see Chapter 16).

Hollindale draws on his own experiences as a child of reading about wildlife and the environment as having a major impact on his adult thinking and ideological bearings. He not only discusses narrative fiction but also non-fiction which often combines strong narrative with powerful pictures. A recent example of this kind of narrative non-fiction is *Into the Unknown: How Great Explorers Found Their Way by Land, Sea and Air* (Ross and Biesty, 2011) which tells the stories of 14 different journeys by explorers from all over the world. The stories comprise strong narratives, often drawing on the words used by the explorers themselves to communicate with other people, taken from journals, diaries and contemporary accounts. However, an equally important part of the text are the illustrations, diagrams and fold-out cross-sections of the craft or equipment the pioneers used. Embedded within the narratives and pictures are scientific, mathematical, historical and geographical ideas which encourage readers to think about how they contributed to these various explorers' achievements. Here, then, is an example of how reading enables communication in many different ways: visually, verbally and interactively.

The extent to which young people's reading of texts such as these might shape their thinking and learning in different disciplines, beyond the mere gleaning of information – as scientists, mathematicians, historians and geographers – is under-explored. Margaret Mallett suggests that this is because 'for a long time informational kinds of reading and writing were relatively neglected. It was assumed that once children had learnt to read and write they could transfer these abilities to all aspects of literacy. Now we recognise that different kinds, or genres, of reading and writing require different strategies' (Mallett, 1999, p. 1). Many teachers are aware of different kinds of information texts and ways of reading them, due to critical studies by researchers such as Margaret Meek in her study, *Information and Book Learning* (1996), and are keen to help students understand ways of both reading and writing non-fiction.

3.4 Reading across the curriculum

Teachers who understand that there are many different ways of reading also know that different ways of teaching about reading are therefore required. As Christine Counsell cautions in her book *History and Literacy in Y7: Building the Lesson Around the Text*, 'A subject is not a collection of information. Subjects are different ways of thinking and ways of knowing. Surely they are also ways of reading?' (Counsell, 2004, p. iv). We are once again reminded that all authentic texts – whether imaginative such as a picturebooks or novels, or real-life texts such as diaries, letters, accounts, memoires – have an audience, purpose, context and style which can (and must) be subject to scrutiny. Heinemann's *History Eyewitness* series reproduces just such texts, for example the reports of an early nineteenth-century Swedish traveller visiting British coal mines to try and discover the perceived successes of the British industrial revolution (Reynoldson, 1995), or a series of articles written by a wealthy American in the mid-nineteenth century based on his journey along the Oregon Trail and his time spent living with Sioux Indians (Shuter, 1993). These texts, used as part of both English *and* history lessons, could be read very differently. In English, the emphasis might be on the style of writing itself as an example of a certain type of non-fiction writing. It might also focus on the viewpoints represented by the writers and consider how the same events or places would have been differently represented had another figure in the account been writing them. In history, meanwhile, knowledge of the period in which the text was produced will be crucial to how the text is read and interpreted as historical evidence. History students therefore need to 'cultivate period-sensitivity' (Counsell, 2004, p. 1) to engage with texts, as well as using those very same texts to cultivate period-sensitivity. If the way texts are read is influenced by disciplinary perspectives, there is much to be gained by teachers working with different subject specialisms to explore distinctions and commonalities in the way knowledge is communicated.

> ### Expert question
>
> **Coherence**: is there clarity in the purposes, content and organisation of the curriculum and does it provide holistic learning experiences?
>
> This question contributes to a conceptual framework underpinning professional expertise (see Chapter 16).

3.5 Reading multimodal texts

In some texts, for example *Ice Trap! Shackleton's Incredible Expedition* (Hooper and Robertson, 2000), which mingle narrative (the true story of how Shackleton's ship *Endurance* became trapped in the Antarctic ice in 1915) with non-narrative (for example information about pack ice and sledge dogs), visual images play a vital part in communicating both story and information. *Ice Trap!* is illustrated with large, vivid watercolour paintings often taking up whole pages on their own, offering many different viewpoints of the Antarctic ice and life onboard ship. However, there are also scale drawings of maps and, at the end of the book, a timeline of the expedition with photographs taken by the ship's photographer, Frank Hurley. Inviting readers to compare the illustrations with the photographs requires analysis and interpretation, demonstrating the value of reading images as well as written text. At the same time, it is possible that the illustrations and pictures may well evoke emotions in the reader as they try to appreciate the horror, fear, courage or despair Shackleton and his companions may have felt when they realised they were trapped in the ice. Focusing on all modes, not just the verbal, develops students' explicit awareness of how ideas are communicated in multimodal texts so that they are better placed to analyse and interpret what is represented.

Increasingly too, written texts are complemented by, or flow from, other media such as film, cartoons, games, digital clips, blogs, tweets, etc. Kress and van Leeuwen's book, *Reading Images: The Grammar of Visual Design* (2006), discusses how 'language, whether in speech or writing, has always existed as just one mode in the ensemble of modes involved in the production of texts' (Kress and van Leeuwen, 2006, p. 41; see also Kress, 2010, Reading 8.6).

3.6 School values and reading

Teachers and their students become acculturated to schooled ways of doing things, including reading, so it can be instructive to step back for a while and consider how taken-for-granted some aspects of reading may quickly become. As teachers, it is valuable to reflect on the explicit and implicit messages we convey to students about reading. The messages they receive may depend on whether we discuss our own reading with them and make recommendations for books or magazines they might explore to support their learning. It may be that students are already familiar with novels, magazines or websites related to the topic we are teaching them and have funds of knowledge teachers can draw on in turn. Sometimes, we favour fiction over non-fiction, sending messages that the non-fiction is somehow inferior. In the following piece of writing, an experienced secondary science teacher, Zoe, reflects on her interest in different kinds of reading and the implications for her students.

Case study 12.1 Zoe's reading and its influence on her teaching

My mother was a biology teacher and the paraphernalia of my childhood consisted of petri dishes, red biros, a formaldehyde preserved sheep heart and a trove of textbooks. My imagination was fired by the world of science and the marvels revealed within its diagrams and orbital cross-sections. My comfort with the informational realm would be a tremendous asset to me throughout my primary education where there was a clear bias by class teachers towards topic work. Topics as varied as 'The Vikings', 'India' or 'Farms' were studied for an entire half term with teachers seamlessly embedding literacy, numeracy, history, music and all else comfortably within them. This may seem a little bizarre, archaic even in a modern primary classroom where subject areas are more discrete but I thrived within an environment which rewarded me for deep reading. To succeed I needed to engage with information in a very personal way. I learnt how to locate the marrow of a topic, some unique factoid which would elevate my writing and engage my teacher's attention.

I started to understand the rules which governed non-fiction books. The inaugural contents page which would set up my expectations as a reader and the terminal index provided me with easy access to the secrets within. Glossaries in particular hold a revered position in my memories. Upon reading a new word for the first time I would refer to the glossary to elucidate the meaning and then in my head I would roll the word around on my tongue manipulating it like a small child with a building block. Frustrated with the lack of similar signposts in fiction works I listed new words on the pasted down endpaper of fiction books.

My fictive diet further aided me in learning the nuances of emotive language. Words are global and like mythological shape-shifters able to traverse between the realms of fact and fiction. I knew what appealed to me and elicited an immediate response and I stored these techniques as part of my own narrative blueprint which would later become the hallmark of my own writing. It is something I advocate to all my pupils: the need to find a distinctive voice. All scientists need to communicate – with the public, funding bodies, their peers. I teach them how the mechanics of non-fiction texts perform an identical role to the beginning, middle and end of fiction tales and help them in writing powerful openings which demand attention.

My experience of working within secondary education has shown me that an impassioned science teacher sharing her love of reading is an unexpected and inspiring hook for pupils. The use of storytelling devices especially has had a very powerful effect on my pupils. At the end of a recent Year 9 class on recycling, my final lesson objective was to impart to the pupils their personal responsibility in caring for the planet. I decided to read them a historical account of the civilisation of Easter Island which at its peak had a population of 7000. There was complete silence as I relayed the eventual grim fate of the islanders with some 'oohs' as the story descended into cannibalism as a direct result of islanders destroying all their natural resources. I told them that like the islanders, the human population on earth has no practical means of escape yet we continue to fatally deplete the resources which are available to us. I questioned them: 'What will your fate be? You are the custodians of our planet. What's your next move?'

Real science is just as fantastic and enthralling as fantasy writing or science fiction. The ability to interweave fiction and non-fiction in the same seamless way as my primary teachers did has helped me to raise aspirations in my own classroom and create that 'buzz' which surely we all want to achieve?

4 Writing

Writing lies on the other side of reading. It offers the ability to communicate outside real time, with people who are not present and whom we may or may not know. It has the potential to endure and thus not only affords the possibility of reflection, but also to extend beyond the present parameters of our lives.

The relationship between reading and writing

The American scholar, Robert Scholes, argues that young people need to acquire textual power by the end of their formal schooling, by which he means they need to become confident readers and writers of texts who have the skills, knowledge and understanding to read for pleasure as well as interpret and take up critical positions towards texts and produce texts for others to do the same. To that end, he writes, we should 'perceive reading not simply as consumption but as a productive activity, the making of meaning, in which one is guided by the text one reads, of course, but not simply manipulated by it … The writer is always reading and the reader is always writing' (Scholes, 1985, p. 8). His point is borne out by research conducted by Barrs and Cork into reading and writing at Key Stage 2 (Barrs and Cork, 2001, Reading 12.5). Barrs and Cork explored the effect on children's writing when high-quality literary texts were their starting point. Evidence from their research showed that children's writing was influenced by several pedagogical approaches, as well as the rich quality of the texts. These approaches included writing in role as characters to encourage empathy and alternative perspectives, reading aloud to hear the sounds and rhythms of the prose, and exploring ideas through drama before committing them to paper. Interesting outcomes may also arise from taking non-literary texts as prompts for writing. Jarman and McClune (2005), for example, have explored newspapers as a resource for extending reading and promoting engagement in the science classroom.

Aim To compare and contrast the writing and reading expectations in the lessons of two different teachers.

Evidence and reflection Join up with another teacher in your school and agree to observe one of each other's lessons with a particular focus on reading and writing. Make a note of all the reading material made available to the students during that lesson: writing that is part of the physical space in which the lesson takes place; writing prepared by the teacher before the lesson (e.g. powerpoint slides or worksheets); published material e.g. text books or class novel, noting with the latter whether photocopied sections or whole texts are used); writing done by the students, including the nature of the task, time allocated, what students are taught about how to accomplish it. Afterwards, discuss the commonalities and distinctions between reading and writing in your two lessons.

Extension What might be the implications for students' reading and writing from the experiences the two of you offer them?

4.1 Teaching writing

Given the complexity of the writing process, all teachers need to make sure that students have sufficient time and support for whatever task they are set. For teachers of students in the early years and primary age, but also often in the secondary years too, this includes supporting students in the transcriptional as well as the compositional elements of writing (Smith, 1994). The transcriptional or secretarial element refers to features of the writing process such as the physical effort of writing, spelling, punctuation and legibility, whereas the compositional element includes the authorial considerations of capturing ideas, selecting words, adapting texts for a particular audience and using appropriate grammar and style. Throughout all phases of schooling, reflective teachers deepen students' understanding across various genres of writing. As teachers in different subject areas, we also need to help students learn what are some of the specific features of writing they will encounter across the curriculum, for example when writing about a science experiment as distinct from a historical explanation. They need encouragement to consider the audience for whom the writing is intended, to think about how its purpose will affect choice of style and format, and to judge the different ways in which the context of the writing affects any decisions they make about how their piece is to be written. Teachers may well offer scaffolding in the form of writing frames or paragraph structures. It is vital to remember that scaffolding is only ever intended to be a temporary form of support to be dismantled once it is no longer needed (see also Chapter 11). As soon as students understand the purpose and diversity of paragraphing in the bigger picture of sustained pieces of writing, they need

Expert question

Personalisation: does the curriculum resonate with the social and cultural needs of diverse learners and provide appropriate elements of choice?

This question contributes to a conceptual framework underpinning professional expertise (see Chapter 16).

to be encouraged to write more independently, confident in their ability to make relevant stylistic choices to achieve particular effects.

4.2 Researching writing

One very influential research study in the field of writing is Bereiter and Scardamalia's *The Psychology of Written Composition* (1987; Reading 12.6). A key idea is that of two models of composing: 'knowledge-telling' and 'knowledge-transforming'. Broadly, the capacity of writers' knowledge-telling is highly dependent on how much they know and can therefore write about. The main point, however, is developing knowledge through writing about it. In knowledge-transforming, on the other hand, the main aim is development of the text, the writer taking into consideration the audience, purpose, context and style in order to create a text which will have maximum impact, not just because of the knowledge the writer is offering, but because of the manner in which it is being represented textually. Teachers who share Bereiter and Scardamalia's ideas about these two models of composition also realise the potential benefit of seeing them as a two-stage process: firstly the writer amasses knowledge then tackles the transformation, rather than trying to undertake both mental operations simultaneously.

Research which looks at writing as a form of design across a range of curriculum areas is a helpful way to conceptualise the task that faces students when they are learning to write. Undertaking research into students' reading and writing in modern foreign languages and English, Maun and Myhill explore the implications of multimodality for teaching writing (Maun and Myhill, 2005). They argue that visual aspects of texts not only affect how they are read but also how writers make choices when writing. Thinking about text-making as design, not simply as writing, can help students to conceptualise it differently. It can also encompass a very wide variety of types of texts that young people need to learn how to write, not just verbal texts such as conventional story narratives but multimodal texts such as newspaper front pages or blogs (Bearne and Wolstencraft, 2007; Cremin and Myhill, 2012). Here, too, we need to ensure students develop a wide enough repertoire of genres, modes and technical proficiency to be able to make choices about how and what to communicate through their writing. Thinking about it as design is an approach that teachers and students often find helpful.

The best marking, feedback and assessment acts as a form of high-quality communication in its own right. In particular, formative feedback on speaking and listening, reading or writing must be dialogic if it is to take effect. When teachers offer formative comments, whether orally or in writing, on young people's work, they act as an actual audience for the piece. To that end, it behoves them to respond genuinely as well as offering formative feedback. To be formative, however, the feedback needs to be acted on by learners in ways which make it clear

Expert questions

Authenticity: do learners recognise routine processes of assessment and feedback as being of personal value?

Feeding back: is there a routine flow of constructive, specific, diagnostic feedback from teacher to learners?

These questions contribute to a conceptual framework underpinning professional expertise (see Chapter 16).

that learning has taken place, not merely that learners are acting as automatons. Thus, at a very simple level, making changes to a draft along lines spelled out by the marker does not make the feedback formative; transforming the marker's feedback to the writer's own ends, does (see Chapter 13).

5 Knowledge about language for communication

5.1 Knowledge about grammar

Debates still rage about whether explicit knowledge about language, such as grammar, makes a difference to the quality of communication. Little evidence has been found to suggest that it does. However, it has been argued recently that research has not looked at instances where students are being taught about writing and about grammar simultaneously (Myhill et al., 2012). There remains no sure answer, but the discussion raises important questions about how language is perceived. Brian Cox and his committee, in their report for the National Curriculum for English in the United Kingdom (UK), stated that:

> Language is a system of sounds, meanings and structures with which we make sense of the world around us. It functions as a tool of thought; as a means of social organisation; as a repository and means of transmission of knowledge; as the raw material of literature; and as the creator and sustainer – or destroyer – of human relationships. It changes inevitably over time and, as change is not uniform, from place to place. Because language is a fundamental part of being human, it is an important aspect of a person's sense of self; because it is a fundamental feature of any community, it is an important aspect of a person's sense of social identity. (DES 1989b, para. 6.18)

If language is a fundamental part of being human, then it is important to teach young people something about how it works and a metalanguage for discussing it. They often find it intrinsically interesting (Crystal, 2002). If students are to learn about language from their teachers, we need to have some understanding of how the everyday language we use to communicate works. One of the concepts we need to teach about is grammar and why it is important in thinking about communication. Grammar comprises word order (syntax), word structure (morphology) and lexis (the vocabulary from which we select). Audience, context and purpose will always affect our grammatical choices.

Expert question

Balance: does the curriculum-as-experienced offer everything which each learner has a right to expect?

This question contributes to a conceptual framework underpinning professional expertise (see Chapter 16).

5.2 Some differences between spoken and written language

A crucial factor affecting our use of grammar is whether we are communicating in spoken or written language. For example, in a newspaper report about a football match we might have said that 'Beckham scored the goal'. A radio commentator, reporting live on the same match might have said 'It's a goal, and Beckham the scorer'. Seen written down, the word order of the radio commentary looks odd, but in the context of reporting a live football match when listeners cannot see for themselves what is happening, the crucial point to communicate is that a goal has been scored; who scored it will be of secondary importance. In a written report, however, there is time for a journalist to adjust the words into more conventional written order. What needs to be understood about these two examples is that the radio commentator's grammar is not wrong, merely different because of the context, audience and purpose.

Understanding some of the differences between spoken and written language can be a valuable way for teachers to think about helping students develop their own communication skills. In spoken language, speakers typically: make use of stress patterns, pitch, speed and volume so listeners can hear what is meant; use gestures and body language to supplement what they say; repeat themselves, make false starts, hesitate, trail off without the listener necessarily losing the thread; interrupt each other or take turns; and link infinite numbers of clauses together (a pattern sometimes known as 'chaining') rather than speaking in sentences with clearly defined beginnings and endings. In *Learning to Write* (1993), Gunther Kress analyses children's speech and writing, drawing out some of the implications for teachers. Kress suggests several areas for consideration, all of which relate closely to the focus on audience, purpose, context and style within this chapter overall. We discuss three of these areas briefly.

First, when we speak we do so for the most part in the physical presence of an audience (phone conversations being one exception). Speakers therefore adjust their talk depending on the immediate response they receive from the listener. When we write, we usually address an audience that is absent. Writers, therefore, need to develop the habit of explicitness in anticipation of how readers might respond. In much spoken language, the word order is often characterised by chaining (e.g. I went to the market *and* I bought some vegetables *and* I went for a coffee). Writing, however, tends to be more hierarchical, with main and subordinate clauses being used to signal to the reader what is key and what is of subsidiary importance (e.g. I went to the market *in order to* get some vegetables, *afterwards* going for a coffee). Writers therefore need to experience as wide a variety of sentence grammar in their reading as possible, with teachers drawing their attention to what different purposes syntax variety can serve, as and when appropriate.

Second, speakers make use of a range of intonation to communicate meaning to listeners. Writers, meanwhile, do not have that option very often. They need, therefore, to be able to use word order to suit their purposes instead. For example, if someone is standing beside a person they are teaching to toss a pancake, they will use intonation as well as words to explain how to move the pan, stress the danger, enjoy the fun. In a written recipe, much closer attention will be paid to word order, vocabulary and sequencing of instructions.

Third, in order to become as versatile a writer as possible, there is a need for an ever-expanding vocabulary. At a market stall I might say to the stallholder, 'One of those, please', indicating a punnet of strawberries. My speech would be minimal since pointing would do the rest. A description of strawberries on a menu to persuade a diner to select them for dessert might read 'Delicious, sun-ripened locally picked juicy strawberries', designed to persuade the diner to choose them without seeing or smelling them in advance.

The more opportunities students are afforded to study the grammar and vocabulary of their own and other people's texts – whether spoken or written – and analyse how they work to achieve particular purposes and address audiences within specific contexts, drawing on particular styles, the greater the textual power that speakers as well as writers will acquire.

5.3 English as an additional language

Language is one of the most significant manifestations of identity and culture, and is thus of enormous significance for the self-respect of individuals and groups. Some 40 years ago the Bullock Report (1975) stated that:

> No child should be expected to cast off the language and culture of home as he [sic] crosses the school threshold, nor to live and act as though school and home represent two totally separate and different cultures which have to be kept firmly apart'. (DES 1975)

Bilingual and multilingual learners face two huge tasks in school: they need to learn to communicate in English as well as any other languages they speak, and they need to learn and communicate within the content of the curriculum. However, Sorace (2010) argues, the ability to communicate with two or more languages brings metalinguistic, cognitive and social advantages. It is essential, therefore, that teachers build on existing language capabilities, recognising the opportunities these bring to enhance the learning of all students.

Cummins (1996) adopted the metaphor of an iceberg to distinguish between basic interpersonal communicative skills (BICS) and cognitive and academic language proficiency (CALP). Children develop communicative skills first, in face-to-face highly contextualised situations, but take longer to develop the cognitive and academic language proficiency that contributes to educational success. Cummins acknowledges that some interpersonal communication can impose considerable cognitive demands on a speaker and that academic situations may also require social communication skills. Generally speaking, children learning an additional language can become conversationally fluent in

Expert question

Connection: does the curriculum engage with the cultural resources and funds-of-knowledge of families and the community?

This question contributes to a conceptual framework underpinning professional expertise (see Chapter 16).

the new language in two to three years but may take five years or longer to catch up with monolingual peers on the development of full language proficiency.

Multilingual children are experts in handling language because they become adept at 'code switching' (switching between languages). Bilingual children are hearing two languages – or two distinct systems – which they have to internalise and respond to. Kuhl (2004) argues that at an early age neither language is likely to interfere with the other, so young children can acquire two languages easily. This does not lead to confusion, on the contrary, it has cognitive, metalinguistic, and communicative advantages. Indeed, bilingual children outperform monolinguals in cognitive flexibility tasks (Bialystok, 2007) because they work constantly with two linguistic systems. These children have considerable language skills on which the teacher can build, and they are likely to have much to offer others, particularly with regards to the subject of language study. Having said this, even if the child may be skilled in language use, he or she may still need particular support and guidance to develop greater proficiency in the use of English at school, especially in terms of written English.

In Reese et al.'s (2000) large-scale study of emergent bilingual students in America, the importance of supporting students' languages was shown:

> … non-English speaking student success in learning to read in English does not rest exclusively on primary language input and development, nor is it solely the result of rapid acquisition of English. Both apparently contribute to students' subsequent English reading achievement … early literacy experiences support subsequent literacy development, regardless of language; time spent on literacy activity in the native language – whether it takes place at home or at school – is not time lost with respect to English reading acquisition. (Reese et al., 2000, p. 633)

> **Expert question**
>
> **Inclusion:** are all learners treated respectfully and fairly in both formal and informal interaction?
>
> This question contributes to a conceptual framework underpinning professional expertise (see Chapter 16).

This means that the use of mother tongue or community languages should be positively encouraged in the classroom, both for children who are new to English and also as they become more fluent. Reflective teachers understand that it is unhelpful to conceive of 'multilingual children' as some kind of homogeneous group. Some children will have been born in this country and their parents may have insisted on a different first language in order to retain the child's sense of ethnic identity and community.

Consequently, the teacher needs to apply great sensitivity to these children: on the one hand, children learning English as an additional language should be encouraged to use spoken English at every possible opportunity; on the other, the teacher needs to employ teaching strategies which ensure that these same children do not begin to lose confidence in their language use because they perceive themselves as underperforming readers and writers. Because language use is closely linked with a person's identity it requires sensitivity and perception by all who work with children (Blackledge, 1994, Reading 12.7).

Conclusion

In this chapter, we have discussed some important aspects of communication in the classroom. We have offered ideas about many of the ways in which teachers and learners communicate with one another. In particular we have stressed what can be learnt by teachers and students when they attend to the audience, purpose, context and style of language use. Although there has been significant emphasis on oral communication, through talk and listening, we have also shown some of the ways in which communication occurs through reading and writing in different modes. We have identified differences between spoken and written language in order to raise awareness of the interesting part they play in the choices we make when we communicate. Many of the young people with whom teachers work in classrooms are bilingual or multilingual, so understanding the advantages and challenges of working with English as an additional language is crucial to the role of any teacher. The Key readings below offer further reading in all these broad areas for those interested in pursuing any of the ideas above further.

Key readings

The classic government report on the significance of language across the curriculum is:

Bullock, A. (1975) *A Language for Life. Report of the Committee of Enquiry into Reading and the Use of English.* London: HMSO.

A National Oracy Project took this further by drawing on the experience of teachers and pupils to emphasise the centrality of talk for learning, see:

Norman, K. (ed.) (1992) *Thinking Voices: The Work of the National Oracy Project.* London: Hodder and Stoughton.

Other influential studies of classroom learning and language in primary and secondary classrooms are:

Edwards, D. and Mercer, N. (1987) *Common Knowledge: The Development of Understanding in Classrooms.* London: Methuen.

Webster, A., Beverage, M. and Reid, M. (1996) *Managing the Literacy Curriculum.* London: Routledge.

The cutting edge of understanding of effective teaching and learning is now focused on 'dialogic teaching', about which Alexander and Mercer have made exceptional contributions. For summaries and applications, see:

Alexander, R. (2008) *Towards Dialogic Teaching: Rethinking Classroom Talk.* Cambridge: Dialogos. (see also Reading 12.3)

Mercer, N. and Littleton, K. (2007) *Dialogue and the Development of Children's Thinking.* London: Routledge. (Reading 11.6)

Approaches to reading are often controversial but there is no dispute about the educational priority that all pupils should achieve competence. For useful surveys of some of the many ongoing debates about the teaching of reading, see:

> Dombey, H. et al. (2010) *Teaching Reading: What the Evidence Says*. Leicester: UKLA.
>
> Harrison, C. (2004) *Understanding Reading Development*. London: SAGE. (Reading 12.4)

For an insightful classic on teaching reading, see:

> Meek, M. (1988) *How Texts Teach What Readers Learn*. Stroud: Thimble Press.

Writing is also essential for success in school and beyond. The books below offer fresh perspectives on writing across the full primary and secondary range:

> Bearne, E. and Wolstencroft, H. (2007) *Visual Approaches to Teaching Writing: Multimodal Literacy 5 – 11*. London: Sage/UKLA.
>
> Cremin, T. and Myhill, D. (2012) *Writing Voice: Creating Communities of Writers*. London: Routledge.

Knowledge about the English language is valuable to any teacher. For a fascinating overview, see:

> Crystal, D. (2002) *The English Language: A Guided Tour of the Language*. London: Penguin.

Excellent reviews of research, theory and practice on linguistic diversity are:

> Conteh, J. (2003) *Succeeding in Diversity: Culture, Language and Learning in Primary Classrooms*. Stoke-on-Trent: Trentham.
>
> Bearne, E. and Marsh, J. (eds) (2007) *Literacy and Social Inclusion: Closing the Gap*. Stoke-on-Trent: Trentham Books

To really drive home the significance of linguistic diversity, take a look at the Greater London Authority website which provides information on the 40 per cent of pupils whose first spoken language at home was other than English, such as Bengali, Urdu and Somali:

> http://data.london.gov.uk/visualisations/atlas/language-2011/atlas.html

reflectiveteaching.co.uk offers additional professional resources for this chapter. These may include *Further Reading*, illustrative *Reflective Activities*, useful *Web Links* and *Download Facilities* for diagrams, figures, checklists, activities.

Assessment
How can assessment enhance learning?

13

Introduction

Assessment has a profound influence on learning. It does not just measure or find out what a student has learnt, it also affects what is learnt, how pupils view themselves as learners, their attitude to school, and possibly their whole future. If these seem startling claims, think about your own experience: perhaps you did well in one subject because it was clear what was required of you and each step was manageable; alternatively you might have disliked another subject and dropped it as soon as possible because everything seemed so confusing and difficult. Maybe you were motivated by the encouragement from one teacher, or humiliated by the comments from another. Possibly you know one of the many people who consider themselves failures because they got lower exam grades than they hoped for, or did not pass the '11-plus' test for secondary school selection; you might be one of the people who thinks they cannot do maths, or sing, or draw or whatever. More positively you might have achieved something you never thought possible, and become confident that given effort and the right support you are able to succeed in many fields. As a teacher, you have undoubtedly helped others to learn and achieve, in formal and informal settings, and across a range of subjects, topics and tasks. Assessment is at the heart of all these scenarios.

Assessment is more than testing, although tests and examinations are clearly very important (see Chapter 14). The word 'assessment' comes from the Latin 'assidere' meaning 'to sit besides', and this broadens the conception of assessment to include collaborative activities, bringing to mind two people in dialogue, looking at something together, one person seeking to understand another's work and suggest improvements. We can also metaphorically sit beside ourselves, reviewing our progress, and planning the way forward.

Assessment that supports learning is referred to as 'Assessment for Learning' (AfL), a term that is often used interchangeably with 'formative assessment'. This chapter deliberately refers to 'Assessment for Learning' with a particular understanding of the term (as discussed in Section 3). In brief, AfL is a whole way of working involving learners and teachers that integrates assessment, learning and teaching. Activities associated with AfL not only provide information to be used for formative purposes, but rather and probably even more importantly they are learning processes in themselves. Not only does AfL support the learning of whatever is being studied at the time, it also promotes learning how to learn. AfL is underpinned by a set of beliefs about learning, which when enacted establish a learning culture in the classroom and help develop learners' metacognitive skills and sense of responsibility.

See Chapter 4

TLRP principles

Two principles are of particular relevance to this chapter on assessment for learning:

Effective teaching and learning needs assessment to be congruent with learning. Assessment should help to advance learning as well as determine whether learning has taken place. It should be designed and carried out so that it measures learning outcomes in a dependable way and also provides feedback for future learning. (Principle 5)

Effective teaching and learning promotes the active engagement of the learner. A chief goal of teaching and learning should be the promotion of learners' independence and autonomy. This involves acquiring a repertoire of learning strategies and practices, developing positive attitudes towards learning, and confidence in oneself as a good learner. (Principle 6)

There are three main sections to this chapter – 'assessment, learning and teaching', 'classroom strategies', and 'affirming assessment for learning'. In the first section key issues, definitions and principles that concern the inter-relationships among assessment, learning and teaching are introduced and discussed. In the second different ways of putting AfL into practice are considered in five groups. It is essential that both these sections are read together since 'doing' AfL divorced from a culture of learning and without understanding the underlying ideas and principles will not bring about the desired results; indeed, doing so could be detrimental to learning. The final section affirms an understanding of assessment for learning and explores how it differs from formative assessment in a little more depth.

The following chapter, Chapter 14, takes as its focus the closely related aspect of assessment in relation to achievement, and issues of evaluating learning outcomes.

Harlen et al. (1992, Reading 13.1) provides an overview of different types and purposes of assessment, and relates to both this chapter and Chapter 14.

1 Assessment, learning and teaching

1.1 Guiding principles

Three key principles about Assessment for Learning were generated through TLRP's *Learning How to Learn* project (James et al., 2007, Reading 2.8; see the **Research Briefing** on p. 156):

- making learning explicit
- promoting learning autonomy
- focusing on learning (as opposed to performance).

'Making learning explicit' involves opening up and making very clear all phases and aspects of learning: what precisely is to be learnt, how it will be judged and what counts as quality; exactly what pupils know and understand, and tellingly what misconceptions they hold; which aspects and parts of their work are evidence of high-quality learning, and how to improve elements that need strengthening. A classroom where learning is made explicit features rich dialogue focused on learning, among pupils and between the teacher and individuals. Exchanges go far beyond closed questions and very short answers, to open questions eliciting extensive responses, with in-depth probing leading to detailed explanation and considered reflection. When marking children's work, learning cannot be made explicit by the occasional tick or an overall mark or grade, but rather by identifying particular strengths and pointing to specific points for improvement.

'Autonomous learning' refers to pupils taking responsibility for their learning and exercising some measure of independence. It does not mean that they work on their own, although there might be occasions when they decide that this is the most appropriate thing to do. For teachers to promote learning autonomy they must grant some level of choice to pupils, and also support them in developing the skills and confidence to make those decisions. A key feature of autonomous learning is being able to evaluate your own work and progress, and decide on your next steps without having to be reliant on a teacher or someone else to tell you, so realistic self-assessment informed by knowledge of the objective and notions of quality is crucial. Self-regulating learning is not age or stage dependent, but is a learnt process: pupils become more autonomous learners with guidance and through practice.

The third principle, 'focusing on learning' (as opposed to performance) draws attention to the nature of the learning that is promoted and valued. It is learning with understanding at its core, and learning for its intrinsic worth and long lasting value, rather than a mechanistic and utilitarian approach to getting marks in a test or examination after which it is forgotten. This principle is closely linked to Carol Dweck's (2006, Reading 2.6) notion of a 'growth' mindset rather than a 'performance' mindset. Focusing on learning includes focusing on the process of learning, as well as the particular subject objective, so that through assessment for learning pupils become better learners.

As well as providing a useful aide memoire to the essential features of AfL, these three principles are very helpful in evaluating putative assessment for learning practices and checking on their actual effect. This is important because as Mary James and her team made clear, 'if practices fail to serve the underlying principles such as making learning explicit and promoting learner autonomy, then they cease to be assessment for learning' (James et al., 2007, p. 215, Reading 2.8, see also the **Research Briefing** on p. 156).

Another helpful reference point is the TLRP principles for effective teaching and learning discussed in Chapter 4. Principle 5, 'Effective pedagogy needs assessment to be congruent with learning' is obviously all about assessment, and stresses that assessment should enhance

Expert question

Congruence: are forms of assessment fit for purpose in terms of overall educational objectives?

This question contributes to a conceptual framework underpinning professional expertise (see Chapter 16).

and advance learning as well as evaluating learning outcomes. This resonates with the third *Learning How to Learn* principle above, drawing attention to the learning process rather than performance per se.

The three principles derived from the *Learning How to Learn* project (making learning explicit, promoting learning autonomy and focusing on learning) serve well as aids to minute-by-minute decisions as well as more considered reflection on practice. Principled decision-making and evaluation are essential if damaging unintended consequences of misrepresentations of AfL are to be avoided, and the powerful benefits of authentic assessment for learning are to be realised.

Reflective activity 13.1

Aim To apply principled reflection to putative assessment for learning practices.

Evidence and reflection Gather evidence and review a lesson in which practices regarded as assessment for learning were evident. To what extent: (a) was learning made explicit? (b) were learners encouraged to be autonomous? and (c) was there a focus on genuine learning (as opposed to performance simply to gain marks)?

Extension Reflect on whether there were any harmful unintended consequences of the practices, and what could have been done differently to enhance the quality of learning.

1.2 Key ideas

Lying beneath any principles and practices are sets of beliefs, values, theories and ideas that shape our actions, whether or not we acknowledge or are even conscious of them. This section draws attention to conceptions of children and of learning, notions of ability, and the interrelated aspects of roles, relationships, agency and identity.

Mary-Jane Drummond (2008) highlighted the 'close and necessary relationship' between assessment and values, arguing that through the practice of assessment educators make 'value-driven choices about children, about learning and achievements' (p. 3). She reminded us that over the years children have been conceptualised in different ways, for example as empty vessels or blank sheets (John Locke), or as passing through stages of development (Jean-Jacques Rousseau, and Jean Piaget). Some conceptualisations are essentially deficit models, where children are viewed as lacking, or yet to develop, the characteristics of a competent learner on the way to adulthood. By contrast, the image of pre-school children held by educators in Reggio Emilia, Italy, is of children as 'rich, strong and powerful' (quoted in Drummond, 2008, p. 9).

In terms of learning and achievement, the construction of curricula, learning activities and recording mechanisms based on pre-specified goals, sequenced steps and check-lists reflect a view of children's learning as standardised, linear and predictable, rather than unique, complex and divergent. The 'Learning Stories' approach to assessment and recording developed in New Zealand (Carr, 2001, 2008; Carr and Lee, 2012) uses narrative to document children's learning not only for recording purposes but more

Promoting learning how to learn

TLRP's Learning How to Learn project, led by Mary James, makes a key contribution to the Personalisation agenda (see page 289). As *2020 Vision* puts it:

> *Too many children drift into underachievement and disengagement and fail to make progress in their learning. Schools should consider how best to integrate 'learning how to learn' into the curriculum – focusing on the skills and attitudes pupils need to become better learners.* (DfES, 2006, p. 21)

Learning How to Learn takes place alongside learning in subject areas – it must be about something. It builds on the explicitness, openness and reflexivity of Assessment for Learning, but goes further to engage with, and influence, the deeper principles and beliefs about learning and teaching held by teachers. INSET, workshops, questionnaire feedback, critical friendship and web-based support were offered to schools. Improvements in pupil learning were found to depend on teacher learning and reflective, classroom-focused, self-improvement activity. For this to succeed required support across the school and could be further enhanced by professional networks. Among the project's 17 secondary and 21 primary schools was one of the top-performing schools in England which had led on 'making learning explicit' and 'promoting learning autonomy'.

Key findings:	Implications:
Assessment for Learning: AfL helps teachers promote learning how to learn (LHTL) in ways which are in line with their own values, and reduces excessive performance orientation. But it is difficult to shift from reliance on specific techniques to practices based on deep principles.	Advice on AfL techniques is useful to teachers in the short term. But progressive professional development requires teachers to re-evaluate their beliefs about learning, the way they structure tasks, and the nature of their classroom roles and relationships.
Classroom enquiry: Classroom-focused enquiry by teachers is a key condition for promoting learner autonomy. Schools that embed LHTL make support for professional learning a priority.	School leaders need to create structures and cultures that focus on learning and support teachers in sharing and evaluating innovations in classroom practice.
New technology: Teachers are optimistic about the value of electronic tools for professional development purposes and networking, but they are not well-used.	There is much still to be done to provide resources, services and online environments that support knowledge creation about teaching and learning, and which align with teachers' professional development needs.
Professional networks: Educational networks are much talked about but little understood. They are subjective phenomena rather than objective structures and the way they are perceived varies according to a person's position.	Building network capacity is complex. It is best understood by analysing the roles and perspectives of those involved and the pathways by which they communicate.

School conditions that foster successful learning how to learn are represented below:

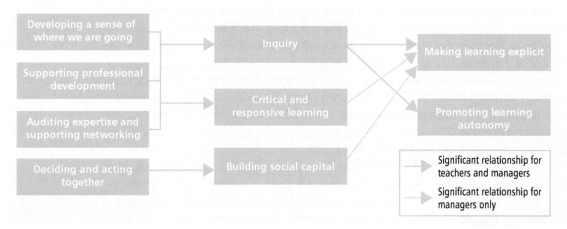

Further information:
James, M. *et al.*(2006) *Learning How to Learn – in Classrooms, Schools and Networks.* TLRP Research Briefing 17. London: TLRP. Available at **www.tlrp.org/pub** (accessed 18 November 2013).
James, M. *et al.*(2006) *Learning How to Learn: Tools for Schools.* TLRP *Improving Practice* Series. London: Routledge.
James M. (2007) *Improving Learning How to Learn.* TLRP *Improving Learning* series. London: Routledge.
An excellent website exists at: **www.learningtolearn.ac.uk**
This project was directed from the Institute of Education, University of London.

importantly as a learning process in itself, shared with friends, teachers, parents and others. Mary James (1998, 2012) has explored the implications for assessment of three theories of learning (behaviourist, constructivist, and sociocultural; see Chapter 2), noting that beliefs about learning are often out of kilter with assessment practices. She advocated reviewing the methods we use for assessment to see the extent to which they align with beliefs and understandings about learning.

What teachers give attention to and what they say indicates to pupils what is valued. If feedback and comments are predominantly about presentation and quantity, rather than the learning intention and quality, these aspects will be seen as the most important. Crucially, if the highest attainment in the class is valued more than the greatest achievement by an individual, and if 'correct answers' appear to be more important than 'having a go', then most of the class will feel they can never succeed and will probably disengage, and the rich learning that comes through effort and risk-taking will be rare. Teachers' language reveals their perceptions of 'ability' and learning potential, and helps shape pupils' learning disposition and mindsets (Dweck, 2006, Reading 2.6). The idea of a 'growth' mindset as opposed to a 'fixed' mindset has been referred to above and in Chapter 2, and the two can be characterised as follows.

Whichever mindset is held has far-reaching repercussions for the disposition of both teachers and pupils. Teachers who ascribe to a fixed mindset try to ascertain pupils' abilities and then match their expectations to this supposed stable and constant entity. Pupils in their turn are concerned how they appear to their peers and teachers, are anxious to look clever not stupid, believe that effort and challenges reveal inadequacies, and because they fear failure they often disengage completely since they would prefer to be thought lazy than stupid. By contrast, a growth mindset fosters effort, engagement, a willingness to tackle new and challenging tasks, and to view failure as part of a learning journey. When growth mindsets characterise a classroom, expectations are high, everyone tries, efforts are valued whatever the outcome, and, in the titles of two powerful books, learning is without limits (Hart et al., 2004; Swann et al., 2012, Reading 1.4).

The roles and relationships of, and among, pupils and teachers that develop in classrooms are closely connected with the prevalent conceptions of children, learning and ability. It makes a huge difference whether children are regarded as rich strong and

Fixed Mindset	Growth Mindset
Intelligence is static	Intelligence is expandable
'I must look clever!'	'I want to learn more'
Avoids challenge	Embraces challenge
Gives up easily	Persists in the face of setbacks
Sees effort as pointless	Sees effort as the way
Ignores useful criticism	Learns from criticism

Figure 13.1 Fixed and growth mindsets

powerful with unlimited possibilities for growth in diverse and complex ways, or of fixed potential with deficiencies yet-to-be remedied by inculcation with the knowledge necessary to succeed in tests. The inter-relationships between assessment practices on the one hand, and roles, relationships, autonomy, agency and identity formation on the other have been explored by a number of researchers (Pollard and Filer, 1999, Reading 14.7; Carr, 2001, 2008; Drummond, 2008, 2012; Stobart, 2008; Swaffield, 2011; Willis, 2011). Gordon Stobart's sketches of students illustrates powerfully how assessment 'creates' learners (2008, Reading 13.6). The essential argument is that the way assessment is practised shapes how learners view

 themselves (which has far-reaching consequences), has a strong influence on their development as successful learners (or not), and determines the culture and interactions of the classroom.

2 Classroom strategies

There have been great advances in the understanding and use of assessment to support learning in the last 15 years. Although there was a considerable amount of research, professional development and practice before that, in 1998 Paul Black and Dylan Wiliam

published an academic article (Black and Wiliam, 1998a) and a summary booklet (Black and Wiliam, 1998b) that led to renewed interest and great activity in the field. Their work was influential because it (a) showed that assessment practice can lead to substantial increases in pupil learning, and (b) identified specific classroom practices.

Since then there has been much development work and many other studies that have further deepened our knowledge and understanding. Most notable were the King's Medway Oxfordshire *Formative Assessment* project (Black, Harrison, Lee, Marshall and Wiliam, 2003), the *Learning How to Learn* project (James, Black, Carmichael, Drummond, Fox, MacBeath, McCormick et al., 2007, see the TLRP **Research Briefing** on p. 156), and work by Shirley Clarke (2005a, 2005b, 2008, 2011) but there have also been many other projects, research studies and development programmes throughout the UK and around the world.

Whilst all this activity has added considerably to our knowledge about how assessment can support learning and has expanded the repertoire of classroom activities, it has also most importantly pointed out some difficulties. Assessment for Learning is not a tool kit to pick and chose from, or a set of techniques that can be put in place almost mechanistically. Indeed, it has been found that when teachers apply the 'letter' rather than the 'spirit' of AfL (Marshall and Drummond, 2006) then it can do more harm than good. Rather, AfL rests on a set of beliefs about learning – notably that the learner has to be actively engaged and that learning is enhanced through working with others (a social constructivist perspective), and that given effort, practice and the right support everyone can achieve (a growth mindset) – and strategies will only be effective when conducted in congruence with these beliefs. Research has also produced sets of principles to guide practice, as discussed in Section 1 of this chapter.

The major features of AfL practice identified by Black and Wiliam (1998a, 1998b) have stood the test of time, and been affirmed by subsequent development and research work.

In this chapter these strategies are considered in five categories, but it should be remembered that they are interrelated. Since AfL is a coherent way of working, any grouping of the practices is to some extent artificial and slightly arbitrary. Also, since AfL is an integral part of learning and teaching there are many connections with other chapters in this book, for example Chapter 4 on principles of effective teaching and learning, Chapter 6 on relationships and classroom climate, Chapter 10 on planning, Chapter 11 on teaching and Chapter 12 on communication.

The approach which was developed in Scotland, 'assessment is for learning' (AiFL), is particularly interesting because of the way in which it integrates assessment principles into holistic, systemic provision (Scottish Government, 2011b, see also Reading 14.2) and is backed by a *National Assessment Resource*. Figure 13.2 gives a sense of AiFL.

Finally, a reminder that it is essential to understand the underpinning beliefs and principles on which the practical strategies rest (see Section 1 above), and to use these as a continual check on the implementation and effect of the practices.

Figure 13.2
Scotland's
'Assessment is for
Learning'

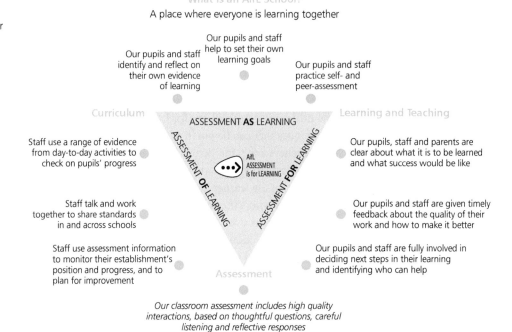

2.1 Sharing goals and identifying quality

Mary Alice White wrote that adults might comprehend what the experience of school is like for pupils if they imagine being:

> … on a ship sailing across an unknown sea, to an unknown destination. An adult would be desperate to know where he is going. But a child only knows he is going to school …The chart is neither available nor understandable to him … Very quickly, the daily life on board ship becomes all important … The daily chores, the demands, the inspections, become the reality, not the voyage, nor the destination. (White, 1971, p. 340)

White is reminding us of the importance of helping children see the bigger picture and knowing how what they are learning today fits in with what they have learnt previously and will do in the future. Not only does this support constructivist learning (see Chapter 2), but it can also capture pupils' interest and increase motivation to learn.

Sharing learning goals, success criteria, notions of quality and information on how their work will be evaluated, all assist pupils to understand what they are trying to achieve. These are all elements of short-term planning – see Chapter 10, section 4. These practices also help learning itself. Experiments by Frederikson and White (1997) showed that students' learning improved when they were involved in discussions about what they were learning, how their work would be assessed and what would count as good work. Moreover, the lower attaining students made greater gains than the previously higher attainers, indicating that some students' previous lack of success may have been because they did not understand what was required.

It is now common practice for the teacher to announce the learning objective at the beginning of the lesson and to write it up so that it is visible and acts as a continual reminder of the aim of the lesson for everyone – pupils, teachers and learning assistants. Referring to it throughout the lesson and in a review at the end helps keep the focus on what the pupils are learning, rather than what they are doing. Shirley Clarke (2008), who through her work with teachers over many years has really deepened understanding of the complexities and subtleties of sharing learning objectives effectively, advocates separating out objective, context, activity and success criteria. For example:

Learning objective:	To produce a travel brochure
Context:	For a place of pilgrimage
Activity (abbreviated):	Introduction, research, planning on paper, discussion, drafting brochure using ICT, self- and peer-assessment, producing final version
Success criteria:	The history of the place
	Features of special interest
	Reasons for visiting
	Places to stay
	Correct presentation

(Adapted from Clarke, 2008, p. 114)

Whilst it helps learners to know what they are aiming for, sometimes stating it too baldly right at the beginning of a lesson can militate against a sense of excitement or surprise. A teacher might want to capture children's interest in any number of creative ways, leading to a statement of the learning objective part way into the lesson. In other cases, when pupils will be investigating or creating something it is inappropriate to give them the 'answer' before they begin. Here an understanding of different kinds of objectives is helpful. Elliott Eisner (2002) distinguished what he called 'curriculum' objectives from 'problem solving' and 'creative' objectives, and these categories suggest phraseology other than a statement of outcome – perhaps in the form of a question or a challenge.

Pupils can be helped to understand what they are aiming for by seeing examples of work generated previously. Single pieces can be discussed to reveal expectations, characteristics and indications of quality, but care must be taken to avoid giving the impression that there is only one way, or that the model should be copied. Several examples could be looked at in sequence, but it can be even more powerful to compare two examples of differing quality as this helps reveal exactly what makes one piece more successful than the other and assists in making characteristics of quality explicit (Clarke, 2008). Examples do not of course have to be limited to written work: different kinds of products including models, artifacts, sound recordings and videos of action, can all be used. Sharing examples of high-quality work and analysing what makes them so can be very powerful, but multiple examples are needed so that pupils realise there are many possible and unique manifestations of excellence.

Once the learning goal has been made explicit, and notions of quality established, it is success criteria that help students attain the objective. Success criteria point out things to attend to, and may be closed instructions ('write down your calculation') or open-ended prompts ('use at least three ways of describing her character, such as likes and dislikes, interests, personality, attitude to others etc.'). Although initially teachers will need to model appropriate success criteria, they are most effective when pupils help generate them. Ways of doing this include asking about key points to remember, comparing examples of products, presenting something that is incomplete, or the teacher 'doing it wrongly' and eliciting ways to improve a piece of work. Helping learners get into the habit and develop the skills of using success criteria enables them to aim for the best and continually improve.

Shared learning intentions, developing a sense of quality, and jointly creating success criteria all enable children to take responsibility for the quality of their work, helping them to become more autonomous learners and assisting them in developing self-regulation. However, it is essential to note that these aspects of assessment for learning only come about when pupils are engaged in the process, as described above; they do not result from the mechanistic writing up of learning objectives. Also, it is crucial that the focus is kept on the learning intention, and that teachers do not unwittingly give the impression that other things (such as behaviour or presentation) are more important than the lesson's learning focus.

2.2 Questioning and dialogue

Questioning and dialogue are central to assessment for learning. It is through dialogue that pupils develop a sense of what they are aiming for, how to get there, and a sense of quality. Questioning and dialogue are integral to feedback and peer-assessment, and are key ways in which teachers ascertain what children have learned, giving insights into their comprehension and misunderstandings. There are many resonances with the research and issues discussed in Chapter 12, and some of the same authors are drawn on in this section.

Crucially for AfL, talk in the classroom not only assesses current understanding but is also an integral part of assessment that supports learning and is itself a thinking and learning process. For this to be the case certain conditions must prevail, and pupils and teachers alike must learn how to engage in effective dialogue. These conditions are discussed below, preceded by a review of the meaning of dialogue.

The word 'dialogue' comes from Greek antiquity and can be interpreted as: 'an exchange of meaning through speech'. So the challenge is how to set up classroom talk, often stimulated by questioning, such that it can generate and distribute meaning and understanding. As we saw in Chapter 12, Robin Alexander (2004) identified five features of 'dialogic teaching':

Expert question

Dialogue: does teacher–learner talk scaffold understanding to build on existing knowledge and to strengthen dispositions to learn?

This question contributes to a conceptual framework underpinning professional expertise (see Chapter 16).

- collective – pupils and teachers learning together rather than in isolation;
- reciprocal – pupils and teachers listening to each other, sharing ideas;
- supportive – pupils supported to voice ideas without feeling there is a single correct response;
- cumulative – pupils and teachers build on contributions to take thinking forward;
- purposeful – teachers plan and facilitate dialogue with particular goals in mind.

For 'meaning to develop through talk' there must first be opportunities for dialogue, in whole-class, small groups or pairs. Instead of what might be considered 'traditional' practice where the teacher asks a closed question, one of the pupils with their hands up gives a short (often one-word) response, and the teacher declares it right or wrong, many ways of engaging more pupils more of the time have been developed. To encourage everyone to think about the issue some teachers have introduced 'no hands up' (Black et al., 2003): every pupil is expected to be engaged and able to respond in some way, even if it is expressing a difficulty or doubt, and knows they can be called on to contribute at any time by the teacher or another pupil. Rather than the 'ping-pong' between teacher and volunteering pupils, whole-class discussions can become more like netball or basketball, where an issue is passed around the group. The next contributor can be selected at random (using named cards or lolly sticks) or nominated by teacher or pupils. Main points about questioning that supports learning are set out by Black et al. (2002).

Other techniques for increasing involvement in dialogue involve the use of small groups. Teachers working with Shirley Clarke (2008; 2011) have explored the practicalities of 'talk partners' in great depth. Key points include keeping discussions very focused and not too long (from 5 or 10 seconds up to 2 or 3 minutes, depending on the task); and frequent changing of randomly selected partners. The quality of dialogue is enhanced by the establishment of protocols and ground rules (Mercer and Littleton, 2007, Reading 11.6), and the modelling of language use by teachers. Being able to engage in effective small group dialogue is a very valuable skill in itself, and needs to be practised and supported: making explicit the learning involved, explaining the value of being able to work with any partner, establishing success criteria and using these to reflect on what went well and how it could be improved, should all be applied to the process.

Along with opportunities to engage, ways of working that enable educative, stimulating initiators of dialogue are required. Questioning is central, but the quality of ensuing dialogue is highly dependent on the nature of the questions. Closed questions used to check children's recall or speed of calculation have their uses, but they do not stimulate dialogue. Instead, open-ended questions, perhaps framed using Bloom's taxonomy or De Bono's 'thinking hats' (see Clarke, 2005a), are more fruitful. 'Why', 'how' and 'what' questions are more likely to lead to discussion than 'when' or 'where' questions, but much depends on the exact phrasing. The format of questions can also be varied with good effect. For example, dialogue can be stimulated by providing a question together with a range of answers, including answers that are definitely right, definitely wrong, and ambiguous ones. Other approaches include asking whether and why pupils agree or

Expert question

Repertoire: is our pedagogic expertise sufficiently creative, skilled and wide-ranging to teach all elements of learning?

This question contributes to a conceptual framework underpinning professional expertise (see Chapter 16).

disagree with a given statement; stating an answer and asking what the question could have been; and asking which statement/shape/object, etc. is the odd one out and why.

Hogden and Webb (2008, p. 83) provide a list of generic questions that dialogue about a problem or task:

- Tell me about the problem
- What do you know about the problem? Can you describe the problem to someone else?
- Have you seen a problem like this before?
- What is similar …? What is different …?
- Do you have a hunch? … a conjecture?
- What would happen if …? Is it always true that …?
- How do you know that …? Can you justify …? Can you find a different method?
- Can you explain … improve/add to that explanation?
- What have you found out about …? What advice would you give to someone else about …?
- What was easy/difficult about this task?

Really good questions and prompts for dialogue often require thinking about in advance, and teachers find it helpful to keep a record of powerful questions, to share them with colleagues, and to plan together.

The final aspect of creating the conditions for dialogue concerns the ways teachers respond to pupils' contributions. Initially they need to allow enough thinking time to produce responses beyond quick recall. Increasing 'wait/think time' even beyond one second takes practice as typically teachers rephrase, ask another question, give a clue, or redirect the question if there is not an immediate response. Dialogue is encouraged by teachers being seen to value all contributions, expected or not. 'As one Year 9 girl said, "When Miss used to ask a question, she used to be interested in the right answer. Now she is interested in what we think"' (Hogden and Webb, 2008, p. 76). This is especially necessary when employing 'no hands up'. Teachers should take the time to carefully consider pupils' contributions, and in so doing model the use of thinking time to enhance dialogue.

Expert question

Authenticity: do learners recognise routine processes of assessment and feedback as being of personal value?

This question contributes to a conceptual framework underpinning professional expertise (see Chapter 16).

2.3 Feedback and marking

A number of researchers have conducted meta-studies of the effects of feedback, including Kluger and De Nisi (1996) and Hattie and Timperley (2007). The key message is that 'feedback is one of the most powerful influences on learning and achievement, but this impact can be either positive or negative' (Hattie and Timperley, 2007, p. 81). Burrell and Bubb's (2000) study of the feedback received by two children in the course of a day helps us understand why this should be so. Kluger and De Nisi reported an average effect size of 0.4 (quite substantial in educational terms) but they found that in over 40 per cent of cases the effect was negative. In other words, in two out of five instances feedback actually lowered performance. So clearly the nature of the feedback is crucial.

It is worth emphasising that authentic feedback has personal implications, and may or may not be welcomed. The quality of relationships and climate in the class is thus significant (see Chapter 6). Spendlove (2009, Reading 13.3) sees the establishment of an appropriate 'emotional environment for feedback' as being essential to an effective process so that pupils are open to learning and receptive to the messages which the feedback conveys (Immordino-Yang and Damasio, 2007, Reading 6.2).

Indicators of good practice can be elicited from the literature (Swaffield, 2008).

1. Feedback should be timely and clear. Feedback should be provided as promptly as possible, when the work to which it relates is fresh in the child's mind. The younger the learner, the greater the imperative that feedback is as immediate as possible, suggesting oral feedback whenever feasible. Oral feedback also has the advantage that the teacher can judge whether the message is being understood, and a fuller dialogue is possible. However, it is often not practical to feed back in this way especially when written work becomes lengthier and the overall quantity increases, hence the age-old practice of teachers marking or providing written feedback. Here again timeliness is important, as well as ensuring that the pupils can read and understand the comments.

2. Use comments alone and avoid marks, grades or levels. The latter all encourage the recipients to focus on performance ('what did I get?') rather than adopt a learning orientation ('what have I achieved and how can I improve my work still further?'). (There is a place for the occasional reference to grades or levels, but these practices do not support learning and so are discussed in the following chapter, not this one.) It is important to note that it is only comments on their own that assist the focus on learning: if they are accompanied by marks or grades pupils again just focus on those as signifiers of performance, and the learning potential of carefully crafted comments is lost (Butler, 1988). Smiley faces, stickers and stars all tend to function as marks or grades, turning children's attention to whether or not they were awarded a symbol of recognition and away from the specific qualities of their work. However, symbols or codes can be useful if they are understood to have a particular meaning, such as 'this point is a particularly good example of demonstrating the success criteria'. Some teachers have also adopted the use of a stamp to indicate that oral feedback has taken place, acting as a record and avoiding the impression that the teacher has not considered the work.

3. Comments on work and possible improvement should be specific. General comments such as 'good', 'well done', or 'you need to work harder' are little more than verbalised marks or grades and do not help the learner improve. Rather, the focus of feedback should be on particular qualities of the work, including information about success in relation to the learning objective and success criteria. Learning is likely to be enhanced if the focus is on the task (as opposed to the learner), and on process and progress (not the product). Comparison with others should be avoided, but instead comparisons should be made with the pupil's own previous work and with shared criteria. As well as acknowledging success, comments should be about next steps and provide specific advice on what and how to improve. This is most likely to support continued learning if couched in terms of questions or prompts rather than direct instruction.

4. Pupils should respond to feedback. The learning potential of high-quality feedback comments will only be realised if pupils take note and act on them. Children should therefore be expected to read (or listen) to feedback, to think about it, and to take some action that is challenging yet achievable. Improving the current piece of work in some way, while it is in progress, is the most meaningful response to feedback. Comments such as 'next time remember to …' are unlikely to be acted upon (even if they are remembered!) since they ask the pupil to do something that they are currently unable or disinclined to do at some indeterminate time in the future. Pupils require time to respond to feedback, which may (and most powerfully) be within the general flow of a lesson, and/or as a routine at the beginning of lessons.

5. Make feedback and marking practice explicit and manageable. To balance quality with manageability, teachers have to be selective about which pieces and aspects of work they mark in detail, ensuring that the focus and pupils rotate. Pupils need to know what to expect in terms of feedback and marking, and policy and practice need to be explained to parents.

Expert question

Feedback: is there a routine flow of constructive, specific, diagnostic feedback from teacher to learners?

This question contributes to a conceptual framework underpinning professional expertise (see Chapter 16).

Shirley Clarke strongly advocates the use of a visualiser to instantly share pupils' work, collectively reviewing and improving work in progress (Clarke, 2008, 2011). These practices model the process of constant review and revision which learners can then adopt themselves.

2.4 Self- and peer-assessment

'All young people need to become their own best self-assessors', declared Earl and Katz (2008, p. 90). The logic behind this is that everyone needs to be continually learning and adapting, becoming more autonomous, self-regulating, self-monitoring learners. The classroom strategies discussed in the sections above help pupils become more self-regulating learners. In particular, understanding the objective, and having a clear sense of success criteria and quality, enable learners to evaluate their own work. The feedback and marking comments they have seen modelled by teachers help pupils give feedback to themselves, essentially 'sitting beside' themselves reviewing their efforts (Muschamp, 1991, Reading 13.4). Self-assessment, as with so many other aspects of assessment for learning, needs support and practice, so to begin with the teacher initiates the activity. However, the aim is for pupils to take control so that they initiate repeated moments of self-assessment, integrating the practice into the continual process of working on a task. This is where the real power of self-assessment lies, not in 'marking' completed pieces of work.

Similarly, peer-assessment is becoming to be seen as 'co-operative improvement' (Clarke, 2011), rather than the swopping of books to be marked in the more traditional sense. Indeed, 'marks' of any kind may be more of a distraction than a help. If peers look at and discuss work together, with improvements being made immediately there is little need for any marks to be made, much less comments written. Too often, especially for less competent writers, peer-assessment has become yet another literacy chore, limited by what can be expressed in writing, with consequent impoverishment of feedback.

Putting the focus on improvement also reduces the emphasis on judgement, and thus lessens some of the more sensitive aspects of peer-assessment including possible threats to self-esteem and opportunities for bullying. Cooperating with a peer in order to make work even better helps pupils appreciate others' strengths and the value of another point of view, and can enhance learning autonomy by assisting the realisation that it can be very useful to seek another person's perspective. Peer-assessment should be focused, with the owner of the work indicating which particular aspect he or she is seeking help to improve.

> ## Reflective activity 13.4
>
> *Aim:* To support pupil development as autonomous self-regulating learners.
>
> *Evidence and reflection:* Consider the opportunities that pupils already have in your classes to improve their learning through self- and peer-assessment. What are the strengths of current practice, and what might be possible negative consequences?
>
> *Extension:* Re-read Section 2.4, and if possible explore other guidance on self- and peer-assessment. Evaluate what you have read against the three principles for AFL (Making learning explicit; Promoting learning autonomy; Focusing on learning rather than performance). Decide what you can do in your practice to help pupils develop as more autonomous self-regulating learners.

2.5 Adjusting teaching and learning

The most important factor influencing learning, according to Ausubel (1968), is what the learner already knows; therefore the teacher should 'ascertain this and teach accordingly'. This seemingly simple yet powerful observation is a key element of assessment for learning with its notion of using assessment to match the next steps to the learner's current position. Records of students' previous attainment in the area can provide useful information, but they should be checked against their current understanding as in the meantime students may have forgotten some things and grasped others.

There are a number of ways in which teachers can check pupils' understanding before starting on a new topic. Concept maps can yield rich information, providing the pupils already know how to draw them. Children could be set a task designed to reveal knowledge and understanding and to highlight areas to be addressed, or given a quick quiz – orally, on paper or using ICT. A teacher in the King's Medway Oxfordshire *Formative Assessment* Project found that a discussion around an open question such as 'If plants need sunlight to make food, how come the biggest plants don't grow in deserts where it is sunny all the time?' (Black et al., 2003, p. 35) allowed all students to participate and enabled him to ascertain their starting point for the upcoming topic of photosynthesis. Another approach for gauging current understanding when pupils already have some knowledge is to ask them to set the questions for a class test at the end. The test itself is not actually taken, but the questions reveal the breadth and depth of current knowledge as well as misconceptions. Some teachers give pupils a list of the items that constitute the forthcoming topic and ask them to indicate their current understanding of each one, typically using 'traffic lights' (colouring items red, orange, green) or smiley faces (happy, neutral or sad). This technique can be very helpful in effectively directing what is always limited teaching time, but there are two necessary conditions. First the items must be phrased in such a way that pupils' responses provide valid information (we don't know what we don't know about something – I may think that I understand 'photosynthesis' for example, but I may have many misconceptions of which I am unaware). Second, pupils must respond honestly, and are more likely to do so if they appreciate the purpose of the task and know the consequences of their responses. If a learning culture is well established in the classroom this is unlikely to be problematic, but may be more so if the emphasis has previously been on 'getting everything right' and being seen to 'be clever'.

Whichever techniques are used to ascertain children's current knowledge and understanding, there must be sufficient time for the teacher to act on what he or she finds out. There is no point using them in the first lesson of a series if the subsequent lessons have already been planned and there is no time to make amendments.

Having established the starting point, thought also needs to be given to the goal. This is often determined by the curriculum, exam syllabi, schemes of work and such like, and of course such statements are very important. However, they must also be realistic given the starting point, and it may be more appropriate to plan some intermediate objectives. Although it is always wise to have some learning intentions in mind, learning is not linear and predictable, so teachers need to be open-minded about unplanned worthwhile learning that may only become apparent during the process.

Some teachers involve the pupils in deciding what they are going to learn, a practice that increases their motivation and effort. However, the 'what do you want to learn?' question generally has to be guided to some extent since children are not aware of all the possibilities, nor of the constraints. One solution is to allow the pupils to select the context within which they explore concepts and skills determined by the teacher – for example the skills of writing persuasively, calculating areas or exercising empathy could be learnt and practised in many different contexts.

Once the starting point and the goal have been ascertained the actual learning journey needs to be planned, and once it is under way continual attention must be given to checking position, keeping track of progress and making necessary adjustments. Teachers should be checking learning and adjusting teaching minute-by-minute, lesson-by-lesson. There are many ways in which teachers can glean information about pupils' learning, for example:

- carefully phrased questioning that elicits important misunderstandings as well as understandings;
- listening attentively to what children say in response to questions and in discussion;
- observing students at work;
- checking written work and other tangible evidence;
- looking at responses on individual white boards;
- using 'ABCD' cards for every pupil to give a response to a multiple choice question;
- setting specifically designed tasks.

There are also many different adjustments a teacher can make in response to what he or she has found out about pupils' learning. In general terms this might involve speeding up or slowing down the learning journey, adding more steps or taking some out, refining the support whether that be from materials or people, setting different tasks, or changing working groups. The practical possibilities are endless, and range from rephrasing a question

or providing a different illustration, to a complete rethink
about the learning goal and ways to achieve it. Many
adjustments are made almost instantaneously while others
may be put into operation the next lesson or the next week.
Continual monitoring and adjusting means the learning
can be kept on track: if position and progress are checked
only occasionally, much greater deviations might be found
requiring a complete change of tack to get back on course.

Students too have an important role to play in
monitoring progress and adjusting learning. The teacher
has responsibility for the whole class, but no one knows
better than the individual pupil whether he or she needs some additional help or has
grasped something and needs to move on. Learners should have a number of strategies they can employ as necessary, such as asking a partner, drawing a diagram, using
equipment, consulting reference material or expressing their understanding in a different
way. Continual review and improvement is the essence of self-regulation, an important
aspect of learning considered in Section 2.4 in relation to self-assessment. When a learning
culture is truly established in a classroom pupils feel comfortable telling their teacher
when a lesson is not going well and together deciding how to improve matters.

Teachers sometimes worry about deviating from set schemes of work. The important
thing to remember is that schemes of work and plans are there to help not hinder learning;
the aim is that pupils will have learnt, not that a pre-determined plan has been followed
step by step. Reviewing a sequence of lessons at the end, thinking about what went well
and what was less successful, will suggest changes that should be made to the plan for the
next time the teacher teaches the same topic.

In summary, learning and teaching will be much more effective if the accuracy of the
assumed starting point is checked, the appropriateness of the proposed finishing point
questioned, and position and progress monitored throughout. Appropriate adjustments can
then be made along the way, rather than when it is too late to rectify any problems.

Reflective activity 13.5

Aim: To reflect on the ways in which teachers aid learning through minute-by-minute
and lesson-by-lesson adjustments.

Evidence and reflection: Think about times when you, or teachers you have observed,
have adjusted teaching on the basis of students' learning. What provided the
evidence of students' learning, or misunderstandings? What was the nature of the
adjustments made?

Extension: What experience do you have of when adjustments should have been made
but were not? What was the result? How could the situation have been handled
differently?

Reading 13.2 from the Assessment Reform Group provides a succinct summary of
characteristics of Assessment for Learning, as does the **Research Briefing** on p. 371.

Research
Briefing Assessment for learning

Many recent developments in formative assessment have been stimulated by the work of the Assessment Reform Group, an offshoot of the British Educational Research Association, whose members have been closely engaged with TLRP. The Assessment Reform Group commissioned Black and Wiliam (1998) to conduct a survey of research literature to answer the following questions:

- Is there evidence that improving formative assessment raises standards?
- Is there evidence that there is room for improvement?
- Is there evidence about how to improve formative assessment?

The answer to all three questions is 'Yes'. Indeed, formative assessment can produce substantial learning gains for all learners, with previously lower attainers improving even more than others. This means that the spread of attainment is reduced whilst attainment is raised overall. The formative assessment processes which lead to these improved performances also equip pupils for taking responsibility for their learning. This Research Briefing draws directly on Black and Wiliam's work.

Key findings:	Implications:
Feedback: Self-esteem and motivation are vital in successful learning, Feedback to any pupil should therefore be about the particular qualities of his or her work, with advice on what he or she can do to improve, and should avoid comparisons with other pupils.	Feedback should focus upon actual work, rather than the pupil. Rewards, such as gold stars, or grades, tend to result in children trying to find ways to obtain the rewards themselves, rather than thinking about their actual learning needs. Some may become reluctant to take try new challenges for fear of failure.
Self-assessment: For formative assessment to be productive, pupils should be trained in self-assessment so that they can understand the main purposes of their learning and thereby grasp what they need to do to achieve.	Self-assessment is concerned with thinking about ones own performance in relation to clearly stated objectives. It is not, as some have interpreted self-assessment, checking work against an answer sheet. Self-assessment is a skill, which like any other skill needs training, coaching and practice.
Expressing understanding: Opportunities for pupils to express their understanding should be designed into any piece of teaching, for this will initiate the interaction whereby formative assessment aids learning.	Classroom practices should really enable children to demonstrate their understanding, and enable teachers to develop authentic insights into children's thinking.
Purposive dialogue: The dialogue between pupils and a teacher should be thoughtful, reflective, focused to evoke and explore understanding, and conducted so that all pupils have an opportunity to think and to express their ideas.	Sometimes the tasks we set mean that it is possible for children to get the right answers for the wrong reasons, and without carefully designed and conducted questioning and discussion these misconceptions may remain undetected, and so become a bar to later learning.
Congruence: Tests and homework exercises can be an invaluable aid to learning, but the exercises must be clear and relevant to learning aims.	Feedback on tests and homework should give each pupil guidance on how to improve, and each must be given opportunity and help to work at the improvement.

Assessment for Learning may seem simple, and elements like clarifying goals, providing feedback, encouraging self-assessment, etc can certainly be promoted. Expert practitioners of AfL argue however, that the approach needs to draw on holistic and principled understanding of teaching and learning in classrooms. It is not just a set of techniques – but becomes an approach to classroom life! When sustained in authentic ways, AfL has the potential to transform classroom experience for both teachers and pupils, as well as underpinning very high standards of attainment.

Further information:
Black. P. and Wiliam, D. (1998b) *Inside the Black Box: Raising Standards through Classroom Assessment.* London: King's College.
Black, P., Harrison, C., Lee, C., Marshall, B., and Wiliam, D. (2003) *Assessment for Learning: Putting It into Practice.* Buckingham: Open University Press.
James, M., Black, P., Carmichael, P., Drummond, M-J., Fox, A., MacBeath, J., Marshall, B., McCormick, R., Pedder, D., Procter, R., Swaffield, S., Swann, J. and Wiliam, D. (2007) *Improving Learning How to Learn: Classrooms, Schools and Networks.* London: Routledge.

ARG
assessment reform group

3 Affirming assessment for learning

The phrase 'Assessment for Learning' (AfL) can be found as the title of chapters, papers and books written by assessment experts first published over a quarter of a century ago (Black, 1986; James, 1992; Sutton, 1995). In recent years the term has been used more and more commonly, yet despite several attempts to define AfL it continues to be understood and interpreted in different ways. It is therefore a good idea to be clear in your own mind what you understand by Assessment for Learning, and to be alert to other interpretations. A key text is an Assessment Reform Group (ARG) pamphlet, *Beyond the Black Box* (ARG, 1999, Reading 13.2).

Mary-Jane Drummond's definition of assessment resonates with the 'sitting beside' notion of assessment referred to in the introduction to this chapter, and it highlights some very important features of AfL. She defined assessment as a process of teachers looking at pupils' learning, striving to understand it, and using that knowledge in the interests of pupils (Drummond, 2012). This is very close to the much quoted definition of assessment for learning produced by the Assessment Reform Group:

> Assessment for Learning is the process of seeking and interpreting evidence for use by learners and their teachers to decide where the learners are in their learning, where they need to go and how best to get there. (ARG, 2002, p. 2)

Both Drummond and the ARG referred to assessment as a process (rather than an event), which involves the need for interpretation and the effort to understand on the part of the teacher, as well as the use of that knowledge. The ARG definition importantly cast learners (as well as teachers) as users of the information. Drummond made clear that the use should be in the interests of the pupils but did not go into specifics, whereas the ARG's definition referred to present position, future goal and moving between the two. Unfortunately some policymakers misinterpreted and distorted this second part of the ARG definition (Klenowski, 2009): they put the emphasis on frequent testing to assess student levels or grades and targeting the next level. This emphasis on performance hinders rather than helps real and sustained learning.

Expert question

Authenticity: Do learners recognise routine processes of assessment and feedback as being of personal value?

This question contributes to a conceptual framework underpinning professional expertise (see Chapter 16).

In order to address this damaging but influential misinterpretation of the definition of AFL, an international conference held in 2009 produced a position paper which included explanation and elaboration of what they called a 'second generation definition of Assessment for Learning' (Klenowski, 2009, p. 264). This read:

> Assessment for Learning is part of everyday practice by students, teachers and peers that seeks, reflects upon and responds to information from dialogue, demonstration and observation in ways that enhance ongoing learning. (Klenowski, 2009, p. 264)

This carefully thought through definition, based on evidence, encompasses many elements each of which were explored in detail. It put students at the centre of the process, and stressed an enquiry process within everyday classroom activity. The elaboration brings out the depth and richness encapsulated in the definition so that it is worth quoting in full:

(1) 'everyday practice' – this refers to teaching and learning, pedagogy and instruction (different terms are used in different regions of the world but the emphasis is on the interactive, dialogic, contingent relationships of teaching and learning).

(2) 'by students, teachers and peers' – students are deliberately listed first because only learners can learn. Assessment for Learning should be student centred. All AFL practices carried out by teachers (such as giving feedback, clarifying criteria, rich questioning) can eventually be 'given away' to students so that they take on these practices to help themselves, and one another, become autonomous learners. This should be a prime objective.

(3) 'seeks, reflects upon and responds to' – these words emphasise the nature of AFL as an enquiry process involving the active search for evidence of capability and understanding, making sense of such evidence, and exercising judgement for wise decision-making about next steps for students and teachers.

(4) 'information from dialogue, demonstration and observation' – verbal (oral and written) and non-verbal behaviours during both planned and unplanned events can be sources of evidence. Observation of these during on-going teaching and learning activity is an important basis for AFL. Special assessment tasks and tests can be used formatively but are not essential; there is a risk of them becoming frequent mini-summative assessments. Everyday learning tasks and activities, as well as routine observation and dialogue are equally, if not more, appropriate for the formative purpose.

(5) 'in ways that enhance ongoing learning' – sources of evidence are formative if, and only if, students and teachers use the information they provide to enhance learning. Providing students with the help they need to know what to do next is vital; it is not sufficient to tell them only that they need to do better. However, such help does not need to provide a complete solution. Research suggests that what works best is an indication of how to improve, so that students engage in mindful problem solving.

(Third Assessment for Learning Conference 2009) (Klenowski, 2009, pp. 264–5)

This elaboration points to features that Sue Swaffield picked up when she made the case for distinguishing assessment for learning from formative assessment (Swaffield, 2011, Reading 13.5). She argued that AfL:

… is characterised by information being used to inform learning and teaching, its focus on learning conceived broadly, and actively engage progressively more autonomous students. It is distinctive in its timescale, protagonists, beneficiaries, the role of students, the relationship between student and teacher, and the centrality of learning to the process – all of which can but may not necessarily be features of formative assessment. (Swaffield, 2011, p. 433)

A classroom where authentic assessment for learning is practised has a particular culture and feeling, far removed from that generated by a relentless and narrow emphasis on scores and teaching to the test.

Conclusion

In focusing on assessment supporting learning, this chapter has sought to acknowledge the complexity of the relationship between assessment and learning. It recognises the profound influence of assessment practices not only on the content of what is being learned, but even more importantly on the process of learning and on the learner's sense of self. Whilst it is a complex area, three research generated guiding principles provided sound direction and useful checks for reflective practitioners.

Teachers would be well advised to be asking themselves continually whether their practices are:

Helping to make learning explicit – making clear the knowledge, understanding and skills that are the focus of each lesson, and providing opportunities for pupils to demonstrate and articulate their learning.

Promoting learner autonomy – providing every opportunity and building an expectation for pupils to become increasingly more self-monitoring and resourceful in taking responsibility for and extending their learning.

Focusing on learning rather than performance – in other words the type of learning that enhances an understanding and valuing of learning not for the sake of a mark or grade but for the development of valuable lifelong attitudes and skills, and for the joy and intrinsic reward of achieving something worthwhile through effort and persistence.

Teachers who are able to answer in the affirmative will likely be practising authentic assessment for learning that genuinely supports pupils in their learning, both for the present and the future.

Key readings

Books that provide overviews of assessment tend to address issues covered in both this and the following chapter, and are included here. They are then followed by texts that are more focused on how assessment is integrated with teaching and learning.

Broadfoot's book is a very clearly written overview covering many aspects of assessment.

Broadfoot, P. (2007) *An Introduction to Assessment.* London: Continuum.
(Reading 14.1)

A comprehensive and authoritative review of assessment to support learning by members of the Assessment Reform Group is:

Gardner, J. (ed.) (2011) *Assessment and Learning.* London: Paul Chapman.

In an eye-opening book, Drummond provides an important critical alternative to mechanistic approaches to assessment:

Drummond, M. (2012) *Assessing Children's Learning.* London: David Fulton.

An enquiring and reflective approach is encouraged in Swaffield's book in which leading figures in assessment explore the values, principles, research and practicalities of assessment:

Swaffield, S. (ed.) (2008) *Unlocking Assessment: Understanding for Reflection and Application.* Abingdon: Routledge. (see also Reading 13.5)

The wide ranging TLRP Learning How to Learn project considered assessment in the classroom as well as issues at the whole school and network levels:

James, M., Black, P., Carmichael, P., Conner, C., Dudley, P., Fox, A., Frost, D., Honour, L., MacBeath, J., McCormick, R., Marshall, B., Pedder, D., Procter, R., Swaffield, S. and Wiliam, D. (2006) *Learning How to Learn: Tools for Schools.* London: Routledge.

James, M., Black, P., Carmichael, P., Drummond, M. J., Fox, A., MacBeath, J., Marshall, B., McCormick, R., Pedder, D., Procter, R., Swaffield, S., Swann, J., and Wiliam, D. (2007) *Improving Learning How to Learn: Classrooms, Schools and Networks.* London: Routledge. (see also Reading 2.8)

Black and Wiliam's influential review of research is summarised in:

Black. P. and Wiliam, D. (1998) *Inside the Black Box: Raising Standards through Classroom Assessment.* London: King's College.

Black and his colleagues at King's College have also published a series of subject and phase specific 'inside the black box' pamphlets:

'Inside the black box' was followed up by a pamphlet that described the key factors needed to put assessment for learning into practice in:

Assessment Reform Group (1999) *Assessment for Learning: Beyond the Black Box.* Cambridge: University of Cambridge, School of Education. (Reading 13.2)

Practice that developed from the Black and Wiliam review is reported in:

Black, P., Harrison, C., Lee, C., Marshall, B., and Wiliam, D. (2003) *Assessment for Learning: Putting It into Practice.* Buckingham: Open University Press.

Wiliam's book providing practical ideas and research evidence is written with US teachers in mind but is equally applicable in the UK.

Wiliam, D. (2011) *Embedded Formative Assessment.* Bloomington, IN: Solution Tree Press. (see also Reading 16.4)

For practical guidance and ideas on developing assessment for learning practices as an integral part of learning and teaching, see:

Blanchard, J. (2009) *Teaching, Learning and Assessment.* Maidenhead: Open University Press.

Clarke, S. (2005a) *Formative Assessment in Action: Weaving the Elements Together.* London: Hodder and Stoughton.

Clarke, S. (2005b) *Formative Assessment in the Secondary Classroom.* London: Hodder and Stoughton.

Spendlove, S. (2012) *Putting Assessment for Learning into Practice.* London: Continuum. (Reading 13.3)

An innovative and internationally acclaimed approach particularly for younger children links assessment practice with the formation of learning dispositions:

Carr, M. and Lee, W. (2012) *Learning Stories: Constructing Learner Identities in Early Education.* London: SAGE.

The social processes influencing assessment in children's lives are the focus of:

Filer, A. and Pollard, A. (2000) *The Social World of Pupil Assessment: Processes and Contexts of Primary Schooling.* London: Continuum. (Reading 14.7)

reflectiveteaching.co.uk offers additional professional resources for this chapter. These may include *Further Reading*, illustrative *Reflective Activities*, useful *Web Links* and *Download Facilities* for diagrams, figures, checklists, activities.

part four

Reflecting on consequences

This part draws attention to what is achieved, and by whom, in our classrooms. What are the consequences of what we do?

Chapter 14 reviews high stakes issues in the assessment of learning outcomes, with particular attention on how schools measure pupil achievement and manage accountability. Whilst some problems are raised, positive uses of summative assessment are also promoted.

'Inclusion' (Chapter 15) asks us to consider various dimensions of difference and also the ways in which routine processes differentiate between people. However, the emphasis is on accepting difference as part of the human condition and on how to build more inclusive classroom communities.

Outcomes
How do we monitor student learning achievements?

14

Introduction

Children and young people should 'fulfil their potential' – this is often cited as a major goal of school teaching. It follows that the measurement and evaluation of learning outcomes is of great importance. The aim should be to assess learning in ways that do justice to students' full achievements, are fair and manageable, can be recorded and certified (if appropriate), and do not have undesirable consequences. Pupil achievements are of great interest to many people – beginning of course with the pupils themselves, but also their parents or carers, teachers and school leaders, employers and admissions officers for the next stages of education or training, as well as politicians and the general public. Indeed, Newton (2007) identified no less than 22 different purposes of assessment, many of which concern summative assessment results. The multiple purposes for assessing learning are also associated with the technical complexities of evaluating diverse achievements – so some complicated issues and dilemmas do arise (Broadfoot, 2007, Reading 14.1).

> ### TLRP principles
>
> Two principles are of particular relevance to this chapter on achievement outcomes:
>
> Effective teaching and learning needs assessment to be congruent with learning. Assessment should help to advance learning as well as determine whether learning has taken place. It should be designed and carried out so that it measures learning outcomes in a dependable way and also provides feedback for future learning. (Principle 5)
>
> Effective teaching and learning demands consistent policy frameworks with support for teaching and learning as their primary focus. Policies at national, local and institutional levels need to recognise the fundamental importance of teaching and learning. They should be designed to create effective learning environments in which all learners can thrive. (Principle 10)

See Chapter 4

This chapter discusses some of the main issues in the assessment of pupils' learning; considers major approaches such as examinations, tests, tasks and teacher assessment; discusses key uses of summative assessment information; and touches on methods of recording and reporting.

The four nations of the United Kingdom have different statutory arrangements for assessing pupils' learning outcomes, and there is a continuing history of change. There are also differences among subjects and depending on the age and stage of the learner. For specific information on the current summative assessment requirements in Scotland, Wales, Northern Ireland and England respectively, please visit:

educationscotland.gov.uk
learning.wales.gov.uk
rewardinglearning.org.uk
education.gov.uk

For the Republic of Ireland, please see:

education.ie

This chapter reviews issues and principles to assist the reflective teacher whatever the jurisdiction or context they work in.

1 Key issues

1.1 Accountability and improvement

In recent years and in most parts of the world, the summative assessment of learning has become more and more important in education. The main reason for this has been the concern of governments to introduce ways of 'measuring' educational outcomes – for performance comparisons of both schools and the educational system as a whole. From this perspective, measurement of outcomes informs accountability procedures and can be seen as forces for improvement.

In comparing schools, governments tend to place particular emphasis on attainment in what are considered to be 'core' subjects, and particularly on standards of literacy and numeracy as measured by tests. Results from key examinations and assessments are used as the basis for judgements about school quality, putting pressure on each school to perform well. Results are likely to inform parents' judgements when choosing schools for their children. Within a context of diverse school types, schools judged to be successful are often granted increased autonomy while those that are deemed to be less adequate or even 'failing' are put under intense pressure to improve. In England, schools which consistently underperform may be *closed*. The rationale for this is that each pupil has just a single opportunity in school and that all schools should provide a good education for all pupils all the time. In other countries, such as Finland, schools which underperform will be *supported* to improve because of the entitlement of all communities to high-quality education in their locality. The ways in which this dilemma is resolved reflects societal values and core assumptions about educational provision.

In terms of comparison of national systems, governments are properly concerned with global economic competition and the effectiveness of the national workforce over the long term. Public education is, after all, funded by taxpayers who rightly expect good use of their considerable investment. In the long run the economic success of the country, including the pensions and welfare for its older citizens, is seen to depend on the education of youngsters. Governments across the world therefore pay great attention to international comparisons of school performance – particularly as portrayed through the Programme for International Student Assessment (PISA) and the Trends in International Mathematics and Science Study (TIMSS) and Progress in International Reading Literacy Study (PIRLS) (Sturman, 2012, Reading 14.6). The interpretation of such evidence can be controversial, but it is often boldly used for political purposes to 'blame' competing parties. In contrast one initiative (see Figure 14.1), presents a strong UK-wide performance – but also highlights the importance of analysing how performance conulsions are reached.

Figure 14.1
International
comparisons: *The
Learning Curve*

The Learning Curve is a project to collate, summarise and analyse international data on the performance of school systems. It is funded by Pearson and uses the expertise of the Economist Intelligence Unit – see **thelearningcurve.pearson.com**
Michael Barber, Pearson's Chief Education Adviser, explains:

Over the last decade, international benchmarking of education systems has become ever more prevalent. More importantly, it has become increasingly influential in shaping education policy at local, regional and national levels. As studies by PISA and TIMSS become more sophisticated and longitudinal time sequences develop, there is ever more to learn about what successful education systems look like and how success can be achieved.

In the early days of international benchmarking, education ministers and other leaders tended to worry more about the media impact than the implications for policy. Increasingly now, what we see is a continuous dialogue among education ministers and top officials around the world about the evidence from international benchmarking and the implications for education reform.

The November 2012 report from *The Learning Curve* reported that the UK's education systems were, in aggregate, sixth best in the world, and second best in Europe. This ranking was not only about performance in school subjects. It owed much to strong science scores and to high literacy, school completion and university graduation rates.

Finland had the top performing system, followed by South Korea, Hong Kong, Japan, Singapore and then the UK. An above-average group included the Netherlands, New Zealand, Canada and Ireland with a middle-ranking group including the United States, Germany and France. The lowest end in 2012 included Mexico, Brazil and Indonesia.

The Learning Curve cautioned against simplistic conclusions but suggested 'five lessons for policymakers':

1   There are no magic bullets
2   Respect teachers
3   Culture can be changed
4   Parents are neither impediments to nor saviours of education
5   Educate for the future, not just the present

No matter how well intentioned, accountability mechanisms based on summative assessment results can have unintended and negative consequences, which detract from the aim of improvement. This phenomenon can be seen at all scales, from the single classroom to the nation state. It is particularly likely when the 'stakes' are high.

Whilst tensions created by assessment attempting to serve multiple purposes will always exist, difficulties can be identified and may be ameliorated by awareness and understanding of key issues discussed below (see also Broadfoot, 2007, Reading 14.1; Stobart, 2008, Reading, 13.6).

1.2 Comparing achievements

The interpretation of any assessment involves some form of comparison about performance in relation to something.

Performance can be judged in relation to:

- performances of others (norm referencing)
- specified, agreed standards (criterion referencing)
- an individual's previous performance (ipsative referencing).

Whilst the terms 'norm', 'criterion' and 'ipsative' may not be commonly used, the practices to which they refer are embedded in the assessment routines of almost all schools.

Norm referencing: With norm referencing, individual pupils are compared with others. Performance may be expressed by ranking, and for much of the last century giving a class position was common ('she came third in the class in maths'). Performance can also be expressed in relation to the rest of the group with statements such as 'he's about average' and 'she's in the bottom third'. In 2013, it was suggested by the Secretary of State that the performance of 11-year-olds in England should be reported in deciles.

Wanting to have a sense of how a pupil is doing in relation to others is understandable, and is necessary when competition and selection are required. However, norm-referenced assessment results give no information about the specifics of what a pupil knows, understands and is able to do, nor do they identify particular difficulties or point to the appropriate next steps in learning. Categorisation can also have significant demotivating effects for weaker learners.

Criterion referencing: Criterion-referenced assessment makes judgements about a pupil's attainment in relation to pre-specified criteria – and this is irrespective of the performance of other pupils. When criteria are made explicit, this form of assessment provides specific information about a pupil's learning. 'Next steps' are implied through the criteria not yet grasped and those at the next level or stage. GCSEs have been norm-referenced for many years and, when criteria are met by many students, it is logical to extend the scale.

Criterion and norm-referenced approaches are interrelated in that the process of establishing criteria takes into account what it is reasonable to expect for pupils at a particular stage of their education. So, notions of norm-referencing do contribute to criterion referencing. Norm and criterion referencing are easily associated with notions of success and failure, whether this be judged in relation to others' performance, or the setting of particular standards, benchmarks or cut-off points in a criterion-referenced system.

Ipsative referencing: The word 'ipsative' comes from Latin 'ipse' meaning 'self'. Although this is not a common term, teachers use ipsative-referenced assessment all the time as judgements are made about a pupil's performance in relation to his or her previous achievements. This works best for detailed assessment when the teacher knows the pupils well, can identify specific improvements, and guide next steps at an appropriate degree of 'stretch'.

Ipsative assessment is very supportive of learning, and seeks to motivate *all* pupils, however they are judged through norm or criterion-referenced assessment. This is the most inclusive and enabling form of assessment, since it values and challenges those at both extremes of the attainment range and everyone in between (see also Chapter 15). It provides direct feedback for a personal learning orientation seeking 'mastery' (Dweck, 1986, Reading 2.6).

In reflecting on the three bases for comparison, it may be helpful to think about the Olympic Games where ipsative, criterion and norm referencing are all in evidence. Ipsative referencing underpins preparation for the Games, as athletes strive to improve on their 'personal best'. Criterion referencing is then often used in relation to qualifying for an event, when athletes do, or do not, satisfy the standard. In the finals, the awarding of medals is norm-referenced as those who beat everyone else are acclaimed. Recognition is also sometimes given to athletes who produce their best ever performance, but it is the norm-referenced brilliance of gold medalists that get paramount attention, rather than ipsative-referenced personal bests, no matter how remarkable these may be.

Reflective activity 14.1

Aim: To consider the bases of comparison used in learning and teaching.

Evidence and reflection: Think of a pupil in your class or whom you know well. Consider when it would be useful and appropriate to use norm, criterion and ipsative-referenced assessment. Now list all the different assessments that the pupil has experienced, and identify the basis of comparison for each. How closely does what happens match what you thought would be useful and appropriate?

Extension: Be aware of the bases of comparison you are using, and explore possibilities for prioritising forms most supportive of learning.

1.3 Validity, reliability and dependability

How do you know that you can trust an assessment outcome? Some endemic issues underlie this question, and we review these below (see also Mansell and James, Reading 14.5).

Validity: This concept is of immense importance. In its traditional, technical meaning, it addresses the question: do assessments actually measure what they purport to measure? This is known as 'construct validity'. So, for example: 'is a whole-class spelling test a valid way of assessing pupils' ability to write effectively? The answer is 'probably not', because many other forms of knowledge, skill and understanding are involved in writing. And even though such a test might be deemed to have higher construct validity as a measure of spelling performance, there may also need to be recognition that some children or young people do not perform consistently in stressful and somewhat artificial situations but may do better, or worse, when applying their knowledge of spelling in a more authentic writing activity.

Understanding of validity has thus evolved so that the answer to whether a test is valid would not be 'yes' or 'no', but rather that whilst some kinds of conclusions may be valid, others would not (Angoff, 1988).

The implication of this is that, whilst we are certainly interested in test results themselves, it is actually the inferences that we draw from outcomes of assessment that make them so crucial. Results of assessment are used to make decisions, for example about: what to teach next; the adequacy of the progress that a pupil is making; appropriate next stages in terms of educational experience; levels of attainment reached; and, of course, the quality of schools and curricula. The quality of these decisions depends on the nature of the assessments on which they are based. As Dylan Wiliam puts it, 'validity is all about the interpretations that we can legitimately draw from assessment results' (Wiliam, 2011, p. 132). For example, Drummond (2003) provides a radical critique of narrow forms of assessment. Illustrating her argument through work with young children, she insists that assessment data are not some form of objective 'evidence', but require interpretation to make sense of them in terms of a teacher's understanding of the child.

Reliability: If a form of assessment is deemed to be valid for a particular purpose, the next question becomes whether it can be used reliably and consistently. Continuing our example, is a spelling test administered by a teaching assistant on a Friday afternoon comparable with a spelling test on a Monday morning led by a class teacher or English specialist? It is important to ensure that irrelevant factors do not interfere in other ways too. A common problem arises when capabilities are interrelated – such as when the reading demand of a particular test may constrain some pupils' ability to demonstrate their under-standing in maths, science, history or some other domain. Assessment processes which conflate different attributes cannot always be avoided, and careful teacher judgement is often required in drawing conclusions.

> **Expert question**
>
> **Validity:** in terms of learning, do the forms of assessment used really measure what they are intended to measure?
>
> This question contributes to a conceptual framework representing enduring issues and teacher expertise (see Chapter 16).

Obtaining adequate reliability is particularly important when achievements are to be certificated or comparisons are to be made with implications for equity. Indeed, it is clearly of enormous significance for major national examination systems where pupil performance is to be measured across schools and when standards are to be maintained from year to year.

Dependability: This is an overarching concept denoting the confidence which stakeholders derive from the assessment system. It reflects outcomes of the struggle to achieve validity and reliability, and the perceived legitimacy of those outcomes. As Mansell, James and the Assessment Reform Group put it:

> **Expert question**
>
> **Dependability**: are assessment processes understood and accepted as being robust and reliable?
>
> This question contributes to a conceptual framework representing enduring issues and teacher expertise (see Chapter 16).

'Together, maximum validity and optimal reliability contribute to the *dependability* of assessments – the confidence that can be placed in them.' (2009, p. 12, Reading 14.5)

The central dilemma is that validity and reliability are interrelated – so strengthening one aspect often weakens another.

- The quest for construct validity tends to lead in the direction of assessment procedures which are designed for routine classroom circumstances, covering a wide curriculum and using a range of assessment techniques such as tasks, course work and continuous assessment. Such approaches resonate with assessment for learning, as discussed in Chapter 13. Modular programmes speak to this concern too.

- However, the drive for reliability tends to suggest simplification in both assessment procedures and the range of curriculum to be assessed, so that there is more chance of comparability being attained. The result of this is an emphasis on methods which can be tightly controlled, such as timed pencil and paper or ICT-based tests and examinations. When the emphasis is on certification of pupil attainment and school accountability, politicians and the media stress this traditional view of reliability and focus on tests and examinations.

Reliability can be increased by using questions to which there is only one correct answer (as in multiple choice questions), since such questions are likely to be marked accurately and consistently. However, multiple choice questions can only assess certain kinds of learning outcomes so cannot be used to assess everything that is considered important. Extended writing, speaking and listening for example require very different assessment arrangements and are more difficult to assess reliably than factual knowledge. Indeed, when National Curriculum assessment was first introduced in England, wide curriculum coverage was endorsed with authentic classroom tasks being used to assess 7-year-olds. However, such assessments were found to be both unmanageable and to have considerable problems of reliability (Shorrocks, 1991; Whetton, 1991). Consider, for example, Lee's interpretation of a mathematics task in Figure 14.2. Required to 'show his working', he did – but not as had been intended.

Figure 14.2 Lee 'shows his working'

The validity and reliability of instruments, tasks, tests, processes, etc. is crucial to overall judgements of the dependability of assessment outcomes. Where construct validity is low, assessments are likely to be regarded as partial, limited and crude because of the elements of learning which they ignore or cannot measure. Where reliability is low, assessments may be regarded as inconsistent and unfair because of the variation in the procedures by which the assessment results were produced.

Reflective activity 14.2

Aim: To highlight dilemmas between construct validity and reliability.

Evidence and reflection: Focus on a specific objective for pupil attainment; for instance, one associated with children's mathematical understanding and computational competence with number. Consider how the competence and understanding of pupils across the country could be assessed with regard to the selected objective. Focus this, perhaps by imagining some individual children whom you know in different schools, or by discussion with teachers or student teachers working in different schools. Do you think your assessment method could reflect what is really involved in understanding and competence (construct validity), and yet be administered in standard and consistent ways by teachers wherever or whoever they are (reliability)?

Extension: Consider any test materials with which you are familiar. How do you feel that the test's designers have tried to resolve the validity/reliability dilemma? What compromises have they made? Do you think it is possible to devise assessment with high validity and high reliability for all subjects?

Decisions about forms of assessment should be related to the primacy of purpose. Thus, for example, in Chapter 13 we focused on the use of assessment to *support learning* itself – a very different goal than the *measurement of attainment* with which this chapter is concerned. Reconciliation of the dilemmas posed by validity and reliability is much more likely if there is absolute clarity about such purposes – and this is the foundation on which confidence in an assessment system can grow. A robust and dependable assessment system will be one in which there is clarity about purposes.

Expert question

Dependability: are assessment processes understood and accepted as being robust and reliable?

This question contributes to a conceptual framework representing enduring issues and teacher expertise (see Chapter 16).

However much care is taken with the technical aspects of assessment, it is worth bearing in mind that outcomes always reflect a series of *social* processes. For example, Pollard and Filer (2000, Reading 14.7) analysed pupils' assessment experiences throughout their primary schooling, and suggested that strict 'objectivity' is a myth. Pupil performance is crucially affected by the context of its production and social and cultural factors have considerable influence over its interpretation, meaning and consequence. A classic study of a similar sort is Becker's *Making the Grade* (1968), which will still have resonance for readers experiencing higher education.

1.4 Effects and consequences

Because assessment outcomes are so significant in our societies, people often adjust their behaviour in attempts to secure 'good results' or to influence the interpretation of outcomes. As we discuss below, this may 'wash back' to directly affect factors such as the curriculum which is taught, teaching and learning processes, classroom relationships and pupil experience.

Curriculum and pedagogical distortion: When summative assessment results are used as measures of performance, the stakes become high for pupils, teachers, school leaders and politicians. In these circumstances there is a well-documented tendency for teachers and pupils to 'work to the test' (Stobart, 2008, Reading 13.6). The result is likely to be a narrowing of the curriculum and, whilst standards in the tested areas of the curriculum may rise, a reduction in overall standards across the broader curriculum may occur. For example, evaluators of the national literacy and numeracy strategies in England expressed deep concerns about the narrowing of the curriculum which they attributed to targets and high-stakes testing (Earl et al., 2003). Whatever is given prominence in high profile assessment understandably comes to dominate teaching, while areas of the curriculum that do not feature in widely reported or significant tests can be sidelined. Thus whole subjects (notably but not only the arts) are devalued, while even within the high-status subjects of mathematics and English key aspects such as investigations and oral capabilities receive very little attention.

Reflective activity 14.3

Aim: To investigate the danger that high-stakes assessment distorts curriculum provision.

Evidence and reflection: Talk to several teachers about the assessments their pupils undertake, in particular those that are reported publicly. Ask them about any concerns they may have. Enquire if it has been necessary to change curriculum provision to ensure that the children can perform respectably in important tests. Ask if public reporting of assessment results broadens, narrows or makes no difference to the curriculum which they provide.

Extension: You could reflect on a potentially very significant dilemma here. A National Curriculum often sets broad curriculum aims, whilst national assessment procedures test only a narrow range. Does one undermine the other?

High-stakes assessment can have a distorting effect not only on what is taught, but also how it is taught. This is an enduring and widespread issue: in relation to the United States where a great deal of testing has been used for many years, Rottenberg and Smith (1990) commented that 'As the stakes become higher, in that more hangs on the results, teaching becomes more "testlike". Teaching to the test in whatever context typically not only focuses on a narrow part of the curriculum but also involves much test preparation concentrating on examination technique, question spotting, mark gaining and practice questions. An extensive inquiry into testing and assessment by the House of Commons Children, Schools and Families Committee concluded that the system of national testing in England was having a detrimental effect on the rounded education of pupils:

> A variety of classroom practices aimed at improving test results has distorted the education of some children, which may leave them unprepared for higher education and employment. We find that 'teaching to the test' and narrowing of the taught curriculum are widespread phenomena in schools, resulting in a disproportionate focus on the 'core' subjects of English, mathematics and science and, in particular, on those aspects of these subjects which are likely to be tested in an examination. Tests, however, can only test a limited range of the skills and activities which are properly part of a rounded education, so that a focus on improving test results compromises teachers' creativity in the classroom and children's access to a balanced curriculum. (House of Commons, 2008, p. 3)

It is important to remember that the 'what' and 'how' of teaching and learning are central daily concerns of teachers – reflective practitioners with values and beliefs who have to make decisions about practice within layered contexts of guidance, expectations and policy. When a professional's values and practices are misaligned for whatever reason, he or she can feel unease and stress. The *Learning How to Learn* project in England (James et al., 2007, Reading 2.8) investigated teachers' beliefs and practices through questionnaires and interviews and found 'many teachers felt constrained by a policy context that encouraged rushed curriculum coverage, teaching to the test and a tick-box culture' (p. 215–16). Teachers' stress is increased by the importance and consequences of assessment results for many stakeholders, which in turn may have distorting effects on their teaching.

Pupil experience of assessment: The early phases of the introduction of national assessment procedures in England and Wales brought enormous protests from primary teachers, many of whom provided illustrations of distressed children (Torrance, 1991). However, more representative samples of teacher opinion did not show the same level of concern (Pollard et al., 1994). Worries from parents were very strong in Scotland, but were relatively small in England and Wales (Hughes, Wikeley and Nash, 1994). Evidence from children themselves on their experience of national testing mostly showed that many of them enjoyed it (Pollard et al., 1994). Indeed, in many classrooms the *early* assessment procedures seemed to have broadened the curriculum, such was its power, and to have been well received by children.

The longer-term picture appears to have changed as testing procedures have been narrowed and tightened by government agencies. Evidence of classroom practice suggests that teaching programmes are being attuned more closely to assessment requirements. The accountability stakes are high for schools in England, and primaries tend to focus on core subjects whilst secondaries are concerned for subjects within the EBacc. The unintended consequence of such decisions is to limit the scope for some pupils to demonstrate other capabilities.

Similarly, there are dangers of stigma emerging from the overt form of some assessment procedures and categoric nature of the results – 'I'll be a nothing', as one child put it (Reay and Wiliam, 1999). Assessment can thus profoundly affect pupils' self-image and identity. Stobart (2008, Reading 13.6) cites not only Hannah, a 6-year-old who featured in Reay and Wiliam's research, but also Ruth, an 18-year-old who far from being 'a nothing' was extremely successful in examinations. However, Ruth had developed an extremely instrumental approach to learning for tests which did little to establish the habits of lifelong learning.

Reflective activity 14.4

Aim: To obtain direct evidence of pupils' feelings about routine assessment.

Evidence and reflection: We suggest that you work with a group of pupils from your class and discuss with them examples of some assessments which you have made. Perhaps you could use some written work that has been produced and look at any comments and corrections which you made. How do the pupils feel about your responses?

You could also self-consciously monitor your verbal feedback during a teaching session. Listen to your comments, observe the children's faces. How do they seem to respond? Are they delighted, wary, confused, anxious, angry, resigned?

Extension: What ways of protecting young people's dignity can you develop, whilst still providing appropriate assessment feedback to them? Could you negotiate with the pupils to establish criteria by which their work will be evaluated? (See Chapter 13)

Expert questions

Expectation: does our school support high staff and student expectations and aspire for excellence?

Inclusion: are all learners treated respectfully and fairly in both formal and informal interaction?

These questions contribute to a conceptual framework representing enduring issues and teacher expertise (see Chapter 16).

The ways in which assessment results influence the expectations which teachers have of pupils, pupils have of each other, and pupils have of themselves are still not yet fully researched. However, the PACE project (Pollard et al., 2000) suggested that pupil motivation, engagement and zest for learning were being adversely affected by an overloaded curriculum and the extent of its assessment (see Figure 14.3, from the PACE project data archive). Despite the rise in measured standards, a significant number of children showed signs of developing negative dispositions towards learning. Harlen and Deakin Crick (2002) also found evidence of the negative impact of testing on pupils' motivation. Repeated testing, including practice tests, seems to undermine the self-image of lower attaining pupils, which widens the attainment gap between pupils. As we will see in Chapter 15, it is likely that the socially differentiating effect of formal assessment will be reinforced by pupils' cultural responses, and the situation may polarise further (see Reading 15.2).

There is little doubt that national assessment procedures have long-term effects on pupils. In part, these may be seen as positive, in that the quality of teaching and learning may be enhanced. Reflective teachers though, will want, prudently, to watch for effects which could both damage the self-image and self-confidence of pupils and have other divisive effects.

Figure 14.3 A child's feelings about SATs (PACE data archive)

2 Summative assessment *of* learning

The assessment of learning for summative purposes can be carried out in a number of ways, and in this section we consider four main approaches.

2.1 Statutory tests and examinations

The education systems of nations and states around the world incorporate statutory tests and examinations to a greater or lesser extent.

Typically, these are scheduled to take place at the end of Key Stages of learning, or at the conclusion of formal education itself. For example, for many years in English primary education, formal testing in the three core subjects of English, maths and science has been carried out at the end of Key Stage 2, age 11 – with data being used to monitor the performance of schools. Similar tests take place in Wales and Northern Ireland. However, Scotland uses a national survey to monitor system performance (see Section 2.2 below) and teachers in non-exam years are thus more able to focus on formative assessment of learning.

Outcomes of secondary education may have enormous implications for individual learners, certifying achievements through official qualifications such as GCSEs, A Levels and Diplomas (in England, Northern Ireland and Wales) and Nationals, Highers and Advanced Highers (in Scotland). In aggregate, such outcomes are also used to track the performance of schools and of education systems as a whole. Examination results are part of contemporary school accountability structures as well as a personal outcome for individual pupils. For both reasons, summative assessment is extremely 'high-stakes', and the policies and practices of most schools are highly attuned to maximise results.

Because of their significance, public confidence in examinations is extremely important and, once established, continuity is prized. However, changes in educational policies and practices may result in qualifications becoming inappropriate over time, and pressure then builds for change. At the time of writing, the governments in Wales and Northern Ireland have confirmed continued faith in their established use of GCSE and A Levels. However, Scotland has announced adjustments to its scheme to improve alignment of its qualifications with its *Curriculum for Exellence* (see Chapter 9 and Reading 14.2), whilst England has decided to change radically the nature of its GCSEs to make them 'tougher'. End of course examinations and a new scale, 1–9, will mark this innovation. At the same time England has packaged its qualifications to emphasise particular subjects through an EBacc. A new school progress measure is based on pupils' average score across a suite of eight qualifications (EBacc, other academic, arts or vocational).

Developing high-quality tests and examinations is a complex and specialised activity. Test development involves not only the trialling and writing of test items but also the production of mark schemes and moderation arrangements, the training and monitoring of markers, the procedures for pupils requiring special arrangements, and much more. Examination boards, awarding bodies and test development agencies typically have great expertise, many years of experience, and are supported by very active research divisions, as well as being regulated themselves.

However, testing is not an exact science, and Black and Wiliam claim the 'very limited reliability of external tests, which command a degree of confidence which they do not deserve' (1998a, p. 158). Undoubtedly some pupils are misclassified, although which individuals and how many in total will always be open to question. Wiliam (2001) estimated that at least 30 per cent of pupils could be given the wrong grade.

The reliability of tests and examinations is also often called into question because of patterns of improvement over time. With the laudable commitment to raise standards, students working hard, and teachers improving their practice and becoming more experienced with the curriculum and the test requirements, it is not surprising that the percentage of students gaining higher grades on criterion-referenced tests might increase year on year. Figure 14.14, for instance, uses official Government data to show that GCSE scores in English and maths rose steadily for many years (DCSF, 2009).

However, while ever-rising standards should ostensibly be a cause for celebration, the risk of 'grade inflation' creates unease: are these students really much better than those of previous years? Is it really that standards are going up, or in another sense are standards actually dropping? To counter such fears, exam boards set grade boundaries using examiners' judgements of the quality of work from year to year. They also work to achieve 'comparable outcomes' across subjects and they use statistical modelling to try to account for other contextual factors.

Despite such efforts, the trend of exam performance is a frequent focus for political debate. The changes to GCSE in England, to be taught from 2015 in English and maths, are one outcome of this.

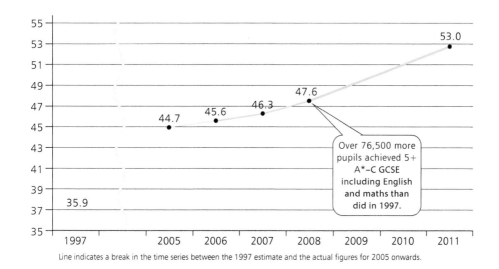

Figure 14.4 The rise in GCSE attainment (DCSF, 2009)

Line indicates a break in the time series between the 1997 estimate and the actual figures for 2005 onwards.

2.2 National surveys of system performance

In the discussion in Section 2.1 above, it will have been apparent how the outcomes of individual pupils are often aggregated and used as measures of the performance of schools or of national systems as a whole. This is common in 'neo-liberal' systems (see Chapter 5, Green and Janmaat, Reading 5.2) where system-wide improvement is expected to come from competition between schools. However, as we have seen, it conflates assessment aims so that judgements about the learning of individuals become entangled in measures of school, local authority, sector or system effectiveness. As Harlen et al. (1992, Reading 13.1) argued, such conflation of aims can have unintended consequences.

An alternative approach is to rely on specific sources of information for each need. For instance, this was the practice in England in the 1970s and 1980s.

- Schools were responsible for the assessment of pupil performance. In primary education, a wide range of commercially available tests was commonly used – with a consequential lack of comparability across schools. In secondary education, exam boards maintained GCSE and A Level qualifications.

- Local authority advisers and inspectors in each local government area supported school improvement, and inspections by HMI were significant accountability events.

- To achieve national monitoring on curricular and other issues, HMI also carried out specific studies and published reports which drew on their extensive professional experience.

However, given the variation in provision and practice in different local authorities, monitoring of national performance prior to examinations at the end of schooling was a problem. This was solved from 1975–89 through the establishment of the Assessment of Performance Unit (APU) to monitor pupil achievement. Rather than tests being necessary in all schools, a sampling frame enabled selection of 1.5 per cent of all pupils at ages 11, 13 and 15 whose test results provided reliable evidence of national performance in selected subjects (including English and maths).

In Scotland a similar national monitoring programme has existed since 1983. It used a nationally representative sample of pupils within primary and secondary schools who undertake assessment activities in a rolling programme to enable a focus on particular subjects, with a three-yearly cycle of surveys in English, maths and science. The system has been refined over the years and the present Scottish Survey of Literacy and Numeracy now monitors performance at Primary 4, Primary 7 and Secondary 2. Results are not reported or recorded at pupil, school or local authority level. Rather, they are used to make judgements about national performance and to produce teaching and learning resources to support teachers in improving the quality of their provision.

National surveys of pupil performance can thus serve this particular purpose in cost-effective and efficient ways, and without unintended distorting effects on school practices.

2.3 Non-statutory tests and tasks

There are many tests that teachers and schools can and do use on an optional basis.

Some of these were developed to assist with the monitoring of progress between points of statutory assessment, and are marked by the teachers of the pupils being tested. This activity itself gives teachers an insight into the statutory assessment process, helps them become more familiar with standards, and provides them with detailed information about each child's performance.

A variety of other externally produced tests are used routinely by schools, although in some cases the reasons for doing so may be questioned. Despite arguments about there being 'too much testing' in schools, teachers appear to do significantly more testing than is formally required. A number of reasons for using additional tests are given, and some, such as the diagnosis of specific reading difficulties, may be laudable. In the main, however, it seems that the high-stakes nature of statutory assessment has a knock-on effect. In particular, it is felt to be necessary to performance more regularly and at other ages.

However, even more serious than the overuse of tests, is the false confidence which may be put in their results, as noted earlier in this chapter. Broadfoot (2007) argues further that educational assessment and the measurement of human achievement 'can never be objective since they are inevitably limited by the social nature of the assessment situation and the values and culture which overlay the interpretation of the quality of a given performance' (p. 28) (Reading 14.1). The issue of reliability is probably greater with non-statutory tests because of the lack of checks and safeguards associated with statutory tests. Filer and Pollard (2000, Reading 14.7) showed how 'objective' assessment practices depend on the contexts and social practices in which performance, judgement and interpretation of judgement are produced, and so are vulnerable to bias and distortion.

2.4 Teacher assessment

Another approach to summative assessment is periodic teacher assessment. Based on their wide knowledge of a pupil's performance in different contexts and over time, teachers make a judgement about the level of attainment against a given standard such as a 'level' as established in a national framework of standards. 'Best fit' judgements, balancing strengths and weaknesses, can be made for different aspects of a subject or a subject as a whole. Where performance 'levels' have been established, judgements can be related to these scales. However, such a classification may provide very little information about what the pupil actually understands and is able to do. In England, the national system of levels was abandoned from 2014 in favour of a more substantive focus by schools on specific learning achievements in relation to programmes of study.

Tests and tasks can be used to inform teacher assessment, but the greatest value of teacher assessment is that a wide range of evidence is taken into account, thus increasing validity.

If teacher assessment is to be used for summative and comparative purposes, then the development of teachers' understanding of standards is crucial for its reliability. Further, once teachers have made provisional judgements, moderation is required to ensure fairness to pupils and that the data produced are useful. Teachers should discuss their assessments of pupils' work with other colleagues in the same school and in other schools, and systems of moderation often involving the local authority help ensure the comparability of assessment across a wider area.

3 Using summative assessment information

An enormous amount of time, energy and money is expended on assessment, yet pupils' learning is only improved if assessment information is actually used, rather than simply collected. As is suggested in this chapter, assessment information is used in a wide variety of ways, by different people, and for different purposes.

3.1 Supporting pupil progress

As we have repeatedly seen in this book, it is crucial to build on pupils' current knowledge and understanding (see also Butt, 2011, Reading 14.3). Thus, at the start of any unit of work teachers need to use assessment information to achieve a cognitive match (see Chapter 10, Section 4 on lesson planning). When meeting a new group of students, teachers are reliant on the assessment information provided by previous teachers, often at an earlier stage of schooling. As time passes, the dependability of records diminishes as pupils will have progressed in their learning, or perhaps forgotten certain things. Recorded information then has to be supplemented by more up-to-date evidence.

When teaching any lesson, teachers will use assessment information formatively to adapt their teaching depending on the children's responses. At the end of each lesson they will be noting, probably on the plans themselves or in a daybook, things that need to be taken into account in the next lesson. These may apply to all or just some of the pupils, and could be about the need to reinforce a particular concept, or omit a planned activity since the learning objective it was designed to support is already well grasped.

Towards the end of a unit the teacher may devise a particular assessment activity focusing on the key learning objectives for that unit, and will use the last period of time to extend the work or review those objectives, as the need is demonstrated. After a unit of work has been completed, notes will again be made to inform both the future teaching of that unit to other groups, and the future teaching of related units to the same group of pupils.

Whilst notes are useful on a day-to-day basis, numerical assessment data, perhaps in the form of levels or grades, are often used for tracking progress over time. Periodically the attainment of both individuals and groups can be compared with both their previous and target attainment, and judgements made about whether they are on an appropriate learning trajectory, falling behind or exceeding expectations. Different scenarios should lead to different actions to support learning – for example, reviewing expectations, providing additional support or extending the challenge. Similarly, when expectations for a unit of work have been set in terms of what 'all', 'most' and 'some' of the students should attain, recording names against each category enables pupil tracking but without recourse to levels or grades. It is important to remember that despite their apparent attractiveness, numbers are a very blunt instrument when trying to represent learning.

3.2 Transfer and transition

Assessment information has a particular and important role in effective transition (moving from one class to another within the same school) and transfer (when pupils move from one school to another). In order that the next teacher and/or school can extend each pupil's present attainment, building on strengths and addressing weaknesses, it is vital that key information from the present teacher's knowledge are passed on in a manageable way and at times when the information can be used effectively. In England there is a Common Transfer Form that must be used when a student moves to another school in England, Wales, Scotland or Northern Ireland. In Scotland a process of profiling is used to support transfer and transition at key points.

Successful transfer and transition goes far beyond the mere passing on of assessment information (Sutton, 2000). In particular principled, professional conversation between past and future teachers at times of transition and transfer is extremely valuable in bringing documentary information to life. However, while this may be possible when a class moves from one teacher to another, it becomes much more difficult when pupils are transferring from many primary schools to a secondary school with different teachers for each subject. Transfer of assessment information and meetings between teachers are the two key strategies in what Galton, Gray and Rudduck (1999) termed the 'managerial/bureaucratic bridge'. They also identified four other 'bridges' used to span the gap – perhaps even more significant but harder to build than the first. These are the social/personal bridge; the curriculum bridge; the pedagogical bridge; and the learning-to-learn bridge. So, important though assessment information is in smoothing pupils' transitions and transfers, it is only one aspect of this crucial process.

When young people complete their schooling, hopefully they move into the world of work or undertake further study. Apprenticeships are a traditional vocational route into the skilled employment, whilst further or university education beckon for some. For many young people however, contemporary economic circumstances are much more challenging and opportunities may be limited.

In any event, it is to be hoped that education will provide them with qualifications of which they can be proud and with the self-confidence and resilience to support them whilst they begin their adult life.

> **Expert question**
>
> **Consequence**: do assessment outcomes lead towards recognised qualifications and a confident sense of personal identity?
>
> This question contributes to a conceptual framework representing enduring issues and teacher expertise (see Chapter 16).

3.3 School improvement and accountability

Assessment has a major role to play not only in the support of individual pupils' learning and progress, but also in improvement efforts at every level from a small group, class or whole school, to an authority or country.

For example, a prominent use of assessment evidence in recent years has been in relation to 'targets', particularly in England. National targets have been set and then cascaded down through local authorities to schools. England's Department for Education put it as follows:

> Schools are required to set statutory targets annually, working with Governors, their School Improvement Partners and using relevant data, which are then reported to the local authority and DfE who may publish this information. Schools often set additional targets as part of effective pupil tracking to keep pupils on trajectory and maintain progress. Key questions are:
> - What does the data and information on pupil targets, attainment, gap-narrowing and progress show?
> - How well are different groups doing? Are tartets sufficiently ambitious for under-performing groups?
> - Are proposed targets stretching and realistic? Do they build on improvements and prior attainment?
> - What strategies and interventions are in place to help achieve the targets?
>
> (Guidance to Local Authorities and Schools, DfE, 2012)

In such ways, performance target and outcome data are hugely influential on school policies and practices as well as being central to accountability mechanisms. This is a worldwide trend, though 'England arguably has more data and more sophisticated data than any other jurisdiction in the world' (Earl and Fullan, 2003, p. 385). National examinations, tests and related assessments of every pupil on many occasions during their school career have generated huge amounts of data, at the same time as developments in information technology have enabled large scale data storage, sophisticated analysis, and detailed reporting. Alongside this, the high profile now given to accountability in education has spawned huge industries using assessment data for school improvement and accountability.

Teachers and headteachers use assessment data for school improvement, sometimes have opportunities to mediate and explain information to pupils, parents and carers, often discuss data with colleagues, and are themselves held accountable by them. Data can be extremely helpful in making informed decisions (Ofsted, 2008, Reading 14.4), but can also be misleading and misinterpreted. A basic understanding of data, their strengths, weaknesses and related issues, is therefore essential for all teachers.

Data derived from assessment is sometimes referred to as 'performance data', a term that encompasses:

- Raw and aggregated attainment data
- Value-added data
- Contextual value-added data.

Attainment data can be generated by teacher assessment, tasks, tests and examinations, and typically attention is given to certain key indicators; for example the attaining of a particular level, or higher grades in a combination of subjects, or the 'point score' from a number of subjects. When raw data from individual pupils are aggregated other indicators are possible; for example the percentage of pupils attaining five or more good grades at age 16. Value added data take account of the fact that pupils have differing starting points, and so two students with the same raw score at the end of a school stage could have made very different progress – or even none at all. Value-added data is applicable for both individuals and large groups of pupils, and is particularly relevant when comparing schools whose pupils on intake were already attaining very differently. Contextual value-added takes the notion further, by not only considering pupils' prior attainment but also taking account of other factors such as gender, ethnicity, special educational needs, and a proxy for social deprivation such as eligibility for free school meals. Many people regard contextual value-added as being a much better measure of school performance than raw scores (Schagen and Hutchinson, 2003), although they do require understanding and care to interpret them appropriately. For this reason the Coalition Government removed the contextual measures from school performance data tables in England saying they were too difficult to understand.

With the amount, complexity and importance of data it is essential for schools to use software packages to handle it all. There are many available and the most commonly used in England are:

- RAISEonline (Reporting and Analysis for Improvement through school Self-Evaluation), **https://raiseonline.org**
- Fischer Family Trust, **http://fischerfamilytrust.org**
- The Data Enabler toolkit, **http://ssatuk.co.uk/ssat/programmes-support/data/data-enabler-toolkit/**
- A whole suite of packages (including Yellis and ALIS) for different ages and countries from the Centre for Evaluation and Monitoring at the University of Durham, **http://cemcentre.org/**.

Whatever the data and the software package, analysis alone will not improve the quality of education or children's learning: it is part of a process that must include action. A five-stage cycle of school improvement encompasses reviewing, planning and acting, and remains a useful framework.

Performance data may be aggregated, analysed and used to produce 'league tables' of schools. Where such tables exist, they often attract considerable media attention and are promoted as enabling parents to make judgements about 'good schools' and thus to inform choice of school. This, in turn, puts market pressure on schools to improve. However, the reliability of such analyses cannot be taken for granted, as Leckie and Goldstein have demonstrated (2009, see the **Research Briefing** on p. 401).

We have seen that the use of pupil assessment data to indicate school performance, whilst superficially attractive, also has many unintended consequences and may not be sufficiently dependable for the purposes to which it is put. As the introduction to this

Figure 14.5 A
five-stage cycle
for school
improvement

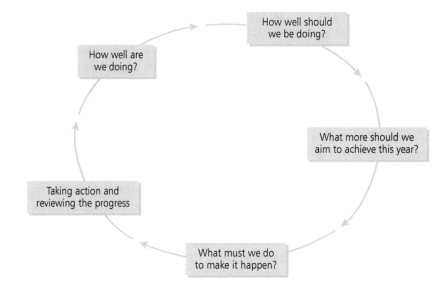

chapter made clear, assessment can be used for such purposes, but to do so weakens its contribution to other educational goals (see also Harlen et al., 1992, Reading 13.1). Using assessment data for accountability purposes can create problems if for example the media, the public and politicians do not understand the limitations of data and draw unwarranted inferences. These issues are discussed in Reading 14.5 by Mansell and James (2009).

In a powerful argument, MacGilchrist (2003) argued that to seek school improvement simply through performance pressure was an approach which was 'past its sell-by date', and she urged more attention to the fundamental processes of teaching and learning themselves. This might be seen as a variation of the folklore that 'you can't fatten a pig by weighing it'. The Scottish curriculum and assessment system exemplifies a more holistic approach (see Scottish Government, 2011b, Reading 14.2).

School league tables: Are they any good for choosing schools?

Key findings
Each year the Government and the media publish league tables of schools' academic performances and encourage parents to use them when choosing a secondary school for their children. Our work shows that these tables are highly misleading when it comes to school choice.

- The most high profile measure – the percentage of children getting five A* to C grades at GCSE – says more about the differences in schools' intakes than it does about the differences in their quality.
- Value-added measures are superior in that they adjust for these initial differences, but deriving from approximately 200 students per school, are so noisy that it is hard to statistically separate many schools' performances from one another.
- Just as with stocks and shares, schools' value-added past performances are not reliable indicators of their future performances and crucially it is these future performances which are relevant when choosing a secondary school.

More should be done by the Government and the media to communicate these important limitations to parents.

The research
Our work focused on a fundamental problem in using school league tables for school choice: school league tables report the past performance of secondary schools, based on children who have just taken their GCSE exams, whereas what parents want to know is how schools will perform in the future when their own children take the exams. Consider parents who chose a secondary school for their child in autumn 2012. Their child will enter school in autumn 2013 and will take their GCSE exams in 2018. Thus, the information parents need when choosing is how schools are predicted to perform in 2018. However, the most recent information available is the school league table for how schools performed in 2011. Thus, there is a seven year gap between the available information and what parents want to know; the most recent league table is always effectively seven years out of date.

School name	School type	% of pupils making expected progress		% achieving 5+ A*-C GCSEs (or equivalent) including English and maths GCSEs				% achieving the English Baccalaureate	% achieving grades A*-C in English and maths GCSEs
		English	Maths	2012	2011	2010	2009		
England - all schools		NA	NA	59.4%	59.0%	53.5%	49.8%	18.4%	60.0%
England - state funded schools only		68.0%	68.7%	58.8%	58.2%	55.2%	50.7%	16.2%	59.3%
Schools (tick the box next to a school/college to select it for comparison - once you have selected all required schools/colleges click here: Compare)									
☐ Bristol Free School	Free School - Mainstream	NA	NA	NA	NA	NA	NA	NA	NA
☐ The Red Maids' School	Other Independent School	NP	NP	99%	97%	97%	93%	80%	99%
☐ Henbury School ⓘ	Academy - Converter Mainstream	No KS4 data available for this school							
☐ Henbury School ⓘ	Community School	68%	58%	52%	46%	39%	27%	5%	53%
☐ Badminton School	Other Independent School	NP	NP	98%	96%	0%	0%	51%	98%
☐ St Bede's Catholic College ⓘ	Voluntary Aided School	81%	81%	71%	69%	72%	65%	25%	71%
☐ St Bede's Catholic College ⓘ	Academy - Converter Mainstream	No KS4 data available for this school							
☐ Orchard School Bristol ⓘ	Academy Sponsor Led	NA	NA	NA	NA	NA	NA	NA	NA
☐ Orchard School ⓘ	Foundation School	67%	57%	38%	36%	37%	35%	1%	38%
☐ Bristol Steiner School	Other Independent School	NP	NP	33%	29%	64%	SUPP	0%	67%

Research design
We focussed on the Government's 'contextual value-added' (CVA) league tables as the Government promoted these as being the most meaningful way to compare schools. Clearly, the more schools' CVA performances change over a seven year period, the less reliable school league tables will be as a guide to schools' future performances. We examined the official school league table data and showed that many schools which were performing in the top quarter of schools in 2002 were below average seven years later. We then proceeded to illustrate just how unreliable the current school league tables are by predicting schools' current performance using data from seven years previously. These predictions are so imprecise that almost no schools can be distinguished reliably from one another. This means that, for choosing a school, the league tables are essentially meaningless and, by not communicating this fundamental problem to parents, they are highly misleading.

References for practitioners, journalists and policymakers
Leckie, G. and Goldstein, H. (2009). School league tables: Are they any good for choosing schools? Research in Public Policy, Bulletin of the Centre for Market and Public Organisation, 8, 6–9.
Goldstein, H. and Leckie, G. (2008). School league tables: what can they really tell us? Significance, 5, 67–9.

This work was carried out at the University of Bristol

4 Records and reporting

4.1 Keeping records

All teachers need to take decisions about *what* aspects of pupil activity and learning achievements should be recorded, and *how* they should be recorded.

What should be recorded?

This question relates to the multiple purposes of assessment and recording. As a minimum, records must meet legal requirements which normally require schools to keep 'curricular' records on every pupil. These formally record academic achievements, skills, abilities and progress, and are a subset of the fuller educational records that must be maintained for each individual. This requirement could probably be met by simply keeping a copy of all annual reports to parents, but this is unlikely to be sufficient to support children's learning, nor satisfy the expectations of school inspectors and others.

Beyond the legal minimum, within any school there could be a number of different records each with particular purposes and uses. These may include:

- to help the teacher plan the next steps in teaching and learning;
- to show what a child knows, understands and can do, and the progress that he or she has made;
- to help children see the progress they are making;
- to provide information for setting targets;
- to inform discussions with parents, and end-of-year reports;
- to provide accurate information about a child's attainment, progress and learning needs that can be passed on to the next teacher or school;
- to assist with end-of-year and statutory teacher assessments;
- to inform revisions to medium-term plans and schemes of work;
- to evaluate the effectiveness of teaching;
- to identify issues for the school improvement plan.
  (Swaffield, 2000)

How should records be kept?

This question concerns manageability and the use of records. It is useful to think of the range of forms that records can take, as in Figure 14.6, on p. 404.

Along with whatever recording systems the school decides upon, individual classroom teachers, and trainee teachers, will keep records to assist in their day-to-day teaching and to contribute to the whole-school system. In most countries there are moves towards increasing access to records. For instance, in England teachers can keep personal records solely for their own use, but any record which may be seen by or transferred to other teachers or other professionals must be made available to parents on request. This can help teachers develop the habit of recording in a positive form – e.g. 'Sally is beginning to participate in group story sessions,' rather than: 'Sally often interrupts story sessions.' The issue reflects general ethical concerns about the central accumulation and recording of information about individuals – whether it is medical information, financial, criminal or anything else. Indeed, most of us would probably want to know what was being kept on us and many people take the view that this is a legitimate right. Continuous awareness of the possible audiences for teacher-created records is thus necessary, and schools should consider the implications of the requirements of the Data Protection Act, 1998, and the Freedom of Information Act, 2000.

Reflective activity 14.5

Aim: To identify information about the children which it is important to know and record.

Evidence and reflection: Make notes, under the following headings, of:

1. What information do you think is important for you to know about children in your class?
2. Why is it important?
3. How would you use it?
4. How would you record it?
5. How would you check on the objectivity and fairness of your records?
6. Who has a right of access to your records?

Extension: Asking such basic questions could provide a check on the keeping of records. Any information which is not demonstrably useful to teaching, manageable, consistent with school policy and ethically sound should be reviewed.

Figure 14.6
Forms of records

Annotated plans	Turn short-term plans into working documents, recording what has actually been taught, and 'next steps' to be fed into the planning for the next lesson or following week.
Children's work and books in different subjects	These show attainment and progress over time, particularly in specific subjects. They are even more useful as records if the learning objective is noted at the top of a piece of work, or incorporated into the teacher's comments.
Teacher's mark book / record file	Mark books or record files can be customised in a whole variety of ways to suit the teacher, different subjects, and various groupings of children. Recording specific learning objectives increases their usefulness.
Children's self-assessment	Children may occasionally record some aspects of their self-assessment, but self-assessment is above all a thinking activity, and an emphasis on recording too often detracts from this.
Unit records	When work has been taught in units, the attainment of children can be recorded in three groups, matching the learning objectives that you would expect *all*, *most*, or *some* of the children to achieve.
Information technology	IT is being used increasingly and is a very powerful tool. Large amounts of assessment data can be stored, analysed, displayed, transferred and reported. As with all assessment and recording, it is essential that IT systems used are manageable and useful, that numbers are treated with the caution they deserve, and that data relates to and informs learning and teaching.
Individual portfolios	Whilst these may be highly valued by children, teachers and parents, the time involved needs to be found and justified. As a whole-school practice, they have been criticised, but they remain important in understanding individuals. Targeted use may be most appropriate.
School portfolios	Annotated examples of work and observations which demonstrate standards agreed by teachers. These complement other forms of records, and are useful for sharing with others (children, parents, inspectors) and for reference by teachers.
Work samples	Regularly collected samples of work, often representing three broad bands of attainment, serving as a record of the type and level of work produced, and useful for monitoring.
Individual Education Plans	Individual Action Plans (IEPs) are records of targets and progress for individual children.
Teachers' day books and personal notes	Teachers' own personal notes. A notebook may be particularly important for Early Years teachers because much of the evidence of children's achievements may be ephemeral – behaviour or comments, rather than recorded 'work'. The habit of jotting down these observations may be difficult to acquire, especially for student teachers who may be preoccupied with management issues. Time has to be planned for observation of children.

4.2 Reporting to parents and carers

Parents and other carers are hugely significant in children's lives as, of course, is informal learning in non-school settings. For these reasons, if the teachers are able to inform, learn from and work with such significant others, the improvement in learning outcomes for pupils is likely to be considerable (Desforges, 2003; Goodall and Vorhaus, 2010).

However, the ways in which teachers report the progress of children and young people to parents are influenced by two seemingly contradictory sets of expectations.

The first makes the assumption that parents are *partners* with teachers in supporting the learning of each child (e.g. Hornby, 2011). Parents may thus be routinely invited into school, particularly in the early years. Parent–teacher discussions are likely to include consideration of the processes and progress of the pupil – perhaps illustrated by reference to their work.

The second expectation is based on an image of parents as *consumers* of education, having contracted with the school for the provision of educational services to their child (e.g. Chubb and Moe, 1990; Woods et al., 1998). They thus require a report of outcomes, through which the school can be held accountable for pupil progress.

Needless to say, most schools make provision which reflects elements of both these approaches. This is not surprising, for, whilst the partnership model is professionally acknowledged as contributing very constructively to pupil learning, the consumer model is increasingly underwritten by legal requirements. For example, for each pupil in England, annual reports to parents are required to include information about:

- achievements
- progress
- attendance.

Additional information is required for pupils who have undergone national assessments, and comparative information about same age pupils at the school and nationally must be available on request. Such requirements feed the 'consumer' model of education. The partnership aspect is most clearly demonstrated by the inclusion within reports of targets for the future, and of advice about specific ways in which parents can help. In England from 2014, maintained schools are required to publish for parents a year-by-year curriculum plan. In principle, this will enable parents to tune support for their children and could be very beneficial educationally.

However, it is by no means certain how this tension between partnership and consumerist models of home–school relationships will develop over time.

One of the most explicit ways of manifesting the partnership model is through the processes which a school adopts in reporting pupil achievements to parents. Annual written reports to parents may be legally required, but most schools offer much more in terms of formal and informal opportunities during the year. Consultation evenings, interim reports, home–school liaison notebooks, phone calls, emails, individual face-to-face discussions and so on can all strengthen the relationship between home and school, while also addressing parental expectations about access and information. Some of the best practice involves the pupils as active participants, for example through attending open days/evenings and contributing to written reports.

> ## Reflective activity 14.6
>
> *Aim:* To develop an informative and constructive procedure for reporting to parents.
>
> *Evidence and reflection:* This activity must be tailored to circumstances. Discuss with appropriate colleagues the aims and scope of a reporting exercise. If you are a student teacher, you might want to limit it to reflect a project which you have completed, or build it into an end-of-term open day.
>
> Consider the following questions:
> How can you best provide information to parents?
> How can you involve the children?
> How can you elicit information and support from parents?
>
> *Extension:* Evaluate your reporting procedure. Did you find consumerist or partnership expectations from parents? How did the children benefit? What will you do when your next opportunity arises?

Conclusion

The assessment of pupils' learning is crucial, complex and, increasingly, controversial.

First and foremost it is of immense importance to the pupils themselves: their life-chances can be significantly affected, both through their results and by the shaping of their self-image and motivation. However, the process of assessing students' learning is complex and requires expert judgement.

Assessment outcomes also often have implications for teachers and headteachers, as their work is increasingly judged on the basis of pupil results in formal assessments. Indeed, in England, schools can even be closed if their performance is deemed to be unsatisfactory by inspectors – with consequences that can spread beyond the school to the surrounding community.

Teachers need a secure understanding of assessment issues so that they can make the best decisions for their pupils' learning, and engage in informed dialogue with colleagues, pupils, parents, policymakers and the public.

Key readings

Books that provide overviews of assessment are listed in the key readings for Chapter 13, but are also relevant to this chapter. Readings given below are more focused on the summative purposes of assessment, but may also relate to the issues discussed in the previous chapter.

For an excellent overview of a wide range of issues, policies and practices in assessment, see:

Broadfoot, P. (2007) *An Introduction to Assessment.* London: Continuum. (Reading 14.1)

A TLRP commentary provides a succinct overview of key issues:

Mansell, W. and James, M. with the Assessment Reform Group (2009) *Assessment in Schools: Fit for Purpose? A Commentary by the Teaching and Learning Research Programme.* London: TLRP. (Reading 14.5)

James' comprehensive book covers many timeless assessment issues:

James, M. (1998) *Using Assessment for School Improvement.* Oxford: Heinemann.

Two pamphlets by the Assessment Reform Group are particularly pertinent:

Assessment Reform Group (2002) *Testing, Motivation and Learning.* Cambridge: University of Cambridge Faculty of Education.
Assessment Reform Group (2006) *The Role of Teachers in Assessment of Learning.* London: Institute of Education.

Drawing on the analysis of more than a dozen research projects, a book that promotes the development of teacher assessment is:

Gardner, J., Harlen, W., Hayward, L. and Stobart, G. with Montgomery, M. (2010) *Developing Teacher Assessment.* Maidenhead: Open University Press.

Stobart provides an insightful analysis of the effects of a variety of tests and assessment practices:

Stobart, G. (2008) *Testing Times: The Uses and Abuses of Assessment.* Abingdon: Routledge. (Reading 13.6)

For a comprehensive discussion of the examination and testing regime in England and its consequences see:

Mansell, W. (2007) *Education by Numbers: The Tyranny of Testing.* London: Politico Publishing.

For a principled guide to classroom assessment, including target setting, see:

Butt, G. (2011) *Making Assessment Matter.* London: Continuum. (Reading 14.3)

Two useful booklets for helping to understand and use assessment and assessment data are:

Swaffield, S. and Dudley, P. (2010) *Assessment Literacy for Wise Decisions* (3rd edn). London: Association of Teachers and Lecturers. (see also Reading 13.5)
Ofsted (2008) *Using Data, Improving Schools.* London: Ofsted. (Reading 14.4)

For developed example of a national assessment system with strong alignment to curriculum objectives, see:

Scottish Government (2011b) Principles of Assessment in *Curriculum for Excellence*. Building the Curriculum 5. A Framework for Assessment. Edinburgh: Scottish Government. (Reading 14.2)

A developed, sociological analysis of assessment practices is offered in:

Filer, A. (ed.) *Assessment: Social Practice and Social Product*. London: Routledge. (see also Reading 14.7)

reflectiveteaching.co.uk offers additional professional resources for this chapter. These may include *Further Reading*, illustrative *Reflective Activities*, useful *Web Links* and *Download Facilities* for diagrams, figures, checklists, activities.

Inclusion
How are we enabling learning opportunities?

15

Introduction

This chapter is primarily concerned with everyday classroom practice: that is, with actions which a reflective teacher can take to promote the inclusion of the children and young people they teach. But inequality is also, in some ways, an *outcome* of education – as we will also see. It is to the credit of the teaching profession that there is considerable awareness of inequalities and of how they can be tackled. The chapter explores the nature of difference and the pedagogical decisions that enable teachers to develop their classes as inclusive learning communities.

The concept of 'inclusive education' is open to many interpretations but our concern here is with the development of classroom practices, and their consequences for learners' lives both in and out of school. Our particular focus is on the ways in which teachers can enable everyone to feel accepted and valued for who they are, make progress in their learning, and have opportunities to participate in a full range of classroom activities. We make two key assumptions:

- diversity amongst a class of learners is to be expected and welcomed;
- *all* learners have the right to achieve.

These assumptions are embedded in enduring, global concerns of social justice and equity. In 1948, Article 26 of the Universal Declaration of Human Rights stated that education 'shall promote understanding, tolerance and friendship among all nations, racial or religious groups'. Nearly 50 years later the Salamanca Statement (United Nations Educational, Scientific and Cultural Organisation (UNESCO), 1994), argued that schools with an 'inclusive orientation are the most effective means of combating discriminatory attitudes, creating welcoming communities, building an inclusive society and achieving education for all'. The countries of the UK are signatories of this Statement and indeed it is embedded in national legislation on inclusion. Meanwhile, recent research indicates that, globally, more than 75 million children are excluded from any form of education at all mainly because of poverty, gender inequity, disability and child labour (UNESCO, 2012). These challenges raise fundamental questions about what it means to be included in a society and about the broader purposes of education. Indeed, Florian (2007) discusses how inclusive education can be understood 'both as a human right and a means of achieving human rights' (p. 8) (see also the discussion in Chapter 17, Section 2 and Reading 17.6).

See Chapter 4

TLRP principles

Three principles are of particular relevance to this chapter on social differences, opportunities and inclusion:

Effective teaching and learning equips learners for life in its broadest sense. Learning should aim to help people to develop the intellectual, personal and social resources that will enable them to participate as active citizens, contribute to economic development and flourish as individuals in a diverse and changing society. This implies adopting a broad view of learning outcomes and ensuring that equity and social justice are taken seriously. (Principle 1)

Effective teaching and learning fosters both individual and social processes and outcomes. Learning is a social activity. Learners should be encouraged and helped to work with others, to share ideas and to build knowledge together. Consulting learners about their learning and giving them a voice is both an expectation and a right. (Principle 7)

Effective teaching and learning recognises the significance of informal learning. Informal learning, such as learning out of school, should be recognised as at least as significant as formal learning and should therefore be valued and used appropriately in formal processes. (Principle 8)

The chapter is divided into five sections. It begins with a discussion of some significant dimensions of difference that inform the ways that we think about identities. In the second section, the ways in which difference may be amplified in schools is examined. The third section explores two related educational concepts: learner diversity and inclusion itself. The fourth section then focuses on particular groups of learners who are identified as needing special or additional support. Finally, we draw on recent research to examine how teachers can enact inclusive pedagogies through the daily routines of their classrooms.

This chapter ranges across many issues and the resources on **reflectiveteaching.co.uk** will help in investigating them more deeply. There is also overlap between this chapter and others in the book, such as Chapter 6 on relationships.

1 Dimensions of difference

In this section we examine diversity as part of the human condition. To do so we consider eight dimensions often used to recognise social differences: social class, ethnicity, gender, sexuality, age, physical appearance and disability. As noted in the introduction, this list is only suggestive of the limitless dimensions of difference that may impact on our educational experiences. Moreover, the ways in which we understand the differences between ourselves and others are interconnected. Contemporary research often examines how social advantages and disadvantages associated with each category may be compounded by the disadvantages associated with another (e.g. Sewell, 1997; Plummer, 2000; Youdell, 2006; Artiles, et al., 2006; Alexander, 2010). Of course, consequential differences in self-confidence and in success in learning accumulate in school settings, as we discuss at the end of the section.

The Equality Act 2010 in England and Wales illustrates the extension off the equality duties of teachers and schools so that key dimensions of difference (named as 'characteristics') are protected (see Richardson, 2009, Reading 15.1, for underlying principles of the legislation and their implications for schools). Similar legislation applies in Northern Ireland, Scotland and the Republic of Ireland.

1.1 Social class

Some commentators argue that social class provides the structures through which gender, race, ability, age and sexuality are played out. Indeed, inequalities of wealth, income and material opportunities remain highly significant in determining life-chances (Feinstein et al., 2008, Reading 1.6) and there has been no 'withering away of class' in the lived experience of UK citizens. For example, for the last 20 years, there has been a consistent trend for the gap between the highest and lowest incomes to widen each year. One consequence was the fact that in 2011 there were 4 million children living in families on or below the 'poverty line' (Office for National Statistics, 2012). However, at the same time, many families were very well off and approximately 8 per cent of school-age children attended private schools. A UNICEF report (2012) compares children's material wellbeing in the UK with other 'economically advanced' nations and warns that child poverty is worsening.

Not all definitions of class are based on income, wealth or economic capital, and some focus more on status and level of education. The concepts of 'cultural capital' (Bourdieu and Passeron, 1977) and 'social capital' (Coleman, 1988) were developed to describe the knowledge, attitudes and experiences which socialisation within a 'higher-class' family may offer, and which complements material wealth. One of their major insights on educational inequality is that students with social and cultural capital are likely to fare better in education than their otherwise comparable peers with less valuable social and cultural assets. For example, parents may deploy their economic, cultural, social and emotional capital by choosing to live in a particular area to access a favoured school and through the nature of the experiences and support which they provide for their children. Such strategies are manifestations of the process of 'social reproduction', in which one generation seeks to pass on the advantages of its social position to another (see, for instance, Connell et al., 1982).

We thus face the challenge of, on the one hand, understanding the economic, social and cultural advantages and disadvantages of particular children; and, on the other hand, of affirming and building on the diverse backgrounds and cultural resources within families and communities.

1.2 Ethnicity

The term 'ethnicity' describes combinations of ancestry, heritage, religion, culture, nationality, language and region. As such, we all have ethnic identities. Globalisation and changing patterns of migration have challenged the idea that ethnicities are fixed. Cultures and social structures, compounded by differences of historical development, can make a considerable difference to people's experience, leading to much variation amongst ethnic groups. Definitions of what constitutes an ethnic group, or ethnic minority are commonly based on a combination of categories including 'race', skin colour, national origins and language (e.g. White British), and information about our ethnicity is routinely collected to understand many current social and economic trends.

The population of the UK is, increasingly, ethnically diverse. Alibhai-Brown (2000) argued that Britain should adopt an approach which accepts the diverse contributions of different cultures and groups, past and present – including those White communities, rich or poor, which also feel excluded from significant aspects of modern society and which may harbour racism (see also Gay, 2010). The recent growth of 'faith schools' in the UK has been associated with some ethnic communities wanting to preserve their own cultural traditions and beliefs. While some view this development as divisive and ultimately discriminatory, it can also be seen as recognition of ethnic diversity and fulfilment of religious rights.

Racism is the term that describes processes in society which adversely affect people according to their identification as members of one ethnic group or another. Racism has a long history in the UK going back to the imperial past and beyond, and it has taken root in the discourse and structure of society. Racial prejudice is also reflected within the cultures of children and young people (Connolly, 1998; Troyna and Hatcher, 1992). Gillborn's (2006) recent analysis of research in the UK using Critical Race Theory offers, in his words, 'a damning critique of the racist nature of the education system'. Such prejudices may be further amplified by the social, cultural, legal and political structures that have developed over time.

1.3 Gender

There is an accepted scientific basis for recognising two sexes: there are differences within the reproductive process and there is also evidence of genetic and neurobiological differences affecting innate behaviours and brain functioning (Greenfield, 1997). The term 'gender', on the other hand, describes the *social definition of sex roles* rather than the biological distinction itself. Indeed, masculinity and femininity should not be considered to be inherent, biological properties, but as socially constructed products of society. They arise from, and condition, social processes (Money, 1995).

'Sexism' is the operation of forces in society by which members of one sex obtain advantages over the other, because of and through their gender. *Patterns* of discrimination prompt us to ask questions such as how school life contributes to restrictive or enabling socialisation. For example, in the last 20 years researchers have asked why it is that girls tend to perform better than boys when in school (e.g. Davies, 1993; Francis, 1998; Gipps and Murphy, 1994; Reay, 2001; Younger et al. 2005; Warrington et al., 2006). The assumption of such research is that, because such patterns in performance are not *inevitable*, the underlying processes that give rise to them should be challenged (Murphy, 2001). This is a complex task because it is important not to inadvertently disadvantage one group in the act of trying to improve the achievements of another.

Sometimes factors beyond schools are also in play, as Arnot, David and Weiner (1999) argued in explaining the performance of girls. Their analysis focused on the political changes of post-war Britain, particularly the welfare state and education reforms under Margaret Thatcher. They argued that: 'successive generations of girls have been challenged by economic and social change and by feminism' (p. 150). The significant aspect of this argument, for our purpose, is recognition of the complexity of social and cultural influences on educational outcomes (Arnot, 2002).

1.4 Sexuality

In some communities there is still considerable social stigma associated with open expressions of sexuality and many teachers may be hesitant about addressing such issues. Yet the recognition and acceptance of such differences may be extremely important to the provision of equal opportunities for some children, young people, teachers or parents.

Discrimination against homosexuality has been common in the past, obliging many to work under the continual stress of pretence and secrecy. The notorious 'Section 28', which became part of the Local Government Act (1986), prohibited the 'promotion' of homosexuality in England and Wales, including 'the teaching in any maintained school of the acceptability of homosexuality as a pretended family relationship', and exerted a strong influence on the content of teaching about sexuality. The Act was repealed in 2003 although there remains controversy and a substantial lack of confidence about how to teach these issues to children and young people within school curricula. Playground myths and legends still exert huge influences on sexual identities.

Motivated to write from personal experience of the need to challenge injustice and inequalities, lesbian and gay activists and educators have made significant contributions to research in this field. Issues of aloneness; secrecy; (in)visibility; heterosexual presumption; and homophobia in schools are common themes (Epstein, 1994; DePalma and Atkinson, 2009). Some useful questions for teachers to reflect on might include: what provision should be made for children who come from families where one or more members are lesbian or gay? Do the ethos and curriculum of the school offer appropriate support to all children and young people's developing awareness of their own sexuality? (How) should primary school pupils be introduced to sexuality as part of peoples' identity?

1.5 Age

The Universal Declaration of Children's Rights establishes the principle that children and young people should not be discriminated against because of their age. Research in the philosophy, history, psychology and sociology of childhood has repeatedly demonstrated how children's perspectives, activities and rights are structured, ignored or constrained by adults (Archard and MacLeod, 2002; James and James, 2004; Miller, 1997). Alternative conceptions of children as being either 'innocent' or 'corrupt' (Aries, 1962; Cunningham, 2006) can be found in popular culture and public policy, with the associated adult responses of both protection and moralising. Indeed, there is a discernible tension around whether the purpose of education is the protection or correction of children during childhood (Linklater, 2010).

In the past, teachers have been accused of constraining children because of a misplaced adherence to Piaget's conception of 'stages of development' (Walkerdine, 1984). Indeed, there remains a risk that linear assumptions of progress or achievement through schools' curricula could have a similarly limiting effect (Hart et al., 2004, see Reading 1.4) (see also Chapter 2, Section 2.3).

More commonly within the profession today, a view of children and young people as active agents, interacting, or co-creating their own childhoods is accepted (Dahlberg Moss and Pence, 1999; Mayall, 2002; John, 2003). Indeed, longitudinal studies of educational experiences year-on-year have shown how children and young people negotiate their circumstances and act strategically to create and pursue their interests (see Pollard and Filer, 1999, for an analysis of 'pupil career').

One aspect of school experience that has received particular attention in the UK and US is how the accident of birth date combined with the start of the school year produces age effects on academic attainment that can be traced throughout primary and secondary school (e.g. Crawford, Dearden and Maghir, 2007). In particular, children who are young in their year can be disadvantaged when immaturity is misinterpreted as a lack of ability, producing an exclusionary effect within the classroom.

1.6 Physical appearance

Physical appearance and perceptions of physical attractiveness have been found to have an important influence on our identities, behaviour and experiences, both in terms of what we expect for ourselves, and how others respond to us.

In the 1960s and 1970s social and psychological research focused on understanding teachers' expectations of pupils. Findings showed that children's attractiveness was significantly associated with how intelligent a teacher expected a child to be, how interested in education their parents were expected to be, how far the child was likely to progress in school and how popular they would be with their peers (Clifford and Walster, 1973; also Seligman, Tucker and Lambert, 1972).

Subsequent research has continued to affirm a correlation between physical appearance, educational outcomes, self-esteem, or motivating factors, and children and young people's standing within their peer group (for example, O'Dea and Abraham, 2000). For this reason, as well as impacting on teachers' expectations, physical appearance is also closely linked to developing a sense of identity.

Those teaching in secondary schools are likely to be particularly aware of the significance of physical appearance throughout the phase of puberty. This takes many forms but, for example, Frances (2004) studied the social and psychological challenges encountered by children and young people who have facial disfigurements, which may be congenital (such as birthmarks or cleft lip) or acquired (burns or scars). She noted that those with visible differences felt a particular need to be affirmed and included.

1.7 Disability

Understanding disability as a question of rights and opportunities has developed in recent years, as a result of people with disabilities articulating a strong voice and rejecting society's traditional views of the disabled as inadequate, damaged, less than whole, or, less than fully human. The success of London's 2012 Paralympic Games reflected this contemporary awareness.

Sociological studies have shifted the analysis of the nature and causes of disability from individualistic frames of reference to an examination of social policies and practice. Barton (2012) describes how this analysis 'provided a framework and language through which disabled people themselves can describe their experiences. Discrimination, exclusion and inequality can be named and challenged. Also, it offers a means through which the question of disability can be explored and understood in terms of wider socio-economic conditions and relations' (p. 115).

Recognising the voice of disabled people has been central to engaging with issues of human rights, respect and active citizenship, as exemplified by Peters in the extract below:

> People with disabilities have been called many things. I have labelled the worst name calling the 'in-words': *in*valid; *in*competent; *in*spirational … I have a dream that someday people won't use a label when referring to me, but that they will call me by the name my parents gave me when I was born: Susan Jeanne Peters. I dream that I will be neither invalid nor inspirational. I want to be just an ordinary person who happens to use a wheelchair. I look forward to the day when it's ordinary to be different; the day when we recognise that our differences are what we all have in common.
> (Peters, 2012, p. 65)

1.8 Learning

For some children, learning is said to 'come easily', whilst for others the acquisition of the knowledge, concepts, skills and attitudes in the school curriculum or beyond is much more difficult. Psychologists, neuroscientists and geneticists study differences in the learning capabilities of individuals, and such abilities are likely to have very significant effects throughout a pupil's school career.

Adults also experience variations in their learning ability – we tend to find it easier to learn things which are of intrinsic, personal interest. One can readily see then, how the factors we have reviewed above, such as social class, ethnicity or gender, can create conditions which may enable or constrain the particular types of learning which are necessary in schools. Social, economic and cultural circumstances often have educational consequences.

Understanding of differences and variations in the self-confidence and learning effectiveness of pupils is essential knowledge for any teacher in planning classroom provision. It enables targeted preparation to match pupil needs. Indeed, teachers tend to be very aware of 'brighter' and 'slower' pupils and many gradations in-between. Whilst such thinking may have a practical purpose in tuning provision, it is potentially dangerous if it leads to a reduction in expectations for some (Hart, et al., 2004, see also Reading 1.4).

Summary

In the discussion above we introduced eight dimensions which are associated with differences between people and with the opportunities that may or may not be made available. These dimensions interact in creating our individual identities. They affect our experiences inside and outside school, and influence the concepts, knowledge and frameworks we use to make sense of the world. As teachers, we have a responsibility to consider how our daily practices may be affected by, and contribute to, such matters.

2 School processes

2.1 Differentiation in routine practices

An integral part of routine schooling is the arrangement of pupils into groups to enable effective teaching and learning to take place and the provision of feedback about learning processes and outcomes (Ireson and Hallam, 2001, Reading 15.4). Indeed, Saljo and Hjorne (2009) describe categorisation in the school context as 'something people do to manage their daily chores' (p. 156). This is nearly always done by taking account of both similarities and differences between learners, so either reducing or extending learner diversity. For example, a thousand students in a co-educational secondary school could not easily be taught all together. A common starting point for organising them into reasonably sized classes would be the age of the students (e.g. all the 11-year-olds together – thereby reducing diversity), with a mixture of genders (e.g. equal numbers of boys and girls – extending diversity). Such decisions are rarely questioned by staff or students, but are part of the taken-for-granted organisational structures of schools. Furthermore, when a group of learners is brought together because they share particular characteristics they are, of course, in many other ways different from each other: hence, Sarason (1996) warns his reader to be wary of the 'myth' of 'homogeneity in the classroom'.

Whilst categorisation is an inevitable part of the organisational and evaluative require-ments of school life, its consequences can be both positive and negative. For example, does including a learner in *this* group, means they are excluded from *that* group? How does the provision of feedback with a whole-class audience affect the feelings of any individuals who may be named? Are some categories of learners more, or less, valued than others in a school? If so, which and why?

Teachers are generally very aware of these dilemmas – but adverse consequences, whilst unintended, can still be real. In particular, forms of grouping, setting, banding, assessment and evaluation constitute overt forms of social differentiation about which pupils will inevitably develop personal perspectives and strategies.

2.2 Polarisation through peer culture

When children and young people share a similar position in relation to school success or failure and regularly come together as a group, they begin to develop subcultures. For example, children who are regularly placed in different 'sets' or groups for particular activities are likely to develop a sense of themselves as a group. This is a common social process. Indeed, whenever people of any age regularly experience being 'differentiated' by organisations or in other circumstances, they tend to share their experiences and provide each other with mutual support. Such groups develop both friendships and their own perspectives – ways of thinking about both themselves and other people. As they bond together, the cultures of each group tend to be affirmed more strongly, particularly if there is rivalry or competition between groups.

In school contexts, this process is termed 'polarisation', for ironically, it involves a reinforcement of the initial differentiation as the children or young people respond to it themselves. In a sense, it is a form of cultural coping strategy, developed in response to experience and circumstances. But it is a strategy that can easily create educational exclusion, even if this is an unintended consequence. There have been many studies of such processes within secondary schools showing how children interpret their experiences of differentiation (e.g. Hargreaves, 1967; Lacey, 1970; Ball, 1981a; Gillborn and Youdell, 2000). There are tendencies for students to identify with or against school, and those who feel that they are 'educational failures' may reject school values in order to protect their own pride and self-esteem. Similar processes have been found in primary school contexts. Indeed, Pollard and Filer (1999) traced the 'school careers' of individual pupils and recorded the social influence of peer, family and teacher relationships as they form increasingly differentiated and unique identities.

This analysis is summarised in Figure 15.1, and a more complete discussion is available in Pollard, 1987a (Reading 15.2).

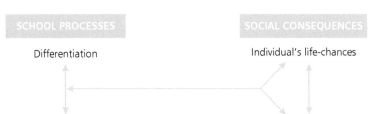

Figure 15.1
Differentiation-polarisation process and its consequences

Polarisation has also been identified in relation to gendered cultures within primary school peer groups, and shows the overlapping of dimensions of difference. For example, Reay's study (2001) of girls' friendship groups – 'Spice Girls', 'Nice Girls', 'Girlies' and 'Tomboys' – showed a common range of responses to school circumstances, but highlighted the way this was overlain by cultures of femininity. As she put it, 'despite widely differentiated practices, all of the girls at various times acted in ways which bolstered boys' power at the expense of their own' (p. 153). Renold (2001) showed how dominant ideas about masculinity shape boys' dispositions to schooling, schoolwork and academic achievement. She found that, even in primary school, high-achieving boys felt the need to use 'disguise' to maintain an apparently masculine disdain for schoolwork, and also clearly wanted to differentiate themselves from girls. In such ways, pervasive cultural differences within our societies are reinforced by social processes within schools, classrooms and playgrounds.

Our challenge as teachers is to monitor the differentiating effect of our routine practices in relation to the polarising processes that may then occur within pupil cultures. Forms of setting, grouping, division, feedback and assessment are particularly relevant here. The key processes lie in a chain, as classroom differentiation is reinforced by polarisation, and then begins to affect the Self-image and self-esteem of pupils. Subsequent effects may be manifest in terms of participation, attainment, exclusion and life-chances.

Lest readers feel overawed by the responsibilities outlined above, we should remember the two principles outlined in the introduction of this chapter. First, we asserted that difference is part of the human condition – so diversity amongst a group of learners is to be expected and welcomed. Second, we noted that all learners have the right to achieve. This brings a responsibility, wherever

> ## Expert questions
>
> **Differentiation**: are curriculum tasks and activities structured appropriately to match the intellectual needs of learners?
>
> **Inclusion**: are all learners treated respectfully and fairly in both formal and informal interaction?
>
> These questions contribute to a conceptual framework underpinning professional expertise (see Chapter 16).

possible, to mitigate adverse or limiting effects – hence the promotion of 'learning without limits' (Hart et al. 2000; Swann et al. 2010, Reading 1.4).

In the sections that follow, we consider the practical implications of this challenge which, fortunately, many teachers seem increasingly skilled at tackling.

3 Difference as part of the human condition

Over the last few decades broad social and cultural shifts have taken place in the countries of the UK that have led to many schools becoming increasingly diverse in their student intake. Alongside these changes, UK governments have introduced policies to encourage more inclusive forms of educational provision. However, research suggests that even though many teachers are highly supportive of the principles of inclusive education there is recognition of the challenge of meeting *all* needs, and especially those identified as having special or additional support needs and disabilities (e.g. Avramidis et al., 2000; Blecker and Boakes, 2010; Ross-Hill, 2009). Indeed, government commitment to inclusive education is of limited value unless teachers feel confident that it can be 'translated into working practices that enable successful learning outcomes to be achieved' (Rose et al., 2010, p. 370).

This section takes as its starting point the principle that difference is part of the human condition and focuses on feelings about learner diversity. It then progresses to explore the meaning of educational inclusion.

3.1 Learner diversity

On the one hand, difference is simply a characteristic of being a person: a positive feature of the human condition to be recognised and celebrated. Certainly, from a teacher's point of view one of the most rewarding aspects of the work is getting to know individual learners. On the other hand, human difference can also produce discomfort, even fear, especially when it is unfamiliar or considered abnormal. Thomas and Loxley (2007) explore these tensions in schools, arguing that: 'Whether difference is seen positively, as diversity, or negatively as deviance or deficit depends on the mindset of the person or group of people who observe that difference' (p. 93) (Reading 15.3). Perhaps, the key questions are, as Minow (1990) has asked: What counts as difference and what difference does difference make?

About half way through their course, a group of trainee teachers were asked to reflect on how they felt about 'teaching a diversity of learners' in relationship to a class they knew well. They were then asked to think of a metaphor which expressed their feelings and to give a reason for their choice. The results were varied and interesting. Four of their metaphors are shown in Figure 15.2, selected because they present a range of different ideas.

Figure 15.2
Metaphors for
teaching diverse
learners

Thinking metaphorically, teaching a diversity of learners is …

1   … *exploring a dark cave, without a torch, I am with a child who is trying to show me the way out. I am too panicked to listen. Then I calm down and listen. The child tells me the way out. We leave the cave together. Because … it is scary teaching such a wide range of children, but when you ask the child for help, they are willing to provide answers.*

2   … *keeping a garden. Because … every plant needs to be nurtured with food, water and warmth, but every plant needs slightly different care. Every plant grows at its own rate and responds differently to the environment it is in and therefore needs caring for.*

3   … *a sea of complexity! Because … all so different. It feels like you need years of experience and expertise in order to understand and provide for the needs.*

4   … *discovering buried treasure. Because … often the children you are teaching are categorised by their diversity and are sometimes simply reduced to this label. I think no matter how informed you are, it is always exciting and surprising to discover the potential, then achievement, of children with diverse needs.*

Reflective activity 15.1

Aim: To reflect on understandings of learner diversity.

Evidence and reflection: Think about the four metaphors for teaching diverse learners in terms of similarities and variations. (a) Are there any that particularly resonate with your own experiences, or that interested, or even surprised you? (b) What are the key ideas they raise about the role of a teacher and the role of learners? (c) Think about a class you know well and reflect on your feelings about teaching the diversity of learners in it. What would your metaphor be and why?

Extension: Reflect on what your metaphor expresses about (a) 'sameness', (b) 'difference' and (c) 'belonging' in the classroom?

3.2 Inclusive education

The meaning of inclusive education is complex, contested, and used in particular ways by different people. Ainscow (2005) identifies three key elements as being 'the presence, participation and achievement of all students' (p. 9).

Meanwhile, Mitchell (2005) analyses 'sixteen propositions' about inclusive education, offering a wide range of perspectives, understandings and definitions, across different national and international contexts. More locally, inclusion is embedded in government documents in all the countries of the UK, although even then there are both important similarities and variations associated with this term.

For example, the following definition is from the National Assembly for Wales (Circular: 47/2006) on *Inclusion and Pupil Support*:

> Inclusive education is an ongoing process concerned with ensuring equality of educational opportunity by accounting for and addressing the diversity present in schools. It requires the commitment of schools and LEAs to develop policies and practices that ensure equality of educational opportunity and access; safeguard vulnerable pupils; and focus on raising the achievement of all learners and increasing their participation in their schools and local communities. (p. 1)

Similar, but not identical, concerns can be found in the proposals put forward by the Northern Irish government in their consultation document *Every School a Good School – The Way Forward for Special Educational Needs and Inclusion* (Department of Education Northern Ireland (DENI), 2009):

> Inclusion is not simply about where a child is taught; it is about the quality of a child's experience of school life, including both the formal and informal curriculum, in and beyond the classroom. These proposals are aimed at ensuring that every child is a valued and valuable member of the school community with equal access to the same opportunities and high quality education. (p. vi)
>
> [And, later in the same document.] Inclusive practices require us to think about the diverse needs of all children. For example, those with SEN, those whose first language is not English, those in alternative education provision (AEP), children from the Traveller community, looked after children (LAC), and those who need help with literacy and numeracy. (p. 7)

Meanwhile, Booth and Smith (2002) examined a number of English government documents to see how the term inclusion was used. Below is a summary of just some of the areas they identified:

- special needs education;
- access to, and participation in, mainstream schools for students identified as having special educational needs and/or disabilities;
- social inclusion/exclusion relating to e.g. truancy, behaviour or looked-after children;
- issues of racial and other forms of discrimination;
- community stresses brought about by poverty, lack of housing, etc.;
- inclusion as an underlying general principle for education;
- supporting the participation of all learners in schools.

These extracts from government documents and the summary above highlight some key themes relating to inclusion but also the complex nature of the concept. This can make implementing and developing policies on inclusion in schools problematic, especially for classroom teachers who are expected to put them into practice. In particular, there is a tension between provision for children and young people considered to be particularly vulnerable to exclusion (those identified as having special needs, likely to experience discrimination, living in poverty, looked after children, etc.) and provision for *all* pupils (which must therefore take full account of diversity).

Of course, in the daily routines of classroom life teachers are expected to engage in both kinds of practices, but this distinction between 'some' and 'all' learners is an important theme that is considered in detail in Sections 4 and 5 of this chapter.

Expert question

Inclusion: are all learners treated respectfully and fairly in both formal and informal interaction?

This question contributes to a conceptual framework underpinning professional expertise (see Chapter 16).

Reflective activity 15.2

Aim To reflect on our understanding of inclusive education and on our provision for *some* or *all* of the learners in the class.

Evidence and reflection Think about a class that you are currently teaching and make notes in response to the following questions.

- What kinds of classroom opportunities and experiences matter to the learners? (What do they want to be included in, or excluded from?)
- How is inclusion assessed and recorded for the class? (For what purposes? Who are its audience?)
- What is the relationship between the inclusion and exclusion of learners?
- What is the relationship between the inclusion of learners and different kinds of special or additional support needs?
- Is the inclusion of some learners in this class more (or less) highly valued than others? (If so, who? Why? By whom?)
- How far is the inclusion of learners in the class influenced by factors that are:
  - within individual learners?
  - related to their peers?
  - relate to you as their teacher and to other professionals?
  - related to the school as an institution?
  - within families and local communities?

Extension Reflecting on your responses what might you do next? Do you need to find out more, perhaps by talking to learners, support staff or other teachers?

Whilst it is clear that there is no straightforward definition of inclusive education, it is important that a reflective teacher considers carefully what inclusion means to them and assesses its implications for classroom practice.

However it is understood, inclusion raises complex questions about how children and young people learn together. In particular, inclusion is concerned with finding ways to respond to learner diversity that do not disadvantage other individuals or groups in the class. It is underpinned by the belief that *all* children and young people should be respected and treated fairly. At the heart of inclusion, therefore, are classroom relationships, between

Research
Briefing

Developing inclusion

Inclusion is one of the major challenges facing education systems around the world. As part of the Personalisation agenda, *2020 Vision*, the English government's analysis of teaching and learning in the future, emphasises 'achievement for all' and 'ensuring a strong focus on progress for *all* pupils':

> *Embedding the concept of progression in personalising learning means instilling in all children and young people the belief that they can succeed, through identifying achievable – but challenging – steps towards clear, shared goals.* (DfES, 2006, p. 37)

However, this depends on teachers themselves having high expectations of all their pupils. TLRP's project on inclusive practices in schools enabled practitioners and researchers to work together to explore ways of achieving inclusion by focusing on learner experiences, pleasure in learning and the development of self-esteem. They adjusted the time spent on formal curricular objectives, particularly concerned with writing, and increased experiential learning, oral work and thinking skills. Pupil perspectives were particularly effective in challenging teacher thinking. An underlying theme concerned the inappropriateness of some National Curriculum requirements for some children and the innovative capacity of teachers to adapt and create constructive alternative provision.

Key findings:	Implications:
Ways of thinking: Many significant barriers to the participation and learning of pupils stem from teachers' misplaced assumptions about what their pupils can do and how best to teach them.	Overcoming barriers requires more than a different way of working – individuals and groups often need to question their accepted ways of thinking, and this takes time.
Engagement of staff: Interruptions to established understandings and practices can be fostered when groups of staff engage with evidence about pupils' experience of school, and about their own practice.	Establishing a focus for school enquiry on a specific issue of genuine concern to many staff is often more productive than imposing whole-school change.
Underlying factors: For many pupils, it is not possible to achieve improved outcomes simply by teaching the curriculum harder and longer. Instead, teachers have to strengthen the factors that underpin learning, such as pupils' pleasure in learning and their self-esteem.	Addressing both underachievement and inclusion requires that the national focus on highly measurable outcomes of school be broadened to include these underlying factors.

The findings of the project were based on understanding gained from teachers and researchers working together in twenty-five schools within three local authorities. They participated in research activities, conferences, exchange visits and workshops over a period of three years. This design allowed relationships to be built which led to data about the social and personal aspects of change in schools, and the interaction of these aspects with technical and managerial development.

Wherever possible, practitioners carried out evaluations of the processes within and outcomes from their own initiatives, supported by university researchers. User engagement and validation thus contributed significantly to the trustworthiness of findings. Researchers invited schools to engage throughout with their accounts of development, and towards the end of the network, time was spent working together on an overview of outcomes.

Further information:
Ainscow, M., Booth, T., Dyson, A., Farrell, P., Frankham, J., Howes, A., Gallannaugh, R., Millward, A. and Smith, R. (2004) *The Development of Inclusive Practices in Schools*. TLRP Research Briefing No 6. Cambridge: TLRP. Available at **www.tlrp.org/pub** (accessed 18 November 2013).
Ainscow, M., Booth, T. and Dyson, A. (2006) *Improving Schools: Developing Inclusion*. TLRP Improving Learning series. London: Routledge.
This project was directed from the University of Manchester.

teachers and learners as well as between learners and learners (Black-Hawkins, Florian and Rouse, 2007, see also Chapter 6).

The research briefing on p. 424 suggests some of the challenges in developing inclusion, including the value of personalising the curriculum and maintaining excellent classroom relationships.

The research briefing on p. 424

> **Expert question**
>
> **Relationships:** are teacher–pupil relationships nurtured as the foundation of good behaviour, mutual wellbeing and high standards?
>
> This question contributes to a conceptual framework underpinning professional expertise (see Chapter 16).

4 'Needs' as a dimension of difference

We began this chapter by examining dimensions of difference that shape the lives of *all* people, both in and beyond school. In contrast, this section focuses on those who are deemed to have special or additional 'needs'. This raises a number of important but difficult questions. Who has such needs and, by implication, who does not? Can such distinctions always be easily made? If doing so is problematic, how useful is it for a teacher to be told that a child or young person in their class has (or does not have) special or additional needs? And, what are the consequences of such decisions?

4.1 Concepts and definitions

Lack of conceptual clarity about needs is commonplace. For example, a large-scale study of mainstream schools in England (Ofsted, 2010) found that the proportion of learners identified as having special educational needs varied from fewer than 5 per cent in some schools to over 70 per cent in others. These differences could not be fully attributed to other variables, such as the socio-economic status of a school's catchment area. These findings led the authors of the report to argue that 'children and young people with similar needs were not being treated equitably and appropriately'. They concluded that it was essential to 'start to think critically about the way terms [like SEN] are used'. Most controversially they noted that about half the schools they visited were using low attainment and relatively slow progress as the main indicators of a special educational need. This led them to make the following criticism of teaching in such schools (emphasis added):

> Inspectors saw schools that identified pupils as having special educational needs when, in fact, their needs were no different from those of most other pupils. They were underachieving but this was sometimes simply because *the school's mainstream teaching provision was not good enough*, and expectations of the pupils were too low. (p. 9)

The complex nature of defining the concept of 'needs' is further highlighted when comparing relevant legislation across the four countries of the UK. Whilst there are shared understandings there are also some important differences. This is reflected in the choice of language used. So, in English policy and practice – as noted above – the most common term is 'special educational needs' (SEN) but 'special educational needs and disability' (SEND) is also in use. Meanwhile, although the governments of Northern Ireland and Wales also use special educational needs, more recently they have both introduced new terms to operate alongside it: 'additional educational needs' (AEN) for Northern Ireland, and 'additional learning needs' (ALN) for Wales. In contrast, in Scottish policy and practice, the term special educational needs is no longer used, having been replaced in 2004 by 'additional support needs' (ASN) as part of the Education (Additional Support for Learning) Act (see Scottish Government, 2010). These recent shifts in language, in the latter three countries, are intended to indicate a concern with a far broader spectrum of learners' needs than the more traditional focus on physical, sensory and cognitive disabilities, and/or behavioural needs. Such developments are to be welcomed as recognition of the complex and often difficult lives of some children and young people.

For example, in Scotland (Scottish Executive, 2010) additional support needs are defined as a 'broad and inclusive term' that applies to children or young people 'who, for whatever reason, require additional support, long or short term, in order to help them make the most of their school education and to be included fully in their learning'. Meanwhile, the Welsh government (2006) explains the relationship between additional learning needs and special educational needs as follows:

> The term 'Additional Learning Needs' includes those learners who require additional support either due to their circumstances or because they have a longer-term disorder or condition. In many cases, for example through sickness or where a family is experiencing temporary difficulties, children and young people may have additional learning needs for a short period only. ... The term 'Special Educational Needs' continues to be used to identify those learners who have severe, complex and / or specific learning difficulties. ... SEN is therefore a sub-category of ALN. (p. 2)

A slightly different understanding in outlined by the government in Northern Ireland (2009). Here additional educational needs are conceptualised as 'four overlapping themes' of which the first is 'SEN'. They are as follows:

1. *Children with SEN*: e.g. 'children with sensory, physical or medical conditions or syndromes';
2. *Learning environment needs:* e.g. 'children who have English as an additional language';
3. *Family circumstances needs:* e.g. 'looked after children';
4. *Social and emotional needs:* e.g. 'those who are suffering from bullying'. (p. 8)

Alongside these generic terms, all four governments offer comprehensive lists of learners who might potentially be identified as having special or additional needs. For example, to return to Scotland, the following reasons why 'children or young people may require additional support' are provided (Scottish Executive, 2010, p. 13):

- have motor or sensory impairments
- are being bullied

- are particularly able or talented
- have experienced a bereavement
- are interrupted learners
- have a learning disability
- are looked after by a local authority
- have a learning difficulty, such as dyslexia
- have English as an additional language

- are living with parents who are abusing substances
- have parents with mental health problems
- are not attending school regularly
- have emotional or social difficulties
- are on the child protection register
- are young carers.

Whilst such lists reflect a broader understanding of the concept of learners' needs, the sheer range can seem overwhelming for practising teachers. Nevertheless, it is important that the many underlying factors that can form barriers to classroom learning are acknowledged. Furthermore, it is also crucial that teachers recognise that individual children and young people often have complex lives that do not fit neatly into one category but may well shift between and overlap with others.

It is not in the remit of this chapter to give a detailed analysis of legislation around children and young people's special or additional needs. It would be difficult to do so because, in all four countries of the UK, this is an area of government policy that is presently in a state of flux. For example, at the time of writing a major review is taking place in England concerning the SEN Code of Practice including arrangements for assessment of and funding for children and young people identified with special educational needs and disabilities. However, there are two key themes across the UK that are worth noting because they are currently shaping legislation on children and young people identified as having special or additional needs. These are first, a strengthening of the role of parents/carers in deciding the educational provision for their children and second, a continuing concern to ensure consistency across education, health and social services. Both these developments are to be welcomed because they acknowledge the holistic nature of the lives of learners and their families.

4.2 Responding to 'needs' in the classroom

There are many categories or conditions of special or additional needs and disabilities, about which specific information will be helpful. Fortunately, there are a huge range of commercially published books that focus on such issues (see **reflectiveteaching.co.uk**) and also many websites that include advice specifically for classroom teachers. Some are run by national governments: for example, the Department for Education (DFE) (England) offers online training materials intended to 'improve teachers' knowledge, skills and understanding of severe learning difficulties (SLD), profound and multiple learning difficulties (PMLD), and complex learning difficulties and disabilities (CLDD)'. Finally, many charities and organisations provide guidance, advice and materials for teachers via their websites. The following links represent just a very small sample of those that are available:

- Autism – **autism.org.uk**
- Down's syndrome – **downs-syndrome.org.uk**
- Dyslexia – **bdadyslexia.org.uk**
- Emotional wellbeing – **youngmindsinschool.org.uk**
- Deafness – **actiononhearingloss.org.uk/**
- Social, Emotional, Behavioural difficulties – **sebda.org**
- Speech, language and communication needs – **speechteach.co.uk**
- Visual impairment – **rnib.org.uk.**

Many adults in and beyond the school also have a particular role in helping to support the learning of children and young people identified as having special or additional needs, and they can be an invaluable source of professional information and advice for classroom teachers. For example, colleagues in school might include the person with overall responsibility for learning support (sometimes called the SENCo), teaching assistants, curriculum leaders and pastoral leaders, and colleagues outside school might include educational psychologists, educational welfare officers, social workers, advisory teachers and, of course, parents and carers (see Chapter 8).

Reflective activity 15.3

Aim: To explore school policy and provision for learners identified as having special or additional needs, and to reflect on their implications for classroom practice.

Evidence and reflection: (a) Identify those who work in, or visit, your school having particular responsibilities for supporting learners identified as having special or additional needs. (b) Make brief notes about their support role and consider how they might support your classroom practice.

Extension: Talk to one of these colleagues about their role and school policy and provision. If there is an individual learner, or group of learners, about whom you are particularly concerned, it might be especially helpful to discuss ideas about classroom practices with them in mind. For example, what changes could you make to your teaching to support their inclusion in classroom activities? What further information can you gather via specialist websites and books?

The Ofsted report (2010) referred to earlier offers a reflective teacher another approach to developing their classroom practices so as to respond to the needs of all learners. The study proposed 11 features likely to support the learning of children and young people identified as having special educational needs (Figure 15.3). The authors argue that, 'Although these features are true for good teaching generally, they are particularly true for the teaching of disabled children and young people and those with special educational needs' (p. 47).

Figure 15.3
Supporting
children with
special educational
needs (Ofsted,
2010)

When children and young people learned best:

1 they looked to the teacher for their main learning and to the support staff for support;
2 assessment was secure, continuous and acted upon;
3 teachers planned opportunities for pupils to collaborate, work things out for themselves and apply what they had learnt to different situations;
4 teachers' subject knowledge was good, as was their understanding of pupils' needs and how to help them;
5 lesson structures were clear and familiar but allowed for adaptation and flexibility;
6 all aspects of a lesson were well thought out and any adaptations needed were made without fuss to ensure that everyone in class had access;
7 teachers presented information in different ways to ensure all children and young people understood;
8 teachers adjusted the pace of the lesson to reflect how children and young people were learning;
9 the staff understood clearly the difference between ensuring that children and young people were learning and keeping them occupied;
10 respect for individuals was reflected in high expectations for their achievement;
11 the effectiveness of specific types of support was understood and the right support was put in place at the right time.

Reflective activity 15.4

Aim To reflect on how far, and in what ways, our classroom practices support all learners including those identified as having special or additional needs.

Evidence and reflection Think about a lesson, or series of lessons, that you have taught recently. (a) Were there any individuals or groups of learners in the class whose progress was of concern? (b) Read each statement from the Ofsted report about when 'children and young people learn best' to help you reflect on the lesson(s). (c) Looking at these statements, what do you think went well? (d) What could you have developed further to support everyone's learning and especially those whose progress was of concern?

Extension Reflect on how you might develop your practice for future lessons with this class, to ensure that all learners make progress.

This section has considered briefly some of the complexities in defining the concept of special or additional 'needs' as well as the variability in the practices of their identification. But what might be the consequences for a learner of being labelled as having a 'need'? Might this discourage them from making progress in their learning? Or, will it support their progress because it ensures that more appropriate provision is made? And, how is a teacher to manage this in the context of their classroom, and in ways that do not marginalise or stigmatise any learner because of their identified needs? Norwich (2008) describes this as the 'dilemma of difference'. He argues:

> The basic dilemma is whether to recognise and respond or not to recognise or respond to difference, as either way there are some negative implications or risks associated with stigma, devaluating, rejection or denial of relevant and quality opportunities. (p. 1)

Teacher judgement and expertise is clearly called for here. In the final section of this chapter we consider how Norwich's dilemma might be addressed, by examining further the practice of teachers who endeavour to respond to learner diversity, not by making special or additional provision for some, but by extending what is ordinarily available to all.

5 Developing inclusive classroom communities

This section considers what we can do as part of our everyday routines and practices to develop our classrooms as more inclusive learning communities. Doing so brings together the main themes from across the chapter as a whole. In particular, it concerns how teachers can enable all learners in their classes to:

- make progress in their learning;
- feel accepted and valued for who they are;
- have opportunities to participate in a full range of classroom activities.

We also engage again with the dilemma, discussed in the previous section, that arises when *some* learners are identified as requiring 'special' or 'additional' provision compared with that made for *most* other learners. This distinction between *all, some* and *most* learners is important. It raises a key question: How can a teacher respect as well as respond to individual differences between learners, and do so in ways that include all learners in the routine, daily life of the classroom? This challenge is at the heart of developing more inclusive classroom communities (see also Chapter 6, section 4.3).

5.1 Inclusive teaching and learning

A starting point for this is to revisit the eleven characteristics of 'best' lessons as set out in the previous section. As noted there, whilst Ofsted (2010) considered these to be essential to supporting the learning of children and young people identified as special educational needs and disability, they acknowledged that they were also highly relevant to 'good teaching generally'. In particular, the significance of good classroom relationships in providing opportunities is well established (see Chapter 6 and Thorne, 1993, Reading 15.5).

Similarly, Kershner (2009) (Reading 15.6) has argued convincingly that 'teaching approaches which seem intrinsic to inclusive learning are already represented in many classrooms'. She places a particular emphasis on the following:

- pupil dialogue

- collaboration
- choice
- exploration
- learning to learn
- the assumption that all pupils are capable of learning.

Of course, Kershner's approaches to inclusive classroom teaching and learning have each been considered elsewhere in this book (see, in particular, Chapters 2, 6, 11 and 12). They are also clearly underpinned by the TLRP principles of effective teaching and learning. Most notable, in terms of developing inclusive classroom communities, is Principle 7. This concerns the importance of fostering 'both individual and social processes and outcomes' because 'learning is a social activity. It demands interaction with other minds'. Kershner reiterates this focus on the collective experience of inclusive practices for *all* learners (and therefore not only *some*):

> Inclusive practice does not just support marginal and potentially disaffected pupils, but these and all the other pupils are collectively the embodiment of inclusive educational activity. … This diversity contributes to a dynamic and creative process of teaching and learning that maintains the schools as a healthy educational context while promoting all pupils' learning in often unpredictable ways. (p. 63)

5.2 The inclusive pedagogical approach

The remainder of this chapter considers key elements of inclusive pedagogy. It draws on a recent research study which worked with teachers committed to the principles of inclusion. Its aim was to understand how these principles informed and shaped the teachers' day-to-day classroom routines and practices (Black-Hawkins and Florian, 2012; Florian and Black-Hawkins, 2011).

Through extended classroom observations and teacher interviews the research explored what teachers 'know, do and believe' about their inclusive practices (Rouse, 2008). Three major themes emerged which encapsulate the inclusive pedagogical approach.

Figure 15.4
Major themes of
inclusive pedagogy

1   *Shifting the focus away from one that is concerned only with individual learners,
    identified as having 'special' or 'additional' needs, to the learning of all children and
    young people in the class.*
    - creating learning opportunities that are sufficiently made available for *everyone*,
      so that all learners participate in classroom life;
    - extending what is ordinarily available for *all* learners (creating a rich learning
      community) rather than using teaching and learning strategies that are suitable
      for *most* learners alongside something 'special' or 'additional' for *some* who
      experience difficulties;
    - focusing on *what* is to be taught (and *how*) rather than *who* is to learn it.

2   *Rejecting deterministic beliefs about ability as being fixed and the associated idea
    that the presence of some will hold back the progress of others.*
    - believing that *all* children will make progress, learn and achieve;
    - focusing teaching and learning on what children can do rather than what they
      can not do;
    - using a variety of grouping strategies to support everyone's learning rather than
      relying on ability grouping to separate ('able' from 'less able' students);
    - using formative assessment to support learning.

3   *Seeing difficulties in learning as professional challenges for teachers, rather than
    deficits in learners, that encourage the development of new ways of working.*
    - seeking and trying out new ways of working to support the learning of all
      children;
    - working with and through other adults that respect the dignity of learners as full
      members of the community of the classroom;
    - being committed to continuing professional development as a way of
      developing more inclusive practices.

(Adapted from Florian and Black-Hawkins, 2011)

Significantly, inclusive pedagogy focuses on the needs of *all* learners working together in the community of the classroom. This requires a subtle but crucial shift in teachers' thinking:

- *away from* traditional approaches to inclusion based on making provision for *most* learners, and then something 'special' or 'additional' for *some* who experience difficulties;

- *towards* enriching and extending the learning opportunities that are ordinarily available for everyone, so that *all* learners are able to participate in classroom life.

As might be expected, the study highlighted considerable connections and overlaps between the three themes in terms of the actual classroom experiences of teachers and learners. The study also showed how putting inclusive pedagogy into practice can be challenging for teachers, not least because of constraints within education systems and across schools that counter teachers' efforts to be inclusive. Certainly, the teachers in the study were sometimes observed engaging in practices that seemed less inclusive than on other occasions.

5.3 Putting inclusive pedagogy into practice

The key overall finding from the study of the teachers' inclusive practices was that inclusive pedagogy is defined not in the teacher's choice of classroom strategies or approaches but in their practical use, including how and why they are chosen. An example of this is provided in the following case study of the inclusive pedagogical approach, which draws on classroom observations and interviews with one teacher, Kate. She had organised the lesson around peer group collaborative learning: a commonly used strategy which is neither essentially inclusive nor exclusive. She arranged the learners into small groups to work on individual tasks and whole-group activities. Kate's choice of 'peer group collaborative learning' is not important *per se*, but the way she uses it to support the learning of *all* the children in her class is notable. This is just one of many strategies that she drew on to enable all the children in her class to participate and achieve, including those identified as having special or additional needs. Her intention was to provide everyone with opportunities to make choices, experience success, take risks, recognise their own and others' strengths, learn from mistakes, and value the support of peers.

Case study 15.1 Kate and the inclusive pedagogical approach

Kate's class comprises children aged eleven and twelve years old. She and Moira (who teaches a parallel class) often combine their classes and team teach, modelling the kinds of collaborative learning they hope to encourage in the children. An extended session was observed: presented (somewhat tongue in cheek) as the 'Ancient Olympics'. The children were arranged into groups of six (mixed girls and boys, from both classes, working with peers outside their usual circle of friends). Each group was given a range of tasks (e.g. problem solving, design, art, music, public speaking, hand-eye coordination): some to be completed individually, others by the whole group.

In the first group activity the children decided who would undertake which individual tasks. Each had to negotiate and agree to one task. Kate described how these activities, were intended to encourage the children to recognise their contribution to the group's work, as well as that of their peers. Because the tasks were so varied, all the children were able to participate and achieve.

Kate: It's all about teamwork and getting them to work collaboratively and decide, 'Well, I'm really good at this so I think I should do this; oh I'm not so good at that, maybe you could do that instead'. … Finding out what your strengths and weaknesses are and how to work as a team. … Depending on the group they were in, they might have been able to find their voice in that group and stand up and do something that they maybe wouldn't have done before.

Kate did not allocate tasks to particular learners according to notions of ability, nor did she provide certain activities for most of the children, whilst offering something 'additional' for some identified as having learning difficulties. She expected children to make judgements about which tasks to engage in, and why. She recognised that there were differences between individual learners, but considered such differences to be part of the ordinary experiences of classroom teaching and learning for all children.

There were children in both Kate's and Moira's classes identified as requiring additional support for learning (specific learning difficulties, English as an additional language, Attention Deficit Hyperactivity Disorder, poor social skills). However, during the observations it was not possible to determine who they were: e.g. teaching assistants were not allocated to their groups. Rather, all staff were observed giving support to individual children or groups in response to requests for assistance, rather than because certain children were identified as having special needs.

One boy, called Thomas, had missed many years of schooling because of his identified social, emotional and behaviour difficulties, including bouts of extreme anger which had been frightening for him and for others. However, nothing in the observations indicated that separate provision was made for him and he participated in all the peer group activities. Kate's view was that Thomas, like all children, needed to participate fully in classroom life, learning with and from his peers: 'He learns, he watches what the other children do and how they are in the class. ... they can teach him better than I can'. Kate did not ignore Thomas's difficulties, but she attended to them in ways that avoided the stigmatising effects of marking him as different. 'He doesn't want to be seen to be as different. And that's a good thing, because he wants to be like everyone else'.

Kate: Thomas's missed out on so many years of school, we still are finding out where his gaps are and where we need to fill in his knowledge. ... He knows time really well, but when we come to symmetry, he just doesn't have a clue ... because he hasn't done it. ... A lot of things are done privately and quietly. ... He had an awful lot to learn ... how to make friends, how to work with people his own age, how to share, how to take turns.

Kate presented Thomas as a person with a complex past, present and future, and not simply as a child with an identified learning difficulty. Whilst her support for Thomas concerned his behaviour, she did not separate this from other aspects of his learning: identifying and helping him to fill the 'gaps' in his skills and knowledge of the curriculum. Kate argued forcefully that such provision must be made in ways that did not isolate him from his peers ('giving him strategies that don't involve him having to remove himself from the classroom') and respected his dignity as a full member of the class. Her attention to his individual differences was always subsumed within the general provision made for all the children, because, as Kate argued, this was pedagogically the best way to support his learning.

(Adapted from Black-Hawkins and Florian, 2012)

The figure opposite draws on the analysis of Kate's articulation of her inclusive practice, using the example of the strategy of peer group collaboration. The first two columns show the traditional approach to inclusion, whereby a teacher makes provision for *most* learners, plus something 'special' or 'additional' for *some* learners who are experiencing difficulties. As demonstrated in the table, the consequence of these 'special' and/or 'additional' practices is both to include but also to exclude some learners from the classroom community. In contrast, the final column illustrates the inclusive pedagogical approach, whereby a teacher enriches and extends the learning opportunities that are ordinarily made available for *all* learners in the class. In this approach, learner diversity is recognised, but without the stigmatising effects of marking some as different or pre-determining the learning that is possible.

Figure 15.5
Analysing Kate's
inclusive pedagogy

Traditional approach to inclusion: Most and Some		Inclusive pedagogy: All
Manifest in terms of inclusion: Individual tasks are differentiated according to learners' identified ability levels. The teacher seeks advice from learning support staff about the appropriateness of tasks/materials for students identified with special educational needs. The teacher selects 'more able' students in each group to lead group tasks. Students work on individual tasks deemed appropriate to their assessed ability levels. Classmates support students with 'additional needs' for both individual and group activities. A learning support assistant works alongside one student, identified with social emotional and behavioural difficulties (SEBD), to facilitate his collaboration in the group.	*Manifest in terms of exclusion:* Students see that individuals are set different tasks according to teacher's assessment of their ability. They notice that 'clever' students are chosen to lead group activities. Some students are perceived as needing help from their classmates, whilst others are perceived as being able to provide that help, thus reinforcing (and sometimes limiting) expectations about different learners. Opportunities for peer collaboration for the student identified with SEBD are restricted by the presence of an adult in the group.	Individual tasks are allocated collaboratively by students through group discussion of their collective skills and knowledge. Group tasks are undertaken collaboratively, including the organisation of the tasks. The teacher fosters a classroom community which encourages all students to work collaboratively, and to value everyone as a resource for learning. Students are encouraged to take risks with their learning, within a supportive group and class environment. Learning support staff are a resource for any individual student or group requesting help. The teacher uses group collaboration to encourage the development of positive peer relationships amongst all learners, (including a student identified with SEBD). The teacher models collaborative learning through her classroom relationships with colleagues

(Adapted from Black-Hawkins and Florian, 2012)

Conclusion

This chapter has explored how teachers can support the inclusion of all children and young people. Every class is diverse in its membership, and inclusion is concerned with understandings of, and attitudes towards, all children and young people in relationship to their age, gender, ethnicity, sexuality, social class, physical appearance, disability and performance at school. Discrimination can be subtle and complex, sometimes unintended, and rarely straightforward. However, the marginalisation or stigmatisation of anyone, for whatever reason, forms a barrier to inclusion. The challenge we face acknowledges differences between learners, but seeks to ensure equity for all. It recognises that diversity is to be expected and welcomed in a class, and that every learner has the right to achieve. At the same time, it is crucial to acknowledge that processes of social differentiation and polarisation are impossible to avoid in school settings. For a reflective teacher, the challenge is how to manage these processes so that their most divisive consequences on the lives of children and young people are mitigated.

Finally, the promotion of inclusion and social justice must also be actively pursued beyond the classroom. Education may not be able to change society (Bernstein, 1970), but teachers should, if possible, try to ameliorate its most divisive effects. These are difficult goals, but working towards them nevertheless remains a continuing educational responsibility. Despite a comprehensive awareness of the risks of exclusion and positive commitments regarding constructive classroom policies and social justice, it is clear that teachers cannot act in isolation from the school in which they work and the society in which they live. As Sarason (1996) asks: What are schools for? And, how shall we live together?

Key readings

There is an enormous literature on topics such as diversity, opportunities, inclusion
and special educational needs, and the list below is indicative only. Consulting
reflectiveteaching.co.uk will expand the suggestions.

We begin with books providing overarching perspectives on equality and difference. See,
for example:

Richardson, R. (2009) *Holding Together: Equalities, Difference and Cohesion.* Stoke-
on-Trent: Trentham. (Reading 15.1)

Solar, J., Walsh, C. S., Craft, A., Rix, J. and Simmons, K. (2012) *Transforming
Practice: Critical Issues in Equity, Diversity and Education.* Maidenhead: Open
University Press.

The analysis of how differentiation by teachers and schools is reinforced by polarisation
within pupil culture can be traced through many sociological studies, including:

Lacey, C. (1970) *Hightown Grammar: The School as a Social System.* Manchester:
Manchester University Press.

Pollard, A. (1985) *The Social World of the Primary School.* London: Cassell. (see
Reading 15.2)

Specific treatment of particular issues with regard to dimensions of difference is
provided in books such as the following classic and contemporary studies.

The influence of social class reaches well beyond the classroom (see also Chapter 5) and
excellent websites providing up-to-date data are available from the Sutton Trust and the
Joseph Rowntree Foundation. See also:

Evans, G. (2006) *Educational Failure and Working Class White Children in Britain.*
Palgrave Macmillan: Basingstoke.

Feinstein, L. Duckworth, K. and Sabates, R. (2008) *Education and the Family:
Passing Success Across the Generations.* Routledge: Abingdon.

Jackson, P. and Marsden, D. (1962) *Education and the Working Class.* London:
Ark.

Sharp, R. and Green, A. (1975) *Education and Social Control.* London: Routledge.

Willis, P. E. (1977) *Learning to Labour: How Working Class Kids Get Working Class
Jobs.* Saxon House: Farnborough.

On gendered experiences, and how these are reproduced, see:

Arnot, M., David, M. and Weiner, G. (1999) *Closing the Gender Gap. Postwar
Education and Social Change.* Cambridge: Polity Press.

Delamont, S. (1990) *Sex Roles and the School.* London: Routledge.

Francis, B., Skelton, C. and Read, B. (2012) *The Identities and Practices of*

High Achieving Pupils: Negotiating Achievement and Peer Cultures. London: Continuum.

Ivinson, G. and Murphy, P. (2007) *Rethinking Single Sex Teaching*. Maidenhead: Open University Press.

Jackson, C. (2006) *Lads and Ladettes in School: Gender and a Fear of Failure*. Maidenhead: Open University Press.

Skelton, C. and Francis, B. (2009) *Feminism and 'The Schooling Scandal'*. London: Routledge.

Plummer, G. (2000) *Failing Working Class Girls*. Stoke-on-Trent: Trentham.

On the apparent underachievement of boys, see:

Lingard, B., Martino, W. and Mills, M. (2009) *Boys and Schooling: Beyond Structural Reform*. Basingstoke: Palgrave Macmillan.

Warrington, M., Younger, M. and Bearne, E. (2006) *Raising Boys' Achievements in Primary Schools: Towards a Holistic Approach*. Maidenhead: Open University Press.

Younger, M., Warrington, M. and McLellan, R. (2005) *Raising Boys' Achievement in Secondary Schools: Issues, Dilemmas and Opportunities*. Maidenhead: Open University Press.

On ethnicity and race, some classic and more contemporary studies include the following. For a pupil-orientated website 'about race, racism and life as seen through the eyes of young people', try: britkid.org.

Connolly, P. (1998) *Racism, Gender and Identities of Young Children: Social Relations in a Multiethnic, Inner-city Primary School*. London: Routledge.

Gillborn, D. (2006) *Racism and Education: Coincidence or Conspiracy?* Routledge: Abingdon.

Gillborn, D. and Youdell, D. (2000) *Rationing Education*. Buckingham: Open University Press.

Mac and Ghaill, M. (1988) *Young, Gifted and Black*. Buckingham: Open University Press.

Nieto, S. (2009) *The Light in their Eyes: Creating Multicultural Learning Communities*. New York: Teacher College Press.

Troyna, B. and Hatcher, R. (1992) *Racism in Children's Lives: A Study of Mainly White Primary Schools*. London: Routledge.

Walters, S. (2011) *Ethnicity, Race and Education*. London: Continuum.

Given the performance pressures of recent years, many schools have returned to the practice of grouping children by attainment (often imprecisely termed 'ability'). The problems were documented many years ago, and remain. Alternative approaches are offered by 'learning without limits'.

Hart, S., Dixon, A., Drummond, M.-J. and McIntyre, D. (2004) *Learning Without Limits*. Maidenhead: Open University Press. (see Reading 1.4)

Ireson, J. and Hallam, S. (2001) *Ability Grouping in Education.* London: SAGE. (see Reading 15.4)

Jackson, B. (1964) *Streaming: An Education System in Miniature.* London: Routledge and Kegan Paul.

Swann, M., Peacock, A., Hart, S. and Drummond, M.- J. (2012) *Creating Learning Without Limits.* Maidenhead: Open University Press. (Reading 1.4)

Introductions to special educational needs include:

Thompson, J. (2010) *The Essential Guide to Understanding Special Educational Needs.* London: Longman.

Wearmouth, J. (2011) *Special Educational Needs: The Basics.* London: Routledge.

For an international overview, see:

Florian, L. (ed.) (2007) *The Handbook of Special Education.* London: SAGE.

On disability and special educational needs, innovative perspectives are provided by:

Lewis, A. and Norwich, B. (2004) *Special Teaching for Special Children? Pedagogies for Inclusion.* Maidenhead: Open University Press.

Thomas, G. and Loxley, A. (2007) *Deconstructing Special Education and Constructing Inclusion.* Buckingham: Open University Press. (Reading 15.3)

On the conceptualisation of inclusive education, see:

Hick, P., Kershner, R. and Farrell, P. (eds) (2008) *Psychology for Inclusive Education: New Directions in Theory and Practice.* Abingdon: Routledge. (see Reading 15.6)

Mitchell, D., (2005) (ed.) *Contextualizing Inclusive Education: Evaluating Old and New International Perspectives.* London: Routledge.

For principled accounts of developing inclusion in primary and secondary classrooms and schools, see:

Ainscow, M., Booth, T. and Dyson, A. (2005) *Improving Schools, Developing Inclusion.* London: Routledge.

Black-Hawkins, K., Florian, L. and Rouse, M. (2007) *Achievement and Inclusion in Schools.* London: Routledge.

Sage, R. (2007) *Inclusion in Schools: Making a Difference.* London: Network Continuum Education.

For exploration of the ways in which all children's social, moral and cultural development can be promoted through debate on issues of social inclusion, see:

Arthur, J. and Cremin, H. (2011) *Debates in Citizenship Education.* London: Routledge.

reflectiveteaching.co.uk offers additional professional resources for this chapter. These may include *Further Reading,* illustrative *Reflective Activities,* useful *Web Links* and *Download Facilities* for diagrams, figures, checklists, activities.

part five

Deepening understanding

This is the final and synoptic part of the book. It integrates major themes through discussion of teacher expertise and professionalism.

'Expertise' (Chapter 16) harvests and integrates powerful ideas from previous chapters into a holistic conceptual framework of enduring issues in teaching and learning. The chapter constructs a framework describing dimensions of expert thinking. In Chapter 17, 'Professionalism', we consider the role of the teaching profession on our societies and suggest how reflective teachers can contribute to democratic processes.

Expertise
Conceptual tools for career-long fascination?

16

Introduction: A conceptual framework for deepening expertise

For extensive supplements to this chapter, see 'Deepening Expertise' at **reflectiveteaching.co.uk**

The contemporary world is complex, challenging and rapidly developing. As Collarbone (2009, Reading 16.1) argues, we have to get used to change itself. And there will certainly be pressure on teachers.

As we saw in Chapter 4 of this book, it is now internationally recognised, more than ever before, that 'teachers matter' (OECD, 2005; Sahlberg, 2012, Reading 4.3; Hattie, 2009, Reading 4.6) – a fact which TLRP's findings and principles embody and promote. As Dylan Wiliam argues, the quality of teaching has a far greater effect than differences caused by type of school. Indeed, 'there is a four-fold difference in the speed of learning between the most effective and least effective classrooms' (Wiliam, 2009, Reading 16.4).

The influence of recent analyses of the 'effect-sizes' of different teaching and learning strategies (see, for instance, Hattie, 2012, Reading 10.7) is to be found throughout this book. Such findings offer wonderful insights on high-quality teaching. However, specific findings also need to be integrated more holistically into teachers' routine practices and ways of thinking. This brings us to a discussion of the progressive development, and deepening, of teacher expertise.

TLRP principles

Effective teaching and learning depends on teacher learning. The need for teachers to learn continuously in order to develop their knowledge and skills, and adapt and develop their roles, especially through classroom inquiry, should be recognised and supported. (Principle 9)

Effective teaching and learning demands consistent policy frameworks with support for teaching and learning as their primary focus. Policies at national, local and institutional levels need to recognise the fundamental importance of teaching and learning. They should be designed to create effective learning environments in which all learners can thrive. (Principle 10)

See Chapter 4

The development of teacher expertise has been studied for many years with the work of Dreyfus and Dreyfus (1986), Glaser (1999) and Berliner (2004) being particularly significant. Glaser (1999) identified three key 'cognitive stages' in the development of expertise – thus highlighting a transition from dependent to independent ways of thinking about classroom practice:

Externally supported > Transitional > Self-regulatory

Whilst this progression makes considerable sense, a further element of expertise lies in contextually appropriate judgement. In other words, it is not enough simply to accumulate a 'box of tricks' or to assemble 'teacher tips' – valuable though these may be. The key capability is to understand when and how to deploy such capabilities. Berliner (2004) picked out the significance of contextual judgement and of practice itself in his elaboration of five stages of teacher development (originally proposed by Dreyfus and Dreyfus, 1986). This is summarised by Eaude (2012, see Reading 16.3) as in Figure 16.1 below.

Figure 16.1 Stages in the development of expertise (Eaude, 2012, after Alexander, 2010, pp. 416–17)

Stage	Strategies	Overall approach	Characteristic
Novice	Context-free rules and guidelines	Relatively inflexible, limited skill	Deliberate
Advanced beginner	Practical case knowledge	Use of rules qualified by greater understanding of conditions	Insightful
Competent	Discrimination of what matters or not	Conscious choices, but not yet fast, fluid or flexible	Rational
Proficient	Accumulated case knowledge enabling key points to be noticed	Degree of intuition based on prediction of pupil response	Intuitive
Expert	Deep reserves of tacit knowledge	Apparently effortless, fluid, instinctive, though able to fall back on a deliberate, analytical approach	Arational

Here we see the rationale for the notion of 'deepening expertise'. The development of advanced forms of expertise requires practice over a long time, so that many cases and circumstances are experienced and a wide range of skills are honed. In some fields, such as music and sport, it has been suggested that 10,000 hours of practice is necessary to achieve intuitive capabilities (Erisson et al, 2006).

The need for contextual understanding and for experience over many years helps to explain the common scepticism of many teachers to the 'latest fad' or to a 'new policy' which may emerge from the media, government or elsewhere. Hargreaves describes such 'presentism' as a conservative force (2007, Reading 16.2) but also recognises it as a founda- tional form of professional knowledge and security, from which new practices can only develop through work *with* teachers and in ways which authentically respect their agency, values, vision and experience.

In summary, the development of teacher expertise occurs over time and is, in essence, concerned with acquiring more sophisticated ways of thinking about teaching and learning as well as the refinement of practical skills and curricular knowledge (Winch, 2012). From a reliance on generic rules for challenges such as classroom management, the expert teacher is able to 'read' a situation and draw intuitively on his or her repertoire of responses. As indicated in Figure 16.1, this appears 'almost effortless', but it is also possible to 'fall back on a deliberate, analytical approach'. The expert teacher has a reper- toire of available strategies (see also Alexander, 2008, Reading 16.3). This developmental process was first introduced in Chapter 3, when it was discussed simply as a career-long 'spiral of professional development' (see Figure 3.1, p. 68). From such foundations, this book has progressed, Part by Part, though educational intentions, conditions for learning, teaching processes and outcomes. Each chapter has focused on practical challenges, but has also been written with an eye to the cumulative development of teacher expertise. To that end too, TLRP's principles, powerful concepts and expert questions for analysing teaching and learning in classrooms have been seeded through the chapters.

Principles, concepts and questions support the interpretation and understanding of classroom experience and of evidence. If we revisit our discussion in Chapter 3, section 1.2 on 'evidence-informed practice', we can see just how vital such tools are. Figure 16.2, below, reproduces an earlier model (see p. 73) – but with one difference. Here, attention is drawn to how evidence has to be *interpreted and understood*. We must 'make sense' of our experience and of the information available to us.

Figure 16.2
Principles, concepts and evidence-informed practice

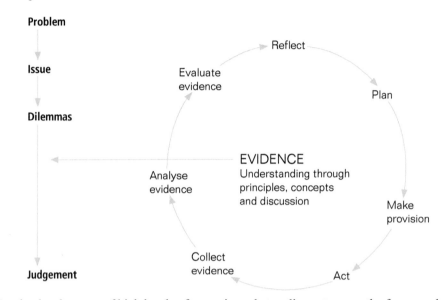

For the development of high levels of expertise, what really matters are the frameworks of deeper understanding and the values which underpin professional judgement.

Indeed, simple 'tips', 'toolkits' or lists of 'what works', whilst useful and worthy of careful attention, are not enough to achieve the highest quality of teaching. They can even be misleading. Hattie (2012, Reading 16.5) recognises this and proposes 'high-level principles' to integrate his otherwise fragmented lists of effective teaching strategies. James (2007, Reading 2.8) makes clear that improvement in pupil outcomes depends on the development of authentic teacher understanding. Put another way, as Bruner stated (1996, Reading 11.3) 'a teacher's conception of a learner shapes the instruction he or she employs'. So at the highest levels of professionalism, there is a key role for overarching, theorised *understanding* of learning and of teaching.

Acknowledging this issue in relation to its 'Teaching and Learning Toolkit', the Education Endowment Foundation is very responsible in drawing attention to limitations:

> The aim of the Toolkit is to support teachers to make their own informed choices and adopt a more 'evidence based' approach. The evidence it contains is a supplement to rather than a substitute for professional judgement. It provides no guaranteed solutions or quick fixes. (**educationendowmentfoundation.org.uk/toolkit/using-the-toolkit**, downloaded 24/12/13).

Of course, TLRP's principles (see Chapter 4) promote a more holistic, multi-dimensional view of Education, within which is nested appreciation of the need to achieve high standards in basic skills and subject knowledge. Indeed, the model of professionalism which underpins this book assumes that teachers will be concerned with issues such as the intrinsic quality of pupil learning experiences, the development of positive learning disposition and self-confidence, the fulfilment of potential and the provision of opportunities for all – as well as achieving very high standards in knowledge, skills and understanding.

Having seeded principles, concepts and questions in each chapter of the book, we are now able to harvest cumulatively from across the whole text and to offer an integrated, conceptual foundation for deepening expertise.

The conceptual framework (see Figure 16.2, overleaf) is based on the proposition is that, in one way or another, teachers inevitably face issues concerning **educational aims, learning contexts, classroom processes** and **learning outcomes** (the rows) and they do so in relation to **curriculum, pedagogy** and **assessment** (the columns) (see also an online, featured version in 'deepening expertise' at **reflectiveteaching.co.uk**).

The 'expert questions' in each cell highlight the enduring issues which reflective teachers need to consider. As we have seen, this calls for evidence-informed professional judgement. However, the analytic capacity of the concepts which are used to think about and discuss such evidence is also absolutely vital. Without such generative power, neither classroom enquiry nor discussion with colleagues will build sustainable professional understanding. If the concepts have sufficient validity, then sustained use will contribute to the development of a professional language to both represent teacher expertise and to challenge those who misunderstand its sophistication.

Having said that, the specific meaning and usage of the identified concepts can certainly be challenged. The framework is simply an analytic device for representing teacher expertise. It could be compiled and re-presented in different ways.

Review of the *columns* of curriculum, pedagogy and assessment are an important way of using the framework. For example, a classroom teacher, staff team or any other group of stakeholders in a school might want to focus on curriculum provision alone, in which case the 'expert questions' in that column would be effective probes for this, enabling considerations of curriculum aims, contexts, processes and outcomes (Chapters 8, 9 and 10 cover this ground too). Pedagogy could be similarly reviewed using the set of expert questions in its column (and chapters 5, 6, 7, 11, 12 and 15 also focus on these issues). Assessment is the subject of the third column (which articulates directly with chapters 13 and 14). On the version of the framework at **reflectiveteaching.co.uk/deepening-expertise**, individual columns open and contract to enable focused consideration.

It is also worthwhile to think of the *rows*. If this is done, the interrelationship of provision for curriculum, pedagogy and assessment is reviewed in relation to each of the enduring issues concerned with aims, contexts, processes and outcomes. This is the approach taken in the remainder of this chapter. Again, to enable simplification, rows open and contract within the version of the framework at **reflectiveteaching.co.uk/deepening-expertise**. Alternatively, it is often insightful to explore connections between the concepts and questions in different parts of the framework. To help in this, **reflectiveteaching.co.uk** provides further ideas and information in relation to each cell.

For more information on how the conceptual framework was created, see the supplementary material for Chapter 16 on **reflectiveteaching. co.uk.**

The framework is simply a tool for thinking and for discussion.

ENDURING ISSUES		Curricular concepts
1 EDUCATIONAL AIMS	**1.1 Society's educational goals** What vision of 'education' is the provision designed to achieve?	**Breadth:** does the curriculum represent society's educational aspirations for its citizens?
	1.2 Elements of learning What knowledge, concepts, skills, values and attitudes are to be learned in formal education?	**Balance:** does the curriculum-as-experienced offer everything which each learner has a right to expect?
2 LEARNING CONTEXTS	**2.1 Community context** Is the educational experience valued and endorsed by parents, community, employers and civil society?	**Connection:** does the curriculum engage with the cultural resources and funds-of-knowledge of families and the community?
	2.2 Institutional context Does the school promote a common vision to extend educational experiences and inspire learners?	**Coherence:** is there clarity in the purposes, content and organisation of the curriculum and does it provide holistic learning experiences?
3 CLASSROOM PROCESSES	**3.1 Process for learners' social needs** Does the educational experience build on social relationships, cultural understandings and learner identities?	**Personalisation:** does the curriculum resonate with the social and cultural needs of diverse learners and provide appropriate elements of choice?
	3.2 Processes for learners' emotional needs Does the educational experience take due account of learner views, feelings and characteristics?	**Relevance:** is the curriculum presented in ways which are meaningful to learners and so that it can excite their imagination?
	3.3 Processes for learners' cognitive needs Does the educational experience match the learner's cognitive needs and provide appropriate challenge?	**Differentiation:** are curriculum tasks and activities structured appropriately to match the intellectual needs of learners?
4 LEARNING OUTCOMES	**4.1 Outcomes for continuing improvement in learning** Does the educational experience lead to *development* in knowledge, concepts, skills and attitudes?	**Progression:** does the curriculum-as-delivered provide an appropriate sequence and depth of learning experiences?
	4.2 Outcomes for certification and the lifecourse Does the educational experience equip learners for adult and working life, and for an unknown future?	**Effectiveness:** are there improvements in standards, in both basic skills and other areas of curricular attainment, to satisfy society's goals?

Pedagogic concepts	Assessment concepts
Principle: is our pedagogy consistent with established principles for effective teaching and learning?	**Congruence**: are forms of assessment fit for purpose in terms of overall educational objectives?
Repertoire: is our pedagogic expertise sufficiently creative, skilled and wide-ranging to teach all elements of learning?	**Validity:** in terms of learning, do the forms of assessment used really measure what they are intended to measure?
Warrant: are our teaching strategies evidence-informed, convincing and justifiable to stakeholders?	**Dependability**: are assessment processes understood and accepted as being robust and reliable?
Culture: does the school support expansive learning by affirming learner contributions, engaging partners and providing attractive opportunities?	**Expectations**: does our school support high staff and student expectations, and aspire to excellence?
Relationships: are teacher–pupil relationships nurtured as the foundation of good behaviour, mutual wellbeing and high standards?	**Inclusion**: are all learners treated respectfully and fairly in both formal and informal interaction?
Engagement: do our teaching strategies, classroom organisation and consultation enable learners to actively participate in and enjoy their learning?	**Authenticity**: do learners recognise routine processes of assessment and feedback as being of personal value?
Dialogue: does teacher–learner talk scaffold understanding to build on existing knowledge and to strengthen dispositions to learn?	**Feeding back**: is there a routine flow of constructive, specific, diagnostic feedback from teacher to learners?
Reflection: is our classroom practice based on incremental, evidence-informed and collaborative improvement strategies?	**Development**: does formative feedback and support enable learners to achieve personal learning goals?
Empowerment: is our pedagogic repertoire successful in enhancing wellbeing, learning disposition, capabilities and agency?	**Consequence**: do assessment outcomes lead towards recognised qualifications and a confident sense of personal identity?

Figure 16.3
A framework for teacher expertise: powerful concepts and expert questions

Society's goals: a opportunity for discussion

We start our review of the conceptual framework for deepening understanding by suggesting a discussion on aims and purposes. Reflective activity 16.1 suggests an initial focus on national priorities. However, such concerns soon have to be transformed into practical action in schools and classrooms. What documentation on overall educational aims is available in your school?

Reflective activity 16.1

Aim: To review national aspirations and consequential links between curriculum breadth, pedagogic principles and congruent assessment.

Evidence and reflection: This activity challenges us to stand back and review our education system as a whole. Four questions might be posed, and could be tackled in discussion with colleagues.

1   Is there a broad consensus on educational purposes for schooling? An indication of this might be the nature of public debate about school provision. What aspects are taken for granted? Which are controversial?

2   How adequately do National Curriculum requirements represent educational goals on which there is broad agreement? For example, is the curriculum regarded as being sufficiently broad to provide an 'all round education' and to foster positive attitudes to learning whilst also ensuring mastery of basic skills and enabling appropriate qualifications to be obtained?

3   Are favoured approaches to teaching justifiable in terms of established, evidence-informed principles? Do these reinforce overall curricular intentions?

4   What sorts of assessment are significant in the school system in which you work? Are these congruent with overall curricular intentions?

Follow-up: These questions are framed above in quite general terms, for consideration of wide-ranging issues across an entire school system. However, they can also be applied much more specifically, to a particular school, department or classroom. If this is done, they become powerful tools for stimulating reflection on overall educational purposes and provision. Our aims and methods should match of course, but do they?

Breadth: Is your subject knowledge adequate in relation to national priorities?

Principle: Is your pedagogic subject knowledge appropriate for national provision well founded in terms of what is known about good teaching?

Congruence: Are you familiar with forms of assessment which will reinforce your aims, and will not inadvertently distort pupil learning?

1. EDUCATIONAL AIMS

1.1 Society's goals

What vision of 'education' is the provision designed to achieve?	**Breadth:** does the curriculum represent society's educational aspirations for its citizens?	**Principle:** is our pedagogy consistent with established principles for effective teaching and learning?	**Congruence:** are forms of assessment fit for purpose in terms of overall educational objectives?

Education connects our past to the future – but exactly what happens is worked out through debate and action in the present.

Children and young people are our most precious asset. They come to embody our culture, and their values and capabilities will determine the ways in which our economy and society will evolve over the twenty-first century. Education both reflects society and contributes to it. Issues such as whether education reproduces social differences or provides new opportunities thus become very important. What vision of education should we adopt?

The Education Reform Act 1988 specified official educational aims for England and Wales. Children are to be offered a 'balanced and broadly based curriculum' which:

- promotes the spiritual, moral, cultural, mental and physical development of pupils; and
- prepares pupils for the opportunities, responsibilities and experiences of adult life.

The law thus formally enshrines a rounded conception of education. However, pressure for short-term performance tends to narrow such goals – and thus we have a major issue of recent decades. The curriculum frameworks for Scotland, Wales, Northern Ireland and the Republic of Ireland promote similarly broad overall aims.

Curriculum: Breadth

There are many views about the areas of learning and experience which should be provided by schools (see Chapter 9). Scotland's *Curriculum for Excellence* proposes eight areas, as does the curriculum in Wales and Northern Ireland. These encompass fields such as: arts and creativity; language and literacy; environment and society; modern languages; mathematics; science and technology; health and physical education; religious and moral education.

In England, very particular emphasis has been given to core subject areas of English, maths and science in primary education and to subjects in the EBacc in secondary. Maintaining breadth in pupils' actual classroom experiences is a big challenge for teachers in any event, and is made difficult in such circumstances. Curriculum, assessment and accountability need to be fully aligned to reinforce breadth of provision.

Pedagogy: Principle

This challenge concerns the extent to which teachers' pedagogic judgement is informed by a deep understanding of learning and teaching and of the factors involved. TLRP's ten principles (see Chapter 4) is one way of representing these factors holistically so that their interconnectedness is emphasised. Such principles often underpin national recommendations but, at best, they should directly inform teacher expertise.

TLRP's principles form four groups. The first concerns the goals and moral purpose of education, knowledge to be learned and the prior experience of the learner. Three aspects of teacher expertise, in 'scaffolding' learning, assessment for learning and active engagement, form another. The role of social processes and informal learning feature next. Finally, the principles emphasise the significance of teacher learning and the need for consistent policy frameworks.

Assessment: Congruence

Assessment activity should support learning objectives – hence 'assessment for learning' (see Chapter 13).

TLRP's project on learning environments (Entwistle, 2009) studied ways in which assessment activity is aligned with learning objectives, appropriate for student backgrounds and fully supported institutionally. Assessment was thus seen as being much more than a narrow technical process, but woven into educational organisations, subjects and their practices. Such congruence supports learning because the learner can more easily understand and engage with available feedback. This work built on the concept of 'constructive alignment' (Biggs, 2007), which asks whether learning activities and forms of assessment are consistent and fit for their purpose.

Elements of learning: a case study

Bringing the curriculum to life

Year 4 teacher Simon Mills took out a tube of sugar-coated chocolate buttons and told the children he was being short-changed. He was certain there were not as many buttons of his favourite colour as the others. Could the children help find out if this was true?

The lesson in data handling had begun and the children were instantly engaged. They worked in groups at their computers, filling in a spread sheet as they counted sweets, and discussing how to solve the problem. Everyone was keen to share their ideas and hear what other people had to say.

The lesson was filmed at a Bristol junior school, to illustrate the TLRP principle 'Teachers should scaffold learning in appropriate ways' – something which demands a secure teaching repertoire to enable the teacher to respond confidently to pupil learning needs. The school was involved in the TLRP's InterActive project, which found that ICT in the classroom will not automatically bring improvements in learning; teachers and children need to choose and use technological tools appropriately.

"One thing I think very carefully about is what tool I'm going to use," says Simon. "I sit down and think, 'am I going to use this book or that book?' 'How do I demonstrate what a full stop is and what a capital letter is?'" For this particular lesson, the questions he asked himself included: am I teaching ICT today or maths? Am I going to use a tool they're familiar with or a new one?

In this case, Simon Mills wanted to ensure the children could access the maths, so he chose technology that would help them do so quickly. Whichever choice he makes, though, "It's important to use real tools with real outcomes."

Simon likened his job to that of an orchestra conductor, and said it was more important to him to have an agenda than a plan. "It's not a passive role. I'm trying to lead the children toward something. I have got an agenda. I have got an outcome, which is an end point. I know I have got to get there."

Significant numbers of children in our schools find it difficult to access the curriculum and may attain at levels below their abilities. Such children may be bored or distracted, unable to concentrate for all sorts of reasons.

However, teachers like Simon bring the curriculum to life for their students by providing an interesting curriculum, varied learning experiences and authentic feedback.

Repertoire: The teacher makes informed decisions about strategies for advancing children's learning and keeping them engaged and autonomous.

A video of this lesson, and commentary upon it, can be viewed in the Chapter 16 resources at **reflectiveteaching. co.uk**.

For more information on the TLRP project see **www.tlrp.org/proj/phase11/phase2i.html** or Sutherland, R., Robertson, S. and John, P. (2008) Improving Classroom Learning with ICT (London, Routledge).

1. EDUCATIONAL AIMS

1.2. Elements of learning

What knowledge, concepts, skills, values and attitudes are to be learned in formal education?	Balance: does the curriculum-as-experienced offer everything which each learner has a right to expect?	Repertoire: is our pedagogic expertise sufficiently creative, skilled and wide-ranging to teach all elements of learning?	Validity: in terms of learning, do the forms of assessment used really measure what they are intended to measure?

Pupils at school acquire knowledge, concepts, skills, values and attitudes, and they do so through their work across the whole curriculum and beyond.

Knowledge and concepts to be learned are often suggested by National Curriculum frameworks, and may be complemented by promotion of the skills and disposition of 'learning-how-to-learn'. Some of these elements of learning, such as the basic skills of literacy and numeracy, are typically given priority in the formal curriculum.

Values and attitudes are no less important. Scotland's *Curriculum for Excellence* is said to be underpinned by the values inscribed on the mace of the Scottish Parliament – wisdom, justice, compassion and integrity. However, the tacit messages that go out from the 'hidden curriculum' of everyday experience may have a particularly direct influence.

Teachers thus have enormous responsibilities not just for the content of what learners may learn, but in contributing to the values and attitudes of our future citizens.

Curriculum: Balance

As HMI (1985, Reading 10.1) put it: 'A balanced curriculum should ensure that each area of learning and experience and each element of learning is given appropriate attention in relation to the others and to the curriculum as a whole' (Chapter 9). If areas of learning are organised in terms of subjects, a balanced allocation of time and resources is crucial.

Elements of learning – knowledge, concepts, skills, values and attitudes – are taught *within* each curriculum area and again need to be balanced. Overemphasis on knowledge or skills sometimes de-motivates learners and should be complemented by support for conceptual understanding and opportunities to develop personal perspectives. Such goals are clearly dependent on having an appropriate pedagogic repertoire.

Pedagogy: Repertoire

Educational objectives are wide-ranging so that a range of teaching approaches is required – from which teachers select having considered the needs of learners, subject-matter goals and other circumstances (Chapter 11). Alexander (2008, Reading 12.3) affirms many variations of pedagogic repertoire, but suggests that three broad aspects can be identified:
- *organisational*: whole-class teaching, collective group work, collaborative group work, one-to-one activity with the teacher, one-to-one activity with peers;
- *teaching talk*: through use of rote, recitation, instruction, discussion, dialogue, etc.;
- *learning talk* (by pupils): such as narrate, explain, speculate, argue, negotiate, etc.

To make provision for all elements of learning to be taught through classroom activities and tasks, teachers need to be confident users of a range of pedagogic approaches.

Assessment: Validity

'Assessing what is easy to measure is not the same as assessing what what is educatonally important – but it is tempting to do so nonetheless (Chapter 14). In classrooms, for example, it is routine to test forms of pupil performance, but much harder to assess deeper understanding. Learning is not always 'on the surface', so we have to find insightful ways of investigating and analysing.

In general, it is easier to assess knowledge and skill than it is to assess understanding and attitudes. The former tend to be more amenable to categoric questions and tests. Understanding and attitudes are likely to be revealed more through dialogue, discussion and demonstration and to require teacher interpretation of the available evidence. Again, to draw out these crucial elements of learning in valid way, a confident pedagogic repertoire is needed.

Community context: a case study

Parents as partners

David and Lucy, 11-year-old twins, were looking forward to their move up to secondary school. David, a sporty, outgoing, but quirky boy, was particularly enthusiastic. His more conformist sister was less keen to leave the comfort of the junior classroom.

But in the event, Lucy thrived and David struggled – he failed to make friends, was bullied, and had to be switched out of his tutor group at the end of Year 7. The twins' parents were unable to provide the support or have the access to school that they had had before, and their mother found this period, and the changes in her children, difficult.

Researchers who followed the twins through their transfer believe a programme from TLRP's Home–school Knowledge Exchange project (HSKE) could have made all the difference. HSKE helped to bridge home and school by valuing the contributions of all parties: parents, children and teachers. Involvement in such a scheme might have enabled David's parents to work with his teachers to help him to develop different coping strategies and to deal with the challenges to his sense of self.

School transfer can challenge children's established identities and force them to reassess who they are and how they interact with others. HSKE enabled parents, teachers and children to engage with this challenge together, and provided a structure that made it easier for parents to share their knowledge of their children with the school.

One of HSKE's three strands was secondary transfer. Action researchers worked with four primary schools in Bristol and Cardiff and their receiving secondaries on improving children's experience of transfer by bringing schools, parents and children together to share the same learning experiences.

For example, videos of Year 7s, their parents and their teachers talking about secondary school life were shown to Year 6s and their parents and teachers. Year 6 children made passports of the skills they might need in secondary school. This meant they had to reflect on themselves as individuals, to imagine themselves in the new setting and to offer themselves advice.

When they started at secondary, children brought in photos of their out-of-school lives. Parents were invited to an informal evening with teachers, and one secondary held an event specifically to discover how the knowledge of the Somali community could be drawn on by the school.

The children involved appeared to adjust more quickly to secondary school and to have better attitudes towards learning. They also made significantly greater progress in literacy between Year 6 and Year 7 than other children.

Connection: Home–school knowledge exchange supports curriculum engagement with the real lives of children and parents.

For more information on the TLRP project, see: **tlrp.org/proj/phase11/phase2e.html**. The case study account above is from: Osborn, McNess and Pollard (2006).

2. LEARNING CONTEXTS

2.1 Community context

Is the educational experience valued and endorsed by parents, community, employers and civil society?	**Connection:** Does the curriculum engage with the cultural resources and funds-of-knowledge of families and the community?	**Warrant:** Are the teaching strategies evidence-informed, convincing and justifiable to stakeholders?	**Dependablity:** Are assessment processes understood and accepted as being robust and reliable?

'Community' is associated with social relationships, cultures and histories and with a collective sense of place and identity (see Chapter 5). Some people and families may feel deeply embedded in their communities and benefit from extensive social networks; such social capital often brings status and advantage. Others, perhaps minority groups, may feel more marginal or even excluded. Such diversity is a very strong feature of contemporary life.

TLRP's research has consistently shown the significance of informal, out-of-school learning: what happens within schools is enriched by understanding of what happened outside schools. Those in the community can thus help considerably, if constructive and trusting connections are made.

However, those beyond the school gate are also positioned as consumers. Parents, employers and others expect children to receive high-quality education, and inspectors and the media are quick to condemn schools when standards fall short. Forms of pedagogy and assessment now have to be justified – hence the concepts of warrant and dependability.

Curriculum: Connection

'Only connect – live in fragments no longer', wrote E. M. Forster. This thought can be applied to the meaningfulness and linkage of the curriculum with the communities which each school serves (see Chapter 10). TLRP's Home–school Knowledge Exchange project affirmed the knowledge of families and devised ways of drawing this into the curriculum. Outcomes in literacy and numeracy improved and transfer between Key Stages 2 and 3 was facilitated (Feiler et al., 2007; Winter et al., 2009). The Royal Society of Arts promotes an 'area based curriculum' (Thomas, 2010, Reading 10.4).

The underlying theme here is about the contextual meaningfulness of the curriculum. Whilst national frameworks exist, local adaption is likely to enhance both the perceived value of schooling and the quality of learning.

Pedagogy: Warrant

The word 'warrant' has several meanings associated with forms of authorisation and justification, ranging from the Royal Warrant to an arrest warrant.

In relation to pedagogy, the concept of warrant challenges us to justify our practice to stakeholders such as parents, employers and learners themselves. We defined pedagogy earlier as 'the act of teaching, together with its attendant theory and discourse' (Chapter 11). Further, it was suggested that maintaining a sound educational rationale and forms of reflective practice can support continuing improvement in the quality of professional judgements (pp. 8–9). This is one clear way of fulfilling the responsibility, set out in the Codes of Conduct and Practice of the UK GTCs and professional associations, for maintaining the quality of teaching.

Assessment: Dependability

How much confidence can we place in different forms of assessment (see Chapter 14)? Technically speaking, high dependability arises when an assessment is both valid and reliable – it measures what is intended and does so with high consistency. Consistent reliability is not easy to achieve. As TLRP's Commentary on assessment pointed out (Mansell and James, 2009, Reading 14.5), it can be undermined by unfair or biased marking and by variations in standards applied by different teachers. Other studies have shown how differences in testing situations or in pupil preparation can affect performance. Electronic marking may achieve consistency in that respect, but struggles on some tests of validity. On the other hand, teacher assessment is likely to strengthen the validity of judgements made, but remains vulnerable to inconsistency unless moderation processes are taken extremely seriously.

For all these reasons, the dependability of school assessments always has to be worked for.

Institutional context: a case study

Pupil consultation is right on target

When Rivington and Blackrod High School consulted with pupils about target setting, it helped to inform teachers' understanding of what school learning felt like for Year 10 and Year 11 students.

By the end of the initiative, the whole-school approach was giving a more active role to students in deciding their targets. Teachers were offering clearer guidance on ways of raising attainment in specific subject areas. Students now had a much clearer understanding of their targets and seemed motivated by the increased ownership and choice, while remaining realistic about their capabilities.

Nine students worked with humanities teachers for two years to investigate pupil views and attitudes towards learning, and how the school's work on target setting could be improved. The teachers and students met regularly to discuss their progress and attainment. During interviews with a researcher from TLRP's 'Consulting Pupils' network, the students indicated that they:

- wanted respect and to be involved in their education;
- did not tolerate poor learning environments;
- had clear ideas about what good teaching and learning looked like;
- had mixed feelings about the value of target setting; and
- wanted to know how to improve their work as well as what required improvement.

Some students felt that being told that they would receive a poor grade affected their confidence. Others made suggestions for improvements:

> 'Someone that knows you should sit down and speak to you and discuss where you are now and what you think you can achieve.' (Y10 student)

> 'It's easier if the teacher has a word with you and says, "Look, you're slipping in this" rather than having to set the grades.' (Y10 student)

Involvement in the project saved one student from being permanently excluded. He now felt he could talk to staff, and the kudos of being involved enhanced his self-esteem and tolerance of school systems.

Under the new process, students were invited to set their own targets based on their average KS3 points and chances graphs. The Head of Year summed up the project's impact.

> 'They had a much clearer understanding of the targets and were motivated by the element of ownership and choice yet realistic about their capabilities ... It is surprising what nine students can achieve and I am sure they are probably unaware of the effect their work has had on school policy ... It certainly opened my eyes toward the effectiveness of "pupil voice" and has influenced the way I now encourage teams of staff to include "pupil feedback" in the departmental procedures.'

Expectations: Being involved in discussing and setting their own targets enhanced aspirations and enabled children to confidently reach for higher goals.

For more information on the TLRP project, see **tlrp.org/proj/phase1/phase1dsept.html,** or consult: Rudduck and McIntyre (2007, also Reading 1.3). The case study above is drawn from Cox (2004).

2. LEARNING CONTEXTS

2.2 Institutional context

Does the school promote a common vision to extend educational experiences and inspire learners?	Coherence: is there clarity in the purposes, content and organisation of the curriculum and does it provide holistic learning experiences?	Culture: does the school support expansive learning by affirming learner contributions, engaging partners and providing attractive opportunities?	Expectations: does our school support high staff and student expectations, and aspire to excellence?

Three points about effective schools are often picked out (Sammons, Hillman and Mortimore, 1995):
- effective headteachers act as leading professionals;
- there is a resolute commitment to the improvement of teaching and learning;
- there is shared vision and goals to lift aspirations and provide consistency in practices.

In complementary ways, a 'learning school' is one in which teachers, pupils and others systematically commit to collaborative self-improvement on teaching and learning. Leaders at all levels within the school work to discover, release, support and spread the expertise of colleagues (James et al., 2007). Pupil learning is thus enhanced.

Curriculum: Coherence

A coherent curriculum is one that makes sense as a whole; and its parts are unified and connected by that sense of the whole. This requires expert selection, planning and presentation of curriculum knowledge. National curricula may structure subject content, but schools must exercise judgement about their specific schemes of work.

Coherence and progression within areas of learning enable students to build their understanding cumulatively. In Scotland, the *Curriculum for Excellence* states that: 'all children and young people have an entitlement to a curriculum which they experience as a coherent whole, with smooth and well-paced progression' (Education Scotland, 2013).

Another dimension of coherence concerns the relationship of one curriculum area to another. In England, cross-curricular studies have been recommended in the curriculum to enable children and young people to apply what they have learned – an approach which 'respects the integrity of subjects but lessens the rigidity of their boundaries' (e.g. Rose, 2009).

Pedagogy: Culture

School culture is often cited as a major influence on teaching and learning. In ideal circumstances, a culture of collaboration would exist among the management and staff of the school, in which the values, commitments and identities of individuals are perfectly aligned with the teaching and learning strategies and aspirations of the institution. Things are usually more complicated – but the ways in which such complexity is handled is crucial.

TLRP's studies of workplace cultures contrasted 'expansive' and 'restrictive' learning environments (Fuller and Unwin, 2003). In the former, staff were engaged in meaningful work, with supportive leadership and opportunities for personal learning and progression. Another TLRP project showed how teachers' sense of wellbeing and job satisfaction is a key factor in their effectiveness (Day et al., 2007, see also Reading 1.1).

Assessment: Expectations

Learners benefit when significant others in their lives believe in them. Parental and teacher expectations are particularly significant for children and young people (Gipps and MacGilchrist, 1999, Reading 6.5; Hattie, 2009, Reading 4.6) and are often based on judgements about capability and potential. Expectations are thus pervasively embedded in perception, relationships and everyday life. As such, although tacit, they are particularly meaningful to learners and influential in the formation of self-belief (Dweck, 1986, Reading 2.6). Expectations are thus a form of ongoing, social assessment. When applied negatively to whole groups, cultural expectations can present significant barriers to learning learning.

Raising expectations is a common recommendation for school improvement. But to be effective, such expectations have to be authentic, because a connection has to be made with the self-belief of learners. Expectations are thus inevitably linked to the leadership of the school as a whole, and to the culture of the communities which it serves.

Processes for learners' social needs: a case study

Removing barriers to learning

Teachers at an East Midlands primary school wanted to find ways to improve the learning of lower attaining pupils, so they asked the children themselves. Their answers, along with the findings from classroom observations by researchers, were used to create a more positive learning environment for all.

The school focused on 12 low-attaining children with special educational needs over a half-term. Pupils were asked questions such as:

- What helps you learn in English?
- What helps you learn in maths?
- What makes it difficult for you to learn?
- Is there anything the teachers or other children can do to make it easier for you to learn?

The most significant findings were that:

- most pupils believed they could only work with the support of adults, especially in English;
- more thought needed to be given to feedback and praise;
- there were only limited opportunities for independent work.

The school acted on these findings. Opportunities for more individual, and more independent, work were provided. Teachers continued to praise pupils for their effort but also reinforced the particular things they had done well, and indicated next steps.

The school built opportunities for greater independence into lesson planning and designed more activities which would enable children to experience success. For example in maths, simpler individual exercises were designed and pairs of pupils were sent to do an activity together without help from an adult. Teachers also began to focus on constructive feedback as well as straightforward praise. For example: 'That's great, you've got the first sound of every word right.' The researchers also talked with support staff about the importance of both making positive comments to the children and prompting the children without giving them answers. On top of all that, pupils saw their comments being acted upon.

TLRP projects (Ainscow et al.. 2006, Howes, 2009) found that the development of inclusive practices requires those within a school to focus collaboratively on how to remove barriers experienced by excluded learners. Becoming more inclusive involves being ready to experiment with new practices which can meet specific personalised needs.

Inclusion: By receiving constructive feedback and opportunities, children with special needs and lower attainers were enabled to develop both confidence and skills.

For more information on the two TLRP projects, see **tlrp.org/proj/phase1/phase1asept.html,** or consult Ainscow, Booth and Dyson (2006). Also view **tlrp.org/proj/smbdavies.html,** or consult: Howes Davies and Fox (2009). The case study is drawn from: Walters, McParland and Lichfield (2008).

3. CLASSROOM PROCESSES

3.1 Processes for learner's social needs

Does the educational experience build on social relationships, cultural understandings and learner identities?	**Personalisation:** does the curriculum resonate with the social and cultural needs of diverse learners and provide appropriate elements of choice?	**Relationships:** are teacher–pupil relationships nurtured as the foundation of good behaviour, mutual wellbeing and high standards?	**Inclusion:** are all learners treated respectfully and fairly in both formal and informal interaction?

Once, teachers aimed to fill the 'empty vessel' of each child's mind. Later, the activity of the pupil in 'making sense' of new knowledge became recognised. In both cases, there was little consideration of social circumstances and relationships.

Now, the enduring role of culture and social processes are better recognised. The ways in which knowledge is understood are cultural, and the processes through which pupils engage with learning are influenced by peer and teacher relationships within the school and by family, community and media beyond. Further, young people are engaged not only in learning specific knowledge and skills, but in a process of personal development. They develop an identity within their network of social relationships in family, school and community. This is not easy, and provision for Personalisation, good relationships and inclusive participation are likely to be greatly appreciated by children and young people.

Curriculum: Personalisation

There has been much discussion in England about the meaning of 'personalised learning' (see Chapter 10). The Chief Inspector explained: 'Personalising learning means, in practical terms, focusing in a more structured way on each child's learning in order to enhance progress, achievement and participation' (Teaching and Learning in 2000 Review Group, 2006, p. 2, Reading 10.7). The Group recommendation was for more responsiveness from teachers, including use of assessment for learning, pupil consultation, learning how to learn and new technologies.

This is not, then, a throwback to 'child-centredness' in the sense of following pupil interests for their own sake. Rather, it proposes customisation of curriculum entitlements so that learners from diverse backgrounds and capabilities are better able to engage with them appropriately. Personalisation thus implies elements of choice. However, for both manageability and effectiveness, many of these choices are likely to be structured around common issues which arise in tackling learning difficulties or extending understanding. This requires expert judgement.

Pedagogy: Relationships

'Good relationships' between the teacher and class are at the heart of pedagogic effectiveness – and every teacher knows this. But what does it really mean? A good relationship is founded on mutual respect and acceptance of ways of getting on together – described technically as a 'working consensus' (Pollard, 1985; Chapter 6, Reading 6.3). This embraces taken-for-granted rules about acceptable behaviour and understandings about how infringements will be dealt with. The teacher leads in establishing such rules, but must be mindful of pupil interests and act fairly and consistently. The understandings which result are the basis of the moral order of the classroom and the foundation of good behaviour. Expectations for standards of work then follow. As successes are achieved, a sense of fulfilment and wellbeing is shared, and a positive classroom climate is created. This climate has to be nurtured and sustained over time.

Assessment: Inclusion

Every child certainly does matter, and ensuring that no one is 'left behind' is not easy (see Chapter 15). Children with special educational needs within mainstream classes require particular attention to ensure that potential barriers to their learning are removed as far as possible. In the case of a physical disability this may require a practical form of provision. Inclusion is more complex for children who have some form of learning difficulty. Careful and sensitive diagnostic work is necessary.

An enduring problem for education systems is that some groups of pupils tend to underperform. The strongest pattern is that of social class but other factors such as ethnicity and gender are important too. TLRP's inclusion projects showed how teacher expectations about capabilities influence learners – sometimes adversely (Ainscow et al. 2006). Engaging positively is thus likely to be very helpful (Howes et al., 2009).

Processes for learners' emotional needs: a case study

Becoming an individual

Hazel had a vivid imagination and considerable artistic skills. When she started primary school, she was also very determined and somewhat egocentric. Her school learning in Reception and Year 1 was disappointing and she tended to reject the curriculum tasks offered by her teachers in favour of the richness and independence of her own imaginative world. For Hazel, school offered little that was meaningful.

In Year 2 there were three important developments. First, Hazel was taught by a teacher who really worked to develop a close relationship. The teacher described the result as 'like opening Pandora's Box'. Second, Hazel began to be aware of her younger sister's progress. Affection and support from parents was now mixed with sibling rivalry, and this focused Hazel's attention on learning to read. Third, Hazel's parents worked closely with her teacher. They read to her, supported her attempts to read and talked to her about her approach to books.

After one bath-time chat about what to do if 'stuck' on a word, Hazel finally began to believe in herself. Her father said, 'Well, you're good at teaching yourself … You're the one that's learning and picking these things up.' Tucked up in bed and with books around her, she found that it was true. She could work things out, and, bit by bit, she began to read. Moving from concern and support, her parents and teacher then had to manage her pride and enthusiasm.

Hazel was one of a group of children whose learning was tracked by TLRP researchers from reception through their entire school careers. The researchers sought to understand the social influences on the children as they learned and developed as individuals.

For Hazel, there was a supplementary discovery – that she could express her imagination through writing. This gave her a medium for success within the core curriculum, and in this respect, the curriculum and the person began to connect. Hazel's learning needs fascinated many of her successive teachers and, when engaged, Hazel was able to realise much of her potential. Sadly, there were no similar developments in mathematics; and she perceived formal testing of performance as 'something done to her'.

In primary school, Hazel formed a strong friendship with Harriet. They shared similar perspectives, independence and humour. By age 11, their culture was distinct, their self-confidence had developed and their individual identities were assured as they moved into secondary education.

Factors such as the school's curriculum plans, Hazel's national test results, her teachers' subject knowledge and pedagogic skill, Ofsted findings and the market position of the school were all relevant to this story. But they are wholly inadequate as a way of understanding what was going on as Hazel learned and developed as a person. In her early twenties, Hazel studied and worked as an artist.

Relevance: As a young child, Hazel was unable to engage with the curriculum until she found ways of expressing herself and succeeding in school terms.

A TLRP **Research Briefing** summarising the implications of the Identity and Learning Programme is at: **tlrp. org/pub/documents/Pollard_RB_23_FINAL.pdf**. For Hazel's story in particular, consult: Pollard with Filer (1997).

3. CLASSROOM PROCESSES

3.2 Processes for learners' emotional needs

Does the educational experience take due account of learner views, feelings and characteristics?	**Relevance**: is the curriculum presented in ways which are meaningful to learners and so that it can excite their imagination?	**Engagement**: do our teaching strategies, classroom organisation and consultation enable learners to actively participate in and enjoy their learning?	**Authenticity**: do learners recognise routine processes of assessment and feedback as being of personal value?

We all, at any age, value our dignity and appreciate it when our individuality is recognised. And we also, as part of our personal development, have to learn to appreciate the needs of others. Goleman (1996) called this 'emotional intelligence' – combining social empathy and skills with personal awareness and capacity to manage one's own feelings. Schools have always worked hard to support such development through curricular provision such as PSHE, drama and the arts.

Feelings about learning itself will directly affect outcomes. Pupils are expert at detecting teacher mood, respect and interest, and research demonstrates the importance of providing a consistent, positive classroom climate. Confidence to tackle new learning challenges is helped by interesting curricula, engaging activities and meaningful feedback. Pitching such learning experiences appropriately is crucial too, with anxiety arising if they are too challenging, and boredom if deemed too easy, repetitive or irrelevant. Such feelings are felt individually but are almost always strongly influenced by peer culture. John Holt's classic book, *How Children Fail* (1964), argued that underperformance is linked to such fear of failure.

Curriculum: Relevance

School inspectors got this right when they wrote: 'The curriculum should be seen by pupils to meet their present and prospective needs. What is taught and learned should be worth learning in that it: improves pupils' grasp of the subject matter; increases their understanding of themselves and the world in which they are growing up; raises their confidence and competence in controlling events and coping with widening expectations; and progressively equips them with the knowledge and skills needed in adult working life' (Her Majesty's Inspectors, 1985, p. 45, Reading 10.1).

In the contemporary world, we have even more diverse and rapidly changing societies. Inequality and underperformance remain intractable for many, so the challenge for schools to offer relevant curricula is very considerable. National frameworks should provide for local adaption, and teachers' knowledge of their learners and communities is vital.

Pedagogy: Engagement

TLRP research on pupil consultation (e.g. Rudduck and McIntyre, 2007, Reading 1.3) and learner identities (e.g. Pollard and Filer, 2007, Reading 1.2) showed that, if pupils feel that they matter in school and are respected, then they feel more positive about themselves as learners. They can understand and manage their own progress better, and feel more included. The underlying driver here is termed 'agency' – the opportunity for self-directed action and fulfilment.

Young people become more engaged if their perspectives, concerns and experiences are taken seriously. The projects found that pupil contributions were invariably practical and constructive – and were thus also beneficial to teachers. Such feedback supported more open, collaborative and communicative relationships and thus had the potential to transform pedagogic strategies and enhance learning outcomes.

Assessment: Authenticity

Traditional assessments measure what a student can recall or do in the formal context of testing. By comparison, authentic assessment puts the emphasis on the meaningful application in *real-life situations* (Wiggins, 1989). Rather than being required to simply demonstrate performance for an artificial purpose, the learner has the opportunity to apply their growing knowledge and capability to genuine activity. The task, and feedback on it, is thus more personally meaningful. Authentic assessment is likely to affirm those who have the deeper levels of skill and understanding which are needed for application.

Overcoming the artificiality of school so that new knowledge can be grounded in the 'real world' is not easy. Project work is a long-standing strategy and new technologies provide wonderful resources. There are many contemporary initiatives to promote 'real-world learning', primarily because transfer of school learning consistently proves to be difficult.

Processes for learners' cognitive needs: a case study

Time to talk

The slogan 'it's good to talk' has become a cliché, but that's because it's true. Projects such as TLRP's SPRinG and Cambridge's Thinking Together have demonstrated how effective pupil dialogue and discussion can boost children's attainment, enthusiasm and self-efficacy.

Examples published by Thinking Together show how teachers who are successful in teaching children to collaborate effectively model the kind of talk that is useful in discussion.

Here, a Key Stage 3 teacher introduces a maths activity to the whole class. The maths activity uses software called 'Function Machine', in which the children are asked to consider what operation might have been done to one number in order to end up with another. As well as deciding on the operation, the groups have to come up with a strategy for discovering it and for testing their ideas.

> Teacher: OK. I'm going to put a number in …
> Louis: One thousand?
> Teacher: OK, Louis immediately said one thousand – is that a good number to put in?
> Child: No
> Teacher: You're shaking your head – but why do you think it is not? … Shall we come back to you? You've got an idea but you can't explain it?
> OK, Louis had one thousand. Anybody think 'yes' or 'no' to that idea? … David.
> David: Start off with an easier number.
> Teacher: Start off with an easier number. By an easier number what kind of number do you mean?
> David: Um. Something like – lower – five.
> Teacher: Fine. A smaller number – a lower number – yes. Louis can you see that point of view?
> Louis: Yes
> Teacher: If we put in a thousand we could end up with a huge number. If we put in five do you think it will be easier to work out what the machine has done?
> Class: Yes
> Teacher: Everyone agree? OK, so I'm going to type in five to start with …

In this discussion the ground rules for talk are embedded in the teacher's demonstration of the activity. The language she uses is full of indicator words, such as 'what', 'how', 'if' and 'why' as she leads them through a line of reasoning. She accepts and discusses the challenges made by David and the class to Louis' suggestion, whilst respecting his contribution in initiating the discussion.

She demonstrates how to consider the validity of alternative suggestions, at the same time as seeking clarification. She invites others to speak so that as many people as possible feel able to join in the discussion. Finally she ensures that an agreement is sought and reached. In this way, the teacher is demonstrating effective collaboration. The children are engaged in the discussion, motivated to participate and are real partners in the learning.

Dialogue: The teacher draws pupils into decision-making about an investigative strategy, respecting their ideas but leading their reasoning.

This case study is adapted with permission from Dawes and Sams (2004). See also TLRP's Commentary, *Assessment in Schools: Fit for Purpose* on **tlrp.org** or **reflectiveteaching.co.uk**

3. CLASSROOM PROCESSES

3.3 Processes for learners' cognitive needs

Does the educational experience match the learner's cognitive needs and provide appropriate challenge?	**Differentiation**: are curriculum tasks and activities structured appropriately to match the intellectual needs of learners?	**Dialogue**: does teacher–learner talk scaffold understanding to build on existing knowledge and to strengthen dispositions to learn?	**Feeding back**: is there a routine flow of constructive, specific, diagnostic feedback from teacher to learners?

Cognition refers to the mental processes involved in gaining knowledge and understanding. These include thinking, knowing, remembering, judging and problem solving. These high-level functions of the brain draw on capabilities such as language and perception. The future promise of neuroscience is considerable (see Howard-Jones, 2007), but social and cultural factors remain crucial in classroom teaching and learning processes.

The brilliance of Vygotsky's psychology derives from his insight in relating cognitive, social and cultural factors together. So we meet each pupil's cognitive needs through social processes of teaching and learning, and the understanding that is developed relates to culturally embedded knowledge. Crucially, the teacher *mediates* between knowledge and learner. A teacher's explanation, questions, discussion, or structured task, provides type of 'scaffolding' it combines challenge and support so that the learner is encouraged to extend their understanding.

Curriculum: Differentiation

Curriculum goals must be converted to tasks and activities and then presented to learners in ways to which they can relate. Too difficult, and frustration often follows; too easy, and boredom may result. The goal is to match the learner and the task so that he or she feels appropriately challenged. Pleasure from success then reinforces learning. But since all learners are different, there is considerable skill in achieving a differentiated match (see Chapter 10).

Three basic strategies can be used to achieve this:

- *vary the task*: so slightly different tasks are set to meet the needs of particular individuals or groups;
- *vary the expected outcomes*: so pupil performance would be judged using specific criteria;
- *vary the level of support*: so a classroom assistant might support some children, whilst others would work alone.

Pedagogy: Dialogue

'Whole-class interactive teaching' describes structured, teacher-controlled but pupil-active methods. Questioning in challenging, engaging and respectful ways is an important way in which pupil understanding can be extended.

Dialogic teaching takes this further to engage the teacher and learner together and to explicitly use language as a tool for learning (Mercer and Littleton, 2007, Reading 11.6). Research suggests that such responsive scaffolding of learning supports longer-term commitment to learning. Alexander (2008, Reading 12.3) identified five characteristics:

- *collective*: teachers and pupils address learning tasks together;
- *reciprocal*: teachers and pupils listen to each other, share ideas and consider alternative viewpoints;
- *supportive*: pupils articulate their ideas freely and confidently;
- *cumulative*: teachers and pupils build on each other's ideas;
- *purposeful*: teachers plan and steer classroom talk in relation to educational goals.

Assessment: Feedback

Providing appropriate feedback to learners has one of the largest measurable effects of any teaching strategy (Hattie, 2009, Reading 4.6; Spendlove, 2009, Reading 13.3). This fact underlies 'assessment for learning' (Black and Wiliam, 1998) which has now been taken up in many school systems across the world. Such formative assessment is an integral part of pedagogy and is designed to help learners grow their capacity to manage their own learning. The TLRP project on *Learning How to Learn* (James et al., 2007, Reading 2.8) showed that the most effective teachers have frameworks of subject and developmental understanding which enable them to respond constructively to pupils' attempts to learn. Such diagnostic and knowledgeable flexibility is essential (see Chapter 13).

Outcomes for continuing improvement in learning: a case study

A cultural revolution in teaching and learning

Mulberry school was formed from the ashes of two secondary closures. Anna, the new headteacher, believed that cultural rebuilding required a concerted move from a teaching-centred view to a learning-centred view. For the Senior Leadership Team (SLT) it was an opportunity to develop a process of reflection on the very process of learning itself – learning how to learn.

When Mulberry joined TLRP's Learning How to Learn Project (LHTL), the most talented teachers in the 1,100-pupil school were already providing Inset sessions for their colleagues, based on their subject expertise. This was complemented by departmental reviews, lesson observations, self-evaluation interviews with staff about lessons observed, and interviews with young people who had taken part in that lesson.

For the SLT, promoting LHTL would 'put learners in the driving seat'. Self- and peer-assessment would be key strategies, and setting learning objectives and understanding criteria would promote learning autonomy. Staff would therefore be able to move beyond routine 'delivery' of the curriculum to more self-aware and reflective teaching.

Creating a 'learning how to learn' mindset in pupils was dependent on teacher feedback, clearly focused on helping pupils to develop their understanding, to think more critically about their learning, and to self-evaluate. Guidelines for staff explained the characteristics of effective feedback.

Mulberry students were taken seriously from the outset. They evaluated lessons through an interactive pupil questionnaire on the school intranet. Examples of questions were: Does your teacher try to find out what you already know before you're starting a new topic? Does your teacher give the class opportunity to make choice and decisions about the work you're doing?

The school also instituted 'lesson study' in which two teachers plan a lesson together with a specific focus in mind (see Chapter 10). In one example, three pupils, chosen across a range of ability or approaches to learning, were observed. Later the teachers talked through what went well and what could be refined, and the lesson was repeated with another group.

For Anna, the goal was to truly become a learning organisation:

> 'A learning organisation would be open to change and develop what it was doing, enthusiastic about reflecting on what it's actually doing and learning about what other people are doing. It would be outward looking to both … academic research and also actual practice in other schools and want to impart [to] the whole educational community. A positive and confident place.'

Asked whether this truly described Mulberry, she replied: 'I'd say we're well on the way.'

Reflection: The school provided both formal and informal structures and processes to help teachers and children think about their learning.

For more information on TLRP's *Learning How to Learn* project, see the **Research Briefing** at p. 356 and **tlrp.org/proj/phase11/phase2f.html**. Two books for teachers are available: James et al. (2007) and James et al. (2006). See also Reading 2.8.

4. LEARNING OUTCOMES

4.1 Outcomes for continuing improvement in learning

Does the educational experience lead to *development* in knowledge, concepts, skills and attitudes?	Progression: does the curriculum-as-delivered provide an appropriate sequence and depth of learning experiences?	Reflection: is our classroom practice based on incremental, evidence-informed and collaborative improvement strategies?	Development: does formative feedback and support enable learners to achieve personal learning goals?

Education is always, in a sense, about the tension between 'what is' and 'what might be'. The expert teacher supports learners in moving forward to higher and higher levels of attainment.

Ensuring progression in the educational experiences provided for pupils is therefore vital. Only through new challenges can they deepen and broaden their knowledge. However, the ultimate educational goal is to support the development of self-motivated and resilient learners who are not only knowledgeable but capable of taking control of their own learning. Through encouragement to achieve personal learning goals at school, we sow the seeds of commitment to lifelong learning.

Reflective processes provide ways of marrying such ambitions, of reconciling what is and what might be. They enable teachers to monitor their own performance, both reflexively and in collaboration with others, and thus to stimulate their own continuing professional development.

Curriculum: Progression

Teaching which consistently achieves cumulative progression for learners requires high levels of subject knowledge, three components of which were identified by Shulman (1986, Reading 9.7; see Chapter 9).

'Content knowledge' is of great importance, because teachers in full command of the raw material of their subject are better able to guide, support and extend the learning of their pupils.

However, it is essential that teachers understand how to use content knowledge in their teaching. Through 'pedagogic content knowledge' expert teachers connect the subject to the learner. The teacher understands the best way of explaining key points, of framing particular tasks, of using examples for their subject. One TLRP project studied the most effective ways of teaching secondary science (Millar et al., 2006). Another investigated 'threshold concepts' (Land et al., 2006).

The third and final form of subject expertise is 'curricular knowledge'. This concerns understanding the way subject material is ordered, structured and assessed by national requirements, institutional policies or other circumstances.

Pedagogy: Reflection

Reflective practice is based on open-minded enquiry and a willingness to use evidence to challenge one's own provision (see Chapter 3). This might be based on external evidence of school or pupil performance, on reading research findings, on small-scale personal enquiries or observations, on discussions or collaborative activities with colleagues. There are many possibilities but, in all cases, evidence is used to generate reappraisal. In this way, taken-for-granted thinking is challenged and professional judgement is refined (see Heilbronn, 2010, Reading 3.6).

Reflective enquiry may be focused on particular problems or issues and is best carried out in systematic ways and for specific purposes. Understanding then becomes embedded in teacher expertise and enables decision-making at other times.

Assessment: Development

Physical, cognitive, social and emotional development all influence and are influenced by educational experiences. This, we know, is an enduring process (see for instance, Blyth, 1984). Resilient and resourceful learners develop when teaching combines appropriate challenge and support – 'building learning power', as Claxton puts it (2002; see Reading 2.9).

Assessment for Learning (Chapter 13) promotes pupil self-assessment so that learners can reflect on where they are, where they need to go next and how to get there (Assessment Reform Group, 2002, Reading 13.2). This requires an understanding of desired outcomes and of appropriate processes of learning, as well as the opportunity and commitment to act on such knowledge. Such self-regulated approaches to learning can be nurtured by encouraging students to set personal learning goals and by providing supportive feedback.

Outcomes for certification and the lifecourse: a case study

'Here's the keys, you're free now'

Tony Wilf was in his fifties, adjusting to the death of his wife, and had two young teenagers still at home. He wanted to look after them properly, and thought it would be nice to make home-made fish and chips.

'I couldn't remember how to do batter so I asked one of the old ladies next door, and she gave me this book,' he told researchers. 'But I could not read.' Tony ended up going to the chip shop because he felt too humiliated to ask the neighbour, or his children, to read the recipe out to him.

Tony had been unfortunate in his schooling. 'I was told time and time again by teachers, "you're thick, you don't understand". If somebody had said, "right, what's the problem?"… that would have been fine.'

Tony had worked as an unskilled labourer for most of his life, and enjoyed learning from the older craftsmen, but he knew his literacy problems had stopped him from advancing.

It was 40 years after leaving school that Tony was finally diagnosed with dyslexia. In fact, this came about because he was trying to help his daughter, Clare, with her own literacy.

Clare had trouble with her handwriting, so Tony decided to get a home computer to print out her work. 'So I went to "Computers for the Terrified". And it worked. I got into it, I really enjoyed that, and then something came up about "insert so and so after the third paragraph" and I thought, "what's a paragraph?" … so that's why I started coming back to doing the English …'

Tony's first English class didn't work out because he and the tutor got into arguments about his use of block capitals to write letters. His school experiences had left him unable to deal with not being listened to. Fortunately he tried again, and this time the tutor dealt with students as individuals. The use of coloured overlays designed for dyslexics led to a big improvement in his reading. Apart from improving his basic skills, the courses provided a focus for his life: 'what I like about it, you know, everybody works as a group; nobody takes the Mickey out of anybody'.

Tony became interested in local history and started writing. 'It's as though I've been locked away for years and somebody's said, "well here you go, here's the keys, you're free now",' he said.

Empowerment: Supportive adult education opened new horizons for Tony, releasing his innate talents and interests.

Tony's case is adapted from Hodkinson et al. (2007). It is available, with much more, from **tlrp.org/proj/phase111/biesta.htm**. An accessible book of the project is: Biesta, Field, Goodson, Hodkinson and Macleod (2010). A comprehensive case for lifelong learning has been made by Schuller and Watson (2009).

Does the educational experience equip learners for adult and working life, and for an unknown future?	Effectiveness: are there improvements in standards, in both basic skills and other areas of curricular attainment, to satisfy society's educational goals?	Empowerment: is our pedagogic repertoire successful in enhancing wellbeing, learning disposition, capabilities and agency?	Consequence: do assessment outcomes lead towards recognised qualifications and a confident sense of personal identity?

What outcomes do we want from education?

We certainly need people who can contribute effectively in economic terms within the labour market. We also need citizens with social and global awareness in response to growing cultural diversity and the ecological challenge. We need those who will become good parents and contribute to their communities and civil society. And then there is the need for future technologists … and the arts ... and so on, and so on. A review of the National Curriculum in Engand proposed an over-riding set of economic, social, cultural, personal and environmental goals (DfE, 2011).

Whilst there is relative continuity in general priorities, specific needs and circumstances do change over time. An enduring priority is that learners should have self-confidence and a positive learning disposition. This relates to empowerment and 'agency' – the intrinsic, personal capacity to adapt to circumstances throughout the lifecourse.

Examinations are the traditional way of certifying capabilities in relation to summative attainment in mainstream school subjects. However, can innovative forms of assessment, such as portfolios, represent broader, developmental achievements.

Curriculum: Effectiveness

School performance is a major public issue and will always be a concern of parents, governors, local authorities, media and politicians (see Chapter 14). The quality of teaching is the single most important factor in realising pupil potential, a fact that is now internationally recognised (OECD, 2005; Hattie, 2009). And the moral commitment of teachers to learners also calls for active monitoring of outcomes. Reviews of performance thus provide a valuable focus for systematic reflective and collaborative enquiry.

Inspection of schools is managed in different ways in each nation of the UK, but there appears to be an increasing focus on the quality of teaching and learning itself and, of course, on pupil outcomes. Significantly, the professional judgement of inspectors has the potential to tackle issues which numeric data cannot reach. For monitoring the performance of school systems internationally performance in key subject areas is sampled, as is done in the OECD's PISA study.

Pedagogy: Empowerment

The first of TLRP's ten principles states that: 'Learning should aim to help people to develop the intellectual, personal and social resources that will enable them to participate as active citizens and workers and to flourish as individuals in a diverse and changing society' (see Chapter 4). So empowerment is the very stuff of 'education' in its broadest sense. But what does this mean in the classroom?

Dweck (2000, Reading 2.6) contrasted pupils with a 'mastery' orientation from those who develop 'learned helplessness'. Experiences of classroom life contribute to such self-beliefs. By creating opportunities for learners to take independent and successful action, teachers support the development of self-confidence and positive learning dispositions.

Assessment: Consequence

In taking stock of their work as a whole, teachers need to consider whether or not they have been able to enrich the lives of the learners in their care and increased learners' life-chances (see Chapter 15).

Are they better able to acquire the qualifications they will one day need to enter the labour market? We need to be sure that new knowledge, understanding and skills are secure. Indeed, it is crucial, that all students acquire good basic skills before they leave school. But have they also developed self-confidence and a strong sense of personal identity?

5 Using the conceptual framework

The conceptual framework represents the issues that teachers face on a day-to-day basis. It is offered as a tool to support professional reflection and deepen expertise. It is a reference point for many of the major questions that must be faced when practical classroom judgements are made.

The framework is an explicit tool for reflecting on theory and practice, as recommended by Timperley et al. in a wide-ranging international review of continuing professional development for teachers (2007, Reading 16.6).

In the 'Deepening Expertise' section of **reflectiveteaching.co.uk**, research and practice underlying each concept is explored further drawing on the work of UK specialists. Please just 'click through' the cell in which you are interested.

Here are some ways in which the framework has been used:

Problem solving during initial training

Student teachers were introduced to the conceptual framework and 'expert questions' before going into schools – but at that stage, it all seemed a bit complicated. During their time in school, they were asked to identify their 'biggest challenge' and to relate it to the framework in discussion with a mentor. The *issues* underlying their *problems* became clearer. When back at college, these experiences were shared in group discussions with other students.

> 'Well, I was in survival mode at school really, but I did the exercise and began to see how the way the children were responding to me related to the curriculum I was providing and to the feedback I was giving them. Once I'd begun to realise how everything fits together, things started to drop into place. The framework is a good device for problem-solving.' (Student Teacher)

Reflecting on professional commitment

Sally Brown had been teaching very successfully for 12 years in primary schools, and had been an advanced skills teacher for several years. What was it that kept her in the classroom?

> 'I've been wondering about applying for management jobs for ages, but the framework showed me why I really prefer to be a hands-on teacher. I enjoy my classroom work immensely but I've found it hard to explain exactly what I do to other people, and even to myself! Now I feel I *can* explain. The framework gives a good overview of why teaching is difficult, but also why it is fascinating!' (Classroom Teacher)

Analysing teaching and learning

To start a discussion about effective teaching at a Special School, each member of staff was asked to write about a successful lesson, describing and analysing what made it work.

Having shared their stories, the staff considered their practice in the light of the conceptual framework. How far were the concepts and questions reflected in narratives of experience? What changes would there have been if certain questions had been asked before planning the lesson?

'The framework offers a way of looking at our practice with a discerning eye, and to really discuss what we're doing. It reveals gaps, and then we collectively develop solutions.' (Deputy Head)

Supporting curriculum development

A primary school redeveloped its approach to foundation subjects to make them more relevant and accessible to the children. The staff team used the conceptual framework to assess and evaluate the content, approach and effectiveness of their ideas.

'I feel the concepts in the framework reflect the important elements of a 21st century school curriculum. For me it asks the questions of why and how we are teaching rather than what – and it offers a structure to think about our provision. Pedagogy, it seems, has for some years not been as important a discussion topic as SATs and results, but I think that effective pedagogy needs to be our principal concern.' (Headteacher)

Reflective activity 16.2

Aim To explore using the conceptual framework to reflect on professional expertise.

Evidence and reflection Consider each of the applications of the framework illustrated above. Do these approaches resonate with you – for problem solving, reviewing professionalism, analysing practice or curriculum development?

Select one of them and identify a particular issue which has challenged you. Does the framework help in reviewing this?

Extension Use the framework when discussing a significant shared issue with a group of colleagues. Does it prevoke new lines of discussion?

Conclusion

This chapter has presented a conceptual framework which holistically represents the major dimensions of teacher expertise. The framework is organised around nine enduring issues associated with educational aims, learning contexts, classroom processes and learning outcomes. Each issue is explored in relation to curriculum, pedagogy and assessment. The chapter then provides both case study illustrations and a brief introduction to some of the research which underpins each concept. Links are also made back to chapters within the book.

The conceptual framework is offered as a contribution to the development of a shared professional language. It is a support for professional thinking and discussion together.

However, the framework also *celebrates* teacher expertise, for the truth is that, whilst it may seem complex, teachers work and succeed within this terrain all the time. Indeed, during a career, a great deal of professional fulfilment is derived from exploring the issues which the framework highlights.

The contemporary challenge is to identify this expertise more explicitly and to find ways of representing it more clearly.

If this can be done, the profession may become more self-confident as well as more effective. The public may become even more appreciative of the skills, knowledge, understanding and moral commitment which good teachers embody.

Key readings

 Many of the Key Readings suggested for Chapters 3 on reflective practice are very relevant for this chapter, including, for example, Schön (Reading 3.2) and Stenhouse (Reading 3.3).

 Key Readings for Chapter 4, on the principles of effective teaching and learning, are also highly pertinent to the enduring issues which have been identified. For example, see OECD (Reading 4.4) or Hattie (Reading 4.6).

 On continuing professional development through a career, the best summary of effective practice is Timperley et al.'s (2007) (Reading 16.6).

We offer supplementary suggestions on the specific issue of expertise itself. For a philosophical overview of the nature of expertise, see:

Winch, C. (2012) *Dimensions of Expertise: A Conceptual Exploration of Vocational Knowledge*. London: Continuum.

Developmental accounts of how expertise evolves through the interaction of practice and analysis are provided by:

Eraut, M. (1994) *Developing Professional Knowledge and Competence.* London: Routledge.

Erisson, K. A., Charness, N., Feltovich, P. and Hoffman, R. R. eds. (2006) *The Cambridge Handbook of Expertise and Expert Performance.* Cambridge: Cambridge University Press.

Flook, J., Ryan, M. and Hawkins, L. (2010) *Professional Expertise: Practice, Theory and Education for Working in Uncertainty.* London: Whiting and Birch.

Loughran, J. (2010) *What Expert Teachers Do: Enhancing Professional Knowledge for Classroom Practice.* London: Routledge.

Shulman, L. S. (2004) *The Wisdom of Practice – Essays on Teaching, Learning and Learning to Teach.* San Francisco: Jossey Bass.

Two books which analyse and apply teacher expertise in primary school contexts are:

Eaude, T. (2012) *How Do Expert Primary Classteachers Really Work? A Critical Guide for Teachers, Headteachers and Teacher Educators.* Northwich: Critical Publishing. (Reading 16.3)

Sangster, M. (2012) *Developing Teacher Expertise: Exploring Key Issues in Primary Pratice.* London: Bloomsbury Academic.

In secondary education, expertise is applied in the context of particular subjects. There are many guides, but for more specific treatment, see:

Goodwyn, A. *The Expert Teacher of English.* London: Routledge.

Li, Y. and Kaiser, G. (2010) *Expertise in Mathematics Instruction.* London: Springer.

Tsui, A. (2003) *Understanding Expertise in Teaching: Case Studies of Second Language Teachers.* Cambridge: Cambridge University Press.

This is an exceptional chapter which integrates the 'expert questions' posed throughout the book into an overarching conceptual framework. To extend this journey, the internet offers many sources for deepening expertise further.

The Deepening Expertise section of reflectiveteaching.co.uk is being developed to provide links to websites which extend understanding and application of particular concepts.

For an excellent guide to the use of the internet for education, see:

Houghton, E. (ed.) (2012) *Education on the Web: A Tool-kit to Help You Search Effectively for Information on Education.* Slough: NFER.

Professionalism

How does reflective teaching contribute to society?

17

Introduction

Historically, there is a strong tradition of civic responsibility among teachers in all parts of the UK, and the contribution to public life of socially aware professional educators has been very strong.

Indeed, teaching reflects moral purpose and has significant social consequences. For these reasons, commitments to educational quality and to social justice have been promoted by the UK General Teaching Councils. For example, the GTC NI's Code of Values and Professional Practice states:

> Teachers will, as reflective practitioners, contribute to the review and revision of policies and practices with a view to optimising the opportunities for pupils or addressing identified individual or institutional needs. (GTC NI, 2007, p. 44)

In our discussion of social contexts, Chapter 5, we introduced the idea of social development being based on a dialectical process, as individuals respond to and act within the situations in which they find themselves (Mills, 1959, Reading 5.1). Actions in the present are thus influenced by the past, but they also contribute to the future (see Archer, 1979, Reading 17.1). All teachers, as individuals, are members of society and we hope that reflective teachers will be particularly capable of acting in society to initiate and foster morally and ethically sound developments as 'imaginative professionals' (Power, 2008, Reading 17.5).

TLRP principles

Two principles are of particular relevance to this chapter on professionalism and teachers' role in society:

Effective teaching and learning depends on teacher learning. The need for teachers to learn continuously in order to develop their knowledge and skills, and adapt and develop their roles, especially through classroom inquiry, should be recognised and supported. (Principle 9)

Effective teaching and learning demands consistent policy frameworks with support for teaching and learning as their primary focus. Policies at national, local and institutional levels need to recognise the fundamental importance of teaching and learning. They should be designed to create effective learning environments in which all learners can thrive. (Principle 10)

See Chapter 4

There are four sections in this chapter. The first discusses the establishment of professional associations and moves on to consider forms of 'restricted' and 'extended' professionalism. The relationship between education and society is then addressed, drawing on the theoretical framework referred to above. The third section considers the classroom responsibilities of a socially aware and reflective teacher and discusses the formation of classroom policies. Finally, we focus on the actions that a reflective teacher could take as a citizen in trying to influence democratic processes of decision-making by local, regional and national governments.

The RT website offers resources that will help with these issues.

1 Professions and professionalism

1.1 Professional and union organisations

Some professions have very long histories. For instance, law and medicine have served enduring needs for social order and personal health. However, from the Enlightenment and industrial revolution onwards, many other professional groups emerged as new demands for specialised expertise developed – engineering, accountancy, nursing and teaching were amongst these. Today, our complex modern societies depend on a very wide range of highly organised professions.

The rationale for professions has a strong moral dimension in fostering collaboration to provide valued services to others, but professional groups also often act to promote and defend the interests of their members – just as trade unions do. Indeed, trade unions developed in a similar historic period in response to the employment conditions of the industrial revolution and as a necessary defence of employee interests. 'Unity', as they say, 'is strength' whether you are a respected professional, such as a doctor, or a lowly paid cleaner on the minimum wage.

Because of this appeal to both the public good and members' interests, there is often some tension in the actual practices of both trade unions and professional associations. This is illustrated for contrastive effect in Figure 17.1 below.

	Unionism	Professionalism
Stakeholders	Members	Clients, society
Foci include	Pay and working conditions	Quality of services
	Member interests	Collective improvement

Figure 17.1
Contrasts between unionism and professionalism

The figure simplifies great complexity, for most trade unions and professional associations partially cross-over in terms of their stakeholders and foci. The British Medical Association (BMA) is an example of a very well-established professional association which articulates the values and moral principles of the National Health Service whilst also defending the material interests of its members. The Royal College of Nursing attempts the same but, as with school teaching, lacks some of the status and cultural capital of the BMA.

In Scottish education, the distinction in functions is relatively clear, with the Educational Institute of Scotland (EIS) having defended the employment interests of teachers since its foundation in 1847. On the other hand, the General Teaching Council for Scotland (GTCS) was founded in 1965 to register teachers, maintain professional standards and enhance the quality of teaching on behalf of all stakeholders. Since 2012, GTCS has become fully independent of government. There are, of course, some boundary negotiations between the EIS and GTCS, but the two major teacher organisations are broadly complimentary.

In England, the situation is more complex. There are a number of trade unions and there has been relatively little cooperation between them historically. Where one may focus on working conditions, another may offer radical critiques of government policy and a third may attempt more cross-over into professional concerns. Some have more members from primary, secondary, further or independent sectors; and others cater for the particular circumstances of headteachers. As teacher unions compete for members, contributions to public debates are often fragmented and it is hard for a positive public impression of the profession to form. The establishment of a General Teaching Council for England (1998 to 2011) was not fully endorsed by teacher unions which left it vulnerable to closure. The teaching profession in England thus lacks a coherent, collective voice at present.

In Wales and Northern Ireland, their General Teaching Councils remain financially vulnerable but are strategically of great importance as teaching continues its struggle to establish itself as an esteemed profession. Perhaps a 'Royal College of Teaching' or something comparable will be established in England. If this happens, then reflective teachers with concerns for the quality of public services should, in principle, strongly support it. A collective organisation to regulate and improve teaching quality and to celebrate and promote teacher expertise is necessary in each country. This should complement the workplace concerns of the unions.

1.2 Professionalism

Eric Hoyle (1974) first drew the powerful distinction between 'restricted' and 'extended' professionalism.

- *Restricted professionalism* describes the competence underpinning core effectiveness. Skills and perspectives are derived from immediate classroom experience; and workplace learning occurs gradually, but largely passively. Consideration of teaching methods tends to be private and personal autonomy may be protected. Involvement in professional development is infrequent and each teacher prefers to develop in his or her own way.

- *Extended professionalism* envisages that skills and understanding are developed from the interaction of practical experience and analysis, including theory; there is awareness of social, economic and political contexts which impinge on education; and workplace events are considered in relation to policies and overall educational purposes. Teaching methods are shared with colleagues and reviewed in terms of research-informed principles. High value is placed on professional collaboration and on networking in sectoral or subject associations. Pedagogic repertoire and subject knowledge are kept up to date in active, committed and open-minded ways.

These contrastive models of teacher professionalism still resonate. For example, a review by Menter et al. (2010) for the Scottish Government used the restricted–extended spectrum in summarising distinctions between four conceptions of professionalism (Reading 17.2). This is summarised in Figure 17.2:

Restricted professionalism	Extended professionalism		
The effective teacher	The reflective teacher	The enquiring teacher	The transformative teacher

Figure 17.2
Models of teacher professionalism and practice

Menter and his colleagues suggested that models of the 'effective teacher' have been favoured by many governments for the last 30 years and linked to the establishment of 'standards' to which teachers are expected to conform. National systems of quality control can thus be established. However, whilst these are necessary, they may not be sufficient. Extended professional models are promoted in many teacher education programmes because of their intrinsic support for innovation and improvement in practice. For example, the GTC for Northern Ireland sets competences for 'Teaching: the Reflective Profession' (GTC NI, 2007, Reading 17.3) and Scotland's Code of Professionalism and Conduct (2012) resonates across the spectrum. A related point about the need for expert teachers, and thus for training which combines theory and practice, was made by an international panel reviewing teacher education for the Government of Ireland (Sahlberg et al., 2012, Reading 17.4).

It seems that there is a broad tension here. Many teachers are committed to the concept of 'extended professionalism' and appreciate the trust and esteem which are enjoyed by colleagues in countries such as Finland. But some governments, despite their protestations that teachers are extremely important, are not yet prepared to really support the full development of the profession. There remains, as Onora O'Neill argued in her Reith Lectures (2002), a crisis of trust in those who provide public services. It is clear from international evidence that this will have to change if overall standards of attainment are to improve. In particular, new relational models of accountability are needed, which recognise mutual responsibilities at all levels of the system (see GTC E, 2011, Reading 5.5). Teachers really do matter. Extended professionalism, with its capacity for intelligent innovation, is the foundation of high-quality education in the modern world.

Reflective activity 17.1

Aim. To consider aspirations for our professional development as a teacher.

Evidence and reflection. Read Sally Power's short article on the 'Imaginative Professional' (Reading 17.5) which draws attention to a distinction between 'private troubles' and 'public issues'. To what extent are you able to identify public issues underlying particular challenges in your professional experience? Share and discuss these with colleagues.

Now consider how your personal and professional development might be facilitated, bearing in mind your circumstances. Strategically review, in other words, the possibilities for your future biography in the light of your work context and the period of history you happen to be living through.

Extension. Is there scope for becoming proactive, in seeking to contribute to policies or practices in your school, or in relation to external policies and practices? How might this be taken forward?

2 Education and society

Education has very often been seen as a means of influencing the development of societies. Two major questions have to be faced.

- What should an education system be designed to do?
- What can actually be achieved through education?

We will address these in turn and draw out some implications for reflective teachers.

2.1 What should an education system be designed to do?

The discussion below is structured in terms of five areas in which education has broad social significance (see Chapter 9 for a related discussion of educational aims). These areas of significance are:

- wealth creation
- cultural reproduction
- social justice
- individual rights
- environmental sustainability.

Wealth creation. One national priority for education is to contribute to economic goals. For instance, in the latter part of the industrial revolution in Great Britain, an important part of the argument for the establishment of an elementary school system was that it should provide a workforce which was more skilled and thus more economically productive. The idea became the linchpin of 'human capital' theory in the 1960s (Schultz, 1961) and many new nations, influenced by analyses such as Rostow's *The Stages of Economic Growth* (1962), put scarce resources into their education systems. The economics of education is still a flourishing area of policy and research.

In Britain, the links between education and economic productivity are constantly being drawn by governments, with particular attention to the standard of basic and vocational skills achieved in schools and to the proportion of young people acquiring advanced knowledge and skills in higher education. This aspiration has provided a rationale for education reforms for several decades – in good times and bad. For example, a Secretary of State for Education for England stated:

> Far from difficult economic times being a reason to scale down our ambitions, the economic challenges we face are a reason to accelerate our reform programme. Already China and India are turning out more engineers, more computer scientists and more university graduates than the whole of Europe and America combined. And the success of other nations in harnessing their intellectual capital is a function of their determination to develop world-beating education systems. (Michael Gove, speech to the National College, June 2010)

As this example illustrates, concern for economic competitiveness has been fuelled by international comparisons between pupil achievement in Britain and that in other countries – most notably those in the Pacific Rim (e.g. Reynolds and Farrell, 1996; Oates, 2010). The inference which is often drawn from such work is that British education is deficient in some way. For example, following publication of the Reynolds and Farrell study, 'interactive whole-class teaching' became a top priority in England, for this appeared to be the pedagogy which was contributing to pupil success and educational achievement in countries such as Singapore and Taiwan. Following publication of Oates's report, the National Curriculum was reviewed to 'sequence core knowledge' in the same way as high performing countries. It is very worthwhile to study other countries, and understanding about effective teaching and learning is accumulating globally as TLRP's principles indicate in Chapter 4 (see also Hattie, 2009, Reading 4.6), but the economic imperative sometimes seems to alarm governments and leads to rather simplistic policy borrowing.

Cultural reproduction. Alternatively, there are those who would highlight the 'function' of education in the production and reproduction of a national culture.

Use of an education system for the production of a sense of shared national identity is common in many parts of the world, particularly where states have been established relatively recently or are growing rapidly. For example, in the US through much of the twentieth century, the country was required to 'assimilate' and 'integrate' successive groups of new immigrants into an 'American culture'. The education system was seen as a vital part of the 'melting pot'. Of course, a highly questionable assumption here was that there was a single American culture, but the notion of the existence of a set of 'central values' was important in this period of the development of the US. Pre-existing identities may be diminished by such use of education to develop or assert a national culture, and these costs are usually borne by minority or less powerful groups. The historical case of the education provided in the colonies of the British Empire provides a particularly graphic example of this last point (Mangan, 1993).

Following UK devolution, the unique culture and history of Scotland, Wales and Northern Ireland has been increasingly prominent. For example, the people of Wales preserve an important part of their culture through the teaching of Welsh in their schools, but, at the same time, their education system inducts Welsh children into the culture of the United Kingdom. In the unique position of Northern Ireland, the education system reflects strong historic and cultural links to England, but also looks towards the Republic of Ireland with its own independent traditions. Scotland, with its exceptional educational and political history, is wrestling to settle its position in relation to England, the UK and European Union – with echoes in its national *Curriculum for Excellence*. In England too, debates about the curriculum often touch on the presence or otherwise of iconic cultural elements. This can be traced back to influence of Arnold (1889) who helped to define the classical curriculum that remains influential today. Indeed, study of Shakespeare and key episodes in English history were deemed essential in the initial 1988 construction of the National Curriculum, and they remain prominent.

Schools also have direct connections to the specific communities in which they are located and to the families from which pupils come. This is reflected in unique decisions on curricular priorities and in local adaption of national curricular requirements. Such tailoring of provision is designed to build on and extend existing learner experiences and understandings. These, of course, reflect the culture, language and funds of knowledge of each family and community (see Thomas, 2010, Reading 10.4).

Education thus plays a part in producing and reproducing culture at each of these levels, and schools have a unique role in managing the formative processes where local cultures and national expectations first meet.

Social justice. Contributing to social justice is a third central purpose which is often identified for education systems. This concern influenced the 1944 Education Act as applied to England, Wales and Northern Ireland and also, following disappointment in the divisions of grammar and secondary modern schools, the subsequent expansion of comprehensive schools from 1965. The issue features prominently in the educational goals which are set by many countries in Europe and across the world (for example, see the UN Millennium Development Goal to 'ensure that, by 2015, children everywhere will be able to complete a full course of primary schooling'). One critical point to make is that 'equality of opportunity' and the meritocratic ideal, which often lie behind policies on this issue, are concepts which are vulnerable to rhetoric. There is a significant difference between articulating a concern, and really contributing to change. Paulo Freire, who was internationally recognised for his advocacy of a 'pedagogy of the oppressed' (Freire, 2000), also insisted on this need to face the structural inequalities of wealth, status and power which exist. If such issues are glossed, then the promotion of social justice through education policy is very unlikely to be successful.

A key issue remains the tail of underachievement which tragically affects almost 20 per cent of young people (see Chapter 5, Section 1.3). This phenomenon has been recognised and studied for many years. For example, Rutter and Madge published their classic analysis of 'cycles of disadvantage' in 1976. The Centre for Wider Benefits of Learning has shown how underperformance can be identified in infancy which grows year on year

so that trajectories can be mapped and, sadly, predicted (Feinstein et al., 2008, Reading 1.6). Twenty-five per cent of children from poor backgrounds do not meet expected attainment at the end of primary, compared with just 3 per cent of pupils from affluent circumstances; and 20 per cent of young people do not achieve five good GCSEs. There is no shortage of knowledge about this phenomenon (Cabinet Office, 2011). At the root of such problems is the extent of inequality within UK societies. Wilkinson and Pickett's (2009) brilliant analysis of 'why more equal societies almost always do better' is just the latest research to demonstrate the fundamental influence of cycles of advantage and disadvantage.

The concern for social justice through education can partly be seen as a desire to ensure that there is a legitimated system for fulfilling potential, certifying capabilities and allocating jobs in democratic societies, and thus for facilitating social mobility based on merit. However, we know too, that there are severe limits on the effectiveness of education in eroding structural inequalities.

However, having recognised the structural realities, we should also affirm that education can change lives and that futures cannot be entirely pre-determined. Indeed, learning depends on the quality of talk and interaction far more that on wealth itself – it's just that patterns do tend to emerge. Commitment to social justice is likely to remain very important.

Individual rights. As we saw in Chapter 9, supporting the personal development of pupils is a fundamental educational objective for teachers. In relation to 'education and society', this commitment is underpinned by international understanding about human rights.

Formal conventions on human rights were developed after the tragic experiences of the Second World War, and are thus based on deep and principled understanding of the need for moral and ethical standards (see Council of Europe, 1985, Reading 17.6). They still frame international law and set principles for the behaviour of governments and others in contemporary societies.

A clear exposition of the relationship between social structures and individual opportunities is contained in the Universal Declaration of Human Rights (United Nations, 1948). Article 1 of the Declaration states that:

> All human beings are born free and equal in dignity and rights. They are endowed with reason and conscience.

These rights are to be enjoyed, according to Article 2:

> Without distinction of any kind, such as race, colour, sex, language, religion, political or other opinion, national or social origin, property, birth or other status.

There then follow many articles dealing with rights and fundamental freedoms of movement, thought, religion, assembly, political participation, work, leisure and an adequate standard of living.

The implications for education of these provisions are made explicit in Article 26. It asserts that:

> Education shall be directed to the full development of the human personality and the strengthening of respect for human rights and fundamental freedoms. It shall promote understanding, tolerance and friendship among all nations, racial and religious groups.

Education was expected to have a crucial role in the dissemination of the UN Declaration across the world, for the document was to be 'displayed, read and expanded principally in schools and other educational institutions' in all member states.

Needless to say, the achievement of social justice and individual rights for all citizens remains a noble and appropriate goal. However, it is one which will probably always be with us for, as discussed earlier in this chapter, it is optimistic to think that educational provision alone can overcome structural inequalities in society. Indeed the necessity of adopting a United Nations Convention on the Rights of the Child in 1989 underlines that fact. The general principles of the Convention focus on providing equal treatment, the child's best interests and giving appropriate weight to the views of the child.

The Human Rights Act 1998 is the most significant UK legislation because it incorporates the European Convention on Human Rights into British law. The struggle to establish and maintain human rights may never be entirely overcome, but teachers, through their daily work, have tangible opportunities to make a difference to the lives of their pupils (Osler and Starkey, 2010).

Environmental sustainability. This educational goal does not have the historical record of the other four, and yet appears to be crucial for the survival of life as we know it. Global warming develops inexorably and appears to be having significant effects on weather, sea levels, flora and fauna – and thence on food supply, energy policies, health and transport, housing, etc. Although politicians demonstrate concern and have established goals for carbon reduction, large scale and sustained action has not been taken across all dimensions of contemporary societies.

When this happens, it is likely that education will be required to give more prominence to environmental education so that the next generation can be better prepared for the future. This is already happening in some countries. For example, New Zealand expresses its educational vision in terms of 'young people who will seize the opportunities offered by new knowledge and technologies to secure a sustainable social, cultural, economic and environmental future for our country' (New Zealand Ministry of Education, 2012).

Education policies and systems can thus be designed to emphasise economic production, cultural reproduction, social justice and individual rights. In the future, environmental sustainability may also become a high priority. Whilst such goals are not necessarily conflicting, various tensions and dilemmas are often posed. One obvious issue concerns the rights of minority groups to maintain an independent culture and sense of identity within a majority culture. Another is the dilemma between the demands of individual development and those of economic production – or, indeed, of environmental sustainability. We raised such value concerns in Chapter 3 and argued that a reflective teacher should make informed and responsible judgements about them. The ways in which action might follow will be discussed further below.

We now move on to the second question: 'What can actually be achieved through education?'

2.2 What can actually be achieved through education?

There has been a long running debate on this topic. Some people, such as Coleman, Coser and Powell (1966), Jenks et al. (1972) and Bowles and Gintis (1976), have argued that education can make little difference to social development. Although coming to the issue from different theoretical perspectives, they argue that educational processes reflect and reproduce major features of existing society, particularly with regard to distinctions related to social class. The suggestion is that relationships of power, wealth, status and ideology are such that education should be seen as a part of the dominant social system, rather than as an autonomous force within it.

Others, such as Berger and Luckman (1967), may be seen as taking a more idealistic theoretical position. They argue that, since our sense of reality is 'socially constructed' by people as they interact together, there is, therefore, scope for individuals to make an independent impact on the course of future social development. For a tangible example, the consequences of the agreements on Human Rights could be considered within schools and classrooms, as suggested by Osler and Starkey (2010). Thus there *is* potential for education to influence change.

We have here the competing positions of those who believe in social determinism ranged against those who believe in individual voluntarism. As we have already seen, education is very often expected to bring about social and economic developments and it is an area which tends to attract idealists. However, we also have to recognise that the major structural features of societies are extremely resistant to change. What is needed then is a theoretical position which recognises the importance of action and of constraint. Such a position would accept that education has a degree of relative autonomy and would thus legitimate action by individuals to contribute to future social development.

Such a theoretical framework is provided by what we call the dialectic of the individual and society (see Chapter 4 for a full discussion and, in particular, Reading 5.1). As Berlak and Berlak (1981) put it:

> Conscious creative activity is limited by prevailing social arrangements, but human actions and institutional forms are not mere reflections of them. (1981, p. 121)

The clear implication is that people can make their own impact and history but must do so in whatever circumstances they find themselves. If this theoretical framework is adopted, social developments can be seen as the product of processes of struggle and contest between different individuals and groups in society. Such processes are ones in which education must, inevitably, play a part.

Our answer to the question of what education can actually achieve must thus be based on a guarded and realistic optimism – as Power suggests, we need 'the imaginative professional' (2008, Reading 17.5). The dialectical model of the influence of individuals and social structures recognises constraints but asserts that action remains possible. This places a considerable responsibility on a reflective teacher whose professional work is both shaped by, and contributes to, society.

3 Classroom teaching and society

As we have seen, one implication of the adoption of a dialectical model of the relationship between individuals and society is that it highlights the possible consequences, for the 'macro' world of society, of actions, experiences and processes which take place in the 'micro' world of the classroom. In Chapter 3, we raised this issue with the assertion that 'reflective teaching implies an active concern with aims and consequences as well as with technical efficiency' and we must pick up the themes again here. One of the most important issues concerns the influence of a reflective teacher's own value commitments.

In Chapter 3, Section 2.1, we argued that reflective teachers should accept democratically determined decisions but should act both as responsible professionals and as autonomous citizens to contribute to such decision-making processes. The 'imaginative-professional' (Power, 2008, Reading 17.5) is called for.

We also suggested that attitudes of 'open-mindedness' and 'responsibility' are essential attributes. Open-mindedness involves a willingness to consider evidence and argument from whatever source it comes. It is thus the antithesis of closure and of habituated or ideological thinking.

Focusing on English examples, there is a link between these attributes and the provisions of the National Curriculum for personal, social, moral and health education (PSME) and citizenship. Children and young people can thus be encouraged through the formal curriculum to review both their personal agency and the social processes that underpin society. They may also be introduced to global issues. The rationale for this provision relates to the development of children's responsibilities in a liberal democracy.

The development of Human Rights' legislation also reinforced the importance of citizenship. In a recommendation to all member states of the European Union, the Council of Ministers reaffirmed the understandings embodied in the United Nations' Universal Declaration of Human Rights and the European Convention of Human Rights (Council of Europe, 1985, Reading 17.6). The Council suggested that study in schools should 'lead to an understanding of, and sympathy for, the concepts of justice, equality, freedom, peace, dignity, rights and democracy'. Osler and Starkey (2007) claim that the United Nations' Declaration is accepted as a worldwide moral standard and that fundamental freedoms are what make effective political democracies possible. Importantly, since 1998, the principles underlying these declarations have been incorporated into the UK's Human Rights Act. These are seen as being fundamental to democratic societies, and all schools, including those for young children, are encouraged to introduce them to their pupils and to develop their understanding (Osler and Starkey, 2010). Additionally, the adoption of the UN Convention on the Rights of the Child (1989) has considerable significance for practice in schools. Beck (1998) reminds us of the enormous influence of Marshall and Bottomore's 1950 classic, *Citizenship and Social Class* (1992). In particular, they set out a number of freedoms – entitlement to welfare, free education and health – which are seen as the essence of the social element of citizenship.

Yet, the political context of recent years suggests that there are some tensions and contradictions. For instance, in England, at the same time as government rhetoric has praised teacher autonomy and the exercise of judgement, the professional work of teachers has continued to be structured centrally, with strong curricular prescription, inspection procedures and sanctions to ensure *compliance*. Unfortunately, successive governments have not yet understood that teachers should be treated as active, thinking, value-driven professionals with whom partnerships to develop the educational system should be created. At times, indeed, teachers were cast as the core 'problem' (HMCI, 1995). This point is illustrated by evidence from the Primary Assessment Curriculum and Experience (PACE) project, which explored the impact of the introduction of the National Curriculum from as far back as 1988. A major conclusion was that changes in curriculum, assessment and pedagogy were mishandled in many ways because of the lack of sincere attempts to work with teachers (Osborn et al., 2000; Pollard et al., 2000). From 1997, Labour governments maintained similar policies, with the result being that there was considerable professional disengagement, with retirement, recruitment and retention problems. From 2010 the Coalition Government maintained constraint, albeit with its own particular priorities ranging from 'core knowledge' to synthetic phonics and examination changes.

We can thus see that the relationship between teacher and society in England has dramatically changed since the inception of the National Curriculum following the Education Reform Act of 1988. From a position of some public esteem and professional recognition, could the role of the teacher now simply be cast as being to comply with centrally defined frameworks? Perhaps not, but as Simco (2000) argues, there is a danger that acceptance of compliance could eventually lead to the teaching profession retreating from consideration of aims, values and their associated pedagogies. This would be deeply damaging, for engagement with underpinning values remains essential to the moral foundations of teaching as a professional vocation. Nor should we ever forget how policy is actually created, and the influence that remains with teachers. As Bowe and Ball with Gold (1992, Reading 17.7) argue, policy is not formed solely through political struggles and through the construction of legislation and official documents. Its operational reality is formed in the 'context of practice' – where it is often reformulated and 'mediated' through the application of professional judgement (see also Osborn, McNess and Broadfoot, 2000; Chapter 3, Section 2.7).

Scotland, Northern Ireland, Wales and England are developing in increasingly distinctive ways and providing some important contrasts as, indeed, does the Republic of Ireland. The basic truth is that, whatever a government may attempt to determine, there are some contentious issues in education that cannot be avoided. In addition to questions about educational outcomes and standards, these include issues concerning individual dignity, equality and freedom, and the influence of sexism, racism and other forms of discrimination based on social class, age, disability or sexual orientation. These are issues upon which, we would argue, children have rights that socially responsible teachers should not compromise. We take this to constitute a 'bottom line', a value commitment to the fundamental rights of citizens in a democratic society and a necessary underpinning for a reflective professional.

4 Reflective teaching and the democratic process

In our discussion of 'reflective teaching' (see Chapter 3), we suggested that, in addition to professional responsibilities to implement democratically determined decisions, teachers as citizens also have responsibilities to act to influence the nature of such decisions. Teachers have rights and it is perfectly reasonable that they should be active in contributing to the formation of public policy. In terms of Bowe, Ball and Gold's model (1992, Reading 17.7), this is about teacher engagement in the 'context of influence'. The role, as Sachs (2003) suggested, is close to that of the activist, and the methods to be utilised are those which have been well developed in recent years by a variety of pressure groups.

There are seven basic elements of successful pressure group activity:

1 Demystifying the democratic process

2 Identifying decision makers

3 Preparing the case

4 Forming alliances

5 Managing the media

6 Lobbying decision-makers

7 Following up.

An exceptional example of pressure group activity in recent years was the campaign orchestrated by the Cambridge Primary Review in England. This was founded on the discontent of many primary school educators with the degree of state control to which they had been subject. The National Curriculum prescribed *what* to teach and National Strategies told them *how* to teach. Standardised assessment tests (SATs) measured pupil performance whilst the inspection regime held schools to account. The groundswell of concern from phase-based associations was strong. These included NPT (the National Primary Trust), NPH (the National Primary Headteachers), NAPE (the National Association for Primary Education), ASPE (the National Association for the Study of Primary Education), NaPTEC (the National Primary Teacher Education Conference) and CASE (the Campaign for the Advancement of State Education). Professional associations such as the National Union of Teachers (NUT), National Association of Schoolmasters Union of Women Teachers (NASUWT) and Association of Teachers and Lecturers (ATL) were also extremely active, though the most influential in recent years had probably been the National Association of Head Teachers (NAHT).

The Cambridge Primary Review team was able to harvest, shape and represent a lot of this concern (Alexander et al., 2010). They obtained funding from an educational charity, consulted in meetings with practitioners across the country, liaised with stakeholder organisations and commissioned reviews of research evidence on a structured range of contemporary topics. These strategies legitimated the voice which they were then able to articulate. Journalistic help was recruited and press releases were issued on a wide range of issues and with considerable success in securing coverage. Civil servants were consulted on proposals as they emerged and lobbying took place of politicians in both the government and opposition parties. This was just as well as the Labour government fell in May 2010, soon after publication of the review report. The Coalition government appeared to be better disposed to the basic thrust of the review. In particular, it was claimed that the extent of state control of schools and of professional practice was to be rolled back. Whilst this headline outcome was consistent with the proposals of the Review, it is noticeable that other aspects of the education policies of the Coalition showed disregard for the evidence and stakeholder opinion which had been marshalled. Perhaps at this point the Review's proposals were too complex, put too stridently, or just inconsistent with the predilection of Ministers – it is hard to tell.

The review delivered a coherent message about an issue of widespread professional and public concern. It was timely in publishing its findings in the run up to an election, and it made many proposals which were broadly consistent with the stated policies of an incoming government. However, where the politicians wished for other outcomes, the review was quietly bypassed.

This example suggests that there is both luck, judgement and vulnerability in pressure group activity and that, whilst some things may be achieved, compromises often have to be accepted. Even with significant resources and expertise, it also sometimes appears to be an uphill struggle to get decision-makers to simply understand all the dimensions of important educational issues. However, when the dust settled in England, the work of the Cambridge Primary Review was significant – not least by establishing conditions for the National Curriculum Review which followed it (DfE, 2011) and the policy development of opposition parties.

Pressure group activity and collective action by individuals can thus both bring about new policy priorities and lead to a reappraisal of existing positions. This is an essential feature of democratic decision-making and we would suggest that reflective teachers have both the right and responsibility to contribute to such processes. Reflective activity 17.2 suggests learning about these processes by studying in depth a single example of political activity and decision-making.

Reflective activity 17.2

Aim To investigate processes of political activity and decision-making with regard to an educational issue.

Evidence and reflection A necessary basic strategy here is to focus on one issue and to trace the debates in the media and elsewhere. This could helpfully be undertaken with colleagues so that the workload is shared. The issue could be local or national.

Newspapers provide useful sources of easily retrievable information. Some, such as *The Times*, publish an index and this is particularly helpful. The BBC and *Guardian*'s websites are also particularly good.

Having gathered a variety of statements about the issue in question, an attempt should be made to classify them so that the competing positions are identified. From this point, it may be possible to gather policy statements directly from the participants, by letter, discussion, interview or library search.

Finally, the decision-point can be studied. Were the public arguments influential? What interests seem to have prevailed when decisions were taken?

Extension Having studied an example of political influence on decision-making, it is worth taking stock of what has been learned. Did you feel that the debate reflected appropriate educational concerns? Could educationalists have made more constructive contributions?

We are conscious, though, that this is a book which is primarily designed to support student teachers during periods of school-based work and that activities to influence wider policies may seem inappropriate. We include them because such activity is a logical consequence of taking extended professionalism and reflective teaching seriously – and because some preparation for such activity is perfectly possible before taking up a full time teaching post. One of the most important aspects of this is to demystify the democratic process itself and we will make various suggestions on this and with regard to the seven elements of pressure group activity which we have identified. These might be followed up by small groups of students or teachers, perhaps by taking an educational issue as a case study, or indeed, by facing a real current issue.

4.1 Demystifying the democratic process

There is a tendency to regard decision-making as something done by 'them' – an ill defined, distant and amorphous body. In fact, decisions in democracies are taken by elected representatives. The connection between the ordinary citizen and decision makers can thus be much more close, direct and personal.

Some possible ways forward here include visiting a relevant meeting of your local or regional council, assembly or parliament. For example, council committee meetings are normally open to the public and attendance at an Education Committee meeting is likely to be very interesting to reflective teachers. Alternatively, you could write to or make an appointment with your local elected representative. Discuss their views on educational issues and get them to explain the constraints and pressures within which they serve. Or, even more locally, you could ask to attend a meeting of the governing body of your school. You could note who the governors are and enquire about their powers in relation to the affairs of your school. Consider the potential for partnership between teachers and governors.

4.2 Identifying decision-makers

Lists of elected representatives, such MPs, MSPs, Assembly Members and Councillors, are normally available in local libraries, official offices and on the internet. It is then necessary to identify those who have a particular interest in education and those who have a particular degree of influence over decisions. Lists of members with an interest in education from the education committee of your council or national parliament will be helpful. The names of school governors will be available in your school.

It is also often appropriate to identify the leaders of political groups and those who speak on education issues. In addition, the chair of the Finance Committee on a local council or Treasury Ministers in government are likely to be worth picking out – depending, of course, on the issue under consideration.

A further group to identify is the education officers, civil servants and special advisers who advise decision-makers and implement many decisions. They can be extremely influential.

4.3 Preparing the case

It is essential to prepare a case well. This requires at least three things:

- appropriate factual information about the issue;
- good educational arguments in support of whatever is being advocated;
- an understanding of the interests and political circumstances affecting those whom it is hoped to influence.

A great deal of factual information can be gathered from the internet by visiting the websites of national, regional or local government agencies and through discussion facilities, blogs and social media. Face-to-face discussion should be sought with people who are be involved locally with the issue under consideration. Sources within your school should be one starting-point. Newspapers also offer a regular source of reports and comment on educational developments and can be monitored for relevant material. If possible, it is worth checking key facts from a number of sources.

To develop coherent educational arguments, the research literature is an important resource (see the suggestions on **reflectiveteaching.co.uk**). Almost all significant educational topics have been researched at some time, and there is much to learn from the experience of others. Of course, one would certainly wish to discuss the issues under consideration with colleagues, and to build a really secure understanding.

Regarding the interests of those whom one wishes to influence, a good place to start is with any published policy statements or manifestos. This could be followed up by discussion and by making judgements regarding the pressures and constraints that they face.

4.4 Forming alliances

Representative democracy is designed as a system which links decision-making with the views of a majority. It follows that the most successful type of campaigning is likely to be one which is broadly based – one which is produced by an alliance of interested parties bringing concerted pressure to bear on policymakers.

Reflective teachers may thus wish to act with others if and when they wish to influence public policy. Obvious places to look for allies are: other colleagues, perhaps through sectoral or subject associations, trade unions or the General Teaching Councils; parents and the importance of parental support cannot be overestimated; other workers in the public services; local community and interest groups who may be directly or indirectly affected by the issues under consideration; and existing national pressure groups such as those listed earlier in this section.

4.5 Managing the media

Important issues here include: clarifying, very clearly indeed, your key message; carrying out a review of the types of media which might be interested in educational issues (press, radio, television, etc.); holding discussions with people who have had experience of managing publicity to learn from them; carrying out an analysis of the types of stories or news that each media outlet is likely to be interested in and, crucially, of the ways in which they are likely to handle educational issues; considering the timing constraints that appropriate media outlets face; holding discussions with selected journalists to get first-hand knowledge of their concerns; preparing press releases and considering suitable images for photographic or filming purposes; and identifying and supporting a spokesperson for press follow-up.

4.6 Lobbying decision-makers

There are any number of possibilities here ranging from discrete lobbying, discussion and letter writing, through to petitions, media campaigns and demonstrations. However, it is important to remember that not many politicians enjoy being forced to change course, but most are open to persuasion if they have not previously taken up a hard, public position.

4.7 Following up

There is no mystery here. If agreement for changes in policy or practice is reached, it is simply necessary to check that the agreement is enacted. One might, for instance, be alert to the possibility of policies being 'watered down' as attention moves onto new issues.

Conclusion

Education is inevitably concerned not just with 'what is' but also with what 'ought to be' (Kogan, 1978). We hope that this book will help teachers and student teachers to develop not only the necessary skills of teaching but also the awareness and commitment which will ensure their contribution as extended and imaginative professionals in the future.

Key readings

Many of the books suggested as further reading for Chapters 3 and 5 will also be relevant here.

An excellent overview of key dimensions of professionalism, including a paper by Sally Power on 'the imaginative professional' (Reading 17.5) is:

Cunningham, B. (ed.) (2008) *Exploring Professionalism*. London: Institute of Education.

Eric Hoyle's classic paper on restricted and extended professionalism can be found in:

Hoyle, E. and Megarry, J. (2005) *World Yearbook of Education 1980: The Professional Development of Teachers*. London: Routledge.

For a historically contextualised account of the development of teachers' professional agency, see:

McCullough, G., Helsby, G. and Knight, P. (2000) *The Politics of Professionalism: Teachers and the Curriculum*. London: Continuum.

On the structural relationships between education and society, with fascinating comparative and historical dimensions, see:

Archer, M. (1979) *The Social Origins of Educational Systems.* London: SAGE. (Reading 17.1)

Interconnections between social structures and pedagogic practices are illustrated in the work of Paolo Freire, such as:

Freire, P. (2000) *Pedagogy of the Oppressed.* London: Continuum.

Stenhouse continues to have much to teach us on the role of the teacher in a democracy and Sachs continues and extends the tradition. Wrigley et al. demonstrate what is possible in schools across the world:

Sachs, J. (2003) *The Activist Teaching Profession.* Buckingham: Open University Press.

Stenhouse, L. (1983) *Authority, Education and Emancipation.* London: Heinemann.

Wrigley, J., Thompson, P. and Lingard, R. (eds) (2012) *Changing Schools: Alternative Ways to Make a World of Difference.* London: Routledge.

The United Nations Convention on Children's Rights is an important international statement. For an excellent account of both it and its implications for the UK, see:

Newell, P. (1991) *The UN Convention and Children's Rights in the UK.* London: National Children's Bureau.

For a child-focused account and more general guidance on Human Rights education, see:

Alderson, P. (2000) *Young Children's Rights.* London: Jessica Kingsley.

Osler, A. and Starkey, H. (2010) *Teachers and Human Rights Education.* Stoke-on-Trent: Trentham Books. (see also Reading 17.6)

For penetrating analyses of how education policy is created in government and may be mediated by teachers, see:

Ball, S. J. (1994) *Education Reform: A Critical and PostStructural Approach.* Buckingham: Open University Press. (see also Reading 17.7)

Ball, S. J., Maguire, M. and Braun, A. (2011) *How Schools Do Policy: Policy Enactments in Secondary Schools.* London: Routledge.

Cunningham, P. (2011) *Politics and the Primary Teacher.* London: Routledge.

Action by reflective teachers within the democratic process calls for some knowledge of political structures and processes. For an excellent UK overview, see:

Leyland, P. (2012) *Constitution of the United Kingdom: A Contextual Analysis.* Oxford: Hart Publishing.

Of course, much of the philosophy which underpins this book as a whole was all set out a century ago by John Dewey:

Dewey, J. (1916) *Democracy and Education: An Introduction to the Philosophy of Education.* New York: Macmillan

reflectiveteaching.co.uk offers additional professional resources for this chapter. These may include *Further Reading, Reflective Activities,* useful *Web Links* and *Download Facilities* for diagrams, figures, checklists, activities.

Reflective activities

9.3   To consider knowledge, concepts, skills and attitudes in planned schemes of work.

9.4   To consider the idea of *transformations* when preparing to teach.

10. Planning. How are we implementing the curriculum?

10.1   To consider the quality of activities in schemes of work.

10.2   To explore the extent to which sharing learning intentions or success criteria influences feelings of engagement for pupils.

10.3   To structure teaching and learning in a curriculum area.

10.4   To evaluate the stimulus and variety of tasks and activities.

10.5   To review existing lesson planning.

10.6   To evaluate a teaching session with particular reference to the appropriate application of subject knowledge.

11. Pedagogy. How can we develop effective teaching strategies?

11.1   To identify aspects of the craft, art and science of pedagogy in our own teaching.

11.2   To reflect from a learner's perspective on aspects of a teacher's pedagogy.

11.3   To explore how principles about pedagogy relate to our own planning and teaching.

12. Communication. How does use of language support learning?

12.1   To investigate who speaks and how much during a lesson.

12.2   To identify question and response patterns in a lesson.

12.3   To analyse and categorise an example of classroom talk.

12.4   To reflect on what messages we, as teachers, communicate about reading to learners.

12.5   To compare and contrast the writing and reading expectations in the lessons of two different teachers.

13. Assessment. How can assessment enhance learning?

13.1   To apply principled reflection to putative assessment for learning practices.

13.2   To reflect on the influence of beliefs and related assessment practices on learner identity and self-efficacy.

13.3   To identify aspects of feedback and marking practice to improve.

13.4   To support pupil development as autonomous self-regulating learners.

13.5   To reflect on the ways in which teachers aid learning through minute-by-minute and lesson-by-lesson adjustments.

PART 4: REFLECTING ON CONSEQUENCES

14. Outcomes. How do we monitor student learning achievements?

14.1   To consider the bases of comparison used in learning and teaching.

14.2   To highlight dilemmas between construct validity and reliability.

14.3   To investigate the danger that high-stakes assessment distorts curriculum provision.

14.4   To obtain direct evidence of pupils' feelings about routine assessment.

14.5   To identify information about the children which it is important to know and record.

14.6   To develop an informative and constructive procedure for reporting to parents.

15. Inclusion. How are we enabling learning opportunities?
15.1   To reflect on understandings of learner diversity.
15.2   To reflect on our understanding of inclusive education and on our provision for *some* or *all* of the learners in the class.
15.3   To explore school policy and provision for learners identified as having special or additional needs, and to reflect on their implications for classroom practice.
15.4   To reflect on how far, and in what ways, our classroom practices support all learners including those identified as having special or additional needs.
15.5   To reflect on inclusive pedagogy and its classroom application.

PART 5: DEEPENING UNDERSTANDING
16. Expertise. Conceptual tools for career-long fascination?
16.1   To review national aspirations and consequential links between curriculum breadth, pedagogy principles and congruent assessment.
16.2   To explore using the conceptual framework to reflect on professional expertise.

17. Professionalism. How does reflective teaching contribute to society?
17.1   To consider aspirations for our professional development as a teacher.
17.2   To investigate processes of political activity and decision-making with regard to an educational issue.

List of case studies, checklists, figures and research briefings

Acknowledgements

Many, many people have contributed to this new edition of *Reflective Teaching in Schools*. An extensive consultation was held and colleagues in schools and teacher education institutions across the UK were engaged through discussion, questionnaires and advice its future development. The book has a long history too, with its first version dating from 1987, and with major contributions to various editions from Sarah Tann, Pat Triggs, Julie Anderson, Janet Collins, Mandy Swann, Neil Simco, Sue Swaffield, Jo Warin and Paul Warwick.

Many educationalists engaged in the UK's Teaching and Learning Research Programme (TLRP, TLRP-TEL, 1999–2012) contributed in one way or another to the thinking which is reflected in these pages, in particular, through the 'ten principles for effective teaching and learning'. TLRP was a very large investment in educational research which coordinated the work of over 100 project, thematic and developmental activities – all based on active engagement between researchers, practitioners and other research users. In 2008, the TLRP Steering Committee, chaired by Bob Burgess, first endorsed the idea of building TLRP findings into these resources on Reflective Teaching. TLRP was funded by UK national governments and by the Higher Education Funding Council for England, and was managed by the Economic and Social Research Council.

The development of the conceptual framework to represent teacher expertise (Chapter 16) took place in active partnership with the GTC E and the other UK Teaching Councils. Thanks, in particular, to Jane Hough and Lesley Saunders. Very helpful consultation also took place at conferences of the: Universities' Council for the Education of Teachers, British Educational Research Association, National Association for Primary Education and the National Association of Primary Teacher Education.

This edition benefits from the work of primary and secondary specialists at the University of Cambridge and from excellent support from colleagues at the Institute of Education, University of London and the Graduate School of Education, University of Bristol. I would also particularly like to thank colleagues from across the UK who read and commented on sample chapters. These included, Tim Cain, Roland Chaplain, Linda Clarke, Jean Dourneen, Mary Jane Drummond, Tony Eaude, Lorna Hamilton, Peter Hick, Steve Kennewell, Tricia Maynard, Ian Menter, Yolande Muschamp, Phil Rigby, d'Reen Struthers and Tatiana Wilson. A very, very long list of colleagues has also assisted with the development of readings to accompany this book. Others are contributing to make the website a comprehensive resource at **reflectiveteaching.co.uk**.

Issues related to the development of the book have been discussed with many classteachers, headteachers, advisers, inspectors and policymakers as a by-product of engagement in research, policy and practice over the past decade. It is appropriate to acknowledge the collegiality of those involved in the review of the National Curriulum in England: Mary James, Tim Oates and Dylan Wiliam, the sincerity of civil servants at the DfE, and the wisdom of many of those consulted for that exercise. Important influence has also derived from those engaged in subject associations for the teaching of English, maths, science, history, geography, etc; major primary education organisations such as the Association for the Study of Primary Education, Cambridge Primary Review and NAPE; and teacher unions such as ATL, NUT and NASUWT. Among important contributions from teachers, are the anonymised case studies in Chapters 11 and 12 and case studies in Chapter 16.

The book has its origins at what is now Oxford Brookes University and responded to the vision of John Isaac. My thanks go also to colleagues at the University of the West of England, University of Bristol, University of Cambridge and at the Institute of Education, University of London, who have significantly influenced my understanding of teaching and learning over the years. They too may find that echoes in this book.

Frances Arnold, Alison Baker, Rosie Pattinson and other members of the Bloomsbury team have been a wonderful source of enthusiasm and practical help throughout the production of this book and its associated reader and website.

The development of new versions of Reflective Teaching for Early Years, Further and Higher Education is extremely exciting and the leadership of Jen Colwell, Yvonne Hillier, Maggie Gregson and Paul Ashwin is exemplary. Amy Pollard has been an enormous help in holding together the different strands of this evolving series.

For permission to reproduce figures or text, thanks are due to:

Susan Hart and Routledge for the text in Figure 1.5, A framework for innovative thinking, from Hart, S. (2000) *Thinking Through Teaching*.

The Government Office for Science for Figure 1.7, Mediating mechanisms for achievement of the wider benefits of learning, from Feinstein, L., Vorhaus, J. and Sabates, R. (2008) *Learning Through Life: Future Challenges*. Foresight Mental Capital and Wellbeing Project.

Mandy Swann for the text of Figure 2.6, Everyday language embodying labelling.

US National Research Council (NRC) for the foundation of Figure 2.9, Factors affecting learner engagement, from NRC (1999) *Improving Student Learning*.

The Teaching and Learning Research Programme for Figure 4.1, Ten evidence-informed educational principles for effective teaching and learning, James, M. and Pollard, A. (2006) *Improving teaching and learning in schools: A commentary by the Teaching and Learning Research Programme*.

Bloomsbury for Figure 5.1, Health and social problems in relation to inequality, from Wilkinson, R. and Pickett, K. (2009) *Why Greater Equality Makes Societies Stronger*.

Routledge for Figure 7.2, Progression in classroom management, from Chaplain, R. (2003) *Teaching Without Disruption in the Primary School.*

Barry Fraser and Darrell Fisher for the short form of the 'My Class Inventory' from their (1983) *Assessment of Classroom Psychsocial Environment: Workshop Manual.*

Guy Claxton and TLO for Figure 9.4, The supple learning mind, from Claxton, G., Chambers, M., Powell, G. and Lucas, B. (2011) *The Learning Powered School: Pioneering 21st Century Education.*

Bloomsbury for Figure 10.3, adapted from Male, B. and Waters, M. (2012) *The Secondary Curriculum Design Handbook.*

Pete Dudley for Figure 10.5, The lesson study cycle, from Dudley, P. (2011) *Lesson Study: a Handbook.*

The Scottish Government for Figure 13.2, Scotland's Assessment is for Learning, from Learning and Teaching Scotland (2007) *Assessment is for Learning.*

Tony Eaude and Critical Publishing for Figure 16.1, Stages in the development of expertise, from Eaude, T. (2012) *How Do Expert Primary Classteachers Really Work?.*

The Teaching and Learning Research Programme for Figure 16.2, from A framework for teacher expertise: powerful concepts and expert questions, from Pollard, A. (ed.) (2010) *Professionalism and Pedagogy: A Contemporary Opportunity.*

The Teaching and Learning Research Programme for Research Briefings on: Teacher careers, Education and neuroscience, Consulting pupils, New technology, Personalised learning, Pupil group work, Learning how to learn, and Assessment for learning and Developing inclusion.

George Leckie and Harvey Goldstein, and the Graduate School of Education, University of Bristol, for two Research Briefings: Are school league tables good for choosing schools? and Family, school, neighbourhood?

Andrew Pollard

December 2013

Bibliography

Abiko, T. (2012) 'A response from Japan to TLRP's ten principles'. In James, M. and Pollard, A. (eds) *Principles for Effective Pedagogy. International Responses to the UK TLRP.* London: Routledge.

Academies Commission, The (2013) *Unleashing Greatness: Getting the Best from an Academised System.* London: RSA/Pearson.

Adey, P. and Shayer, M. (1994) *Really Raising Standards: Cognitive Intervention and Academic Achievement.* London: Routledge.

Adler, A. (1927) *The Practice and Theory of Individual Psychology.* New York: Harcourt.

Ainscow, M., Booth, T. and Dyson, A. (2006) *Improving Schools, Developing Inclusion.* London: Routledge.

Alderson, P. (2000) *Young Children's Rights.* London: Jessica Kingsley.

Alexander, R. J. (1984) *Primary Teaching.* London: Holt, Rinehart and Winston.

—(2000) *Culture and Pedagogy. International Comparisons in Primary Education.* Oxford: Blackwell.

—(2004) 'Still no pedagogy? Principle, pragmatism and compliance in primary education'. *Cambridge Journal of Education,* 34 (1), 7–34.

—(2008a) *Essays on Pedagogy.* London: Routledge.

—(2008b) *Towards Dialogic Teaching: Rethinking Classroom Talk.* Cambridge: Dialogos.

—(ed.) (2010) *Children, Their World, Their Education. Final Report and Recommendations of the Cambridge Primary Review.* London: Routledge.

Alexander, R. J., Rose, J. and Woodhead, C. (1992) *Curriculum Organisation and Classroom Practice in Primary Schools: a Discussion Paper.* London: Department of Education and Science.

Alibhai-Brown, Y. (2000) *Who Do We Think We Are? Imagining the New Britain.* London: Allen Lane.

Allal, L. (2012) 'Pedagogy, didactics and the co-regulation of learning'. In James, M. and Pollard, A. (eds) *Principles for Effective Pedagogy. International Responses to the UK TLRP.* London: Routledge.

Altback, P. G. and Kelly, G. P. (eds) (1986) *New Approaches to Comparative Education.* Chicago: University of Chicago Press.

Althusser, L. (1971) 'Ideology and the ideological state apparatus'. In Cosin, B. R. (ed.) *Education, Structure and Society.* Harmondsworth: Penguin.

Alur, M. and Hegarty, S. (2002) *Education and Children with Special Educational Needs.* London: Paul Chapman Publishing.

Americal Psychological Association (1997) *Learner-centred Psychological Principles: A Framework for School Reform and Redesign.* New York: APA.

Anderson, B. (1991) *Imagined Communities: Reflections on the Origin and Spread of Nationalism.* London: Verso.

Anderson, P. M. (2008) *Pedagogy. A Primer.* New York: Peter Lang.

Andrew-Power, K. and Gormley, C. (2009) *Display for Learning*. London: Continuum.

Angoff, W. H. (1988) 'Validity: an evolving concept'. In Wainer, H. and Braun, H. I. (eds) *Test Validity*. Hillsdale, NJ: Lawerence Erlbaum Associates.

Anning, A. (1991) *The First Years at School, Education 4 to 8*. Buckingham: Open University Press.

Archard, D.and MacLeod, C. M. (2002) *The Moral and Political Status of Children*. Oxford: Oxford University Press.

Archer, M. (1979) *The Social Origins of Educational Systems*. London: SAGE.

Aries, P. (1962) *Centuries of Childhood*. Harmondsworth: Penguin.

Arnold, M. (1889) *Reports on Elementary Schools 1852–1882*. London: Macmillan.

Arnot, M. (2002) *Reproducing Gender? Critical Essays on Educational Theory and Feminist Politics*. London: RoutledgeFalmer.

Arnot, M. and Barton, L. (eds) (1992) *Voicing Concerns: Sociological Perspectives on Contemporary Education Reforms*. Wallingford: Triangle.

Arnot, M., David, M. and Weiner, G. (1999) *Closing the Gender Gap. Postwar Education and Social Change*. Cambridge: Polity Press.

Arthur, J. and Cremin, H. (2011) *Debates in Citizenship Education*. London: Routledge.

Askew, M., Brown, M., Rhodes, V., Wiliam, D. and Johnson, D. (1997) *Effective Teachers of Numeracy: Report of a Study Carried out for the Teacher Training Agency*. London: King's College, University of London.

Assessment Reform Group (1999) *Assessment for Learning: Beyond the Black Box*. Cambridge: University of Cambridge School of Education.

—(2002) *Testing, Motivation and Learning*. Cambridge: University of Cambridge Faculty of Education.

—(2006) *The Role of Teachers in Assessment of Learning*. London: Institute of Education.

Atkinson, T. and Claxton, G. (eds) (2000) *The Intuitive Practitioner: On the Value of Not Always Knowing What One is Doing*. Buckingham: Open University Press.

Aubrey, C. (1994) *The Role of Subject Knowledge in the Early Years of Schooling*. Lewes: Falmer Press.

Ausubel, D. P. (1968) *Educational Psychology: A Cognitive View*. New York: Holt, Rinehart and Winston.

Avramidis, E., Bayliss, P. and Burden, R. (2000) 'A survey into mainstream teachers' attitudes towards the inclusion of children with special educational needs in the ordinary school in one local education authority', *Educational Psychology*, 20(2), 191–211.

Baines, E., Blatchford, P. Kutnick, P., Chowne, A., Ota, C. and Berdondini, L. (2008) *Promoting Effective Group Work in the Primary Classroom. A Handbook for Teachers and Practitioners*. London: Routledge.

—(2009) *Promoting Effective Groupwork in the Classroom*. London: Routledge.

Baker, K. (ed.) (2013) *14–18: A New Vision for Secondary Education*. London: Bloomsbury.

Baker, R. and Berger, J. G. (2007) 'Improving educational research: TLRP's projects and themes'. International commentary. *British Educational Research Journal*, 33 (5), 781–804.

Baker, R. G. (1968) *Ecological Psychology. Concepts and Methods of Studying the Environment of Human Behaviour*. Stanford: Stanford University Press.

Ball, S. (1981a) *Beachside Comprehensive*. Cambridge: Cambridge University Press.

—(1981b) 'Initial encounters in the classroom and the process of establishment'. In Woods, P. F. (ed.) *Pupil Strategies*. London: Croom Helm.

—(1990) *Politics and Policy Making in Education: Explorations in Policy Sociology*. London: Routledge.

—(2006) *Education Policy and Social Class*. London: Routledge.

—(2008) *The More Things Change ... Educational Research, Social Class and 'Interlocking' Inequalities*. Inaugural lecture. London: Institute of Education.

Ball, S. J. (1994) *Education Reform: A Critical and PostStructural Approach.* Buckingham: Open University Press.

Ball, S. J., Maguire, M. and Braun, A. (2011) *How Schools Do Policy. Policy Enactments in Secondary Schools.* London: Routledge.

Bandura, A. (1995) *Self-efficacy in Changing Societies.* New York: Cambridge University Press.

Banister, J. (2004) *Word of Mouse: The New Age of Networked Media.* Berkeley, CA: Agate.

Barber, M. and Mourshead, M. (2007) *How the World's Best Performing School Systems Come Out on Top.* London: McKinsey and Company.

Barnes, D. (2008) 'Exploratory talk for learning'. In Mercer, N. and Hodgkinson, S. (eds) (2008) *Exploring Talk in School.* London: SAGE.

Barnes, D., Britton, J. and Rosen, H. (1986) *Language, the Learner and the School.* Harmondsworth: Penguin.

Barrow, R. (1984) *Giving Teaching Back to Teachers.* Brighton: Wheatsheaf.

Barrs, M. and Cork, V. (2001) *The Reader in the Writer: The Link Between the Study of Literature and Writing Development at Key Stage 2.* London: Centre for Language in Primary Education.

Bartlett, S. and Burton, D. (2012) *Introduction to Education Studies.* London: SAGE.

Bartley, K. (2010) 'Preface'. In Pollard, A. (ed.) *Professionalism and Pedagogy: A Contemporary Opportunity.* London: TLRP.

Barton, L. (2012) 'Response'. In *The Sociology of Disability and Inclusive Education: A Tribute to Len Barton.* London: Routledge.

Bates, J. and Lewis, S. (2009) *The Study of Education: An Introduction.* London: Continuum.

Bearne, E. and Marsh, J. (eds) (2007) *Literacy and Social Inclusion: Closing the Gap.* Stoke-on-Trent: Trentham Books

Bearne, E. (ed.) (1996) *Differentiation and Diversity in the Primary School.* London: Routledge.

—(2002) *Making Progress in Writing.* London: Routledge.

Bearne, E. and Wolstencroft, H. (2007) *Visual Approaches to Teaching Writing: Multimodal Literacy 5–11.* London: Sage/UKLA.

Beauchamp, G. (2012) *ICT in the Primary School: From Pedagogy to Practice.* Harlow: Pearson.

Beauchamp, G. and Kennewell, S. (2013) 'Transition in pedagogical orchestration using the interactive whiteboard', *Education and Information Technologies,* 18 (2) ACM Digital Library.

Becker, H. S. (1968) *Making the Grade. The Academic Side of College Life.* New York: Wiley.

Benn, M. (2011) *School Wars. The Battle for Britain's Education.* London: Verso.

Bennett, N., Desforges, C., Cockburn, A. and Wilkinson, B. (1984) *The Quality of Pupil Learning Experiences.* London: Lawrence Erlbaum.

Bennett, T. (2012) *Mastering the Art and Craft of Teaching.* London: Continuum.

Bereiter, C. and Scardamalia, M. (1987) *The Psychology of Written Composition.* Hillsdale, NJ: Lawrence Erlbaum Associates.

Berger, P. L. and Luckman, T. (1967) *The Social Construction of Reality.* New York: Doubleday.

Berlak, A. and Berlak, H. (1981) *Dilemmas of Schooling.* London: Methuen.

Berliner, D. (1991) 'What's all the fuss about instructional time?' In M. Ben-Peretz and R. Bromme (eds) *The Nature of Time in Schools: Theoretical Concepts, Practitioner Perceptions.* New York: Teachers College Press.

—(2001) 'Learning about and learning from expert teachers', *International Journal of Educational Research,* 35, 463–82.

—(2004) 'Describing the behavior and documenting the accomplishments of expert teachers', *Bulletin of Science, Technology and Society,* 24 (3), 200–12.

Bernstein, B. (1970) 'Education cannot compensate for society', *New Society,* 387, 344–7.

—(1971) 'On the classification and framing of educational knowledge'. In Young, M. F. D. (ed.) *Knowledge and Control.* London: Collier–Macmillan.

Bevan, R. (2007) *From Black Boxes to Glass Boxes: On-screen Learning in Schools with Concept maps.* Research Briefing 21. London: TLRP.

Bialystok, E. (2007) 'Cognitive effects of bilingualism: how linguistic experience leads to cognitive change', *International Journal of Bilingual Education and Bilingualism*, 10 (3), 210–23.

Biesta, G., Field, J., Goodson, I., Hodkinson, P. and Macleod, F. (2010) *Improving Learning through the Lifecourse.* London, Routledge.

Black, H. (1986) 'Assessment for learning'. In D. Nuttall (ed.) *Assessing Educational Achievement.* London: Falmer Press.

Black, P. (1998) *Testing Friend or Foe? Theory and Practice of Assessment and Testing.* London: Falmer.

Black, P., Harrison, C., Lee, C., Marshall, B. and Wiliam, D. (2003) *Assessment for Learning: Putting It into Practice.* Buckingham: Open University Press.

Black, P. and Wiliam, D. (1998a) 'Assessment and classroom learning', *Assessment in Education*, 5 (1), 7–74.

—(1998b) *Inside the Black Box: Raising Standards through Classroom Assessment.* London: King's College.

Black-Hawkins, K. and Florian, L. (2012) 'Teachers' craft knowledge of their inclusive practice', *Teachers and Teaching: Theory and Practice.* On-line.

Black-Hawkins, K., Florian, L. and Rouse, M. (2007) *Achievement and Inclusion in Schools.* London: Routledge.

Blackledge, A. (ed.) (1994) *Teaching Bilingual Children.* Stoke-on-Trent: Trentham.

Blakemore, C. (2000) 'It Makes You Think.' (December) *Independent on Sunday.*

Blanchard, J. (2009) *Teaching, Learning and Assessment.* Maidenhead: Open University Press.

Blanden, J., Gregg, P. and Machin, P. (2005) *Intergenerational Mobility in Europe and North America.* London: The Sutton Trust.

Blatchford, P. (2003) *The Class Size Debate: Is Small Better?* Maidenhead: Open University Press.

Blatchford, P., Galton, M. and Kutnick, P. (2005) 'Improving group work in classrooms: A new approach to increasing engagement and learning in everyday classroom settings at Key Stages 1, 2 and 3', *TLRP Research Briefing 11*. London: TLRP.

Blatchford, P., Russell, A. and Webster, R. (2011) *Reassessing the impact of Teaching Assistants.* London: Routledge.

Blecker, N. S. and Boakes, N. J. (2010) 'Creating a learning environment for all children: are teachers able and willing?', *International Journal of Inclusive Education*, 14(5), 435–47.

Blenkin, G. M. and Kelly, A. V. (1981) *The Primary Curriculum.* London: Harper and Row.

Blishen, E. (1969) *The School that I'd Like.* Harmondsworth: Penguin.

Bloom B. S. (1956) *Taxonomy of Educational Objectives.* New York: David McKay.

Blundell, D. (2012) *Education and Constructions of Childhood.* London: Continuum.

Blyth, A. (1976) *8–13: Place, Time and Society: Curriculum Planning in History, Geography and Social Science.* London: Schools Council.

—(1984) *Development, Experience and Curriculum in Primary Education.* London: Croom Helm.

Boas, G. (1986) *The Cult of Childhood.* London: Warburg Institute.

Bolster, A. (1983) 'Towards a more effective model of research on teaching', *Harvard Educational Review*, 53 (3), 294–308.

Booth, T. and Smith, R. (2002) 'Sustaining inclusive education development: learning about barriers and resources in a London borough'. Revision of paper presented at the British Educational Research Association Annual Conference, University of Exeter.

Bourdieu, P. and Passeron, J. C. (1977) *Reproduction in Education, Society and Culture.* London: SAGE.

Bowe, R., Ball, S. and Gold, A. (1992) *Reforming Education and Changing Schools*. London: Routledge.

Bowles, S. and Gintis, H. (1976) *Schooling in Capitalist America*. London: Routledge.

Bransford, J. D., Brown, A. I. and Cocking, R. R. (eds) (2000) *How People Learn: Brain, Mind, Experience and School*. Washington, DC: National Academy Press.

Breakwell, G. (1986) *Coping with Threatened Identities*. London: Methuen.

Bridges, D. (2009) *Evidence-based Policy. What Evidence? What Basis? Whose Policy?* TLRP Research Briefing No. 74. London: TLRP.

Britton, J., Burgess, T., Martin, N., McLeod, A. and Rosen, H. (1975) *The Development of Writing Abilities (11–18)*. London: MacMillan Education.

Britzman, D. P. (2003) *Practice Makes Practice: A Critical Study of Learning to Teach*. Albany: State University of New York.

Broadfoot, P. (2007) *An Introduction to Assessment*. London: Continuum.

Bronfenbrenner, U. (1979) *The Ecology of Human Development: Experiments by Nature and Design*. Cambridge, MA: Harvard University Press.

—(1993) 'Environments as contexts of development'. In 'Ecological models of human development'. In Gauvain, M. and Cole, M. (eds) *Readings on the Development of Children*. New York: Freeman.

Brophy, J. E. and Good, T. L. (1974) *Teacher–Student Relationships*. New York: Cassell.

Brown, M. E. and Precious, G. N. (1968) *The Integrated Day in the Primary School*. London: Ward Lock Educational.

Brown, S. and McIntyre (1993) *Making Sense of Teaching*. Buckingham: Open University Press.

Bruner, J. (1966) *Towards a Theory of Instruction*. Cambridge, MA: Harvard University Press.

—(1972) 'The nature and uses of immaturity', *American Psychologist*, 27, 1–28.

—(1977) *The Process of Instruction*. Cambridge, MA: Harvard University Press.

—(1986) *Actual Minds, Possible Worlds*. Cambridge, MA: Harvard University Press.

—(1990) *Acts of Meaning*. Cambridge, MA: Harvard University Press.

—(1996) *The Culture of Education*. Cambridge, MA: Harvard University Press.

—(2006) *In Search of Pedagogy 1 and II: The Selected Works of Jerome S. Bruner, 1957–1978 and 1979–2006*. London: Routledge.

Buckingham, D. (2000) *After the Death of Childhood: Growing up in the Age of Electronic Media*. Cambridge: Polity Press.

—(2008) *Youth, Identity and Digital Media*. Cambridge, MA: MIT Press.

Buckingham, D. and Willett, R. (eds) (2006) *Digital Generations. Children, Young People and the New Media*. London: Routledge.

Burrell, A. and Bubb, S. (2000) 'Teacher feedback in the reception class: associations with pupils' positive adjustments to school', *Education 3–13*, 28 (3), 58–64.

Butler, K. A. (1998) *Learning and Teaching Style: In Theory and Practice*. Columbia: Learner's Dimension.

Butler, R. (1988) 'Enhancing and undermining intrinsic motivation: the effects of task-involving and ego-involving evaluation on interest and performance', *British Journal of Educational Psychology*, 58, 1–14.

Butt, G. (2011) *Making Assessment Matter*. London: Continuum.

Cabinet Office (2011) *Opening Doors, Breaking Barriers: A Strategy for Social Mobility*. London: HM Government.

Calderhead, J. (1988) *Teachers' Professional Learning*. London: Falmer.

—(1994) 'Competence and the complexities of teaching'. Mimeo. ESRC seminar series on teacher competence.

Callaghan, J. (1976) 'Towards a national debate', *Education*, 148 (17), 332–3.

Campbell, J. and Neill, S. R. St J. (1992) *Teacher Time and Curriculum Manageability at Key Stage 1*. London: AMMA.

Canter, L. and Canter, M. (1992) *Assertive Discipline: Positive Behavior Management for Today's Classroom.* Santa Monica, CA: Canter and Associates.

Carr, M. (2008) 'Can assessment unlock and open the doors to resourcefulness and agency?'. In Swaffield, S. (ed.) *Unlocking Assessment: Understanding for Reflection and Application,* 36–54. Abingdon: Routledge.

Carr, M. and Lee, W. (2012) *Learning Stories: Constructing Learner Identities in Early Education.* London: SAGE.

Carr, W. and Kemmis, S. (1986) *Becoming Critical: Knowing Through Action Research.* London: Falmer.

Central Advisory Council for Education (CACE) (1967) *Chidren and their Primary Schools.* London: HMSO.

Chaplain, R. (2003a) *Teaching Without Disruption in the Primary School.* London: Routledge.

—(2003b) *Teaching Without Disruption in the Secondary School.* London: Routledge.

Chubb, T. E. and Moe, T. M. (1990) *Politics, Markets, and America's Schools.* Washington, DC: Brookings.

Clark, C., and Phythian-Sence, C. (2008) *Interesting Choice: The (Relative) Importance of Choice and Interest in Reader Engagement.* Available at http://www.literacytrust.org.uk/assets/0000/0541/Interesting_choice_2008.pdf (accessed 17 June 2012).

Clarke, S. (1998) *Targeting Assessment in the Primary Classroom.* London: Hodder and Stoughton.

—(2001) *Unlocking Formative Assessment: Practical Strategies for Enhancing Pupils' Learning in the Primary Classroom.* London: Hodder and Stoughton.

—(2005a) *Formative Assessment in Action: Weaving the Elements Together.* London: Hodder and Stoughton.

—(2005b) *Formative Assessment in the Secondary Classroom.* London: Hodder and Stoughton.

—(2008) *Active Learning through Formative Assessment.* London: Hodder and Stoughton

—(2011) 'The Power of Formative Assessment: Self-belief and Active Involvement in the Process of learning' (DVD). Shirley Clarke Media Ltd.

Clarricoates, K. (1987) 'Child culture at school: a clash between gendered worlds?' In Pollard, A. (ed.) *Children and Their Primary Schools.* London: Falmer.

Claxton, G. (1999) *Wise Up: the Challenge of Lifelong Learning.* London: Bloomsbury.

—(2002) *Building Learning Power: Helping Young People Become Better Learners.* Bristol: TLO.

—(2004) *Building 101 Ways to Learning Power.* Bristol: TLO.

Claxton, G., Chambers, M., Powell, G. and Lucas, B. (2011) *The Learning Powered School: Pioneering 21ˢᵗ Century Education.* Bristol: TLO.

Clegg, D. and Billington, S. (1994) *The Effective Primary Classroom: Management and Organisation of Teaching and Learning.* London: David Fulton.

Cliff Hodges, G. (2010) 'Reasons for reading: why literature matters', *Literacy,* 44 (2), 60–8.

Clifford, M. M. and Walster, E. (1973) 'The effect of physical attractiveness on teacher expectations', *Sociology of Education,* 46(2) (Spring, 1973), 248–58.

Coffield, F., Mosley, D., Hall, E. and Ecclestone, K. (2004) *Learning Styles and Pedagogy in Post-16 Learning: A Systematic and Critical Review.* London: LSDA.

Cole, M. and Walker, S. E. (1989) *Teaching and Stress.* Buckingham: Open University Press.

Coleman, J. S. (1988) 'Social capital in the creation of human capital', *American Journal of Sociology,* 94 (Supplement), 95–120.

Coleman, J. S., Coser, L. A. and Powell, W. W. (1966) *Equality of Educational Opportunity.* Washington, DC: US Government Printing Office.

Collerbone, P. (2009) *Creating Tomorrow: Planning, Developing and Sustaining Change in Education and Other Public Services.* London: Continuum.

Collins, J. (1996) *The Quiet Child.* London: Cassell.

Collins, R. (1977) 'Some comparative principles of educational stratification', *Higher Education Review*, 47 (1), 1–27.

Connell, R. W., Ashden, D. J., Kessler, S. and Dowsett, G. W. (1982) *Making the Difference: Schools, Families and Social Division.* Sydney: Allen and Unwin.

Connolly, P. (1998) *Racism, Gender and Identities of Young Children: Social Relations in a Multiethnic, Inner-city Primary School.* London: Routledge.

Conteh, J. (2003) *Succeeding in Diversity: Culture, Language and Learning in Primary Classrooms.* Stoke-on-Trent: Trentham.

Cooper, H. and Hyland, R. (eds) (2000) *Children's Perceptions of Learning with Trainee Teachers.* London: Routledge.

Cordon, R. (2000) *Literacy and Learning through Talk: Strategies for the Primary Classroom.* Buckingham: Open University Press.

Corsaro, W. A. (2011) *The Sociology of Childhood.* London: SAGE.

Council for the Curriculum Examinations and Assessment (CCEA) (2007) The Northern Ireland Curriculum. http://www.rewardinglearning.org.uk/curriculum (accessed February 2013).

Council of Europe (1985) *Teaching and Learning about Human Rights in Schools,* Recommendation No. R (85) 7 of the Committee of Ministers. Strasbourg: Council of Europe.

Counsell, C. (2004) *History and Literacy in Y 7: Building the Lesson Around the Text.* London: John Murray.

Cowie, H. (2012) *From Birth to Sixteen. Children's Health, Social, Emotional and Linguistic Development.* London: Routledge.

Cowie, H. and Wallace, P. (2000) *Peer Support in Action: From Bystanding to Standing By.* London: SAGE.

Cowley, S. (2010) *Getting the Buggers to Behave.* London: Continuum.

Cox, I. (2004) *Developing Student Leadership in a Networked Learning Community.* London: NTRP.

Crawford, C., Dearden, L. and Meghir, C. (2007) *When You Are Born Matters: The Impact of Date of Birth on Child Cognitive Outcomes.* London: Institute for Fiscal Studies.

Crawford, C., Johnson, P., Machin, S. and Vignoles, A. (2011) *Social Mobility: A Literature Review.* London: BIS.

Cremin, T. (2009) *Teaching English Creatively.* London: Routledge.

Cremin, T. and Myhill, D. (2012) *Writing Voice. Creating Communities of Writers.* London: Routledge.

Croll, P. and Moses, D. (2000) *Special Needs in the Primary School.* London: Cassell.

Crozier, G. (2000) *Parents and Schools: Partners or Protagonists?* Stoke-on-Trent: Trentham.

Crozier, G. and Reay, D. (eds) (2005) *Activating Participation: Parents and Teachers Working Towards Partnership.* Stoke-on-Trent: Trentham Books.

Crozier, G., Reay, D. and Clayton, J. (2010) 'The socio-cultural and learning experiences of working-class students in higher education'. In David, M. (ed.) *Improving Learning by Widening Participation in Higher Education.* London: Routledge.

Crystal, D. (2002) *The English Language: A Guided Tour of the Language.* London: Penguin.

Cummins, J. (1996) *Negotiating Identities: Education for Empowerment in a Diverse Society.* Los Angeles: CABE.

Cunningham, B. (ed.) (2008) *Exploring Professionalism.* London: Institute of Education.

Cunningham, H. (2006) *The Invention of Childhood.* London: BBC Books.

Cunningham, P. (2011) *Politics and the Primary Teacher.* London: Routledge.

Curriculum and Assessment Authority for Wales (ACCAC) (2003) *Developing the Curriculum Cymreig.* Cardiff: ACCAC.

Curriculum Council for Wales (CCW) (1991) *The Whole Curriculum in Wales.* Cardiff: CCW.

Dadds, M. (1995) *Passionate Enquiry and School Development: A Story about Teacher Action Research.* London: Falmer.

—(2001) 'The politics of pedagogy', *Teachers and Teaching: Theory and Practice*, 7 (1), 43–58.

Dahlberg, G., Moss, P. and Pence, A. (eds) (1999) *Beyond Quality in Early Childhood Education and Care: Postmodern Perspectives.* London: RoutledgeFalmer.

Darling Hammond, L. (1996) *The Right to Learn: A Blueprint for Creating Schools that Work.* San Francisco: Jossey-Bass.

—(2007) *Testimony Before the House Education and Labor Committee on the Re-authorization of the NCLB legislation.* 10 September.

Darling Hammond, L., Barron, P. D., Pearson, A., Schoenfeld, E. et al. (2008) *Powerful Learning. What we Know About Teaching for Understanding.* San Francisco: Jossey-Bass.

Darling-Hammond, L. and Lieberman, A. (2012) *Teacher Education Around the World: Changing Policies and Practices.* London: Routledge.

Darmon, A. (2007) 'Improving educational research: TLRP's projects and themes'. International commentary. *British Educational Research Journal*, 33 (5), 781–804.

Darvin, J. (2009) 'Make books, not war: workshops at a summer camp in Bosnia', *Literacy*, 43 (1), 50–9.

Davies, B. (1982) *Life in the Classroom and Playground.* London: Routledge and Kegan Paul.

—(1993) *Shards of Glass: Children Reading and Writing Beyond Gendered Identities.* Sydney: Allen and Unwin.

Dawes, L. (2004) 'Talk and learning in classroom science', *International Journal of Science Education,* 26 (6), 677–95.

Dawes, L. and Sams, C. (2004) 'Developing the capacity to collaborate'. In Littleton, K., Miell, D. and Faulkner, D. (eds) *Learning to Collaborate: Collaborating to Learn.* New York: Nova Science.

Dawkins, R. (1978) *The Selfish Gene.* London: Granada.

Day, C. and Gu, Q. *(2010) The New Lives of Teachers.* London: Routledge.

Day, C., Kington, A., Stobart, G. and Sammons, P. (2006) 'The personal and professional selves of teachers: stable and unstable identities', *British Educational Research Journal*, 32 (04), 601–16.

Day, C., Sammons, P., Stobart, G., Kington, A. and Gu, Q. (2007) *Teachers Matter: Connecting Work, Lives and Effectiveness.* Maidenhead: Open University Press.

Deakin Crick, R. (2006) *Learning Power in Practice.* London: Paul Chapman.

Dean, J. (2008) *Organising Learning in the Primary School Classroom.* London: Routledge.

Delamont, S. (1990) *Sex Roles and the School.* London: Routledge.

DePalma, R and Atkinson, E. (eds) (2009) *Interrogating Heteronormativity in Primary Schools: The Work of the No Outsiders Project.* Stoke on Trent: Trentham Books.

Department for Education (DfE) (2010) *The Importance of Teaching – Schools White Paper.* London: DfE.

—(2011) *The Framework for the National Curriculum. A Report by the Expert Panel for the National Curriculum Review.* London: DfE.

—(2012) *Guidance for Local Authorities and Schools on Setting Education Performance Targets for 2012.* London: DfE.

Department of Education for Northern Ireland (DENI) (2009) *Every School a Good School – The Way Forward for Special Educational Needs and Inclusion.* Belfast: DENI.

Department for Education and Science (1975) *A Language for Life (The Bullock Report).* London: HMSO.

—(1985) *The Curriculum from 5 to 16. Curriculum Matters 2, an HMI Series.* London: HMSO.

—(1989a) *Discipline in Schools, Report of the Committee of Enquiry,* chaired by Lord Elton. London: HMSO.

—(1989b) *English for Ages 5–16.* London: HMSO.

Department for Education and Skills (2003a) *Excellence and Enjoyment: A Strategy for Primary Schools.* London: DfES.

—(2003b) *Every Child Matters.* London: DfES.

—(2004) *Personalised Learning: Adding Value to the Learning Journey through Primary School.* London: DfES.

—(2006) *The Five Year Strategy for Children and Learners: Maintaining the Excellent Progress.* London: DfES.

Department for Work and Pensions (DWP) (2011) *A New Approach to Child Poverty. Tackling the Causes of Disadantage and Transforming Families' Lives.* London: DWP.

Desforges, C. with Abouchaar, A. (2003) *The Impact of Parental Involvement, Parental Support and Family Education on Pupil Achievement and Adjustment: A Literature Review.* London: DfES.

Devine, D. (2003) *Children, Power and Schooling. The Social Structuring of Childhood in the Primary School.* Stoke-on-Trent: Trentham.

Dewey, J. (1916) *Democracy and Education: An Introduction to the Philosophy of Education.* New York: Macmillan.

—(1933) *How We Think: A Restatement of the Relation of Reflective Thinking to the Educative Process.* Chicago: Henry Regnery.

Dillow, C. (2010) *Supporting Stories. Being a Teaching Assistant.* Stoke-on-Trent: Trentham Books.

Dixon, A., Drummond, M. J., Hart, S. and McIntyre, D. (2004) *Learning Without Limits.* Maidenhead: Open University Press.

Dochy, F., Segers, M. and Buehl, M. (1999) 'The relation between assessment practices and outcomes of studies: The case of research on prior knowledge', *Review of Educational Research,* 69 (2), 145–86.

Doddington, C. and Hilton, M. (2007) *Child-Centred Education: Reviving the Creative Tradition.* London: SAGE.

Dombey, H. et al. (2010) *Teaching Reading: What the Evidence Says.* Leicester: UKLA.

Donaldson, G. (2010) *Teaching: Scotland's Future.* Report of a review of teacher education in Scotland. Edinburgh: Scottish Government.

Donaldson, M. (1978) *Children's Minds.* London: Fontana.

Dowling, M. (1992) *Education 3–5.* London: Paul Chapman.

—(1999) *Neurons and Networks: An Introduction to Behavioural Neuroscience.* Cambridge, MA: Harvard University Press.

Doyle, W. (1977) 'Learning the classroom environment: an ecological analysis', *Journal of Teacher Education,* 28 (6), 51–4.

—(1986) 'Classroom organization and management'. In Wittrock, M. C. (ed.) *Handbook of Research on Teaching* (3rd edn). New York: Macmillan.

Drews, D. and Hansen, A. (2007) *Using Resources to Support Mathematical Thinking.* Exeter: Learning Matters.

Dreyfus, H. L. and Dreyfus, S. E. (1986) *Mind Over Machine.* New York: Free Press.

Drummond, M. J. (2008) 'Assessment and values: a close and necessary relationship'. In Swaffield, S. (ed.), *Unlocking Assessment: Understanding for Reflection and Application.* Abingdon: Routledge.

—(2012) *Assessing Children's Learning.* London: Routledge.

Dudley, P. (2011) *Lesson Study: A Handbook.* Cambridge: Dudley. Available at lessonstudy.co.uk.

Dudley, P. and Gowing, G. (2012) 'Reflection through lesson study'. In Hansen, A. (ed.) *Transforming QTS: Reflective Practice.* London: Sage.

Dumont, H., Istance, D. and Benavides, F. (2010) *The Nature of Learning. Using Research to Inspire Practice.* Paris: OECD.

Dunham, J. (1992) *Stress in Teaching.* London: Routledge.

Dunkin, M. and Biddle, B. (1974) *The Study of Teaching.* New York: Holt, Rinehart and Winston.

Dunn, J. (1988) *The Beginnings of Social Understanding.* Oxford: Blackwell.

Dweck, C. S. (1986) 'Motivational processes affecting learning', *American Psychology,* 41, 1040–8.

—(2000) *Self-Theories: Their Role in Motivation, Personality and Development.* London: Psychology Press.

—(2006) *Mindset. The New Psychology of Success.* New York: Ballantine.

Earl, L. (2012) 'A response from Canada to TLRP's ten principles for effective pedagoy'. In James, M. and Pollard, A. (eds) *Principles for Effective Pedagogy. International Responses to the UK TLRP.* London: Routledge.

Earl, L. and Katz, S. (2008) 'Getting to the core of learning: using assessment for self-monitoring and self-regulation'. In Swaffield, S. (ed.) *Unlocking Assessment: Understanding for Reflection and application,* 90–104. Abingdon: Routledge.

Earl, L., Watson, N., Levin, B., Leithwood, K., Fullan, M. and Torrance, N. with Jantzi, D., Mascall, B. and Volante, L. (2003) *Watching and Learning 3: Final Report of the External Evaluation of England's National Literacy and Numeracy Strategies.* Toronto: Ontario Institute for Studies in Education.

Eaude, T. (2012) *How Do Expert Primary Classteachers Really Work? A Critical Guide for Teachers, Headteachers and Teacher Educators.* Northwich: Critical Publishing.

Education Scotland (2013) *Principles for Curriculum Design.* At www.educationscotland.uk/thecurriculum (accessed 9 November 2013).

Edwards, A. (2012) *New Technology and Education,* London: Continuum.

Edwards, R. and Alldred, P. (2000) 'Children's understanding of home–school relations', *Education 3–13,* 28 (3), 41–5.

Egan, K. (1988) *An Alternative Approach to Teaching and the Curriculum.* London: Routledge.

Egan, M. and Bunting, B. (1991) 'The effects of coaching on elevenplus scores', *British Journal of Educational Psychology,* 61 (1), 85–91.

Eisner, E. (1996) *Cognition and Curriculum Reconsidered.* London: Paul Chapman.

—(2002) *The Arts and the Creation of Mind.* New Haven and London: Yale University Press.

Elliott, G. (1976) *Teaching for Concepts. Place, Time and Society 8–11.* London: Schools Council.

Elliott, J. (1991) *Action Research for Educational Change.* Buckingham: Open University Press.

Elliott, J. and Vaitilingam, R. (2008) *Now We Are 50.* London: Centre for Longitudinal Studies, Institute of Education.

Entwistle, N. (2009) *Teaching for Understanding at University.* London: Palgrave Macmillan.

Epstein, D. (1993) *Changing Classroom Cultures: AntiRacism, Politics and Schools.* Stoke-on-Trent: Trentham Books.

—(ed.) (1994) *Challenging Lesbian and Gay Inequalities in Education.* Buckingham: Open University Press.

Eraut, M. (1994) *Developing Professional Knowledge and Competence.* London: Routledge.

—(2007) *Early Career Learning at Work.* Research Briefing 25. London: TLRP.

Ernest, P. (1991) *The Philosophy of Mathematics Education.* London: Falmer.

Etzioni, A. (1961) 'A basis for the comparative analysis of complex organisations'. In Etzioni, A. *A Sociological Reader on Complex Organisations.* New York: Holt, Rinehart and Winston.

Evans, G. (2006) *Educational Failure and Working Class White Children in Britain.* Basingstoke: Palgrave Macmillan.

Evans, K., Hodkinson, P., Rainbird, H. and Unwin, L. (2006) *Improving Workplace Learning.* London: Routledge.

Ewing, R. and Manuel, J. (2005) 'Retaining quality early career teachers in the profession: new teacher narratives', *Change: Transformations in Education,* 8 (1), 1–16.

Eysenck, H. J. and Cookson, C. D. (1969) 'Personality in primary school children: ability and achievement', *British Journal of Educational Psychology,* 39 (2), 109–22.

Facer, K. (2011) *Learning Futures. Education, Technology and Social Change.* London: Routledge.

Facer, K., Furlong, J., Furlong, R. and Sutherland, R. (2003) *Screenplay: Children and Computing in the Home.* London: Routledge.

Feiler, A., Andrews, J., Greenhough, P., Hughes, M., Johnson, D., Scanlan, M. and Yee, W. (2007) *Improving Primary Literacy: Linking Home and School.* London: Routldge.

Feinstein, L., Duckworth, K. and Sabates, R. (2008) *Education and the Family: Passing Success Across the Generations.* Abingdon: Routledge.

Feinstein, L., Vorhaus, J. and Sabates, R. (2008) *Learning Through Life: Future Challenges.* Foresight Mental Capital and Wellbeing Project. London: The Government Office for Science.

Feuerstein, R., Hoffman, M. and Miller, R. (1980) *Instrumental Enrichment: an Intervention for Cognitive Modifiability.* Baltimore, MD: University Park Press.

Fielding, M. and Moss, P. (2011) *Radical Education and the Common School: A Democratic Alternative.* London: Routledge.

Filer, A. (ed.) *Assessment: Social Practice and Social Product.* London: Routledge.

Filer, A. and Pollard, A. (2000) *The Social World of Pupil Assessment: Processes and Contexts of Primary Schooling.* London: Continuum.

Fisher, R. (2008) *Teaching Thinking. Philosophical Enquiry in the Classroom.* London: Continuum.

Flavell, J. H. (1970) 'Developmental studies of mediated memory'. In Reese, H. W. and Lipsett, L. P. (eds) *Advances in Child Development and Behaviour.* New York: Academic Press.

—(1979) 'Metacognition and cognitive monitoring', *American Psychologist*, 34 (10), 906–11.

Flitton, L. (2010) *Developing the use of Talk as a Tool for Learning: From Classroom Analysis to School Development.* Unpublished Masters thesis: University of Cambridge.

Flitton, L. and Warwick P. (2012) 'From classroom analysis to whole school professional development: promoting talk as a tool for learning across school departments'. Available online at: http://www.tandfonline.com/doi/abs/10.1080/19415257.2012.719288 (accessed 9 November 2013).

Flook, J., Ryan, M. and Hawkins, L. (2010) *Professional Expertise: Practice, Theory and Education for Working in Uncertainty.* London: Whiting and Birch.

Florian, L. (ed.) (2007) *The Handbook of Special Education.* London: SAGE.

Florian, L. and Black-Hawkins, K. (2011) 'Exploring inclusive pedagogy', *British Educational Research Journal*, 37 (5), 813–28.

Frances, J. (2004) *Educating Children with Facial Disfigurement: Creating Inclusive School Communities.* London: RoutledgeFalmer.

Francis, B. (1998) *Power Plays: Primary School Children's Constructions of Gender, Power and Adult Work.* Stoke-on-Trent: Trentham.

—(2000) *Boys, Girls and Achievement: Addressing, the Classroom Issues.* London: RoutledgeFalmer.

Francis, B., Skelton, C. and Read, B. (2012) *The Identities and Practices of High Achieving Pupils: Negotiating Achievement and Peer Cultures.* London: Continuum.

Fraser, B. (1986) *Classroom Environment.* London: Routledge.

Fraser, B. J. and Fisher, D. L. (1984) *Assessment of Classroom Psychosocial Environment: Workshop Manual.* Bentley: Western Australia Institute of Technology.

Frederiksen, J. R. and White, B. J. (1997) 'Reflective assessment of students' research within an inquiry-based middle school science curriculum', paper presented at the Annual Meeting of AERA Chicago.

Freire, P. (2000) *Pedagogy of the Oppressed.* London: Continuum.

Frieberg, H. J. (1999) *School Climate: Measuring, Improving and Sustaining Healthy Learning Environments.* London: Psychology Press.

Frijda, N. H. (2001) 'The laws of emotion'. In Parrott, G. W. (ed.) *Emotions in Social Psychology.* Hove: Psychology Press.

Fuller, A. and Unwin, L. (2003) 'Learning as apprentices in the contemporary UK workplace:

creating and managing expansive and restrictive participation', *Journal of Education and Work*, 16 (4): 407–26.

Gage, N. and Berliner, D. C. (1975) *Educational Psychology*. Boston: Houghton Mofflin.

Gagné, R. M. (1965) *The Conditions of Learning*. New York: Holt, Rinehart and Winston.

Galton, M. (1989) *Teaching in the Primary School*. London: David Fulton.

—(2007) *Learning and Teaching in the Primary Classroom*. London: Paul Chapman.

Galton, M., Gray, J. and Rudduck, J. (1999) *The Impact of School Transitions and Transfers on Pupil Progress and Attainment*. London: DfEE.

Galton, M., Hargreaves, L., Comber, C., Wall, D. and Pell, A. (1999) *Inside the Primary Classroom: 20 Years On*. London: Routledge.

Galton, M., Simon, B. and Croll, P. (1980) *Inside the Primary Classroom*. London: Routledge and Kegan Paul.

Galton, M. and Williamson, J. (1992) *Group Work in the Primary Classroom*. London: Routledge.

Gardner, H. (1985) *Frames of Mind: The Theory of Multiple Intelligence*. London: Paladin Books.

—(1999) *Intelligence Reframed: Multiple Intelligences for the Twenty-first Century*. New York: Basic Books.

Gardner, J. (ed.) (2011) *Assessment and Learning*. London: Paul Chapman.

Gardner, J., Harlen, W., Hayward, L. and Stobart, G. with Montgomery, M. (2010) *Developing Teacher Assessment*. Maidenhead: Open University Press.

Gay, G. (2010) *Culturally Responsive Teaching: Theory, Research and Practice*. New York: Teachers College Press.

Geographical Association (2012) *Thinking Geographically. Response to the Consultation on the National Curriculum Review*. London: Geographical Association.

Gibson, E. J. (1977) 'The theory of affordances'. In Shaw, R. and Bransford, J. (eds) *Percieving, Acting and Knowing*. Hillsdale, NJ: Lawrence Earlbaum.

Giddens, A. (1984) *The Constitution of Society: Outline of the Theory of Structuration*. Berkeley: University of California Press.

Gilbert, I. (2002) *Essential Motivation in the Classroom*. London: RoutledgeFalmer.

Gilborn, P. (1995) *Racism and AntiRacism in Real Schools*. Buckingham: Open University Press.

Gillborn, D. (2006) *Racism and Education. Coincidence or Conspiracy?* Abingdon: Routledge.

Gillborn, D. and Youdell, D. (2000) *Rationing Education*. Buckingham: Open University Press.

Gillis, J. R. (1997) *A World of Their Own Making: Myth, Ritual, and the Quest for Family Values*. Cambridge, MA: Harvard University Press.

Gipps, C. and MacGilchrist, B. (1999) 'Primary school learners'. In Mortimore, P. (ed.) *Understanding Pedagogy and its Impact on Learning*. London: Paul Chapman.

Gipps, C. and Murphy, P. (1994) *A Fair Test? Assessment, Achievement, and Equity*. Buckingham: Open University Press.

Gipps, C., McCullum, B., McAllister, S. and Brown, M. (1991) 'National assessment at seven: some emerging themes'. In Gipps, C. (ed.) *Developing Assessment for the National Curriculum*. London: Kogan Page.

Glaser, R. (1999) 'Expert Knowledge and Processes of Thinking'. In McCormick, R. and Paechter, C. (eds) *Learning and Knowledge*. London: Paul Chapman.

Glass, G. V. (1982) *School Class Size, Research and Policy*. Beverley Hills, CA: SAGE.

Goleman, D. (1996) *Emotional Intelligence: Why it Can Matter More than IQ*. London: Bloomsbury.

—(1998) *Working with Emotional Intelligence*. London: Bloomsbury.

Gonzalez, N., Moll, L. and Amanti, C. (eds) (2005) *Funds of Knowledge: Theorizing Practices in Households, Communities and Classrooms*. Mahwah, NJ: Lawrence Erlbaum Associates.

Good, T. and Brophy, J. (2008) *Looking in Classrooms*. Boston: Pearson.

Goodhall, J. and Vorhaus, J. (2010) *Review of Best Practice in Parental Engagement*. London: DfE.

Goodwyn, A. *The Expert Teacher of English*. London: Routledge.

Goswami, U. (2008) *Cognitive Development. The Learning Brain*. Hove: Psychology Press

Goswami, U. and Bryant, P. (2010) 'Children's cognitive development and learning'. In Alexander, R. J. et al. (eds) *The Cambridge Primary Review Research Surveys*. London: Routledge.

Grainger, T., Goouch, K. and Lambirth, A. (2005) *Creativity and Writing: Developing Voice and Verve in the Classroom*. London: Routledge.

Gramsci, A. (1978) *Selections from Political Writings*. London: Lawrence and Wishart.

Grant, L. (2011) '"I'm a completely different person at home": using digital technologies to connect learning between home and school', *Journal of Computer-Assisted Learning*, 27, 292–302.

Green, A. and Janmaat, J. (2011) *Regimes of Social Cohesion: Societies and the Crisis of Globalization*. Basingstoke: Palgrave Macmillan.

Green, A., Preston, J. and Janmaat, J. G. (2006) *Education, Equality and Social Cohesion. A Comparative Analysis*. London: Palgrave.

Greenfield, S. (1997) *The Human Brain: A Guided Tour*. London: Weidenfeld and Nicolson.

GTC E (2010) 'Pedagogy matters'. In Pollard, A. (ed.) *Professionalism and Pedagogy: A Contemporary Opportunity*. London: TLRP.

—(2011) *Teaching Quality:* Policy Papers. London: GTC E.

GTC NI (2007) *Teaching: The Reflective Profession*. Belfast: GTC NI.

GTC S (2012) *Scotland's Code of Professionalism and Conduct*. Edinburgh: GTC S.

Gu, Q. (2007) *Teacher Development: Knowledge and Context*. London: Continuum.

Hagger, H. and McIntyre, D. (2006) *Learning Teaching from Teachers – Realizing the Potential of School-Based Teacher Education*. Maidenhead: Open University Press.

Hall, C. and Coles, M. (1999) *Children's Reading Choices*. London: Routledge.

Halpin, D. (2001) 'Hope, utopianism and educational management', *Cambridge Journal of Education*, 31 (1), 103–18.

Halsey, A. H. (1986) *Change in British Society*. Oxford: Oxford University Press.

Hampson, S. E. (1988) *The Construction of Personality: An Introduction*. London: Routledge.

Hardy, B. (1977) 'Towards a poetics of fiction: an approach through narrative'. In Meek, M., Warlow, A. and Barton, G. (eds) *The Cool Web*. London: Bodley Head.

Hargreaves, A. (1998) 'The emotional practice of teaching', *Teaching and Teacher Education*, 14 (8), 835–54.

—(2008) *The Persistence of Presentism and the Struggle for Lasting Improvement*. Inaugural lecture. London: Institute of Education.

Hargreaves, D. H. (1967) *Social Relations in a Secondary School*. London: Routledge.

—(1972) *Interpersonal Relationships and Education*. London: Routledge.

Hargreaves, D. H., Hestor, S. K. and Mellor, F. J. (1975) *Deviance in Classrooms*. London: Routledge and Kegan Paul.

Harlen, W. (2006) 'Teachers' and childrens' questioning'. In Harlen, W. (ed.) *ASE Guide to Primary Science*. Hatfield: Association for Science Education.

Harlen, W. and Bell, D. (2010) *Principles and Big Ideas of Science Education*. London: Association for Science Education.

Harlen, W. and Deakin Crick, R. (2002) 'A systematic review of the impact of summative assessment and tests on students' motivation for learning' (EPPICentre Review). In *Research Evidence in Education Library*. Issue 1. London: EPPI Centre, Social Science Research Unit, Institute of Education.

Harlen, W., Gipps, C., Broadfoot, P. and Nuttall, D. (1992) 'Assessment and the improvement of education', *Curriculum Journal*, 3 (3), 217–25.

Harris, A., Andrew-Power, K. and Goodall, J. (2009) *Do Parents Know They Matter? Raising Achievement Through Parental Engagement*. London: Continuum.

Harrison, C. (2004) *Understanding Reading Development*. London: SAGE.

Harrison, C. and Howard, S. (2009) *Inside the Primary Black Box: Assessment for Learning in Primary and Early Years Classrooms.* London: GL Assessment.

Hart, S. (2000) *Thinking Through Teaching* London: David Fulton Publishers.

Hart, S., Dixon, A., Drummond, M-J. and McIntyre, D. (2004) *Learning Without Limits.* Maidenhead: Open University Press.

Hartley, D. (1985) *Understanding the Primary School.* London: Croom Helm.

Hascher, T. (2003) 'Well-being in school – why students need social support'. In Mayring, P. and Von Rhoeneck, C. (eds) *Learning Emotions: The Influence of Affective Factors on Classroom Learning.* Frankfurt: Peter Lang.

Hashweh, M. Z. (1987) 'Effects of subject matter knowledge in the teaching of biology and physics', *Teaching and Teacher Education,* 3, 109–20.

Haste, H. (1987) 'Growing into rules'. In Bruner, J. S. and Haste, H. (eds) *Making Sense: The Child's Construction of the World.* London: Metheun.

Hastings, N. and Wood, C. K. (2001) *Reorganising Primary Classroom Learning.* Buckingham: Open University Press.

Hattie, J. (2009) *Visible Learning. A Synthesis of Meta-Analyses Relating to Achievement.* London: Routledge.

—(2012) *Visible Learning for Teachers: Maximising Impact on Learning.* London: Routledge.

Hattie, J. and Timperley, H. (2007) 'The power of feedback', *Review of Educational Research,* 77, 81–112.

Haviland, J. (1988) *Take Care, Mr Baker!* London: Fourth Estate.

Hay McBer Consultancy (2000) *Research into Teacher Effectiveness: A Model of Teacher Effectiveness.* London: DfEE.

Haydn, T. (2007) *Managing Pupil Behaviour.* London: Routledge.

Hayes, D., Mills, M., Christie, P. and Linguard, R. (2006) *Teachers and Schooling Making a Difference.* Sydney: Allen and Unwin.

Haynes, A. (2010) *The Complete Guide to Lesson Planning and Preparation.* London: Continuum.

Heilbronn, R. (2010) 'The nature of practice-based knowledge and understanding'. In Heilbronn, R. and Yandell, J. (2011) *Critical Practice in Teacher Education: A Study of Professional Learning.* London: Institute of Education.

Hellige, J. B. (1993) *Hemispheric Asymmetry: What's Left and What's Left.* Cambridge, MA: Harvard University Press.

Her Majesty's Inspectors (HMI) (1985) *The Curriculum from 5 to 16.* Curriculum Matters 2. An HMI Series. London: HMSO.

Heuston, B. and Miller, H. (2011) *Academic Learning Time: The Most Important Educational Concept You've Never Heard Of.* Salt Lake City: Waterford Institute.

Hick, P., Kershner, R. and Farrell, P. (eds) (2008) *Psychology for Inclusive Education: New Directions in Theory and Practice.* Abingdon: Routledge.

Higgins, S. (2003) *Does ICT Improve Learning and Teaching in Schools?* Nottingham: British Educational Research Association.

Higgins, S., Katsipataki, M., Kokotsaki, D., Coleman, R., Major, L. E. and Coe, R. (2013) *The Sutton Trust-Education Endowment Foundation Teaching and Learning Toolkit.* London: Education Endowment Foundation.

Hirsch, E. D. (1987) *Cutural Literacy: What Every American Needs to Know.* New York: Houghton Mifflin.

HMCI (1995) *The Annual Report of Her Majesty's Chief Inspector of Schools.* London: HMSO.

Hodgson, C. and Pyle, K. (2010) *Assessment for Learning in Science: A Literature Review.* Slough: NfER.

—(2007) Improving educational research: TLRP's projects and themes'. International commentary. *British Educational Research Journal,* 33 (5), 781–804.

Hogan, D. (2012) 'Yes Brian, at long last, there is pedagogy in England – and in Singapore too'.

In James, M. and Pollard, A. (eds) *Principles for Effective Pedagogy. International Responses to the UK TLRP.* London: Routledge.

Hogan, D., Chan, M., Rahim, R., Kwek, D., Aye, K. M., Loo, S. C., Sheng, Y. and Luo, W. (2013) 'Assessment and the logic of instructional practice in Secondary 3 English and Mathematics classes in Singapore', *Review of Education*, 1 (1), 57–106.

Hogden, J. and Webb, M. (2008) 'Questioning and dialogue'. In S. Swaffield (ed.) *Unlocking Assessment: Understanding for Reflection and Application,* 73–89*.* Abingdon: Routledge.

Hohmann, M., Banet, B. and Weikart, D. (1979) *Young Children in Action.* Ypsilanti, MI: High Scope Educational Research Foundation.

Holt, J. (1982) *How Children Fail.* London: Penguin.

Hooper, M. and Robertson, M. P. (2000) *Ice Trap! Shackleton's Incredible Expedition.* London: Frances Lincoln.

Hopkins, D., Harris, A., Singleton, C. and Watts, R. (2000) *Creating the Conditions for Teaching and Learning.* London: David Fulton.

Hornby, G. (2011) *Parental Involvement in Childhood Education: Building Effective School-Family Partnerships.* London: Springer.

Houghton, E. (ed.) (2012) *Education on the Web: A Tool-kit to Help You Search Effectively for Information on Education.* Slough: NFER.

House of Commons (2008) *Testing and Assessment.* Third Report of Session 2007–08, Children, Schools and Families Committee. London: House of Commons.

Howard-Jones, P. (ed.) (2007) *Neuroscience and Education: Issues and Opportunities.* A TLRP Commentary. London: TLRP.

Howe, C. and Mercer, N. (2007) *Children's Social Development, Peer Interaction and Classroom Learning.* The Primary Review: Research Survey 2/1b.

Howe, M. J. A. (1990) *The Origins of Exceptional Abilities.* London: Blackwell.

Howes, A., Davies, S. M. B. and Fox, S. (2009) *Improving the Context for Inclusion: Personalising Teacher Development through Collaborative Action Research.* London, Routledge.

Hoyle, E. (1974) 'Professionality, professionalism and control in teaching', *London Educational Review*, 3 (2).

Hoyle, E. and Megarry, J. (2005) *World Yearbook of Education 1980: The Professional Development of Teachers* (reprinted). London: Routledge.

Huberman, M. (1993) *The Lives of Teachers.* London: Cassell.

Hugdahl, K. (1995) *Psychophysiology: The Mind–Body Perspective.* Cambridge, MA: Harvard University Press.

Hughes, M., Desforges, C., Mitchell, C. and Carre, C. (2000) *Numeracy and Beyond: Applying Mathematics in the Primary School.* Buckingham: Open University Press.

Hughes, M. and Pollard, A. (2000) 'Home–school knowledge exchange and transformation in primary education', *ESRC Project L139251078.* Bristol: University of Bristol.

Hughes, M., Wikeley, F. and Nash, T. (1994) *Parents and Their Children's Schools.* Oxford: Blackwell.

Humphreys, T. (1995) *A Different Kind of Teacher.* London: Cassell.

Hunter, R. and Scheirer, E. A. (1988) *The Organic Classroom: Organizing for Learning 7 to 12.* London: Falmer.

Immordino-Yang, M. H. and Dmasio, A. (2007) 'We feel, therefore we learn. The relevance of affective social neuroscience to education', *Mind, Brain and Education*, 1 (1), 3–9.

Ingram, J. and Worrall, N. (1993) *Teacher–Child Partnership: The Negotiating Classroom.* London: David Fulton.

Inhelder, B. and Piaget, J. (1958) *The Growth of Logical Thinking from Childhood to Adolescence.* New York: Basic Book.

Ireson, J. and Hallam, S. (2001) *Ability Grouping in Education.* London: SAGE.

Ivinson, G. and Murphy, P. (2007) *Rethinking Single Sex Teaching.* Maidenhead: Open University Press.

Jackson, B. (1964) *Streaming: An Education System in Miniture.* London: Routledge and Kegan Paul.

Jackson, B. and Marsden, D. (1962) *Education and the Working Class.* London: Ark.

Jackson, C (2006) *Lads and Ladettes in School: Gender and a Fear of Failure.* Maidenhead: Open University Press.

Jackson, C. and Warin, J. (2000) 'The importance of gender as an aspect of identity at key transition points in compulsory education', *British Educational Research Journal,* 26 (3), 375–91.

Jackson, P. W. (1968) *Life in Classrooms.* New York: Holt, Rinehart and Winston.

James, A. and James, A. L. (2004) *Constructing Childhood: Theory, Policy and Social Practice* Hampshire: Palgrave Macmillan

James, A., Jenks, C. and Prout, A. (1998) *Theorising Childhood.* Cambridge: Polity Press.

James, D. and Biesta, G. (2007) *Improving Learning Cultures in Further Education.* London: Routledge.

James, M. (1992) *Assessment for learning.* Paper presented at the Annual Conference of the Association for Supervision and Curriculum Development (Assembly session on 'Critique of Reforms in Assessment and Testing in Britain') held at New Orleans, LA, April.

—(1998) *Using Assessment for School Improvement.* Oxford: Heinemann.

—(2005) 'Insights on teacher learning from the Teaching and Learning Research Programme (TLRP)', *Research Papers in Education,* 20 (2), 105–8.

—(2008) *Only Connect! Improving Teaching and Learning in Schools.* Inaugural lecture. London: Institute of Education.

—(2012) 'Assessment in harmony with our understanding of learning: problems and possibilities'. In Gardner, J. (ed.) *Assessment and Learning,* 2nd edn, 187–205. London: SAGE.

James, M., Black, P., Carmichael, P., Conner, C., Dudley, P., Fox, A., Frost, D., Honour, L., MacBeath, J., McCormick, R., Marshall, B., Pedder, D., Procter, R., Swaffield, S. and Wiliam, D. (2006) *Learning How to Learn: Tools for schools.* London: Routledge.

James, M., McCormick, R., Black, P., Carmichael, P., Drummond, M-J., Fox, A., MacBeath, J., Marshall, B., Pedder, D., Procter, R., Swaffield, S., Swann, J. and Wiliam, D. (2007) *Improving Learning How to Learn: Classrooms, Schools and Networks.* London: Routledge.

James, M. and Pollard, A. (2004) *Personalised Learning.* London: TLRP

—(2006) *Improving Teaching and Learning in Schools: A commentary by the Teaching and Learning Research Programme.* London: TLRP.

—(2012a) *Principles for Effective Pedagogy. International Responses to Evidence from the UK Teaching and Learning Research Programme.* London: Routledge.

—(2012b) 'TLRP's ten principles for effective pedagogy: rationale, development, evidence, argument and impact', *Research Papers in Education,* 26 (3), 275–328.

Jarman, R. and McClune, B. (2005) 'Space Science News: Special Edition: A resource for extending reading and promoting engagement with newspapers in the science classroom', *Literacy,* 39 (3), 121–8.

Jenks, C. (1972) *A Question of Control: A Case Study of Interaction in a Junior School.* London: Institute of Education, University of London.

Jewitt, C. and Parashar, U. (2011) 'Technology and learning at home: findings from the evaluation of the Home Access Programme Pilot', *Journal of Computer Assisted Learning,* 27 (4), 303–13.

John, M. (2003) *Children's Rights and Power: Charging Up for a New Century.* London: Jessica Kingsley.

Johnson, D. W. and Johnson, F. (1997) *Joining Together: Group Theory and Group Skills.* Boston: Allyn and Bacon.

Jones, P. (2009) *Rethinking Childhood: Attitudes in Contemporary Society*. London: Continuum.

Joseph Rowntree Foundation (2000) *Poverty and Social Exclusion in Britain*. York: JRF.

Joyce, B., Weil, M. and Calhoun, E. (2009) *Models of Teaching*. New York: Pearson.

Kagan, J. (1964) 'Information processing in the child: significance of analytic and reflective attitudes', *Psychological Monographs*, 78 (1), 1–37.

Karoly, L. A., Greenwood, P. W. and Everingham, S. (eds) (1998) *Investing in Our Children: What We Know and Don't Know about the Costs and Benefits of Early Childhood Intervention*. New York: RAND.

Katz, L. (1998) 'A development approach to the curriculum in the early years'. In Smidt, S. (ed.) *The Early Years: A Reader*. London: Routledge.

Kehily, M. J. (2002) *Sexuality, Gender and Schooling: Shifting Agendas in Social Learning*. London: RoutledgeFalmer.

Kennewell, S., Tanner, H. et al. (2008) *Interactive Teaching and ICT*. Research Briefing 33. London: TLRP.

Kent, N. A. and Facer, K. L. (2004) 'Different worlds? Children's home and school computer use', *Journal of Computer Assisted Learning*, 20 (6), 440–55.

Kerry, T. and Kerry, C. (1997) 'Differentiation: teachers' views of the usefulness of recommended strategies in helping the more able pupils in primary and secondary classrooms', *Educational Studies*, 23 (3), 439–57.

Kershner, R. (2009) 'Learning in inclusive classrooms'. In Hick, P., Kershner, R. and Farrell, P. (eds) *Psychology for Inclusive Education: New directions in Theory and Practice*. Abingdon: Routledge.

Kettle, B. and Sellars, N. (1996) 'The development of student teachers practical theory of teaching', *Teaching and Teacher Education*, 12 (1), 1–24.

Kincheloe, J. L. (2008) *Critical Pedagogy Primer*. New York: Peter Lang.

King, R. (1978) *All Things Bright and Beautiful? A Sociological Study of Infants' Classrooms*. Chichester: Wiley.

Kirsch, I., de Jong, J., LaFontaine, D., McQueen, J., Mendelovits, J. and Monseur, C. (2002) *Reading for Change: Performance and Engagement across Countries*. Paris: OECD Development.

Klenowski, V. (2009) 'Assessment for Learning revisited: An Asia-Pacific perspective', *Assessment in Education: Principles, Policy and Practice*, 16 (3), 263–8.

Kline, P. (1991) *Intelligence: The Psychometric View*. London: Routledge.

Kluger, A. N. and De Nisi, A. (1996) 'The effects of feedback interventions on performance: a historical review, a meta-analysis, and a preliminary feedback intervention theory', *Psychological Bulletin*, 119, 254–84.

Kogan, M. (1978) *The Politics of Educational Change*. London: Fontana.

Kohlberg, L. (1976) 'Moral stages and moralization: the cognitive-developmental approach'. In Lickona, T. (ed.) *Moral Development and Behavior*. New York: Holt, Rinehart and Winston.

Kounin, J. S. (1970) *Discipline and Group Management in Classrooms*. New York: Holt, Rhinehart and Winston.

Kress, G. (1993) *Learning to Write*. London: Routledge.

—(2010) 'The profound shift of digital literacies'. In Gillen, J. and Barton, D. (eds) *Digital Literacies*. London: TLRP TEL.

Kress, G. and van Leeuwen, T. (2006) *Reading Images: The Grammar of Visual Design*. London: Routledge.

Kress, K. (2012) *Literacy in the New Media Age*. London: Routledge.

Kuhl, P. (2004) 'Early language acquisition: cracking the speech code', *Nature Neuroscience*, 5, 831–43.

Kuno, H. (2011) 'Lesson Study from Japanese school leadership perspective'. Paper presented at the International Practical Science conference, 'Teacher professional development: traditions and changes', 5–6 December, Astana, Kazakhstan.

Kutnick, P., Blatchford, P. and Baines, E. (2002) 'Pupil groupings in primary school classrooms: sites for learning and social pedagogy?', *British Educational Research Journal*, 28 (2), 187–206.

Kutnick, P., Ota, C. and Berdondini, L. (2008) 'Improving the effects of group working in classrooms with young school-aged children: facilitating attainment, interaction and classroom activity', *Learning and Instruction*, 18 (1), 83–95.

Kyriacou, C. (2009) *Effective Teaching in Schools. Theory and Practice.* Cheltenham: Nelson Thornes.

Kyriacou, C. and Issitt, J. (2008) 'What characterizes effective teacher–pupil dialogue to promote conceptual understanding in mathematics lessons in England in Key Stages 2 and 3?', *EPPI-Centre Report no. 1604R.* Social Science Research Unit: Institute of Education, University of London.

Lacey, C. (1970) *Hightown Grammar. The School as a Social System.* Manchester: Manchester University Press.

Land, R., Meyer, J. and Smith, J. (eds) (2008) *Threshold Concepts within the Disciplines.* Rotterdam: Sense Publishers.

Lareau, A. (1989) *Home Advantage: Social Class and Parental Intervention in Elementary Education.* London: Falmer.

Laslett, R. and Smith, C. (1992) *Effective Classroom Management: A Teacher's Guide.* London: Routledge.

Lave, J. and Wenger, E. (1991) *Situated Learning: Legitimate Peripheral Participation.* Cambridge: Cambridge University Press.

Lawn, M. and Grace, G. (eds) (1987) *Teachers: The Culture and Politics of Work.* London: Falmer.

Lawn, M. and Ozga, J. (1986) 'Unequal partners: teachers under indirect rule', *British Journal of Sociology of Education*, 7 (2), 225–38.

Lawrence, D. (1987) *Enhancing Self-esteem in the Classroom.* London: Paul Chapman.

Lazarus, R. S. (1991) *Emotion and Adaption.* Oxford: Oxford University Press.

—(1999) *Stress and Emotion: A New Synthesis.* London: Free Association Books.

Leach, J. and Moon, B. (eds) (1999) *Learners and Pedagogy.* London: SAGE.

—(2008) *The Power of Pedagogy.* London: SAGE.

Leckie, G. and Goldstein, H. (2009) 'The limitations of using school league tables to inform school choice', *Journal of the Royal Statistical Society: Series A.,* 172, 835–51.

Lees, S. (1993) *Sugar and Spice: Sexuality and Adolescent Girls.* Harmonsworth: Penguin.

Levin, B. (2008) *How to Change 5000 Schools.* Cambridge, MA.: Harvard Eduction Press.

Lewin, K. (1935) *A Dynamic Theory of Personality.* New York: McGraw-Hill.

Lewis, A. and Norwich, B. (2004) *Special Teaching for Special Children? Pedagogies for Inclusion.* Maidenhead: Open University Press.

Leyland, P. (2012) *Constitution of the United Kingdom: A Contextual Analysis.* Oxford: Hart Publishing.

Li, Y. and Kaiser, G. (2010) *Expertise in Mathematics Instruction.* London: Springer.

Light, P. and Littleton, K. (1999) *Social Processes in Children's Learning.* Cambridge: Cambridge University Press.

Lingard, B. (2008) 'Pedagogies of indifference: in research, policy and practice'. In Linguard, B., Nixon, J. and Ranson, S. *Transforming Learning in Schools and Communities.* London: Continuum.

Lingard,B., Hayes, D., Mills, M. and Christie, P. (2003) *Leading Learning:Making Hope Practical in Schools.* Maidenhead: Open University Press.

Lingard, B., Martino, W. and Mills, M. (2009) *Boys and Schooling: Beyond Structural Reform.* Basingstoke: Palgrave Macmillan

Linklater, H. (2010) *Making Children Count? An Autoethnographic Exploration of Pedagogy.* Unpublished PhD thesis, University of Aberdeen, Scotland.

Lipman, M., Sharp, A. M. and Oscanyan, F. S. (1980) *Philosophy in the Classroom.* Philadelphia: Temple University Press.

Loughran, J. (2010) *What Expert Teachers Do: Enhancing Professional Knowledge for Classroom Practice.* London: Routledge.

Lucas, D. and Thomas, G. (2000) 'Organising classrooms to promote learning for all children'. In Clipson-Boyles, S. *Putting Research into Practice.* London: David Fulton.

Luehmann, A. L. (2007) 'Identity development as a lens to science teacher preparation', *Science Education,* 91, 822–39.

Mac an Ghaill, M. (1988) *Young, Gifted and Black.* Buckingham: Open University Press.

—(1994) *The Making of Men: Masculintities, Sexualities and Schooling.* Buckingham: Open University Press.

MacBeath, J. and Mortimore, P. (eds) (2001) *Improving School Effectiveness.* Buckingham: Open University Press.

MacGilchrist, B. (2003) *Has School Improvement Passed Its Sell-by date?* Inaugural lecture. London: Institute of Education.

MacGilchrist, B., Myers, K. and Reed, J. (2004) *The Intelligent School.* London: SAGE.

Maclure, M. (2000) 'Arguing for yourself: identity as an organising principle in teachers' jobs and lives', *British Educational Research Journal,* 19 (4), 311–22.

Male, B. and Waters, M. (2012a) *The Primary Curriculum Design Handbook.* London: Continuum.

—(2012b) *The Secondary Curriculum Design Handbook.* London: Continuum.

Mallett, M. (1999) *Young Researchers: Informational Reading and Writing in the Early and Primary Years.* London: Routledge.

Manen, M. van (1991) *The Tact of Teaching: The meaning of Pedagogical Thoughtfulness.* London, Ontario: The Althouse Press.

—(1999) 'The language of pedagogy and the primacy of student experience'. In Loughran, J. (ed.) *Researching Teaching: Methodologies and Practices for Understanding Pedagogy,* 19–22. London: Falmer Press.

Mangan, J. A. E. (1993) *The Imperial Curriculum: Racial Images and Education in the British Colonial Experience.* London: Routledge.

Mansell, W. (2007) *Education by Numbers: The Tyranny of Testing.* London: Politico Publishing.

Mansell, W. and James, M. with the Assessment Reform Group (2009) *Assessment in Schools: Fit for Purpose? A Commentary by the Teaching and Learning Research Programme.* London: TLRP.

Marsh, J. (2005) *Popular Culture, New Media and Digital Literacy in Early Childhood.* London: Routledge.

Marsh, L. (1970) *Alongside the Child.* London: Black.

Marshall, B. and Drummond, M. J. (2006) 'How teachers engage with assessment for learning: lessons from the classroom', *Research Papers in Education,* 21 (2), 133–49.

Marshall, T. H. and Bottomore, T. (1992) *Citizenship and Social Class.* London: Pluto.

Marzano, R. J. (2009) *Designing and Teaching Learning Goals and Objectives.* Bloomington: Solution Tree.

Maslow, A. H. (1954) *Motivation and Personality.* New York: Harper and Row.

Maude, P. (2001) *Physical Children, Active Teaching: Investigating Physical Literacy.* Buckingham: Open University Press.

Maun, I. and Myhill, D. (2005) 'Text as design, writers as designers', *English in Education,* 39 (2), 5–21.

Mayall, B (1994) *Negotiating Health: Children at Home and Primary School.* London: Cassell.

—(2002) *Towards a Sociology for Childhood: Thinking from Children's Lives.* Milton Keynes: Open University Press.

—(2009) 'Children's lives outside school'. In Alexander R (ed.) *Children, Their World, Their Education*. London: Routledge.

Maynard, T. and Furlong, J. (1993) 'Learning to teach and models of mentoring'. In McIntyre, D., Hagger, H. and Wilkin, M. (eds) *Mentoring: Perspectives on School Based Teacher Education*. London: Kogan Page.

McCullough, G., Helsby, G. and Knight, P. (2000) *The Politics of Professionalism: Teachers and the Curriculum*. London: Continuum.

McDermott, R. P. (1996) 'The acquisition of a child by a learning disability'. In Chaiklin, S. and Lave, J. (eds) *Understanding Practice*. Cambridge: Cambridge University Press.

McGregor (2007) *Developing Thinking; Developing Learning: A Guide to Thinking Skills in Education*. Maidenhead: Open University Press.

McGuinness, C. (1999) *From Thinking Skills to Thinking Classrooms*. Research Report 115. London: DfEE.

McLaughlin, C., Black Hawkins, K., Brindley, S., McIntyre, D. and Taber, K. (2006) *Researching Schools. Stories from a Schools-University Partnership*. Maidenhead: Open University Press.

McNally, J. and Blake, A. (eds) (2010) *Improving Learning in a Professional Context. The New Teacher at School*. London: TLRP.

McNiff, J. (1988) *Action Research: Principles and Practice*. London: Routledge.

McPherson, A. and Raab, C. D. (1988) *Governing Education: A Sociology of Policy since 1945*. Edinburgh: Edinburgh University Press.

Mead, G. H. (1934) *Mind, Self, and Society*. Chicago: University of Chicago Press.

Meek, M. (1988) *How Texts Teach What Readers Learn*. Stroud: Thimble Press.

—(1996) *Information and Book Learning*. Stroud: Thimble Press.

Meighan, R. (1978) 'The learner's viewpoint', *Educational Review*, 30 (2).

Meighan, R. and Siraj-Blatchford, I. (1981) *A Sociology of Educating*. London: Cassell.

Mental Health Foundation (2005) *A Bright Future for All*. London: Mental Health Foundation.

Menter, I., Elliot, D., Hall, J., Hulme, M., Lewin, J. and Lowden, K. (2010) *A Guide to Practitioner Research in Education*. Maidenhead: Open University Press.

Menter, I., Hulme, M., Elliot, D., Lewin, J. et al. (2010) *Literature Review on Teacher Education in the 21st Century*. Edinburgh: The Scottish Government.

Mercer, N. (1992) 'Culture, context and the appropriation of knowledge'. In Light, P. and Butterworth, G. (eds) *Context and Cognition: Ways of Learning and Knowing*. Hemel Hempstead: Harvester Wheatsheaf.

—(1995) *The Guided Construction of Knowledge: Talk amongst Teachers and Learners*. Clevedon: Multilingual Matters.

—(2000) *Words and Minds: How We Use Language to Think Together*. London: Routledge.

Mercer, N., Dawes, L., Wegerif, R. and Sams, C. (2004) 'Reasoning as a scientist: ways of helping children to use language to learn science', *British Educational Research Journal*, 30 (3), 359–77.

Mercer, N. and Hodgkinson, S. (2008) (eds) (2008) *Exploring Talk in School*. London: SAGE.

Mercer, N. and Littleton, K. (2007) *Dialogue and the Development of Children's Thinking*. London: Routledge.

Mercier, C., Philpott, C. and Scott, H. (2012) *Professional Issues in Secondary Teaching*. London: SAGE.

Merrett, F. and Wheldall, K. (1990) *Identifying Troublesome Classroom Behaviour*. London: Paul Chapman.

Meyer, J. W. and Kamens, D. H. (1992) 'Conclusion: accounting for a world curriculum'. In Meyer, J. W., Kamens, D. H. and Benavot, A. with Cha, Y. K. and Wong S. Y. (eds) *School Knowledge for the Masses: World Models of National Primary Curricular Categories in the Twentieth Century*. London: Falmer.

Meyer, J. W., Kamens, D. H. and Benavot, A. with Cha Y. K. and Wong S. Y. (eds) (1992) *School Knowledge for the Masses: World Models of National Primary Curricular Categories in the Twentieth Century*. London: Falmer.

Millar, R., Leach, J., Osborne, J. and Ratcliffe, M. (2006) *Improving Subject Teaching: Lessons from Research in Science. Education*. London: Routledge.

Miller, J. (1997) *Never Too Young: How Young Children Can Take Responsibility and Make Decisions*. London: Save the Children.

Mills, C. W. (1959) *The Sociological Imagination*. New York: Oxford University Press.

Minow, M. (1990) *Making All the Difference: Inclusion, Exclusion and American Law*. Ithaca: Cornell University Press.

Mitchell, D., (2005) (ed.) *Contextualizing Inclusive Education: Evaluating Old and New International Perspectives*. London: Routledge.

Mitchell, J. (2012) *Devolution in the United Kingdom*. Manchester: Manchester University Press.

Mitchell, N. and Pearson, J. (2012) *Inquiring in the Classroom. Asking the Questions that Matter about Teaching and Learning*. London: Continuum.

Moll, L. C. and Greenberg, J. B. (1990) 'Creating zones of possibilities: combining social contexts for instruction'. In Moll, L. C. (ed.) *Vygotsky and Education*. Cambridge: Cambridge University Press.

Money, J. (1985) *Gendermaps: Social Constructionism, Feminism, and Sexosophical History*. New York: Continuum.

Moore, A. (2004) *The Good Teacher: Dominant Discourses in Teaching and Teacher Education*. Abingdon: Routledge.

Morange, M. (2001) *The Misunderstood Gene*. Cambridge, MA: Harvard University Press.

Mortimer, E. F. and Scott, P. H. (2007) *Meaning Making in Secondary Science Classrooms*. Maidenhead: Open University Press.

Mortimore, P., Sammons, P., Stoll, L., Lewis, D. and Ecob, R. (1988) *School Matters: The Junior Years*. Wells: Open Books.

Moyles, J., Hargreaves, L., Merry, R., Peterson, F. and Esarte-Sarries, V. (2003) *Interactive Teaching in the Primary School: Digging Deeper into Meaning*. Buckingham: Open University Press.

Moyles, J. R. (ed.) (2005) *The Excellence of Play*, 2nd edn. Maidenhead: Open University Press.

Muijs, D. and Reynolds, D. (2011) *Effective Teaching: Evidence and Practice*. London: SAGE.

Murphy, P. (2001) 'Gendered learning and achievement'. In Collins, J. and Cook, D. (eds) *Understanding Learning: Influences and Outcomes*. London: Paul Chapman.

Muschamp, Y. (1991) 'Pupil self-assessment', *Practical Issues in Primary Education*, No. 9. Bristol: NPC SW.

—(1994) 'Target setting with young children'. In Pollard, A. and Bourne, J. (eds) *Teaching and Learning in Primary Schools*. London: Routledge.

Myhill, D., Jones, S., Lines, H. and Watson, A. (2012) 'Re-thinking grammar: the impact of embedded grammar teaching on students' writing and students' metalinguistic understanding', *Research Papers in Education*, 27 (2), 139–66.

Nash, R. (1976) *Teacher Expectations and Pupil Learning*. London: Routledge.

National Assembly for Wales (NAfW) (2006) *Inclusion and Pupil Support*. Circular 47. Cardiff: NAfW.

National Audit Commission (2001) *Tackling Obesity in England*. London: The Stationery Office.

National Curriculum Council (NCC) (1990) *The Whole Curriculum*. York: NCC.

National Foundation for Educational Research (NFER) (2011) *Report on Subject Breadth in International Jurisdictions. Review of the National Curriculum in England*. London: DfE.

National Research Council (1999) *Improving Learning: A Strategic Plan for Education Research and its Utilisation*. Washington, DC: National Academy Press.

Neelands, J. and Goode, T. (eds) (2000) *Structuring Drama work: A Handbook of Available Forms in Theatre and Drama*, 2nd edn. London: David Fulton.

Neimi, H., Toom, A. and Kallioniemi, A. (eds) (2012) *Miricle of Education: The Principles and Practices of Teaching and Learning in Finnish Schools*. Rotterdam: Sense Publishers.

Newell, P. (1991) *The UN Convention and Children's Rights in the UK.* London: National Children's Bureau.

Newmann, F., Bryk, A. and Nagaoka, J. (2001) *Authentic Intellectual Work and Standardized Tests: Conflict or Coexistence.* Chicago: Consortium on Chicago School Research.

Newton, P. (2007) *Techniques for Monitoring the Comparability of Examination Standards.* London: Qualification and Curriculum Authority.

New Zealand Ministry of Education (2012) *The New Zealand Curriculum Online.* Available at http://nzcurriculum.tki.org.nz (accessed February 2013).

Nias, J. (1989) *Primary Teachers Talking: A Study of Teaching at Work.* London: Routledge.

Nias, J., Southworth, G. and Campbell, P. (1992) *Whole-school Curriculum Development in the Primary School*. London: Falmer Press.

Nias, J., Southworth, G. and Yeomans, R. (1989) *Staff Relationships in the Primary School: A Study of Organisational Cultures*. London: Cassell.

Niemi, H. (2007) 'Improving educational research: TLRP's projects and themes'. International commentary, *British Educational Research Journal*, 33 (5), 781–804.

Nieto, S. (2009) *The Light in their Eyes: Creating Multicultural Learning Communities.* New York: Teachers College Press.

Norman, K. (ed.) (1992) *Thinking Voices: The Work of the National Oracy Project.* London: Hodder and Stoughton.

Norwich, B. (2008) *Dilemmas of Difference, Inclusion and Disability: International Perspectives and Future Directions,* London: Routledge.

Nystrand, M., with Gamoran A., Kachur, R. and Prendergast, C. (1997) *Opening Dialogue: Understanding the Dynamics of Language and Learning in the English Classroom.* New York: Teachers College Press.

Oates, T. (2010) *Could Do Better. Using International Comparisons to Refine the National Curriculum in England.* Cambridge: Cambridge Assessment.

O'Brien, T. and Garner, P. (2001) *Untold Stories: Learning Support Assistants and Their Work.* Stoke-on-Trent: Trentham Books.

O'Dea, J. and Abraham, S. (2000) 'Improving the body image, eating attitudes and behaviours of young male and female adolescents', *International Journal of Eating Disorders.* 28, 42–57.

OECD (2005) *Teachers Matter: Attracting, Developing and Retaining Effective Teachers.* Paris: OECD.

—(2011) *The Nature of Learning. Using Research to Inspire Practice.* Paris: OECD.

Office for National Statistics (2012) *Britain: The Official Yearbook of the United Kingdom.* London: The Stationery Office.

Ofsted (2008) *Using Data, Improving Schools.* London: Ofsted.

—(2009a) *Twelve Outstanding Secondary Schools – Excelling Against the Odds.* London: Ofsted.

—(2009b) *Twenty Outstanding Primary Schools – Excelling Against the Odds.* London: Ofsted.

—(2010) *The Special Needs and Disability Review.* London: Ofsted.

—(2011) *ICT in Schools 2008–11.* London: Ofsted.

—(2012) *The Framework for School Inspection.* London: Ofsted.

O'Neill, A. (2002) *A Question of Trust.* The Reith Lectures. London: BBC.

Opie, I. and Opie, P. (1959) *Children's Games in Street and Playground.* Oxford: Oxford University Press.

Osborn, M., McNess, E. and Broadfoot, P. with Pollard, A. and Triggs, P. (2000) *What Teachers Do. Changing Policy and Practice in Primary Education.* London: Continuum.

Osborn, M, McNess, E. and Pollard, A. (2006) 'Identity and transfer: a new focus for home–school knowledge exchange', *Educational Research – Special Issue*, 58 (4), 415–33.

Osler, A. and Starkey, H. (2010) *Teacehrs and Human Rights Education.* Stoke-on-Trent: Trentham Books.

Parker-Rees, R. (1999) 'Protecting playfulness'. In Abbott, L. and Moylett, H. (eds) *Early Education Transformed*. London: Falmer.

Pate-Bain, H., Achilles, C., Boyd-Zaharias, J. and McKenna, B. (1992) 'Class size does make a difference', *Phi Delta Kappa*, November, 253–5.

Paterson, L. (1998) 'The civic activism of Scottish teachers: explanations and consequences', *Oxford Review of Education*, 24 (3), 279–302.

Pea, R. D. (2004) 'The social and technological dimensions of scaffolding and related theoretical concepts for learning, education and human activity', *Journal of the Learning Sciences*, 13, 423–51.

Perrot, E. (1982) *Effective Teaching: A Practical Guide to Improving Your Teaching*. London: Longman.

Peters, S. J. (2012) 'The heterodoxy of student voice: challenges to identity in the sociology of disability and education'. In M. Arnot (ed.) *The Sociology of Disability and Inclusive Education: A Tribute to Len Barton*. London: Routledge.

Petty, G. (2009) *Teaching Today. A Practical Guide.* Cheltenham: Nelson Thornes

Piaget, J. (1926) *The Language and Thought of the Child*. New York: Basic Books.

—(1950) *The Psychology of Intelligence*. London: Routledge and Kegan Paul.

—(1951) *Play, Dreams and Imitation*. New York: Norton.

—(1961) 'A genetic approach to the psychology of thought', *Journal of Educational Psychology*, 52, 51–61.

Pianta, R. C. (1999) *Enhancing Relationships Between Children and Teachers*. Washington, DC: American.

Plummer, G. (2000) *Failing Working Class Girls*. Stoke-on-Trent: Trentham Books.

Pointon, P. and Kershner, R. (2000) 'Children's views of the primary classroom as an environment for work and learning', *Research in Education*, 64, 64–77.

Pol, J. van de, Volan, M. and Beishuizen, J. (2012) 'Promoting teacher scaffolding in small group work: A contingency perspective', *Teaching and Teacher Education,* 28 (2), 193–205.

Polanyi, M. (1962) *Personal Knowledge. Towards a Post-critical Philosphy.* London: Routledge.

Pollard, A. (1982) 'A model of coping strategies', *British Journal of Sociology of Education*, 3 (1), 19–37.

—(1985) *The Social World of the Primary School*. London: Cassell.

—(1987a) 'Social differentiation in primary schools', *Cambridge Journal of Education*, 17 (3), 158–61.

—(1987b) 'Primary school teachers and their colleagues'. In Delamont, S. (ed.) *The Primary School Teacher*. Lewes: Falmer.

—(ed.) (1987) *Children and their Primary Schools: A New Perspective*. London: Falmer.

—(ed.) (2010) *Professionalism and Pedagogy: A Contemporary Opportunity.* London: TLRP.

Pollard, A., Broadfoot, P., Croll, P., Osborn, M. and Abbott, D. (1994) *Changing English Primary Schools? The Impact of the Education Reform Act at Key Stage One*. London: Cassell.

Pollard, A. and Filer, A. (1996) *The Social World of Children's Learning: Case Studies of Pupils from Four to Seven*. London: Cassell.

—(1999) *The Social World of Pupil Career: Strategic Biographies through Primary School*. London: Cassell.

—(2007) *Education, Schooling and Learning for Life.* Reserch Briefing 23. London: TLRP.

Pollard, A. and James, M. (2004) *Personalised Learning: A Commentary by the Teaching and Learning Research Programme*. Cambridge: TLRP.

Pollard, A. and Triggs, P. (1997) *Reflective Teaching in Secondary Education*. London: Cassell.

—(2000) *What Pupils Say: Changing Policy and Practice in Primary Education*. London: Continuum.

Power, S. (2008) 'The imaginative professional'. In Cunningham, B. *Exploring Professionalism*. London: Institute of Education Publications.

Pring, R. (2010) *Philosophy of Educational Research*. London: Continuum.

—(2012) *The Life and Death of Secondary Education for All.* London: Routledge.

Pring, R., Hayward, G., Hodgson, A., Johnson, J., Keep, E., Oancea, A., Rees, G., Spours, K. and Wilde, S. (2009) *Education for All: The Future of Education and Training for 14–19 Year Olds in England and Wales*, London: Routledge.

Pringle, M. and Cobb, T. (1999) *Making Pupil Data Powerful: A Guide for Classroom Teachers*. Stafford: Network Educational Press.

Prutzman, P., Burger, M. L., Bodenhamer, G. and Stern, L. (1978) *The Friendly Classroom for a Small Planet*. New York: Avery Publishing.

Putnam, J. and Burke, J. B. (1992) *Organising and Managing Classroom Learning Communities*. New York: McGraw Hill.

Putnam, R. D. (1995) 'Bowling alone: America's declining social capital', *Journal of Democracy*, 6 (1) 65–78.

Qualifications and Curriculum Authority (QCA) (2007) *The Big Picture of the Curriculum*. London: QCA.

Raffe, D., Brannen, K., Croxford, L. and Martin, C. (1999) 'Comparing England, Scotland, Wales and Northern Ireland: the case for "home internationals" in comparative research', *Comparative Education*, 35 (1), 9–25.

Raphael-Read, L. (1995) 'Working with boys: a new research agenda', *Redland Papers*, 3. Bristol: University of the West of England.

Rawling, E. (2006) 'A shift in the zeitgeist? Are we witnessing the return of curriculum development?', *Nuffield Review of 14–19 Education*, Working Paper. Oxford.

Reay, D. (1998) *Class Work: Mothers' Involvement in Children's Schooling*. London: University College Press.

—(2000) 'A useful extension of Bourdieu's conceptual framework? Emotional capital as a way of understanding mothers' involvement in their children's education?', *Sociological Review*, 48 (4), 568–85.

—(2001) ' "Spice Girls", "Nice Girls", "Girlies" and "Tomboys": gender discourses, girls' cultures and feminities in the primary school classroom', *Gender and Education*, 13 (2), 153–66.

Reay, D. and Wiliam, D. (1999) ' "I'll be a nothing": structure, agency and the construction of identity through assessment', *British Educational Research Journal*, 25 (3), 343–54.

Reese, L., Garnier, H., Gallimore, R. and Goldenberg, C. (2000) 'Longitudinal analysis of the antecedents of emergent Spanish literacy and middle-school English reading achievement of Spanish-speaking students', *American Educational Research Journal*, 37 (3), 622–33.

Reid, I. (1998) *Class in Britain*. Cambridge: Polity.

Renold, E. (2001) 'Learning the "hard" way: boys, hegemonic masculinity and the negotiation of learner identities in the primary school', *British Journal of Sociology of Education*, 22 (3), 369–86.

Reynolds, D. and Farrell, S. (1996) *Worlds Apart? A Review of International Surveys of Educational Achievement Involving England*. London: OFSTED.

Reynoldson, F. (1995) *Svedenstierna and the Industrial Revolution*. Oxford: Heinemann.

Richards, M. and Light, P. (eds) (1986) *Children of Social Worlds*. Oxford: Blackwell.

Richardson, R. (1990) *Daring to be a Teacher*. Stoke-on-Trent: Trentham.

—(2009) *Holding Together. Equalities, Difference and Cohesion*. Stoke-on-Trent: Trentham.

Richardson, R. and Miles, B. (2008a) *Equality Stories: Recognition, Respect and Raising Achievement*. Stoke-on-Trent: Trentham.

—(2008b) *Racist Incidents and Bullying in Schools*. Stoke-on-Trent: Trentham.

Richardson, V. (2001) *Handbook of Research on Teaching*. Washington, DC: American Educational Research Association.

Riding, R. J. and Rayner, S. (1998) *Cognitive Styles and Learning Strategies*. London: Fulton.

Rist, R. (1970) 'Student social class and teacher expectations', *Harvard Education Review*, 40, 411–51.

Roberts, R. (2002) *Self-esteem and Early Learning*. London: Paul Chapman.

Robertson, J. (1996) *Effective Classroom Control: Understanding Teacher–Pupil Relationships*. London: Hodder and Stoughton.

Robertson, S. and Dale, R. (2009) 'Aliens in the classroom: when technology meets classroom life'. In Sutherland, R., Robertson, S. and John, P. *Improving Classroom Learning with ICT*. London: Routledge.

Robinson, E. (1983) 'Metacognitive development'. In Meadows, S. (ed.) *Developing Thinking*. London: Methuen.

Robinson, G., Sleigh, J. and Maines, B. (1995) *No Bullying Starts Today*. Portishead: Lame Duck.

Rogers, B. (2011) *Classroom Behaviour*. London: SAGE.

Rogers, C. (1969) *Freedom to Learn*. New York: Merrill.

Rogers, C. R. (1961) *On Becoming a Person*. London: Constable.

—(1980) *A Way of Being*. Boston: Houghton Mifflin.

Rogoff, B. (1990) *Apprenticeship in Thinking: Cognitive Development in Social Context*. Oxford: Oxford University Press.

Rogoff, B., Goodman Turkanis, C. and Bartlett, L. (2001) *Learning Together: Children and Adults in a School Community*. Oxford: Oxford University Press.

Rose, J. (2009) *Independent Review of the Primary Curriculum*. Final Report. London: DCSF.

Rose, R., Shevlin, M., Winter, E. and O'Raw, P. (2010) 'Special and inclusive education in the Republic of Ireland: reviewing the literature from 2000 to 2009', *European Journal of Special Needs Education*, 25 (4), 359–73.

Rosen, H. (1988) 'The irrepressible genre'. In Maclure, M., Phillips, T. and Wilkinson, A., (eds) *Oracy Matters*. Milton Keynes: Open University Press.

Rosenberg, M. (1989) *Society and the Adolescent Self-image*. Middletown, CT: Wesleyan University Press.

Rosenblatt, L. M. (1978/1994) *The Reader the Text the Poem: The Transactional Theory of the Literary Work*. Carbondale and Edwardsville: Southern Illinois University Press.

Ross, A. (2001) 'What is the Curriculum?' In Collins, J., Insley, K. and Soler, J. (eds) *Developing Pedagogy*. London: Paul Chapman.

Ross, S. and Biesty, S. (2011) *Into the Unknown: How Great Explorers Found Their Way by Land, Sea and Air*. London: Walker Books.

Ross-Hill, R. (2009) 'Teacher attitude towards inclusion practices and special needs students', *Journal of Research in Special Educational Needs*, 9 (3), 188–98.

Rostow, W. W. (1962) *The Stages of Economic Growth*. Cambridge: Cambridge University Press.

Rottenberg, C. and Smith, M. L. (1990) *Unintended effects of external testing in elementary schools*. Conference of the American Educational Research Association. Boston, April.

Rouse, M. (2008) 'Developing Inclusive Practice', *Education in the North* 16, 6–13.

Rowe, N., Wilkin, A. and Wilson, R. (2012) *Mapping of Seminal Reports on Good Teaching*. Slough: NFER.

Rowland, S. (1987) 'Child in control: towards an interpretive model of teaching and learning'. In Pollard, A. (ed.) *Children and their Primary Schools*. London: Falmer.

Rowland, T., Turner, F., Thwaites, A. and Huckstep, P. (2009) *Developing Primary Mathematics Teaching: Reflecting on Practice with the Knowledge Quartet*. London: SAGE.

Royal Society, The (2011a) *Neuroscience, Society and Policy*. Brain Waves Module 1. London: The Royal Society.

—(2011b) *Neuroscience: Implications for Education and Lifelong Learning*. Brain Waves Module 2. London: The Royal Society.

Royal Society of Arts, The (RSA) (2013) *Opening Minds: The Competence Framework*. London: RSA.

Rubin, Z. (1980) *Children's Friendships*. London: Fontana.

Rudduck, J. and Flutter, J. (2003) *Involving Pupils, Improving School*. London: Continuum.

Rudduck, J. and McIntyre, D. (2007) *Improving Learning Through Consulting Pupils*. London: Routledge.

Rutter, M. and Madge, N. (1976) *Cycles of Disadvantage*. London: Heinemann.

Ryle, G. (1945) 'Knowing how and knowing that', *Proceedings of the Aristotelian Society*, 46, 1–16.

Sachs, J. (2003) *The Activist Teaching Profession*. Buckingham: Open University Press.

Sage, R. (2007) *Inclusion in Schools. Making a Difference*. London: Network Continuum Education.

Sahlberg, P. (2012) *Finnish Lessons: What Can the World Learn from Educational Change in Finland?* Boston: Teachers' College Press.

Saljo, R. and Hjorne, E. (2009) 'Symptoms, categories, and the process of invoking labels'. In Daniels, H., Lauder, H. and Porter, J. (eds) *Knowledge, Values and Educational Policy: A Critical Perspective*. London: Routledge.

Sammons, P., Hillman, J. and Mortimore, P. (1995) *Key Characteristics of Effective Schools: A Review of School Effectiveness Research*. London: Ofsted.

Sangster, M. (2012) *Developing Teacher Expertise: Exploring Key Issues in Primary Practice*. London: Bloomsbury Academic.

Sarasin, L. C. (1999) *Learning Style Perspectives: Impact in the Classroom*. Madison, WI: Atwood Publishing.

Sarason, S. B. (1996) *Revisiting the Culture of the School and the Problem of Change*. New York: Teachers College Press.

Sawyer, R. K. (2006) *The Cambridge Handbook of the Learning Sciences*. Cambridge: Cambridge University Press.

Scardamalia, M. and Bereiter, C. (1983) 'Child as coinvestigator: helping children gain insight into their own mental processes'. In Paris, S. G., Olson, G. M. and Stevenson, H. (eds) *Learning and Motivation in the Classroom*. Hillsdale, NJ: Lawrence Erlbaum.

Schagen, I. and Hutchison, D. (2003), 'Adding value in educational research – the marriage of value-added measures for school improvement data and analytical power', *British Educational Research Journal*, 29 (5), 749–65.

Schmidt, W. and Prawat, R. (2006) 'Curriculum coherence and national control of education. Issues or non-issue?', *Journal of Curriculum Studies*, 38 (6), 641–58.

Scholes, R. (1985) *Textual Power*. New Haven: Yale University Press.

Schön, D. A. (1983) *The Reflective Practitioner: How Professionals Think in Action*. London: Temple Smith.

—(1987) *Educating the Reflective Practitioner*. San Francisco: Jossey Bass.

Schuller, T. and Watson, D. (2009) *Learning Through Life*. London: NIACE.

Schultz, T. (1961) 'Investment in human capital', *American Economic Review*, 51, 1–17.

Schwab, J. (1978) 'Education and the structure of the disciplines'. In Westbury, I. and Wilkof, N. J. (eds), *Science Curriculum and Liberal Education*, 229–72. Chicago: University of Chicago Press.

Scott, D. and Usher, R. (1996) *Understanding Educational Research*, London: Routledge.

Scottish Government (2006) *A Curriculum for Excellence: Building Curriculum Series*. Edinburgh: The Scottish Government.

—(2008) *A Curriculum for Excellence: Building the Curriculum 3*. Edinburgh: The Scottish Government.

—(2009) *A Curriculum for Excellence: Curriculum Guidelines*. Edinburgh: The Scottish Government.

—(2010) *Supporting Children's Learning: Code of Practice*. Edinburgh: The Scottish Government.

—(2011a) *Review of Post-16 Education and Vocational Training.* Edinburgh: The Scottish Government.

—(2011b) *Principles of Assessment in Curriculum for Excellence. Building the Curriculum 5. A Framework for Assessment.* Edinburgh: The Scottish Government.

Sedgwick, F. (1988) *Here Comes the Assembly Man.* London: Falmer Press.

SEED (Scottish Executive) (2000) *The Structure and Balance of the Curriculum: 5 to 14 National Guidelines.* Edinburgh: Learning and Teaching Scotland.

Seligman, C. F., Tucker, G. R. and Lambert, W. E. (1972) 'The effects of speech style and other attributes on teachers' attitudes towards pupils', *Language in Society,* 1, 131–42.

Sewell, T. (1997) *Black Masculinities and Schooling. How Black Boys Survive Modern Schooling,* Stoke-on-Trent: Trentham.

Sfard, A. (1998) 'On the two metaphors of learning and the dangers of choosing just one', *Educational Researcher,* 27 (2), 4–13.

Sharp, R. and Green, A. (1975) *Education and Social Control.* London: Routledge.

Shayer, M. and Adey, P. (eds) (2002) *Learning Intelligence: Cognitive Acceleration Across the Curriculum from 5 to 15 Years.* Maidenhead: Open University Press

Shorrocks, D. (1991) *The Evaluation of National Curriculum Assessment at Key Stage One, Final Report.* Leeds: University of Leeds

Shulman, L. S. (1986) 'Those who understand: knowledge and growth in teaching', *Educational Researcher,* 15, 4–14.

—(2004) *The Wisdom of Practice – Essays on Teaching, Learning and Learning to Teach.* San Francisco: Jossey Bass.

Shuter, J. (1993) *Francis Parkman and the Plains Indians.* Oxford: Heinemann.

Sibieta, L. (2011) *Inequality in Britain: An Explanation of Recent Trends.* London: Institute for Fiscal Studies.

Siegler, R. S. (1997) *Emerging Minds: The Process of Change in Children's Thinking.* Oxford: Oxford University Press.

Sikes, P. (1997) *Parents Who Teach: Stories from Home and School.* London: Cassell.

Sikes, P., Measor, L. and Woods, P. (1985) *Teacher Careers: Crises and Continuities.* London: Falmer.

Silver, H. (1980) *Education and the Social Condition.* London: Methuen.

Simco, N. (2000) 'Learning to comply: the impact of national curricula for primary pupils and primary trainee teacher on the ownership of learning', *Forum,* 42 (1), 33–8.

Simon, B. (1953) *Intelligence Testing and the Comprehensive School.* London: Lawrence and Wishart.

—(1981) 'Why no pedagogy in England?' In Simon, B. and Taylor, W. (eds) *Education in the Eighties.* London: Batsford Educational.

—(1985) *Does Education Matter?* London: Lawrence and Wishart.

—(1992) *What Future for Education?* London: Lawrence and Wishart.

Siraj-Blatchford, I. and Clarke, P. (2000) *Diversity and Language in the Early Years.* Buckingham: Open University Press.

Siraj-Blatchford, J. and Siraj-Blatchford, I. (1995) *Educating the Whole Child: Crosscurricular Skills, Themes and Dimensions.* Buckingham: Open University Press.

Skelton, C. (2001) *Schooling the Boys. Masculinities and Primary Education.* Buckingham: Open University Press.

Skelton, C. and Francis, B. (2009) *Feminism and 'The Schooling Scandal'.* London: Routledge.

Skinner B. F. (1953) *Science and Human Behaviour.* New York: Macmillan.

—(1954) 'The science of learning and the art of teaching', *Harvard Educational Review,* 24, 86–97.

—(1968) *The Technology of Teaching.* New York: Appleton.

Slukin, A. (1981) *Growing Up in the Playground.* London: Routledge and Kegan Paul.

Smith, F. (1994) *Writing and the Writer,* 2nd edn. Hove: Lawrence Erlbaum Associates.

Smith, F., Hardman, F., Wall, K. and Mroz, M. (2004), 'Interactive whole class teaching in the National Literacy and Numeracy Strategies', *British Educational Research Journal*, 30 (3), 395–411.

Solar, J., Walsh, C. S., Craft, A., Rix, J. and Simmons, K. (2012) *Transforming Practice. Critical Issues in Equity, Diversity and Education.* Maidenhead: Open University Press.

Solomon, J. (1987) 'New thoughts on teacher education', *Oxford Review of Education,* 13 (3), 267–74.

Sood, K. (2005) 'Working with Other Professionals'. In Cole, M. (ed.) *Professional Values and Practice: Meeting the Standards.* London: David Fulton.

Sorace, A. (2010) 'Two languages, one brain: advantages of bilingualism across the lifespan', at http://www.bilingualism-matters.org.uk/ (accessed December 2013).

Sotto, E. (2007) *When Teaching Becomes Learning.* London: Continuum.

Spendlove, S. (2012) *Putting Assessment for Learning into Practice.* London: Continuum.

Squibb, P. (1973) 'The concept of intelligence: a sociological perspective', *Sociological Review*, 21 (1), 147–66.

Stenhouse, L. (1975) *An Introduction to Curriculum Research and Development.* London: Heinemann.

—(1983) *Authority, Education and Emancipation.* London: Heinemann.

Stobart, G. (2008) *Testing Times: The Uses and Abuses of Assessment.* London: Routledge.

Stone, C. A. (1998) 'The metaphor of scaffolding: Its utility for the field of learning disabilities', *Journal of Learning Disabilities,* 31, 344–64.

Straughan, R. (1988) *Can We Teach Children to be Good? Basic Issues in Moral, Personal and Social Education.* Buckingham: Open University Press.

Sturman (2012) 'Making best use of international comparison data', *Research Intelligence*, 119 (Autumn/Winter). London: BERA.

Sutherland, R., Robertson, S. and John, P. (2009) *Improving Classroom Learning with ICT.* London: Routledge.

Sutton, R. (1995) *Assessment for Learning.* Salford: RS Publications.

—(2000) *Undoing the Muddle in the Middle.* Salford: RS Publications.

Swaffield, S. (2000) 'Record keeping', *Primary File*, 38, 61–4.

—(2011) 'Getting to the heart of authentic assessment for learning', *Assessment in Education: Principles, Policy and Practice,* 18 (4), 433–49.

—(ed.) (2008) *Unlocking Assessment: Understanding for Reflection and Application.* Abingdon: Routledge.

Swaffield, S. and Dudley, P. (2010) *Assessment Literacy for Wise Decisions.* London: Association of Teachers and Lecturers.

Swaffield. S. and MacBeath, J. (2005) 'Self-evaluation and the role of a critical friend', *Cambridge Journal of Education,* 35 (2), 239–52.

Swann, M., Peacock, A., Hart, S. and Drummond, M. J. (2012) *Creating Learning Without Limits.* Maidenhead: Open University Press.

Sylva, K., Melhuish, E., Sammons, P., Siraj-Blatchford, I. and Taggart, B. (2010) *Early Childhood Matters. Evidence from the Effective Pre-school and Primary Education Project.* London: Routledge.

Tabachnick, R. and Zeichner, K. (eds) (1991) *Issues and Practices in Inquiry Oriented Teacher Education.* London: Falmer.

Tanner, J. M. (1978) *Education and Physical Growth.* London: University of London Press.

Tattum, D. P. and Lane, D. A. (1989) *Bullying in Schools.* Stoke-on-Trent: Trentham.

Teaching and Learning in 2020 Review Group (2006) *2020 Vision: Report of the Teaching and Learning in 2020 Review Group.* London: DfES.

Tharp, R. and Gallimore, R. (1988) *Rousing Minds to Life: Teaching, Learning and Schooling in Social Context.* New York: Cambridge University Press.

Thomas, A. and Pattison, H. (2007) *How Children Learn at Home.* London: Continuum.

Thomas, G. and Loxley, A. (2007) *Deconstructing Special Education and Constructing Inclusion.* Buckingham: Open University Press.

Thomas, L. (2010) *The RSA Area Based Curriculum: Engaging the Local.* London: RSA.

—(2012) *Thinking About an Area Based Curriculum.* London: RSA.

Thompson, J. (2010) *The Essential Guide to Understanding Special Educational Needs.* London: Longman.

Thompson, M. (1997) *Professional Ethics and the Teacher.* Stoke-on-Trent: Trentham.

Thorndike, E. L. (1911) *Human Learning.* New York: Prentice Hall.

Thorne, B. (1993) *Gender Play: Girls and Boys in School.* Buckingham: Open University Press.

Tickell, C. (2011) *The Early Years: Foundations for Life, Health and Learning.* London: DfE.

Timperley, H. (2011) *Realising the Power of Professional Learning.* Maidenhead: Open University Press.

Timperley, H., Wilson, A., Barrar, H. and Fung, I. (2007) *Teacher Professional Learning and Development.* Best Evidence Synthesis Iteration [BES]. New Zealand: Ministry of Education.

Tizard, B. and Hughes, M. (1984) *Young Children Learning: Talking and Learning at Home and School.* London: Fontana.

Tizard, B., Blatchford, P., Burke, J., Farquhar, C. and Plewis, I. (1988) *Young Children at School in the Inner City.* London: Lawrence Erlbaum.

Tomlinson, P. (1999a) 'Conscious reflection and implicit learning in teacher preparation: implications for a balanced approach', *Oxford Review of Education*, 24 (4), 533–44.

—(1999b) 'Conscious reflection and implicit learning in teacher preparation: recent light on old issues', *Oxford Review of Education*, 25 (3), 405–25.

Torrance, H. (1991) 'Evaluating SATs: the 1991 pilot', *Cambridge Journal of Education*, 21 (2), 129–40.

Training and Development Agency for Schools (2008) *Continuing Professional Development Guidance.* London: TDA.

Troyna, B. and Hatcher, R. (1992) *Racism in Children's Lives: A Study of Mainly White Primary Schools.* London: Routledge.

Tsui, A. (2003) *Understanding Expertise in Teaching: Case Studies of Second Language Teachers.* Cambridge: Cambridge University Press.

Turbull, J. (2007) *9 Habits of Highly Effective Teachers. A Practical Guide to Empowerment.* London: Continuum.

Turner, F. (2009) 'Growth in teacher knowledge: individual reflection and community participation', *Research in Mathematics Education,* 11 (1), 81.

Turner-Bisset, R. (2000) 'Reconstructing the primary curriculum', *Education 3–13: International Journal of Primary, Elementary and Early Years Education*, 28 (1), 3–8.

UNESCO (1994) *The Salamanca Statement on Principles, Policy and Practice in Special Needs Education.* Salamanca: UNESCO.

—(2012) *Inclusive Education.* Available at http://www.unesco.org/new/en/ education/themes/strengthening-education-systems/inclusive-education (accessed July 2012).

UNICEF (2012) *Measuring Child Poverty. New League Tables of Child Poverty in the World's Rich Countries.* Florence: UNICEF.

United Kingdom Literacy Association (2004) *Raising Boys' Achievements in Writing.* London: UKLA.

United Nations (1948) *Universal Declaration of Human Rights.* New York: United Nations.

—(1989) *Convention on the Rights of the Child.* New York: United Nations.

Unwin, L. (2009) *Sensuality, Sustainability and Social Justice Vocational Education in Changing Times.* Inaugural lecture. London: Institute of Education.

Vincent, C. (1996) *Parents and Teachers: Power and Participation.* London: Falmer.

—(2000) *Including Parents? Education, Citzenship and Parental Agency.* Buckingham: Open University Press.

Vygotsky, L. S. (1962) *Thought and Language*. Cambridge, MA: Massachusetts Institute of Technology.

—(1978) *Mind in Society: the Development of Higher Psychological Processes*. Cambridge, MA: Harvard University Press.

Walkerdine, V. (1981) 'Sex power and pedagogy', *Screen Education*, 38, 1–24.

—(1983) 'It's only natural: rethinking Child-centred pedagogy'. In Wolpe, A. M. and Donald, J. (eds) *Is There Anybody There from Education?* London: Pluto Press.

—(1984) 'Cognitive development and the Child-centred pedagogy'. In Henriques, D. (ed.) *Changing the Subject: Psychology, Social Regulation and Subjectivity*. London: Methuen.

—(1988) *The Mastery of Reason: Cognitive Development and the Production of Rationality*. London: Routledge.

Waller, W. (1932) *The Sociology of Teaching*. New York: Russell and Russell.

Walters, E., McParland, J. and Lichfield, G. (2008) *How Inclusive are our Classrooms?* London: NTRP.

Walters, S. (2011) *Ethnicity, Race and Education*. London: Continuum.

Walton, J. (ed.) (1971) *The Integrated Day: Theory and Practice*. London: Ward Lock.

Ward, S. (ed.) (2012) *A Student's Guide to Education Studies*. London: Routledge.

Warin, J. (2010) *Stories of Self: Tracking Children's Identity and Wellbeing Through the School Years*. Stoke-on-Trent: Trentham Books.

Warrington, M., Younger, M. and Bearne, E. (2006) *Raising Boys' Achievements in Primary Schools: Towards a Holistic Approach*. Maidenhead: Open University Press.

Warwick, P., Hennessy, S. and Mercer, N. (2011) 'Promoting teacher and school development through co-enquiry: developing interactive whiteboard use in a "dialogic classroom"', *Teachers and Teaching: theory and practice*, 17 (3), 303–24.

Watkins, C. (2003) *Learning: A Sense Maker's Guide*. London: ATL.

—(2004) *Classrooms as Learning Communities*. London: Routledge.

—(2011) *Managing Classroom Behaviour*. London: ATL.

Watson, A. and Mason, J. (2005) *Mathematics as a Constructive Activity. Learners Generating Examples*. London: Routledge.

Wearmouth, J. (2011) *Special Educational Needs. The Basics*. London: Routledge.

Webb, N. M., Ing, M., Nemer, K. M. and Kersting, N. (2006) 'Help seeking in cooperative learning groups'. In Newman, R. S. and Karabenick, S. A. (eds) *Help Seeking in Academic Settings: Goals, Groups and Contexts*, 45–88. Hillsdale, NJ: Lawrence Erlbaum Associates.

Webb, R. and Vulliamy, G. (2002) 'The social work dimension of the primary teachers' role', *Research Papers in Education*, 17 (2), 165–84.

Wegerif, R. and Dawes, L. (2004) *Thinking and Learning with ICT: Raising achievement in Primary Classrooms*. London: RoutledgeFalmer

Wells, G. (1999) *Dialogic Inquiry: Towards a Socio-cultural Practice and Theory of Education*. New York: Cambridge University Press.

—(2008) 'Dialogue, inquiry and the construction of learning communities'. In Lingard, B., Nixon, J. and Ranson, S. *Transforming Learning in Schools and Communities*. London: Continuum.

Welsh Government (2008) *The School Curriculum for Wales*. Cardiff: Welsh Government.

Wenger, E. (1999) *Communities of Practice. Learning, Meaning and Identity*. Cambridge: Cambridge University Press.

Wertsch, J. V. (1985) *Vygotsky and the Social Formation of Mind*. Cambridge, MA: Harvard University Press.

—(1991) *Voices of the Mind: A Socio-cultural Approach to Mediated Action*. Cambridge, MA: Harvard University Press.

West, A. and Pennell, H. (2003) *Underachievement in Schools*. London: RoutledgeFalmer.

West-Burnham, J., Farrar, M. and Otero, G. (2007) *Schools and Communities: Working Together to Transform Children's Lives*. London: Continuum.

Wheldall, K. (1991) *Discipline in Schools: Psychological Perspectives on the Elton Report.* London: Routledge.

Whetton, C. E. A. (1991) *National Curriculum Assessment at Key Stage One: 1991 Evaluation, Report 4.* Slough: NFER.

White, J. (1978) 'The primary teacher as servant of the state', *Education 3–13*, 7 (2), 18–23.

White, M. A. (1971) 'The view from the student's desk'. In Silberman, M. L. (ed.) *The Experience of Schooling*, 337–45. New York: Rinehart and Winston.

Whitebread, D. and Pino Pasternak, D. (2010) 'Metacognition, self-regulation and meta-knowing'. In Littleton, K., Wood, C. and Kleine, J. Staarman (eds) *International Handbook of Psychology in education.* Bingley: Emerald.

Wiggins, G. (1989) 'A true test: toward more authentic and equitable assessment', *Phi Delta Kappan*, 70 (9), 703–13.

Wiliam, D. (2001) *Level Best? Levels of Attainment in National Curriculum Assesment.* London: Association of Teachers and Lecturers.

—(2009) *Assessment for Learning: Why, What and How?* Inaugural lecture, Institute of Education, University of London, 24 January.

—(2011) *Embedded Formative Assessment.* Bloomington, IN: Solution Tree Press.

Wilkinson, R. and Pickett, K. (2009) *The Spirit Level. Why Equality is Better for Everyone.* London: Penguin.

Willis, J. (2011) 'Affiliation, autonomy and Assessment for Learning', *Assessment in Education: Principles, Policy and Practice*, 18 (4), 399–415.

Willis, P. E. (1977) *Learning to Labour: How Working Class Kids Get Working Class Jobs.* Farnborough: Saxon House.

Wilson, C. and Powell, M. (2001) *A Guide to Interviewing Children.* London: Routledge.

Wilson, E. O. and Lumsden, C. J. (1981) *Genes, Mind and Culture.* Cambridge, MA, and London: Harvard University Press.

Wilson, J. (2000) *Key issues in Education and Teaching.* London: Cassell.

Winch, C. (2012) *Dimensions of Expertise: A Conceptual Exploration of Vocational Knowledge.* London: Continuum.

Winter, J., Andrews, J., Greenhough, P., Hughes, M., Salway, L. and Yee, W. (2009) *Improving Primary Mathematics: Linking Home and School.* London: Routledge.

Winterbottom, M. and Wilkins, A. (2007) 'Lighting and visual discomfort in the classroom', *Journal of Environmental Psychology*, 29, 63–75.

Withall, J. (1949) 'The development of a technique for the measurement of social–emotional climate in classrooms', *Journal of Experimental Education*, 17, 347–61.

Wolf, A. (2011) *Review of Vocational Education.* London: DfE.

Wolf, M. (2008) *Proust and the Squid: The Story and Science of the Reading Brain.* Cambridge: Icon Books.

Wolf, M. K., Crosson, A. C. and Resnick, L. B. (2004) 'Classroom talk for rigorous comprehension instruction', *Reading Psychology*, 26 (1), 27–53.

Wood, D. (1986) 'Aspects of teaching and learning'. In Richards, M. and Light, P. (eds) *Children of Social Worlds.* Cambridge: Polity Press.

—(1997) *How Children Think and Learn. The Social Contexts of Cognitive Development.* London: Wiley-Blackwell.

Wood, D., Bruner, J. S. and Ross, G. (1976) 'The role of tutoring in problem solving', *Journal of Child Psychology and Psychiatry,* 17 (19), 89–100.

Woods, P. (1990) *The Happiest Days? How Pupils Cope with School.* London: Falmer.

Woods, P. and Jeffrey, B. (1996) *Teachable Moments: The Art of Teaching in Primary Schools.* Buckingham: Open University Press.

Woods, P. A., Bagley, C. and Glatter, R. (1998) *School Choice and Competition: Markets in the Public Interest.* London: Psychology Press.

Woolland, B. (2010) *Teaching Primary Drama*. Harlow: Pearson Education.

Woolner, P., Hall, E., Higgins, S., McCaughey, C., Wall, K. et al. (2007a) 'A sound foundation? What we know about the impact of environments on learning and the implications for Building Schools for the Future', *Oxford Review of Education, 33* (1), 47–70.

Wragg, E. C. (2000) *Class Management*. London: Routledge.

Wragg, E. C. and Brown, G. (2001a) *Explaining in the Primary School*. London: RoutledgeFalmer.

—(2001b) *Questioning in the Primary School*. London: RoutledgeFalmer.

Wright, C. (1992) *Race Relations in the Primary School*. London: David Fulton.

Wrigley, J., Thompson, P. and Lingard, R. (eds) (2012) *Changing Schools. Alternative Ways to Make a World of Difference*. London: Routledge.

Wyse, D., Baumfield, V., Egan, D., Hayward, D., Mulme, M., Menter, I., Gallagher, C., Leitch, R., Livingston, K. and Lingard, R. (2012) *Creating the Curriculum*. London: Routledge.

Youdell, D. (2006) *Impossible Bodies, Impossible Selves: Exclusions and Student Subjectivities*. Dordrecht: Springer.

Young, M. (2008) *Bringing Knowledge Back In*. London: Routledge.

Young, M. F. D. (ed.) (1971) *Knowledge and Control*. London: CollierMacmillan.

Younger, M., Warrington, M. and McLellan, R. (2005) *Raising Boys' Achievement in Secondary Schools: Issues, Dilemmas and Opportunities*. Maidenhead: Open University Press.

Zeichner, K. and Liston, D. (1996) *Reflective Teaching: An Introduction*. Mahwah, NJ: Lawrence Erlbaum Associates

Zipes, J. (1995) *Creative Storytelling: Building Communities, Changing Lives*. London: Routledge.

Index

This index categorises reflective schools, classrooms, teachers, pupils, teaching and learning, and related concepts under different headings, including Teaching and Learning Research Programme (TLRP) findings; it covers Chapters 1–17 but not personal names or key reading lists. Letters and typographical elements with page numbers signify various features: an 'f' indicates a figure; an '(RA)' indicates a reflective activity (in boxed text); an '(RB)' indicates a figure in a research briefing; a '(CS)' indicates a case study; bold type indicates TLRP principles (in boxed text); italic type indicates framework concepts (in boxed text); underlined type indicates principal coverage of these principles and concepts (Chapters 4 and 16).

Readings for Reflective Teaching in Schools: Contents list

The reflective teaching series

This book is one of the *Reflective Teaching Series* – applying principles of reflective practice in early years, schools, further, higher and adult education.

The *Reflective Teaching Series* supports improvements in outcomes for learners through:

- The development of high quality, principled expertise in teaching;
- Partnership between those involved in the academic study and the practice of education.

With adaptions for early years, schools, further, higher and adult education, the series endorses the aspirations of the Teaching Councils of Scotland, Wales, Northern Ireland and the Republic of Ireland. As they put it:

> We view teaching as a complex profession which requires high standards of competence, professional skills and commitment. We consider that high quality teaching is necessary to deliver high standards of learning for our students. We believe that quality teaching is achieved when teachers commit themselves to lifelong learning and ongoing reflection on their professional practice; when they have excellent knowledge of the curriculum which they are expected to teach; when they have deep and detailed understanding of how pupils learn; and when they have the confidence to apply and vary their pedagogical skills to meet the needs of learners in different and sometimes challenging contexts.
>
> We require that teachers are suitably qualified, both academically and professionally, and that they have appropriate values and a commitment to maintaining and improving their professional practice as they progress throughout their careers. *(Joint Statement, April 2013)*

The series is supported by a website, **reflectiveteaching.co.uk**. For each book, this site is being developed to offer a range of resources including reflective activities, research briefings, advice on further reading and additional chapters. The site also offers generic resources such as a compendium of educational terms, links to other useful websites, and a conceptual framework for 'Deepening Expertise'. The latter will also showcase some of the UK's best educational research.

The series is coordinated through meetings of the volume and series editors: Paul Ashwin, Jennifer Colwell, Maggie Gregson, Yvonne Hillier, Amy Pollard and Andrew

Pollard. Each volume has an editorial team of contributors whose collective expertise and experience enable research and practice to be reviewed and applied in relation to early years, school, further, adult, vocational and higher education.

The Pollard Partnership

The series is the first product of the Pollard Partnership, a collaboration between Andrew and Amy Pollard to enable the long-term development of this series and to maximise the beneficial use of research and evidence on public life, policymaking and professional practice.

In the long term, we may undertake activities in a range of policy areas. This initiative focuses on education – building on Andrew's longstanding publishing record, research and professional engagement. In this arena, we seek to support teacher professionals in deepening their expertise and in developing policy contexts in which evidence-informed judgement can flourish.

In relation to education and when appropriate, Amy will act as custodian of Andrew's literary legacy. As Andrew's daughter, she is in a unique position to safeguard the value commitment of his work – and will engage with education professionals and associations as appropriate to ensure that future outputs, including **reflectiveteaching.co.uk**, are underpinned by the necessary expertise.

Amy Pollard specialises in the application of social science to policy and practice and has worked on education projects at Demos (demos.co.uk), the Overseas Development Institute (odi.org.uk) and Anthropology Matters (anthropologymatters.com). She is currently Deputy Director of Involve (involve.org.uk), the public engagement charity. With a PhD in social anthropology, she has worked in charities, think tanks, government and international agencies for over ten years. She was co-founder and chair of Beyond 2015 (beyond2015.org), a major civil society campaign bringing together over 400 civil society groups from more than 80 countries.

Andrew Pollard taught in schools for ten years before entering teacher education and developing a career in educational research. His research interests include learner perspectives, teaching-learning processes, the role of curriculum, pedagogy and assessment, and the development of evidence-informed classroom practice. He has been a Professor of Education at the universities of Bristol, Cambridge, London and West of England. He was Director of the ESRC Teaching and Learning Research Programme (tlrp.org), the UK Strategic Forum for Research in Education (sfre.ac.uk) and of ESCalate (escalate.ac.uk), the Education Subject Centre of the UK's Higher Education Academy. He is Chairman of William Pollard & Co. Ltd. (pollardsprint.co.uk), a print and communications company, founded in 1781.